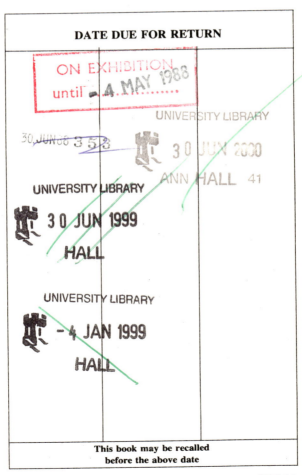

Kings, Bishops, Nobles and Burghers in Medieval Hungary

Professor Dr Erik Fügedi

Erik Fügedi

Kings, Bishops, Nobles and Burghers in Medieval Hungary

Edited by J. M. Bak

VARIORUM REPRINTS
London 1986

British Library CIP data

Fügedi, Erik
Kings, bishops, nobles and burghers in medieval
Hungary.
1. Hungary — Social life and customs
I. Title   II. Bak, János M.
943.9′02   DB.920.5

ISBN 0–86078–177–1

Copyright © 1986 by

Variorum Reprints

Published in Great Britain by

Variorum Reprints
20 Pembridge Mews London W11 3EQ

Printed in Great Britain by

Galliard (Printers) Ltd
Great Yarmouth Norfolk

VARIORUM REPRINT CS229

CONTENTS

vi

This volume contains a total of 346 pages.

PUBLISHER'S NOTE

ERIK FÜGEDI SEPTUAGENARIO:
AD MULTOS ANNOS!

In making Professor Fügedi's foreign language works easily accessible to a wider public, we present this volume of selected studies on social history as a gift for the author's seventieth birthday.

Erik Fügedi belongs to that generation which inherited both the values and problems of historical Hungary and tried to rescue its intellectual achievements while overcoming its national and social prejudices. Faced with war, destruction, persecution and upheavals, they had to exert unique efforts to not only keep their humanistic and 'European' standards alive, but even attempt to pass them on to the next generations.

Born on 22 September 1916 in Vienna, where his father served in the Austro-Hungarian army, Erik Fügedi went to school in Budapest and after graduation from the Piarist's Gymnasium, he studied at the Péter Pázmány University under some of the best historians of inter-war Hungary, those like Elemér Mályusz, Imre Szentpétery and Imre Hajnal. Students in Mályusz's seminar held that the understanding of history is better served by detailed study of the society than by grand rhetoric, and that the problems of the Danubian Basin are better solved if students learn to appreciate the culture and language of the neighbouring nations.

The young Dr Fügedi had hardly obtained his first post — in the National Archives, as was usual with future scholars — when the war broke out and he was called up to active service. Discharged after several years at the Russian front, he had the privilege of obtaining a scholarship in Bratislava: the family originated in "Upper Hungary" (Slovakia) and Fügedi had learned the language while working on his dissertation about the settlement of one of the northern counties of historic Hungary. After the end of the Second World War Dr Fügedi received an important government commission: from 1945 to 1949 he was in charge of the rescue and conservation of endangered private collections, libraries and archives. It may have been from the experiences of those years, when Dr Fügedi visited castles and manor houses, some still inhabited, others looted and in desperate shape, that he received a major impetus to study the history and structure of the nobility of old Hungary, since he had had the chance to meet its last representatives.

In 1950, when the country's archives were centralized, Dr Fügedi became the head of the research division of the Archival Centre. However, only a few years later, the Stalinist Rákosi-regime denounced members of the intelligentsia, especially those whose careers began before the war, as potential 'enemies'. Fügedi lost his position in the Centre and worked for nearly a decade as a clerk in a canning factory. It was only in 1961 that he was able to return to scholarly work as a research fellow with the Historical Association.

In 1965 Dr Fügedi joined the newly established Historical Demography Research Group in the Library of the Central Statistical Office. For ten years, until his retirement from the Office in 1980, he was the head of the Research Group. A small but very important institution, it was first among the centres in Hungary where the methods of 'new history' — quantification, complex analysis, application of demographic and sociological perspectives — were pursued and propagated.

Immediately after his return to scholarly work, Dr Fügedi concentrated on a field barely plowed before by historians in Hungary: urban development. Due to their primary concern with politics and with the noble republic, historians had devoted little attention to the — mostly German or Italian — townsmen of the medieval kingdom. Fügedi has done yeoman work in this field, following the footsteps of his teacher, Elemér Mályusz. A number of his articles (nos. IX–XIII below) are still seminal, even though new archaeological data and comparative studies have updated (and in some cases corrected) his theses.

The author himself noted recently in the preface to a Hungarian collection of his articles that his first scholarly visit to Paris introduced him to that area of research, which became his 'home ground': sociological and psychological approaches to the history of society, especially of its élites. Following studies on economic aspects and demographic-prosopographical explorations (see nos. II, III and VII) he has now summarized his insights into the development of aristocracy in medieval Hungary (no. IV), on which a major monograph is in preparation, and presented a pioneering study on the oral culture of the nobility in his recent "Verba volant ... " (no. VI). The contacts with France and the *Annales* school further suggested the combination of ecclesiastical, social and urban history (no. XII). The methodological advances are also reflected in the reports Dr Fügedi presented to foreign audiences about the rôle of 'immigrants' in medieval Hungary (no. VIII), the hitherto little-known agrarian towns (no. XIII) and the medieval 'intelligentsia' (no. VI). The study on the coronation of kings in Hungary (no. I) grew out of his Hungarian-language books on kingship and royal insignia.

From 1979 Dr Fügedi was frequently invited to lecture at the University and after his retirement, when he also assumed the chairmanship of the Medieval Research Commission of the Hungarian Academy of Sciences, he was made professor of history at the Eötvös Loránd University. This belated invitation, part of the University's attempt to remedy its damaging failure of having left the best scholarly forces isolated from teaching for many years, will finally permit students to grow up in Professor Fügedi's seminars. For his eightieth birthday. I am sure, it will be their studies which can be collected into a *Festschrift* for their teacher.

The studies presented here reflect only a part of Dr Fügedi's work: his papers on social history available in foreign languages. The bibliography at the end of this volume contains the titles of his contributions to other fields and those published only in his native language. For the development of the author's approach to history, it might have been interesting to follow the chronological order of the articles' publication; a topical arrangement however, offered a better overview of his field of study. This order follows a 'descending theme': beginning with king and coronation, proceeding with prelates, aristocrats, nobles, intellectuals, immigrant *hospites* and closing with urban history from the major cities down to the semi-urban market-towns. Could we have included the author's important study on the miracles at the grave of St. John Capestrano (published only in Hungarian), commoners and peasants would also have been properly represented.

I am grateful to the editors of the journals and collective works in which the articles first appeared for permission to reprint copyright material; to Mrs Edina Fügedi and Dr Gyula Benda for their editorial assistance; and to Mrs Eileen Turner, not only for including this volume in the Variorum Collected Studies series, but also for the kindness and patience with which she helped me put this collection together.

Dr Fügedi recently formulated his own, and his generation's, tasks in these words: "to aid by means of scholarly inquiry that process by which Hungarian society makes peace with its own past,

with both its glorious and dark ages, with its successes and failures."
For those reading these papers outside the borders of Hungary, the
author performs another important task: to present the society of the
kingdom of Hungary with a keen eye to its specific characteristics
without losing sight of its place in medieval Europe. If these articles
were to encourage readers to widen their research interests by
including Hungary in their historical horizon — that would be a
fitting tribute to Professor Fügedi's achievement.

J. M. BAK

Vancouver,
Fall 1985

I

CORONATION IN MEDIEVAL HUNGARY

On Christmas Day, 1000 A.D., St. Stephen, the first Christian king of Hungary was crowned: to quote the bishop of Merseburg, *coronam et benedictionem accepit.*[1] The crown used at the ceremony had been sent to Hungary by Pope Silvester II and from that date until the end of the medieval Hungarian kingdom in 1526, thirty-six rulers were crowned with it. In fact, the actual number of coronations was even greater, for some kings such as Béla IV (1252-1270) were consecrated twice: first he was crowned as an infant and then again when he inherited the throne. Such coronations took place in childhood in order to ensure the succession, and in all they occurred five times, bringing the total to forty-one over a period of five centuries. Despite this high number, as well as the importance attached to the ceremony, emphasized by the fact that the royal Chancery reckoned a reign from the day of a king's coronation[2] and the chronicles regularly recorded the date,[3] only a few late sources refer to the ceremony itself.

In 1440 the Holy Crown, which was already considered the sacred property of the "nation", was stolen, and an infant of twelve weeks, Ladislas V, was crowned. His nurse gave a short account of the coronation in her memoirs, and this is the first extensive description that has come down to us.[4] A few weeks later, Wladislas I, king of Poland, was elected by the majority of the barons, and inaugurated. This time, two of his attendants, his tutor, the Italian humanist Filippo Buonaccorsi — better known by his literary name Callimachus — and the canon, Jan Dlugosz wrote somewhat contradictory reports of the event.[5] The first detailed and reliable account of a Hungarian coronation dates from 1490, when another Italian

The editors wish to thank J.M. Bak and K. Lawrence for their assistance in preparing this text for publication.

1   Thietmarus episcopus Merseburgenisis, ed. Pertz, MGH SS III.784.
2   I. Szentpétery; *Magyar oklevéltan* (Hungarian diplomatics) (Budapest: M. Történelmi Társ.,1931) pp. 86-87.
3   E. Szentpétery, ed., *Scriptores Rerum Hungaricarum tempore ducum regumque stirpis Arpadianae* (Budapest: Academia Litter. Hungarica, 1937), I, pp. 453, 464, 467, etc. from Géza II on.
4   K. Mollay, ed. *Die Denkwürdigkeiten der Helene Kottannerin (1439-1440).* (Wien: Österreichischer Bundesverlag, 1975).
5   J.G. Schwandtner, ed. *Scriptores rerum Hungaricarum veteres et genuini.* (Viennae, 1746) I, pp. 463-464.

humanist, Antonio Bonfini described Wladislas I's consecration. For the coronations that followed, those of Louis II (1515), János Szapolyai (1526) and Ferdinand I (1527), we have written descriptions, though they are vague and unreliable. Some of the authors were well-educated and informed, like Tubero, who was present at the coronation of Louis II,[6] and Ursinus Velius, an eyewitness of Ferdinand's,[7] but they preferred literary elegance to precise detail, while another author, the court chaplain Szerémy who described the coronation of Szapolyai, was much more interested in gossip and scandal than in the ceremony.[8] Other sources are not much more reliable. The liturgical text, that is the pontifical used for the event, has been preserved only for Albert's coronation (1428), in Latin as well as in a contemporary German translation. The former was published by B. Petz in the eighteenth century;[9] the latter, recently, by J.M. Bak.[10] Apart from these texts there are fragmentary sources at our disposal: casual remarks in the royal charters as well as some studies on objects by art historians.

All the sources mentioned above were known to Emma Bartoniek, a Hungarian medievalist in the inter-war years, who studied the *ordines* and, in particular, the coronation oaths.[11] However, due to the work of P.E. Schramm and his school and to more recent research in the field of ecclesiastical history, especially early medieval liturgy, her results have been rendered partially obsolete. In the last few years J.M. Bak has reconsidered the data used by Bartoniek,[12] and in many aspects I shall follow him. Both Bak and Bartoniek proceeded along the traditional line of historians, beginning with the earliest data, and continuing in chronological order. I shall reverse the procedure, and start at the point where there is plenty of evidence and proceed to the earlier periods where we have only fragments at our disposal.

---

6   *Scriptores* (*v* n. 5), II, pp. 145.

7   G. Ursinus Velius: *De bello Pannonico...libri decem,* ed. A.F. Kollár. (Viennae, 1762).

8   G. Wenzel Pest, ed., *Szerémi György...emlékirata Magyarország romlásáról 1484-1543.* (Mon. Hung. Hist. Cl. II. Vol. I.) Budapest: Magyar Tudományos Akadémia, 1857) pp. 136-137.

9   B. Pez, *Thesaurus anecdotorum novissimus.* Augsburg 1729) Tertia pars, pp. 288.

10 J.M. Bak, *Königtum und Stände in Ungarn im 14-16. Jh.* (Quellen und Studien zu Geschichte des östlichen Europas,Hg. v.M. Hellmann VI) (Wiesbaden: F. Steiner, 1973) pp. 177-178.

11 E. Bartoniek, *A magyar királykoronázások története (The History of Hungarian Coronations)* (Budapest: M. Történelmi Társ.,s.d. 1939), where she summed up her earlier studies.

12 Bak, op. cit.

1. THE CORONATION CEREMONY IN 1490 AND 1527

Antonio Bonfini, a Florentine writer who spent many years at the court of King Matthias Corvinus (1458-1490), engaged, among other things, in writing a "modern" history of Hungary from ancient days to his own time. His *Rerum Ungaricarum Decades* is based on the older chronicles of the thirteenth to fifteenth centuries and is a particularly valuable source for the age of Matthias and his immediate successor. Bonfini had not yet finished his work when Matthias died suddenly in Vienna, but though he may have left Buda for a while, he returned to Hungary to complete his history. In *Decas IV* he gives a detailed description of the coronation of Wladislas II on September 23, 1490 which either he witnessed himself or about which he received reliable information soon afterwards. Bonfini also had access to all official records, and these certainly included the liturgical books used at the ceremony.[13]

Wladislas, the Jagiello king of Bohemia, was elected king of Hungary in a tumultuous diet of June, 1490. A delegation of barons and prelates was sent to Prague, whence they accompanied him to Buda. The date for the coronation was set, and the elected king arrived a few days before, in Féhervár (Alba Regia), the ancient royal city where the kings of Hungary had been crowned since the time of St. Stephen and where most of them were also buried, in the Basilica of the Holy Virgin. According to Bonfini, Wladislas fasted three days, passing his time in religious meditation in order to prepare himself for his consecration and the royal office. On Sunday morning he walked in a solemn procession to the Basilica. The insignia carried in front of him by bishops and barons were: two processional crosses, the royal standard, the naked sword, the sceptre, another sword (in its scabbard), the orb and the Holy Crown of Hungary. As the king walked, his horse was led behind him as part of the procession.

Arriving at the Basilica, the twelve bishops of Hungary gathered at the altar where the crown, sceptre, orb, and the sword in its scabbard had been placed. Wladislas took his seat on a specially prepared pulpit (not the throne). The burghers of the cities of Buda and Fehérvár stood guard in full armour at the Basilica's doors during the entire ceremony.[14] Wladislas

---

13 A. de Bonfinis, *Reum Ungaricarum decades.* ed. I. Fógel, B. Iványi et L. Juhász, Bibliotheca Scriptorum Medii Recentisque Aevorum, Red. L. Juhász, XV. (Lipsiae-Budapestini: K.M. Egyetemi Nyomda, 1941.)

14 According to the statutes of Buda § 6. "Zu des küniges oder kunigin knönung sol derr Stat Richter mit etlichen herren des rats und mit anderen erberen statleuten erlichen ziehen mit yrem folk gen weissenburg (= Fehérvár) do dy kronung sol geschehen. Vnd zu weissenburg süllen sy wol vnd zirtlich geharnascht sten pey der vorderen thüerr an der kirchen, do man den künig vnd dy kuniginn kron. Vnd sullen derr kirchtür jüetten eben so lang, vntz das dy kronung gantz vnd gar geschen ist ..." *Ofner Stadtrecht,* ed. K. Mollay, Mon. hist. Budapestiensia 1. (Budapest: Akadémiai Kiadó, 1959), p. 61.

was ushered to the altar by two bishops, one on either side. The celebrating pontiff's opening speech outlined an honest ruler's duties, whereupon Wladislas, his hand on the Bible, took an oath to defend the Church, protect the weak, widows and orphans, and to maintain the privileges of his subjects.

The king, now lying in *venia* among the bishops on the steps of the altar, was consecrated and, — again surrounded by the bishops — was anointed between his shoulders, and on the wrist of his right hand. After the function, mass was celebrated, during which the canons of the Basilica took charge of the king, leading him into the sacristy where he was undressed and invested with St. Stephen's mantle, gloves and boots. Brought back to the church, Wladislas was again taken to the altar where he was first given the naked sword, and then girded with it, sheathed in its scabbard. He bared the sword, brandished it, wiped it on his sleeve and then returned it to its sheath.

The most important scene followed. The bishops formed a circle around the king and put the Holy Crown on his head. The sceptre, and then the orb were given to him, and finally he was enthroned. The ceremony ended with the *Te Deum*.

After the ceremony the king, his prelates and barons formed a solemn procession; the two processional crosses, the naked sword and the royal banner were carried in front of the ruler. The new king mounted his horse, crown on his head and sceptre and orb in his hands, and rode to the church of St. Peter. There, seated on the throne, he dubbed some privileged subjects "Knights of the Golden Spur" and passed judgement on two exceptionally difficult legal cases. He again mounted his horse, and rode to a hill outside the city walls where he took another oath, three fingers lifted to the sky, to maintain the law, in particular the so-called "Golden Bull" of Andrew II, issued in 1222. Henceforth we shall refer to this oath as the "coronation oath." Next, the king climbed to the top of the hill, unsheathed his sword and made four strokes in the four cardinal directions.

Upon his return to the city a feast brought the solemnities to an end.

This series of acts corresponds with passages in the *Pontificale Romanum* compiled by the French bishop Guillaume Durand (Durandus) in 1292-95 (henceforth PRD). Below these passages are indicated in parentheses, according to Andrieu's edition[15] of ordo no. XXVI. The acts are as follows:

15   M.Andrieu: *Le Pontifical Romain au moyen-âge,* I-IV. Studi i testi, 86-88, 99. (Citta del Vaticano, 1939, 1941), III. Le Pontifical de Guillaume Durand, pp. 441.

1. Fasting of the candidate
2. Procession to and entry into the Basilica
3. Placing the insignia (PRD 1-2)
4. Acclamation (PRD 3-5)
5. Enumeration of the king's duties (PRD 6)
6. Ecclesiastical oath of the king (PRD 7)
7. Consecration (PRD 8-12)
8. Anointing (PRD 13-15)
9. Vesting (PRD 16-17)
10. Girding with the sword
11. Unsheathing the sword
12. Coronation (PRD 21-22)
13. Handing over the sceptre and orb (PRD 23)
14. Enthroning (PRD 24-25)
15. *Te Deum* and closing prayers (PRD 26-29)
16. Moving to St. Peter's, dubbing of knights and passing of judgments
17. Coronation oath
18. Four sword strokes

In the following analysis we shall refer to this sceme by the numbers 1-18.

The first question is whether Ferdinand's coronation in 1527 corresponded to the report left us by Bonfini of the 1490 ceremony. Two sources are at our disposal: the description of Ursinus Velius and a pamphlet in German,[16] which Bartoniek called "the official report." The latter, while much shorter, is clearer and contains more evidence than the story by the learned humanist.

The "official report" does not mention the fasting. If Ferdinand kept it at all, he surely did not do it at Fehérvár, where he arrived with a huge train of Austrian and Czech lords and knights just a day before his coronation. The description of the procession that entered the church and of the placing of the insignia on the altar correspond almost completely to that given by Bonfini. The report differs, however, from Bonfini's description in omitting the sword in its sheath and the two crosses. While mention of the royal standard is also missing in the description of the procession, we do learn that when Ferdinand took his seat in the Basilica, the flags of the vassal countries were displayed by peers on the four corners of the pulpit, and a fifth peer held the royal standard in the middle. It is likely that the royal standard already had a part of the procession, but that the reporter

---

16 Országos Széchenyi Könyvtár, Régi és ritka nyomtatványok tára. Röplap 78.

forgot it. He may have considered too unimportant to mention because it was not placed on the altar and, consequently, played no part in the ceremony itself. I will come back to the question of the missing insignia later.

We do not find any mention of the acclamation at the opening part of the ceremony (Scene 4). Scenes 5-9 followed one another in the sequence reported by Bonfini. The acclamation took the place of the girding of the sword (10). The first secular peer of the country, the count palatine, put the question — in Hungarian — to those present as to whether they wanted Ferdinand to become their king; to which all answered in Hungarian and by a show of hands.[17] Thus the acclamation was not dropped but only transferred to a point immediately before the coronation. Also it was not led by the officiating bishop, but by a secular officer of the realm.

The coronation (12) differed, inasmuch as it was not the bishops, but the officiating metropolitan and the count palatine who jointly placed the crown on Ferdinand's head.[18] The coronation was followed by the handing over of the sceptre, the orb (13) and the sword, and the unsheathing and brandishing of the sword in the manner described by Bonfini (11). Thus only the sequence of the acts was changed. The remaining scenes of the ecclesiastical ceremony followed in the predetermined order (14-15).

Ferdinand also moved to St. Peter's church, but there he contented himself with the creation of the Knights of the Golden Spur. There is no mention of his passing judgments (16). The execution of the coronation oath and the four sword strokes were again identical with the acts of Wladislas III.

A comparison between the two inaugurations leads to the conclusion that both rulers were crowned roughly according to the same ceremonial order. There are only four minor differences: a) the ecclesiastical acclamation was replaced by a lay acclamation within the ecclesiastical ceremony; b) perhaps the sequence of the girding with the sword was altered to insert the acclamation; c) the coronation proper was done by the acting pontiff and the first lay peer; and d) in St. Peter's the passing of judgments was omitted.

In discussing this change of the girding with the sword, we should

---

17 According to the leaflet: "Vnd nachwolgend der Gross Graf zu dreyeñ malen nach einander allweg etwas in Hungarisch zu den Hungeren geredt vnnd gefraget,ob sy Ferdinandum zu einen Künig begeren oder haben wollen, darauff sy all mit grosser stymb vnnd aufreckung yren hennd in jrer sprech durch einander geschrien, Ja er gefellt vns wol, oder wir wollen in haben".

18 ibid. "Vnd der Bischoff von Neytra hat dy Kron von dem Alter genommen, daran vil grosser hungarischen Herren gegriffen vnnd di Kü. Mie. damit gekrönt."

point out that Durand put this act in his *Pontifical Romanum* immediately before the coronation, but not in a mandatory fashion; that is, he left it up to the custom of the country. He did not attach a special prayer to the act and wrote: "Metropolitanus dat gladium sub forma in eodem titulo — De coronatione imperatoris scripta, ubi sic fieri mos est." Bonfini is not quite clear on the matter. He writes: "Tunc ille i.e. metropolitanus sumpto ex ara stricto gladio, quem diximus, 'Accipe, inquit, gladium' . . . Cum ita dixisset, ensem in vagina reconditium illi sc. regi accinxit, 'Super femur', inquit, 'tuum'. . . ."[19] Taking Bonfini's report in the strict sense, there seem to have been two swords, one naked which was handed to the king with the prayer "Accipe gladium" and another, sheathed, which was girded on his waist accompanied by the prayer "Super femur tuum." Logically there must have been two swords because the king could not unsheath a naked one. This fits well with Wladislas I's coronation since, in his description of the procession into the Basilica, Bonfini mentioned two swords, one sheathed and the other unsheathed. He also explicitly referred to these (*quem diximus*) in his description of the coronation.

According to Durand's ordo for the imperial inauguration (no. XXV) the pope was supposed to give the emperor a naked sword taken from the altar while reciting the prayer "Accipe gladium." Hereupon "ense in vaginam reposito accingit illi ensem cum vagina," praying "Accingere gladio tuo." The emperor has to unsheath the sword, brandish and wipe it on his sleeve before enclosing it in the sheath.[20] The text leaves no doubt that only one sword was intended, though it was used twice: once naked and once sheathed. A later source gives evidence that, in Hungary as well, the same procedure had been used. Following the ceremonial order of Matthias II (1608), the sword was taken from the altar by the acolyte, given to the celebrating bishop who unsheathed it and handed it over naked, to the king saying the prayer, "Accipe gladium." Having finished the prayer, the king returned the sword to the bishop, and the acolytes put it in the scabbard. After that, the king was girded with the sword, which he drew, brandished, wiped, and returned to its sheath.[21] These two independent sources then, allow for the assumption that although two swords were carried in front of the king during the procession, only one played a role in the ceremony. Bonfini's description does not allow us to decide whether in 1490 this may or may not have been the case. If we assume there was only

---

19   A. de Bonfinis, op. cit. 4 X 98-101.
20   Andrieu, op. cit., III, pp. 430-431.
21   Országos Levéltár (= Hungarian National Archives). Hofkanzleiakten. Fremde Gegenstände 1. f-o. 327-331, 343-347.

one sword in the ceremony then the difference between the two inaugurations lies merely in the sequence of the acts; the acts themselves remained the same. Nevertheless, given the fact that a century later the girding took place immediately before the coronation, an error of the reporter of 1527 is conceivable.

At this point, we must return to the question of the insignia missing in the "official report" of 1527. As has already been mentioned, four pieces of the royal emblems were not noted: the two crosses, the naked sword and the royal standard. None of these was used in the ceremony. They were not given to the king, but simply displayed inside the Basilica, or carried in front of the monarch in processions outside the church. While they were as much indispensable parts of the royal paraphernalia as sceptre, orb and crown, there is a considerable difference between the two groups. Let us take a look at the parts of the first group separately.

Two of the four emblems were closely connected. The king was commander-in-chief of the country's army; therefore, a naked sword was carried before him. In the early middle ages, the sword as the sign of war played an important role. When war broke out, particularly when the country was invaded, the king sent messengers all around the country with a sword dipped in blood to call up the host.[22] The standard stood for the same royal obligation: the force of barons, knights and warriors gathered under the king's banner when called to arms. It was carried in front of the army held by one of the barons, the standard-bearer (*signifer* or *vexillifer regis*) who was an important dignitary especially in war-time.[23] It was the custom — as we learn from a description of the battle at Mohács in 1526[24] — for the standard-bearer to take off his spurs before going into battle, so that he would not be able to retreat in the face of attack. This was supposed to be "an old custom" of the country. A royal charter of 1291 tells us that in peacetime the standard was kept in the Fehérvár basilica, where it was solemnly raised by the king himself when he was about to announce a war. One cannot help comparing this *vexillum elevatum* with the famous ceremonies surrounding the French oriflamme. Unfortunately, we have no

---

22 Werbőczy I. Hármaskönyve (*The Tripartitum of Werbőczy*) ed. D. Márkus, (Budapest, Franklin 1897). Pars. I. Tit, 3. & 2.

23 The first person, who bore the title was "Laurentius signifer domini regis" Codex diplomaticus Hungariae Andegaviensis, ed. I. Nagy. Mon. Hung. Hist. Cl. I (Budapest, Magyar Tudományos Adakémia, 1881), No. 474, pp. 553.

24 "ingens vexillum Divae Virginis ... a Joanne Dragffio sustentur, cui veteri more calcaria detracta erant ... ne de fuga cogitaret." N. Istvanffy, Regni Hungarici Historia... (Colonia Aggrippinae: H. Rommerskirchen 1724), p. 80 a.

precise information about the later fate of the royal standard, although it is mentioned at the coronation of Charles of Durazzo (1385) and both Dlugosz and Callimachus maintain that a standard was handed to King Wladislas I during his coronation. The use of the banner in the ceremony itself seems to have been a exception, and we shall come back to it later. Banners are also mentioned as part of the coronation procession in 1508, but no special royal standard is identified in the sources.[25]

One of the two crosses was called *aurea pax* and may have symbolized the king as supreme guardian of the peace in his realm. The other was called the "apostolic cross" in reference to St. Stephen, who had been credited with the conversion of the Hungarians to Christianity, and who was supposed to have been invested with the authority and rights of a papal legate. This was the basis for the claim to "apostolic" status of the Hungarian kings and to the privilege of presenting their candidates to the pope for the episcopal sees.[26]

All four objects were, thus, symbols of the rights and duties of the sovereign, but they were different from the insignia used at the coronation. They did not play any role in the ceremony. No ideological or constitutional importance was attached to them as they signified only some of the king's qualities, but not the very essence of his personal rule over the country. It is not surprising, therefore, that in the mid-fifteenth century, when mighty barons secured themselves a share in the safe-keeping of the royal insignia, only the Holy Crown, the sceptre and the orb were put into a chest sealed jointly by the ruler and the barons.[27] Henceforth I will call the former group of signs "royal emblems" in contrast to the insignia proper of rulership *(Herrschaftszeichen).*

---

25 "cum contra Albertum ducem Austrie filium regis Romanorum iniuria nobis illata movissemus et ad venerabilem ecclesiam nostram Albensem pro elevando vexillo nostro accessissemus". Codex diplomaticus Arpadianus continuatus, ed. G. Wenzel, Mon. Hung. Hist. Cl. I., X. (Budapest: M. Tudományos Akadémia 1873) No. 18, pp. 29. For 1385, L. de Monacis (*Carmen seu historia de Carlo II cognomento Parvo Rege Hungariae,* ed. F. Cornelius, Venetiis 1758, pp. 355) reports that the flag broke, when the procession left the Basilica and this was taken as a bad omen. Dlugosz (op. cit. 664) mentions a *banderium vetustum Regni Hungariae* carried by the burghers and guarded during the ceremony but also refers to a *vexillum* in the description of the ceremony. The *Streitfahn* (war-banners) of 1508 are mentioned in a manuscript source and are described as having the image of the Virgin on them by a Venetian observer (cf. Bak n.10, pp. 119, n.42).

26 The idea was first expressed by Bishop Hartwich in his *Vita S. Stephani* (c. 1112-1116). "Crucem insuper ferendum regi velut in signum apostolatus misit" (sc. papa) *Scriptores (v* n. 3) II. p. 1112.

27 Denkwürdigkeiten (*v* n. 4), pp. 260-261.

In summary, then, the 1490 and 1527 ceremonies do not show any essential differences; indeed, we may regard them as identical. Though the ceremony consisted of many acts, there were two clearly discernible parts: an ecclesiastical and secular ritual.

2. THE QUESTION OF THE ORDO.

Besides the "official report," on which we have so far based our study, we have another piece of evidence for Ferdinand's coronation: the pontifical used at the occasion. The ceremony was celebrated by bishop Stephen Podmaniczky, at that time almost the only consecrated bishop in the country, since the great majority of the prelates had lost their lives in the battle of Mohács a year before. We also know that at the time of Ferdinand's coronation, Podmaniczky was already in possession of the beautifully illuminated pontifical, originally made for bishop John Filipec, and presently in the Diocesan Library of Esztergom.[28] The pontifical had been produced before 1490, the year Filipec abdicated and retired into a Franciscan friary in Moravia. Polykarp Radó, who has examined the codex, points out that the script shows two hands. On the basis of a reference to "brother John" in the latter part, he concludes that probably Filipec himself continued to work on the codex after his retirement.[29] Nothing proves this assumption save the identity of the first name, and John is too common a name to warrant such a hypothesis. Even if we accept Radó's argument, we may be sure that the *ordo* for the king's consecration was already finished in 1490, the year of Wladislas's inauguration, as it was written by the first hand.[30] The art historian, Edith Hoffmann, came to the same conclusion, stating that the illuminator of the Filipec pontifical was the same artist who worked on a codex of bishop Kálmáncsehy and on another of the outstanding volumes of the Corvina Library, in both cases prior to 1490.[31] According to Bonfini, Filipec acted as master of ceremonies at the inauguration of Wladislas in 1490.[32] Therefore there is good reason to assume — although we cannot prove it — that Wladislas' coronation was celebrated on the basis of Filipec's pontifical. However, it is quite certain that Podmaniczky used it when he presided at Ferdinand's inauguration in 1527.

The pontifical of John Filipec is, however, a copy of Durand's

28 D. Radó, *Libri liturgici manuscripti bibliothecarum Hungariae et limitropharaum regionum.* *(Budapest: Bibl. Nat. Hung., 1973), p. 459.*

29 V. Bunyitay, *A váradi püspökség története* (The history of the Diocese Várad) (Nagyvárad: Franklin, 1883), III, pp. 320-322.

30 Radó, op. cit. p. 459.

31 E. Hoffmann, *Régi magyar bibliofilek,* (Early Hungarian bibliophiles) (Budapest, 1929), pp. 122-124.

32 Bonfini, 4, X:78 *"Ceremoniarum ordinis prefectura Ioanni episcopo Varadiensi tradita".*

Pontificale Romanum. [33] This implies that Ferdinand was consecrated according to Durand's royal coronation *ardo*. Still, since in the case of Wladislas we could not prove, even if we had reason to suppose, the use of the Filipec codex, then the question is which *ordo* was used in 1490?

The answer may come from Bonfini who quoted the following nine prayers of the ceremony (following in parentheses are the numbers of the scene as listed above that belong to the prayer):

Omnipotens sempiterne Deus, Creator omnium . . . (8)
Christus optimus maximus, filius Dei vivi . . . (14)
Omnipotens et sempiterne Deus, qui reges populi tui . . . (14)
Accipe gladium . . . (20)
Super femur tuum . . . (20)
Coronam sacram accipe . . . (22)
Virtutis et veritatis vergam accipe . . . (23)
Sta hic, rex inclyte . . . (25)
Firmetur manus tua . . . (27)

The best way to demonstrate how Bonfini treated ecclesiastical texts is to compare the prayers in his version with Durand's text. We choose three of the above cited prayers:

Bonfini 4 X 95	Durand, Pont.Rom XXVI.15.
Omnipotens et sempiterne Deus,	Omnipotens sempiterneque Deus, qui Azabel super Syriam et Ieu super Israel per Helyam, David quoque et
qui reges populi tui, ut sacro	Saulem per Sameulem prophetam in reges inungi fedisti, tribue
misericordie oleo tue inungerentur, edixisti; manibus nostris vim tue benedictionis concede quesumus, et Wladislao famulo tuo sub tuo numine regem unungimus, dignam unctionis eficaciam et virtutem in funde, ut munita dextera et corroborato humero fortiter iuste ac sapienter delegatum sibi regnum tuis auspiciis gubernare videatur tuamque sacrosanctam fidem longe lateque tueatur, quod ut a clementia tua impetremus, te per filium tuum unigentum exoramus	quesumus manibus nostris opem tue benedictionis et huic famulo tuo quem hodie licet indigni regem sacro unigimine delinimus, dignam delibationis huius efficaciam et virtutem. Constitue domine, principatum super humerum eius, ut sit fortis, iustus, fidelis, providus et indefessus regni huius et populi tui gubernator, infidelium expugnator, iustitioe cultor, meritorum et demeritorum remunerator, ecclesie tue sancte ac fidei christiane defensor, ad decus et laudem tui nominis gloriori. Per.

33 Hoffmann (*v* n.31), 123.

4 X: 105-106

Virtutis et veritatis virgam
accipe, qua te facinorosos
protere fovere pios et errantes
dirigere, collabantes data
dextera remorari deprimere
superbos et humanos effere,
tueri probitatem et iniqui-
tatem insectari scias oportere.
Divinum illud dictu tecum quo-
tidie repute: virga equitatis,
virga regni tui. Et ideo
dilige iusititiam et iniqui-
tatem odio habe quin propterea quidem te unxit deus
exultationis oleo pre participibus suis, ut sua unctionis
iura servando cum herede suo
filio te perpetuo regnare
posse sentimus

Durand, Pont.Rom. XXVI.23.

Accipe virgam virtutis atque veritatis,
qua intelligas te obnoxium mulcere
pios, terrere reprobos et relevare
humiles et aperiat tibi hostium Iesus
Christus dominus noster, qui de sem-
etipso ait: "Ego sum hostium per me si
quis introierit salvabitur", qui est clavis
David et sceptrum domus Israel, qui
aperit et nemo claudit, claudit et nemo
aperit. Sitque tibi auctor qui educit
vinctum de domo carceris, sedentem
in tenebris et umbra mortis et in
omnibus sequi merearis eum, de quo
David propheta ce init: "Sedes tua,
Deus in seculum seculi, virga equitatis virga regni tui" et imitando ipsum
diligas iustitam et odio habeas iniquit-
atem, quia propterea unxit te deus,
deus tuus ad exemplum illius, quem
ante secula unxerat oleo exultationis
pre participibus suis, Iesum Christum
dominum nostrum. Qui cum eo.

4   X: 101

Super femur tuum accingere
gladio tuo, potentissime,
illudque menti altius imprime
sacrosanctos viros non gladio,
sed fide regna vicisse.

Durand, Pont.Rom. XXV, 15.

Accingere gladio tuo super femur
tuum potentissime et attende, quia
sancti non in gladio, sed per fidem
vicerunt regna . . .

These comparisons suggest that Bonfini did not copy the prayers
word for word but followed their main ideas. He "corrected" their Latin and
did not hesitate to do so even if the Bible was at stake, as in the last of the
texts cited above where the whole passage is taken from the Vulgate (Ps.
45:4). He was not very well versed in theology either and was eager to
replace Christian motifs with classical ones. On the other hand, there can
scarcely be any doubt that he had Durand's *Pontificale Romanum* in front of
him because the first prayer quoted above (Omnipotens et sempiterne
Deus) is not included in the forerunners of Durand. The sequence of the

acts also corresponds exactly with the Durandus-ordo, so we may conclude that between 1490 and 1527 Hungarian kings were inaugurated according to Durand's *Pontificale Romanum*. This leads us to the second question which is how far back can we trace the use of this *ordo*?

We have already mentioned the *ordo* used at Albert's coronation. Andrieu, the most eminent expert, has stated that it was one of the variants of the royal coronation ordo from Durand's *Pontificale Romanum*,[34] that is, essentially the same as had been used in 1490 and 1527.

After Albert's death two inaugurations took place in rapid succession: that of the infant Ladislas V and of Wladislas I. Both were held under extraordinary circumstances. The crown, but only the crown, was stolen and used at the ceremony for Ladislas V, while all the other emblems and insignia remained at their place in the fortress Visegrád. On the other hand, all the paraphernalia were at hand for Wladislas' coronation except the Holy Crown itself.

Wladislas' coronation has been described, as already mentioned, by two learned authors, Callimachus and Jan Dlugosz but they give slightly different accounts of the event. According to Callimachus, first the ruler's duties were enumerated, then the king was consecrated, anointed, vested and given the "apostolic" cross, the sceptre, orb and standard. Next he took an oath to maintain the constitution of the country "coronation oath") and created knights. It was only then that he moved to St. Peter's where he gave judgments in two legal cases. Finally Wladislas made the four sword strokes from the steeple of St. Martin's church, leaning out of the window as far as he could.[35] Dlugosz began his report with the consecration, followed by the anointing and vesting. Afterwards cross, standard, sceptre and orb were given to Wladislas is that order. The coronation oath and the coronation proper followed. The acts in the two other churches are described in the same way as in Callimachus' report.[36]

These two descriptions allow us to reconstruct the following sequence of acts (in parentheses are the numbers of our scheme):

Enumeration of the king's duties...(5)
Consecration...(7)
Anointing...(8)
Vesting...(9)

34 Andrieu III; p. 436, cf. ibid, pp. 319f.
35 *Scriptores* (v n. 5), I. pp. 463-464.
36 ibid, p. 742-743.

Handing over of the apostolic cross and the royal standard...(9)
Handing over of sceptre and orb...(13)
Coronation...(12)
Coronation-oath...(17)
Passing judgments in St. Peter's church...(16)
Four sword strokes...(18)

It seems obvious that an acclamation took place before the enumeration of the ruler's duties. However this is not mentioned by either source, perhaps because the same ritual was also observed at the Polish coronation. The most impressive, and later unknown, acts were the handing over of the apostolic cross and the royal standard. Further, it must be noted that the knights were created not in St. Peter's but in the Basilica within the framework of the liturgy.

For an explanation we should look at the main features of the political situation at the time of the coronation. King Albert died without a male heir, and the majority of the barons decided to exercise their right to elect a ruler who would be able to defend the country against the growing Ottoman threat. They chose the young king of Poland, Wladislas Jagiellonczyk and invited him to the throne of Hungary. At first Albert's widow, Queen Elisabeth, pregnant at the time, agreed to the election, but later when she gave birth to a son, she changed her mind, had the Crown stolen and her son crowned on May 14, 1440. The barons who had elected Wladislas stuck to their choice, justifying it with the argument that an infant could not defend the country. Needless to say, a political reason lay behind this patriotic argument. Young Ladislas' coronation was supported by a minority of ecclesiastical and secular lords; the celebrating pontiff, Denis Széchi, archbishop of Esztergom and primate of Hungary, also belonged to the group of the queen's personal adherents. Nevertheless changes in politics and chiefly the military success of Wladislas compelled the very same prelate to celebrate Wladislas' coronation not two months later.

The most striking innovations, the inclusion of the apostolic cross and of the royal standard in the ceremony, were obviously chosen to express the significant ideas of Wladislas' party, as the comments of the two Polish writers make it perfectly clear. The handing over of the cross was to signify the possession of legatine privileges in "designating" bishops, which, according to Callimachus, the Hungarian kings had enjoyed from the beginning.[37] Dlugosz goes even further, by writing that the cross has been given to St. Stephen by the pope because the Hungarian kings had the right

37   ibid, p. 463.

to "invest" his bishops.[38] Reading these comments, one has the impression that by inserting the apostolic cross into the ceremony, Wladislas' barons wanted to put pressure on Archbishop Szécsi. As to the handing over of the royal standard and the creation of knights within the frame of the main ecclesiastical ceremony, one has to consider the circumstances in 1439 when the military situation was both central for the realm and for the arguments of Wladislas' electors. As Callimachus emphasized: "ut intelligatur regnum ab armis auspicari."[39]

Bartoniek was convinced that Wladislas was not inaugurated with the same ceremony as Albert. She thought that the *ordo* used at the coronation of 1439 was to be found in the ceremonial of Esztergom, now in the Széchenyi National Library.[40] At the time of Bartoniek's research, there was far less information available on medieval liturgies than there is now, and, so she had to proceed by comparing the acts and their sequence with known *ordines*. A comparison of the two Polish reports with the codex in the National Library was obvious.

Since then, Radó has examined the codex. He found there a gloss in which the archbishop of Esztergom was asked to consecrate the bishop of Veszprém. It is probable that these bishops were really consecrated by the archbishop, but this is merely conjecture. Radó has pointed out that the content of codex does not correspond with other pontificals which were definitely made for and used by the archbishops of Esztergom. The weightiest argument he has presented is that St. Adalbert, the patron of Esztergom, is not mentioned anywhere in the entire text. Radó has concluded his examination by stating that it seems almost certain that the codex did not belong to any archbishop of Esztergom.[41] On the other hand we know very well that Wladislas was consecrated by archbishop Szécsi and therefore we may safely exclude this codex from our investigation.

So we are left with the report of the two Polish spectators and can at least state that the acts and their sequence, as set down, do not contradict the use of Durand's *Pontificale Romanum,* with additions motivated by the extraordinary conditions. Moreover, the fact that Wladislas was anointed between his shoulders and on the right arm, in the same way as Wladislas II was to be in 1490 and Ferdinand I in 1527, strengthens the assumption of the use of the same *ordo*.

38   ibid, p. 743.
39   ibid, p. 463.
40   Bartoniek, op. cit. (*v* n. 11), p. 40.
41   Radó, op. cit. pp. 446-447.
42   ibid, p. 447.

Tracing further into the past, we find an interesting peculiarity in the Filipec pontifical. The oath formula for the *rex coronandus* begins with the words "Ego Ludovicus. . ." Radó therefore concluded from the name of the Hungarian ruler, Louis I (1343-1382) and from the fact that the oath of the imperial *ordo* begins with "Ego Karolus. . ." (referring probably to Emperor Charles IV, 1346-1378) that the Filipec pontifical was copied from a text that had been written some time before 1372.[42]

Thus we may dare to say that Louis I was also inaugurated according to the Durand *ordo* on July 21, 1342. At this point we find ourselves in disagreement with Bartoniek,[43] who denied that the name of Ludovicus in the *ordo* implies the use of its original at this coronation. She argued that while copying codices scribes were accustomed to put the name of the ruler at the time into the formulae. However, with the exception of two manuscripts containing the name of Emperor Sigismund of Luxemburg (1410-1437) — one of them with the name of his queen, Barbara, as well — none of the texts collated by Andrieu insert a name into the ordines, but instead write the usual N.[44] Based on this "statistical probability" one has to consider the likelihood of the *ordo's* use in 1342.

There is, however, good reason to believe that this was the first time that a Hungarian king was crowned according to Durand's text, which was, as we have tried to demonstrate, to become the standard *ordo* for the later Middle Ages. The Filipec codex opens with these words: "Incipit pontificale secundum novum ordinem Romane ecclesie compositum per sanctissimum patrem dominum Johannem papam XXII."[45] The reference is to Pope John XXII (1316-1334) who, although he did not compose it, by his recommendation furthered the spread of Durand's compilation which, according to Andrieu, became widely accepted during his pontificate.[46] It could not have reached Hungary for any of the coronations preceding that of Louis I because of the chronology of the inaugurations. Louis' father, Charles Robert I of Anjou was crowned three times: first, as a claimant to the throne in 1301 by the archbishop-elect of Esztergom in Esztergom (and incidentally not with the traditional crown), second in 1309 with a crown made specially for the occasion when he was consecrated by the papal legate to Hungary, and third in 1310, when the traditional "Holy Crown" had been recovered from adherents of other pretenders, because the mighty

43 E. Bartoniek: "A magyar királlyáavatáshoz" ("Contributions to Hungarian inaugurations"), *Századok,* 57-58 (1923-1924), 303.
44 Andrieu, op. cit., III, p. 430.
45 Radó, op. cit., p. 459.
46 Andrieu, op. cit., III.

barons of the realm refused to recognize the validity of either previous coronation. Although we have no evidence to suggest which *ordines* were used in these ceremonies, it is highly unlikely that Durand's work, finished in 1295 and more generally accepted only after 1316 when Rome lent its support, would have already been used in faraway Hungary in 1309 or 1310.

At this point we exhaust our knowledge even to the point of probably conjecture. There is no evidence on the *ordines* of earlier coronations. Bartoniek persisted in thinking that in the case of Salomon (1064) the *ordo* could be identified.[47] She based her belief on the remark in the Hungarian Chronicle that the sentence "Esto dominus fratrorum tuorum..." used in a prayer at the coronation raised discord between Salomon and his uncle. This sentence, a quotation from Genesis (12:29), is indeed part of the prayer "Omnipotens det tibi Deus..." Bartoniek found this prayer in the so-called Egbert *ordo* and assumed that this *ordo* had been used in 1064. Even Schramm accepted this assumption. More recent research has proven that the prayer was used in several *ordines* so the statement loses its absolute validity.[48]

3. HUNGARIAN CHARACTERISTICS WITHIN THE ORDO.

Helen Kottaner, the wet nurse of Ladislas V, wrote in her memoirs: "There are three laws in the Kingdom of Hungary. They believe that if any one of them is disregarded, the claimant is not a legal king. The first law is that which says the king of Hungary has to be crowned with the Holy Crown. The second is that he must be crowned by the archbishop of Esztergom. The third is that the coronation must be held at Fehérvár."[49]

Let us first examine the second of these laws. The archbishop of Esztergom had been ever since the establishment of Christianity the head of the Hungarian church. His preeminence was never seriously questioned, though he only became *primas Hungariae* under pope Boniface IX in 1393.[50]

---

47 Bartoniek, in *Századok* 57-58, (1923-24), 297.
48 Bak, op. cit., pp. 165-166.
49 *Die Denkwürdigkeiten* (v n. 4), p.272. "Wann sy habent drew geseczin dem Kunigreich zu Ungern. Vnd wo der aine abgeet, da mainen Sie, daz er nicht rechtleich Kunig sey. Das ain gesecz ist, daz vnd das Haisst, daz ain Kunig sey. Das ain gesecz ist, daz vnd das Haisst, daz ain Kung zu Vngern sol gekront werden mit der heiligen kron. Das ander, daz in sol kroenen der Ercz Bishoue zu Gran. Das dritt, daz die kronung sol beschehen zu Wissenburg."
50 *Monumenta Vaticana historiam Hungariae illustrantia*, Ser. I., III. Bullae Bonifacii IX. (Budapest 1888), p. 249, no. 280.

I

176

We do not know what year the archbishop of Esztergom received the exclusive right and the privilege to undertake the coronation but an incident furnishes at least one *terminus ante quem*. When in 1172 Stephen III suddenly died, his younger brother Béla succeeded. Béla had lived since his youth at the Byzantine court and, until the birth of Emperor Manuel's son, in 1169 was regarded as presumptive heir. The archbishop of Esztergom refused to consecrate him, perhaps because he suspected schismatic leanings due to Béla's Byzantine education. The Hungarian lords wrote a letter to the pope asking him to grant permission to the other archbishop of the country, that of Kalocsa, "to convocate the bishops to the place where kings are usually crowned and anoint the elected king Béla and put the crown on his head." They promised, however, that Béla would assure in a charter that "this will not prejudice the privilege of the church of Esztergom." The charter was actually issued and, although the original got lost, it was fortunately later (1207) inserted in a papal bull.[51] In 1172, the archbishop was the strict reformer, Lukas, who came from a family of the old nobility and had studied at the University of Paris. Ten years earlier, he had refused to crown the rival king Ladislas II and suffered imprisonment for his determined stance.[52] These facts enable us to state that the right of Esztergom at the coronation dated from before 1162.

Of course, the right of the archbishop of Esztergom is not a special Hungarian characteristic. The medieval church used the coronation to strengthen its own power and control over the monarch. Therefore in every country the question had to be decided as to who had the exclusive right to consecrate the king. Sooner or later it was settled even in those countries where several sees competed for the privilege. In Hungary it seems to have been a foregone conclusion.

The archbishop's seat had been Esztergom. At the beginning of the eleventh century the political centre of Hungary and the royal residence was also Esztergom. On a hill in front of the royal castle stood an impressive and, as far as one can judge from the remaining ruins, beautiful church in which St. Stephen was consecrated. Nevertheless his successors until 1527 were all inaugurated at Fehérvár which probably by the end of the eleventh century counted as the coronation city *par excellence*. Fehérvár,

51 Gy. Pauler: *A magyar nemzet története az Árpádházi királyok alatt* (The history of the Hungarian nation under the rule of the Árpáds), (Budapest: Athenaeum, 1899) I, pp. 320-322.
52 *Monumenta ecclesiae Strigoniensis,* ed. F. Knauz, (Strigonii 1874), I, p. 114.

of course, had been the centre of the ruling dynasty's domains ever since the Hungarian conquest. A small hill amidst a huge marsh had been fortified in the beginning or middle of the tenth century. The church of St. Peter's was built soon afterwards, and Prince Géza, the first Christian ruler, was buried there in 997. About 1015 St. Stephen had a basilica built beside the hill where first his son Emerich (c.1030) and later he himself (c.1038) were buried.[53] When both of them were canonized in 1083 the Basilica became a place of national pilgrimage and, as expected, miracles took place at the tombs. Soon some constitutional acts were also attached to Fehérvár, for example, a session of the court on St. Stephen's day (August 20) is mentioned as early as 1046. All coronations prior to 1527 were held there with the exception of two. The first two coronations of Charles I, as already mentioned, were celebrated elsewhere and this was one of the reasons for challenging their validity. thus both practice and legal expectation support the statement of Kottaner emphasizing the importance of the place. In all likelihood it was the national saints' tomb that had lent particular importance to the Fehérvár Basilica. The vesting of the king points in the same direction.

Vesting, as an act of the king's inauguration, appears in many *ordines*, including Durand's in the *Pontificale Romanum*.[54] The ceremonies we have studied so far stress the importance of the "mantle of St. Stephen." The official report on Ferdinand's coronation is the only one that describes the "royal robe" in general terms as an old ceremonial vestment, richly embroidered.[55] Dlugosz underlines its antiquity and the fact that it was prepared for the first king's coronation.[57] The robe is mentioned for the first time in an Austrian chronicle describing the inauguration of Andrew III in 1290. There, "according to Hungarian custom:"

---

53   J. Deér, "Aachen und die Herrschersitze der Arpaden," MIÖG, 79 (1971), 1-56. "Der Stadtplan von Stuhlweissenburg und die Anfänge des Büngertums in Ungarn," *Acta Historica Acad. Sc. Hung.* 15, (1969), 110-117; by Eric Fügedi.
54   Andrieu, op. cit., III, p. 46.
55   "ainan küniglichen habit. So von Prauner Seyden, vnnd guldinen heiligen pildern vnd plvmewerchen darein gewürckt schier ainem alten Chormantel gemess gemacht, ist angelegt"
56   Bonfini, 4 X 96: "Interea rex in sacrarium relatus deposito paludamento regali divi Stephani regis habitu auresque cothurnis induitur. . ."
57   "Haec autem omnia ornamenta vetustate attrita, pro primi regis beati Stephani coronatione praeparata. . ."

"A holy garment
is put on the king
which St. Stephen had
worn on his body."[58]

The next earlier evidence on the royal insignia is in a royal charter of Ladislas IV (1272-1290) in which land is granted to a canon of Fehérvár "qui ipso
die coronationis nostre nos beatorum progenitorum nostrorum sacris
regalibus ad coronationem consecratis induit indumentis."[59] However a
foreign Cistercian staying in Hungary in 1240 already knew about the "objects of St. Stephen" when he wrote:

"Reges usque hodie
quando coronantur
in prefati Stephani
solio locantur
suis armis inclitis
illi decorantur
qui per regni presules
in reges consecrantur."[60]

As J. Deér points out, the word *arma* can mean all the utensils and insignia,
not just a weapon or weapons.[61]

Finally, the earliest reference to the interest in the first king's
garments occurs soon after his death. In 1046 a revolt broke out which aimed at restoring the "good old customs," chiefly the pagan rites. When the
revolt was crushed, Andrew I (1046-1060) gave orders to a bishop "ut in-
quireret ornamentum et supellectilem regiam."[62] J. Deér attaches great importance to this piece of evidence; surely, he argues, it was a decisive step to
save Stephen's paraphernalia, but it had a different character from the later
reverence for his "relics" since Stephen was not yet regarded as a saint.

If the place of coronation and the vestments used for it pointed to
St. Stephen, even more does Kottaner's "first law," that the kings of

---

58 Ottokar von Horneck, *Oesterreichische Reimchronik*. MGH, SS ling. vernac. V/L. 41,
    222-41, 225.
59 G. Fejér, *Codex diplomaticus Hungariae ecclesiasticus et civilis*. (Budae 1829-1844) VII./2, p.
    54.
60 *Scriptores* (*v* n. 3) II, p. 607.
61 J. Deér, *Die Heilige Krone Ungarns*, Österreichische Akademie der Wissenschaften. Phil-
    hist. Klasse. Denkschriften 91. (Wien: Böhlau, 1966), p. 209.
62 Fundatio ecclesiae s. Albani Namucensis, MGH, SS, SV/2, p. 964.

Hungary have to be inaugurated with the Holy Crown. Its association with the first king goes back at least to the late thirteenth century. The first to emphasize that the Holy Crown belonged to Stephen I was king Andrew III (1290-1301) who wrote in 1293 that he wanted "coronari apud Albam Regalem, prout moris est, corona et dydemate sanctissimi regis Stephani."[63] With the death of Andrew III the native dynasty of Hungary, the Árpáds, became extinct in the male line. The great lords of the country were anxious to elect the new king from the female descendants of the last Árpáds.[64] First they invited Venceslas III, the son of king Venceslas II of Bohemia, to the Hungarian throne. He accepted the offer and was duly crowned at Fehérvár. But since he could not stabilize his position he left in 1304 for Prague taking the crown and other insignia with him. The archbishop-elect of Esztergom excommunicated his adherents because they helped to carry away "coronam sacram beati regis Stephani, ipsius utique regni lugubris gloriam et honorem cum ceteris pertinentibus ad eandem regalibus insignis in Bohemiam."[65]

The theft of the Holy Crown in 1440 by the queen's lady-in-waiting had, as was already mentioned, put almost insurmountable difficulties in the way of Wladislas's party. An elected king was not considered the legal ruler of that country until he had been inaugurated with the Holy Crown and that crown was in the hands of the opposing faction. Wladislas' adherents decided upon an important step. They had another crown made from the crown that was on the head-reliquary of St. Stephen and declared in a solemn document that the newly-made crown would have the same *signamentum, mysterium et robur* as the Holy Crown itself.[66] This document is characterized by two different trains of thoughts. First, it expressed the political concept that the Holy Crown represented the whole nation, and belonged to the whole nation and that it was the right of the nation to

---

63 Fejér, op. cit. VI.1, p. 237.
64 "Demum etiam domino Andree illustri rege Hungarie divina vocante clementia rebus humanis exempto, ultimo avero ramusculo a progenie, sitpre ac sanguine santi regis Stephani primi regis Hungarorum per paternam lineam descendenti extincto, cum universi ecclesiarum prelati ... et barones, proveres ac universi nobiles et cuiuscis status homines regni Hungarie cum se veri ac naturali domino desoltos sentirent, scirent et intellegerent, de morte eiusdem more Rachelis deplorantes et immensum perturbati et admodum soliciti qualiter et quemadmodum sibi divina desuper disponente clementia futurum dominum de sanguine sancti regis populatum possent et valerent invenire" says the palatine. Cod. dipl. Hung. Andegavenisis (v n. 23) I., p. 52.
65 Fejér, op. cit. , VIII.1, p. 187.
66 S. Katona, *Historia critica regum Hungariae* XIII. (Pest: Landerer, 1790), pp. 91-100.

find a suitable person to rule the country and to wear its crown.[67] The second aspect is of greater interest to our inquiry. Although the *praelati, barones, milites, proceres et nobiles totius regni Hungariae* decided to have another crown made to replace the missing Holy Crown, they nevertheless considered the Holy Crown to have been sent by the pope to the first Christian ruler and national saint. Thus, they were not content with a newly-made diadem. They wanted to transfer "the virtues and the mystery" of the old to the new by using the crown from the reliquary of St. Stephen, a crown which had been "in touch with" the saint's body.

The Holy Crown and the mantle used at the coronation which was to take place at the tomb are coherent parts of one idea: that a symbolic and mystical contact had to be established between the *rex coronandus* and the founder of the kingdom, St. Stephen. Hungarians did not compile a special coronation *ordo* like most other nations of medieval Europe, or if they did, they abandoned it at the beginning of the fourteenth century when they accepted a general "official" *ordo* from Rome. Yet beginning in the twelfth century they filled the coronation ceremony, and kept on filling the new *ordo* of the fourteenth century with special references to St. Stephen. Based on the Christian belief in the saints uninterrupted intervention after death, these references placed the national saint right in the centre of the *ordo*.

At this point, however, the critical historian encounters a mire of contradictions. The tomb in Fehérvár was certainly St. Stephen's. The throne in the Basilica could have been his. But neither could the Holy Crown have belonged to him, nor could he have "worn on his body," the mantle associated with him.

Of course it is quite likely that, on the recommendation of emperor Otto III, Stephen received crown and insignia from pope Silvester II.[68] Yet, no evidence for that has come down to us. When Stephen's immediate successor, Peter Orseolo, was driven away by a local rebellion in 1042, he asked for help from the emperor who came with an army to Hungary, and defeated the rival king Aba in 1044. Crown and insignia became part of the booty, and Henry III sent them to Rome.[69] The events were summed up by pope Gregory VII, who, in 1074 in a letter to the Hungarian king, wrote: "Henricus piae memoriae imperator. . . victo rege et facta victoria ad corpus beati Petri lanceam coronamque transmisit et

---

67   "quod semper regum coronation a regnicolarum voluntate dependet" says the document, ibid, 94-95.

68   B. Hóman, "Szent István megkoronázásának időpontja" (The date of St. Stephen's coronation) *Magyar Nyelv* 23, (1927) 443, 452.

69   Pauler, op. cit. I., pp. 88-89.

pro gloria triumphi illuc regni direxit insignia."[70] A recently discovered description of Rome in 1693 mentioned these insignia explicitly as being on show in St. Peter's cathedral. It is very likely that the crown shown on St. Stephen's only contemporary portrait is a fairly authentic representation. There, he wears a crown consisting of a band ornamented with precious stones and four outstanding lilies. The Holy Crown of the later Middle Ages, the one we know today, could not be that of St. Stephen.[72]

Experts who have examined the Holy Crown differ very much on its origin and date,[73] but most agree that no part of it could go back to the beginning of the eleventh century. It would be tedious to report here all the arguments and less than useful, as we can now hope that a scientific examination, made possible by the return of the crown to Hungary, will soon lead to new and more reliable results. For our inquiry it is sufficient to state that the crown of the Hungarian kings is called *sacra corona* in documents from the middle of the thirteenth century. Ascribed to St. Stephen, it has been considered as the sacred property of the nation ever since.

The mantle of St. Stephen is, however, a garment from the early eleventh century. It was not a lay but an ecclesiastical vestment, more precisely a *pluviale,* made in the workshop of king Stephen's queen, Gisella, for the Basilica in Fehérvár.[74] We do not know how and when it acquired

70   A.F. Gombos, *Catalogus fontium historiae Hungaricae aevo ducum et regum ex stirpe Arpad descendentium,* (Budapest, 1937), pp. 1081-1082.

71   P.J. Kelleher, *The Holy Crown of Hungary,* (Roma: American Academy of Rome, 1951. p. 47-48. Kelleher cited J. Ciampini as follows: "Fuit etiam eadem jànua Porta Veronicae . . . sive Sudarii . . . denominata: supra eam autem appensa erant corona, lancea et insignia regis Hungariae ad corpus beati Petri transmissa ab Henrico caesare. . ." This statement of 1693 does not seem to be in concert with other sources of the eleventh century. Arnulph, archbishop of Milan wrote (ca. 1085) in his *Gesta* dealing with the emperor's victory: "Cuius (victoriae) unum insigne tropheum aurata indicat lancea Ungrorum rego violenter extorta et Rome in apostolorum templo suspensa" (MG XX VIII. p. 18). Bonizo says: ". . .capta est Ungarici regis lancea, que per eosdem nuncios Romae delata est et usque hodie ob signum victoriae ante confessionem beati Petri apostoli apparet" (MG Libelli de lite imperatorum et pontificum I. P. 523). Deér (op. cit., pp. 198-200) refused to accept the conjectures regarding the capture of St. Stephen's crown. Gy. Györffy, *István király és müve* (King Stephen and his work), (Budapest: Gondolat, 1977), p. 550, also rejects Ciampini's statement, because the nearly contemporary sources (cited above) speak only of the royal lance, but adopts the view that the crown had been sent to Rome too.

72   Gy. Györffy; "Mikor készülhetett a szent korona?" (= When was the Holy Crown made?) *Élet és Tudomány,* 1971, no. 2.

73   T.v. Bogyay: "Ungarns Heilige Krone. Ein kritischer Forschungsbericht," *Ungarn-Jahrbuch* 8, (forthcoming).

74   E. Kovács: "Casula Sancti Stephani regis." *Acta Historiae Artium Acad. Sc. Hung. 5,* (1958), 181-182.

the role of a royal mantle. We know only that by 1240 according to the Cistercian's verses, it was regarded as such. The cult of St. Stephen could not long antedate 1083, when he was "elevated" at Fehérvár. The 1160's is probable date since by that time the coronation right of the archbishop of Esztergom had already been established and thus the ceremony itself, or at least its outstanding features, must also have been well established. Perhaps we can narrow the gap to between 1083 and 1162 by pointing out that the beginning of the twelfth century seems to be the most likely date. On the one hand some who had known Stephen personally were still alive in 1083, and could scarcely be persuaded to accept the *pluviale* as the royal mantle. On the other hand, the fight against papal claims of sovereignty over Hungary reached its climax at the turn of the twelfth century, and Stephen's "apostolic rights" were certainly used as a weapon in those controversies.[75]

As we know the Durand *ordo* was compiled between 1292-1295. Thus, when Durand's Pontifical was put into practice in Hungary, in all likelihood in 1342, there was a break in the *ordines* used at the coronation. In spite of changing the *ordo* the Hungarian characteristics originating from the twelfth century continued to be manifest. They had been chosen to establish a close contact between the actual ruler and the saint who was both the founder of Christianity and of kingship in Hungary. They aimed to hold the inauguration at his tomb (which was surely his), to enthrone the king on his throne (which may have been his), to vest the king in "his" mantle (which it was not) and to put "his" crown (which could not be his) on the ruler's head. But for the historian beliefs may be as important as facts. It is obvious that from the beginning of the thirteenth century Hungarians believed that they possessed St. Stephen's insignia and so strengthened the actual ruler's charisma by using them at the coronation. In medieval Europe, every dynasty had its patron saint: the Merovingians revered St. Martin, the Capetians St. Denis, the German kings the Three Magi. The newly inaugurated German king had to undertake a pilgrimage after his coronation to the shrine of the Three Magi in Cologne. Their Hungarian counterparts did not need to go anywhere as the spiritual contact with the patron saint was established by the coronation itself.

We have tried to determine the Hungarian characteristics within the *ordo*, yet we have left one feature aside: the role of the palatine in leading the acclamation and placing the crown on the king's head. As we have al-

---

75   Z. Tóth: *A Hartvik legenda kritikájához* (To the critique of Hartwich's legend) (Budapest, Ranschburg, 1942).

ready learned, at Ferdinand's coronation in 1527, the palatine put the question to all present, and after the acclamation, not the bishops — as foreseen in Durand's Pontifical — but the metropolitan and several lords performed the coronation proper. Unfortunately the offical report speaks only of "many" lay peers and leaves us in the dark as to their identity. A year before at the inauguration of János Szapolyai it was the guardian of the crown, an important dignitary since the middle of the fifteenth century, who played the same role. He led the acclamation since the palatine, an adherent of Ferdinand, was not present.[76] Tracing these aspects, we find that the acclamation was led by the palatine at the coronation of Louis II in 1508, but the coronation proper was done by the archbishop of Esztergom.[77] This was the first time that the question preceeding the acclamation was put by the palatine, as we know that no secular officer had any role in the inauguration of Wladislas II in 1490.

4. THE SECULAR PART OF THE INAUGURATION.

The coronation ceremonies did not end with the ecclesiastical service. An additional lay part was subsequently performed that consisted of three acts:

  (16) moving into St. Peter's church, creating of knights and passing of judgments;
  (17) swearing the coronation oath, and
  (18) performing the four sword strokes.

As a matter of fact two acts took place in St. Peter's: the creation of knights and the passing of judgments. However, we consider them as one action not only because at times only one was undertaken, as in the case of Wladislas I who passed judgments only in St. Peter's, or in the case of Ferdinand I who dubbed only knights, but also because the two acts represented together the solemn beginning of effective rule. The spot for these acts was, in fact, a smaller church, where St. Stephen's father, Géza, lay buried. He was the first Hungarian ruler to accept Christianity, though he apparently did not abandon the old pagan rites entirely. In any event, he was the common ancestor of all later Árpáds. We hear first of this grave in

76 Szerémi, op. cit. (v n. 8). V. Fraknói claimed, that according to a Hungarian report of the coronation of Louis II in 1508 the crown was placed on the head of the king together by the archbishop of Esztergom and the palatine. The report could not be traced in the Modena archives (Bak, op. cit., 1973) and I personally have strong doubts about this alleged innovation in 1508.
77 Tubero's report in: *Scriptores*... (v n. 5) II, p. 145: "in qua sepultus fuisse Geysa pater sancti Stephani..."

I

184

St. Peter's from Dlugosz.[78] Up to now, there has always existed an apparent contradiction between his information and a passage in the Hungarian Chronicle that claims St. Peter's in Fehérvár was founded by Béla IV.[79] The building itself, though rebuilt in Baroque style, was constructed originally as an early Gothic church.[80] Recent archeological research by Alan Kralovánszky has solved the apparent problem. Beneath the foundation of the existing church, he found the ruins of another that dates from the tenth century.[81] While the present church may indeed have been founded by Béla IV, this building was placed next to the older one, whence, apparently, Géza's grave was moved.

The relevant passage of the Chronicle tells us that in 1235, Béla IV was inaugurated in St. Peter's but this does not seem likely. The chronicler emphasizes that Béla's younger brother, Koloman, carried the naked sword in front of the king and that his horse was led by his vassal, Danilo, Duke of Ruthenia. These details fit more with the procession from the Basilica to St. Peter's. Though Béla IV had been in opposition to his father before inheriting the throne, it is most unlikely that he would have been uninterested in the mysterious bond that was created between him and St. Stephen during coronation in the Basilica. It is, however, not impossible to consider that, since Béla had been crowned as a child, his second inauguration was held in a different form. Theoretically a man could not be consecrated and anointed twice for the same office; so it is possible that the ceremony in the Basilica was not repeated at all, and only the lay inauguration, that began in St. Peter's, took place.

The history of the coronation oath has been expertly written by Bartoniek and needs little addition. Such an oath is first mentioned in a papal letter to the archbishop of Kalocsa who was ordered to remind Andrew II (1204-1223) of his oath taken at the coronation, to maintain the dignity of the crown and the integrity of the royal domain. Ernest H. Kan-

78 Scriptores (v n. 3) I. 467: "in cathedrali ecclesia Beati Petri Albe, quam ipse consecrari fecit..."
79 Scriptores... (v n. 3) I., p. 467.: "in cathedrali ecclesia Beati Petri Albe, quam ipse consecrari fecit..."
80 J. Fitz, L. Császár, I. Papp, Székesfehérvár. (Budapest: Müszaki Kiadó, 1966) p. 93.
81 The validity of the information of Dlugosz had been questioned by J. Göckenjahn (Beiträge zur Stadt - und Reginalgeschichte Ost - und Nordeuropas. Wiesbaden 1971, pp. 146-147.) Dr. Kralovánszky has not publish yet the results of the excavation.
82 (v n. 79) "Rex Bela ... coronatus est ... in cathedrali ecclesia Beati Petri ..., Colomanno duce fratre eiusdem ensem regalem ad latus ipsius honorifice tenente, Daniele vero duce Ruthernorum equum suum ante ipsum summa cum reverentia ducente"

torowicz points out that this does not prove that Andrew II actually swore such an oath, but only that this was supposed by the papal court.[83] György Bónis, who dealt with the question more recently, comes to the same conclusion.[84]

Reliable evidence is only furnished about fifty years later when Stephen V (1270-1272) admitted in a royal charter that he promised under oath to maintain the rights of all his subjects.[85] The so-called "coronation cross," one of the outstanding pieces in the treasury of Esztergom, originated in the twelfth century but received later additions. The middle of the cross contains a small *staurotheka*, a reliquary with a piece of the "true cross."[86] Thus, it is a fairly correct rendering of the event when Stephen V writes that he took the oath "tactis sacrosanctis reliquiis necnon vivifice crucis ligno interposito."

Subsequently, there is more dubious evidence, when in 1276, the queen says that she promised "iuramento, quod iura nobilium per antecessores nostros alienata et iniuste occupata reddi faciemus et restitui."[87] She did not say that the oath was taken at the coronation, and it seems probable that it was an *ad hoc* oath, such as rulers occasionally made on some laws or pacts.

The first event where we get any information on the content of the oath is the coronation of Andrew III in 1290. According to the Austrian Chronicle already mentioned, the king was asked by the Hungarian magnates to make a promise under oath. The chronicle enumerates seven items altogether, of which the first six were repetitions of the ecclesiastical oath. The seventh was a slightly altered formula of inalienability. The king engaged himself to recapture the territory of the "Virgin's possession" (Hungary) that had fallen into the hands of Austrian lords.[88] Inalienability,

83 E.H. Kantorowicz: *The King's Two Bodies. A study in medieval political theology*, (Princeton, Princeton U.P., 1957) p. 355.
84 Gy. Bónis: "A decretalis 'Intellecto' " (= The decretalis "Intellecto") *Történelmi Szemle*, (1974), p. 23, 31.
85 "cum ad regni nostri gubernacula coronarique accessissemus et per universale edictum omnes barones nostri seu quicunque et qualescunque comitatus dignitates et honores regni nostri tenentes in Albensem civitatem convenissent et nos eisdem inviolabilis fidei firmitatem tactis sacrosanctis reliquis necnon vivifice crucis ligno interposito observaturos promissemus ut singulos singulariter et universos universaliter in suis iuribus illesos conservaremus. . . ." *Zichy oklevéltár* I., (Pest 1871), No. 26, p. 20.
86 *Esztergom müemlékei* (= The monuments of Esztergom), ed. I. Genthon. (Budapest, 1948) I, p. 222.
87 Fejér, op. cit. V.1, p. 237.
88 Ottokar von Horneck, op. cit. 41, 282-41291.

or integrity of the realm was not a special Hungarian idea. Kantorowicz demonstrates how it became a part of the royal oaths, taken over from the duties of bishops.[89] But since the *promissio* of the ecclesiastical *ordo* contained no mention of integrity, it was added to the "secular" oath and became the starting point of the development of the coronation oath, so much so, in fact, that traditional research often called this oath the "oath of integrity".

Unfortunately we do not have sufficient evidence to follow this development step by step. Although the oath of Charles I is known to us, it is an *ad hoc* mixture taken from the ecclesiastical *promissio* and compiled for the special conditions of the papacy vis-à-vis the Anjou king. The king swore:

(1) to keep the Church and the prelates in their rights,
(2) not to oppose the pope,
(3) "regnum sibi commissum et iura regalia non minuere nec alienare,"
(4) "Nobiles regni sui Ungarie in approbato et antiquo iure servare,"
(5) "legitimo coniugio tantum uti"
(6) "populo Dei...sibi commendato prodesse."[90]

Among these promises the third was already known in Hungary — as the reported oath of Stephen V proves — but a new item was added by the fourth, and this one was to last.

After a gap of more than one hundred years, the next coronation which has been described in detail, is that of Wladislas I. We are told that the king "prolatis in medium regni legibus institutisque exigit ut in verba ipsorum sc. Hungarorum iuret."[91] Concerning these *leges institutaque,* we know that in the case of Albert (1438) and Wladislas II (1490), they included essentially the Golden Bull of 1222, which, together with some additions, had been regarded, at least since 1351, as the foundation of the nobility's privileges. When Ladislas V came into actual possession of the throne, he had to swear an oath that was enacted into the law in 1453 stating: "primo dominus rex iurabit, quod regnum suum Hungarie cum suis regnicolis in omnibus et singulis iuribus, libertatibus et legibus ac approbatis consuetudinibus inviolabiliter conservabit, in quibus predecessores sui...tenuerunt et conservaverunt et quod metas regni Hungarie non alienabit sed pro posse defendet et alienata recuperabit."[92]

89   Kantorowicz, op. cit. pp. 347-357.
90   Bak, op. cit. pp. 129-130.
91   *Scriptores* (*v* n. 5), p. 464.
92   F. Döry, G. Bónis, V. Bácskai: *Decreta Regni Hungariae.* (Budapest: Akadémiai Kiadó, 1976), p. 376.

Evaluating the scanty evidence, we may state that in Hungary a solemn oath was introduced at the time that the content of the episcopal oath had been transferred into the royal *promissio*. Yet between 1290 and 1440 the content was enlarged so that, besides the oath of integrity, the fundamental laws of the country were also included and these two items became the core of the coronation oath. Unfortunately our sources do not permit us to offer a more precise chronology.

We know least of all about the four sword strokes. The first observers to report the act were two Polish scholars, present at the inauguration of Wladislas I in 1440. Since that date the four strokes were always the closing act of Hungarian coronations. From the fact that in 1440 they were executed from a tower, while in 1490 and ever afterwards, they were performed from the top of a hill, we may perhaps conclude that in the middle of the fifteenth century, this custom was still *in statu nascendi*. This seems even more likely if we consider that the detailed description of the coronation in 1290 does not mention the act, though it would have surely made an impression on any foreign observer. We do not fare much better with the origins of the act. The four cardinal points play an important role in many coronations, even in the liturgy, but in our case, an obviously pagan rite was introduced, a sheer act of sorcery, based on the belief that a naked sword is able to drive away or to stop the oncoming enemy or any other evil.

5. THE IDEOLOGICAL SIGNIFICANCE OF THE CORONATIONS.

The purpose of the acts performed in the ceremonies of inauguration was to express ideas about power, and the way royal power was to be legally exercised. Hungary, a part of Europe, and bound to Europe by all the ties of Latin Christianity, was also bound in the form and substance of coronations. As we have demonstrated, there must have been a break in the use of the coronation *ordo* some time in the fourteenth century when the *ordo* of Árpád coronations, unknown to us, was abandoned and the new "official" *ordo* of Rome introduced. This was an *ordo* that did not aim at expressing any national peculiarities but was to be suitable for the inauguration of any Christian king. When, after three hundred years of use, an *ordo* is abandoned, we have the right to assume that, from the Hungarian point of view, it had been as uncharacteristic as the new Durand *ordo* was. We have the same right to think that the characteristics to which the nation became most devoted were not a part of the original liturgy. At the beginning of the fourteenth century, the characteristics were implied and in the custom which prescribed the place of coronation and the objects used for it. Both were closely connected with the national saint. They served as ties by which the new ruler established symbolic contact with St. Stephen, and received his strength and virtues. Place and objects were faithfully tranferred into the new *ordo*. It is not important whether the objects (crown and mantle) actually did belong to Stephen. The important thing was that the whole country believed they did.

Before the fourteenth century, an additional ceremony had developed, a secular one, in which the newly-crowned king created knights and passed judgments in St. Peter's church where the first Christian ruler of Hungary lay buried. It was a visible demonstration of the ruler's first and foremost activities: *defensio* and *iustitia*. The introduction of St. Stephen's cult into the *ordo* and the additional ceremony mark the first period in the history of coronations in Hungary. We hardly need argue that it must have been the work of rulers from the Árpád dynasty. They considered, and often included into the text of royal charters,[93] St. Stephen as their spiritual progenitor and used his saintliness in order to strengthen their own charisma. In the same spirit they used the church with Géza's tomb to solemnly and officially begin their reign. Until the fourteenth century these exclusively monarchical features favoured in their whole development the supreme status of the king. The only antagonistic feature was the introduction of a special oath at the end of the ceremony. In all likelihood this occurred in 1270. At first it followed European customs by imitating the episcopal oath. By 1290 it had already become the *conditio sine qua non* for the barons' oath of allegiance.

During the fifteenth century, when royal power was diminishing, the barons took the initiative and filled the old acts with new meaning or created new ceremonies. First the coronation oath received a new dimension. While before 1290 it had contained only the promise to maintain or restore the country's integrity, modelled on the episcopal oath, it now became more political and more detailed by promising the maintenance of the "constitution," that is the older laws and chiefly the Golden Bull. This change was certainly not unconnected to the fact that from the end of the Anjou period hereditary succession became the exception as kings were elected by the nobility and mostly from abroad. With the four sword

---

93 "inherentes felicibus sanctissimi regis Stephani progenitoris nostri vestigiis" says Béla IV in 1270. *Codex patrius* (ed. I. Nagy), IV, No. 28, p. 48. Let me point that Stephen had no male descendants, all later Árpáds were descendants of his cousin.

strokes, another ceremonial act was also introduced, emphasizing that the defense of the country was the king's duty, and only his.

The second trend, reflecting the interests of the aristocracy, carried the day. After the death of Mathias Corvinus in 1490, the true rulers were the barons. This fact left is mark now not in the secular, but in the ecclesiastical part of the ceremony. First, the leading role in the acclamation was taken over by the count palatine. Later, he was to take part in the coronation proper as well. The first step was in line with East European developments and was paralleled in neighbouring Bohemia where the same change had been introduced at about the same time. Still, the Czech king was crowned by the bishops alone in Prague, and the lay peers played no role in placing the "crown of St. Venceslas" on his head. Thus, the victory of the Hungarian aristocracy was more complete. They elected the king, they guarded the crown and the insignia, and, they claimed the right to place the crown on his head. The aristocratic "constitution" of late medieval and early modern Hungary found a forceful and impressive reflection in the major acts of the coronation ceremony.

II

Hungarian Bishops in the Fifteenth Century
(Some Statistical Observations)[1]

In the following few lines I have summed up some facts about Hungarian bishops in the 15th century because, in my opinion, these observations may be of interest for medieval demography, social life and the relation between Church and state. In the Middle Ages the prelates belonged to the feudal ruling class not only on account of their church dignity but, in most cases, also by their origin. However, the extant archives of the Hungarian nobility are generally one-sided: they contain a great number of documents of legal interest, but notes of a family character are almost completely lacking and therefore it is rather difficult to establish the particulars of the secular personalities (date of birth, of marriage, name of spouse etc.). The appointment of bishops involved a complicated procedure like everywhere in medieval Europe and the written records pertaining to it are left over not only in the domestic but also in the Vatican archives, and more than once they contain personal data (e.g. age) which are usually lacking about the members of the secular Hungarian ruling stratum. The monographs of the different dioceses had been usually drawn up earlier and more thoroughly than the history of the worldly dignitaries and thus also the career of the bishops can be easier followed up than e.g. of those who held the office of the *comes palatinus* ranking next to the king. The unevenness in our material is the sin of our earlier historians; beside outstanding monographs, the history of several dioceses has not even reached the phase of a preliminary study.[2]

[1] The present article is the abridged translation of a paper published in Hungarian in the 1965 edition of the Történelmi Szemle (Historical Review).

[2] The material of this paper was actually collected in the course of the preparation of the Hungarian Biographical Encyclopedia in progress. In the Hungarian historical literature biographies were last compiled for the "Pallas Nagy Lexikon" (Pallas Great Encyclopedia) at the turn of the century. This enterprise often used excellent historians (e. g. J.Karácsonyi) It is doubtless that the biographies published in the Encyclopedia encompassed the material of the age and J. Karácsonyi often made use of unpublished archive material. The material of the Hungarian Biographical Encyclopedia under preparation relies on these biographies. My task was to bring them up to date on the basis of sources published since. I did not use any unpublished archive material because it would have prolonged the work by several years. Only bishops Tamás Ludányi and György Berzeviczy formed an exception; in connection with their persons I made use of my earlier archive work.

As an appendix to the Hungarian text of my present paper I added a list of the bishops who held office in the 15th century, to facilitate the checking of the statistical tables. This list contains the name of the bishops, the years of their birth and death, the ecclesiastic offices held by them and the appointments, their origin and the number of their brothers and sisters. E. g. Tamás Bakócz b. 1442 d. 1521; 1480—1521 Provost of Titel; 1486—1491 Bishop of

376

The paper deals with the governing Hungarian bishops of Hungary in the 15th century but, obviously, the lives and work of the first bishops of the 15th century include also the last decades of the 14th century. The same applies to the 1500 year limit which owing to the battle of Mohács and the beginnings of the Reformation has been shifted to 1520. Hence we have extended our investigation to the bishops born between 1325 and 1499. When compiling the data it was my chief endeavour to find out the age, the beginning of the career, the duration of the work and the origin of the person in question. I considered only bishops who actually ruled. I did not include in the list the governors appointed by the Pope, cardinal John of Aragon who held the title of archbishop of Esztergom for some years. As to the duration of their rule I tried to establish the actual dates. The right of patronage was exercised by the king in Hungary and the bishops had often been in actual possession of the episcopate before having received their appointment from the Holy See. According to canon law, the *electus* was practically the same sort of bishop as the *confirmatus* if, with the King's help, he actually enjoyed the income of the diocese. Owing to the "white spots" in my material, I could not choose a smaller time limit than one year as a basis. Medieval Hungary had 15 dioceses, two of the bishops of which were leaders of a *prcvincia* each, in the rank of an archbishop, and all of them belonged under the archbishop of Esztergom who was primate of the Hungarian church-province. My paper contain only 12 dioceses of the medieval Hungarian church-province. I have left out the bishoprics of Szerém, Nándorfehérvár, and Bosnia. All the three of them were situated on the southern border of the country and suffered very early heavy losses in the Turkish wars and therefore the task to collect their material would have been overwhelming. Besides the bishopric of Nándorfehérvár was only titulary in the second half of our period and the Bosnian episcopate was often filled by Franciscans whose origin can be established only in the rarest cases. Even so there are, unfortunately, doubtful cases, underterminable data galore.

*

To judge from 27 cases when the dates of birth and death are known, the average lifespan of the Hungarian bishops in the Middle Ages was strikingly high: 54 years. Although out of the 27 bishops five were killed in action; the average obtained without them yields a lifespan of 57 years. Those who fell in action were not young people. The classification of the average duration of life by the social origin is even more interesting. It is 50 for barons, 51 for noblemen, 59 for commoners and 66 for bishops of peasant origin. If somebody fought up his way from serfdom to the peak of the ruling class he surely must have had a tough body.

The age of the beginning of the career and the average duration of life show an inverse ratio. The average age of their appointment, computed from the 27 known cases, was 26 years. The extreme values are represented by a seven-year old bishop and an eight-year old archbishop. Bishops who were

---

Győr; 1491—1492 Bishop of Eger; 1498—1521 Archbishop of Esztergom; 1500 — Cardinal 1507 — Patriarch of Constantinople. Attended university. In 1487 still *"in minoribus"*. Peasant origin. Had four brothers and two sisters.

barons began their careers at the age of 22 years, noblemen at 24, commoners at 29, and the three prelates who were of peasant origin began it at the age of 37. The extreme value is represented here by Ferenc Bakócz who, following his brother, began his career at the age of 42.

The same inverse ratio can be seen also in the age of reaching the prelacy. Those of our prelates whose age is known were on an average 25 years old, the noblemen 34, the commoners 39 and the peasant bishops were 47. The extreme values are represented also here by a seven-year old aristocrat and, at the other end, by a 55-year old prelate of peasant origin.

At first sight it appears that prelates who had risen from the peasantry offset the drawbacks of beginning their career late and of late episcopal appointment by a long life. However, if we compare the classified data we obtain quite a different picture. Though the bishops of peasant origin survived the barons by 17 years on an average, their long life could not make up for the disadvantage of late beginning. Their rule of 20 years was 5 years shorter than that of the baron bishops. The long life represented an advantage only over prelates from the nobility and of burgeois origin. So far we have examined prelates whose dates of birth are known and found the average to be 26 years when they began their career, viz. earliest at the age of 22, latest at 37, subject to their origin. Let us now take this as a basis. Beside the listed 27 prelates the year of beginning the career can be established in case of 43 persons. If we subtract cautiously 22 years we obtain their assumed date of birth and, together with it, also their assumed length of life. Hereby the number of the examined individuals increases to 70 which enables us to analyse them also by generations. Since we have to deal with very small numbers we have taken intervals of 25 years for a generation as a basis. In our period (1375—1499), out of the five generations the most populous are those between 1375—1474. On examining the presumed and known lifespans we find that the age of the prelates who fell on the battlefield (and now their number is not 5 but 8) causes a significant deviation only in the generation of 1475—1500. Let us bear in mind that three members of this generation fell in the battles agains the Turks and the oldest of them was not more than 45 years whereas the age of the bishops killed in action in the earlier generations was 45—70 years, which means that the youngest of them was of the same age as the oldest of those. If we disregard this generation which perished in the tragic battle of Mohács concluding the Hungarian Middle Ages, or in other Turkish battles, the averages of the four generations whose numbers are higher (12—16 persons), are found to fluctuate between 54 and 50 years, i.e. do not significantly deviate from the average of the total values (57 years). The cause of the deviation lies in the social position. The higher the number of the prelates of baronial origin, the lower the average length of life of the generation in question. The highest value is attained when the ratio of prelates of peasant origin is the highest. This means that in the 15th century the average duration of life did not change and any change in the average lifespan of the different generations can be attributed to the change in the social structure. In the feudal age peasants seemed to live longest, aristocrats, shortest. Obviously their living conditions should be investigated. It clearly follows from the tables that, with the exception of the battle of Mohács, it was not the military actions and not the epidemics but, in my opinion, primarily the nutritional conditions that tended to shape the duration of life.

In connection with age we can rise one further question: how far was the composition of the Hungarian episcopacy constant by the age of bishops. Three cross-sections yield the following ages:[3]

1433:		38, 44, 50, 52, 55, 56, 58, 59, 60
1466:	27, 30, 32, 39, 43, 47, 55, 58, 58, 58, 59
1499:	20, 41, 42, 47, 49, 49, 51, 55, 57, 58, 59, 63

It strikes us at first sight that generally the age of the Hungarian bishops was above 45 (they form the majority), and young bishops were rather rare. The three series reveal also another trend. In 1433, at the end of the rule of King Sigismund, the episcopates were held by persons belonging to the old-established (1402!) ruling stratum,[4] and even the youngest bishop belonged to this stratum. The middle position of the series is held by the 55 years old archbishop of Esztergom, and most of the bishops were over 50. In 1466, King Matthias (then 23) reinforced the Bench of Bishops with members faithful to the Hunyadi clan. This is where the three youngest prelates belong. The middle age (47 years) is represented by the Chief Chancellor whereas the "old" were left over from the time of King Ladislaus V (1452—1457). Then the majority of the bishops were not yet quite 50 years old. In 1499, again the older persons prevailed; we find nobody from the generation of the 30 year old. Bishop György Szatmári who had risen in the Jagello period (1490—1525) was also as old as 42 years. With the exception of four prelates they belonged, to the legacy of King Matthias' age; the middle value (50) is still five years lower than in 1433.

*

In the development of the stratum of secular officials the Hungarian historians recently attribute great importance to university studies. Out of our 75 bishops 36 (i.e. 48.0%) had attended university. We find no significant deviation as to the length of ruling the dioceses; in fact those, who had attended university spent less time in the pontifical see than the others. It is not surprising that the highest number of university graduates can be found the bishops of peasant origin (only one of them had not attended the university). In the endeavour to achieve higher social positions they had to make use also of this opportunity. As far as the nobility is concerned a strange situation arose: though the career of university graduates was longer, the term of their office was shorter which means that their term of expectation was prolonged. Of the 15 prelates of noble origin who had attended university ten were in the king's service: they were royal secretaries, officials at the Chancery or treasurers. They had to serve the King for a long time to get a bishopric. It is especially striking that out of the prelates of burgeois origin none had attended university.

[3] All bishoprics were filled only in 1499. In 1466 there was one, in 1433 there were three vacancies.
[4] The rule of King Sigismund met with a strong resistance of the barons and it was not before 1402 that the king could consolidate his rule by making a pact with one of the aristocratic leagues (headed by the Garai family). The king passed over the rule of the country to the members of the league and, devoting the last 30 years of his long rule to the problems of world politics, he lived mostly abroad.

Concerning university attandance by generations all we can venture to say is that the barons and the landed nobility studied in increasing numbers. This statement, however, can also mean that for episcopal appointments university degrees were increasingly required and so this problem cannot be solved definitively without compiling and studying the statistics about Hungarian students attending foreign universities.

*

Let us now reverse the course of our studies and examine each leader of a diocese as a separate person and the length of their rule. Instead of the average of 19 years computed above we obtain an average term of 11 years and instead of 100 bishops we get 131. It becomes, however, apparent even from this table that the bishops of baronial origin spent the longest time in office, and most of the prelates came from the ranks of the nobility. If the barons and the nobility are taken to form one single layer of the feudal ruling class then, by the number of bishops of such origin and by the duration of their rule, this will be found to be by far largest group. This is emphasized all the more by reducing the number of bishops to their actual number (100), i.e. by counting each person governing several bishoprics, as one. In this case more than half the number and roughly 2/3 of the years of rule are accounted for by persons belonging to the nobility. The group of commoners displays the most interesting features. It contains only 11 persons which in itself sufficiently proves that the Hungarian townships had no weight in the leadership of the country. But the insignificance of the Hungarian burgeoisie is stressed even more if we realise that out of the 11 persons only four hailed from Hungary whereas the others came from Czech, German, Italian or Dalmatian bourgeois families in the Monarch's service. It is obvious that our foreign bishops had earned merits in the service of the king and even though they may have shown greater understanding for our towns than the barons or the noble Hungarians they could not feel so much attachment to the single towns as the Hungarians to their own native towns. In other words: our towns had no advantage from the diocese being headed by a prelate of commoner origin.

Hence the low number and the even lower term of office of the peasant bishops are not surprising. What is more interesting is the chronology of their appearance. The first prelate of peasant extraction György Handó appeared in 1479, during King Matthias. No bishop of serf origin can be traced before him, not even during the rule of King Matthias (1458—1490). Up to 1476 the King asked for the appointment of 11 bishops in which group we find barons and noblemen faithful to the Hunyadi clan in the sixties. In 1465 the first real favourite, János Beckensloer from Silesia appeared. In 1471, a plot was hatched by against the King those who did not wish him to abandon the fight against the Turks and to conquer the West. The plot was headed by János Vitéz, archbishop of Esztergom, who had supported the father of King Matthias, János Hunyadi, for many years in his fight against the Turks. Beside the old archbishop there were two other bishops involved which sped up the sudden advance of the favourites. In 1472 Beckensloer was followed by the Italian Gábor Rangoni and in 1476 by the Moravian János Filipec. In the meanwhile two other big-landowners obtained bishoprics but we still do not find any prelates of serf origin. In 1479 Beckensloer who had in the meantime become archbishop of Esztergom escaped and in 1486 again a man of serf origin became a prelate. Handó was then followed by Tamás Bakócz. This shows the chronological background of the transformation brought about by the Monarch, heading for centralization, but it also points to the necesarry recessions imposed on him by the political situation of the country.

After the death of King Matthias not more than three persons of serf origin succeded in becoming prelates. Tamás Bakócz helped his brother Ferenc to become a prelate, the second became a bishop as a reward for his long state service. About 20 years later another gifted man, free of moral inhibitions like Tamás Bakócz, made the big leap: László Szalkai became bishop of Vác in 1513. He was the last prelate of serf origin; in the Jagello age again the members of the nobility played the leading role although the archepiscopate of Esztergom continued to remain in the possession of prelates of bourgeois and of peasant origin. Before 1526 the members of serf families had the opportunity to reach the episcopal see, only during the period of centralization of King Matthias; the others were individual exceptions.

The position of the different social classes was reflected not only in the over-all changes but also in individual fates. True, the term of office of the baronial descendants was shorter but taken together they spent more in the pontifical see than the rest. The year of 1465 i.e. the appointment of Beckensloer is the turning point. Before 1465 we do not come across any prelate of peasant origin, but after this year their waiting time was the longest (52.1% of their term of office). Although before 1465 prelates of bourgeois origin had to wait a longer time for their episcopal appointment (58.3%), after 1465 they, too, reached the bishopric much quicker, their waiting time fell to more than a half (23%). The commoners appointed before 1465 were members of King Sigismund's Chancery and were appointed bishops only after a long service, and this ratio could not be changed even by the sudden appointment of two of the three Florentine commoners. If we compare this fact with the burgeois prelates of King Matthias and of the Jagellos we find a striking difference. Filipec had not held any lower church office. The longest waiting time was 12 years i.e. three years less than the shortest in the age of King Sigismund. Also the waiting time of bishops coming from the landed mobility became shorter, in fact after 1465 two of them became bishops without any waiting. Before 1465, only two barons belonging to the highest social stratum began their career as bishops, after 1465 there were already four. Nothing could be more characteristic of the development of feudalism in Hungary than the fact that also the waiting time of the barons decreased. In this respect the change set in during the reign of King Matthias. Out of the four prelates of baronial origin appointed in the time of King Matthias only two had to wait in a lower office but even these two only for a minimum time (one and four years, respectively). In the Jagello age out of four prelates two had to wait five and nine years respectively for the pontifical appointment.

On the whole our tables confirm our observation made in respect of bishops whose age was known that baronial bishops spent the longest term in office (67.3%) and the peasant ones the shortest (47.9%).

When examining the episcopal appointments by dioceses we found it striking that 100 bishops had held 131 bishoprics. This number will be even higher if we include the episcopates of Szerém, Bosnia and the other small bishoprics at the southern border: we have found 38 pontiffs who held not one but several bishoprics each, sometimes two or three or even four. Out of eight bishops of Eger only two, out of 16 bishops of Várad only eight, and out of 12 archbishops of Kalocsa only seven who had not been bishops earlier somewhere else. Out of the "transitory" dioceses Szerém holds the leading position: six bishops of Szerém were transferred to some other dioceses. Szerém was followed by Vác and Veszprém but even from the diocese of Transylvania five bishops went over to some other bishoprics. And the time needed for a person to hold several bishoprics, was not very long either! There were bishops who held two episcopates over six years and three episcopates over five. Migration is probably to be attributed to the difference in the income.

Though it is impossible to establish accurately the revenues of the Hungarian episcopates, the interrelation of the incomes and their average amounts can still be determined from approximate data. Our first source is the amount of the papal servitia.[5] This amount was fixed for each bishopric and since the same rate was applied it shows in equal ratio the incomes of the different dioceses. However, the extant servitium-list requires a certain correction just in this respect. First, because it was drawn up at an age when the sources of income were still quite different, second, and this is the most striking, the income of one of the bishoprics, that of Eger, was set rather low. This latter may have had several reasons. Partly it was the duty of the bishop of Eger to provide about the education of the fourth son of the King and this duty involved an enormous loss of income — if the King really had several sons; besides it is possible that the income of the bishopric of Eger increased, as time went by, together with agricultural productivity.[6] Owing to these reasons instead of using the papal servitium as our basis we resorted to the data included in the report of the envoys of Venice. Disregarding sporadic data the report of Vincenzo Guidotto of 1525 deals in greatest detail with the episcopal incomes.[7] On some points we can check his data and we find that, on the whole, he was correctly informed about the incomes of the Hungarian bishops. The maximum deviation can be that he overestimated the income of the archbishop of Esztergom (35.000 florins) and somewhat underestimated that of the bishop of Eger. In our opinion the Venetian diplomat included in the income of the archbishop of Esztergom also the revenue of 10.000 florins paid out to him in his capacity of Chancellor and thus what he computed was not the archepiscopal income but that of Szalkai personally.

In case of Eger we must point out that, according to the accounts left over,[8] the revenue amounted to about 18.6 to 17.7 thousand florins but this does not include the value of the produce (wine, cereals, lambs, etc.) received as tithe. Hence it must have been much higher. In a report from 1516, likewise

[5] B. MAYER: *Pápai bankárok szerepe Magyarországon a középkor végén* (Role of Papal bankers in Hungary in the late Middle Ages). Századok 57—58/1923—1924, p. 651, note 3.
[6] Mainly because in the diocese, round Tokaj, intensive wine-growing developed, and this increased the income from tithes.
[7] I. BALOGH: *Velencei diplomaták Magyarországról (1500—1526)* [Venetian Diplomats about Hungary (1500—1526)]. Szeged 1929 p. LXXIX.
[8] From the period of the rule of Tamás Bakócz a book of accounts covering two years was left over. K. KANDRA: *Adatok az egri egyházmegye történelméhez. II. Eger 1887* (Some data about the history of the diocese of Eger II). Eger 1887. pp. 33—458.

by a Venetian diplomat, Eger figures with 32 thousand florins which is again an overstatment. In 1516, the bishop was Hippolit of Este and it is mentioned that at the time of report, owing to the absence of Hippolit, the income did not amount to more than 4 thousand florins. In the bishop's absence the revenue obviously significantly declined but the amount of 32 thousand florins must have been suggested by optimistic reminiscences of the age of Tamás Bakócz. We assess the revenue of the archbishop of Esztergom at 25 thousand florins, leaving the revenue of the bishop of Eger at 22 thousand florins as we had no figure from another source to substitute it with. The tabulation confirms what we have said about episcopal appointments with the additional statement that bishops from baronial families had an advantage in respect of the income and that the favourable position of the nobility was even more oppressive. We have also seen in cases of prelates who held office in several dioceses that, with one or two exceptions, all of them made a change to the better. The exceptions can be traced back either to some external impact (e.g. Szatmári was compelled to renounce the bishopric of Transylvania), to the obtention of the title of archbishop or to such a case when e.g. the diocese of Szerém threatened by the Turks was exchanged for a bishopric with a smaller income but situated farther away from the frontier. It further follows from the table that the dioceses with the greatest turnover (Esztergom, Eger, Várad, Kalocsa) yielded, at the same time, the greatest income.

*

It is clear from the foregoing that in the Hungarian episcopal appointments people from baronial and noble families played a leading part. Our last task is to examine this problem from the angle of the noble families. Owing to our scanty genealogical knowledge, we could only clear up the family background of 60 prelates out of 100. It follows from the very nature of things that most of the data refer to barons. If we compile the number of brothers and sisters the first thing that strikes us is that, with one exception, we do not know of a single prelate to have been an only child. The bishops of baronial origin had the highest number of brothers and sisters (3.7), and the commoner prelates the lowest (1.5). In most cases three or more brothers or sisters remained at home in the bishops' families. This was the case in 19 families of baronial bishops, in 11 families of noble ones, in one family of a commoner in three families of serfs. This represents more than one half (56.9%) of all known cases.

Let us resort now to the cases when one family gave more than one bishop in the 15th century, in the Héderváry family, one son of three chose the ecclesiastic profession but at the turn of the 15th and 16th centuries not one of five brothers took the orders. This could be observed in the Kanizsai family even earlier: in the 14th century one of four and five brothers became a bishop, but in the next generation out of the four male members not one did so.

In the Báthory family of the 14th century out of three and four brothers there was always a priest but in the 15th century the ecclesiastic career was chosen only if there were many children (seven and ten brothers). Let us take the Váradi family who were commoners: out of three brothers there was always one to become a bishop even at the end of the 15th century. The Rozgonyi family hardly fits into the picture: its members begin to embrace ecclesiastic professions at a later date and the family ist not very populous then. From all this we can conclude, for the time being, that the baronial families always had a chance to send one of their numerous children to become a priest. Among the simple noblemen, even with fewer children, there was a certain inclination to have one family member in the ecclesiastic profession and whenever one of them succeeded in reaching a higher church dignity, he helped a priest member of the next generation to follow his example. Another conclusion would be that the financial position of the middle nobility demanded the reduction of the number of male members in the family i.e. the prevention of the division of land.[9] It would be, however, one-sided to ascribe the choice of career exclusively to demographic factors, especially in case of the barons. Here we must partly point out that also other aspects influenced the matter, such as corporal unfitness to military life, vocation (Ferenc Perényi was considered a fool for his attachment to arts), the political position or other possibilities of the family (one of the bishops of Csanád received the bishopric from his uncle upon whom the king had conferred the right of patronage as a favour).

Besides we must also examin the interconnection between the secular clerical stratum and the ecclesiastic grants of the central authority. If somebody took only the lower orders, he did not bar himself from a secular career. This is why there are so many not ordained priests among the appointed bishops. During the rule of King Matthias 24 bishops were appointed of which exactly one quarter (six) were not consecrated (not to speak of archbishop Hippolit who, being a child, could not be consecrated). Out of the six persons in question, three were employed at the Chancery. In the age of King Sigismund, these employees received rather the incomes of abbeys and more than one of them did not take the ecclesiastic orders. In the time of King Matthias a distinct type of bishopric was due to officials of the Chancery who did their work well. In other words: even in King Matthias's centralized finances there was no other possibility than to cover the salary of the employees from ecclesiastic revenues. And it is characteristic that Tamás Bakócz, creature of King Matthias, made the greatest career even in financial respect. It was he who established one of the most significant family fortunes of the 16th century from his ecclesiastic income.

[9] The Law of the Hungarian nobility did not know the institution of primogenitura; the family estate was equally divided among the grown-up sons.

1. Bishops of known age

Name	Age at			Term of office in years	Origin
	death	beginning of career	episcopal appointm.		
1. Hippolit of Este	41	8	8	33	ruling class
2. Miklós Báthory	71	34	34	37	baron
3. László Geréb	50	19	23	27	,,
4. Ferenc Perényi*	26	·7	7	19	,,
5. István Podmanicki	50	—	—	18	,,
6. János Szokoli	54	26	27	27	,,
7. Ferenc Váradi	50	26	35	15	,,
8. János Csezmicei	38	17	26	13	nobleman
9. Ferenc Csaholyi*	30	18	18	12	,,
10. János Erdődy	45	28	40	4	,,
11. Simon Erdődy	54	16	29	25	,,
12. György Lépes*	67	27	52	15	,,
13. Zsigmond Thurzó	47	30	37	10	,,
14. Osvát Tuz	63	30	30	33	,,
15. János Vitéz	64	25	37	27	,,
16. János Beckensloer	62	37	38	25	commoner
17. Péter Beriszló*	45	25	37	8	,,
18. János Buondelmonte	59	19	34	24	,,
19. János Filipec	78	45	45	15	,,
20. György Szatmári	67	37	42	25	,,
21. János Uski	51	15	48	3	,,
22. Péter Váradi	51	24	30	21	,,
23. Ferenc Bakócz	64	42	55	13	peasant
24. Tamás Bakócz	79	37	44	35	,,
25. László Szalkai*	54	32	41	13	,,
26. Máté de la Bischino	42	23	23	19	unknown
27. Gábor Veronai	66	32	50	16	other

* = fell in action

2. *Average lifespan, age at beginning of career, at appointment, term of office*
(Based on data of table 1.)

Origin	Average lifespan	Average age at beg. of career	Average age at appointment	Average term of office in years
Baron (2—7.)	50	22	25	24
Nobleman (8—15.)	51	24	34	17
Commoner (16—22.)	59	29	39	17
Peasant (23—25.)	66	37	47	20
Total (1—27.)	54	26	34	19

3. *Average lifespan by generation*
(Based on known and assumed age)

Date of birth	Number of persons	Average term of life	Average term of life without those who fell in action
1325—49	2	76	76
1350—74	7	64	62
1375—99	14	57	57
1400—24	16	56	56
1425—49	13	60	60
1450—74	12	54	54
1475—99	7	43	50

4. *Average lifespan and origin*
(Based on known and assumed age)

Date of birth	Average lifespan	Total	barons	noblemen	commoners	peasant	unknown
					by origin		
a) *In absolute numbers*							
1375—99	57	14	5	5	3	—	1
1400—24	55	16	6	7	—	—	3
1425—49	60	13	2	5	2	4	—
1450—74	54	12	5	3	3	1	—
b) *Percentage*							
1375—99	57	100.0	35.7	35.7	21.4	—	7.2
1400—24	55	100.0	37.5	43.8	—	—	18.7
1425—49	60	100.0	15.4	38.5	15.4	30.7	—
1450—74	54	100.0	41.7	25.0	25.0	8.3	—

5. *Term of office of bishops*

Origin	Total	Term of office total	Term of office as prelate
Barons	26	35	24
Noblemen	25	31	17
Commoners	11	25	15
Peasants	5	29	14
Total	67	31	19

6. *Distribution of term of office*

Origin	Appointed before and after 1465 total office	Appointed before and after 1465 waiting time	Appointed before and after 1465 as prelate	Appointed before 1465 total office	Appointed before 1465 waiting time	Appointed before 1465 as prelate	Appointed after 1465 total office	Appointed after 1465 waiting time	Appointed after 1465 as prelate
a) *In absolute numbers*									
Barons	913	292	621	627	259	368	286	33	253
Noblemen	827	385	422	570	285	265	257	100	157
Commoners	280	111	169	132	77	55	148	34	114
Peasants	144	75	69	—	—	—	144	75	69
Total	2164	863	1281	1329	621	688	835	242	593
b) *Percentage*									
Barons	100.0	32.0	68.0	100.0	41.3	58.7	100.0	11.7	88.3
Noblemen	100.0	46.6	53.4	100.0	50.0	50.0	100.0	38.9	61.1
Commoners	100.0	39.6	60.4	100.0	58.3	41.7	100.0	23.0	77.0
Peasants	100.0	52.1	47.9	100.0	—	—	100.0	52.1	47.9
Total	100.0	39.9	60.1	100.0	48.2	51.8	100.0	29.0	71.0

7. *Distribution of waiting time per head*

Origin	Waiting time in year for total	canons	abbots	provosts	others
a) *Appointed before 1465*					
Barons	16	5	2	7	2
Noblemen	18	7	1	9	1
Commoners	26	3	5	18	—
Peasants	—	—	—	—	—
Average	18	6	2	8	2
b) *Appointed after 1465*					
Barons	3	1	—	1	1
Noblemen	10	5	—	5	1
Commoners	6	2	—	4	—
Peasants	15	—	—	13	2
Average	8	2	—	5	1

8. *Term of office of bishops having attended university*

Origin	Number	Term of office in years	
		total	as prelate
Barons	14	38	24
Noblemen	15	30	14
Commoners	1	27	21
Peasants	4	30	14
Unknown	2	12	7
Average		32	18

9. *Bishops having attended university, by generations*
(Based on known and assumed age)

Time of birth	Total	Social origin				
		barons	noblemen	commoners	peasants	unknown
1325—49	2	2	—	—	—	—
1350—74	3	2	1	—	—	—
1375—99	4	2	2	—	—	—
1400—24	8	3	5	—	—	—
1425—49	8	1	3	—	4	—
1450—74	7	3	3	1	—	—
1475—99	3	1	2	—	—	—

10. *Bishops of four generations having attended university*

Time of birth	Barons		Noblemen		Commoners	
	total	university graduates	total	university graduates	total	university graduates
1375—99	5	2	5	2	3	—
1400—24	6	3	7	5	—	—
1425—49	2	1	5	3	2	—
1450—74	5	3	3	3	3	1

11. Episcopal appointments

Diocese	Total		Barons		Noblemen		Commoners		Peasants		Unknown	
	numb.	years	numb.	years	numb.	years	numb.	years	numb.	years	numb.	years
a) *In absolute numbers*												
Esztergom	7	122	2	57	2	24	1	6	1	24	1	11
Eger	11	112	4	42	2	12	1	6	1	7	3	45
Győr	9	127	2	46	4	58	1	4	2	19	—	—
Nyitra	14	125	4	48	4	13	—	—	—	—	6	64
Pécs	8	146	4	104	2	15	1	16	—	—	1	11
Vác	10	113	2	36	4	40	—	—	1	10	3	27
Veszprém	12	104	4	27	4	62	3	14	—	—	1	1
Kalocsa	12	109	3	26	2	22	3	49	1	2	3	10
Csanád	9	124	3	53	2	21	1	7	—	—	3	43
Erdély	14	119	3	42	6	48	—	—	1	1	4	28
Várad	16	120	2	18	3	38	4	39	1	6	6	19
Zágráb	9	119	1	12	4	74	2	11	—	—	2	22
Total	131	1440	34	511	39	427	17	152	8	69	33	281
b) *Percentage*												
Total number		100.0		26.3		30.0		13.1		6.1		24,5
Total years		100.0		35.5		29.7		10.6		4.7		19,5
c) *Corrected*												
Total number	100		26		31		9		9		30	

12. Persons holding several bishoprics

Number of episcopal appointments	Number of bishops					
	total	barons	noblemen	commoners	peasants	unkown
1	63	10	20	6	2	25
2	26	13	8	—	1	4
3	8	2	3	2	1	—
4	3	1	—	1	1	—
Total	100	26	31	9	5	29

13. *Migration among bishoprics*

Name	Origin	Income of bishoprics in 1000 florins			
		1	2	3	4
D. Csupor	baron	?	?	?	13
Gy. Szatmári	commoner	26	12	25	25
L. Szalkai	peasant	20	4	22	25
J. Albeni	baron	25	12	18	
D. Szécsi	baron	22	4	25	
M. Bácskai	nobleman	4	5	24	
Zs. Thurzó	nobleman	24	4	26	
J. Gosztonyi	nobleman	13	4	24	
J. Beckensloer	commoner	22	26	25	
L. Szegedi	commoner	3	?	18	
T. Bakócz	peasant	22	13	25	
M. Báthory	baron	4	5		
M. Csáky	baron	3	5		
G. Frangepán	baron	20	12		
L. Geréb	baron	20	24		
R. Herceg	baron	20	?		
D. Jakcs	baron	26	?		
J. Kanizsai	baron	25	22		
G. Kun	baron	4	5		
J. Ország	baron	4	5		
E. Perényi	baron	26	24		
P. Rozgonyi	baron	22	12		
S. Rozgonyi	baron	22	12		
F. Váradi	baron	24	4		
M. Gatalóci	nobleman	12	4		
M. Kápolnai	nobleman	12	4		
T. Ludányi	nobleman	22	5		
Gy. Pálóci	nobleman	25	24		
A. Vetési	nobleman	12	4		
J. Vitéz	nobleman	25	26		
O. Nagylucsei	nobleman	22	13		
Kálmáncsehi D.	peasant	24	26		
J. Dominis	unknown	26	?		
Miklós	unknown	4	?		
G. Veronai	unknown	22	24		
P. Agmándi	unknown	20	4		

14. Income of Hungarian bishoprics

Dioceses	Papal servitium	Report of 1525	Corrected income
Esztergom	4,000	35,000	25,000
Eger	800	22,000	
Győr	800	13,000	
Nyitra	275	—	4,000
Pécs	3,300	25,000	
Vác	500	4,000	
Veszprém	900	12,000	
Kalocsa	2,000	20,000	
Erdély	1,500	24,000	
Csanád	900	3,000	
Várad	2,000	26,000	
Zágráb	2,000	18,000	
Bosznia	200	—	
Szerém	100	5,000	

15. Distribution of total income of dioceses

Diocese	Annual income	Total		Barons		Noblemen		Commoners		Peasants		Unknown	
		years	income	years	income	years	income	years	income	years	income	years	inc.
Esztergom	25	122	3050	57	1425	24	600	6	150	24	600	11	275
Eger	22	112	2464	42	924	12	264	6	132	7	154	45	990
Győr	13	127	1651	46	598	58	754	4	52	19	247	—	—
Veszprém	12	104	1248	27	324	62	744	14	168	—	—	1	12
Pécs	25	146	3650	104	2600	15	375	16	400	—	—	11	275
Vác	4	113	452	36	144	40	160	—	—	10	40	27	108
Nyitra	4	125	500	58	192	13	52	—	—	—	—	64	256
Kalocsa	20	109	2180	26	520	22	440	49	980	2	40	10	200
Csanád	3	124	372	53	159	21	63	7	21	—	—	43	129
Várad	26	120	3120	18	468	38	988	39	1014	6	156	19	494
Erdély	24	119	2856	42	1008	48	1152	—	—	1	24	28	672
Zágráb	18	119	2142	12	216	74	1332	11	198	—	—	21	396
Total		1440	23685	521	8578	427	6924	152	3115	69	1261	280	3807

16. Number of brothers and sisters

Number of brothers and sisters	Total	Barons	Noblemen	Commoners	Peasants	Unknown
			number of cases			
9	1	1	—	—	—	—
8	1	1	—	—	—	—
7	1	1	—	—	—	—
6	3	3	—	—	—	—
5	7	3	1	—	2	1
4	7	1	6	—	—	—
3	13	8	4	1	—	—
2	13	3	9	—	1	—
1	13	4	4	3	1	1
0	1	—	1	—	—	—

17. Schemes of descendancy

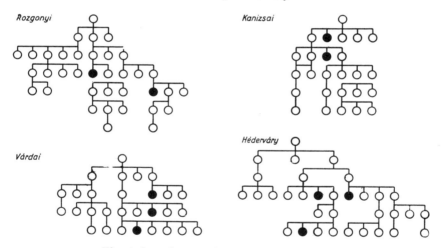

Rozgonyi

Kanizsai

Várdai

Héderváry

The circles refer to males, the full ones to prelats

III

Die Wirtschaft des Erzbistums von Gran am Ende des 15. Jahrhunderts

1486 wurde der Neffe der Königin Beatrice, Herzog Hippolyt von Este zum Erzbischof von Gran (ung.: Esztergom) ernannt. Der neue Metropolit war zur Zeit seiner Ernennung sechs Jahre alt, die erzbischöfliche Wirtschaft wurde von seinen italienischen Beamten verwaltet. Über die Verwaltung führten die Beamten ausführliche Rechnungen, die an den fürstlichen Hof in Ferrara gesandt wurden. Diese Rechnungsbücher — die in der ungarischen wissenschaftlichen Literatur Hippolyt-Kodexe oder Modenaer Kodexe genannt werden — entgingen der Verheerung während der Türkenherrschaft. Wir besitzen zwar auch andere Verrechnungen einiger Domänen aus der Zeit vor der Schlacht bei Mohács (1526), doch enthalten diese in der Regel nur die Einnahmen und Ausgaben der betreffenden Domäne, nicht aber die persönlichen Ausgaben des Grundherrn. Der große Vorteil der Hippolyt-Kodexe besteht eben darin, daß sie die einzigen Rechnungen sind, die die gesamte wirtschaftliche Tätigkeit eines Feudalherren aus dem 15. Jh. umfassen.

Die Rechnungsbücher wurden von A. Nyáry vor hundert Jahren in Italien, im Staatsarchiv von Modena entdeckt. Ihre eingehende Besprechung, die in der Zeitschrift *Századok* erschien,[1] weckte rasch das Interesse an ihnen und die Ungarische Historische Gesellschaft ließ das Material teilweise kopieren. Die ersten Abschriften erwiesen sich jedoch als fehlerhaft;[2] deshalb wurde 1908 A. Veress nach Modena geschickt und auf Grund seines Berichtes[3] mit der Abschrift der Rechnungsbücher von neuem begonnen, diesmal im Staatsarchiv von Venedig, wo fachkundige Kopisten die Arbeit vornehmen

---

[1] A. NYÁRY: *Az esztergomi érsekség és az egri püspökség számadási könyvei a XV—XVI. századból* (Die Rechnungsbücher des Erzbistums von Gran und des Bistums von Erlau aus dem 15. u. 16. Jh.). Századok I/1867. 378—384, und: *A modenai Hippolyt kódexek* (Die Hippolyt-Kodexe in Modena). Századok III/1870. 275, 355, 661; V/1872. 288, 355; VII/1874. 1 u. 73.

[2] Die in den sechziger Jahren des vorigen Jahrhunderts verfertigten Abschriften nahmen keine Rücksicht auf den Unterschied zwischen der Soll- u. Habenseite, sondern kopierten den Text fortlaufend (den einzelnen Seiten nach), wodurch das Buchungssystem verwirrt wurde.

[3] Der Bericht von A. VERESS in der Handschriftensammlung der Ungarischen Akademie der Wissenschaften.

konnten.[4] Die Abschriften, die bis zum Ausbruch des ersten Weltkrieges fertiggestellt wurden, befinden sich heute in der Bibliothek der Ungarischen Akademie der Wissenschaften und bilden die Unterlage der vorliegenden Studie. In ihr sollen — auf Grund von fünf Rechnungsbüchern aus den Jahren 1488—1490 — 1. die Einkünfte der Jahre 1488—1490, 2. die Ausgaben der Jahre 1489—1490, schließlich 3. jene wichtigsten wirtschaftsgeschichtlichen Fragen untersucht werden, die mit den erwähnten Einkünften und Ausgaben in engstem Zusammenhang stehen.

I. Das Quellenmaterial

In Modena sind heute 29 Bände der erzbischöflichen Rechnungen zu finden, die aber keineswegs eine einheitliche Serie identischer Rechnungen bilden, sondern Bücher verschiedener Natur darstellen. Der überwiegende Teil der Bände besteht aus den von ungarischen Beamten lateinisch geführten Rechnungen und italienisch geführten Hauptbüchern. Außer diesen blieben ein Inventar, ein Tagebuch und zwei sog. Salarienbücher erhalten.

Die wichtigsten Angaben enthalten die Hauptbücher (insgesamt 18 Bände).[5] Ursprünglich wurde jeder Band mit einer aus der Jahreszahl und einem Kreuz, oder einem Buchstaben bestehenden Signatur versehen, u. zw. so, daß der Buchstabe die Jahreszahl trennte, z. B. 14 B 88. Bei den Hauptbüchern gab man außerdem noch an, ob in dem betreffenden Band die Einkünfte *(libro di intrada)* oder die Ausgaben *(libro di usita)* gebucht wurden. Die volle Signatur eines Bandes war also *libro di usita 14 B 88* oder nur *libro di usita B*. Das System der Buchstaben konnte aus den verfügbaren Abschriften nicht ermittelt werden, doch dürfte der Band *A* immer eine Art Memorial gewesen sein, in dem man sich die Auszüge verschiedener Verträge und andere wichtige Geschäftsakten notierte.

Die zwei Bücher der Einkünfte und Ausgaben *(libro di intrada* und *libro di usita)* müssen als zwei Teile des Hauptbuches angesehen werden. Die Art der Buchführung und der Ausfertigung ist in beiden Teilen ein und dieselbe. Beide werden von einem Register eingeführt. Die zeitgenössische italienische Buchhaltung legte großes Gewicht auf die Führung der Register und das ließen sich auch die italienischen Rechnungsbeamten in Gran angelegen sein.[6] Das Register enthält die Titel der Konten (ungeachtet dessen,

---

[4] I. LUKINICH: *Az MTA történettudományi bizottsága másolat- és kéziratgyűjteményének ismertetése* (Die Abschrift- u. Handschriftensammlung der Hist. Kommission der Ung. Akademie der Wiss.). Budapest, 1935, 33—36.

[5] Die erhalten gebliebenen Hauptbücher enthalten die Ausgaben der Jahre 1487, 1489—1490, 1495 u. 1497 und die Einnahmen der Jahre 1487—1491, 1493—1495.

[6] Vgl. R. BROWN: *A history of accounting and accountants.* Edinburgh, 1905. 93—123; B. PENNDORF: *Geschichte der Buchhaltung in Deutschland.* 1913, 40—46; F. EDLER: *Glossary of Mediaeval Terms of Business.* Italien series 1200—1600. Cambridge (Mass.), 1934, 370

ob es sich um ein Personal- oder Sachkonto handelt) und die Seite, wo das Konto steht. Die alphabetische Ordnung ist natürlicherweise unkonsequent, die Fürstin von Ferrara figuriert z. B. unter dem Buchstaben *D*, als *Ex-ma Duchesa da Ferrara*. Auf der ersten Seite des Einnahmenbandes wurden die Pächter und der Betrag der Zehnten aufgezeichnet, um die Arbeit des Rechnungsbeamten zu erleichtern.

Alljährlich wurden neue Hauptbücher eröffnet, wie dies aus dem Texte, der mit dem Datum anfängt, klar zu ersehen ist. In diesem Texte rief der Rechnungsbeamte Gott, die hl. Jungfrau und den hl. Adalbert (den Schutzpatron der Diözese) zur Hilfe und gab an, welche Posten (Einkünfte oder Ausgaben) im betreffenden Band gebucht wurden, welche Signatur der Band bekam, wieviel Folien er enthält und wer der verantwortliche Rechnungsbeamte war.[7]

Nach dem Eröffnungstext folgen im Hauptbuch die Konten. Die linke Seite des Buches war die Soll-, die rechte die Habenseite, was übrigens durch die in der oberen Ecke der linken Seite stehende Anschrift *dare* und durch die Anschrift des rechten Seite *havere* bestätigt wird.

Die einzelnen Posten enthalten links das Tagesdatum, in der Mitte den nötigen Text und rechts den Wert in Ziffern geschrieben. Der Wert wurde im Text fast immer auch mit Buchstaben angeführt, die ungarischen Gulden (lat. *florenus*) wurden italienisch konsequent *ducati*, die Pfennige (lat. *denarius*) konsequent *dinari* genannt. Der Text des Postens wurde mit der Berufung auf das Gegenkonto abgesperrt.[8]

Jedes Konto ist mit der Jahreszahl, dem Datierungsort (z. B. *1489 Strigonjo*) und dem Titel des Kontos eingeführt.[9] Konten, die ausschließlich Forderungen oder ausschließlich Schulden enthalten, sind mit einer *summa* abgeschlossen, die Personalkonten (die Soll- und Habenposten enthalten) sind regelrecht saldiert. Überschritt der Umfang des Kontos eine Seite, so wurden die Posten unten auf dem Blatt summiert und auf dem nächsten Blatt Jahreszahl, Datierungsort und Kontotitel aufs neue angeführt, sowie die Teilsummierung des vorangehenden Blattes regelrecht übertragen.

Die Einnahmen wurden detailliert in Konten zerlegt, bei den Ausgaben ist eine gewisse sachgemäße Gruppierung zu beobachten. So finden wir z. B. besondere Konten für die Frachtkosten, die Baukosten, usw. In anderen Fällen scheint das Prinzip des Kostenträgers zur Geltung gelangt zu sein,

---

[7] Z. B. »El quale libro servire per usita generale« »Chiamase questo libro B de usita 1489« (Usita 1489 f. 1.)

[8] Z. B. »Como in questo ala partita de le decime magior charta 18.« (Intrada 1489 f. 100.)

[9] Z. B. »1489 Strigonjo. Spesa menuda dela Cuisina fatta per mano del provisore: como apare per uno suo libro, sotto scritto de mja mano a di per di «(Usita 1489 f. 1.)

so z. B. bilden die Erhaltungskosten des Preßburger Hauses ein selbständiges Konto, das auch die vom Preßburger Offizial bezahlten Frachtkosten enthält.

Das Hauptbuch kennt kein Kassenkonto, statt dessen werden die Geldeinnahmen der Person zu Lasten geschrieben, die das Geld tatsächlich übernahm und die Ausgaben der gutgeschrieben, die das Geld tatsächlich ausgab. Da prinzipiell alle Einnahmen an barem Geld von dem Verwalter *(provisor)* empfangen und alle Ausgaben von ihm ausgezahlt werden mußten,[10] ist sein persönliches Konto das Kassenkonto im heutigen Sinne des Wortes. Als z. B. M. Kis am 3. Juli 1489 als einen Teil seiner Zehntenpacht 800 Gulden zahlte, wurden die 800 Gulden auf dem Konto *decimae maiores* auf der Soll- und auf seinem eigenen Konto auf der Habenseite gebucht, gleichzeitig aber auch auf dem Personalkonto dem Verwalter zu Lasten geschrieben. Dieser Zusammenhang ist zugleich ein Beweis, daß die Buchung von der heutigen doppelten Buchführung in gewissem Maße abweicht, weil die Pachtsumme der Zehnten auf der Habenseite der *decimae maiores* bei der Eröffnung nicht gebucht wurde.

Das Konto des Verwalters bildet auch den Abschluß des Hauptbuches, da im venezianischen Buchführungssystem des 15. Jhs. keine jährliche Bilanz aufgestellt wurde, vielmehr scheinen die erzbischöflichen Finanzen überhaupt keine Bilanz gezogen zu haben. Die Graner Hauptbücher widerspiegeln auch in dieser Hinsicht treu das Verfahren der zeitgenössischen italienischen Buchhaltung.

Außer dem Hauptbuch wurde auch ein Tagebuch *(giornale)* geführt; das vom Jahre 1495 ist erhalten geblieben und steht in Abschrift zur Verfügung.[11] Dieses Tagebuch wurde ohne Eröffnungstext in zwei Teilen fortlaufend geführt, in dem ersten Teil wurden die Einnahmen, im zweiten Teil die Ausgaben in chronologischer Ordnung von Tag zu Tag gebucht. Die Ausfertigung der einzelnen Posten stimmt mit der des Hauptbuches vollkommen

---

[10] »Notto che generalmente ogni intrada venera nela mane de missere Stephano Bachiano, provisore di questo castello« (Intrada 1490. f. 1.)

[11] Ein Beispiel der Übertragung eines Postens aus der *pisetum*-Rechnung des Jahres 1488:

> Item nona die mensis novembris Michael famulus Georgii litterati pisetary de Rivulodo-
> 45 minarum attulit in auro fl. 200 et comparavit etiam scribano aliquas res pro fl. 13, qui positi sunt ad compotum ipsius scribani, faciunt in toto   fl. 213

Derselbe Posten im Hauptbuch des Jahres 1488:   duc. din.

> 9 novembrjo per conta di al provisore duc. dozento et tredezj d oro, i qualli presento Michaelle famje del ditto Giorgjo literato pisetarjo li mando per conto de la intrada di questo anno ny va debitor el provisore per farny nota zoe   213

überein und auf dem linken Rand der Seite ist die Seitenzahl angegeben, auf die der Posten übertragen wurde. Z. B.

Martedi a die 5 di magio

carte 65   *Da la villa Tardaskedi fiorini nove et denari settanta per lo censo di sancto Giorgio proximo passato, porto Giovanni Piccolo loro giudice f. 9 d. 70*

Da das Hauptbuch von 1495 nicht zur Verfügung stand, war es unmöglich festzustellen, auf welches Buch sich die Seitenzahl beruft, jedoch ist es wahrscheinlich, daß die Ausgabeposten des Tagebuches nicht unmittelbar ins Hauptbuch, sondern in ein Kostenbuch *(libro di spese)* eingetragen wurden, wo sie schon nach Konten und innerhalb dieser in chronologischer Reihe gebucht wurden. Wahrscheinlich hatten auch die Einnahmen ein dem Kostenbuch ähnliches Buch, wo sie in Konten gruppiert wurden.

Die Unterlagen des Tagebuches waren — zumindest teilweise — die von den ungarischen Beamten geführten Rechnungen. Diese Rechnungen wurden — nach der allgemeinen Praxis im damaligen Ungarn — im System der einfachen Buchhaltung geführt, u. zw. zuerst die Einnahmen *(introitus)* und danach die Ausgaben *(exitus)*. Die Bücher sind in lateinischer Sprache gehalten, die Ziffern sind römische Zahlen, die Datierung richtete sich in mittelalterlicher Weise nach den kirchlichen Festtagen, die Summen wurden im Buchungstext in Worten nicht angegeben. Nach diesem System wurden die Rechnungen des Preßburger Beamten aus dem Jahre 1489 und die des Verwalters des sog. *pisetum* aus dem Jahre 1488 geführt. Eine Übergangserscheinung zwischen den ungarischen und italienischen Rechnungen stellen die dem Kostenbuch verwandten Bücher dar, in denen zwar der Text noch lateinisch ist, die Ziffern aber teilweise schon arabisch und die Posten bereits in Konten gruppiert sind.

Die in den ungarischen Rechnungen gefundenen Posten wurden in das Tagebuch, Kostenbuch oder möglichenfalls in das Hauptbuch übertragen. Dies wurde am Rand des Blattes bemerkt, indem man die Seitenzahl notierte und den Posten ausstrich.

Das Verhältnis zwischen den Hauptbüchern und anderen Rechnungen kann folgenderweise geschildert werden:

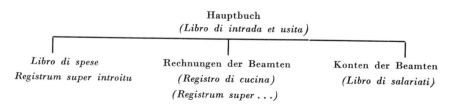

Hauptbuch
(Libro di intrada et usita)

Libro di spese   Rechnungen der Beamten   Konten der Beamten
Registrum super introitu   *(Registro di cucina)*   *(Libro di salariati)*
(Registrum super ...)

II. Die erzbischöflichen Einnahmen 1488—1490

Der Erzbischof von Gran genoß seine Einkünfte auf Grund zweier verschiedener Rechtstitel: einerseits gebührten ihm als einem der größten Grundbesitzer im mittelalterlichen Ungarn die grundherrschaftlichen Renten von seinen umfangreichen Gütern, andererseits gebührten ihm, als dem Erzbischof von Gran die Zehnten der Einwohner seiner ausgedehnten Diözese, die beinahe die ganze heutige Slowakei umfaßte. Die Verteilung des Gesamteinkommens war prozentmäßig folgende:

	1488	1489	1490
grundherrschaftliche Einkünfte ..	28,5	18,2	34,0
kirchliche Einkünfte	71,5	81,8	66,0
Insgesamt	100,0	100,0	100,0

Die große Abweichung im Verhältnis der grundherrschaftlichen zu den kirchlichen Einkünften kann durch das Schwanken der kirchlichen Einkünfte erklärt werden. Während nämlich die grundherrschaftlichen Einkünfte sich in absoluten Ziffern zwischen 4—5000 Gulden bewegten, war die Summe der kirchlichen Einkünfte 1489 auffallend hoch, 1490 demgegenüber auffallend niedrig. Unserer Meinung nach zeigt sich das übliche Verhältnis der beiden Einnahmequellen am besten 1488.

1. *Allgemeiner Stand der erzbischöflichen Güter*

1488 gehörten zu den erzbischöflichen Gütern insgesamt 112 Ortschaften, darunter 98 Dörfer und 14 Marktflecken. Die 112 Ortschaften lagen überwiegend in der heutigen Südslowakei auf einem großen Territorium zerstreut. Den geographischen Gegebenheiten gemäß waren in den verschiedenen Dörfern verschiedene Zweige der Landwirtschaft (Getreide-, Weinproduktion, Schafzucht, Fischerei, usw.) am höchsten entwickelt, Rosenau (Rozsnyó, Rožňava) war das einzige Bergstädtchen, wo sich die Bevölkerung mit Industrie und Handwerk befaßte.

Im mittelalterlichen Ungarn besaßen viele weltliche Feudalherren einen ebenso großen oder noch größeren Grundbesitz und diese waren in ähnlicher Weise zerstreut wie die des Erzbistums, doch war ihre Organisation verschieden. Die Domänen der weltlichen Großgrundbesitzer gruppierten sich um eine Burg und der Kastellan war als Stellvertreter des Besitzers der Verwalter der betreffenden Domäne. In organisatorischer Hinsicht waren von den erzbischöflichen Gütern nur die Domäne Driegel (Drégely) und Heiligenkreuz (Szentkereszt, Sv. Kríž n/Hronom) den weltlichen Gütern ähnlich, doch bildete nur im Fall von Driegel eine Burg den Mittelpunkt der Domäne. Die überwiegende Mehrheit der erzbischöflichen Güter war in sog. *officiolatus* organisiert. Die benachbarten Dörfer wurden einem Beamten *(officialis)* untergeordnet und die so entstandene Organisationseinheit wurde *officiolatus* genannt. In dem von uns untersuchten Zeitraum standen an der Spitze eines *officiolatus* je zwei Beamte, ihr Wirkungskreis konnte aber auf Grund der Rechnungen nicht ermittelt werden.[12]

2. Census—munera — servitium

Die grundherrschaftliche Rente hatte im 15. Jh. drei Erscheinungsformen: der in barem Geld bezahlte Erbzins *(census, terragium)*, das in Naturalien gelieferte »Geschenk« *(munera, prandium)*, und die Fronarbeit *(servitium)*. Die auf den Grundsassen lastenden Verpflichtungen wurden in sog. Urbarien aufgezeichnet. Das Urbarium des Erzbistums wurde *Liber S. Adalberti* genannt; wir besitzen zwei Fassungen desselben aus 1527 und 1553.[13] Die Posten der Rechnungsbücher erklären und ergänzen die Vorschriften des Urbariums; darum waren wir bemüht, die Forderungen des Urbariums den tatsächlichen Verhältnissen der Rechnungen gegenüberzustellen.

Das größte Einkommen bildete der Erbzins. Im allgemeinen war dieser Zins jährlich an zwei oder drei Terminen im Frühjahr und im Herbst (am Georgstag, 24. April und Michaelistag, 29. September) fällig. Die Dorfrichter und Schöffen waren von dem Erbzins ganz oder teilweise befreit, ebenso die Einwohner abgebrannter Häuser. Da die Zahl der besiedelten und bebauten Hufen einem fortwährenden Schwanken ausgesetzt war, wurde jährlich ein Beamter aus Gran mit der Aufgabe entsandt, die Zahl der zinspflichtigen Hufen zu bestimmen. Der Zins wurde dann vom Dorfrichter eingetrieben und nach Gran geschickt. In gewissen Fällen wurde das Ausmaß des Zinses nicht nach Hufen, sondern für das ganze Dorf in einer Pauschalsumme bestimmt. Aus den Rechnungsbüchern geht eine viel größere Anzahl im Pauschale zinsender Dörfer hervor als aus dem Urbarium. In unserem Falle scheint aber die allgemeingültige Auffassung nicht bestätigt, daß das Pauschale eine Begünstigung war, die vorwiegend den Marktflecken gewährt wurde.

---

[12] Aus den Rechnungen sind 9 *officiolatus* zu rekonstruieren, von denen vier ihren Bestand bis 1578 nicht änderten. Scheinbar war das *officiolatus* eine spezielle Organisationsform des kirchlichen Großgrundbesitzes, da wir es auch auf den Gütern des Bistums von Weszprim (Veszprém) finden. Vgl. J. HOLUB: *Egy dunántúli egyházi nagybirtok élete a középkor végén* (Das Leben eines kirchlichen Großgrundbesitzes in Transdanubien am Ausgang des MAs) (Pannónia könyvtár, 62.) Pécs, 1943. 17.

[13] Ein Exemplar des *Liber S. Adalberti* aus 1527 ist im Primatialarchiv in Gran unter der Signatur *Archivum saeculare. Acata protocollata. Urbarium Olahi.* zu finden, die Photokopie desselben im Országos Levéltár [Ung. Staatsarchiv, des weiteren: OL.]. Das Exemplar von 1553 ebenfalls OL. *Urbaria et Conscriptiones* 45—25. Dieses Exemplar wurde seit dem Erscheinen unseres Artikels in ungarischer Sprache in einer slowakischen Quellenpublikation veröffentlicht, samt einer Fassung aus 1578, die ebenfalls im OL. bewahrt wird. S. R. MARSINA—M. KUSIK: *Urbáre feudálnych panstiev na Slovensku* (Die Urbare der feudalen Grundherrschaften in der Slowakei) I. Bratislava, 1959, 278 ff.

Es ist überraschend, in welchem Maße die Größe, die Zahlungstermine des Zinses und die Zahl der befreiten Personen in den verschiedenen Marktflecken und Dörfern voneinander abweichen. Bei dieser Mannigfaltigkeit scheint nur der Grundsatz durchgedrungen zu sein, daß der Zins in jedem Fall für eine Vollhufe festgesetzt wurde (die im Pauschal zinsenden Ortschaften ausgenommen) und daß sich die Höhe des für eine Vollhufe festgesetzten Zinses und der Zahlungstermine desselben im Laufe der Jahrhunderte nicht geändert hat. Auf Grund dieser Erscheinung sind wir zur Schlußfolgerung gelangt, daß im 13—14. Jh. in Ungarn eine der böhmischen und polnischen Regelung ähnliche Regelung stattfand. Die Regelung erstreckte sich auf die Bestimmung der Größe einer Vollhufe, des danach zu zahlenden Zinses und dessen Zahlungstermine. Wahrscheinlich wurde im Laufe des 13. Jhs. eher nur ein jährlicher Zahlungstermin festgesetzt, am Ende des 13. und am Anfang des 14. Jhs. waren zwei, im zweiten Drittel des 14. Jhs. drei jährliche Zahlungstermine zur Regel geworden. Die Regelung war eine Erscheinung des Überganges von der Natural- zur Geldwirtschaft und die Höhe des Erbzinses war gewiß ein Resultat, bei dem mehrere heute noch unbekannte Faktoren (die Qualität des Ackers, die Größe der Hufe, die Absatzmöglichkeiten, usw.) mitwirkten. Gelangte ein Dorf in den Besitz des Erzbischofs, so wurde der festgesetzte Zins nicht geändert, infolgedessen zeigte der Zins auf den erzbischöflichen Gütern am Ausgang des Mittelalters ein sehr mannigfaltiges Bild.[14]

*

Die Verpflichtung, ein »Geschenk« zu geben, haftete ebenfalls an der Bauernhufe. Dem Grundherrn wurden meistens Geflügel, Käse und Eier geleistet, manchmal gaben die Dorfbewohner gemeinschaftlich ein gemästetes Schwein oder einen Ochsen. Der praktische Zweck der Naturalienabgaben — ein Relikt der Naturalwirtschaft — bestand darin, den Grundherren an den größeren Feiertagen mit Lebensmitteln zu versorgen; deswegen waren sie meistens auch zu Weihnachten oder zu Ostern fällig, doch sind uns auch andere Termine bekannt. Einige Dörfer waren nicht abgabepflichtig. Die Ursache dieser Erscheinung ist uns nicht ganz klar, vielleicht stand sie ebenfalls mit der Einführung der Geldwirtschaft im Zusammenhang. Wo nämlich die Bauern imstande waren, statt Naturalien Geld zu geben, dort erhob der Grundherr wahrscheinlich schon im 13. Jh. keinen Anspruch auf das Geschenk.

In dem von uns untersuchten Zeitraum wurden in überwiegendem Teil die Naturalienabgaben mit entsprechendem Bargeld erlöst. Die Summe

---

[14] In bezug auf Einzelheiten der verwickelten Frage des grundherrschaftlichen Zinses, des Geschenks und der Fronarbeit weisen wir auf das ungarische Original unseres Artikels hin, wo das Material der Rechnungsbücher eingehend analysiert wurde. S. Századok, Jhg. 94, 1960, 1—3., S. 4.

des Lösungsgeldes wurde aber von den Tagespreisen unabhängig festgesetzt. Statt einem Schwein z. B. zahlten die Dorfbewohner gemeinschaftlich
einen Gulden, obzwar der Durchschnittspreis eines Schweines zwischen 1489
und 1490 nur 0,59 Gulden betrug und statt eines Ochsen zahlten sie ebenfalls
einen Gulden, obzwar der Preis im erwähnten Zeitraum zwischen 1,45 und
2,44 Gulden schwankte. Vielleicht deutet dies darauf hin, daß das Lösegeld
des Geschenks aus der Zeit der Hufenregelung stammte und seitdem unverändert blieb.

*

Selbst auf Grund der Rechnungen waren wir nicht imstande, die verwickelte Frage der Arbeitsrente, der Fronarbeit zu klären. Aus den Vorschriften des Urbariums geht sicher hervor, daß die Fronarbeit noch keine
so drückende Last war wie sie es später, am Ende des 16. Jhs. wurde. Die
Rechnungen bestätigen, daß für die Fronarbeit ein gewisser Lohn bezahlt
wurde. Leider ist die Frage der Löhne noch nicht genügend untersucht worden, um zu ermöglichen, daß wir die für die Fronarbeit ausbezahlten Löhne
mit den allgemeingültigen Löhnen vergleichen können; so vermögen wir
nicht zu entscheiden, ob es sich hier um richtige Löhne oder nur um eine Art
Vergütung handelt.

2. Die grundherrschaftliche Nona

Das Gesetz von 1351 verordnete, daß die Grundsassen einen weiteren
Teil *(Nona)* ihren landwirtschaftlichen Produktion ihrem Grundherren abzuliefern haben. Die Frage, ob und wie das Gesetz tatsächlich durchgeführt
wurde, wird in unserer wissenschaftlichen Literatur nicht eindeutig beurteilt.
G. Székely behauptet, daß das Eintreiben der Nona vereinzelt schon vor
1351 üblich war, und sich zwischen 1351 und 1381 im ganzen Lande durchsetzte.[15] E. Mályusz wies nach, daß auf Grund des Gesetzartikels 17 vom Jahre
1492 in den Marktflecken des Ungarischen Tieflandes die Nona tatsächlich
eingetrieben wurde.[16] Derselbe Verfasser wies auf ein richterliches Urteil aus
dem Jahre 1481 hin, in dem verordnet wurde, daß alle Fremden, selbst städtische Bürger, die den Boden eines Feudalherren bebauen, ihm die Nona abzuliefern haben, weiterhin, daß der Gesetzartikel 41 v. J. 1498 auf diesem Urteil
beruhte.[17] Demgegenüber brachte die Untersuchung der Urbarien durch
I. Szabó den Beweis, daß in Transdanubien am Ende des 15. und am Anfang

---

[15] *Tanulmányok a parasztság történetéhez Magyarországon a 14. században,* szerk. Székely
Gy. (Studien zur Geschichte des Bauerntums in Ungarn im 14. Jh. red. v. G. Székely). 1953.
S. 276—287.
[16] E. MÁLYUSZ: *Az 1514. évi jobbágyháború okai* (Die Ursachen des Bauernkrieges
von 1514). Társadalomtudomány VII/1926. 375—378.
[17] E. MÁLYUSZ: *Az 1498. évi 41. törvénycikk* (Der Gesetzartikel 41 v. J. 1498). Századok
LXIII—LXIV/1929—1930. 821 ff.

des 16. Jhs die Nona in den Marktflecken noch immer nicht eingetrieben wurde. In einem später erschienenen Artikel wies I. Szabó darauf hin, daß das Gesetz von 1351 ursprünglich eine Errungenschaft des Kleinadels war, der mit dem Gesetz den Abzug seiner Grundsassen zu verhindern versuchte, die Großgrundbesitzer aber waren gegen die Einführung der Nona.[18]

Die Graner Rechnungen und das *Liber S. Adalberti* beweisen einstimmig, daß die im 14. Jh. grundsätzlich eingeführte grundherrschaftliche Nona vom Erzbischof weder systematisch gefordert, noch eingetrieben wurde. Nach den Vorschriften des Urbariums waren von den 112 Ortschaften 27 von der Nonapflicht vollkommen befreit, andere 3 Dörfer sollten nur eine Weinnona leisten, das heißt 24,1% der Ortschaften waren überhaupt nicht, 2,7% nur teilweise mit der grundherrschaftlichen Nona belastet.

Aus den Rechnungen können wir feststellen, daß tatsächlich noch weniger Ortschaften die Nona lieferten. Insgesamt waren es nur 49 Dörfer und Marktflecken, die die Nona tatsächlich leisteten, also nur 43,8% aller Ortschaften. Von diesen waren 46 nur der Getreidenona pflichtig, die anderen 3 nur der Weinnona. Tatsächlich lieferten 56,2% der Ortschaften überhaupt keine Nona.

Der entscheidende Grund für die Einführung der Nonapflicht war unseres Erachtens die Entwicklung der Marktverhältnisse. Am frühesten wurde die Weinnona eingeführt, da der Wein im mittelalterlichen Ungarn sich immer einer großen Nachfrage erfreute. Es kann nicht als Zufall angesehen werden, daß das Urteil von 1481 im Zusammenhang mit den Gütern Szentgyörgyis gefällt wurde, die dieser Zeit ihre Weinausfuhr nach Mähren steigerten. Zur Einführung der Getreidenona kam es dann, als der Getreidemarkt sich stark entwickelte, d. h. im 16. Jh. Vor dem Ende des 15. Jhs. kann also — unseres Erachtens — von einem allgemeinen Durchdringen der Nona eben deshalb nicht gesprochen werden. Wenn wir in dieser Frage weitere Fortschritte erzielen wollen, so müssen wir in erster Reihe die statistische Methode anwenden.

3. *Sonstige grundherrschaftliche Einnahmen*

In der Reihe der grundherrschaftlichen Einnahmen nimmt die sog. *taxa extraordinaria* einen wichtigen Platz ein. In dem von uns untersuchten Zeitraum wurde sie nur einmal, 1490 eingehoben, jedoch können wir uns aus diesen spärlichen Angaben kaum ein klares Bild über die Größe der *taxa* schaffen. Im großen und ganzen betrug sie etwas mehr als die Hälfte des Zinses, doch ist es nicht klar, wie diese Summe erzielt wurde: ob man die

---

[18] I. Szabó: *Hanyatló jobbágyság a középkor végén* (Verfall des Bauerntums am Ende des MAs) Századok LXXII/1938. 55—56.

taxa nur aus einem Teil der Ortschaften eintrieb, oder ob alle Ortschaften etwa die Hälfte ihres Zinses zahlen mußten. Die Detailangaben deuten auf eine sehr abwechslungsreiche Praxis hin.

*

Ein Drittel der Einkünfte der Mühlen gebührte ebenfalls dem Erzbischof. Die Einnahmen der kleinen Mühlen waren sehr bescheiden, 1489 nur 10—13, 1490 4—5 Gulden. Der Ertrag der Mühle in der Bergstadt Kremnitz (Körmöcbánya, Kremnica) war dagegen sehr hoch, diese wurde jährlich für 300 Gulden an die Stadt verpachtet.

*

Zu den kleineren Einkünften gehörten die Einnahmen aus der Maut. Auf den erzbischöflichen Gütern standen insgesamt acht Mauten, von denen zwei, die von Mautneudorf (Nyergesújfalu) auf der Straße Wien—Ofen und die von Heiligenkreuz a. d. Gran am Wege von Gran nach den niederungarischen Bergstädten bedeutend waren. Die Mauteinnahmen der Jahre 1488 und 1489 wurden zum Teil in gewissen Zeitabständen gebucht, so war es uns möglich, die zeitliche Verteilung zu bestimmen. In Heiligenkreuz scheint die Maut völlig von der landwirtschaftlichen Produktion abhängig gewesen zu sein. Die Einkünfte waren hier in beiden Jahren zur Zeit der großen landwirtschaftlichen Arbeiten (1488 21. VI.—5. IX., 1489 3. VII.—9. IX.) am niedrigsten, das Maximum des Verkehrs fiel auf das Jahresende. Dieser Zeitraum umfaßte 1488 die Monate Oktober—Dezember, 1489 den Monat September, d. h. der Ertrag der Ernte wurde 1488 im letzten Vierteljahr in den Bergstädten verkauft, 1489 wurde aber der Ertrag der schlechten Ernte im September abgesetzt. Gegenüber dem Maximum am Ende des Jahres 1488 steht im ersten Vierteljahr 1489 ein sehr niedriger Verkehr. Grund dieser Erscheinung ist nicht nur, daß die schlechte Ernte einen früheren Absatz fand, sondern vielleicht auch die Tatsache, daß der Winter mild war und die primitiven Wege unbefahrbar waren.

Die Maut von Mautneudorf war von der landwirtschaftlichen Produktion unabhängiger. Das Schwanken der täglichen Einnahmen richtet sich eher nach dem Schwanken der Preßburger Dreißigsteneinnahmen, an beiden Stellen fiel das Maximum des Verkehrs auf August—September, das Minimum auf das erste Vierteljahr.

4. *Die kirchlichen Zehnten*

Die Zehnten der Diözese von Gran, die den ganzen westlichen Teil der heutigen Slowakei umfaßte, gebührten dem Erzbischof. In der von der Zeit der Einführung der Zehnten in Ungarn (11. Jh.) bis zu unserem Zeitraum vergangenen Periode unterlag die Zehntenwirtschaft einer langen Entwicklung. Ursprünglich war der Erzbischof der einzige Inhaber der Zehnten, doch während der Jahrhunderte verschenkten sie einen beträchtlichen Teil derselben an das Domkapitel von Gran und andere kirchliche Institutionen, obzwar auch weiterhin sie im Besitz des größten Teiles der Zehnten blieben.[19] Die eingewanderten fremden »Gäste« und die Einwohner der zu Städten erhobenen Dörfer steuerten ihre Zehnten in einer von den übrigen Dörfern abweichenden Weise. Die Art der Buchung der Zehnteneinnahme steigerte noch die Verwickeltheit der Lage. Die Zehnten der Komitate, in denen die Zehnten gänzlich oder überwiegend im Besitz des Erzbischofs waren, wurden im Konto *decimae maiores* geführt, demgegenüber wurden die Zehnten der kleineren Kreise, oder einzelnen Marktflecken, die in das Territorium anderer Zehntenbesitzer eingekeilt waren, im Konto *decimae minores* gebucht. Dieses Unterscheiden der *decimae maiores* und *minores* entsprach also nicht der allgemeinen Praxis der mittelalterlichen Kirche.[20]

Die Zehnten wurden nach altem Brauch mit Ausnahme derer des Komitates Preßburg verpachtet. Die Pächter der *decimae maiores* pachteten meistens die Zehnten mehrerer Komitate, die Pächter der *decimae minores* waren in den meisten Fällen erzbischöfliche Beamte. Die Pachtverträge wurden am Anfang des Jahres abgeschlossen, der Vertrag enthielt zwei Zahlungstermine. Der erste Termin ging der Ernte voraus und bildete manchmal 35%, in anderen Fällen 85% der gesamten Pachtsumme. Der andere Termin wird als der »gewohnheitsmäßige Zeitpunkt« erwähnt, konnte aber näher nicht bestimmt werden.[21]

Tatsächlich sind die gesamten Pachtsummen nie eingegangen, beinahe jeder Pächter blieb mehr oder weniger schuldig. Noch 1490 wurden die Konten der Personen geführt, die mit Pachtsummen aus 1488 schuldig geblieben waren. Die Zahlungstermine wurden auch nicht eingehalten, so daß in den

---

[19] Das Monopol des Zehntenbesitzes wurde zu der Zeit gebrochen, als der Haushalt des Domkapitels von dem des Erzbischofs getrennt wurde. Die Zehnten aus dem Besitz des Kapitels sind am pünktlichsten in der Visitation des Jahres 1396 angeführt. Vgl. F. KOLLÁNYI: *Visitatio capituli Strigoniensis*, Tört. Tár II/1901. 101. ff. Die Zehntenbesitzer der erzbischöflichen Güter werden im *Liber S. Adalberti* ausführlich angegeben. Ein gutes Beispiel der Zehntenverschenkung gibt uns eine Urkunde aus d. J. 1156. Vgl. I. KNIEZSA: Századok LXXIII/1939. 167—187.

[20] Das *Liber S. Adalberti*, die Rechnungen und die verfügbaren Urkunden beweisen eindeutig, daß in der Graner Diözese am Ende des 15. Jhs. nur Getreide-, Wein-, Schafs- u. Honigzehnten eingetrieben wurden. Demgegenüber werden in älteren Urkunden auch andere Zehntenarten (z. B. Geflügelzehnten) erwähnt (Mon. Strig. III. 656.), diese waren aber — wie darauf MÁLYUSZ hingewiesen hat — wahrscheinlich nur eine vereinzelte Erscheinung. In den Diözesen, wo eine großzügige Schweinezucht betrieben wurde, hat man auch nach Schweinen Zehnten eingehoben. Vgl. K. KANDRA: *Adatok az egri egyházmegye történetéhez* (Beiträge zur Geschichte der Diözese von Erlau) II. 393.

[21] Die Bedingungen der Pacht wurden am ausführlichsten im Rechnungsbuch von 1488 aufgezeichnet, z. B. im Falle von M. Kis »che al presente debia disborsare duc. millj e zento, el resto ... ali tempi consueti«, im Falle von Gosztonyi »che al presente i pagano duc. 1500, el resto a tempi consueti« (Intrada 1488 f. 125).

betreffenden Jahren das Eintreiben der Pachtsumme nur bis zu 53—69% gelang.

Die Pacht wurde nicht immer in barem Gelde beglichen, vielmehr scheint es aus den Angaben, daß die Pächter nur am Anfang des Jahres bares Geld zahlten, als sie einen »Vorschuß« gaben: später kam es nur zur Abrechnung, weil die Pächter ihre Verpflichtungen mit Warenlieferungen und mit Übernahme von Verbindlichkeiten beglichen.

Die Pacht der Zehnten hatte vom Standpunkt des kirchlichen Verpächters drei Vorteile: *1.* mußte der Verpächter die Kosten des Eintreibens und des Absatzes nicht tragen, *2.* erhielt er die Einnahme statt in Naturalien in barem Gelde, *3.* die Einnahme wurde rascher erzielt, als wenn der Verpächter sich mit dem Absatz befaßt hätte. Wenn wir nach den Angaben der Rechnungsbücher urteilen dürfen, so genoß das Erzbistum nur den ersten Vorteil, Kosten des Eintreibens und Absatzes belasteten die Zehnteneinnahme wirklich nicht. Die Einnahmen erhielt es aber nur teilweise in barem Gelde, teilweise mußte es sie in Waren oder in Schuldübertragungen übernehmen. Der Zeitpunkt der Übernahme konnte auch nur teilweise vorverlegt werden. Zweifellos lief ein Teil der Pachtsumme früher ein als am Zeitpunkt des Absatzes nach der Ernte, ein anderer Teil kam aber nur in den folgenden Jahren zur Abrechnung, ganz zu schweigen von den Summen, deren Eintreibung noch nach Jahren nicht gelang.

*

Die Untersuchung der wirtschaftlichen Tätigkeit der Pächter stellt uns einige interessante Typen des Wirtschaftslebens des mittelalterlichen Ungarns dar. Die Zehnten der Komitate Sohl (Zólyom, Zvolen), Turtz (Turóc, Turiec), Liptau (Liptó, Liptov) und Árva (Orava) wurden während dreier Jahre an den Gespan des Komitates Turtz, an M. Kis von Cece verpachtet. Wenn wir seine im Anhang veröffentlichten Konten überblicken, dann sehen wir, daß er 1488 die Pachtsumme bis zu 104,50 Gulden in barem Gelde beglich. 1489 zahlte er nur mehr 800,— Gulden in barem Gelde, im Werte von 661,— Gulden lieferte er Waren, im Werte von 4,50 Gulden übernahm er eine Verpflichtung des Erzbistums, 100,— Gulden wurden ihm wegen der schlechten Ernte gestrichen. Dennoch blieb er mit 89,— Gulden schuldig, obzwar er im selben Jahr 500,— Gulden als Vorschuß der Pacht des Jahres 1490 zahlte und sich zur Lieferung von 2000 Schindeln verpflichtete. 1490 bezahlte er die rückständigen 700,— Gulden in barem Gelde. Mit 89,— Gulden blieb er für immer schuldig, da er im Jahr 1490 starb und die Schulden von seinen Erben nicht bezahlt wurden.

Dem anderen Pächter, B. Szakácsi wurden zwei Jahre hindurch die Zehnten der Komitate Gömör und Torna verpachtet. 1488 zahlte er nur 39,5% der Pacht aus, doch tilgte er seine Schulden bis zum Mai des folgenden

266

Jahres. 1489 zahlte er nur 610 Gulden in barem Gelde, er übernahm die Verpflichtungen des Erzbistums gegenüber verschiedenen Ofner Kaufleuten und
Handwerkern zuerst im Werte von 441,07 Gulden, später, bei der Schluß-
abrechnung von noch 537,— Gulden.

Die Tätigkeit der beiden Pächter kann mit anderen Angaben ergänzt
werden. M. Kis war ein adeliger Grundbesitzer, befaßte sich außerdem in
beträchtlichem Ausmaß mit Handel.[22] Als er starb, blieb er dem königlichen
Salz- und dem Dreißigstamt schuldig, dem letzteren mit dem Zoll für Waren
im Werte von 6664,— Gulden.[23] Dem Erzbistum lieferte er teils Waren aus
Krakau, teilweise Bauholz und Schindeln aus seinen eigenen Wäldern. Er erwarb zwei Domänen und zwei andere Güter, für das eine zahlte er 200,—,
für das andere 8000,— Gulden.[24]

Allen Anzeichen nach stammte Szakácsi nicht aus einer alten bürgerlichen Familie, er war vielmehr der Vertreter der ersten Generation in Pest.[25]
Er erwarb sein Vermögen im Dienst der Königlichen Kanzlei, und — soweit
man es aus den lückenhaften Angaben beurteilen kann — im Wege der Pacht
von Regalien und Zehnten. Wahrscheinlich ging er auch daran zugrunde,
da er 1504 mit einer Schuld von 2890 Gulden gegenüber dem Graner Erzbischof Bakóc bankrott wurde. In seiner Person sehen wir den Typ vor uns,
der im Laufe seiner amtlichen Karriere reich geworden ist, vom Dorfe oder
von einem Marktflecken sich in die Reihe der städtischen Bürger emporarbei-
tete und in der Stadt eine große Rolle spielte.

Die wirtschaftliche Tätigkeit beider Pächter beweist uns, daß die
Pächter eigentlich nur über ein Anfangskapital verfügten und dieses Kapital
zur Bezahlung der ersten Rate der Pacht verwendet wurde. Die nächsten
Raten wurden dann so gezahlt, wie es die Stellung des Pächters in dem Kredit-
system der mittelalterlichen Wirtschaft ermöglichte. M. Kis beglich seine
Schulden teilweise mit seinen eigenen Waren (Holz), teils mit dem Waren-
kredit, den er im Handelsleben genoß. Szakácsi besaß keine Waren eigener
Produktion, seine Beziehungen zu den Ofner Kaufleuten machten ihn in
Ofen kreditfähig, er übernahm eben deswegen die Schulden des Erzbistums
gegenüber Ofner Kaufleuten und Handwerkern.

Die Pächter der *decimae minores* zeigen uns denselben Typ *in statu
nascendi*. Wie schon gesagt, waren die Pächter der *decimae minores* in der
Regel Beamte des Erzbistums. Sie hatten natürlich die Pacht nicht zu be-

---

[22] M. Kis galt als Sachverständiger in Handelsangelegenheiten, da er auch an den
ungarisch—polnischen Handelsverhandlungen teilnahm. B. IVÁNYI: *Bártfa sz. kir. város levéltára* [Das Archiv der kgl. Freistadt Bartfeld (Bardejov)] Nr. 2751, 2756, 2757, 2758).
[23] Familienarchiv Révay, Blatnica III. Nr. 9. u. Nr. 15. (Fotografie im OL.)
[24] Ebd. Blatnica II. 11, 12.
[25] A. KUBINYI: *A kincstári személyzet a XV. sz. második felében* (Das Personal des
Schatzmeisters in der zweiten Hälfte des 15. Jhs). Tanulmányok Budapest múltjából XII/1956.
32, 34.

zahlen, die Pacht war nur nominell, eigentlich eine Abrechnung, im Laufe derer ihr Lohn mit der Pachtsumme verringert wurde. Wenn wir nun von der Tatsache ausgehen, daß diese Beamten die Vorgesetzten der Grundsassen, also in der Lage waren, die Zehnten gänzlich einzutreiben, und wenn wir andererseits in Erwägung ziehen, daß die Pachtsumme der *decimae minores* jahrhundertelang unverändert blieb,[26] so müssen wir behaupten, daß die Zehnten nicht nur im Werte der nominellen Pachtsumme, sondern in größerem Werte eingetrieben werden und die Pächter in Besitz einer größeren Warenmenge kommen konnten. Man denke hier nicht gleich an Mißbrauch der Amtsgewalt. Im Falle einer ständig gewordenen Pachtsumme bestand immer die Möglichkeit, daß der Wert der tatsächlich eingetriebenen Warenmenge höher war. Unter entsprechenden Umständen konnte diese Ware mit Gewinn abgesetzt werden, d. h. der Pächter konnte sich einen Gewinn verschaffen, der höher war als die Pachtsumme. Die Pächter der *decimae minores* konnten unter glücklichen Umständen ebensolche handeltreibende Gutsbesitzer werden, wie M. Kis, dessen Vater ebenfalls ein Beamter einer Grundherrschaft war.

Die Zehntenpächter stellen also einen Typ in seinem anfänglichen und entwickelten Stadium dar.[27] Den Beginn der Laufbahn des Typs bildet das Erwerben der elementaren lateinischen Bildung und die Verschaffung einer Stellung in der feudalen Amtshierarchie. Unter feudalem Amt verstehen wir nicht nur die königlichen Ämter, die Beamtenorganisation eines Großgrundbesitzes war auch entsprechend. Die schriftliche Arbeit war an allen Punkten des Großgrundbesitzes unentbehrlich, und die Wirtschaftsbeamten erwarben sich meistens einen gewissen Überfluß an landwirtschaftlichen Produkten. Ihre Versorgung übernahm die Domäne; so bedurften sie nicht der Produkte ihrer eigenen kleinen Güter. Der Überfluß an Produkten wurde zur Ware und die Besitzer bemühten sich diese abzusetzen. Vom Ende des 15. Jhs. begegnen uns im Archiv der Stadt Bartfeld (Bártfa, Bardiov) des öfteren Briefe, in denen die benachbarten Kastellane ihre Produkte zum Verkauf anboten.[28] Diese Form des Eintritts in das Handelsleben ist uns hauptsächlich deswegen so gut bekannt, weil die Korrespondenz dieser Stadt am besten erhalten blieb. Es ist aber klar, daß die Beamten der Domäne sich nicht nur über die Städte in das Handelsleben einschalten konnten. Die Vorbedingungen des Eintritts waren einerseits die Waren, andererseits die Zugehörigkeit zu einem Amtssystem. Der Warenkredit war ein unentbehrlicher Faktor des mittelalter-

---

[26] Der Abt von Pilis besaß das Dorf Csákány und die Zehnten des Dorfes waren an ihn verpachtet. Der Pachtvertrag stammt aus d. J. 1341 (R. Békefi: *A pilisi apátság története* [Die Geschichte der Abtei von Pilis] I. 535). 1431 zahlte er als Pachtsumme 68 Gulden (Ebd. I. 404) und 1488—1490 belief sich die Pachtsumme noch immer auf 68 Gulden.
[27] Gy. Bónis: *Egy Jagelló kori magyar jogász* (Ein ungarischer Jurist der Jagellonenzeit). A Szegedi Tud. Egy. Állam- és Jogtudományi karának Évkönyve 1953.
[28] Iványi, a. a. O. Nr. 1739, 3013, 3338 und OL. Dl. 47.140.

lichen Handels, und wer den Warenkredit in Anspruch nahm, mußte zu einer Körperschaft gehören, die ihn zur Tilgung seiner Schulden zwingen konnte. Für den städtischen Bürger bürgte die Stadt, gegen den Beamten konnte man vor seinem *dominus* eine Klage erheben.

Nach Anhäufung eines bescheidenen Anfangskapitals pachtete dieser Typ meistens eine Einnahme der Feudalherren. In dieser Hinsicht war die Pacht der kirchlichen Zehnten und am häufigsten die der Weinzehnten das beliebteste Unternehmen. Wein konnte hohe Regiespesen tragen und fand immer guten Absatz. Dem Pächter war es möglich, seine Warenbasis zu erweitern und den in der Zehntenpacht erhaltenen Wein zu verkaufen. Wenn der Absatz mit Erfolg und Gewinn abgeschlossen war, konnte es zu noch größeren Pachten kommen. Der Fall Szakácsis zeigt, daß im Falle eines Mangels an nötigem Kapital mit einer Vereinbarung geholfen wurde. Es ist durchaus kennzeichnend, daß der mit jahrelanger Arbeit geschaffene und sich in der Form verschiedener Kredite anhäufende Gewinn letzten Endes zur Erwerbung liegender Güter verwendet wurde. Wir besitzen wenig Angaben über Geldgeschäfte,[29] umso mehr über Güterankauf.

Die Verbindung zu den Städten begleitet die ganze Tätigkeit dieses Pächters. Die städtischen Bürger waren die Abnehmer ihrer Ware, in mehreren Fällen erwarben sie sich das Bürgerrecht, gelangten sogar zu einer führenden Stellung in der Stadt.[30] Unter den Pächtern der grundherrschaftlichen Einnahmen kommen in dieser Zeit die städtischen Bürger nicht mehr vor. Auch im Falle des Erzbischofs von Gran bildeten die Angehörigen des Kleinadels und die kirchlichen Würdenträger die Mehrheit. Anscheinend spielte diese Schicht am Ende des 15. und am Anfang des 16. Jahrhunderts eine immer bedeutendere Rolle in der Wirtschaft des Landes.[31]

Zwei Pächter der *decimae minores* waren vom hier dargestellten Typ verschieden. Der eine war Perotto Visach, der Gespan des Komitates Sohl, der Vertraute der Königin Beatrice. Seine wirtschaftliche Tätigkeit bestand im Ankauf von Grundbesitz *en gros*, der schon beinahe den Charakter der

---

[29] Der Stadt Schemnitz [Banská Šťiavnica] wurde von J. Horváth eine Anleihe von 200 Gulden gewährt (Stadtarchiv II. 536). Es ist durchaus möglich, daß dieser J. Horváth mit jenem J. Horváth identisch ist, der in den Hippolyt-Kodexen als Genosse von Szakácsi auftaucht.

[30] Ein ähnlicher Fall wird von KUBINYI (a. a. O. 34.) erwähnt. Außer Szakácsi gehörte vielleicht auch der Graner Stadtrichter Ambrosius zu diesem Typ, er wird Ambrosius litteratus genannt und war wahrscheinlich eine Zeitlang ein Angestellter des königlichen Schatzmeisters.

[31] Wenn wir hier von der Handelstätigkeit der kirchlichen und weltlichen Beamten sprechen, so muß hervorgehoben werden, daß sie in erster Reihe mit landwirtschaftlichen Artikeln Handel trieben und in dieser Hinsicht das städtische Bürgertum anscheinend verdrängten. Der viel bedeutendere Handel mit Waren des Handwerks und des Bergbaus blieb aber weiterhin in den Händen des Bürgertums. Das Übergewicht der städtischen Bürger wurde durch die Tätigkeit der zu Kaufleuten gewordenen Beamten nicht gebrochen, da im Außenhandel der Verkehr der landwirtschaftlichen Produkte unbedeutend war.

Immobilienspekulation trug. Alle angekauften Güter hat er dann 1500 verkauft, als er mit der Königin das Land verließ.[32]

1488 wurden die Zehnten des Dorfes Bény den Einwohnern von Bény verpachtet. Sie beglichen die Pachtsumme noch im selben Jahre mit barem Geld. Wir können zwar nicht näher bestimmen, wer diese »huomini di Bény« waren, doch ist die Erscheinung desto auffallender, als 1511 — laut einer Aufzeichnung — im Komitate Hont 13 Ortschaften ihre eigenen Zehnten in Pacht nahmen.[33] Diese Angaben beweisen uns, daß der Warenverkehr sich erweitert hatte und für die Einwohner oder Dörfer, die in der Nähe eines größeren Absatzzentrums (Bergstädte, Gran, die königliche Residenz in Plintenburg [Visegrád] usw.) lagen, es vorteilhafter war, die Pacht der Zehnten zu bezahlen, als die Zehnten in Naturalien abzuliefern.

5. Die Zehnten des Komitats Preßburg

Die Zehnten des Komitats Preßburg wurden nicht verpachtet, sondern vom Erzbistum selbst verwaltet. In den Weinbergen des Komitats wurde Wein in großen Mengen und von guter Qualität gefechst, die Stadt Preßburg (Bratislava) war ein Handelszentrum, in dem die Vorgänger Hippolyts schon im 14. Jh. ein Haus kauften.[34] Glücklicherweise sind uns die Rechnungen der Preßburger Hausverwalter unter den Hippolyt-Kodexen erhalten geblieben und so sind wir über ihre Tätigkeit ziemlich gut unterrichtet.[35]

Die Preßburger Zehnten wurden teilweise in Naturalien (Wein und Getreide), teilweise in Geld geliefert. Aus den Rechnungsbüchern geht die Tendenz klar hervor, nur die Weinzehnten in Naturalien zu behalten, die Getreidezehnten dagegen in kleineren Bezirken zu verpachten.

Die Rechnungen führen den Ertrag der Getreidezehnten jährlich an, 1488 war der Ertrag 13.099 Hocken, 1489 13.745 und 1490 10.913 Hocken. Allerdings überrascht, daß sich 1489 die Zahl der Hocken trotz der schlech-

[32] Perotto kaufte 1482 um 6.000 Gulden die Domäne Szenyér im Komitat Somogy (Graner Kapitelarchiv Lad. 27. fasc. 6. no. 13.), 1484 um 750 Gulden ein Teilgut im Dorfe Libád im Komitat Bares (ebd. Lad. 27. fasc. 2. no. 15.). 1489 den Marktflecken Szob um 1.800 Gulden ebenfalls im Komitat Somogy (ebd. Lad. 28. fasc. 2. no. 13.). Von diesen verkaufte er Libád um 2.000 Gulden dem Domkapitel von Gran (ebd. Lad. 27. fasc. 3. no. 1.), die Domäne Szenyér um 6.000 Gulden dem Erzbischof von Gran, T. Bakóc (ebd. Lad. 28. fasc. 3. no. 1.).

[33] Diese Aufzeichnung enthält die Zehnten der Hl.-Jungfrau-Kapelle in Gran im Komitat Hont. Unter den Zehntenpächtern finden sich Gutsbesitzer (Mitglieder des niederen Adels und der Prämonstratenserprobst v. Bozók), ein Pfarrer, ein Graner Domherr und die Einwohner einiger Ortschaften (ebd. Lad. 46. fasc. 4. no. 5.).

[34] T. ORTVAY: *Pozsony város története* (Die Geschichte der Stadt Preßburg) II/2. S 27. u. 74.

[35] Diese Rechnung trägt den Titel »*Registrum Bernaldi*« und wurde augenscheinlich von dem Preßburger Hausverwalter Bernhard Tomori geführt. Die in lateinischer Sprache geführte Rechnung enthält zuerst die Verrechnung des Weines nach Fässern, sodann die Geldeinnahmen und schließlich die Geldausgaben, natürlich nach den Regeln der einfachen« Buchhaltung.

ten Ernte nicht verringerte. Demgegenüber waren in diesem Jahre die Einnahmen aus den Pachten niedriger. Die Erklärung dieser Erscheinung dürfte sein, daß 1489 angesichts der schlechten Ernte das Erzbistum weniger Getreidezehnten verpachtete und so den Ertrag im Gleichgewicht halten konnte. Der Wert des Ertrags wurde in jedem Jahr mit dem gleichen Preis verrechnet, zwölf Hocken waren einen Gulden wert. Leider können wir wegen Mangel an vergleichendem Material nicht beurteilen, wie weit dieser Preis real war.[36]

Die Weinzehnten wurden nach Fässern verrechnet. Wir wissen, daß sich der Ertrag 1488 auf 314, 1489 auf 318, 1490 auf 294 Fässer belief. Aus der hier angeführten Verteilung ist es ersichtlich, daß ein bedeutender Teil des Weines vom Erzbistum selbst verbraucht wurde. Zwar dürfte von den 1490 nach Gran geschickten Fässern ein gewisser Teil noch verkauft worden sein, doch müssen wir den Prozensatz des verkauften Weines 1489 mit 29,4%, 1490 mit 33,6% schon als reell ansehen. Viel Wein wurde im Preßburger Haus von den Gästen verbraucht, viel wurde z. B. der Königin geschenkt. Nach dem Abzug dieses Verbrauches blieben 1488 nur 62,0%, 1489 nur 49,6%, 1490 noch weniger für den Handel übrig.

Die größte Kundschaft für den Wein war der König, der nicht zu den besten Schuldnern gehörte. 1489 bezahlte er auf einmal 2490 Gulden, doch wissen wir leider nicht, welche Menge Weines damit bezahlt wurde. Die andere Form des Absatzes war der Ausschank in den grundherrschaftlichen Weinstuben des Erzbistums. 1488 erhielt der Preßburger Verwalter für eine unbekannte Menge 115,53 Gulden, 1489 wurden 76 Fässer Wein in einem Gesamtwerte von 764 Gulden ausgeschenkt, das bedeutet also 10,05 Gulden je Faß. 1490 konnte ein noch höherer Preis erzielt werden, 21 Fässer wurden in einem Gesamtwerte von 268,66 Gulden, also 12,79 Gulden je Faß ausgeschenkt. 1489 wurden außer den schon erwähnten Mengen 16 Fässer den erzbischöflichen Beamten für 5 Gulden je Faß verkauft. Gegenüber diesem niedrigen Einheitspreis finden wir einmal einen sehr hohen. Als 1490 die Familie Szentgyörgyi auf ihren Gütern die Zehnten beschlagnahmte, wurden auf ihrem Konto 117 Fässer im Gesamtwerte von 1404 Gulden zu Lasten geschrieben, was einem Einheitspreis von 12,— Gulden entspricht. Einen so hohen Preis konnte das Erzbistum nur mit dem Ausschank erreichen, nicht aber im Handel.

Der Einheitspreis von 5,— Gulden pro Faß war auf die Regiespesen der Preßburger Zehnten begründet. Die Regiespesen des Jahres sind uns genau und detailliert, die des Jahres 1490 in großen Zügen bekannt. Regiespesen waren demnach alle das Preßburger Haus belastenden, in einem sehr weiten Sinne des Wortes genommenen Spesen, unter denen die Verwaltungs-,

---

[36] Die Verrechnung der Preßburger Zehnten erwähnt den Verkauf von Getreide nur ein einziges Mal, doch ist die Menge des Getreides nicht angegeben.

Fracht- und Erhaltungskosten des Hauses (z. B. eine Monstranz für die
Kapelle im Haus) auffindbar sind. Den größten Teil der Regiespesen bildeten
die Verwaltungskosten des Weines. Große Mengen von Fässern waren nötig:
1489 wurden 222, 1490 199 neue Fässer gekauft, u. zw. zu sehr verschiedenen
Preisen, 1489 für 0,50 Gulden, 1490 für 0,77 Gulden das Faß. Die Frachtkosten waren ebenfalls hoch, obzwar diese nicht die gesamten Frachtenkosten
des Preßburger Weines darstellen, denn 1489 erscheinen noch auf dem Frachten-
konto 29,— Gulden für die Lieferung Preßburger Weines nach Ofen. Alles
in allem ergaben die Regiespesen auf ein Faß umgerechnet 1489 4,65, 1490
2,89 Gulden. Aus diesen Ziffern dürfen wir zwei Folgerungen ziehen: *1.* daß
die Regiespesen sehr veränderlich waren, *2.* daß man den Angestellten den
Wein — im heutigen Sinne des Wortes — für den Selbstkostenpreis verkaufte.

Wir haben die mit den Preßburger Weinzehnten im Zusammenhang
stehenden Angaben deswegen so ausführlich erwähnt, weil sie die Wirtschaft
des Erzbistums sehr gut charakterisieren. Das Erzbistum war nicht geneigt,
eine aktive Rolle im Weinhandel zu spielen. Nur zwei Drittel der gesamten
Weinmenge wurden verkauft, und selbst diese zwei Drittel wurden in der
traditionellen Auffassung des mittelalterlichen Großgrundbesitzes teilweise
an den größten Verbraucher des Landes, doch an den schlechtesten Schuldner,
den König verkauft, teils den Grundsassen ausgeschenkt. Die Verwaltung
und die Fracht ließen die Regiespesen ansteigen. 25—40% des höchsten
erzielbaren Verkaufspreises waren die Regiespesen und das bei einer Ware,
deren Produktion dem Erzbischof keinen Heller kostete. Dieser Regieschlüssel
ist nicht nur nach unserer heutigen Meinung hoch, er schien es auch im Auge
der Zeitgenossen. Die Regiekosten der staatlichen Steuer waren 1495 im
Komitate Preßburg nur 5,3%.[37]

Teils der hohe Regieschlüssel, teils die nach dem Tode des Königs Matthias
einsetzenden politischen Wirren waren die Motive des Entschlusses, daß das
Erzbistum der langjährigen Praxis ein Ende machte, die Preßburger Zehnten
verpachtete, u. zw. dem Großgrundbesitzer, der die größten Unannehmlichkeiten beim Eintreiben der Zehnten verursachen konnte, dem Peter Szentgyörgyi. Es ist durchaus kennzeichnend, daß die Pachtsumme sich auf 4000
Gulden belief, auf eine Summe, die das Erzbistum selbst nicht erreichen
konnte, die aber mit einer rationellen Verwaltung und mit einer nach Mähren
gerichteten Weinausfuhr wahrscheinlich zu erreichen war.

6. *Sonstige kirchliche Einnahmen*

Hierher gehört in erster Reihe die Einnahme aus der Münze, das sog.
pisetum. Im mittelalterlichen Ungarn durfte nur der König Münzen prägen

---

[37] Die staatliche Steuer des Komitates Preßburg betrug 1495 3.786 Gulden, 201 Gulden
wurden zum Eintreiben derselben verwendet.

lassen, und die Zehnten der Münze gebührten dem Erzbischof von Gran. Die ungarische wissenschaftliche Literatur befaßte sich ausführlich mit dem *pisetum*, deshalb können wir von einer Darstellung desselben hier absehen.[38] Der *census plebanorum* war eine spezifische Einnahme. Die Pfarrer waren grundsätzlich der Aufsicht des Archidiakons unterstellt, doch konnten sie von dieser befreit werden, und in diesem Falle übte der Erzbischof als Diözesan bzw. als Metropolit der ungarischen Kirchenprovinz die Aufsicht aus. Die Befreiung hatte aber auch ihre materiellen Konsequenzen. Die Zehnten gebührten grundsätzlich dem Diözesan, doch im Falle enthobener Pfarreien überließ er sie öfters dem Pfarrer und behielt sich nur einen Teil derselben. Dieser vorbehaltene Teil der Zehnten ist der *census plebanorum*. Aus den lückenhaften Angaben kann weder die Frage, welche Pfarren des Amtsgewalt des Archidiakons entzogen wurden, noch das Verhältnis des *census plebanorum* zu den Einkommen der Pfarrer beantwortet werden. Diese Fragen müssen der künftigen Forschung überlassen werden.[39]

In unserer Tabelle haben wir unter »sonstige Einnahmen« ein durch den Probst von Gran gezahltes *subsidium caritativum* aus d. J. 1488 und den Nachlaß eines Graner Domherren aus d. J. 1489 eingefügt.

7. *Allgemeine Charakteristik der erzbischöflichen Einnahmen*

Das Hauptmerkmal der erzbischöflichen Einnahmen besteht darin, daß historische Elemente sowohl bei den grundherrschaftlichen wie bei den kirchlichen Einnahmen oft zur Geltung gelangten. Ein ansehnlicher Teil der grundherrschaftlichen Einkünfte war ein historisches Gebilde, das wahrscheinlich während einer langen Zeit, vielleicht Jahrhunderte hindurch unverändert blieb. Der Erbzins, dessen Zahlungstermine, das Geschenk und das als Grundlage des Geschenkerlöses dienende Preissystem waren alles historische Gebilde. Wir finden diese unter den kirchlichen Einnahmen in geringerer Zahl, obzwar die Art der Zehntenleistung und der Besitz der Zehnten, sowie der *census plebanorum* solch ein historisches Gebilde war. Daß die Zehnten-

---

[38] Die Geschichte des *pisetums* wurde von A. Kollányi verfaßt: *Az esztergomi érsek pisetum-joga* (Das *pisetum*-Recht des Erzbischofs von Gran). Kath. Szemle III/1889. F. Kováts versuchte auf Grund der Einnahmen aus dem *pisetum* die ungarische Goldproduktion zu berechnen: *A magyar arany világtörténeti jelentősége és kereskedelmi összekötteteseink a nyugattal a középkorban* (Die weltgeschichtliche Bedeutung des ungarischen Goldes und unsere Handelsbeziehungen mit dem Westen im MA). Történeti Szemle 1922, 115.

[39] Mit den Pfarren, die zur Bezahlung des *census plebanorum* verpflichtet waren, befaßte sich A. Gárdonyi: *Városi plébániák kiváltságos állása a középkorban* (Die privilegisierte Stellung der Stadtpfarreien im MA). Károlyi Emlékkönyv. 163—182.; und M. Jankovich: *Budakörnyék plébániáinak középkori kialakulása és a királyi kápolnák intézménye* (Die Entwicklung der Pfarreien in der Umgebung von Ofen im MA und die Institution der königlichen Kapellen). Budapest Régiségei XIX/1959. S. 57—94. Über die ganze, ziemlich verwickelte Frage s.: S. Fügedi: *Kirchliche Topographie und Siedlungsverhältnisse im MA in der Slowakei.* Studia Slavica V/1959. S. 396—397.

wirtschaft rationeller war als die grundherrschaftlichen Einnahmen, fällt umso mehr auf, da die Kirche als Körperschaft durch einen Konservativismus gekennzeichnet war, der selbst unter den mittelalterlichen Verhältnissen hochgradig schien.

Der andere Charakterzug wurde schon von Nyáry hervorgehoben, als er vom vollkommenen Mangel an »produktiver Kraft« sprach.[40] Die Einnahmen kennzeichnen die Periode des Feudalismus, in der die Geldwirtschaft das Übergewicht erlangte, die Geldrente die vorherrschende Form geworden war und die Eigenproduktion der Grundherren noch nicht in Gang kam. Die Einnahmen des Erzbischofs bestanden — ungeachtet dessen, ob es sich um kirchliche oder grundherrschaftliche Einnahmen handelte — aus den von Grundsassen geleisteten Renten oder Geld, das als Erlös von Naturalien einlief. Gegenüber der grundherrschaftlichen Rente war die grundherrschaftliche Warenproduktion beinahe völlig unbedeutend. Die erzbischöflichen Meierhöfe waren nicht der Warenproduktion, sondern nur der Selbstversorgung dienende landwirtschaftliche Betriebe, deren Aufgabe es war, die Pferde des Erzbistums mit Futter zu versehen. Das produzierte Heu wurde nicht einmal für Zwecke der Viehzucht verwendet, obwohl die Güter an der Grenze der Komitate Neutra und Komorn hierfür besonders geeignet waren.[41]

Die Merkmale der Einnahmen hatten ihre notwendigen wirtschaftlichen Konsequenzen. Das Erzbistum war zweifellos bemüht, möglichst alle Einnahmen an Naturalien in barem Gelde einzutreiben. Dieses Bestreben stand nicht nur zur Lage der Bauernwirtschaften sondern auch zur ganzen ungarischen Wirtschaft in Gegensatz. Darum mußte der Erzbischof einen Teil der Naturalieneinnahmen in der Form von Abrechnungen übertragen.

Die Merkmale der Einnahmen hatten noch eine andere Konsequenz. Die erzbischöflichen Einkünfte konnten mit sorgfältigem oder selbst mit gewaltsamem Eintreiben nicht in großem Maße gesteigert werden. Dies hätte man nur auf zwei Wegen erreichen können: 1. durch rationelle Regelung der bereits bestehenden Renten, was nach mittelalterlicher Denkweise unvorstellbar war und erst im 18. Jh. durchgeführt wurde; 2. durch Einführung neuer Renten. Wir wissen, daß die feudalen Grundherren sich der letzteren Methode bedienten und 1490 tat das Erzbistum dasselbe *(taxa extraordinaria)*.

Der Typ des Zehntenpächters weist darauf hin, daß sich am Ende des 15. Jhs. der Verkehr von landwirtschaftlichen Produkten belebte und daß sich der Kleinadel und die niederen kirchlichen Würdenträger mit Vorliebe in diesen Verkehr einschalteten. Dazu bot sich auch dem Erzbistum eine gute

[40] Századok III/1870. 282.
[41] Die ausgedehnten erzbischöflichen Güter, die an der Grenze der Komitate Komorn und Neutra auf einem sumpfigen Gebiet lagen, waren ausgezeichnete Heuproduzenten, wo die Haupteinnahmsquelle der Einwohner noch im 18. Jh. das Heu war *(Magyarország vármegyéi és városai, Komárom megye monografiája)* [Die Monographie des Komitates Komorn].

Gelegenheit, u. zw. vor allem durch die in Naturalien gelieferten Zehnten, und doch zeichnet sich aus den Rechnungsbüchern ein grundverschiedenes Bild ab. Das Erzbistum dachte nicht daran, sich in den Getreidehandel einzuschalten, vom Preßburger Wein wurden nur etwa 60% auf den Markt gebracht, d. h. die große Menge des Getreides und Weines diente in erster Reihe der Selbstversorgung. Wenn wir aus dem Gewinn der Preßburger Weinzehnten die Summe abrechnen, die für Weineinkauf verwendet wurde, dann bleibt aus den Weinzehnten, die bei rationeller Verwaltung und zeitgemäßem Absatz für 4000 Gulden verpachtet werden konnten, in dreijährigem Durchschnitt ein Gewinn von 1300—1400 Gulden übrig. Die Pächter und Beamtem des Erzbistums schlossen sich dem Warenverkehr an, die Familie Szentgyörgyi ging den gleichen Weg, das Erzbistum selbst aber nicht.

Alles in allem war das Erzbistum am Ende des 15. Jhs. derselbe Großgrundbesitz wie hundert Jahre früher, seine Einnahmen stammten aus Renten und Zehntenpachten, die Waren wurden mit konservativen Methoden abgesetzt.

III. Die Ausgaben des Erzbistums

Der Erzbischof von Gran war das Haupt der ungarischen Kirche, einer der größten Grundbesitzer in Ungarn und besaß eine gewisse politische Autorität. In unserem Zeitraum hatte er neben der Burg in Gran und Driegel ein Haus in der Hauptstadt Ofen, in Wien, in Preßburg, in Plintenburg (Visegrád) und in Marót, ein Schloß in Berzence und Verpécs. Eine große Zahl von Angestellten, mehr als zweihundert Personen wurden zur Instandhaltung der Burgen und Häuser, sowie zur Verwaltung der Güter angestellt. Der Erzbischof mußte die Angestellten verköstigen und teilweise mit Kleidung versehen, den Lohn der zeitweiligen Angestellten zahlen und die Kosten tragen, die ihm im Zusammenhang mit seinen kirchlichen, politischen und militärischen Aufgaben erwuchsen.

Wir haben die Angaben der Jahre 1489—1490 den hier erwähnten Funktionen entsprechend gruppiert, indem wir die ursprünglichen Konten der Hauptbücher zusammenzogen und die Ausgaben nach diesen Gruppen untersuchten.

1. *Die Ausgaben für Verpflegung*

Die Verköstigung des Personals, das Futter für die Pferde und das Brennholz für die Küche bildeten die Ausgaben der Verpflegung. Die größte Summe wurde für den Einkauf von Futter verwendet, in großer Menge wurde Schlachtvieh, hauptsächlich Schweine und Ochsen, gekauft. Es ist auffallend, wie wenig Wild in die Küchen des Erzbistums kam, obschon es große Wälder besaß. In den sehr ausführlichen Rechnungen von 1489 finden wir nur ein Wildschwein, 4 Hirsche, 3 Hasen und 2 Fasane. Als der König in Gran weilte, wurden viele Südfrüchte (Orangen, Zitronen und Feigen) gekauft. Unter den Gewürzen stehen Pfeffer und Safran in der ersten Reihe. Außer dem Preßburger Wein wurden 1489 noch 34 Faß Wein gekauft, von denen 5 Fässer syrmischer Wein waren, der im mittelalterlichen Ungarn als der beste galt.

Die zur Verpflegung nötigen Waren bildeten mit Ausnahme des Pfeffers und der Südfrüchte landwirtschaftliche Produkte des Inlandes. Von der gesamten Einkaufssumme kennen wir bloß den Einkaufsort von Ware im Werte von 1447,03 Gulden. Von dieser Summe wurde eingekauft

auf den erzbischöflichen Gütern	um	945,22 Gulden	65,3%
in Ofen	um	492,62 Gulden	34,0%
andernorts	um	9,19 Gulden	0,7%
insgesamt:		um 1 447,03 Gulden	100,0%

Das Erzbistum kaufte das Getreide, den Wein und das Brennholz zu überwiegendem Teil auf seinen eigenen Gütern. Es ist interessant zu beobachten, daß der Mittelpunkt des landwirtschaftlichen Warenverkehrs nicht Gran, sondern der am anderen Ufer der Donau, Gran gegenüber gelegene Marktflecken Kakat war. Gran war im 12—13. Jh. ein reger Handelsplatz, doch verfiel es später derart, daß man in der Stadt nur Wein und Brennholz kaufen konnte und selbst um ein halbes Pfund Pfeffer nach Ofen schicken mußte. In Ofen wurden auch die Südfrüchte und die Gewürze, also die Importartikel besorgt.

2. *Kleidung*

Hohe Summen wurden vom glänzenden erzbischöflichen Hof für Kleidung ausgegeben. Die gekauften Stoffe waren überwiegend italienisches, in erster Reihe Veroneser und Florentiner Tuch, außerdem gab es in größeren Mengen Aachener Tuch. Zur Herstellung der Kleidung der Söldner wurden schlesische und süddeutsche Tuche verwendet.[42] In großer Menge wurde inländisches Grobtuch (sog. *pannus griseus*) für die Kleidung der Dienerschaft angekauft, doch war dieses Tuch sehr billig. Eine Elle Grobtuch kostete 3,3 Pfennige, eine Elle Veroneser 0,34 Gulden, eine Elle Londoner Tuch 2,— und eine Elle Florentiner Scharlachtuch 2,50 Gulden. Nach den zur Verfügung stehenden Angaben urteilend blieb der Preis des teueren italienischen und englischen Tuches im 15. Jh. in Ungarn unverändert, während

---

[42] Statt der Steuer wurde von den Städten Kaschau und Bartfeld ebenfalls um Görlitzer und Nürnberger Tuch gebeten (*Tört. Tár* 1902. 346, 349; IVÁNYI, a. a. O. Nr. 2402.). Auch nach unseren Rechnungen »pro panno Gerliczer peciis 6 pro vestitura familiarum domini provisoris« (Usita et intrada 1491. f. 72.).

der Preis der billigeren und hauptsächlich der süddeutschen und schlesischen Tuche sank.

Viel Geld kostete die Herstellung des mit Silber reich beschlagenen Pferdegeschirrs. Auf denselben Konten wurden auch andere Luxusartikel gebucht. Gobelins aus Flandern, Kristallbecher und Spielkarten gehörten ebenfalls zu den Bedürfnissen des Hofes eines hohen Geistlichen der Renaissance.

Die Gesamtsumme des Kontos betrug 1955,99 Gulden, von denen 1558,51 Gulden den Gegenwert der Importartikel bildeten. Diese Artikel wurden überwiegend in Ofen von den dortigen italienischen und deutschen Kaufleuten erstanden, doch wurden italienische Tuche auch unmittelbar aus Italien importiert. 1489 behob der Dominikaner-Inquisitor Maestro Gianetto 3000 Gulden, um dafür in Ferrara Tuch zu kaufen. Die ausländischen Pelze wurden von M. Kis aus Krakau importiert, die Wolfspelze auf dem Markt von Kakat gekauft.

3. Bau- und Instandhaltungskosten

Mit dem baugeschichtlichen Material der Rechnungen befaßte sich P. Voit ausführlich,[43] so beschränkt sich unsere Untersuchung nur auf einige wirtschaftliche Feststellungen. Aus der Aufschlüsselung der sehr ausführlichen Posten geht hervor, daß der Lohn der Bauarbeiten wahrscheinlich höher war als die Kosten des verwendeten Materials. Beim Anschaffen des Rohmaterials kann auch hier beobachtet werden, daß in gewissen Produktionszweigen einige Dörfer und Marktflecken zu ständigen Lieferanten geworden waren. Das Erzbistum kaufte den Kalk, die Holzkohle, das Weidengeflecht zum Binden der Fässer stets in ein und demselben Dorf, wie auch die zum Bau nötige Eisenware aus Rosenau geholt wurde.

4. Die Gehälter

Die Gehälter der erzbischöflichen weltlichen Angestellten können auf Grund der Rechnungen untersucht werden, die Untersuchung kann auf die kirchlichen Angestellten nicht ausgebreitet werden, da sie nicht vom Erzbischof bezahlt wurden, sondern Inhaber unabhängiger kirchlicher Einnahmen (Benefizien) waren. Das Einkommen der weltlichen Angestellten können wir auch nicht vollkommen berechnen, weil der Wert der in Naturalien erhaltenen Deputate uns nicht bekannt ist.

[43] P. Voit: Gyarmati Dénes mester és a régi magyar építőművészet (Meister Dénes Gyarmati und die alte ungarische Baukunst). Művészettörténeti Tanulmányok (szerk. Dávid K.) Budapest, 1956. S. 46—87., Magyar kerámiaitörténeti tanulmányok. I. Kaza György, Estei Hippolyt esztergomi érsek kályhása (Studien zur Geschichte der ungarischen Keramik. I. Georg Kaza, Der Graner Ofensetzer des Hippolyt von Este). Művészettörténeti Értesítő, 1954.

Das Gefolge der Feudalherren war eben in dieser Zeit einer starken Umgestaltung unterworfen. Das traditionelle feudale Gefolge des 14—15. Jhs. hieß *familia*, deren Angehörige waren die *familiares*. Die *familiares* spielten nicht nur in der Leitung des Großgrundbesitzes eine wichtige Rolle, sondern waren in jeder Hinsicht die Stellvertreter des Grundbesitzers. Sie zogen mit ihrem *dominus* gemeinsam in den Krieg, verteidigten seine Interessen mit ihren Bewaffneten nicht nur gegen fremden Angriff, sondern auch gegen seine eigenen Grundsassen. Im Namen des *dominus* fällten und vollstreckten sie Urteile.[44] Von den *familiares* waren es die Offizialen genannten Gutsverwalter oder Kastellane, die an der Spitze der Angestellten einer Domäne standen und die Verwalter der Meierhöfe, der Maut, die Wirtschafter und letzten Endes auch die Dorfrichter zusammenfaßten. In der Person eines Offizials verflochten sich die militärischen und wirtschaftlichen Funktionen, so daß wir zwischen den beiden Funktionen keine scharfe Grenze ziehen können.

Am Ende des 15. Jhs. gesellte sich zu diesem traditionellen Gefolge ein neues Element, die repräsentative Gruppe des Hofstaates. Zur Entwicklung des neuen Elementes gab der glanzvolle Hof des Königs Matthias die erste Veranlassung, im Falle Hippolyts haben wir auch noch mit unmittelbaren italienischen Einflüssen zu rechnen. Die Aufgabe dieser Gruppe war es, den Glanz des Hofes zu steigern, der Macht des Großgrundbesitzers einen entsprechenden Rahmen zu verleihen. Dementsprechend hatten die Mitglieder dieser Gruppe keine militärischen Aufgaben und mischten sich nicht in die Angelegenheiten der wirtschaftlichen Leitung.

Auch das Personal des Erzbischofs von Gran kann in zwei verschiedene Gruppen geteilt werden: in die Gruppe der traditionellen *familia* und in die des Hofstaates. Der Unterschied zwischen den beiden Gruppen wurde durch den nationalen Gegensatz gesteigert: die Mitglieder des Hofstaates waren Italiener, die übrigen waren Ungarn. Das traditionelle Gefolge kann wiederum in drei Untergruppen zerlegt werden: die mit militärischen Aufgaben betrauten, die Offizialen und die Angestellten der wirtschaftlichen Leitung des Großgrundbesitzes.

Die bewaffnete Gefolgschaft — oder wie es in Ungarn genannt wurde — das *banderium* bestand einerseits aus Adeligen, die zur Unterhaltung bewaffneter Reiter verpflichtet waren, andererseits aus Berufssöldnern. Diese Gruppe hatte den größten Stand und das größte veranschlagte Gesamtgehalt. Sie bestand aus 48 ständigen Angestellten (6 adelige »*homo d'arme*«, die 29 Mann starke Graner Wache, 3 Artilleriefachleute und 1 Trompeter) und aus 117 bewaffneten Reitern, die von Adeligen des *banderiums* oder von den Offizialen nur im Notfall in Sold genommen wurden. Solang die Reiter in Waffen stan-

---

[44] I. SINKOVICS: *A magyar nagybirtok a XV. század elején* (Der ungarische Großgrundbesitz am Anfang des 15. Jhs.) Tanulmányok a magyar mezőgazdaság történetéhez. 8. Bp. 1933, S. 6—7.

III

den, erhielt der Adelige oder der Offizial, der sie gestellt hatte, monatlich 3 Gulden je Reiter. Die militärischen Ausgaben waren eigentlich sehr niedrig, wenn die Auffüllung des Kaders nicht nötig war.

Die Offizialen waren 24 an der Zahl. Mit Ausnahme des italienischen Kastellans von Gran waren sie alle Angehörige des ungarischen mittleren oder niederen Adels. Ihr Gehalt schwankte zwischen 60—80 Gulden jährlich, ihr Einkommen war aber viel höher, da sie in Naturalien Getreide und Wein, in barem Geld die Strafgelder der Grundsassen auf der von ihnen verwalteten Domäne erhielten.

An der Spitze der Gutsverwaltung finden wir auch die Vertreter der weltlichen Intelligenz. Zu ihnen zählten der Rechnungsbeamte, der Notar, der Anwalt und die Verwalter des sog. *pisetum*.

Zur selben Untergruppe müssen wir auch die Handwerker des Graner Hofes zählen. Die ständigen Instandhaltungsarbeiten, die Versorgung der Gefolgschaft mit Kleidung erforderte die Anstellung von 12 ständigen Handwerkern. Ihre Anstellung war häufig von vertraglichem Charakter. Das Personal der Graner Burg wurde durch Nachtwärter *(vigilatores)*, Kutscher, Stallknechte, Köche und Küchenjungen, Gärtner, Hirten und Taglöhner ergänzt. Das zur Erhaltung der Burg und des Hofes nötige Personal belief sich auf 67 Personen.

Die andere Gruppe des erzbischöflichen Personals bildete der Hofstaat. An der Spitze des Hofes stand der apostolische Protonotar und Verweser des Erzbistums, Beltramo di Costabili. Zur italienischen Hofhaltung gehörte der Hauskaplan, der Kämmerer, der Mundschenk, der Truchseß, der Arzt des Erzbischofs, der Unterkämmerer, der Untermundschenk, der Stallmeister und der Mesner. Der Verwalter des Ofner Hauses und das Personal des Wiener Hauses waren ebenfalls Italiener. Diese Gruppe des Gefolges wurde durch einen ungarischen *maestro di sala*, einen ungarischen Stallmeister, die (ebenfalls italienischen) Diener des Erzbischofs, das ungarische Personal der Küche und des Stalles, sowie durch die Diener, die den Tragstuhl trugen, ergänzt. All dies waren unerläßliche Voraussetzungen und Elemente des Prunkes, der dem ersten Würdenträger der ungarischen Kirche und dem italienischen Fürsten der Zeit gebührte. Mit Rücksicht auf das Alter des Erzbischofs (er war zu dieser Zeit zehn Jahre alt) mußte das Personal um zwei italienische Lehrer vermehrt werden. 1489 verließ Frau Cassandra, die ursprünglich Hippolyts Amme war, den Hof.

Die führenden Personen des Hofhaltes genossen die höchsten Gehälter. Selbst das letzte Mitglied des persönlichen Gefolges erhielt jährlich 30,— Gulden, weniger bekam nur der ungarische Stallmeister. Das Küchenpersonal und die Stallknechte hatten dagegen auch in dieser Gruppe kein höheres Gehalt als die ähnlichen Angestellten der Graner Burg.

*

In den Rechnungsbüchern wurde die Dienstzeit eines jeden Angestellten angeführt. Der überwiegende Teil des Hofstaates begann den Dienst noch am 18. Juni 1487 in Ferrara, d. h. als Hippolyts Hof aufgestellt wurde, die Adeligen des *banderiums* gesellten sich im August desselben Jahres zu Hippolyt. Die Dauer der Dienstzeit kann für die Zeitspanne 1487—1490 gut beobachtet werden. Selbst wenn wir die bewaffneten Reiter, die nur im Notfall gestellt wurden, außer acht lassen, zeigt uns die Verteilung der Dienstzeit, daß die lange Dauer des Dienstes umso wahrscheinlicher schien, je größer der Gehalt war. 1489 traten insgesamt 13 Personen aus dem Dienst Hippolyts, doch nur drei von ihnen gehörten zur persönlichen italienischen Gefolgschaft, und alle drei zu den schlechter bezahlten. Von den gut bezahlten verließen den Erzbischof nur ein Adeliger des *banderiums* und ein Offizial. Es ist durchaus kennzeichnend, daß dieser das kleinste Gehalt unter den Offizialen hatte.

*

Trotz den riesigen Einnahmen war das Erzbistum nicht in der Lage, die Angestellten pünktlich, zur rechten Zeit zu bezahlen, darum kam das Erzbistum seinen Verpflichtungen so nach, daß es einen Teil der Einkommen den Angestellten überließ. Besonders auffallend ist diese Tatsache im Falle der Offizialen, deren Gehalt nicht nur teilweise, sondern beinahe gänzlich durch Überlassen einer Einnahmequelle beglichen wurde. Einen beträchtlichen Teil der Zinsen, der *decimae minores*, des Einkommens aus den Mühlen und der Maut erhielten die Offizialen unmittelbar. Die Anweisung der tatsächlichen Einnahmen erreichte bei den Offizialen 71,5%. Die Form der Abwicklung ist nicht immer ganz klar. Im Falle der *decimae minores* wurden die Pachtsummen vom Gehalt abgeschrieben, in anderen Fällen wurden die tatsächlich eingetriebenen Einnahmen gutgeschrieben.

Auch bei den Mitgliedern der persönlichen Gefolgschaft begegnen wir öfters dem Fall, daß der betreffende Hofmann vom Erzbischof ein Tuch, einen Pelz oder ein anderes Kleidungsstück auf das Konto des Gehaltes bekam. Eigentlich stellt dieser Fall auch nichts anderes als die Anweisung einer Einnahme dar. Denn das Tuch oder der Pelz wurde vom Erzbischof auch nicht in barem Geld bezahlt, sondern die erwachsene Schuld bei einem Ofner Kaufmann wurde einem Pächter auf das Konto der *decimae maiores* übertragen. Es kam vor, daß der Pächter die Auszahlung des Gehaltes unmittelbar übernahm. Wenn dieser zweite Fall auch einen kürzeren Weg bedeutete als der über den Ofner Kaufmann, waren dem Wesen nach beides Anweisungen.

So ist es kaum überraschend, daß die Gehälter vom Erzbistum nie vollkommen bezahlt wurden. Das Personal der Gutsleitung erhielt auch nicht ihren ganzen Gehalt, obzwar die Angaben auf unserer Tabelle es so erscheinen lassen, als hätte es mehr denn die vertraglich festgesetzte Summe bekommen. Der Grund für diese Erscheinung ist aber die Tatsache, daß das Gehalt einiger Angestellter nicht im vorhinein pünktlich festgesetzt wurde, sondern sie bekamen so viel, wie es dem Erzbischof »gefiel«. So war das z. B. im Falle des Verwalters, der aber tatsächlich 514,25 Gulden erhielt.

Hinter dem verwickelten Tilgungssystem der Gehälter verbirgt sich also die ständige Geldverlegenheit des Erzbistums.

*

Unter den Angestellten finden sich sechs Personen, die das lateinische Attribut »*litteratus*«, oder das ungarische »*deák*« führen, d. h. sie hatten eine Domschule absolviert und waren im Besitz der elementaren lateinischen Kultur des Mittelalters. In den letzten Jahren befaßte sich die ungarische Geschichts- und Literaturgeschichtsforschung eingehend mit ihnen, weil man in ihnen die Vorgänger der späteren weltlichen Intelligenz erblickte, doch kümmerte man sich wenig um die materiellen Grundlagen ihrer Existenz.[45] Wenn wir die Lage der sechs Personen untersuchen, so sehen wir, daß nur zwei von ihnen den höheren Grad der Angestellten erreichten, einer war *homo d'arme*, der andere war der Verwalter des *pisetums*. Die übrigen waren alle Diener.

Die Kehrseite der Münze war, daß im ganzen Personal nur fünf Männer ihr Brot mit geistiger Arbeit verdienten, u. zw. die Kanzleibeamten, der Anwalt und die beiden Verwalter des *pisetums*. Sicherlich waren sie geschulte Männer, ansonsten hätten sie ihre Plätze nicht behaupten können. Außer ihnen hätte anstelle des italienischen Buchhalters noch ein ungarischer *litteratus* beschäftigt werden können. Wenn aber ein so großer Grundbesitz nur sechs geschulte Männer anstellen konnte, dann wurden im mittelalterlichen ungarischen Schulsystem viel mehr Schüler ausgebildet, als das Land unterhalten konnte. Zwangsläufig konnten viele *litterati* keine entsprechende Anstellung finden und sie waren gezwungen, die verschiedensten Berufe auszuüben, die ihrer Bildung nicht entsprachen. Die Dauer ihrer Dienstzeit beweist, daß sie keine Aussicht auf eine bessere Stellung hatten.

5. *Frachtkosten*

Die Versorgung der Residenzhäuser in den verschiedenen Städten, die Aufrechterhaltung der Verbindung und die Warenbeförderung bedeuteten besondere Spesen für das Erzbistum. Das Frachtkonto wurde 1489 so ausführlich geführt, daß wir die Frachtkosten dieses Jahres analysieren können. Die Gesamtsumme betrug 452,81 Gulden, von denen 184,72 auf den Wagen-, 157,87 auf den Schifftransport entfielen, während 110,22 Gulden für Waren ausgegeben wurden, die man zu Fuß oder mit Pferd befördert hatte.

---

[45] S. Anm. 27.

Mit Wagen wurde in erster Reihe von Preßburg transportiert, u. zw. jene Waren, die auf dem Wasserwege nicht transportiert werden konnten. Der Grund dafür lag offenbar darin, daß die Frachtkosten eines Wagens viel höher als die eines Schiffes waren. Der Transport eines Fasses von Preßburg nach Gran kostete mit Wagen 1,31, mit Schiff 0,57 Gulden. Über die Wagen können wir aus den Rechnungen nur so viel erfahren, daß sie zu dem ungarischen Wagentyp aus »Kocs« gehörten, mit Eisen beschlagen und mit Strängen aus Seil versehen waren. Ein Wagen wurde von zwei-drei Kutschern vom Sattel aus gefahren, also nach ungarischem System bespannt.[46] Einer der Kutscher war für den Wagen und die Pferde verantwortlich.

Von der Donauschiffahrt verraten unsere Rechnungen überraschend viel. Die Schiffe waren im Besitze des Erzbistums, sie waren teilweise große Schiffe, auf denen eine Hütte aufgebaut wurde, teilweise kleinere, den heutigen Kähnen ähnliche Schiffe. Über ihr Fassungsvermögen besitzen wir zwar keine Angaben, doch wurden — wie nach der Praxis zu urteilen ist — von zwei Schiffern 6—10 Faß Wein mit einem Schiff flußabwärts befördert. Die Schiffe wurden in Wien und in Preßburg gekauft.[47]

Die Frachtkosten hingen von der Länge des Weges und der Zahl der Schiffer ab. Die Frachtkosten von Gran nach Ofen betrugen pro Schiffer 0,20 Gulden, wenn also das Schiff mit vier Leuten bemannt war, ergaben die Frachtkosten 0,80 Gulden. Dieser Tarif war von der transportierten Ware unabhängig. Es war ganz einerlei, ob das Gefolge des Königs, ein fremder Gesandter, Holz, Wein, Mehl oder Fische befördert wurden. An der Spitze der Schiffer stand ein Meister, italienisch »*procurator de la nave*« genannt, der ein ständiger Angestellter der Graner Burg war. Die Schiffer stammten aus den Reihen der Grundsassen von Kövesd.[48]

Die Schifftransportkosten verteilten sich 1489 je nach der beförderten Ware folgenderweise:

Personen	5,62 Gulden
Brennholz	12,37 Gulden
Wein	79,38 Gulden
Heu	35,10 Gulden
sonstige Waren	25,40 Gulden
insgesamt	157,87 Gulden

Die Kosten des Transportes mit menschlicher Kraft bestanden hauptsächlich aus dem Lohn der sog. Faßzieher, die 10 Pfennige für das Heraufziehen eines Fasses aus dem Keller bekamen. Für den Transport durch mensch-

---

[46] PETTKO—SZANDTNER: *A magyar kocsizás* (Die ungarische Kutsche) Budapest 1931.
[47] G. CSERMÁK: *A magyar hajózás múltjából* (Aus der Vergangenheit der ungarischen Schiffahrt). Budapest, 1956. 21. ff.
[48] Laut des *Liber S. Adalberti* war es ihre Pflicht, in Fronarbeit Ruderer zu stellen.

liche Kraft finden wir auch andere — unserer heutigen Auffassung nach abschreckende — Beispiele, in Ofen wurden z. B. die Weinfässer mit menschlicher Kraft von der Donau in die Burg gebracht, 8 Fässer um 2,— Gulden.

6. Administration

Die Kosten der erzbischöflichen Administration erscheinen bei zwei verschiedenen Posten. Auf dem einen Konto wurden die Spesen der Kanzlei (Papier, Bucheinband, usw.) gebucht; diese beliefen sich auf 15,50 Gulden. Das andere Konto war — mit einem heutigen Ausdruck — das Diätenkonto, das 1489 mit einer Gesamtsumme von 295,28 Gulden abgeschlossen wurde. Die Unkosten des offiziell reisenden Angestellten wurden ihm ersetzt. Die Angestellten mußten in überraschend vielerlei Angelegenheiten entsandt werden, mag es sich nun um die Verwaltungsprobleme eines Gutes, um ein richterliches Verfahren, oder nur um die Zustellung eines Briefes gehandelt haben.

7. Die kirchlichen Ausgaben

Die sog. Servitien des Erzbischofs von Gran, die er für die päpstliche Ernennungsbulle zu zahlen hatte, beliefen sich in der zweiten Hälfte des 15. Jhs. auf 4714,30 Gulden.[49] Laut der Rechnungen schickte Hippolyt in zwei Jahren unter diesem Titel 7530 Gulden nach Italien. Leider erfahren wir aus den Rechnungsbüchern nicht, ob er mit dieser Summe seiner Verpflichtung vollkommen nachgekommen ist oder nicht, und welche Posten diese Summe enthielt (Zinsen, Schulden des Vorgängers, usw.).[50]

Mit den Servitien verglichen, waren die übrigen kirchlichen Ausgaben verschwindend gering. Den übrigen Teil der kirchlichen Ausgaben bildeten Almosen, die zu den Zeremonien nötigen Kerzen und Wachs; die Herstellung der Kerzen wurde einem Graner Handwerker überlassen.

Man muß das Mißverhältnis bemerken, das zwischen den kirchlichen Einnahmen und den kirchlichen Ausgaben bestand. Etwa 66—80% der Gesamteinnahmen gebührten dem Erzbischof als kirchlichem Würdenträger; obendrein waren diese Einnahmen leichter und schneller zu beheben, als die grundherrschaftlichen. 1489 bildeten die kirchlichen Ausgaben trotz der

[49] B. MAYER: A pápai bankárok szerepe Magyarországon a középkor végén (Die Rolle der päpstlichen Bankherrn am Ende des MAs). Századok LVII—LVIII/1923—1924. S. 648—669.

[50] Die Geschichte der Ernennung Hippolyts wurde von FRAKNÓI (Magyarország egyházi és politikai összeköttetései a római szentszékkel [Die kirchlichen und politischen Verbindungen Ungarns mit dem Hl. Stuhl] Budapest, 1902. S. 229—236) verfaßt, auch wurde eine Urkunde im Zusammenhang mit der Ernennung veröffentlicht (Oklevéltár a magyar királyi kegyúri jog történetéhez [Urkundenbuch zur Geschichte des Patronatsrechtes der ungarischen Könige]. Budapest, 1889. 53.). FRAKNÓI behauptet, daß der Gesandte des Königs Matthias für die Kosten der Ernennungsbulle 6.000 Gulden Anleihe behob, doch ist es nicht klar, in welcher Valuta das zu verstehen ist.

ungeheueren Servitien (in diesem Jahre 5000 Gulden) nur 23,6%, 1490 nur 2,8% der Gesamtausgaben. Von Kirchenbauten, von Ausgaben zur Hebung des Glanzes der kirchlichen Zeremonien ist hier keine Rede, wie es mit Ausnahme eines Orgelspielers auch keine Angestellten gibt, die bei den Zeremonien mitgewirkt hätten. Von den kulturellen Ausgaben, von der Pflege der Renaissancekultur fehlen ebenfalls jegliche Angaben, Hippolyts Hof kaufte 1489 bloß ein Buch in Ofen um 14 Gulden. Riesige Summen wurden von den Empfängen und von der Unterhaltung der Gäste, durch die Ausgaben für ausländische Tuche und Seiden, von glänzenden Gefolge verschlungen, aber zu kirchlichen oder religiösen Zwecken so gut wie nichts zurückerstattet.

8. Sonstige Ausgaben

Unter diesem Titel haben wir das Konto der »außerordentlichen Ausgaben« mit einigen anderen, kleineren gemischten Konten zusammengezogen. Die »außerordentlichen Ausgaben« waren dem Wesen nach Repräsentationskosten, die infolge des Besuches des Königs oder eines Gesandten, wegen der ihnen überreichten Geschenken erwuchsen. Hier wurden auch die Zinsen nach der Anleihe eines Juden und die Zinsen einer Anleihe von 50,— Gulden gebucht. Die Spuren von Schulden sind aber nicht nur hier zu finden. Die »alten«, noch 1486—1487 gemachten Schulden wurden auf einem besonderen Konto geführt. Von der Gesamtsumme der Schulden schweigt das Hauptbuch, nur die Tilgungen wurden aufgezeichnet.

9. Allgemeine Charakteristik der Ausgaben

Der erste Charakterzug der Ausgaben ist die Tatsache, daß der Erzbischof alles, was zur Verpflegung des Personals nötig war, für bares Geld kaufen mußte. Die angekauften landwirtschaftlichen Artikel waren offenbar teuerer, als wenn sie die erzbischöflichen Güter produziert hätten. Der teuerste Preßburger Wein kostete 5,— Gulden, für den in Gran gekauften und dort bebauten Wein zahlte der Erzbischof im besten Fall 6,37 Gulden je Faß. So ist es nicht überraschend, daß für landwirtschaftliche Produkte 1489 nicht weniger als 4238,48 Gulden, d. h. 18,8% der Ausgaben ausbezahlt werden mußten.

Der glänzende Hofstaat war überdimensioniert. Der Graner Erzbischof besaß auch schon vor Hippolyt ein Haus in Ofen und Preßburg. Hippolyt fügte aber diesen noch ein Haus in Wien hinzu und unterhielt überall ein ständiges Personal. Ein großer Teil des persönlichen Gefolges hielt sich ständig in Wien oder in Ofen auf, dies steigerte die Unterhalts- und Frachtkosten.

Das Personal des Hofes war auf jeden Fall zu groß. Dies gilt nicht für die Zahl der Angestellten in der Gutsverwaltung oder im bewaffneten Gefolge, sondern für die der Angestellten, die in Ferrara rekrutiert wurden und überhaupt keine produktive Arbeit leisteten. Der Erzbischof mußte ihre Verpflegung decken und jährlich rund 1000 Gulden Gehalt bezahlen. Die Tatsache, daß das Erzbistum den vollen Jahresgehalt nicht auszahlen konnte, ist ein glänzender Beweis der Überdimensionierung.

Die Lebensweise des Hofes war ebenfalls überspannt. Nyáry hatte recht, als er davon sprach, daß man zuviel Gäste empfing und unterhielt, zuviel Geschenke für sie kaufte und daß der Prozentsatz der »außerordentlichen« Ausgaben zu hoch war.

Die Überdimensionierung ließ ihre negativen Früchte reifen. Der großartigen Bautätigkeit des Erzbischofs Johann Vitéz — des Vorgängers von Hippolyt — folgte die Herabsetzung der Investitionen. 1489 wurde noch am Haus in Marót gebaut, 1490 beschränkten sich die Bauarbeiten auf das Nötigste, der Wert der Investitionen sank um ein Drittel.

Bei der Charakterisierung der Einnahmen haben wir behauptet, daß das Erzbistum in der Entwicklung zurückblieb. Die Ausgaben kennzeichnen das Erzbistum als einen glänzenden feudalen Hof der Renaissance. Der Gegensatz zwischen den für das 14. Jh. charakteristischen Einnahmen und den für das Ende das 15. Jhs charakteristischen Ausgaben war nicht zu überbrücken.

*

Der ungeheuere Grundbesitz und die hohen Einnahmen des Erzbistums gestalteten es zu einem Großverbraucher, der mit seinen Ausgaben und Käufen auf das ungarische Wirtschaftsleben auswirkte. Die Rechnungen des Jahres 1489 ermöglichen uns, fast alle Ausgaben des Erzbistums zu qualifizieren und so die Frage zu beantworten, wofür die Einnahmen — und sogar noch etwas mehr — ausgegeben wurden. Demnach wurden ausgegeben:

für Importwaren	2 355,02 Gulden	32,6%
für das päpstliche Servitium	5 000,00 Gulden	
für einheimische Waren	6 235,47 Gulden	27,6%
für Arbeitslöhne und Gehälter	7 920,05 Gulden	35,1%
unbestimmbar	1 058,39 Gulden	4,7%
insgesamt	22 568,93 Gulden	100,0%

Aus dieser Tabelle geht klar hervor, daß ein Drittel von Hippolyts Einnahmen als Arbeitslohn und Gehälter, ein Drittel für einheimische Waren, ein Drittel für ausländische Waren verausgabt wurde. Da aber nicht in jedem Jahre eine so hohe päpstliche Steuer bezahlt werden mußte, sind wir gezwungen, unsere Zusammenstellung ohne das päpstliche Servitium zu wiederholen:

für ausländische Ware	2 355,02 Gulden	13,4%
für einheimische Ware	6 235,47 Gulden	35,5%
für Arbeitslöhne und Gehälter	7 920,05 Gulden	45,1%
unbestimmbar	1 058,39 Gulden	6,0%
insgesamt	17 568,93 Gulden	100,0%

Man fragt sich jedoch, ob Hippolyt und sein italienischer Hof nicht mehr für ausländische Waren ausgegeben hat, als die übrigen hohen Würdenträger der Kirche und des Landes in Ungarn. Wir kennen den Warenverkehr an der Westgrenze Ungarns aus den Jahren 1457—1458. Wenn wir nun die Verteilung dieses Zolls mit der Verteilung der Ausgaben Hippolyts vergleichen, bekommen wir folgendes Resultat.

	Hippolyt		Preßburger Zoll	
Gewürze, Südfrüchte	156,35 Gl.	6,6%	396,21 Gl.	4,0%
Rohwaren	3,28 Gl.	0,1%		
Textilien	1 517,01 Gl.	64,4%	7 717,17 Gl.	78,8%
Andere Gewerbeprodukte ...	678,28 Gl.	28,9%	1 684,87 Gl.	17,2%
insgesamt:	2 355,02 Gl.	100,0%	9 798,25 Gl.	100,0%

Zwischen den beiden Prozensätzen ist kein großer Unterschied. Hippolyts Hof verbrauchte zwar weniger ausländische Textilien, als rund dreißig Jahre früher an der Westgrenze des Landes eingeführt wurden, doch war der Prozentsatz bei Gewürz und Südfrüchten seitens des Erzbistums etwas höher als der des Preßburger Zolls, und auch der Prozentsatz der Industrieprodukte war bei dem Erzbistum höher als an der Westgrenze. Im Großen wurde in beiden Fällen die überwiegende Mehrheit vom Wert der Textilien gebildet. So scheint der Importprozentsatz von 13,4 nicht zu hoch zu sein.

Wir kommen zum selben Resultat, wenn wir bedenken, daß Hippolyt eigentlich keine besonderen luxuriösen Leidenschaften hatte. Er baute nicht in so großem Maße wie sein Vorgänger und sein Nachfolger, kaufte nicht so viele Bücher. Statt dessen ging er den Weg der zeitgenössischen ungarischen Magnaten und gab das meiste für die Kleidung aus. Doch wurde in dieser Hinsicht am Ende des 15. und Anfang des 16. Jhs. von den ungarischen Prälaten und Magnaten ein Luxus und Prunk entfaltet, daß es jeden Diplomaten bestürzte, der über die tatsächliche politische und wirtschaftliche Lage des Landes im Bilde war. Wenn wir zu der Summe, die für Importwaren ausgegeben wurde, noch die päpstliche Steuer hinzurechnen, die ebenfalls außer Landes ging, dann müssen wir feststellen, daß ein bedeutender Teil der erzbischöflichen Einnahmen ins Ausland wanderte. Der ungarische Wirtschaftshistoriker F. Kováts schätzte die Passivität unseres mittelalterlichen Handels

auf 300.000, O. Paulinyi auf 400.000 Gulden. 0,5% dieser Summe, bzw. die
päpstliche Steuer mit inbegriffen 1,0%, wurde vom Erzbistum exportiert.
Gänzlich unbestimmbar ist die Summe, die vom Gehalt der italienischen
Angestellten ins Ausland mitgenommen wurde. Wir haben gesehen, daß
Perotto Vesach alle seine Güter verflüssigte, bevor er nach Italien zurückkehrte, er nahm also wahrscheinlich ungarische Goldgulden mit sich. Wir
können für sicher halten, daß er nicht der einzige Italiener war, der ungarisches Gold in Münzen »exportierte«.

Es ist also zweifellos, daß 1489 ein Drittel der erzbischöflichen Ausgaben
in der Form von Goldgulden ins Ausland gingen. 1489 war dieses Verhältnis
wegen der hohen päpstlichen Steuer so schlecht, in anderen Jahren schwankte
es um 13% der Gesamtausgaben, was 0,5% der jährlichen Goldausfuhr des
Landes betrug.

*

Ein zweites Drittel wurde für den Kauf inländischer Ware ausgegeben.
Die Verteilung dieser stattlichen Summe ist folgende:

Landwirtschaftliche Rohprodukte	4238,48 Gl.	68,0%
Sonstige	695,28 Gl.	11,1%
Gewerbeartikel	1301,71 Gl.	20,9%
insgesamt	6235,47 Gl.	100,0%

Auf den überaus hohen Prozentsatz der landwirtschaftlichen Rohpro-
dukte wurde schon hingewiesen. Hier können unsere Folgerungen höchstens
damit ergänzt werden, daß die Einkäufe des erzbischöflichen Hofes und
anderer Magnatenhöfe vielleicht bei der Steigerung der Nachfrage an landwirtschaftlichen Produkten mitgewirkt haben. Die Steigerung der Ansprüche
seitens der feudalen Höfe war offenbar nicht der einzige Grund, doch einer
der vielen Gründe, die die Nachfrage erhöhten.

Laut der Rechnungen war der Anspruch auf inländische Gewerbeartikel
sehr niedrig. Auf Gewerbeartikel entfielen bloß 20,9% des Wertes der inlän-
dischen Ware.

Metallhandwerk	539,28 Gulden	41,4%
Beleuchtung	166,18 Gulden	12,8%
Textilien	99,47 Gulden	7,6%
Leder	191,17 Gulden	14,7%
Holzverarbeitung	152,42 Gulden	11,7%
Lebensmittel	13,29 Gulden	1,0%
Kleidung	15,70 Gulden	1,2%
Baumaterial	68,45 Gulden	5,3%
sonstige Handwerksartikel	55,75 Gulden	4,3%
insgesamt:	1301,71 Gulden	100,0%

An der Spitze steht das Metallhandwerk, doch gereichte der hohe Prozentsatz hauptsächlich den Goldschmieden zum Vorteil, da von den 538,28
Gulden der Gesamtsumme z. B. ein dem König geschenkter Becher allein
412,— Gulden kostete. Als Vertreter des Lederhandwerks erscheinen die
Sattler und Kürschner, die Erzeuger der luxuriösen Pferdegeschirre und der
Pelzmäntel. Die von der ausländischen Konkurrenz zugrunde gerichteten
Handwerker des Textilien- und Kleidungshandwerks figurierten mit einem
minimalen Prozentsatz. Die hier figurierende Summe des Lebensmittelsge-
werbes gibt uns kein reales Bild. Auf dem Küchenkonto, das näher nicht
bestimmbare Posten in einem Gesamtwerte von 2422,— Gulden enthält,
war offenbar der Wert von einer Menge fertiger Lebensmittel geführt, obzwar
die Anstellung eines Bäckers und Müllers die Aussichten dieses Handwerks-
zweiges stark verminderte. In landesgültiger Hinsicht kann auch der Prozentsatz des Beleuchtungshandwerks nicht als kennzeichnend betrachtet werden,
weil die für religiöse Zwecke verwendeten Kerzen und Leuchter diese Ausgaben in hohem Maße steigerten. Dies ist auch einer der Punkte, wo die
Zahlen uns daran erinnern, daß Hippolyt eine hohe geistliche Würde innehatte.
All dies bestätigt die allgemeine Auffassung, daß das Handwerk in
Ungarn im Mittelalter unentwickelt war. Doch begegnen wir auch noch anderen Merkmalen, die auf die Unentwickeltheit des ungarischen Handwerks
hindeuten. Ein bedeutender Teil der Produkte des Bau- und Holzgewerbes
wurde von den Bauern als Hausgewerbe betrieben (Schindeln, Kalk, usw.).
Diese Produkte wurden nicht von einem städtischen Handwerkertum, sondern von der Agrarbevölkerung als Nebenbeschäftigung erzeugt.
Die Versorgung der Angestellten mit Kleidern weist auf die Ansprüche
hin, die gegenüber dem Handwerk gestellt wurden. Es erscheint als natürlich,
daß die Angehörigen des *banderiums* und des persönlichen Gefolges im allgemeinen ausländische Tuche oder aus solchem genähte Kleider erhielten,
doch überrascht es zu hören, daß auch der Schmied Urban und der Polier
Peter auf ein Kleid aus Veroneser Tuch und auf einen Lammpelz Anspruch
haben konnten. Wenn selbst diese Handwerker darauf bestanden, ein aus
ausländischem Stoff verfertigtes Gewand zu bekommen, für wen wurde dann
eigentlich das inländische Grobtuch und Leinen gekauft? Für die Kutscher,
Stallknechte, für das Küchenpersonal und für die Taglöhner. Unwillkürlich
taucht die Frage auf: welche Aussichten hatte das ungarische Textilhand-
werk, wenn selbst die Handwerker nicht geneigt waren seine Produkte zu
tragen und diese nur von der Dienerschaft und der armen Schicht des Bauerntums gekauft wurden?
Wenn wir das vom Handwerk entworfene Bild mit den Löhnen ergänzen, die den Handwerkern ausbezahlt wurden, bekommen wir die folgende
Verteilung:

Metallhandwerk	26,50 Gulden	1,8%
Lederhandwerk	746,69 Gulden	49,7%
Holzverarbeitung	5,69 Gulden	0,4%
Lebensmittel	16,66 Gulden	1,1%
Kleidung	286,80 Gulden	19,1%
Baumaterial	398,50 Gulden	26,5%
sonstige Handwerker	20,71 Gulden	1,4%
insgesamt:	1501,55 Gulden	100,0%

Im Großen bleibt das Bild unverändert, obzwar die Gesamtsumme höher ist, als die für die Waren ausgezahlte Summe war. An der Spitze steht auch hier das Lederhandwerk (Pferdegeschirr und Fertigung der Pelze). Der Prozentsatz der Bauindustrie ist ein wenig verzerrt, da im Lohn auch der Lohn von drei Hilfsarbeitern inbegriffen ist. Der den Meistern des Textilhandwerks ausgezahlte Lohn ist ausschließlich der Lohn des Tuchscherers.

Wenn wir uns vergegenwärtigen, daß gegenüber der Gesamtsumme von 2803,21 Gulden, die den einheimischen Handwerkern bezahlt wurde, die Summe von 2195,39 Gulden steht, die für ausländische Gewerbewaren bezahlt wurde, dann können wir nicht nur feststellen, daß das ungarische Handwerk — abgesehen von einigen Zweigen, die Luxuswaren erzeugten — unentwickelt war (was schon von der bisherigen Forschung hervorgehoben wurde), sondern auch, daß die Ursache der Unentwickeltheit der Mangel an Nachfrage seitens der einheimischen Verbraucherschicht war.

*

Nach der ausführlichen Analyse versuchen wir in groben Zügen die Frage zu beantworten, zu wem Hippolyts Einnahmen gelangten. Ein beträchtlicher Teil ging ins Ausland. Zwei Drittel floß aber im Inland in den Blutkreislauf des Wirtschaftslebens zurück. Zum größten Teil gelangte es zu den Bauern zurück. Zu diesem Teil gehörten die 4238,76 Gulden, die für landwirtschaftliche Rohstoffe bezahlt wurden, und die 166,66 Gulden Lohn, der den Arbeitern ausgezahlt wurde, weiterhin ein Teil des für inländische Handwerkerwaren ausgegebenen Geldes. Die städtischen Handwerker erhielten im besten Fall 2803,21 Gulden. Der Gehalt der italienischen Hofbeamten und der ungarischen Wirtschaftsbeamten betrug insgesamt 5800 Gulden. Im Spiegel dieser Zahlen ist es leicht zu verstehen, warum die Handwerker in unseren mittelalterlichen Städten so wenig prosperierten, warum man mit Handel, und besonders mit dem Handel ausländischer Tuche so viel verdienen konnte.

Die Wirtschaft des Erzbistums von Gran   289

IV. Die Bilanz des Erzbistums

Die Bilanz zeigt uns folgende Summen:

	1489	1490
Einnahmen	22 275,05 Gulden	15 005,91 Gulden
Ausgaben	22 568,03 Gulden	15 566,24 Gulden
Defizit	292,98 Gulden	560,33 Gulden

Das Defizit wurde auf zwei Wegen beseitigt: einerseits blieb das Erzbistum den Hauptbeamten schuldig, andererseits behob es Anleihen. Wenn wir diese Frage eingehender beleuchten wollen, so muß unser Ausgangspunkt die Tatsache sein, daß ein beträchtlicher Teil der Einnahmen aus der jährlichen landwirtschaftlichen Produktion stammte. Die Bauern waren verpflichtet, nach der Ernte den grundherrschaftlichen Zins, die Zehnten in Getreide, Wein, usw. zu leisten.

In Gulden:	1488	1489	1490
Von der Landwirtschaft abhängige Einnahmen	12 974,39	18 996,75	13 392,83
Einnahmen aus dem Bergbau	2 975,75	3 278,30	1 613,08
insgesamt:	15 950,14	22 275,05	15 005,91

In Prozenten:	1488	1489	1490
Von der Landwirtschaft abhängige Einnahmen	81,3	85,3	89,3
Einnahmen aus dem Bergbau	18,7	14,7	10,7
insgesamt:	100,0	100,0	100,0

Im mittelalterlichen Ungarn war in der zweiten Hälfte des Sommers der Ertrag der Ernte ein *fait accompli*, die Getreidepreise wurden Ende Juli oder Anfang August stabilisiert. In den großen Verbraucherzentren, in den Städten finden wir im allgemeinen überall die Jahrmärkte, die gegen Ende des Sommers oder im Herbst gehalten wurden und an denen die Bauern ihre Waren absetzten, die städtischen Handwerker und Kaufleute ihre Waren verkauften. Doch weder die Handwerker noch die städtischen Bürger hatten das nötige Bargeld, um die gekaufte Ware sofort auszuzahlen. Die uns bekannten Transaktionen wurden ganz, oder wenigstens teilweise in Form eines Kredites abgeschlossen. Oft war ein ganzes Jahr nötig, um die im Sommer oder Herbst abgeschlossenen Transaktionen liquidieren zu können. Im Warenverkehr hat der Ertrag der Ernte rasch den Besitzer gewechselt (das bestätigen die Mauteinnahmen), doch dauerte die finanzielle Abwicklung noch lange.

Die grundherrschaftliche Rente mußte sich wohl oder übel an diese Abwicklungsweise halten. Vom Standpunkt des Grundherren hieß dies, daß die Einnahmen nur nach der Ernte fällig wurden, und ihr Eintreiben sich bis zum nächsten Frühling hinzog. Das Erzbistum konnte natürlich nicht warten, die Ausgaben waren dringend. Es half sich auf zweierlei Art. Erstens nahm es bei der Verpachtung der Naturaleinnahmen keine Rücksicht auf den Zeitpunkt des Absatzes des Ernteertrages, zweitens überwies es einen Teil der Naturaleinnahmen unmittelbar an den Gläubiger. 1489 erhielt das Erzbistum vor dem 1. Juli 2000 Gulden aus den Zehntenpachten, und im selben Jahr beglich es 2055,93 Gulden mit Anweisungen. Im Werte von 765,31 Gulden wurden auch die Kreditübertragungen in Anspruch genommen. Dem Wesen nach stehen wir im Fall der unmittelbaren Anweisungen und der Kreditübertragungen der Erscheinung gegenüber, daß das Erzbistum das Tempo des Absatzes des landwirtschaftlichen Ertrages sowohl seinen Gläubigern, wie auch seinen Angestellten aufgezwungen hat.

Auch der Geldschonungsverkehr (geldsparende Zahlungsverkehr) wurde in Anspruch genommen. Dieser Verkehr erscheint 1489 unter den Einnahmen mit einem Wert von 971,46 Gulden. Ein Beispiel dieses Verkehrs war die Ware, die von M. Kis geliefert wurde und die Gehälter der Offizialen, denen eine Einnahmsquelle unmittelbar zugewiesen wurde.

Diese Mittel wurden vom Erzbistum angewendet, um die Einnahmen zeitlich besser zu verteilen und hauptsächlich, um sie vom Zeitpunkt der Ernte unabhängig zu machen. Im Grunde genommen können das schleppende Tempo der landwirtschaftlichen Produktion und alle damit zusammenhängenden Fragen auf einen einzigen Charakterzug der ungarischen Wirtschaft im Mittelalter zurückgeführt werden: der mittelalterliche Geldverkehr war geringer, als es zur Abwicklung des tatsächlichen Warenverkehrs nötig gewesen wäre. Hinter dem regen Verkehr war unsere mittelalterliche Wirtschaft durch einen Mangel an barem Gelde gekennzeichnet.

1. Die Einnahmen des Erzbischofs von Gran

In Gulden

1. Grundherrschaftliche Einnahmen

Grundzins	2 138,32	2 194,95	2 191,69
Taxa extraordinaria	—	—	1 226,27
Munera	184,39	153,52	284,37
Grundherrschaftliche Nona	684,06	427,11	510,00
Fronarbeit	12,00	12,00	12,00
Zoll- u. Mauteinnahmen	204,29	251,78	367,46
Einnahmen aus den Mühlen	60,08	24,48	—
Zins der Kremnitzer Mühle	600,00	300,00	300,00
Urbura	444,25	310,46	136,85
Verkauf von Agrarprodukten	216,64	387,87	74,24
Insgesamt	4 544,03	4 062,17	5 102,88

2. Kirchliche Einnahmen

Decimae maiores	5 914,60	9 647,81	5 788,15
Decimae minores	689,00	938,46	836,72
Pisetum	2 531,50	2 967,84	1 476,50
Preßburger Zehnten	1 175,02	4 321,77	1 432,66
Census plebanorum	393,00	62,00	369,00
Sonstige Einnahmen	703,00	275,00	—
Insgesamt	11 406,12	18 212,88	9 903,03
Insgesamt	15 950,15	22 275,05	15 005,91

Im Prozentsatz

1. Grundherrschaftliche Einnahmen

Grundzins	47,1	54,0	43,0
Taxa extraordinaria	—	—	24,0
Munera	4,1	3,8	5,6
Grundherrschaftliche Nona	15,1	10,5	10,0
Fronarbeit	0,3	0,3	0,2
Zoll- und Mauteinnahmen	4,5	6,2 }	
Einnahmen aus den Mühlen	1,3	0,7 }	7,2
Zins der Kremnitzer Mühle	13,2	7,4	5,8
Urbura	9,7	7,6	2,7
Verkauf von Agrarprodukten	4,7	9,5	1,5
Insgesamt	100,0	100,0	100,0

2. Kirchliche Einnahmen

Decimae maiores	51,9	53,0	58,4
Decimae minores	6,0	5,2	8,4
Pisetum	22,2	16,3	14,9
Preßburger Zehnten	10,3	23,7	14,6
Census plebanorum	3,4	0,3	3,7
Sonstige Einnahmen	6,2	1,5	—
Insgesamt	100,0	100,0	100,0

2. Die Konten des M. Kis von Cece

Soll   Haben

1488

Zehntenpacht	1 300,—	20.3. Barzahlung	1 100,—
		26.10. Barzahlung	95,50
		Saldo	104,50
Insgesamt	1 300,—	Insgesamt	1 300,—

1489/I.

Schuld des vorigen Jahres .	104,50	3.6. Barzahlung	800,—
Zehntenpacht (1489)	1 550,—	13.12. Preis des gelieferten Holzes	135,—
		24.12. Preis des gelieferten Holzes	100,—
		28.12. Preis von Pferden	50,—
		28.12. Preis eines Pelzmantels	80,—
		31.12. Preis eines Pelzmantels	36,—
		31.12. Preis von Fell	155,—
		31.12. Preis von Fell	22 —
		31.12. Frachtkosten	1,12
		31.12. Preis von Fell	14,88
		31.12. Preis von Biberfell	67,00
		31.12. Gehalt des G. Sáfár	4,50
		31.12. Die Entlassung der Zehntenpacht	100,—
		Saldo	89,—
Insgesamt	1 654,50	Insgesamt	1 654,50

1489/II.

Zehntenpacht des Jahres 1490	1 200,—	28.9. Barzahlung	500,—
		Saldo	700,—
Insgesamt	1 200,—	Insgesamt	1 200,—

1490

Zehntenpacht	700,—	6.4. Barzahlung	150,—
		29.2. Barzahlung	250,—
		29.2. Barzahlung	50,—
		20.6. Barzahlung	250,—
Insgesamt	700,—	Insgesamt	700,—

3. Die Konten des B. Szakácsi

Soll   1488   Haben

Zehntenpacht	2 250,—	24.6.	Barzahlung	600,—
		3.10.	Barzahlung	100,—
		25.10.	Barzahlung	88,—
		10.11.	Barzahlung	99,76
			Saldo	1 362,24
Insgesamt	2 250,—		Insgesamt	2 250,—

1489

Schulden des vorigen Jahres	1 362,24	1.3.	Barzahlung	137,—
Zehntenpacht (1489)	2 300,—	2.3.	Barzahlung	1 161,—
		3.3.	Barzahlung	40,—
		? 5.	Barzahlung	24,24
		9.6.	Barzahlung	400,—
		? ?	Barzahlung	150,—
		? ?	Barzahlung	50,—
		18.11.	Übernahme der erzbischöfl. Verpflichtungen gegenüber R. Bontempi (Ofen)	226,22
		23.11.	gegenüber Arbar (Ofen)	130,15
		23.11.	gegenüber Antonio (Ofen)	39,70
		31.12.	gegenüber Piller (Ofen)	26,—
		31.12.	Barzahlung	10,—
		31.12.	Übernahme der erzbischöfl. Verpflichtungen gegenüber J. Libarius	16,—
		31.12.	Für Ausstellung einer Urkunde	3,—
			Saldo	1 248,93
Insgesamt	3 662,24		Insgesamt	3 662,24

1490

Schuld des vorigen Jahres	1 248,93	15.2.	Übernahme der erzbischöfl. Verpflichtungen gegenüber dem Goldschmied Emericus	159,—
		6.4.	Barzahlung	90,—
		29.2.	Barzahlung	600,—
		29.2.	Übernahme der erzbischöfl. Verpflichtungen gegenüber Piller	34,—
		29.2.	gegenüber Cavalkanti	300,—
		29.2.	gegenüber Johannes (Kürschner)	26,—
		29.2.	gegenüber Goldschmied Emericus	18,—
			Saldo	21,93
Insgesamt	1 248,93		Insgesamt	1 248,93

4. Die Ausgaben des Erzbischofs von Gran

In Gulden	1489	1490
Versorgung	4 325,59	4 848,56
Kleidung	3 300,93	1 000,57
Baukosten	917,49	653,—
Gegalte	5 531,50	6 027,83
Frachtkosten	225,23	239,94
Administration	310,78	350,57
Kosten des Preßburger Hauses	551,94	563,51
Außerordentliche Ausgaben	2 087,37	1 448,40
Ausgaben für kirchliche Zwecke	5 318,10	433,86
Insgesamt	22 568,93	15 566,24

In Prozentsatz		
Versorgung	19,2	31,1
Kleidung	14,6	6,4
Baukosten	4,1	4,2
Gehalte	24,5	38,7
Frachtkosten	1,0	1,6
Administration	1,4	2,3
Kosten des Preßburger Hauses	2,4	3,6
Außerordentliche Ausgaben	9,2	9,3
Ausgaben für kirchliche Zwecke	23,6	2,8
Insgesamt	100,0	100,0

IV

THE ARISTOCRACY IN MEDIEVAL HUNGARY
(THESES)

> *Having studied the various aspects of Hungarian nobility in the past decades, I found it useful to summarize the results of these inquiries for further discussion and future research. References to sources and literature can be found in the studies listed in the bibliography at the end of this volume, esp.* items *1963/c; 1965/g; 1970/c; 1972/e; 1974/d; 1977/g; 1979/a, d; 1982/a; 1984/b; 1984/c [=* **VI** , below] , *and will be expanded in my monograph under preparation.*

I. Questions of Method and the Sources

1.   The availability and character of sources define to a great extent the feasibility of historical research on a given topic. For the history of the aristocracy in the medieval kingdom of Hungary it is the dearth of reliable and explicit sources which prescribes the parameters of inquiry.

For a working hypothesis I shall regard the aristocracy as that group of great landowners (precisely: landowning families, see below) whose members claimed and received a part in political decisions through their participation in the royal council. The two elements of this definition — landownership and political office — are susceptible to separate analysis. I shall begin with the latter, for it is still better documented, and shall confront the results with a study of the former.

2.   No list of the members of the royal council has come down to us from before the sixteenth century. It is clear, however, that this body included besides the prelates (two archbishops and ten bishops):

(a) the high officers of the realm, i.e. the count palatine, the voivode of Transylvania and the bans of Croatia, Slavonia and some of the banates along the southern frontier;

(b) the high justices (judge royal and Master of the Treasurers, as appeal judge of certain cities);

(c) the household officers of the king and the queen (lords ostiary, gentlemen carvers, chamberlains, cupbearers, masters of the horse).

A list of these men — henceforth to be called barons, following the usage of the fourteenth and fifteenth centuries — offers some insight into the aristocracy at large, although it remains to be explored, to what extent were they identical with it. Such lists, i.e. archontologies of the kingdom, can be complied from five types of sources of very different value:

(i) list of dignitaries inserted in the eschatocols of royal charters;

The listing of witnesses, usual in the charters preceding the mid-twelfth century, was replaced by lists of spiritual and secular office holders regardless of their presence at the issue under King Stephen V (1270-72), but became neither continuous nor consistent in chancery practice until 1356. While between 1272 and 1276 the dignitaries were always listed, this usage was discontinued for half a century, only to be taken up again by King Charles I Robert (1308-42) in 1323. From that date on the naming of the prelates, barons and certain counts became mandatory for every privilegial charter. However, the officers included remained rather unsystematic until 1356. After that time little had been changed, and if so, it reflected the changing role of certain offices in the course of the fifteenth century.

Unfortunately, we have no indication about the principle of selection for these lists. They probably originated in some foreign model, but diplomatists so far were unable to trace its descent. A few trends appear obvious:

(a) not all barons were intended to be listed, as reflected in the usual closing formula: *et aliis quampluribus comitatus et honores regni tenentibus;*

(b) two groups, counts of counties (*comites*) and barons *(honores regni)* were distinguished;

(c) the barons of the queen's household were not included, with the exception of three decades (1323-55) during which time some of them were;

(d) first there was a tendency to shorten the list: under Stephen V fourteen names are mentioned, under Charles I twelve, under Louis I (1342-82) eleven; in the fifteenth century the list again increased to fourteen at the expense of the *comites.*

(ii) adressees of royal charters and mandates;

(iii) notes on *relationes* of charters, i.e. the name of the officer who had presented the case to the king and/or council;
(iv) introductions on baronial charters;
(v) references in other, local or private, records.
Among these records, royal charters, of course, deserve highest credence. Records issued by local authorities (counties, *loca credibilia*) or private individuals often "overstyle" or forget to include references to the fact that the person does not hold the office any more *(pridem, alias)*.

3.   While the group of barons can thus be fairly well reconstructed, the question arises, to what extent the counts of counties *(comites parochiales, comites civitatum;* in Hungarian: *ispán*, Pl.: *ispánok)* should be included in the aristocracy. If we were able to add them to the barons, the majority of the aristocracy would be included in our inquiry. However desirable this may be, the system of government in medieval Hungary on the one hand, and the scarcity of sources on local administration on the other, preclude a thorough and systematic survey of the group of the *comites*.
   To begin with, there was always some overlapping between baronial and comital offices. From ca. 1320 on certain royal offices were regularly connected with the comital post of one or more counties, such as the banate of Macsó/Mačva with six southern counties, the voivodship of Transylvania with county Szolnok, the palatinate with county Pest, the royal castellanship of the residential castle Visegrád with county Pilis. There may have been other counties administered by barons, regularly or occasionally. As to the sources: we have no complete list of counts of counties for any one year before the end of the fifteenth century.
   We can assume that in the fourteenth century only 47 counties remained under the king's immediate jurisdiction; some of these were entrusted to retainers holding baronial offices. If we count the counties and the royal castles administered by barons (in five-year intervals) from 1330 and 1375, we find that until 1350 usually four barons held 7-8 counties and 13-26 castles; after 1350 only three barons held 4-7 counties with no more than 22 castles. After 1370 these numbers fell drastically to two barons holding two counties and only one single royal castle. The trend is not only numerical, but is also reflected in the fact that the commissions were given individually.
   No statistical table can be constructed for the Angevin period, but for the early fifteenth century the data permit us to draw up a

table for most counties (the *comites* of five counties are not known).

TABLE I:
BARONS AND COUNTS GOVERNING COUNTIES IN 1407

	families	counties held
barons	9	12
ispánok	15	30
Total	24	42

The concentration of power in the hands of a few dozen baronial and comital families is also apparent from their ownership of castles. I shall return to that below (see Table II).

Table I above — and Tables II-III, below — are formulated in terms of families and not of individuals. This is reasonable, because, I argue, from the thirteenth century on the aristocracy consisted of families. No useful archontology can be compiled (as far as at all possible) without considering that usually several members of the same family held baronial or comital offices at the same time.

The combined study of baronial and comital families is the prerequisite for any meaningful social history of the medieval élites. It is also true, however, that the barons, i.e. those members of the aristocracy who regularly participated in political decisions, acted as a kind of pressure group for the interests of their entire estate, while the *ispánok* (if not also barons) played the role of supporting cast on the political stage.

4. Turning to the other characteristic of the aristocracy, its landed property, we have less unequivocal evidence at our disposal. Some twenty years ago I believed that an adequate inquiry into this aspect cannot be conducted at all, because both the relevant analytical concepts (such as the definition and structural description of the great estate) and the necessary historical-geographical surveys are lacking. However, my studies on the thirteenth and fourteenth centuries suggested to me that the erecting and holding stone-built castles sufficiently reflects the political potential of the great landed estates. The owners of such castles cum estates can be safely regarded as members of the aristocracy.

The following tables demonstrate the concentration of castles in the hands of aristocratic families (Table II) and the correlations between castle-ownership and political office (Table III).

TABLE II:
CASTLE OWNERSHIP

	1355		1407	
	family	castle	family	castle
baronial	13	11	12	48
comital*	20	20	13	33
TOTAL	33	31	25	81
in % of all castles**		10.3		27.0

NOTES:

* the five unknown counts may change this figure slightly

** of which the owner is known, including royal castles

This table demonstrates that in the course of the later fourteenth century not only fewer families came to hold the politically significant positions in their hands (see Table I), but also that these families had acquired significantly more castles and estates. Of the mid-fourteenth-century baronial families six owned no castle at all and only half of the comital families had a castle to their name. In 1407 only one baron did not have (yet!) a castle and only three of the thirteen comital families owned no fortified residence.

TABLE III:
CASTLE OWNERSHIP AND POLITICAL OFFICE

	1355	1407
Castle owning families	68	65
Of these:		
barons	13	13
ispánok	10 (16)*	9
office holders total	23 (29)*	22
in % of total	33.8	33.8
	(42.9)*	

NOTE: *The numbers in brackets include the unknown counts, assuming that they came from six different families.

Even if considering the uncertain factors, the ratio of office holding families with castles to the total number of castle owners (aristocrats) remained roughly the same: one third or somewhat higher. Thus in the mid-fourteenth to early fifteenth century about a third of the aristocratic families participated in daily political decisions as barons or counts of counties. The rest joined them only in emergencies, such as wars. It is questionable, though, whether the considerable number of families with one castle to their name, who were neither barons nor counts (such as the Cseklészi-Apponyi, Szegi, Szinnyei &cet.) should be at all counted to the aristocracy. Were we to discount them, then most of the families owning more than one castle would appear as office holders. On the other hand, in the later fifteenth and early sixteenth centuries the number of castle owners without public office declined decisively, and at the end of the medieval period (before 1526) very few lords of castles lived the retired life of a seigneur, without being part of the "political" aristocracy.

II. Beginnings

1.   It has been suggested that participation in a Crusade, such as that of Andrew II (1204-1235) in the Fifth Crusade, indicates the consolidation of a feudal society. Coincidentally, our sources allow us for the first time to reconstruct the background and career of barons and counts under King Andrew II. We are able to identify twenty-six clans among the lords whose names occur in these three decades. Though fragmentary, the evidence is sufficient to establish that they constituted a unified aristocracy, which is also suggested by the few marriages known to us from this age. The unity was the result of a longer period of assimilation, for nine of the twenty-six clans descended from "immigrants": six German knights and one French, Italian and Spanish family each. The beginning of this immigration goes back to the age of Prince Géza (d. 977) and St. Stephen (977-1038), when the ancestors of the Ják and Hontpázmány clans had come to Hungary. Many, later influential, families descended from knights who arrived under King Coloman (1095-1116), Géza II (1141-1162) and Imre (Henry) (1196-1204). The majority, two thirds of the known clans, was of Hungarian origin, some of them — according to the research of György Györffy — descendants of tribal and clan chiefs of the original conquering Magyars of the ninth century.

   The merger of the two groups was above all a political assimilation , while certain clans or branches of clans (such as the Héder clan or the Szentgyörgyi branch of the Hontpázmány clan) seem to have retained their mother tongue and foreign habits for quite a number of generations.

The process of assimilation could be best studied by analysing intermarriage patterns. Unfortunately, we know very little about these. There is evidence for a marriage of Lampert *de genere* Hontpázmány and a girl from the royal Árpád family, and eight other marriages are known to have been contracted between members of clans that had arrived before 1240 and the ancient *genera*. These marriages suggest that assimilation was well under way. Similar results emerge from the study of Christian names: I found that among two German clans, the Hahót and Héder, the German given names declined in the course of a century; Hungarian (Magyar) names appear already in the third generation.

Another useful indicator of assimilation is the spread of chivalric way of fighting. The foreign knights fought from the beginning in heavy armour, in Western chivalric form, and this was gradually adapted by the indigenous clans as well. Otto of Freising noted in 1147 that most Hungarians fought with "ugly weapons", excepting those who were trained by "foreigners". Ágnes Kurcz has tentatively dated the beginning of tournaments, a necessary element of chivalric life, to the turn of the twelfth to the thirteenth century. The Anonymous Notary (author of the *Gesta Ungarorum* c. 1200), who usually projects the conditions of his times into the past, describes the chiefs of the conquering Magyars as knights; this suggests that the dating of chivalric combat to his times is to be accepted. Hungarian knights who took the cross a few years later must have appeared in the crusading army as well as in the king's camp for domestic campaigns in chivalric armour. Chivalry also came to dominate the literary taste, as witnessed by the reception of the Alexander romances, and the choice of images on seals.

A significant element in the assimilation of Hungarian and Western clans, or, in other words in the Europeanization of the Magyar warrior élite, was Christianity. Two approaches of research might offer insight into the Christianization of the nobility: the history of clan-founded monasteries and the clerical careers of noble clan members. Unfortunately, neither of these problems has been hitherto sufficiently studied. So much is, however, clear, that both indigenous and immigrant noble clans had founded Benedictine monasteries as sepulchral and sacral centres of the clan, and at least six bishops of the twelfth and early thirteenth centuries came from the ancient clans. Their ecclesiastical career does not betray that only a century or so before their ancestors were still pagans.

The main characteristics of this unified aristocracy had developed before the beginning of the thirteenth century and were to last for quite some time. Most important among these was that Hungarian aristocrats were bound to their king not by feudal (vassalic) ties, but by the fidelity due to the chief of an armed retinue by its members. Although the aristocrats of the thirteenth century were great landowners, their military obligations followed from their membership in the royal retinue and not from contractual-feudal arrangements.

Since the selection of members into the retinue is a par excellence sovereign right of every ruler or even magnate, no attempts were made to define who was or could be an aristocrat, i.e., a member of the king's retinue. Also, the Hungarian Middle Ages were not particularly eager to codify customary law until the sixteenth century. Latin sources preceding the Golden Bull of 1222 style the aristocrats *nobiles*, some charters as *regni nostri nobiles sub vexillo regis militantes*, which points to their function as members of the armed retinue. This usage was, of course, also parallel to Central and Western European Latin and vernacular nomenclature ('nobility', *Adel*).

III. Developments in the Thirteenth and Fourteenth Centuries

1. The fist wave of growth in the power of the aristocracy was based on the building of castles. The process had begun in a time of demographic upswing, mainly due to immigration, in the early thirteenth century. It was enhanced by Andrew II's lavish donations in perpetuity which for the first time gave castles to the king's supporters, and was continued by Béla IV (1235-70) whose policy of encouraging additional settlement and the construction of well defendable fortifications was due to the lessons learned from the unimpeded conquest of Hungary by the Mongols in 1241-42. Between 1242 and 1270 private lords erected thirty four castles.

The trends are fairly obvious:

(a) the basis of the castle is the closed body of great landed estate;

(b) castle breeds (opponent) castle, which leads to a fortification race;

(c) the network of castles was defined by the interests of the great estates — and the access of lords to royal licence — and in no ways by the defense needs of the country;

(d) by obtaining a defendable castle, the dormant political (and military) power of the aristocracy became a real basis for

autonomy and expansion;

(e) through service in their castles (as castellans or constables) the aristocrats were able to mediatize the lesser noble clans.

By the time of King Béla's death the type of aristocrat emerged who owned more than one castle. In the following decades, during which the central authority declined and finally collapsed, these multi-castle-owner lords became oligarchs with virtual petty principalities in which they exercized semi-royal powers based on fictional official titles (palatine, voivode). It is, however, a peculiar trait of Hungarian development that none of them was able to transform his estates into true territorial polities comparable to French or German duchies. Even the most powerful oligarch, Máté Csák (d.1321), who controlled north-western Hungary for several decades, governed his properties in terms of castle-estates *(provinciae)* entrusted to lesser noble retainers *(familiares)*, who aped the royal counts of counties in their capacity as castellans. The unit of landed estate was never moulded into a politically autonomous principality.

2.   King Charles I Robert not only created a new aristocracy as new dynasties usually attempt to do, but also created a new governmental system. The vanguard of the aristocracy consisted still of the barons, but they now received regular tasks and new attributes. After the restoration and enhancement of royal authority, the barons were styled by the king and other chancelleries as *viri magnifici* and the king made sure that they were "kept busy" in governmental and household offices. The banderial system of defense came to be regulated and systematized: the barons and prelates were held to appear with their retainers under their own flags in the royal camp. (Hence the name from the Italian *bandiera*.) With the introduction of banners, crests and coats of arms the outward appearance of barons was enhanced. With the king's personal participation in tournaments and the foundation of the knightly Order of St. George the chivalric style of the court was elaborated upon.

Following his victory in the struggle for succession, Charles confiscated the castles of the oligarchs. Some of the violently usurped ones seem to have been returned to their original owners, but many were retained by the king's new supporters (such as the French Drugeth family). In the long run, Charles recovered many of these as well, together with the castles on the Western border from powerful families and Austrian owners. After 1327 many a royal castle, usurped during the anarchical decades, was reunited with the king's estates and led to the re-establishment of extensive royal domains. The growth of the number of royal castles cum estates enabled the king to change both the mechanism of government and the social hierarchy. The barons, at the top of the ladder, were now followed by the second rank of counts of counties *(ispánok)* and the third of royal castellans. The custom of combining offices did not change essentially: there were barons who were in charge of counties or of royal castles. In some counties the office of *ispán* and castellan of the central castle merged, e.g. in the case of the important western border-fortification of Pozsony (Pressburg, today: Bratislava). The practice of entrusting several castles to the same person was also continued; this makes sense in the case of adjacent fortifications but is puzzling when castles far remote from each other are granted to the same person for administration.

The reigns of the Angevin kings are characterized by the development of a small inner circle of magnates. The rather conservative policies of Louis I, preferring to retain the sons of his father's barons in the major offices, only enhanced the development of this leading clique. The members of these ten families are notable by

(a) having held several baronial and other royal offices,

(b) mostly for life;

(c) retained their title *magnificus*, as members of the royal council, even if they were temporarily out of office;

(d) their sons, if they chose ecclesiastical careers, became all prelates.

On the other hand, this "new nobility" was not so very new either. About half of the barons and one third of the *comites* came from families which belonged to ancient clans that had held office in the thirteenth century. They were either from the same "office-holding" branches (whom I shall call "old branches") or from branches that had supplied no office-holders under the Árpád kings but were part of an otherwise politically active ancient clan ("new branches") Only 22.5 % came from such ancient clans of which no branch had held royal office in the preceding century ("new clans").

TABLE IV:
ORIGIN OF THE ANGEVIN ARISTOCRACY

	barons	ispánok	total	in % of all
From "old" branches	15	7	22	17
From "new" branches	16	10	26	20
From "new" clans	18	11	29	22.5
Ancient clans total	49	28	77	59.5
From lesser nobility	19	19	38	29.5
Foreigners	5	9	14	11
TOTAL	73	56	129	100

The table demonstrates that a good part of the old aristocracy was able to retain their properties and political offices, thus the Angevin kings were not able to create an entirely new aristocracy. The dependence of the aristocrats on the king's favour did not diminish essentially: for example, even though the favourite Lackfi-clan were Masters of the Horse for fourty and voivodes of Transylvania for twenty years in a row, baronial offices did not become hereditary.

3. The royal domains were placed in charge of castellans who were in the same way *(nomine honoris regis)* appointed by the king as *ispánok* to counties or barons to their offices. The castellan was commander of the castle and its guard, steward of the pertinent estates and judge of the dependent peasants *(jobagiones)* in all, including major (capital), cases. The elements of this system had developed from the thirteenth century onward; the administrative and economic functions have been performed by castellans of private castles as well. A new feature was the jurisdiction over the peasants which earlier belonged only to noblemen with *ius gladii* (high justice). There is a debate between my view of the castellans' position and Pál Engel's assumption about their rights to the domains' income. The difference is partially due to his concentration on the age of Louis I and my focussing on the reign of Charles I. However, I believe that there is ample evidence that the king kept his right to the domains' income and a few exceptional cases (esp. the income of castle Temesvár's estates under Benedek Himfy) do not prove the opposite. The matter is worth further discussion.

4.   The four years of virtual civil war under Queen Mary and the dowager Queen Elisabeth (1382-86) are unfortunately poorly researched, although during these open confrontations between aristocratic factions important events took place above all in the development of closed baronial cliques. As far as we can see, the men who emerged in these anarchic years came from older baronial or comital families, or were helped by — mostly clerical — relatives to higher positions.

IV. From Sigismund to Matthias

1.   The factional wars did not end with the accession of Sigismund of Luxemburg (1387-1437), not even with the physical liquidation of one party by the murder of the Lackfi brothers (1395).   The consolidation was only achieved after the failure of the 1403 rebellion which finally secured the king's position as "president" of a league of magnates. This faction was formalized in 1409 by the foundation of the Order of the Dragon.

The great majority of Sigismund's barons and counts came from the aristocracy, particularly from among the Knights of the Dragon. Barons of lesser noble background were named only to the onerous military offices of certain banates. During his reign the aristocracy gained strength and — in spite of its *de jure* openness — became more closed than before. Baronial families not only held baronial posts in every generation but usually more than one member held a baronial position at the same time. The intermarriage among baronial families became more prevalent and the prelatures were mostly reserved for scions of these families. Also, the styling with *magnificus* was usually retained even after the commission of a baron to a distinct office had ended. On the other hand, among the upwardly mobile lesser nobles usually only one family member made it into the baronage and their descendants sank back into the group of *moyenne* nobility.

Nevertheless, Sigismund succeeded in

(a) precluding that offices, even if held by members of the same family for some time, became hereditary;

(b) retaining and upgrading the castles of the southern frontier, by appointing Pipo Scolari (Ozorai) and the Tallóci-brothers as their administrators;

(c) breaking the hegemonial power of the Garai-family by granting the Palatinate to Mátyusz Pálóczi and later to Lörinc Hédervári after the death of Miklós Garai (1433), and the banates of Slavonia, Croatia and Severin to the Tallóci brothers after the death of Hermann Cillei/Cilly (1435).

(d) limiting the privileges and prestige of the "chartered members" (his former electors) by transforming the Order of the Dragon into a typical late medieval international knightly order.

2.   Sigismund was thus able to stop the trend that all power passed into the hands of the aristocracy.   In the two decades following his death the dynastic continuity was broken and during the interregna (esp. in 1440) aristocratic parties vied for power under the flag of loyalty to the one or the other "legitimate" ruler.   In the decade between 1444 and 1453 the vanguard of the aristocracy took over the governance even pro forma: they occupied the royal domains and usurped the crown's revenues.   The *homo novus* János Hunyadi, was unable even at the zenith of his career as regent (1446-52) to curtail the power of the aristocrats.

3.   In the fifteenth century only Matthias I Corvinus (1458-90) ruled long enough to be able to attempt, just as Sigismund did, restricting the baronial rule.   Although he came to power on the basis of a baronial agreement — between the Hunyadi and Garai families — he consistently named newcomers for the governmental offices (ban, voivode), preferably from the Hunyadi retainers and relatives.   He went even further in the ecclesiastical sphere, where his hands were bound less, and made some commoners into bishops. However, the household officers and high judiciary posts remained in the hands of the old families.   Although a number of the old baronial families became extinct during his long reign, Matthias did not achieve his aim, because,

(a) he could not touch the foundation of the baronial families' power, the great landed estates;

(b) even the newly risen nobles proved to be fickle in their loyalty to the king; and

(c) through granting more than one baronial post to his favourites, he gave away too much royal power.

4.   Ironically, Matthias is also to be credited with the formal establishment of the estate of magnates in Hungary.   The precedent

was the advancement of his father, János Hunyadi, to count perpetual of Beszterce (in Transylvania) in 1453, but this title ended with Matthias' election and his uncle's, Mihály Szilágyi's death in 1461. The Szentgyörgyi family, who also became titled "counts", had obtained their charter from the emperor Frederick III.

These precedents might have remained isolated cases, had Matthias himself not taken up the practice. From 1463 onwards he created several perpetual comital familes: 1463 Vitovec, 1465 Szapolyai/Zápolyai, 1483 Alsólendvai Bánfi and 1487 Vingárti Geréb. In the peace treaty of Sankt Pölten (1487) the king acknowledged not only these, but an additional nineteen families as *barones naturales* in contrast to the *barones ex officio* (palatine, judge royal, master of the horse, master of the treasurers, lord treasurer). If this is indeed the first official use of these expressions — which needs confirmation by additional research — then 1487 is the birthdate of the estate of magnates in Hungary.

Translated by the editor from a Hungarian original,
revised by the author for this volume.

V

The *avus* in the Mediaeval Conceptual Framework of Kinship in Hungary

The aim of this paper is to draw the attention of all experts (historians, ethnographers and linguists) concerned to the questions of middle-Latin kinship conceptual framework of Hungary. To deal with these questions with the help of a cross-section, covering one or two generations became a habit with the anthropologists ever since L. H. Morgan's epoch-making work has been published.[1] Perhaps it seems strange to begin with a vertical section, but historical sources — and chiefly those referring to the Hungarian nobility — abound usually in descriptions of ascendant lines.

In the mediaeval kingdom of Hungary the documents, royal charters as well as judicial records or those of the collegiate churches, acting as notars, were written in Latin. Most of the documents were drafted by clergymen, even in the 14th century, many of whom took their degree in canon law. They surely knew the nomeclature of canon law, and what is more, kinship terms were taught according to canon law even in such town-schools as that of Sáros-patak, where one of the pupils was to become later archbishop of Esztergom and besigned an arbor consanguineitatis and arbor affinitatis in his copy-book.[2] In spite that they knew the kinship terms of canon law, they did not use it, but translated Hungarian expressions into Latin, when making a document. I hope the reader will be satisfied with only one example. In 1416 George, dean of the Collegiate Church of Pozsega, son of the late Ladislas of Csorna, let made a record of his deed of transfer, whereas he gave away one estate »nobili domine Ilko vocate, filie condam Johannis filii eiusdem Ladislai de dicta Chorna, sorori sue«.[3] The kinship link is beyond doubt.

---

[1] L. H. MORGAN, Systems of Consanguineity and Affinity of the Human Family (Smithsonians Contributions to Knowledge XVII). Washington 1871.
[2] MÉSZÁROS I., A Szalkai kódex és a XV. század végi sárospataki iskola [The Szalkai manuscripts and the school of Sárospatak at the end of the 15th c.]. Budapest 1972, 129—138.
[3] ZÁVODSZKY L., A Héderváry család oklevéltára, I—II. Budapest, 1922, I. 150.

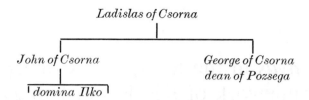

Ladislas of Csorna

John of Csorna   *George of Csorna*
                                    dean of Pozsega
domina Ilko

Nevertheless, it is clear too that Ilko had not been the sister of the dean, but his niece, the correct expression would have been »filie fratris sui«. But in Hungarian every female relative has been called *hug* (younger) or *néne* (older sister than the ego) and so the expression *hug* was translated into the Latin *soror*.

Besides the problem of translation from the Hungarian, an important role must have been played by the legal system of the nobility, according to which the noble status was transferred from father to child (the mother's status being irrelevant) and the father's estate equally divided between his sons (primogeniture being unknown), while daughters were paid out in cash. I try to prove, how very much these two factors were interwoven.

The word *avus* had been used in two meanings in the antiquity : »1. father's or mother's father ; 2. Interdum tamen avos dicunt poetae quoscunque majores, sive consanguinei, sive non.«[4] Both were adopted by the middle ages.[5] In the second meaning the word was declined as *aves-avum* instead of the regular *avi-avorum*, at least in Poland.[6]

Hungarian mediaeval records reflect these two meanings.

1. The meaning 'father's or mother's father' appears so often that I present only a few examples of them, indicating the date, the maker and the relevant part of the text.

111. 1270. Stephen younger king. »*quod castrum . . . rex Andreas clare memorie avus noster ab Andronico ceco . . . pretio comparasset*« (ÁUO VIII. 255, RA 1908).

112. 1272. King Ladislas IV. »*privilegium domini Bele illustris regis Hungarie felicis recordationis, karissimi avi nostri*« (ÁUO IX. 4, RA 2332).

113. 1295. Collagiate Church of Zalavár. „*Nicolaus, Fabianus, Sebastianus et Stephanus filii Leustachii filii Kurtuyld de Bagala . . . possessionem eorum hereditariam . . . sub eisdem metis, quibus . . . Kurtuyld prefatus, avus eorum possedissent . . .*" (Df. 233 154).

114. 1334. King Charles I. „*Nicolaus et Johannes filii Thome filiii Leurenthe de Seguar . . . detexerunt querulose, quod cum Johannes filius Herrici bani . . . prefatum Leurenthe avum ipsorum captivasset*" (AO III. 78).

---

[4] A. FORCELLINI—J. BAILEY, Totius Latinitatis lexicon. Londini 1828, I. 233.
[5] Mittellateinisches Wörterbuch, hg. von O. PRINZ. Berlin 1967, I. 1288.
[6] Lexicon mediae et infimae Latinitatis Polonorum. Wroclaw—Kraków—Warszawa 1953—1958, I. 1002.

115. 1344. Collegiate Church of Eger. „*Nicolaus filius Andree . . . pro se et pro Beke fratre suo . . . pretextu quarte filialis condam nobilis domine matris ipsorum, filie scilicet Mark filii Stephani . . . adversus Nicolaum* [filium Moysi de Zentkyral] *avunculum ipsorum et successorem dicti Mark avi eorum litem movissent"* (AO IV. 391).

116. The town Torda 1424. „*Valentinus Kerekes unacum provida domina Katherina consorte sua ac filio suo Stephano nomine . . . portionem ipsorum molendinariam per Egidium parvum, videlicet avum ipsius Stephani et patrem ipsius domine ipsis devolutam . . . vendidissent"* (Dl. 62 808).

2. The second meaning (majores, sive consanguinei, sive non) seems to be more important, so I divided the occurences at my disposal into three sub-categories.

21. A progenitor, but not grandfather.

211. 1285. King Ladislas IV. „*nos visis tenoribus privilegiorum Andree et Bele avorum nostrorum illustrium regum Hungarie"* (RA 3358). King Béla IV was the grandfather, Andrew II the great-grandfather of Ladislas IV.

212. 1307. King Charles I. „*exhibuit nobis litteras . . . Andree regis continentes tenorem privilegii domini regis Ladizlai karissimi fratris nostri patruelis, in quo continetur forma collationis . . . Stephani quondam . . . regis Hungarie, avi nostri"* (AO I. 156). Stephen V was a great-grandfather of Charles I (his grandmother's father).

214. 1326/1359. Charles I. „*exhibuit nobis duo privilegia, unum scilicet domini Bele et aliud Stephani filii eiusdem quondam . . . regum Hungarie . . . karissimorum avorum nostrorum"* (Df. 226 349). King Béla IV was Charles' great-great-grandfather (his grandmother's grandfather), Stephen V his great-grandfather.

215. 1328. Charles I. „*per dominum illustrem regem Bela felicis recordationis Hungarie, avi nostri data* [sc. littera]*"* (ZO I. 221). See **214**.

216. 1334. Paul Chief Mustice. „*Johannes filius Salomonis filii Ekch filii Elex . . . contra Ladislaum et Fabianum filios Johannis filii Laurentii filii Pauli proposuit eo modo, quod prior avus ipsius, scilicet Elex et avus ipsorum Ladislai et Fabiani, Nandor ab uno patre, videlicet Farkasio procreati extitissent"* (AO III. 88).

217. 1358. Ladislas chancellor. „*Lorandus procurator nobilis domine Sebee vocate filie Johannis filii Dominici filii Pertoldi de Stupan, neptis videlicet Salomonis de Darow . . . proposuit . . . quod quedam possessio . . . ex donatione condam Salomonis filii Nicolai gratiosi avi sui domine ave sue, filie videlicet eiusdem Salomonis facta . . . titulo successionis . . . ad ipsam deberet pertinere"* (AO VI. 43).

218. 1368. Stephen Bebek Chief Justice. „*Nam annotatus Pyssa avus eorum* [sc. Nicolai filii Johannis filii Laurentii filii Andree] *filium nomine Pancratium ipse vero Pancratius tres filios, scilicet Vrmand, Endre et Hernand successive generasset, predictus vero Johannes pater suus ac Ivan pater dicti Andree patris* *ipsius Laurentii filii dicti condam Vrmand . . . extitissent''* (ZO II. 22). Pyssa was in the fifth generation of one of the concerned (great-grandfather of Laurentius' grandfather), in the fourth of the other (the grandfather of Nicolaus' grandfather).

219. 1384. Queen Maria. *,,exhibuerunt quasdam litteras genitoris nostri . . . litteras privilegiales principis domini Andree, tertii Bele regis filii, olim incliti regis Hungarie, avi et predecessoris nostri''* (Decreta 142). Andrew II was Maria's great-grandfather's grandfather.

220. 1407. Frank Szécsényi Chief Justice. *,,magister Emericus litteratus filius Petri filii Stephani filii Bartholomey . . . proposuit eo modo, quod quedam littere, que videlicet pretactum Bartholomeum filium Ompud avum suum . . . nominarent . . . habere vellet''* (HO III. 226).

22. A consaguineal, but not in the direct line.

221. 1290. King Andrew III. *,,quasdam particulas terre . . . a gloriosisiimo Bela rege avo nostro . . . fuissent . . . assecutus . . .''* (ÁUO X. 1). Though Andrew III calls Béla IV several times his *avus* (1291 : ÁUO XII. 505, 1295 : ÁUO X. 180), Béla was his father's elder brother.

222. 1291. Andrew III. *,,quas ex collatione regis Stephani carissimi avi nostri se habuisse . . . dixerunt''* (ÁUO X. 34). Stephen V was Andrew's first cousin.

23. A predecessor, but not consanguineal.

231. 1424. King Sigmund. *,,litteras olim . . . domini Karoly regis . . . avis nostri karissimi''* (Zichy VIII. 219). Charles I was Sigmund's wife's grandfather.

24. An unnamed progenitor.

241. Paul dean of Fehérvár, delegated justice. *,,Ex adverso Larigrab et Bartholomeus . . . responderunt, quod illa eadem silva semper fuerit patris ipsorum comitis Remigy videlicet et avorum suorum''* (ÁUO XI. 519).

242. 1280. Collegiate church of Háj. *,,cum omnibus utilitatibus et pertinentiis suis, prout proavi et avi possederunt''* (ÁUO XII. 313).

243. 1325. Alexander Chief Justice. *,,avos et priores eorum ac se dictam possessionem usquemodo . . . possedisse''* (AO II. 186).

244. 1329. Peter, count of Pozsony. *,,responderunt, ut ab antiquo tempore sancti regis et avorum suorum incipiens nobiles fuissent et extitissent''* (HO IV. 144).

245. 1341. Charles I. *,,dicunt nobis . . . quod quedam possesio . . . ab avo et protavo Pauli filii Sech hominis sine herede defuncti fuisset hereditaria''* (AO IV. 112).

246. 1346. King Louis I. *,,quod quedam possessio . . . ab avo et prothavo ipsorum fuisset et esset hereditaria''* (AO IV. 584).

247. 1354. Louis I. *,,quod ipsi ab avo et prothavo incipiens . . . nobiles in comitatu Pestiensi extitissent et nunc existerent''* (Dl. 69 679).

248. 1366. Collegiate church of Vasvár. *,,quia ipsi ab uno avo progressi et propagati sint et existant''* (ZO II. 11—13).

249. 1381. Collegiate church of Győr. ,,*quod ipsi ab uno avo propaginis extitissent progressi*'' (Sopron vm. I. 457).

250. 1388. Stephen Count Palatine. ,,*quod ab uno avo et prothavo originem duxissent*'' (Dl. 7 400).

From the given cases only two (214, 218) use the word *avus* in the plural, as it had been used in the classical and mediaeval Latin, meaning more than one progenitor. In all the other cases any of the progenitors of the 3—6th generation is called *avus*, be it the grandfather's father (211, 212, 216, 217, 220), his grandfather (215) or his grandfather's father (213, 219). In the cases 241—250 not progenitors generally, but one certain progenitor (usually the common ancestor) is mentioned; he could be any of the 3—6th generation or even further away.

Taking for granted that the *avus* was a translation of a Hungarian word, let us look it up in the mediaeval vocabularies, to see, how their authors translated *avus*.

Vocabulary		Expressions
Fragment of Gyöngyös	1380—1390	*ős* [ancestor]
Fragment of Brassó	cca 1395	*atyámatyja* [father's father]
Schlägli's word-list	cca 1405	*ük!* [ancestress]
Murmelius	1533	*ős* [ancestor]
Calepinus	1585	*jobatya* [grandfather]
Sz. Fabricius	1590	*ős, szépapa* [ancestor, grandfather]

The majority translated *avus* as *ős* (i.e. 'ancestor') into Hungarian, some of them *szép/jóbatya* (i.e. 'grandfather'). The first meaning of *ős* was 'a far away ancestor' and the word belongs to the most pristine layer of the Hungarian language.[7] A further step forward would be the collection of the Hungarian expressions of the progenitors up to the seventh generation.

Vocabulary	3rd avus	4th proavus	5th abavus	6th atavus	7th generation tritavus
Gyöngyös	*ős*	—	—	*ősöd atyja*	—
Schlägli	*ük*	—	—	*déd ős*	—
Calepinus	*job atya*	—	*job atyám atyjának atyja*	*4. job atya*	—
Fabricius	*ős, szépapa*	*nagyapád apja*	*nagyapád nagyapja*	*ük*	*atavi pater!*

[7] A magyar nyelv történeti-etimológiai szótára, III. Budapest 1976, 39—40.

The table enables us to draw the following conclusions : (i) only Fabricius gives a coherent system ; (ii) he does not know the Hungarian expressions corresponding to the Latin, except the *avus* and the *atavus* ; (iii) the meaning of *ük* seems uncertain, it is likely that first it denoted the father's or mother's mother, i.e. an ancestress and only later was used to the ancestor in the sixth generation ; (iv) all other Latin notions are expressed by a possessive construction ; (v) the word-list of Gyöngyös uses also possessive construction, while Calepinus made use of the generations' serial number (taking grandfather as a base). In one word, there was no special name in Hungarian denoting different ancestors, all were called *ős*. Later one of the ancestors became to be distinguished with the help of a Slavic loan-word *déd*.[8] It seems doubtful which ancestor was denoted with it, up to the 15th century it might have been corresponding to the *atavus*, i.e. a very far ancestor in the 6th generation. Anyhow, vocabularies and written documents seem to agree fully with one an other.

The legal system of the nobility claimed to know the ancestors and noblemen were always ready in court to enumerate 5—6 progenitors, though sometimes not without mistakes. But none of the indicated progenitors was endowed with special rights or duties. All were bound to continue their clan, have sons and hand over the inherited estates to them. So there was no need to make any difference between them. Practically it was sufficient to know the third "ancestor" *(abavus)* to avoid difficulties arising from choosing a wife, as marriage between blood relatives to the fourth degree was forbidden. To know and specify more was only a matter of prestige.

Abbreviations

AO	Anjoukori okmánytár — Codex diplomaticus Hungariae Andegavensis. Ed. by I. NAGY, I—VII. Budapest 1879—1920
ÁUO	WENCZEL G., Árpádkori új okmánytár — Codex diplomaticus Arpadianus continuatus, I—XII. Pest 1860—1874
Decreta	Decreta Regni Hungariae. Ed. F. DŐRY, GY. BÓNIS, V. BÁCSKAI. Budapest 1976
Df	OL, diplomatikai fényképgyűjtemény [collection of filmed documents, dated before 1526]
Dl	OL, diplomatikai gyűjtemény [collection of documents, dated before 1526]
HO	Hazai Okmánytár — Codex diplomaticus patrius Hungaricus, I—VIII. Győr — Budapest 1865—1891.
OL	Magyar Országos Levéltár [Hungarian Record Office], Budapest
RA	SZENTPÉTERY I.—BORSA I., Az Árpád-házi királyok okleveleinek kritikai jegyzéke — Regesta rerum stirpis Arpadianae critico-diplomatica, I—II. Budapest 1923—1961
Sopron vm.	Sopron vármegye története, Oklevéltár. Ed. by NAGY I. Sopron 1889
Zichy	A zichi és vásonkeői gróf Zichy-család idősb ágának okmánytára — Codex diplomaticus domus senioris comitum Zichy de Zich et Vasonkeő. Ed. by E. NAGY, J. B. NAGY, etc., I—III. Pest [later] Budapest 1871—1931
ZO	Zala megye története, Oklevéltár. Ed. by NAGY I., VÉGHELY D. and NAGY GY., I—II. Budapest 1886—1890

[8] KNIEZSA I., A magyar nyelv szláv jövevényszavai, I/1. Budapest 1955, 156.

VI

VERBA VOLANT...

ORAL CULTURE AND LITERACY AMONG THE MEDIEVAL HUNGARIAN NOBILITY

On Epiphany 1345 the Nagymihályi clan declared in front of King Louis that castle Nagymihály together with its appurtenances in the counties Zemplén and Ung had been their hereditary property ever since the time of their forebear and their forebear's forebears, and this was well known to the nobles and non-nobles of the region. The king thereupon ordered three ecclesiastical institutions, as places of authentication, and the magistrates of two counties to send emissaries, who, together with the king's bailiff should establish the "whole truth". The convents and counties duly reported to the king in the course of the following two months, the counties being the last, submitting their report only in early March. The chapter of Eger reported that its men spoke to the inhabitants of eight counties, the chapter of Szepes, the convent of Lelesz, the magistrates of County Ung, and in the city of Kassa to the parish priest, the Dominican convent and the council. They emphasized that besides the neighbours of the Nagymihályi, the emissaries interviewed several aged (annosus) noblemen, who claimed to have lived in King Béla's times (1235-1270) or who fought with King Ladislas IV (1272-1290) in the battle of Marchfeld and "served the Holy Crown" together with the ancestors of the Nagymihályi in the battle of 1280 against the Cumans, or knew about the grandfather of the clan's having been an officer of King Andrew III (1290-1301).[1] The officer of the Várad chapter visited not only five counties but also the Franciscan house in Szatmár, where he met an old friar who had said Mass in

1 Gy. Nagy, ed. *A ... gróf Sztáray család oklevéltára* [Diplomatarium of the Count Sz. family] (Budapest, 1887) [henceforth Szt. O.] I: 184-5; cf. also, G. Fejér, *Codex diplomaticus Hungariae eccl. et civ.* (Buda, 1829-44) [henceforth: CD] IX/1: 315.

the Nagymihály church on St. Mary's Day preceding the second Mongol invasion. The counties' reports are more laconic, listing the magistrates and the emissaries and confirming, just as the ecclesiastical inquirers did, the ancient rights of the Nagymihályi.[2]

This procedure was a routine one and we shall return to it later. Let us first look at the interviews with the "old men". If one was alive when King Béla died on 3 May 1270, even if only a child of, say, five years, then in 1345 he must have been around 80 years old. If the participants of the battles of 1278 and 1280 were only young knaves in those times, say fifteen years' old, they, too would have been in their eighties. The same holds true for the friar, who, if he had been ordained as a priest in 1284 (assuming that he had reached canonical age) was then at least 25 years' old, which makes him over 80 at the time of the *inquisitio*. In comparison to them, the men who served with the Nagymihályi grandfather under Andrew III may not have been older than 60-75 years at the time the convent's man spoke to them. György Györffy, while investigating the traditions about St. Stephen, concluded that in the early twelfth century the memory of old men went back some seventy years;[3] a similar figure also seems to have been valid 200 years later as well.

The search for aged witnesses was the most important part of the procedure, be it done by clerical or secular authorities. Their recollections served as the basis and also the temporal boundary beyond which "the memory of men does not reach" *(cuius non extat memoria)*. For example, when two priests in 1380 were ordered by the vicar of Eger to interrogate some witnesses, whether the village Budafalva was in fact the property of the descendants of the daughter of a certain Buda, they looked for "such men of both sexes afflicted by age, namely noble men and women", whose memories preserve the relevant facts even in the present",[4] and found among others, several clergy of this description: two parish priests, four monks and a cleric who had been notary of county Ung for three years. No ages were recorded here, but we have them for another inquiry about a mortgage among members of the chapter of Buda and nobles from county Pest. In this group of

---

2 Szt. O. I:185.

3 "Zu den Anfängen der ungarischen Kirchenorganisation", *Archivum Historiae Pontificiae* 7 (1969) 109-12.

4 Archives of Lelesz, Hungarian National Archives, Microfilms [henceforth: Df] 219 919.

witnesses the oldest was Benedek Szentmártoni, *cantor*, declaring to be 66 years' old, followed by a nobleman of 60. The declared ages are, of course, unreliable and approximate, as half of the twenty-nine witnesses named round figures for their age, six maintained to be 40 and six to be 50. Characteristically, none of them was younger than 26, and half of them were older than 40, although the transaction they were to confirm happened only a year before the inquiry.[5] In another inquiry the vicar charged the priests to establish, whether a clerk and some noblemen were truly the grandchildren of a certain Martonos Pelejtei, so that they should first ask those whom the parties name as witnesses and then other old noblemen and noblewomen. The vicar expected that some of the witnesses may not be able to travel to his see and permitted that affidavits be sworn locally.[6]

It is obvious that the selection of old persons had very practical reasons, but one should also remember that the status of age is always high in societies where average life expectancy is low. Thus it is understandable that in 1335, in a property case involving a grant of 1256 and 1271, the chapter of Fehérvár first sought the testimony of "three such old and aged men who remembered well King Béla of blessed memory" and of "two other old neighbours and abutters", and had their statements discussed by other witnesses who then confirmed the findings of the old men.[7] In general we may state that medieval nobles relied on the knowledge of persons who in the given average lifespan counted as old for establishing facts and events from the past. That old women were also included in these inquiries is a consequence of the laws of demography. Ecclesiastical courts regularly had recourse to old women, but they were heard also in secular cases, where otherwise female witnesses were not regarded as equal partners.[8]

Clergy enjoyed a privileged position among the witnesses. As we have seen in the Nagymihályi case, not only members of the

---

5 Hungarian National Archives, Diplomatic Collection [henceforth: Dl] 15476.
6 I. Nagy *et al.*, eds., *A ... gróf Zichy család idösb ágának okmánytára/Codex diplomaticus domus senioris comitum Zichy...* (Pest/Budapest, 1871-1931) [henceforth: Zichy O.] III: 610-11.
7 *Ibid.*, I: 454.
8 I. Hajnik, *A magyar bírósági szervezet...* [The Hungarian court system and procedural law in the age of the kings from the Árpád and mixed dynasties] (Budapest, 1899) 299, n.70.

4

Lelesz convent, but also the priests and Dominican friars in Kassa and the Franciscan of Szatmár were heard, and in the mortgage case the canons of Buda served as priority witnesses. This tendency is clear in those reports of *inquisitiones* as well, where the witnesses are listed by numbers only; priests and religious always feature in impressive numbers.[9] Apparently, clergy in general, members of chapters and convents (as places of authentication) and parish priests in particular, were expected to remember the events and conditions of their parishes and regions, including such matters which we would now regard as private affairs.

A casual comment regarding a last will and testament sheds light on the mechanics of memory. In 1448 László Kővári called witnesses about the last will of his wife who had died twenty-two years before. Six witnesses were cited to the notary, five of them women, three of those widows. Even if widowhood did not imply high age in the Middle Ages, all of them must have been at least "middle aged", since they were present at the event two decades earlier.[10] The first witness testified that Mrs Kővári left her dowry *(dos et paraphernalia)*, in front of witnesses, especially of János, then parish priest of Csomja, to her husband. The second witness, Péter, successor of János in the parish of Csomja, tells us something interesting. He testifed that when his predecessor returned from hearing Mrs Kővári's confession, he turned to him, his chaplain, and his other clerics, and said: *"Fratres mei, attendite et memoramini* that today in her deathbed lady Dorottya, wife of László, son of Master Pál made such and such a will..." and recited the testament.

Thus the clergy seems to have had special methods to be able to respond to the social demand of registering and retaining important events and affairs; not only did they try to remember them themselves, but charged their fellows to do so, thus, in a way, institutionalizing remembrance. It is unlikely that the parson of Csajta introduced this technique on his own, rather he had learned it when he was a chaplain. With such methods and others, not known to us, medieval men were able to bridge the gap of

9 E.g. in a charter printed in I. and Gy. Nagy, eds., *Codex diplomaticus Hungariae Andegavensis* (Budapest, 1873-1925) [henceforth: Cod. dipl. Andeg.] IV: 274-5, the numbers of witnesses are given as: 13 priests, 90 nobles and 114 commoners.

10 K. Géresi, ed., *A ... gróf Károlyi család oklevéltára* [Diplomatarium of the Count K. family] (Budapest, 1882-97) [henceforth: Kár. O.] II: 286.

considerable timespans, apparently at least seven decades. Certain elements of life stuck in their minds and were handed down to assure the survival of information in the memory of men.

To judge the significance of this type of memory, let us return to the Nagymihályi case for a moment. The castle was in fact not a hereditary property of the Kaplonyclan in the sense of Hungarian noble property rights. They did not receive it as a royal grant and it was not passed down in the male line, they had acquired it together with its sizeable estates by marriage with the last Nagymihályi daughter around 1250.[11] They held several charters about this acquisition which they produced at the trial in 1346. The castle was built after 1275, lost by the family in the anarchical decades after 1300, but recovered later.[12] Thus, in 1345 the Nagymihályi were in the possession of both castle and written legal title, but they did not use these, rather the testimony of numerous people from an enormous area of the north-eastern part of the country.

The Nagymihályi were not threatened by anybody or challenged in their possession: the testimonies were acquired and kept for security's sake. This was not a typical case: most inquiries were aimed at settling conflicting claims. In 1359 the king's bailiffs, searching for usurped royal property, accused the nobles of Jóka at a meeting of the county that they did not have noble title to their village, because they had been castle-warriors (jobagiones castri). Five from among the numerous members of the Jókai family appeared at the meeting and retorted that their ancestors were indeed castle-warriors, but in 1197 had received nobility from King Imre.[13] They produced the charter and the count palatine acknowledged its authenticity. But their descent from the ennobled ancestor had still to be demonstrated. This was done by the emissaries of the chapter of Pozsony, who "ascertained the truth ... from all such noble and non-noble person from whom it was useful and suitable, primarily from neighbours and abutters" regarding the descent of the Jókai family from Zerzivoj, the

11 J. Karácsonyi, *Magyar nemzetségek a XIV. század közepéig* [Hungarian clans to the mid-fourteenth century] (Budapest, 1900) II: 297-8.
12 E. Fügedi, *Vár és társadalom* [Castle and society in thirteenth-fourteenth C. Hungary] (Budapest, 1977) 169.
13 CD II: 388; cf. I. Szentpétery, *Regesta hist.-dipl. regum Arpad.* [henceforth: RA] no. 169.

ennobled warrior of 1197. [14] The chapter does not list the number of witnesses, but seems to have "found the truth" to the satisfaction of the count palatine. The king's officers had to admit that the Jókai held their property legally and by noble title. Had they not been vindicated, the whole family would have lost house and status alike, because the charter of their ancestor was not sufficient: the descent had to be proven. In the records of this procedure the ennobled Zerzivoj is called *prothavus*, an unusual expression in Hungarian charters. King Béla IV referred to St. Stephen with this word, [15] but in fact he (just as all other medieval kings of Hungary) was not a blood descendant of the first king at all. It is more helpful to note that King Louis I called Andrew II his *prothavus*: [16] the Arpadian king stood five generations above the Angevin on the family tree (in the female line). If the ennobled Zerzivoj of 1197 was in fact six generations removed from the mid-fourteenth-century Jókais, then a generation covered roughly 27 years. Only charters could have bridged a gap of 162 years or more; and however efficient medieval nobles were in remembering genealogical details, the line of descent could be established only by the many witnesses. And they vindicated the Jókais.

These kinds of inquests were classified by the historian of medieval Hungarian legal procedure, Imre Hajnik, in four types: *inquisitio simplex, communis inquisitio, inquisitio generalis* and *inquisitio per modum proclamatae congregationis*. [17] The first two were done by trustworthy persons and the last two at regular or special meetings of the noble county. For our purpose the "common inquest" is of great importance. The reports expected by the judge from such inquiries had to list the names, sometimes also the properties, of all witnesses; record whether they spoke as neighbours, fellow villagers or fellow county-men; whether they were nobles or not, and whether they testified from personal knowledge or by hearsay. Sometimes single testimonies were cited verbatim. Such detailed reports allowed the weighing of the evidence: naturally, the word of neighbours and abutters was more valuable than that of *comprovinciales*; testimony *ex scitu* more than *ex auditu*. The listing of the witnesses by categories also enabled

14 Dl 38 817.
15 *Zala megye története, Oklevéltár* [Hist. of county Zala: Diplomatarium] (Budapest, 1886) I: 29.
16 Df 227 132.
17 Hajnik [as above, n. 8] 298f.

the parties to object to the commissioners, to witnesses or to the whole procedure. Another important form was the "general inquest", requested by anyone present at a judicial meeting of the county nobility. Two kinds of inquiries could be asked for: either that the viscount, the magistrates and elected jurors should be asked to testify, or that all nobles present should be required to do so. In the former case the office-holders deliberated *in camera*, and upon their return made a statement "with one common mouth, on their faith, their fidelity to the king and the Holy Crown that bound them to tell the truth, having touched the Crucifix". Hajnik emphasized, however, that neither form of the inquest was sufficient to decide a trial, it only led to the decision about the definitive judicial proof, the oath.[18]

Needless to say that such *inquisitiones* were held in all possible trials, including those which we would call "criminal" cases and still try by questioning witnesses. But for our inquiry these are less important than those which in later times would have been decided by the presentation of written evidence, such as cases regarding property, nobility or inheritance. The preceding examples were taken from such cases and we shall concentrate on these. One more restriction may be mentioned: the "typical" noble in the following will be a member of the lesser nobility, excluding both the small number of aristocrats and the larger number of poor nobles without serfs *(nobiles unius sessionis)* . In spite of the oft-cited principle of *una et eadem nobilitas*, in fact the medieval nobility of Hungary was highly stratified, the "common noblemen" constituting the typical representative of the estate.

Hajnik's summary needs correction in a minor and a major point. It was not as general to list the names of witnesses in the "common inquest" as he would have us believe.[19] I have already cited an example from county Bars,[20] which contains only the number of witnesses from the different estates. In 1360 the chapter of Győr conducted a "common inquest" in a property dispute between two ecclesiastical landlords. The testimonies were contradictory, hence the details on the witnesses would have been very important. Nevertheless, the canons did not include them, "because the writ

18 *Ibid.*, 282-302.
19 True, a fourteenth century formulary, ed. by G. M. Kovachich (*Formulae solennes styli...* , Pest, 1820, p.29,§127) also prescribes this.
20 See above, n. 9.

ordering the inquest did not prescribe so."[21]
There are many examples that at least qualify Hajnik's statement about the inquests' not having been decisive, even though this may have been the general rule. In 1335 the convent of Fehérvár held a common inquest regarding the property of a certain estate Ete (county Komárom). The result was favourable to the plaintiff (actually, the witnesses' names are not listed), yet he had to swear an oath with 68 oath helpers, the value of the estate having been 68 Mark silver.[22] In 1330 part of the estate Zsibó (county Baranya) was taken away from the sons of Lancret, claiming that this was the property of royal servitors. The neighbours and abutters testified that Lancret's sons held the land as nobles, which was accepted by the judge royal, nevertheless an oath according to the value of the property was ordered "for the avoidance of any suspicion, the clarity of the matter and the preservation of justice".[23] In 1340 the judge royal granted seizin for a property explicitly on the basis of an *inquisitio simplex* that had proven the rights of the owners.[24] Sometimes the decision was not as explicit; in the example cited about the Jókais the royal bailiffs dropped the case after the "simple inquest". Or a more complex instance: in 1339 László Rozgonyi charged Lukács Sárolyi that the latter had been a serf and bailiff on his estate Sároly, caused him 100 Marks damage and occupied Sároly. Lukács seems to have known of the accusation, because he presented charters of the chapters of Esztergom and Fehérvár in which these places of authentication, on the basis of an *inquisitio simplex*, declare that Sároly is Lukács's hereditary land, and that he is innocent in the 100-Mark damage. The judge royal ordered a common inquest by the chapter of Buda, which in due course reported (again, without listing the witnesses) that there were two Sároly estates in county Fejér, clearly marked by signs: one of these belongs to Lukács, who has never been a serf of the Rozgonyi, but "served them as neighbouring nobleman out of free will and for payment". The trial ended in settlement, fully vindicating Lukács. [25]

21 L. B. Kumorowitz, *Veszprémi regeszták: Regesta Vesprimiensia 1301-1387* (Budapest, 1953) no. 540.
22 Zichy O., I: 451-4, 467-8.
23 Cod. dipl. Andeg. II: 468-70.
24 *Ibid.* IV: 61.
25 *Ibid.* III: 599-602.

In summary, then: oral testimony was usually decisive in the fourteenth-fifteenth centuries on noble status, descent and matters of property. Witnesses were instrumental in deciding matters of genealogy and privilege, but, due to the close connection of status and property oral testimony was often crucial in disputes about *possessiones* as well. Thus we may state that it was the groups of the nobility who, through their testimonies, decided about nobility, about status and the right to property based on noble descent. It is well known that medieval nobles in Hungary lived not in nuclear families but in kinship- or territory-based larger units. In the sixteenth century customary law-book of Werbőczy this kin-group is called *genus*, which I shall translate (even though I am aware of the different usage of this term in anthropology) as "clan". The territorial groupings are reflected in the references to abutters *(commetanei)*, neighbours *(vicini)* and fellow nobles of the county *(comprovinciales)*.

These groups were active not only at inquests but other acts as well. As we have seen, the inquest often led to oath taking, and judges frequently defined, how many nobles of each group should serve as oath helpers. If the case ended with a compromise, the arbitrators were also chosen from these groups. In the case of induction into a property, the new owner could probably always select a fellow nobleman as royal officer for this procedure.[26] These groups are well-known to social historians, but their development and function have not been systematically studied, although the workings of local administration are incomprehensible without doing so. True, it is not easy to reconstruct the details, but the fragmentary and highly formulaic sources offer some insights.

The existing literature on inquest permits the assertion that through these procedures the county had the right to decide major matters, and, apparently, the crown recognized this right. In 1386 Queen Mary ordered county Bars to call a meeting of the nobles to establish, whether the owners of the estate Hecse — recently seized by Ladislas of Opolie and attached to the castle Gimes — were in fact descendants of that Márton, son of Mihály, to whom King Béla IV had granted the property in 1268.[27] We can only guess the outcome of the inquest, because the county's report did not survive. However, when a few weeks later the queen granted castle Gimes

26 *A nagykállói Kállay csalá levéltára* [Diplomatarium of the K. family of N.] (Budapest, 1943) [henceforth: Káll. O.] no. 354.
27 Dl 58 651; the original charter is to be dated to 1268, cf. RA. no. 1581.

to the Forgách family, those of Hecse went to court, which would suggest that they had been vindicated in the earlier procedure.[28] Regardless of subsequent events, the queen could have ordered that those of Hecse be introduced to the property on the basis of the 1268 charter and let opponents raise objections at that occasion. But she obviously found it necessary to establish the descent of the family from the grantee, and for that the proper procedure was inquest with witnesses. This was the task of the county, where the local nobility had a chance to have its voice heard. The Hecse example is not an isolated case. In 1439 István Rozgonyi, *comes* of Pozsony and Szepes wrote to Queen Elisabeth that a judgment in favour of the Tarkői family "was against the customs of the realm", because the queen did not observe, so Rozgonyi argued, the usual procedure to have the nobles of the appropriate county asked, or rather obligated to state under oath, what they knew about the matter.[29] The ruler was thus seen as having to consult the nobles of the county in every case related to a nobleman.

Inquest by witnesses is based on individual memory. Sociologists have established that memory is a social fact: it retains such things as are expected to be remembered and forgets those which are not socially required. Hence we may assume that medieval Hungarian nobles remembered the events and conditions related to those persons with whom they were connected by kin or by locality. In his own best interest a nobleman had to be able to recall his ancestors at least to the fourth grade and also the forebear who had played the crucial role in the clan's history. In the case of the Jókai this meant the warrior of 1197, who had been granted nobility; even if they could not list the five generations that connected them to him, they all knew that they were Zerzivoj's descendants. The nobleman had to know quite a lot about the genealogy of his clan, for that defined the order of inheritance. He had to know the title for every piece of property and be able to describe, or at least show, its borders.

Logically, what he knew of his own clan and its properties, he also knew, even if less precisely, of his neighbours and abutters. For this he had a good chance at legal procedures, such as the

---

28 L. Bártfai Szabó, *A Hunt-Pazman nemzetségbeli Forgách család története* [History of the Forgach-family d.g. Hontpázmány], (Budapest, 1910) 109-10.

29 *Hazai Okmánytár: Codex diplomaticus patrius Hungaricus*, I. Nagy *et al.*, eds., (GyörBudapest, 1865-91) VII: 457.

"beating of bounds" of neighbouring properties, where he had to be present for his own best interest, or even further in the county, where he may have served as a royal bailiff. Other local offices, such as that of magistrate, would have carried him to the farthest end of his county and made him deal with legal cases not immediately pertaining to his estate. Again, logically, as the circle widened, the details of his knowledge decreased. Still, if a nobleman lived a long life, the bulk of information he was able to amass could be quite considerable. He was able to hand down some of it to his children, extending the natural boundaries of human memory. Thus it is not surprising that nobles were capable of making declarations under oath about events of 100-150 years before their birth.

Legal thinking was well aware of the social and topographical parameters of memory and testimony. Werbőczy, in his great collection of customary law, explained why it was necessary to note the names and conditions (neighbour, abutter etc.) of the witnesses:

> First, because the testimony of two or three neighbours or abutters is more valuable before law than that of twenty nobles from the county at large, since by their proximity they have a more truthful and better knowledge of the merit of the case and the sequence of events than the *comprovinciales* in general.[30]

In the light of these considerations, the inquest by witnesses appears as a logical system, even as a genuine social institution. It accomodated the biological limitations on the existence of man, hence questions were addressed mainly to the older ones. It also made allowance for the decrease in precise knowledge by increased distance, hence greater weight was given to closer neighbours. It took into account the fact that the magistrates and viscounts commanded more knowledge than anyone else, therefore, the practice of *generalis inquisitio* was introduced. In this the best-informed office holders gave testimony, but only after having had a chance to "compare notes" and ponder their judgment. If the example of the priest and vicar of Csomja can be regarded as typical, we may add that specific methods were also found to assure the survival of individual pieces of information.

---

30 *Tripartitum opus iuris consuetudinarii...* (Vienna, 1517, facsimile ed. Glashütten/Taunus, 1971) Pars II: tit. 29.

It is not surprising that all this was connected to the county. As early as *circa* 1300, a legal collection charged the counties with the *inquisitio* and ordered that twelve "conscientious and trustworthy" nobles be elected, including the four magistrates, and these should be obligated to make statements under oath on "all facts and lawsuits emerging in the county".[31] The county was the largest community, comprising the greatest number of clans and the widest territorial expanse, within which memory remained workable. When witnesses were heard in the county, this procedure often tapped not merely individual recollections but rather collective memory. Even more explicitely "collective memory" is summoned in the *generalis inquisitio*, which implies that the office-holders are omniscient in their counties. At some county meetings they made sworn statements on descent, kinship, robbery, criminals, titles and boundaries of estates. Even though we frequently do not know their names, higher courts seem to have trusted them.[32]

I mention it only *en passant* that this collective memory, insitutionalized in the inquests of different sorts, also implied power for the county's nobility, and they knew how to use it. When, for example, in 1368 János, son of István Vatai asked the congregation of county Pozsony to confirm Kisvata, which had been occupied by the men of the nuns from Óbuda, as his hereditary estate, the magistrates and jurors stated under oath that Kisvata was never the hereditary possession of János, because his father had been a servile tenant of László Gutori, and acquired his possession in Kisvata as the "filial quarter" of his noble wife.[33]

While the institution had a collective character, it was based on individual memory, and carried all the faults and shortcoming of the latter with it. There are cases of contradicting testimonies, even by members of the very same clan.[34] There could emerge

31 F. Döry, Gy. Bónis, V. Bácskai, eds., *Decreta Regni Hungariae 1301-1457* (Budapest, 1976) 389-90.
32 G. Iványi, "Generalis congregatio", *Levéltári Közlemények* 17 (1939) 69, suggests that they were regarded as representatives of the nobility. Names are usually not listed, except in documents of *proscriptio*, see e.g. Zichy O. III: 236; Szt.O., I: 366.
33 Count J. Eszterházy, ed., *Az Eszterházy család ... oklevéltár* [Diplomatarium to the description of the E. family and its branches] (Budapest, 1901) [henceforth: Eszt. O.] 24, n.1.
34 G. Wenzel, ed., *Árpádkori új okmánytár: Cod. dipl. Arpadianus contin.*

linguistic problems as well: in 1513 the parish priest of Novák asked a travelling priest to hear the confession of the landlord's wife, because he did not know Hungarian, and had then to inquire from him about the last will of the lady of the manor. 35 But these problems did not seem to question the validity, and even less the survival of the institution. King Matthias was right when he wrote to county Vas, à propos an inquest, that the hearing of oral testimony was "a particular pillar of the commonwealth, of the law and of the customs of the realm, and a force of truth". 36

The essential prerequisite for the efficacy and significance of the system of oral testimony was that the nobility lived in an oral culture, with a very weak writing practice, if any. Studies on archival history seem to confirm that the coffers of noble families, and even of ecclesiastical institutions, contained only charters of title. Great care was taken to preserve the records of the acquisition of property, be they royal donations, gifts or mortgage deeds, together with the minutes about the induction into the estates. These parchments and papers were handed over to the new proprietors if the property was alienated in any way. Also preserved were the writings about lawsuits, from summonses and prorogatory decisions to the sentence. But this was virtually all that the archives contained. The inventories of the archbishopric of Esztergom of c. 1417 and of the bishopric of Veszprém from 1352 prove this fact beyond doubt. 37 Private landowners, especially in larger clans, often made arrangements for the safekeeping of charters, entrusted them to ecclesiastical institutions or to barons with castles. 38

(Pest/Budapest, 1860-74) IV: 274-5 contains the record of two opposing testimonies, one by István son of Ugod of Ugodháza, the other by Iván and Péter, sons of Ugod. While they were probably not brothers, they were clearly descendants of a certain Ugod, who had acquired the property.

35 *Magyar Nyelv* **55** (1959), 425-66.

36 *...huiusmodi attestatio rei publicae, legique et regni nostri consuetudini sit speciale firmamentum et robur veritatis.* Hajnik, [as above, n.8] 293, n. 38.

37 *Levéltári Közlemények* **37** (1966), 113-37; **20-23** (1942-45), 384-8.

38 A. Czobor, "Családi levéltárak" [Family archives in the Middle Ages] *Ibid.* **20** (1940), 380-440.

In contrast to the handful of charters the gaps are immense. The genealogy and history of the clan was clearly not passed on in writing, but by word of mouth. Gergely Bethlen, around A.D. 1600 is the first person I know of, who noted down the birth of his children.[39] The few genealogical tables, which survived from the late fifteenth century are all ex post compilations, aimed exclusively at proving property rights and disregard all members who were not important for the hereditary succession, however significant they may have been in the history of the country. [40] Genealogical literature, comparable to this genre in western Europe, never developed in medieval Hungary, even though King Matthias Corvinus had his own fictional genealogy, tracing it back to a Roman *gens*, compiled by his Humanist courtiers. But when the barons in his court gave information to the historians Bonfini and Thúróczy, they spoke about single members, who were major figures in the past, and did not tell them continuous family histories. [41] That the deeds of some great men were recorded at all is due to the royal chancellery's preference for extensive *narrationes* in charters of royal donations. [42] These are of course, in no way comprehensive and do not "cover" family histories systematically.

If it was not the family archives, was it then the *loca credibilia* which kept family records? We have seen that extensive knowledge of family affairs was expected from the staff of these ecclesiastical institutions, which served as places of authentication. So much so that, for example, Miklós Csáky, voivode of Transylvania inquired from the provost of Lelesz, whether he was related to his wife and, if so, to what degree. [43] Besides the records

39 I. Lukinich, *A bethleni gróf Bethlen család története* [History of the family of the Counts B. of B.] (Budapest, s.d.) 38, 52.
40 So, for example, a genealogical table for the family Szentgyörgyi Vincze from c. 1482 disregards several lateral branches, which became extinct in the earlier fifteenth century; *A Veszprém megyei múzeumok közleményei* 11 (1972), 266-8.
41 E. Mályusz, *A Thúróczy krónika forrásai* [Sources of the Chronica of Th.] (Budapest, 1967) 99, 140; P. Kulcsár, *Bonfini Magyar Történetének forrásai és keletkezése: Fonti e genesi della storia ungherese di Bonfini* (Budapest, 1973) 185-8.
42 E. Mályusz, "La chancellerie royale et la rédaction des chroniques dans la Hongrie médiévale" *Moyen Age* 71 (1969), 59-69.
43 *Oklevéltár a ... gróf Csáky család történetéhez* [Diplomatarium for the

originating from their own official participation in inquests and other legal procedures, many *loca credibilia* served as depositories of family archives, entrusted to them for safekeeping.[44] Thus, there were sufficient data at their disposal for writing up some kind of genealogies, yet the fairly extensive records from the surviving archives of major *loca credibilia*, such as Jászó, Lelesz, Pozsony or the cathedral chapter of Veszprém, do not contain any writing of this kind. [45] It is unlikely that if there had been some, none would have survived, at least in a fragment. The same holds true for the monasteries of families or clans, although they belonged to the same monastic orders that have produced extensive genealogical writings in western Europe. When the Hungarian order of St. Paul the Hermit compiled a calendar of their charters in the early sixteenth century, they too registered only the property deeds, without any reference to the person and family of the founders.

Clearly, the genealogical tradition of the nobility of medieval Hungary was an oral and not a written one. But why should one concentrate so much on writings about family history when such writings would not have been legally valid in medieval courts anyhow? The reason is, paradoxically, a legal one. Hungarian nobles lived in the legal system of *aviticitas* ("entail"), which ensured unlimited inheritance in the male line of descent. Hence, every nobleman had to be thoroughly familiar with all the ramifications of his paternal descent, but he also had to know about the property transactions and loans related to his maternal family. Lack of knowledge in these matters could cause material loss. I have found that among the aristocracy the paternal genealogy was indeed well known, while their information on the descent in the female line was often surprisingly poor. [46] The same also seems to have been the case with the lesser noblity. In 1402 a certain Mrs Sebestyén sued the Várdai family for an inheritance, but was unable to state the name of her great-grandmother. The defendants successfully argued that they do not know about a sister of their great-grandfather and have no knowledge of Mrs

history of the Cs. family] (Budapest, 1919) [henceforth: Csáky. O.]
200.

44 Czobor [as n. 38, above] 390-94.

45 *Történelmi Tár*, 1886: 571-4.

46 See my *A 15. sz.-i magyar arisztokrácia mobilitása* [Social mobility of fifteenth-century Hungarian aristocracy] (Budapest 1970) 78f.

Sebestyén's relationship to them. [47] Some lesser noblemen from county Pozsony did not know the name of their grandmother, and when Mihály Károlyi in 1592 wanted to draw up a family tree, he had to inquire from a relative the name of his father's sister. [48]

Not only the danger of material loss should have encouraged genealogical interest. The noblity is an élite, which guards its prestige. When the charter granting baronage to the Károlyi family in 1698 displayed that dragon on the coat of arms that had been worn by their family in the fifteenth century but which was not in fashion two hundred years later (and actually had vanished from the sixteenth-century seals of the family members), then this was an attempt at demonstrating both the ancient descent and the high status of the family. [49]

The oral survival of genealogical information, so necessary for a number of purposes, was threatened by many dangers. Epidemics, wars or other demographic catastrophies extinguishing all adult male members of a family were not rarities in the Middle Ages. In such cases considerable segments of the tradition, maybe first the less important ones, on farther branches, could easily be lost. When Mihály, son of Dezső Elefánti challenged a perfectly legal property transaction of his father, he lost the case, because he was not aware of certain orally existing traditions, since he had lost his father while still a child.[50] Even more was lost when a family died out in the male line, because the descendants "on the distaff side" kept only those traditions alive, which were relevant to their properties.

Besides genealogical writings, we also lack data on the nobles' properties. The main definition of the estate was its boundaries, and these were contained in the record about the induction. Usually only the name of the estate was named in other

47 Zichy O., V: 314.

48 Eszt. O., 143. With the exception of the family book of the Haller family — which belongs to the burgher tradition of South Germany and not to Hungarian noble usages — the first genealogical notations begin in the late sixteenth century. One of the earliest was started by Ferenc Eszterházy, viscount of Pozsony in 1567, continued by his son, Dániel to 1653 (Ibid., 178 ff.). For the Károlyi project, see Kár. O., III: 574, 576.

49 Kár. O., 574; cf. G. Éble, A ... gróf Károlyi család leszármazása [Genealogy of the Counts K.] (Budapest, 1913) Tb. II.

50 Cod. dipl. Andeg., IV: 252-5.

transactions, very rarely noting the size or the type of the land, the number of tenants, or any other quantitative or qualitative information. In the early years of Sigismund there was some interest in counting the tenancies, but in significant numbers these surveys were done only when an estimation of the property was ordered. Not too many such records survived. *Urbaria* (customals, surveys) were rarely drawn up, usually only on the largest estates. [51] The administration was obviously based on memory, maybe on some simple system of tallies.

To write last wills and testaments was not much more frequent either. Inherited property descended in the prescribed way of *aviticitas*, hence there was no need to make decisions. The nobleman's testament may have contained his will regarding acquired property, debts and outstanding loans, some personal goods and perhaps his choice of burial site. Hence, it is understandable that last wills were not written before the late fifteenth century, when some great "collectors" of estates in particular, who also held several properties in mortgage, found it most useful and necessary to draw up a will. But even these documents are rather dissatisfying. The testator may have named a ward for his minor children, but he never had words of guidance for his successors. Besides naming the burial site, little is said about otherwordly matters before the late fifteenth century. [52] Neither was there any need for *post mortem* inventories, because the mobile property was divided between widow and children, with the exception of armour, which went to the sons, and the dowry of the wife, which was kept by her.

Let us finally turn to a "personal" type of writing, the letter. From the fifteenth century onwards many Latin letters are known and letter-writing did in fact develop, at least among the aristocracy. Even special types, such as invitations and letters of condolence were formulated. [53] Unfortunately letters have often not been analyzed by internal criteria, but summed up under an archival term of the eighteenth century as *missiles*. Let us

51 I. Szabó, *A falurendszer kialakulása Magyarországon* [Development of the village system in Hungary] (Budapest, 1966) 192f.
52 E.g. in a will of 1465, B. Radvánszky, L. Závodszky, eds., *A Hédervéry család oklevéltára* [Diplomatarium of the family H.], (Budapest, 1909-12) I: 331; or in another of 1495, Eszt. O., 107.
53 E.g. an invitiation in Csáky O., I: 200; a condoleance in Zichy O., XII: 279.

scrutinize a set of forty-nine "letters" written by István Várdai, archbishop of Kalocsa, between 1448 and 1470.[54] Two of these could be called mandates, as they resemble royal mandates, but they are letters close, not letters patent like the usual royal ones. They are addressed on the outside, have no *intitulatio*, hence resemble fairly closely the family letters among the *missiles*. Almost half of the letters contain barely more than an introduction for the bearer of the writing (the editors styled them "letters of credence") and, even if some details of the matter at hand are mentioned, the point is that the addressee should "give credence to the retainer, who delivers it." [55] We may say, then, that more than half of the letters do not in fact belong to a culture of written communication, but rather to an oral culture, in which the writing serves merely as an authentication for oral messages. And one should consider that Várdai was a learned man, doctor of Canon Law, a rising member of the better-off lesser nobility, even if not a Humanist, as his contemporary, Johannes Vitéz de Zredna. The letters of lesser nobles were in a much larger percentage "letters of credence", mandates to stewards and reeves, or other writings granting powers for oral deliberation.

All this could be simply explained by assuming that Hungarian noblemen did not know how to write, and knew Latin even less. It is well known that the regent János Hunyadi (d. 1453) and the famous commander of the royal army István Báthory (d. 1493) were illiterates. And it is also true that deliberations at courts, counties and on the Diet were conducted not in Latin but in Magyar. But the matter is not as simple as that.

A short excursus on writing may be proper here. It is well known that book-hands, i. e. the writings in ecclesiastical codices, liturgical books, etc. are much easier to read than court hands, or cursives. People learned to read in church codices. For our inquiry the literate person is the one who can read the cursive of economic, political and legal records, and not he who may manage to read a missal or psalter. Literate noblemen in this sense included a good number of clerks in royal and baronial offices, who were not *clerici* but secular persons. For example, a few related noble families which lived in a quite small region of county Nyitra supplied three chancellery clerks within 50 years. That they knew both Latin and writing is self evident. Their official activity left its mark on the

54 Printed in Zichy O., vols. IX-XII *passim*.
55 Zichy O., XII: 276, 286.

life of the clan: they acquired a charter granting them a coat of arms to enhance their ancient nobility, recovered lost properties and procured a licence for holding fairs. [56] The nobles from Nyitra fit well into the over-all picture drawn by György Bónis who established the names of scores of lesser nobles in judicial offices, where not only Latin and writing, but a fair knowledge of customary law also was necessary. [57]

When scanning the genealogical literature, one has the impression that almost every noble family had its *literatus*. But let us try to quantify once more. Assuming that the thesis of Bernát L. Kumorowitz about notaries in the *loca credibilia*[58] can be generalized for all the convents and chapters so qualified, and that the proposition[59] of Géza Istványi, about every county having a notary is correct, then, counting 60 counties in Hungary, 7 in Slavonia and about 40 *loca credibilia*, there could have been over hundred active notaries in these places.[60] To the local officials we have to add the staff of the chief justices (count palatine, judge royal), of the voivode of Transylvania and of the ban of Slavonia. Estimating one deputy, a protonotary and a dozen scribes and notaries, these would amount to some 50-60 persons. A great number of clerks were employed by the treasury: following András Kubinyi's studies,[61] one may take that some 200-250 people worked there at any one time. If we detract the likely number of non-noble

---

56 The notary in the secret cancellery was Márton Bosányi, the letters patent for the coat of arms is Dl 95 680. Péter Elefánti, notary, was a relative of his. Polycarpus/György Kosztolányi is a well-known official, see V. Fraknói, in *Századok* **33** (1898), 214.

57 *A jogtudó értelmiség a Mohács előtti Magyarországon* [Men trained in the law in pre-1526 Hungary] (Budapest 1971), 175-218, 265-308.

58 "A leleszi prépostság tagjai és hiteleshelyi személyzete 1569-ig" [Members and legal staff of the collegiate church of Lelesz before 1569], *Emlékkönyv Szt. Norbert...* (Gödöllő 1934), 47f.

59 "A megyei írásbeliség..." [Beginnings of written records in the counties] *Századok* **71** (1937), 549f.

60 A. Oszvald, in the above quoted St. Norbert *Festschrift* (p. 99) mentions that the notary of the convent of Ság was at the same time the notary of the magistrates' court *(sedria)* of Co. Hont. Thus the number 107 may be a maximum.

61 "A kincstári személyzet a XV. sz. második felében" [Treasury staff in the second half of the 15th C.], *Tanulmányok Budapest múltjából* **12** (1957), 29.

employees (just as we have disregarded the staff of the *magister tavarnicorum*, which also consisted to a great extent of burghers)', we still should count 80-150 nobles in Treasury service. The royal chancellery has to be left out, because we have no figures on its size, and the majority of its staff was still clergy. But there were clerks at the centres of the great estates as well: since we know about some 350 castles from the early fifteenth century, and there were estates without castle (but hardly castles without estates), we may assume the existence of 400 seigneurial notaries.

Counting in all categories the highest estimate, we arrive at 700 writing officers in the medieval kingdom. Hungary at that time had a population of ca. four million, of which 40 000 persons were nobles (about 6-8000 families in some 1700 clans). This means, therefore, that every third noble clan had at least one *literatus*. Essentially the same results were arrived at by Bónis, who analysed the place of origin of the notaries and other clerks in the higher courts. Besides Slavonia, thirty-three counties feature in his tables, in a rather uneven geographical distribution, and those regions supplying the most names, which also sent most immigrants to the capital cities.[62] Among the clerks at court we encounter members of 96 clans. All these calculations are very incomplete and certainly contain many mistakes. But even if we doubled the assumed number of literate nobles, it would still be safe to state that the overwhelming majority of medieval nobles in Hungary did not have any interest in writing, and this fact explains the dearth of written documents of all types.

So far we have disregarded all those nobles, who chose an ecclesiastical career, although one may argue that they, some of whom even graduated from universities, represented a significant segment of literate nobility. However, even though only monks were legally disabled to hold property — and were usually left out of the late medieval genealogies[63] — priests could not have legal heirs either, hence all clergy counted as having "left the clan". They could and did help to raise the status of their clan, procured prebends for cousins and nephews, intervened in lawsuits, but did not take part in the life of the noble county, the very locus of noble politics. If we would add them to the literate nobility, we would

---

62 Bónis, [as n. 57 above] 305; cf. A. Kubinyi "Déldunántúli parasztok...."
[Migration of peasants from southern Transdanubia to the cities],
Somogy megye múltjából 3 (1972), 16.
63 See my note in *Veszprém megyei* [as n. 40, above], 266.

gain considerable numbers. Elemér Mályusz compiled statistics for the cathedral and collegiate chapters in medieval Hungary, [64] on the basis of which, assuming that the dignitaries of every chapter (provost, lector, cantor, guardian) were nobles, we arrive (for 49 chapters) at some 200 noble canons. The archdeacons, of which there were about a hundred, came also mostly from the nobility. Some greater, well-endowed parishes may also have had noble *plebani*, which add another 100 to our count. Thus some four hundred nobles among the clergy, i. e., at least one in every four clans, should be added to the secular *literati*. Even so, the number of nobles able to write — that is, being fluent in cursive, as discussed above — was still a small fraction of the total privileged population. Whichever way we count, we cannot even be sure that every clan had a literate person among its members. This fact is suggested also by the survival of the custom of sending one's seal as an authentication.

Before we leave statistics, one more figure should be considered. Although I doubt that the number 800 for the market towns, *oppida*, as proposed in the older literature, is correct, a few hundred such semi-urban centres did certainly exist. Many of these market towns also had notaries, as the Latin letters of the town of Patak[65] prove. Although we have no idea about how many *literati* may have been active in commercial life, it is quite likely that "peasant scribes" existed in numbers equal to, or larger than, that of literate noblemen. If we consider that about half of the canons — maybe 300-350 altogether — came from the market town *civis* population, than the number of "intellectuals" with peasant background would be quite impressive. This aspect of literacy has not yet been studied.

In the fifteenth century this literate élite, slim as it may have been by any count, advanced literacy in all three major centres of writing: in the *loca credibilia*, in the counties and on the large estates. Convents and chapters began to keep registers (*protocolla*), instead of preserving single writs, mandates and chirographs. [66] The counties tended to have more regularly established notaries, and in 1500 the first *protocollum* was started in

---

64 *Egyházi társadalom a középkori Magyarországon* [Ecclesiastical society in medieval Hungary] (Budapest, 1971) 115-18.

65 Df 219 563.

66 The earliest extant is from the convent of Kolozsmonostor, beginning in 1438; Dl 36 390.

county Zólyom.[67] On the great estates Latin surveys and records also became more widespread. The three types of records developed in parallel, reflecting the mobility of the *literati*, who served equally in county, convent and castle, wherever employment was available. However, it is important to stress that the fifteenth-century development remained strictly within the limits of the older types and institutions. One may say that it was a growth in depth, not in width: no significant new types of writing, no new centres of literacy were established, and the existing ones were not expanded beyond traditional confines either.

I should like now to place all these developments in a larger historical context. The majority of Hungarian nobility acquired its status, together with landed property, by the grace of the king. In the last quarter of the thirteenth century the merits that led to status and estates were almost exclusively military ones. Letters of ennoblement invariably refer to chivalric warfare, knights in armour and the royal banner under which the meritorious warrior fought. Before the century ended, the main definition of the noble had shifted to the aspect of property, and he is referred to as *homo possessionatus*. By the 1330s the "propertied man" had virtually replaced the "warrior". Under King Charles I Robert, when conditions of property holding were extensively revised, the principle that royal donation is the sole source of noble property became generally established. This also implied that an estate is incomplete without a charter of donation. The royal chancellery produced these in great numbers, and issued, if the charters were lost, records on induction to property. Yet many families, noble beyond doubt, still did not have any written deed, because their land came from purchase, exchange or private donation. For them the *loca credibilia* had to satisfy the need for written proof of possession. In minor matters a lawsuit in the county, with a letter issued in the chancellery of the *comes*, could also serve the purpose; the county notary later inherited this practice from the seigneurial scribes of the count. These three instances, together with the writing offices of the high justices of the realm, sufficed for producing those title deeds which the nobility expected to acquire.

---

67 A. Föglein, "A vármegyei jegyzőkönyv" [The county minutes], *Levéltári Közlemények* **16** (1938), 167. Even though the surviving minutes are mostly from the later sixteenth century, there is evidence for earlier, now lost, ones.

The problems became serious when the gap between the original charter and the fourteenth-fifteenth-century descendants had to be bridged, or the charter got lost — if it ever existed at all. It became clear that all these writing offices had worked *ad hoc* and, although there may have been some early registers in some of them, no reliable record existed of the written transactions of preceding decades and centuries. We have some about surveys of the castle-lands under the Árpádian kings, but no details. Two references suggest that some kind of list of noble properties was drawn up in the fourteenth century as well. In a mandate of 19 November 1364, issued by King Louis I, on the *relatio* of Benedek Himfi, addressed to the chancellery, we read that a charter of the chapter of Szepes was produced about the seizin granted on an estate in county Liptó, near the rivulet Kalina, and a renewal under the king's new seal was requested. The king ordered the chancellor to search "for the said property's name in the register existing with you about the possessions in the said county Liptó for greater security's sake", and if found, to issue a confirmation for the charter of Szepes. [68] This "Liptó register" features in another charter of the same year (24 October 1364), in which Louis states that he had read in the register prepared at the revision of the charters of the nobles in Liptó that his father, King Charles, had acknowledged the authenticity of a charter by King Ladislas the Cuman and ordered the *comes* of Liptó to enter the property of Lazan into the register.[69] However, all this is contained in a later transcript, while neither of these charters have come down to us, hence all that we know is that there was some kind of register in county Liptó about noble titles to land.

The *loca credibilia* could not keep systematic surveys, because more than one of them was active within a given territory, nothing said of the chapters of Buda and Fehérvár, which had the right to issue documents for the entire country. Neither did the county nobility keep appropriate records; the earliest extant registers of the nobility date from the mid-sixteenth century.

The emergence of the territorially closed great estate in the later thirteenth century had a definite impact on the growth of written documentation. The policies of King Sigismund, which enhanced considerably the concentration of properties, above all of the great landed estates, were crucial in this development. Several

68 Dl 41 605.
69 *Történelmi Tár*, 1904.

great lords owned major tracts of land in different, often quite remote, parts of the realm. In these cases, written communication and accounting became a necessity, as the castellans and stewards rarely met their lord personally. For the guidance of the frequently changing administrative personnel, the tenants' dues had to be put into writing as well. These needs triggered the production of those estate records, which permitted the detailed study of manorial administration in the fifteenth century.[70]

In summary, then: the demands of medieval Hungarian nobles to written documents did not go beyond the need for securing their landed property and administering their estates. Everything else, be it family tradition or major events in the life of the country, was passed on by the word of mouth. Werbőczy, whose law-book contains the most vivid picture of the noble clan, fully supports this assumption. He writes that it is a cardinal duty of the father to "educate" his son, and as a gloss to *educare* he adds, that this means to feed and clothe him. No cultural demands are placed on the parents; had there been any, Werbőczy, a man who rose by his legal and literary training, would have certainly included them.

Let us close with a brief look at the literacy of the nobility in the century that followed the end of the medieval kingdom of Hungary in the battle of Mohács. Scholars of that period make one believe that the world changed very much during the sixteenth century. Studies on letters in the vernacular propose that qualitative and quantitative changes occurred because "in the latter part of the century ... all types of official writings (although not those of the major offices) came to be translated into Magyar, almost all legal technical terms appear in the vernacular, and Hungarian legal formulations are able to describe all manners of business". [71] The authors of these studies, based on eastern Hungarian records and on documents written before 1533, respectively, propose that the reasons are to be found in the preceding century. Enhanced by the incentives of the royal court and by increased schooling, Latin writing spread in the fifteenth century.

---

70 I. Sinkovics, *A magyar nagybirtok élete a XV. sz. elején* [The life of the great estates in early fifteenth-century Hungary] (Budapest, 1933).

71 L. Papp, *Magyar nyelvű levelek és okiratok a XVI. sz.-ban* [Letters and documents in Hungarian in the sixteenth century], (Budapest, 1964, Nyelvtud. ért. 44); cf. also G. Istványi, *A magyar nyelvű írásbeliség ki-alakulása* [Development of Hungarian-language literacy] (Bu-da-pest, 1934).

This was followed by the upsurge of writing in the vernacular, first quite rapidly, than between 1530 and 1540 at a slower pace, and after 1540 almost as an explosion of Hungarian-language literacy. In a publication of the Nádasdy archives, Elemér Mályusz collected the Hungarian letters before 1550, because, he wrote, extensive "vernacular letter-writing begins after the mid-century".[72] It was logical to select the letters, because this genre grew most conspicuously. Among the letters of Ferenc Sennyei there was one in Hungarian in 1540, one again in 1543, but nineteen in 1551 and seventy-six in 1552: a truly exponential growth. However, as Istványi correctly noted, "the vernacular did not conquer the entire field of writing at all. Only private writing changed more or less to Hungarian." [73] No new type of writing emerged, only the language of some of the old ones was changed. In a list of records studied by Istványi, appended to his study, out of 97 authentic pieces 57 are *missiles*, of which again five are Latin letters with a Magyar post-script. Title deeds (including last wills) are still in great numbers present: sixteen of them. Only 27 pieces are of other types, most of them, however, successors of fifteenth-century precursors, such as petitions to landlords, accounts and surveys of different sorts. The same picture — change of language but not of attitude to letters — also emerges from the tables of L. Papp. [74] Out of 385 dating lines, two thirds are in Latin, and half of all writings dated by church holidays are dated in a medieval, Catholic fashion, while the population of eastern Hungary was already overwhelmingly Protestant.

The literacy of late sixteenth-century Hungary does not differ significantly from the preceding century: merely the language has changed from Latin to the vernacular.

(Translated from the Hungarian by the editor.)

72 "A Nádasdylevéltár magyar levelei 1531-1549" [Hungarian-language
    letters of the N.archives], *Levéltári Közlemények* 1 (1922), 129.
73 See n. 71, above.
74 See n. 71, above.

VII

LES INTELLECTUELS ET LA SOCIÉTÉ
DANS LA HONGRIE MÉDIÉVALE

Communication présentée au colloque Franco-Hongrois
sur l'histoire des intellectuels, Mátrafüred, Octobre, 1980.

Je tenterai ci-dessous de donner une réponse à la question de
savoir comment le sort des intellectuels a évolué jusqu'à la fin du
XVe siècle dans un pays qui, situé à l'extrèmité est de l'Europe, a
adopté le christianisme à une époque tardive — très tardive du point
de vue occidental — et a vécu dans un système social différant de
celui de l'Europe Occidentale. La longueur et la profondeur de mon
exposé, concentré sur l'histoire sociale, sont limitées par les cadres
habituels des rapports présentés à l'occasion d'un colloque.

A la fin du IXe siècle, au moment de la conquête et de
l'unification du bassin des Karpathes, les Hongrois constituent un
peuple d'une composition mixte. Politiquement, ils vivent en
confédération tribale ; la couche dirigeante de la société poursuit sans
aucun doute le mode de vie des cavaliers nomades, mais dans les
couches inférieures on trouve un grand nombre d'agriculteurs
partiellement sédentarisés. L'ensemble du peuple hongrois est païen
au point qu'une partie des Slaves sur place qui s'étaient déjà
convertis au christianisme, reviennent au paganisme. Comme tous
les peuples nomades, les Hongrois avaient une culture fondée sur la
tradition orale, bien qu'ils aient eu une écriture runéiforme et qu'ils
l'aient utilisée, comme en témoignent les monuments. Toutefois ce
n'est pas cette écriture, mais l'art des raconteurs qui a maintenu
dans la conscience du peuple les hauts faits des héros.

Cent ans plus tard une grave crise politique oblige le peuple
et son prince à prendre une décision lourde de conséquences. La
crise ne peut être résolue que par l'adoption du christianisme,
notamment de sa branche romaine. La religion des Hongrois
conquérants est mal connue, néanmoins il est certain qu'elle fut
assez forte pour qu'en 1046, une génération après l'organisation de
l'Eglise, elle déclenche une révolte de grande envergure, conduite, si
l'on en croit les récits laconiques de nos chroniqueurs, par les chefs de

clan. La révolte fut réprimée. Une remarque de Delumeau m'a suggéré l'idée d'attribuer le triomphe total de l'Eglise au fait qu'elle avait pu s'assurer le soutien des chefs de clan en leur arrogeant le droit de patronage des monastères privés et réservant aux plus petits propriétaires le droit de patronage des paroisses, ce qui leur permettait d'occuper dans la vie religieuse une place correspondant à leur statut social. Si cette idée reste pour l'instant une hypothèse incertaine, il n'en est pas moins sûr qu'en trois générations le pays fut entièrement évangélisé. Les protocoles de canonisation de fin du XIIIe siècle (Marguerite de la maison d'Árpád) et du milieu du XVe (Jean de Capistrano), montrent que toute la société, couches inférieures comprises, fait preuve d'une attitude sincèrement chrétienne. Le succès est donc complet, bien qu'une partie des pratiques païennes se soit indéniablement maintenue. Le peuple hongrois venait de surmonter la plus grave crise culturelle de son existence.

Les conséquences de ce qui vient d'être dit me semblent être si logiques que je m'abstiendrai de les commenter. Avant le XIIe siècle, on ne peut pas parler d'intellectuels hongrois. Au XIe siècle la culture et le produit intellectuel sont dûs presque entièrement à l'élite de l'Eglise, missionnaires venus de l'étranger, apportant un produit sacral étranger à la société. Le nombre de documents est réduit, ce qui n'est pas surprenant : il s'agit de quelques légendes du "saint roi, fondateur du pays" (Etienne I, 997-1038) ou d'ouvrages théologiques, tels que le *Deliberatio super hymnum trium puerorum* de l'évêque Gérard qui mourut martyr de la foi pendant la révolte païenne. Le XIe siècle en Hongrie n'est pas l'époque de la "réaction à l'écriture" mais celle de la réaction au christianisme.

Le triomphe du christianisme porte ses premiers fruits au XIIe siècle. Il y a toujours beaucoup d'ecclésiastiques venus de l'étranger; nombre de sièges épiscopaux sont occupés par des immigrés, le Français Robert par exemple, archevêque d'Esztergom au début du XIIIe siècle. Mais on remarque déjà l'apparition d'un petit groupe dont les membres se recrutent parmi les fils des grands lignages toujours aussi puissants et ces jeunes gens, après avoir fréquenté des écoles hongroises, poursuivent leurs études à l'Université de Paris . Le rayonnement de celle-ci est transmis à la Hongrie d'une part par les écclésiastiques français (prêtres et ordres fraîchement fondés), d'autre part grâce aux deux mariages du roi de Hongrie, Béla III qui eut pour première femme Anne de Châtillon, puis épousa Marguerite Capet, en seconde noces, en 1186. Les données relatives à ce petit groupe sont très fragmentaires, mais en recourant à une méthode inverse, István Hajnal a néanmoins réussi à évaluer leur nombre. A l'aide de la graphie des chartes qui nous sont parvenues des XIIe et XIIIe siècles, il a constaté qu'en général, on doit voir dans un scribe moderne, distingué, bien formé, un ancien élève de l'Université de Paris, ce qui permet d'estimer qu'ils étaient cent ou deux cent.

Les étudiants de retour de l'Université de Paris ont fourni un travail de grande envergure. A la fin du XIIe siècle ils établirent la chancellerie royale. En effet, en 1181, Béla III ordonna qu'on mette par écrit les affaires et les procès qui se déroulaient devant lui. Pour constituer leur chancellerie les souverains eurent recours à l'Eglise. Les employés de la chancellerie sont des clercs ; leur supérieur, le chancelier, est en général le prévôt d'un grand chapitre qui, au terme d'un long service auprès du roi se voit récompensé par un évêché, et dans ce cas quitte la cour. Les bases matérielles du travail des notaires et du chancelier sont fournies par l'Eglise et non par le roi. Deux décennies plus tard les clercs revenus de Paris créeront une des institutions caractéristiques du développement hongrois, les *loca credibilia*. Ce sont des chapitres et des couvents qui possèdent un sceau authentique, reconnu, et qui, établissent sous ce sceau les documents des affaires juridiques qui se concluent devant eux et en gardent la copie. Ils assument ainsi les fonctions des notaires publics italiens. Disons tout de suite qu'au cours du XIIIe siècle ils seront intégrés à la juridiction royale : c'est en leur présence que "l'homme du roi" *(homo regius)* convoque et exécute les sentences et ce sont les *loca credibilia* qui en établissent la charte. Au XIIe siècle on commence aussi à se préoccuper du renouvellement des cadres. Près des *loca credibilia* les plus importants, on organise des écoles dont les élèves apprennent le *trivium* et même, exceptionnellement, le *quadrivium*.

Cette première période se termine en 1241 par l'invasion des Mongols qui détruisent une partie des églises et massacrent plus d'un clerc. Si l'on veut dresser le bilan de ce siècle on peut dire que la Hongrie a organisé son Eglise, s'est ralliée à la culture européenne, et a créé les centres qui assuraient les bases matérielles de l'existence des intellectuels (chancellerie royale et chapitres) et réhaussaient leur prestige par l'autorité de l'Eglise. L'énergie des intellectuels s'épuise à cette époque, dans l'organisation du pays et de l'Eglise. Très peu d'ouvrages littéraires ou scientifiques apparaissent à cette époque, et encore moins dans la période qui suit l'invasion des Mongols. On ne connaît en fait que les premières rédactions de chroniques dues à des Hongrois. Ce que nous savons des misères causées par l'invasion mongole provient également des mémoires d'un chanoine italien. Néanmoins tout ce cela crée une première base de la carrière intellectuelle, une possibilité de faire accepter l'intellectuel comme membre utile de la société. En ce qui concerne son caractère général, la performance intellectuelle de l'époque ne diffère en rien de celle de l'Occident: l'écriture et le travail intellectuel entrent parmi les activités de l'Eglise, leur but est d'assurer son fonctionnement. A l'exception de la chancellerie royale, les institutions appartiennent toutes à l'Eglise et leurs membres sont, bien entendu, des clercs.

Au cours des cent ans succédant à l'invasion des Mongols, la société subit des changements radicaux qui ne tarderont pas à influencer la situation des intellectuels. Bien que les origines des trois processus dont il sera question dans ce qui suit remontent à la période avant 1241, leur essor se situe dans la seconde moitié du XIIIe siècle.

Le premier évènement important est l'apparition des ordres mendiants. Au moment de l'invasion des Mongols, il y avait en Hongrie environ 170 à 180 couvents et monastères, auxquels il faut ajouter, jusqu'en 1300, les dix-sept couvents des Pauliniens, le seul ordre hongrois, qui s'organisa en partie grâce à l'intervention de Bertrand, évêque de Pecs, d'origine française. Le premier ordre mendiant apparu en Hongrie en 1221 sous la direction de Paulus Hungarus, enseignant de l'Université de Bologne, est l'ordre des Dominicains. Après une première période de grande influence, leur élan retombe, et dès 1265 ce sont les Franciscains qui prennent la tête. En 1350, les Dominicains auront fondé trente-huit couvents; les Franciscains cinquante et un, et les ermites augustiniens quinze, presque exclusivement dans les villes. De ces deux ordres, c'est celui de Saint Dominique qui semble être supérieur intellectuellement ; les Dominicains se servant de la Hongrie comme base pour leur travail d'apostolat en Orient, et leur école à Buda déploie une activité intense.

Avec la fondation d'une série de nouvelles villes, le réseau des agglomérations de caractère urbain s'élargit. Après l'invasion des Mongols, le roi fonda de nouvelles villes dans lesquelles vinrent s'établir des colons étrangers. Comme les bourgeois citadins ont encore davantage besoin de l'écriture que les nobles, la rédaction de chartes prend rapidement son essor. La langue des chartes est le latin dans les villes où vit une population mixte du point de vue ethnique : à Esztergom, habitée par des Français et des Hongrois, et à Fehérvár, par exemple. Ailleurs, là où la population est entièrement ou en majeure partie allemande, les chartes sont rédigées en allemand.

Au XIIe siècle on entendait par *nobilis* les grands propriétaires terriens du pays dont la fortune et le pouvoir augmentèrent d'une façon inouie, au détriment du roi, pendant le XIIIe siècle. La conscience accrue qu'ils ont de leur importance se réflète dans les sceaux pontificaux des évêques. Au XIIe et XIIIe siècles, ces sceaux représentaient uniformément un évêque assis en chape et en mitre sur le *distorsium* mural; au début du XIVe siècle — sans doute sous l'influence de l'Occident — on introduit le sceau à compartiment: le prélat est représenté en bas, et à côté de lui, à peu près de la même taille, apparaissent les armoiries du lignage. Les propriétaires terriens qui sont encore libres sont appelés à cette époque *servientes regis*, terme qui souligne — en contraste avec les aspirations des grands seigneurs — leurs rapports directs avec le souverain. Mais cette appellation disparait au XIIIe siècle pour céder la place au terme *nobilis*, et, en 1351, la noblesse unie obtient définitivement le droit de vivre selon le système social des grands propriétaires. L'unité fondamentale du système social est le lignage (et non la famille), soit l'ensemble des descendants en ligne paternelle d'un ancêtre commun. La terre assurant les bases de l'existence matérielle est répartie à chaque génération en proportion égale entre les fils, mais la succession réciproque se maintient également. Les filles ne pouvaient pas hériter des terres, et si l'on ajoute que le revenu des terres est grevé de l'obligation de fournir des soldats, il est clair que l'on a affaire à une élite militaire, bien que dès le début du XIVe siècle l'épithète principal du noble exprime qu'il est propriétaire *(homo possessionatus)* par opposition au serf qui ne possède rien *(homo impossessionatus)*.

Une des caractéristiques importantes du système qui nous intéresse ici est que toute la noblesse possède une culture orale et que ses institutions maintiennent jusqu'au XVe siècle la validité de la tradition orale. Voyons un exemple: chaque noble énumère sans peine ses ancêtres au cinquième ou sixième degré en ligne paternelle. Ce n'est pas uniquement son prestige qui l'exige, mais aussi le système de succession selon lequel le statut, le rang ou le domaine se transmettent de père en fils. Le noble cependant ne faisait pas tenir de registre de ses ancêtres. Cette abscence de documents écrits était un fait que même la procédure devait accepter. Au cours du procès, les parties pouvaient présenter des documents prouvant la descendance, mais dans la majorité des cas on la justifiait par l'attestation sous la foi du serment de la noblesse du comitat, autrement dit, on s'appuyait sur la mémoire collective de la communauté nobiliaire *(communitas nobilium)*. Comme le montre cet exemple, il ne s'agit pas ici d'une aversion de la noblesse guerrière pour la lettre et l'écriture, mais d'une préférence accordée par la société à la tradition orale. Cette manière de procéder est encore généralement admise au XVe siècle et n'est nullement une particularité du haut moyen-âge. Il est aisé de comprendre que le principe de la procédure orale assignait à priori des restrictions au développement du groupe des intellectuels. Pour rédiger par écrit les documents indispensables, le personnel des *loca credibilia* et un notaire par comitat étaient largement suffisants.

Nous venons de constater le rétrécissement des possibilités des intellectuels, toutefois — paradoxalement — on est en droit d'affirmer en même temps que c'est précisément ce système qui, dès le début du XIVe siècle, a produit la fleur des intellectuels. Pour rendre ceci plus clair, nous devons faire un petit détour. Connaissant le système social de la noblesse, on comprend que la terre, base matérielle de son existence, se comportait comme la marmite de Papin dans laquelle la pression démographique de la vapeur est soumise à un changement constant. Si dans les générations successives il y avait de nombreux garçons qui atteignaient l'âge adulte, la pression démographique supportée par la propriété terrienne augmentait proportionnellement, en d'autres termes, le domaine se morcelait de plus en plus, et ce morcellement entraînait d'abord l'abaissement du niveau de vie, puis rendait impossible qu'on satisfasse à l'obligation du service militaire et finalement entamait même le prestige. Il fallait donc ménager des soupapes qui permettaient de diminuer la pression. On connaît deux soupapes de ce genre: la carrière ecclésiastique et le système des *familiares*.

Que de temps en temps la famille décide de destiner un des garçons à la carrière ecclésiastique, n'a en soi rien de particulier. Nous avons bien vu que dès le XIIe siècle les lignages aristocratiques suivaient le même chemin. Il n'est pas non plus surprenant que les fils d'aristocrates ne soient pas restés dans les rangs du bas clergé, mais que, conformément à leur statut social, ils aient obtenu une place distinguée dans la hiérarchie de l'Eglise, ce qui leur donnait également un revenu plus important. Bien entendu, chaque prêtre d'origine aristocratique ne devint pas évêque, puisqu'il n'y avait en Hongrie que douze évêchés. Mais les dignitaires des chapitres *prepositus, custos, cantor, lector*, et les *archidiacones* exerçant le droit de regard de l'évêque, étaient tous largement rémunérés. Il existait déjà deux cent soixante dix bénéfices de ce genre dans le pays, et nous n'avons pas encore parlé de l'accumulation des bénéfices. Quelle que soit la méthode qu'on applique à l'étude des dignitaires d'un chapitre (en coupe horizontale de tous les chapitres d'une époque, ou en coupe verticale d'un seul chapitre pendant une période plus longue), on constate que ces postes étaient remplis au XIVe et XVe siècles d'une part par les membres de la haute noblesse, d'autre part par ceux de la noblesse locale. Toutefois, il en restait un nombre suffisant pour les favoris du roi venus de l'étranger et pour les prêtres issus des couches inférieures de la société. Le phénomène est d'autant plus surprenant que selon une déclaration de l'ambassadeur du roi de Hongrie datant de 1475, il y a à cette époque en Hongrie mille sept cent lignages nobiliaires, ce qui correspond à vingt-trois ou vingt-quatre personnes par lignage, et en admettant que la moitié en était masculine, on arrive au chiffre de vingt mille.Cela signifierait donc que sur vingt mille hommes, moins de deux cent soixante dix étaient des ecclésiastiques de rang moyen. Dans l'intérêt de la clarté de ce qui va suivre, ce fait demande à être souligné. J'ajouterais encore que suite aux recherches généalogiques, on peut affirmer qu'il y eut effectivement peu de membres de la couche nobiliaire qui choisirent la vocation de prêtre. La raison en était, entre autres, qu' avec le fils entré dans les ordres le lignage perdait un filiateur potentiel ce qui ne pouvait pas ou ne pouvait que rarement se permettre dans les conditions démographiques de l'époque.

Le système des *familiares* — un autre phénomène typique de l'histoire hongroise — offrait moins de difficultés. Les membres moins aisés de la noblesse s'engageaient au service des grands seigneurs. En cette qualité, on les appelait *familiares* et le seigneur était leur *dominus*. Le *familiaris* prêtait serment de fidélité au seigneur et dans les affaires touchant à son service, il devait répondre devant la juridiction seigneurale, en échange de quoi il recevait salaire et protection. Il s'agit là indubitablement d'un lien vassalique, mais en Hongrie le seigneur gardait davantage de despotisme et le *familiaris* davantage de liberté que dans le système féodal européen; parce que premièrement le lien qui unissait le *familiaris* au seigneur pouvait être rompu même de leur vivant et n'était pas héréditaire ; deuxièmement, il ne touchait pas le statut et le prestige du *familiaris* qui restait un noble de plein droit ; troisièmement, il restait sans effet sur la propriété terrienne que le *familiaris* détenait de par sa noblesse et indépendamment de son seigneur; enfin, le pouvoir juridique du seigneur n'était pas réglementé en détail par le droit coutumier. Les *familiares* présentaient pour les familles nobiliaires de gros avantages parce qu'ils accroissaient les revenus, plus exactement les revenus en argent dont elles avaient grand besoin, la rente foncière s'étant aussi dévaluée en Hongrie, parce que les *familiares* assuraient la protection du lignage, et qu'ils pouvaient éventuellement gravir l'échelle hiérarchique.

Les *familiares* étaient une institution généralement répandue dans la vie politique et économique hongroise. Le personnel des chancelleries des dignitaires du pays et des grands juges se composait de *familiares*, qui quittaient leurs postes avec leurs patrons, tout comme la direction administrative et économique de la grande propriété. Il va sans dire que dans une sphère d'activité comme dans l'autre, le *familiaris* devait savoir lire, écrire et posséder une solide culture. Au début du XIVe siècle, on voit apparaître dans les chartes un terme nouveau de *literatus* appliqué au noble laïque. Le recueil de formulaires mis au point vers 1350 à l'intention des *loca credibilia* et des tribunaux contient une définition exacte de ce terme:

> ...est notandum: quod inter clericum scholarem et literatum talis differentia, quia clerici in iure scripto vocantur sacerdotes ... qui ideo ad laycalem habitum non possunt declinari... scholares autem sunt studentes in scolis, vel qui in minoribus ordinibus sont positi ... literati autem sunt illi, qui nec clericari voluant, sed scolas frequentant, omnino proposuerant laycatum.

Il est intéressant de noter que le *literatus* est défini ici par rapport au *clericus* et désigne un homme sachant lire et écrire, voire même ayant fréquenté une école, qui n'est pas prêtre et ne veut pas l'être. Les chartes nous révèlent aussi que c'est des rangs des *literati* que sont sortis les notaires des comitats et des *loca credibilia*, les avocats et les employés de toute une série d'institutions, dont les grands domaines. On constate donc la naissance d'un groupe d'intellectuels laïques qui, paradoxalement, est tributaire d'un système dont la culture est restée invariablement orale. Dès cette époque, il faut tenir compte de deux sortes d'intellectuels : les uns restent dans la voie traditionnelle de l'Eglise et jouissent de bénéfices, les autres appartiennent au monde laïque.

Nous possédons plus de renseignements sur les clercs de statut ecclésiastique, et on sait qu'il s'est produit dans ce milieu un changement important. Nous avons mentionné plus haut Paulus Hungarus qui après avoir enseigné à l'université de Bologne et écrit une *Summa penitentie* entra dans l'ordre des Dominicains et, en 1221, devint le fondateur de la province hongroise. Le personnage marque en lui-même le changement qui surviendra dans la fréquentation des universités de l'étranger. Dans la seconde moitié du XIIIe siècle, l'Université de Paris non seulement perd son rôle exclusif, mais elle passe même au second plan, bien que le rapport avec elle soit maintenu. Les clercs hongrois commencent à s'orienter de plus en plus vers l'Italie où ils se rendent en premier lieu pour étudier le droit canon. A titre d'illustration, je citerai deux exemples. A l'école du chapitre de Veszprém, détruite en 1276, les études de droit étaient tenues en estime particulière, et sur les trente deux chanoines du chapitre, quinze portaient le titre de *decretorum doctor*. C'est un cas exceptionnel évidemment; plus caractéristique est le fait qu'à Esztergom la moitié des anciens étudiants d'université, dix pour cent de l'ensemble des chanoines connus, ont une licence en droit canon. Cette prédominance des études de droit est un fait indéniable, mais ses raisons ne sont malheureusement pas suffisamment connues. On peut, à la rigueur, admettre que l'activité des *loca credibilia* vint renforcer le rôle général du droit canon observé dans les affaires ecclésiastiques.

L'exemple d'Esztergom indique aussi que pas tous les prêtres d'origine aristocratique, ou noble, avaient poursuivi des études universitaires, et à la première moitié du XIVe siècle on en trouve qui ne savent même pas tracer leur propre nom. Jusqu'au XIVe siècle, seules les universités italiennes et celles de Paris et de Prague, puis de Vienne et Cracovie, permettaient aux clercs hongrois d'acquérir une formation supérieure. Toutefois l'occasion d'en profiter dépendait de la situation matérielle. Il n'était pas indifférent que le bénéfice fût ou non suffisant pour couvrir les frais et tout le monde ne disposait pas d'autres ressources. A ce propos, on relève un autre phénomène caractéristique : le fils que la famille avait confié à l'Eglise assurait plus d'une fois les frais de l'éducation d'un membre de la génération suivante qu'on destinait également à la carrière ecclésiastique. Il arrivait souvent que quelqu'un qui lui-même n'avait pas pu faire des études supérieures ou n'avait pas pu les terminer, assurait le financement des études de son neveu. Voici deux exemples concrets : la famille Pálóczi commença à la fin du XIVe siècle à s'élever dans les rangs de la noblesse, dans ceux de l'aristocratie notamment, grâce à un de ses membres qui était prévôt de l'ordre des Prémontrés. Il fit nommer son neveu chanoine de

Szepes, l'envoya étudier à l'Université de Vienne d'où le jeune homme rentra muni du titre de *doctor decretorum*, devint prévôt de Szepes, puis évêque de Transylvanie et enfin archevêque d'Esztergom. Le grand humaniste János Vitéz, pût commencer ses études à l'université de Vienne, mais il ne les termina jamais. En revanche, il assuma les frais d'études de son neveu Janus Pannonius en Italie. La première génération de prêtres pût se rendre compte de par ses propres expériences de l'importance des études universitaires et de la formation intellectuelle, et elle était désireuse d'en faire profiter les autres. Dans les dernières années du XIVe siècle, un des dignitaires du chapitre d'Esztergom reçut l'approbation du siège pontifical à Rome pour fonder avec ses propres revenus et sa propre fortune un *Collegium Christi* dont le but était de donner à l'église d'Esztergom des prêtres bien formés. L'archévêque était tenu de doter d'une prébende le clerc qui avait fait des études universitaires aux frais du *Collegium*, tandis que celui-ci, après son retour devait rembourser les frais de ses études et envoyer quelqu'un d'autre dans une université à l'étranger.

Le parcours habituel était donc le suivant: le jeune homme noble destiné à la carrière ecclésiastique était envoyé à l'université, après quoi on cherchait à lui procurer une charge bien rémunérée qui pouvait aussi bien signifier une carrière laïque à la chancellerie royale ou à la chancellerie dite secrète qui, établie au début du XIVe siècle, s'occupait des relations diplomatiques du roi, ou encore dans une autre office de l'administration du pays, comme le trésor. Le roi ménageant ses propres revenus s'en remettait aux institutions ecclésiastiques pour ce qui concerne le salaire de ses employés, et, partant des exemples cités, on peut même dire qu'il faisait payer leur formation à l'Eglise. Ainsi, la couche supérieure des intellectuels hongrois qui possède une culture écclésiastique, maintient la langue latine dans l'usage écrit, les procès et négociations se faisant en hongrois. Du point de vue du roi, ce système présente l'avantage d'exclure l'hérédité, d'assurer une relève plus rapide et d'offrir un choix plus large. Son inconvénient est que ceux qui occupent les postes élevés ne sont pas initiés dès leur enfance à la vie bureaucratique, mais commencent leur carrière par un apprentissage, à l'âge adulte, auprès de leur maître. Le système s'accompagne du reste d'un autre désavantage : les capacités intellectuelles ne peuvent s'épanouir en science et en lettres, parce que le travail administratif sollicite toute l'énergie de ces hommes. Aucune oeuvre scientifique ne paraît en Hongrie, et, à l'exception du seul Janus Pannonius, il n'y a personne vraiment qui cultive la littérature.

On connaît encore un autre type de carrière. Il semble que ceux qui éprouvent la nécessité de s'adonner à la science préfèrent ne pas rentrer en Hongrie et déploient leur activité à l'étranger, dans la plupart des cas dans des universités. Le premier d'entre eux, une fois de plus, est Paulus Hungarus, mais il y a aussi Alexander de Hungaria qui resta à Paris et enseigna à l'université, et dans la seconde moitié du XIVe siècle, le Dominicain Nicolaus de Mirabilibus, né à Kołozsvár, devient régent des études de l'ordre à Florence, et c'est là qu'il écrit son ouvrage en langue italienne, *Libello de conscientia*. Je voudrais insister en particulier sur la carrière d'Andreas Pannonius. Nombre de détails de sa vie ne nous sont pas connus. Issu très probablement de la petite noblesse, il passe cinq années de sa jeunesse auprès de János Hunyadi comme *familiaris*. C'est en cette qualité qu'il participe aux campagnes de son seigneur et qu'il assiste au baptême de son fils, le futur roi de Hongrie. Pour des raisons inconnues, il interrompt bientôt cette carrière laïque, entre dans l'ordre des Chartreux à Venise, puis passe à Ferrare où on le retrouve supérieur du couvent. C'est là qu'il rédige son *Libellus de virtutibus Matthiae Corvino dedicatus*.

C'est des universités italiennes célèbres par leur enseignement du droit canon que l'étincelle de l'humanisme atteint la Hongrie au milieu du XVe siècle. Le premier qui l 'accueille avec enthousiasme est János Vitéz, évêque de Várad, qui à son tour le transmet au roi Mathias qui accède au trône en 1458. Une fois de plus il se forme un groupe restreint qui participe à la vie intellectuelle du pays : elle produit un poète latin de talent en la personne de Janus Pannonius, évêque de Pécs, et elle crée aussi la bibliothèque Corvina, la seconde en importance dans l'Europe de l'époque. Ses relations sont plus étroites avec le miliieu international des humanistes qu'avec la société hongroise, quoique le renouvellement des cadres soit assurée par la noblesse et la paysannerie hongroises. Au centre de ce cercle humaniste de Hongrie, on retrouve d'abord János Vitéz, puis le roi Mathias et son épouse d'origine italienne. C'est ce qui explique l'esprit conservateur de l'humanisme en Hongrie. A l'exception des italiens invités (Galeotto, Bonfini, etc.), chaque membre du cercle humaniste a une charge ecclésiastique, tout comme les intellectuels du XIIe siècle, et plus d'un est, malgré ses dispositions et son intérêt pour les lettres, docteur en droit. Ce cercle dont l'influence s'excerce par le haut sur la société, contribue au renforcement des phénomènes qui, au XVe siècle, donnent une nouvelle orientation au développement. Pour la première fois, la

bourgeoisie et les serfs apparaissent parmi les grands du pays, pour
la première fois ils deviennent partenaires égaux des descendants
des familles aristocratiques et nobles.

Et même ce cercle-là restait à moitié enraciné dans la culture
orale. Voici comment Galeotto décrit un repas chez le roi:

> Semper enim in eius convivio disputatur aut sermo de re honesta
> et iocunda habetur aut carmen cantatur. Sunt enim ibi musici et
> citharoedi, qui fortium gesta in lingua patria ad mensam in lyra
> decantant... apud Hungaros... eadem loquendi forma vel exigua
> admodum differentia est, unde fit, ut carmen lingua Hungarica
> compositum rusticis, mediis et extremis eodem tenore intelligatur.

Devant le niveau culturel élevé des humanistes on peut, une
fois de plus et à juste titre, poser la question de savoir pourquoi il n'y
avait pas d'université en Hongrie. Les tentatives de fondation, en
1367, au début et à la fin du XVe siècle, restèrent embryonaires, et
périclitèrent bientôt. La réponse quelque peu banale est que le pays
n'en avait tout simplement pas besoin. Les quelques centaines de
jeunes gens désireux de poursuivre des études universitaires
pouvaient trouver les fonds nécessaires, sinon autrement, par
l'intermédiaire de l'Eglise. Leur savoir ne servait qu'à
l'administration de l'Etat et à l'Eglise. Les besoins des grandes
masses, de la noblesse et des villes étaient pleinement satisfaits par
les écoles du pays.

J'ai esquissé plus haut la genèse de la couche des intellectuels
laïques, les *literati*. En dehors des travaux mineurs nécessitant leur
connaissance de l'écriture, ils ne se trouvaient de sphère d'activité
d'un niveau plus élevé que dans la justice. Le personnel des bureaux
des grands juges du pays se constituait, comme je l'ai dit, des
familiares nobles du juge. Ces *literati* acquirent, en dehors des
aptitudes à lire, à écrire et à rédiger des textes en latin, une grande
pratique des connaissances théoriques dans le domaine des coutumes
juridiques hongroises, ce qui les rendait capables d'assumer des
fonctions d'avocat et de juge. En général, ils ne faisaient pas
d'études universitaires, ne disposant pas des moyens matériels
nécessaires, mais ils n'en n'avaient en réalité pas besoin; la
connaissance du droit romain ou du droit canon était parfaitement
superflue pour l'exercice du droit en Hongrie. Leur formation
reposera encore longtemps sur la pratique, et on ne trouve aucune
trace d'un essai d'enseignement institutionalisé du droit en Hongrie,
même à la fin du XIVe siècle, lorsqu'il se forme dans les tribunaux

un groupe de juristes, appelés *prothonotarii*, qui préparent les sentences, rédigent les considérants et les documents correspondants. Leur situation subit à cette époque un changement radical. Les protonotaires ne quittent plus leurs fonctions en même temps que leur patron, mais restent sur place à la disposition du juge suivant. Mais qu'on ne s'y trompe pas : la profession, la carrière intellectuelle ne s'hérite pas. Les protonotaires connaissent bien les ficelles du métier, ils réussissent en général à amasser une fortune, et leurs descendants retournent dans les rangs de la noblesse aisée des comitats, éventuellement en se mettant à la tête du nouveau parti nobiliaire qui s'organise à la fin du XVe siècle.

La langue de la procédure était le hongrois (seuls les documents sont rédigés en latin), et à en croire Galeotto, grands seigneurs, nobles, bourgeois et paysans, parlaient et comprenaient tous cette langue. Aussi bien les bourgeois qui vivaient dans les villes royales libres que les paysans qui habitaient dans les agglomerations appelées *oppida*. En effet, à partir du milieu du XVe siècle, il y eut de plus en plus de villages qui se transformèrent de communes directement soumises au seigneur en *oppida*, c'est à dire une petite ville disposant d'une certaine autonomie. C'étaient eux qui, pour reprendre les termes d'Elemér Mályusz, "conduisaient la paysannerie vers la vie urbaine", et ceci non seulement sur le plan économique mais encore dans le domaine culturel. Le processus n'est pas encore entièrement clair; on sait cependant qu'entre 1440 et 1514 plus de deux mille jeunes gens venant de presque cent *oppida* furent envoyés aux Universités de Vienne et de Cracovie. Il y avait parmi eux certainement beaucoup de clercs de statut ecclésiastique, mais il y avait aussi de plus en plus de commerçants et d'artisans. Ce n'est certainement pas un effet du hasard que lorsque le roi Mathias élève pour la première fois de l'histoire hongroise un prêtre d'origine paysanne à la dignité de prélat, celui-ci est originaire d'un *oppidum* de Transdanubie et qu'il ne tarde pas à être rejoint par d'autres membres cultivés de sa famille. On relève d'ailleurs d'autres signes de l'aspiration de la paysannerie à gravir l'échelle sociale. En étudiant les listes des chapitres de la fin du XVe siècle, on constate que si les dignitaires sont en général toujours des nobles, les simples chanoines sont presque toujours issus de différents *oppida*. L'ordre des Franciscains occupe déjà à cette époque une place importante dans la vie spirituelle du peuple hongrois. Une partie considérable de leurs couvents se trouve dans les *oppida*, ce qui explique que leurs directeurs soient également originaires de ces petites villes. Une source qui nous est parvenue par hasard prouve que les écoles de ces villes présentaient un niveau d'enseignement élevé. Les cahiers scolaires de László Szalkai, archevêque d'Esztergom, tombé à la bataille de Mohács en 1526, et qui avait fait sa scolarité à l'école de la ville de Sárospatak, sont conservés aujourd'hui à Esztergom. On ne peut s'empêcher d'admirer le large éventail de ses connaissances acquises à l'école et son latin impeccable quoi que pas toujours exempt de vulgarismes. A la fin du XVe siècle, plus exactement après la grande réforme financière du roi Mathias, la bourgeoisie des bourgades s'infiltre dans l'administration publique. Les *literati* travaillant auprès du trésor, de la chambre de la gabelle, des ateliers de la monnaie et aux offices de la douane sortent en majeure partie de leur rangs. Leur carrière leur assure aussi l'élévation sociale. Ils se procurent un titre de noblesse ou entrent dans la bourgeoisie des grandes villes. La seule branche de l'administration publique qui reste entre les mains des bourgeois — le plus souvent allemands — des villes minières est l'exploitation des mines.

Si les gens provenant des *oppida* font des études scolaires — comme on l'a vu dans le cas de Szalkai — ils apprenent le latin et rédigent les chartes dans cette langue. Le latin reste donc la langue du service d'Etat. Mais en même temps, la classe en question fait partie de la culture orale dont parlait Galoetto. Et c'est ici qu'interviendra le facteur décisif, car cette couche commencera à noter et à mettre par écrit ce qu'elle entend. Les premiers essais sont encore timides, ce qui explique qu'il n'y a guère que deux exemples parmi les genres chantés avant 1490, dont il a été question, qui nous ont été transmis. Il faut attendre la réforme pour que s'épanouisse la langue nationale écrite, et pour que naisse la poésie lyrique mondaine écrite, celle que — à l'exception de Janus Pannonius — les intellectuels hongrois du moyen-âge n'avaient pas sû créer.

*(D'après le rapport dactylographié de la conférence;
une publication, augmentée d'annotations, est prévue.)*

VIII

Das mittelalterliche Königreich Ungarn als Gastland

Es ist für einen ungarischen Forscher wirklich nicht leicht, der ehrenvollen Einladung des Konstanzer Arbeitskreises folgend über die deutsche Ostsiedlung das Wort zu ergreifen. Das Thema ist schon an sich außerordentlich groß; die Klärung einer nach zeitlichem, geographischem oder sachlichem Gesichtspunkt abgegrenzten Spezialfrage stellt noch immer eine große Aufgabe dar. Es stellen sich auch gewisse Informationsschwierigkeiten. In der letzten Zeit hat die ungarische Geschichtswissenschaft eben in bezug auf die erste Periode des Königtums neue Ergebnisse erzielt, welche im Ausland wenig bekannt sind, nicht zuletzt wegen der absoluten Isoliertheit unserer Sprache. Wir trauen uns auch nicht zu behaupten, daß wir die neueste deutsche Fachliteratur zu diesem Thema kennen; sicherlich sind uns bedeutungsvolle neuere Arbeiten unbekannt geblieben.

Die Zielsetzung ist nicht weniger schwer. Es wäre sicherlich sehr interessant, die Historiographie zur Frage der Ostsiedlung zu untersuchen, den Einfluß der vielen und mannigfaltigen Ideen und der Zeitverhältnisse auf die Geschichtsschreibung zu analysieren. Dies zieht den Historiker von heute schon deswegen an, weil mit Hilfe einer solchen Analyse die Denkart und Forschungsmethoden unserer Vorgänger besser kennengelernt werden könnten, doch würde u. E. eine solche Analyse die Frage der Ostsiedlung kaum fördern. Statt dessen schien es uns angemessener, diesmal eben auf Grund der neuen Ergebnisse ein umfassendes Bild der deutschen Siedlung in Ungarn zu geben und die wichtigsten politischen, sozialen und wirtschaftlichen Kennzeichen hervorzuheben. Bewußt haben wir das Wort »Auswertung« vermieden. Wir glauben der gemeinsamen wissenschaftlichen Aufgabe mit einem Versuch, Tatsachen festzustellen und Zusammenhänge aufzuhellen, weitaus besseren Dienst zu leisten.

Prinzipiell war jener Teil der Ostsiedlung, der sich in Ungarn abspielte, ein bilateraler Vorgang; politisch betrachtet die Angelegenheit des österreichischen Markgrafen bzw. Herzogs und des ungarischen Königs oder — falls wir das Problem erweitern — die Angelegenheit des Römischen Reichs und des Königreichs Ungarn; siedlungsmäßig betrachtet die Angelegenheit des deutschen Volkes und der Völker Ungarns. Insofern gehört die Ostsiedlung in den Rahmen der Geschichte Ungarns

472

und der deutschen Länder; wir sind aber fest überzeugt — so paradox es auch klingen mag —, daß die deutsche Ostsiedlung nur im Rahmen der europäischen Geschichte untersucht werden kann. Daher hoffen wir das Bild der deutschen Ostsiedlung in Ungarn so entwerfen zu können, daß es sich in die Bevölkerungs- und Siedlungsgeschichte Europas nicht nur einordnen läßt, sondern einen organischen Teil des europäischen Gesamtvorgangs bildet.

Wir bedienen uns des Ausdrucks »Königreich Ungarn« und tun das ebenfalls zielbewußt. Das Wort »Staat« wurde zwar seit jeher auf die politischen Bildungen des Mittelalters übertragen, doch kann es einerseits nicht auf die frühmittelalterlichen Monarchien angewendet werden [1], andererseits klingen in diesem Wort auch heute noch die Ideen und Vorstellungen des Staates des 19. Jahrhunderts nach, und wir sollten uns, soweit nur möglich, von diesen Vorstellungen befreien, um die Ostsiedlung in ihrer historischen Bedeutung sehen zu können.

Wir haben uns auch zeitlich feste Grenzen gesteckt, indem wir das verhängnisvolle Jahr 1526 nicht überschreiten. Für den ausländischen Leser soll hierzu nur soviel bemerkt werden, daß in der Schlacht bei Mohács das mittelalterliche Königreich Ungarn tatsächlich unterging, obwohl es der Form nach weiter bestand und obwohl die Türken die Folgerungen erst rund fünfzehn Jahre später zogen und das Land besetzten.

1526 soll allerdings als die äußerste zeitliche Grenze unserer Untersuchung dienen. Wir werden die bis zu diesem Ereignis verflossenen rund fünf Jahrhunderte nicht mit der gleichen Intensität behandeln. Unserem Ziel gemäß wollen wir vor allem die Anfangsphase der Entwicklung, also die Zeit der eigentlichen deutschen Besiedlung erfassen, die um die Mitte des 14. Jahrhunderts zu Ende ging. Der Schwerpunkt liegt auf diesem Zeitraum. Das spätere Schicksal der Deutschen in Ungarn möchten wir hier nur soweit berühren, als es zur Erhellung der ersten Phase beiträgt. Daß dabei Verlauf und Kennzeichen in erster Linie von seiten der ungarischen Entwicklung besprochen werden, muß kaum erwähnt werden.

1.

Um den Rahmen für unsere Betrachtung der deutschen Ostsiedlung in Ungarn abstecken zu können, müssen wir weit zurückblicken, bis zur ungarischen Landnahme. Am Ende des 9. Jahrhunderts eroberte das Ungarntum das Karpatenbecken, das von da an sechs Jahrhunderte hindurch — von einer ganz kurzen Periode abge-

---

[1] »L'idée de l'Etat, concept et organisme contenant, définissant et coordonnant les devoirs et les droits des individus et des groupes et forçant ceux-ci les accomplir et à les respecter, était absente de la réalité du Moyen Age naissant ... « M. PACAUT, Les structures politiques de l'Occident médiéval (Collection U. Série »Histoire médievale«, dir. par G. Duby), Paris 1969, S. 36.

sehen — eine politische Einheit und sogar die weitaus stabilste politische Einheit
Europas bildete.

Das landnehmende Ungarntum war vom Gesichtspunkt der wirtschaftlichen
Lebensform her gesehen kein einheitliches Volk. Die führende Schicht bestand zwei-
felsohne aus Reiternomaden; sie erschien im Auge der westlichen Nachbarn als
unmittelbarer Nachkomme der Hunnen und Avaren [2]. Doch in den niederen Sozial-
schichten waren auch Ackerbauern vertreten. Der Anteil der letzteren ist durch die
im Karpatenbecken vorgefundenen Slawen und die in Transdanubien lebenden romanisierten Völkerreste der Völkerwanderungszeit gestiegen [3]. Von den übriggebliebenen Avaren wissen wir ziemlich wenig, doch ist es sicher, daß sie im Schatten
der fränkischen Herrschaft in Raab einen Kagan hatten [4]. Ein großer Teil der hier
vorgefundenen Bevölkerung wurde in auffallend kurzer Zeit assimiliert. Dies gilt
vor allem für Transdanubien und die Gegenden östlich der Theiß, während die im
Norden des Landes lebenden Slawen, die Ahnen der heutigen Slowaken, ihr selbständiges Volkstum weiterhin behielten. Die landnehmenden Ungarn werden von
G. Györffy auf 400 000 Seelen, die hier lebenden Völker auf 200 000 Seelen geschätzt, insgesamt eine viel zu kleine Zahl, um das Karpatenbecken auch nur einiger-
maßen auszufüllen [5]. Das Ungarntum verschloß sich gegenüber seinen westlichen
Nachbarn und verharrte in jenem osteuropäischen Wirtschaftskreis, zu dem es vor
der Landnahme gehörte und dessen Mittelpunkte Kiev und Byzanz waren. Die Los-
lösung von diesem Wirtschaftsraum erfolgte schrittweise; es dauerte beinahe drei-
hundert Jahre, bis der Prozeß abgeschlossen war [6]. Es nimmt also nicht Wunder,

2) So z. B. das Chronicon Eberspergense: *Eodem tempore Hunni, qui et Hungari ... vastant,*
MGH SS XXV, S. 868. — Widukind von Korvei: *Avares, quos modo Ungarios vocamus* und
Avares autem, ut quidam putant, reliquiae erant Hunnorum, hg. H.-E. LOHMANN u. P.
HIRSCH, SS rer. Germ. in us. schol., 1935, S. 28.
3) E. FÜGEDI, Pour une analyse démographique de la Hongrie médiévale. In: Annales.
Economies, Sociétés, Civilisations (Paris). 24, 1969, S. 1299–1312.
4) P. VÁCZY, A város az ókor és a középkor fordulóján [Die Stadt an der Wende des
Mittelalters]. In: Győr. Várostörténeti tanulmányok [Raab. Stadtgeschichtliche Studien],
Győr 1971, S. 55–59.
5) G. GYÖRFFY; Einwohnerzahl und Bevölkerungsdichte in Ungarn bis zum Anfang des
XIV. Jh. (Études historiques), Budapest 1960, Bd. I, S. 171.
6) Diese Tatsache kann am besten an Hand zweier Erscheinungen bewiesen werden. Einerseits sind die Handelsbeziehungen fast ausschließlich byzantinische oder osteuropäische.
Ungarische Kaufleute werden in Prag, Byzanz und Pereslavec erwähnt; die Münzfunde
zeigen die Verbreitung der auf dem Handelsweg ins Land gekommenen Dirhems und byzan-
tischen Münzen gegenüber den im Kriege erbeuteten westeuropäischen. Das früheste ungarische Münzsystem beruht auf byzantinischem Muster *(pensa auri).* Werke ungarischer
Silberschmieden sind in den archäologischen Funden Südrußlands anzutreffen. Andererseits
kann dieselbe Isolation aus den Vorschriften über die Bewachung der Grenze ermittelt
werden. Vgl. E. FÜGEDI, Die Entstehung des Städtewesens in Ungarn. In: Alba Regia 10,
1969, S. 103–106, wo auch die entsprechenden Literaturhinweise zu finden sind.

daß im 9. Jahrhundert vor allem östliche Einwanderer aufgenommen wurden, Donaubulgaren, verschiedene Mohammedaner und Petschenegen. Um die Jahrtausendwende erreichte die Bevölkerungszahl Ungarns eine Million [7]. Das Land war noch immer äußerst spärlich besiedelt.

955 verlor das ungarische Heer bei Augsburg eine entscheidende Schlacht, und damit war es auch mit der starren Isolationspolitik zu Ende. Es stellte sich die Alternative: untergehen wie die Vorgänger (Hunnen, Avaren) oder sich Europa anpassen. Das Anpassen bedeutete vor allem den Übertritt zum Christentum (das übrigens damals bei den Ungarn schon weithin nicht unbekannt war [8]), und so ergab sich noch eine andere Alternative: ob man sich an die lateinische oder an die griechische Kirche anschließen sollte. Die Wahl scheint umso schwerer gewesen zu sein, als im Lande damals schon Missionäre der byzantinischen Kirche tätig waren [9]. Tatsächlich blieben Reste der östlichen kirchlichen Institutionen noch zwei Jahrhunderte lang erhalten [10], doch steht es außer Zweifel, daß sich der ungarische Fürst für Rom entschied; das Ungarntum sollte nach lateinischem Ritus getauft werden. Dazu waren Missionäre und Krieger nötig, die einerseits die Bekehrung durchführten, anderseits den Fürst gegen renitente, an dem Heidentum festhaltende Stammeshäuptlinge unterstützten. Männer verschiedener Nationalität strömten in das Land, unter ihnen erschienen in der Gefolgschaft der Königin Gisela die ersten Deutschen [11].

---

7) GYÖRFFY (wie Anm. 5) S. 174.

8) GY. MORAVCSIK, A honfoglalás elötti magyarság és a kereszténység [Das Ungarntum und das Christentum vor der Landnahme]. In: Szent István emlékkönyv [St. Stephan-Gedenkgabe], hg. J. SERÉDI, Budapest 1938, Bd. I S. 173–212; P. VÁCZY, Magyarország kereszténysége a honfoglalás korában [Das Christentum in Ungarn zur Zeit der Landnahme]. Ebd. Bd. I S. 215–265; J. L. CSÓKA, A magyarok és a kereszténység Géza fejedelem korában [Die Ungarn und das Christentum zur Regierungszeit des Fürsten Gejza]. Ebd. Bd. I, S. 269–291.

9) GY. MORAVCSIK, Görögnyelvü kolostorok [Die griechischen Klöster zur Zeit Stephans des Hlg.]. In: Szent István emlékkönyv (wie Anm. 8) Bd. I, S. 402–422; G. FEJÉR, A bolgár egyház kisérletei és sikerei hazánkban [Die Unternehmungen und Erfolge der bulgarischen Kirche in Ungarn]. In: Századok 71/72, 1927/28, S. 1–20.

10) MORAVCSIK (wie Anm. 8); DERS. (wie Anm. 9), S. 390–422.

11) Die ersten Deutschen in der Gefolgschaft der Königin Gisela dürften natürlich Ritter und Kleriker gewesen sein. Nur in einer einzigen Stadt, nämlich in Szatmár, blieb eine Tradition lebendig, daß die Einwohner *se ... in fide domine regine Keysle ad Hungariam convenisse*, G. FEJÉR, Codex diplomaticus Hungariae ecclesiasticus et civilis, Budae 1829–44, tom. III/2, S. 211. Diese Tradition wurde aber von deutscher und ungarischer Seite gleichermaßen abgewiesen. Vgl. K. SCHÜNEMANN, Die Deutschen in Ungarn bis zum XII. Jh., 1923, S. 41 sowie F. MAKSAY, A középkori Szatmár megye [Das Komitat Szatmár im Mittelalter], Budapest 1940, S. 67–70.

Doch war mit Taufe und Königtum die Isolation gegenüber dem Westen noch immer nicht ganz vorbei. Von nun an gab es im Osten Europas ein christliches Königtum, das sich zu Rom bekannte, wo man mit dem König und dem Hofe verhandeln konnte, das Land blieb jedoch praktisch weiterhin versperrt. Die Isolation war aber nicht mehr so starr, es gelang fremden Klerikern, Kriegern, Pilgern und Kaufleuten, nach Ungarn zu kommen [12]. Die ersten Nachrichten [13] über das Land sickerten durch, doch gingen sie noch in einem sehr begrenzten Kreis um. Es verflossen wiederum hundert Jahre, bis eine grundlegende Wandlung eintrat. Nachdem der zweite Kreuzzug Ungarn durchquert hatte, wurden die ersten Einwanderer ins Land gerufen. Zwischen Einwanderern anderer Nationalitäten erschienen die Vorfahren der Siebenbürger und Zipser Sachsen.

Die Einwanderung war — angesichts der Bevölkerungszahl des Landes und an den Verhältnissen des 12. Jahrhunderts gemessen — massenhaft und bedeutete somit den Anfang eines wirtschaftlichen Vorganges, den wir als Landesausbau bezeichnen dürfen. Es wurden Urwälder gerodet, neue Siedlungen ins Leben gerufen, neue Wege ausgebaut. Der Prozeß wurde 1241 durch den Tatareneinfall unterbrochen, doch eben die Verwüstungen der Tataren schufen neue Gelegenheit für die Einwanderer und beschleunigten den Prozeß. Es entstanden Siedlungen, die im westeuropäischen Sinne des Wortes Städte genannt werden können, nach langen inneren Kämpfen stabilisierte sich die Sozialstruktur. Ungarn war jetzt ein Königreich Europas mit zwei Millionen Einwohnern, die hinsichtlich ihrer Nationalität ein buntes Bild zeigten. Eigentlich war nur die Aristokratie rein ungarisch. In den Reihen des niederen Adels findet man schon Angehörige anderer Nationalitäten; die Bürger waren *Latini* oder Deutsche mit Ungarn und Slawen vermischt; die Hörigen gehörten zu den verschiedensten Nationalitäten; die ehemaligen nomadischen Hilfsvölker genossen eine besondere Rechtsstellung (Sekler und Kumanen).

---

12) Über die Pilger s. F. GALLA, Szent István apostoli tevékenysége és e téren ismertebb munkatársai [Das Apostolat des Hlg. Stephan und seine bekannteren Mitarbeiter auf diesem Feld] Szent István emlékkönyv (wie Anm. 8), Bd. I S. 297; S. ÉCKHARDT, András király francia zarándokai [Die französischen Pilger unter Andreas I.]. In: Magyar Nyelv 1935, S. 38—40; MGH SS XII, S. 230. — Über die Kaufleute vgl. FÜGEDI, Entstehung (wie Anm. 6) S. 105 und die dort angegebene Literatur.
13) Sicherlich stammten die Informationen, auf Grund deren Idrisi sein geographisches Werk verfaßte und fünf ungarische Städte beschrieb, von Fernhandelskaufleuten. Vgl. T. LEWICKI, Polska i kraje sąsiednie w świetle »Księgi Rogera« geographa arabskiego z XII. w. Al Idrisiego [Polen und seine Nachbarländer im »Buch des Rogers« von dem arabischen Geographen Al Idrisi aus dem 12. Jh.] (= Prace Komisji Orientalistycznej 34), Kraków 1945.

2.

Bevor wir auf dieses sehr flüchtig skizzierte Bild weitere Einzelzüge auftragen, lohnt es sich, die Anfänge des Näheren zu untersuchen.

Nach den Schätzungen belief sich die Bevölkerungszahl um das Jahr 1000 auf eine Million [14] und dürfte auch zur Zeit des zweiten Kreuzzuges nicht viel höher gewesen sein, da nach den zur Verfügung stehenden Angaben höchstens mit einem jährlichen natürlichen Zuwachs von 4 Promille gerechnet werden darf [15]. Diese Behauptung stimmt mit den Ergebnissen der ungarischen Siedlungsgeschichte überein, die besagen, daß im Lande noch riesige Wälder fast menschenleer geblieben sind und daß außer Transdanubien und der Tiefebene nur die Flußtäler besiedelt waren. Diese Feststellung betrifft hauptsächlich die nördlichen und östlichen Gebiete; im Hinblick auf die Bevölkerungsdichte lag der Schwerpunkt des Landes in Transdanubien [16]. Wir vermeiden absichtlich die heute übliche Ziffer der Bevölkerungsdichte pro Quadratkilometer, da wir die Lage aus dem Gesichtspunkt der damaligen Menschen beurteilen wollen. Lesen wir die Beschreibung Ottos von Freising oder anderer Zeitgenossen, die entweder selbst mit den Kreuzfahrern durch Ungarn gezogen sind oder ihre Informationen aus erster Hand erhielten, so ist vor allem die Betonung der Fruchtbarkeit des Landes auffallend [17]. Otto von Freising sieht sogar das Zeichen der göttlichen Geduld in der Tatsache, daß ein so garstiges Volk ein so schönes und fruchtbares Land bewohnen darf, das dem Ägypten des Alten Testaments oder dem Paradies gleicht [18]. Ungefähr zur selben Zeit weilte ein spanischer

14) GYÖRFFY (wie Anm. 5), S. 174.
15) FÜGEDI (wie Anm. 3).
16) Die wirtschaftliche (und kulturelle) Überlegenheit Transdanubiens kann mit Hilfe von drei Beobachtungen gezeigt werden. – a) Von den zehn Diözesen, die durch Stephan I. gegründet wurden, befinden sich vier (Gran, Raab, Veszprém und Fünfkirchen) in Transdanubien. Die später erfolgten zwei weiteren Bistumsgründungen verursachten Verschiebungen, doch blieb ein Drittel der Bischofsitze noch immer hier. – b) Ungefähr die Hälfte der frühen Städte befand sich ebenfalls in Transdanubien, vgl. FÜGEDI, Entstehung (wie Anm. 6) S. 109. – c) Auch der größte Teil – und zugleich die größten – der Klöster befand sich in Transdanubien (E. FÜGEDI, La formation des villes et les ordres mendiants en Hongrie. In: Annales. Economies, Sociétés, Civilisations (Paris) 25, 1970, S. 968.) – Transdanubien behielt stets eine seine geographische Größe übersteigende Bedeutung, obwohl die Bergstädte alle außerhalb lagen.
17) So Ansbert in seiner Historia de expeditione Friderici imperatoris, Fontes Rerum Austriacarum SS V, 1863, S. 18, sowie Guibertus abbas in seiner Historia Hierosolymitana, MIGNE, Patr. lat. Bd. CLVI, 1880, S. 705.
18) Gesta Frederici I, 33, hg. FR.-J. SCHMALE (= Ausgewählte Quellen zur Geschichte des Mittelalters Bd. 17, 1965), S. 192: *Hec enim provincia ... tam innata amenitate faciei leta quam agrorum fertilitate locuples esse cognoscitur, ut tamquam paradisus Dei vel Egyptus spectabilis esse videatur ... potius divina patientia sit ammiranda, que, ne dicam hominibus, sed talibus hominum monstris tam delectabilem exposuit terram.*

Mohammedaner namens Abu Hamid al Andalusi in Ungarn, der nicht nur die Fruchtbarkeit des Landes rühmte, sondern auch einen sehr wichtigen Hinweis gab, indem er das Silber- und Goldvorkommen in Ungarn erwähnt [19]. Autoren des 12. Jahrhunderts sprechen nicht von der dünnen Besiedlung des Landes, darüber konnten sie sich bei einem Durchzug keine Vorstellungen machen; doch war sie für einen westlichen Beobachter noch am Anfang des 14. Jahrhunderts auffallend, wie es die Schilderung Ungarns in der Beschreibung von Osteuropa eines unbekannten französischen Dominikaners belegt [20]. Es kann keinerlei Zweifel bestehen, daß die Kreuzfahrer die Fruchtbarkeit Ungarns wahrgenommen und diese Beobachtung in ganz Europa verbreitet haben. Dadurch war der eine Partner des künftigen Siedlungsprozesses gewonnen.

Auf der Kehrseite der Medaille steht der ungarische König, für den die dünne Besiedlung des Landes keine besondere Sorge bedeutete, solange sein Heer aus leichter Reiterei bestand und sich der Taktik der Reiternomaden bediente. Diese Heeresorganisation konnte sich nicht lange halten. 1099 wurde der ungarische König bei Kiev von den Kumanen mit einem ganz einfachen Trick der Reiternomaden (den übrigens die Ungarn selbst noch anderthalb Jahrhunderte früher erfolgreich praktiziert hatten) geschlagen [21], und das hatte eine Wandlung im ungarischen Heerwesen zur Folge, das sich auf schwer gepanzerte Ritter umstellte.

Abgesehen von der Notwendigkeit, das Land dichter zu besiedeln, war der ungarische Herrscher auch in einer anderen Hinsicht auf die Aufnahme fremder Siedler vorbereitet. Wie wir oben schon erwähnten, empfing das Land im 10. Jahrhundert aus der östlichen Nachbarschaft Fremde und gewährte ihnen das Recht, sich geschlossen anzusiedeln. Ob dieser Zug wirklich auf die nomadische politische Struktur zurückzuführen ist — wie es einige Forscher behaupteten [22] — oder nicht, bleibe

---

19) Acta Orientalia Acad. Sc. Hung. 5, 1955, S. 20.

20) Höchstens dürfte man die Bemerkung des Odo de Deuil *terra haec tantum pabulosa est*, MGH SS XXVI, S. 62, als Wahrnehmen einer dünnen Bevölkerungsdichte hinnehmen. Dagegen gibt die Descriptio Europae Orientalis (Anonymi Descriptio Europae orientalis. Imperium Constantinopolitanum, Albania, Serbia, Bulgaria, Ruthenia, Ungaria, Polonia, Bohemia. Anno MCCCVIII exarata. Ed. O. Górka, Cracoviae 1916, S. 49. Vgl. J. DEÉR, Ungarn in der Descriptio Europae Orientalis. In: MIÖG 45, 1931, S. 1—22) einen direkten Hinweis: *sunt tamen multa oppida, castra seu fortalitia et ville innumerabiles in dicto regno et cum hoc toto videtur prefatum regnum esse vacuum propter magnitudinem eiusdem.*

21) A. HODINKA, Kálmán királyunk 1099-i peremysli csatája az orosz őskrónika nyomán [Die Schlacht des Königs Koloman bei Peremysl im Jahr 1099 auf Grund der russischen Urchronik]. In: Hadtörténeti Közlemények 14, 1913, S. 325—346, 524—544.

22) J. DEÉR; Pogány magyarság, keresztény magyarság [Heidnische Ungarn, christliche Ungarn], Budapest 1938, S. 267. Vgl. die Zusammenfassung der einschlägigen Literatur bei K. GUOTH, A nem-magyar népelemek helyzete a középkorban [Die Lage der nicht-ungarischen Völker im Mittelalter]. In: Hitel 8, 1943, S. 723—735.

hier dahingestellt. Ohne auf diese Frage weiter einzugehen, möchten wir aus den geschichtlichen Prämissen nur zwei Tatsachen von besonderer Bedeutung hervorheben: 1.) daß nicht alle im Lande vorgefundenen Völkerschaften assimiliert werden konnten, das Land also niemals sprachlich einheitlich war; 2.) daß Fremde schon vor der westeuropäischen Einwanderung aufgenommen wurden, und zwar in einer Weise, aus der klar hervorgeht, daß man sie weder magyarisieren noch — was noch auffallender ist — christianisieren wollte. Die einheimischen Mohammedaner, mit denen Abu Hamid 1150–1152 verkehrte, waren seit anderthalb Jahrhunderten hier und waren Muselmanen geblieben, während die Ungarn gezwungen wurden, ihr Heidentum aufzugeben und sich zum Christentum zu bekehren. Es kann nicht genug unterstrichen werden, daß das frühe Königreich Ungarn in seine politische Struktur Völker aufnahm, deren Nationalität und sogar Religion abweichend war. Es kann keine Spur einer nationalen oder — vor dem Anfang des 13. Jahrhunderts — einer religiösen Intoleranz entdeckt werden. Im Hinblick auf die deutsche Ostsiedlung darf diese Tatsache nicht aus den Augen gelassen werden. Zusammenfassend kann festgestellt werden, daß zwei Faktoren zur Geltung kamen, nämlich die Kreuzfahrer, die Ungarn kennen gelernt haben, und das Umstellen des ungarischen Heerwesens. Diese zwei Faktoren verbanden sich im 12. Jahrhundert und schufen eine Lage, in der selbst eine gemäßigte Isolation des Landes nicht weiter aufrechterhalten werden konnte, weil:

a.) eine zu große demographische Spannung zwischen Westeuropa und Ungarn zutage getreten war;

b.) der ungarische König gezwungen war, sein Einkommen zu erhöhen, d. h. seine Güter besser auszunützen — und das ging nicht anders, als durch rasche Vermehrung der Bevölkerung, also durch Herbeirufung fremder Siedler. Dies fiel dem ungarischen König umso leichter, als er seit jeher daran gewöhnt war, über Völker verschiedener Sprache zu gebieten.

Es entstand also eine Lage, in der auf der einen Seite der ungarische König gezwungen und bereit war, die Initiative zu ergreifen und Siedler in sein Land zu rufen, auf der anderen Seite die Völker Europas auf diesen Ruf prompt und positiv antworteten. Es wäre wirklich ganz natürlich gewesen, daß dieser Ruf ausschließlich oder fast ausschließlich von den Nachbarn, also von den Deutschen, besser gesagt von den Süddeutschen beantwortet würde. Es gehört aber zur Charakteristik dieser Lage, daß die Gelegenheit von allen Völkern ergriffen wurde, in deren Reihen sich unternehmungslustige Männer fanden, und daß Ungarn alle fremden Siedler ohne Unterschied der Nationalität freundlich aufnahm.

Ein Blick auf die westlichen Einwanderer genügt, um sich davon zu überzeugen, daß es nicht allein Deutsche waren, die nach Ungarn kamen. Halten wir uns an die Hierarchie des Mittelalters und richten wir unseren Blick zuerst auf die Kirche. Die

Benediktiner waren anfangs wahrscheinlich hauptsächlich Böhmen und Deutsche [23]), doch schon am Ende des 11. Jahrhunderts erschienen in Transdanubien Benediktiner aus St. Gilles [24]). Die Zisterzienser gründeten ihre Häuser hauptsächlich von Frankreich, teils aber von dem Römischen Reich aus [25]). Die Prämonstratenser stammten fast ausschließlich aus Frankreich [26]). Die entstandene Lage wird in einer an den ungarischen König gerichteten päpstlichen Bulle vom Jahr 1204 klassisch beschrieben: *nec novum est, nec absurdum, ut in regno tuo diversarum nationum conventus uni Domino sub regulari habito famulentur* [27]).

Die nächste Welle, die der Bettelorden, ist ebenfalls heterogen zusammengesetzt, und zwar schon auf etwas kompliziertere Weise. Die Dominikaner kamen zwar aus Italien, doch das Haupt der ersten kleinen Schar war ein Ungar, der früher in Bologna Universitätsprofessor war [28]). Die Franziskaner kamen aus Deutschland, die ungarischen Klöster gehörten anfangs zur deutschen Ordensprovinz, doch war der erste Provinzial der selbständigen ungarischen Ordensprovinz allem Anscheine nach ein Franzose, und die ersten Gründungen erfolgten meistens dort, wo die *Latini*

23) G. Györffy, Zu den Anfängen der ungarischen Kirchenorganisation auf Grund neuer quellenkritischer Ergebnisse. In: Archivum historiae pontificiae 7, 1969, S. 86–101.
24) P. Sörös, Az elenyészett bencés apátságok [Die aufgehobenen Benediktinerabteien] (= A Pannonhalmi Szent Benedek rend története (künftig: PRT) 12 [Die Geschichte des Benediktinerordens von Pannonhalma, Bd. 12]) Budapest 1912, S. 151.
25) Die ungarischen Zisterzienserabteien wurden größtenteils unmittelbar von Frankreich aus gegründet. Das Affiliationssystem zeigt das folgende Bild:
Von Clairvaux aus Zirc (1182), Pilis (1184), Sankt Gotthard (1184), Topuszko (1205). Von diesen Klöstern aus weitere fünf Häuser in Ungarn. – Von Pontigny aus Egres (1177–1179), von da aus Kerz (1202) in Siebenbürgen. – Von Troisfontaines aus Bélakut (1234). – Morimond war die Mutterabtei von Styavnik (in der Zips, 1223). – Die deutsche Linie repräsentiert Heiligenkreuz in Österreich, das Marienberg (Borsmonostora) gründete, von wo aus zwei weitere Häuser gegründet wurden (Telki 1224, Siklós 1303). – Insgesamt bestanden 17 Zisterzienserhäuser in Ungarn. Obzwar die Affiliation nicht in allen Fällen festgestellt werden kann, scheint es doch kennzeichnend, daß die unmittelbaren französischen Filien 13 neue Abteien, die eine deutsche aber nur zwei weitere Klöster ins Leben rufen konnten. Vgl. F. van de Meer, Atlas de l'Ordre cistercien, Paris-Bruxelles 1965, S. 26.
26) Auf Grund der frühesten Klosterverzeichnisse hat F. Oszvald, Adalékok a magyarországi premontreiek Árpád-kori történetéhez [Beiträge zur Geschichte der Prämonstratenser in der Zeit der Arpaden]. In: Müvészettörténeti Értesítő 6, 1957, S. 231–254, das Affiliationssystem festgestellt. Prémontré gründete 3 Häuser in Ungarn; von diesen aus wurden 30 weitere Gründungen vorgenommen. Die einzige Ausnahme war Bozók, das von Gradec (Mähren) aus gegründet war und keine Filien hatte. Leider ließ sich mit Hilfe dieser Verzeichnisse die Herkunft der uns am meisten interessierenden Frauenklöster, von denen sich zwei in Siebenbürgen befanden (Kronstadt und Hermannstadt), nicht ermitteln.
27) J. Bárdosy, Supplementum Analectorum terrae Scepusiensis, Leutschoviae 1802, S. 196. Anm. b.
28) N. Pfeiffer, Die ungarische Dominikanerprovinz von ihrer Gründung 1221 bis zur Tatarenwüstung 1241–1242, Zürich 1913.

VIII

lebten [29]). Das allgemein europäische Wesen der westlichen Ansiedlung kommt selbst bei den Ritterorden zur Geltung: neben den Johannitern erscheint am Anfang des 13. Jahrhunderts der Deutschritterorden.

In die Städte ziehen *Latini* und Deutsche. Daß die *Latini* hauptsächlich Wallonen und Franzosen waren, war der ungarischen Geschichtswissenschaft schon längst bekannt [30]). Seit dem Aufsatz Ammanns ist es aber klar [31]), daß sie Ungarn im Laufe einer zielbewußten Ostwanderung erreichten. Das französische Sprachgebiet gab eben im 12.–13. Jahrhundert seine Auswanderer nach dem Osten ab, bis dann die spanische Reconquista sie nach dem Süden Europas abzog.

Zusammenfassend dürfen wir feststellen, daß es zwei Partner gab: Ungarn und Westeuropa. Europa dehnte sich aus, zog das Karpatenbecken an sich. Nichts ist natürlicher, als daß die Deutschen, die in der Nachbarschaft Ungarns unter ähnlichen Klimaverhältnissen lebten, an diesem Vorgang lebhaft teilgenommen haben und alles mitbrachten, was sie bisher geschaffen und gelernt hatten.

Diese Feststellung hat ihre Folgen für die Erforschung der deutschen Ostsiedlung. Die deutsche Auswanderung war — wenigstens in Ungarn — ein Teil eines gesamteuropäischen demographischen und wirtschaftlichen Vorgangs, in dessen Verlauf westeuropäische Bevölkerung nach dem Osten des Kontinents zog, um dort neue Dörfer und Städte ins Leben zu rufen. Dadurch wurde die Europäisierung Ungarns beschleunigt. Deswegen scheint es angemessen zu behaupten, daß im Laufe des 12. und 13. Jahrhunderts Ungarn europäisiert wurde und daß zu dieser Leistung die Deutschen samt anderen Völker Europas viel beigetragen haben. Wir möchten diese Worte »viel beigetragen« mit drei Zielsetzungen untersuchen, und zwar in politischer, sozialer und wirtschaftlicher Hinsicht.

Zuvor muß hier noch kurz eine andere Frage aufgegriffen werden. Auf der ersten Tagung versuchte man, bei der Beurteilung der deutschen Ostsiedlung die Auswanderung öfters durch einen Zwang (relative Übervölkerung, Naturkatastrophe) zu begründen [32]). Ob Westeuropa übervölkert war oder nicht, sei dahingestellt; sicher ist es aber, daß die Bevölkerungsdichte zwischen Westeuropa und Ungarn sehr unterschiedlich gewesen sein muß. Ein solcher Unterschied läßt sich

29) J. KARÁCSONYI, Szt. Ferencz rendjének története Magyarországon 1711–ig [Die Geschichte der Franziskaner in Ungarn bis 1711]. Budapest 1922, Bd. I, S. 13–16.
30) Schon bei GY. PAULER, A magyar nemzet története az Árpádházi királyok alatt [Geschichte der ungarischen Nation unter den Arpaden]. Budapest 1900², Bd. II, S. 487 (auf Grund des Aufsatzes von E. BORCHGRAVE, Essai historique sur les colonies belges qui s'établirent en Hongrie et en Transylvanie pendant les XIe, XIIe et XIIIe siècles. Bruxelles 1871). Vgl. M. AUNER, Latinus. In: Századok 50, 1916, S. 28–41.
31) H. AMMANN, Die französische Südostwanderung im Rahmen der mittelalterlichen französischen Wanderungen. In: Südostforschungen 14, 1955, S. 406–428.
32) Konstanzer Arbeitskreis für mittelalterliche Geschichte e. V. Protokoll über die Arbeitstagung vom 17.–20. März 1970 auf der Insel Reichenau. Nr. 160, S. 124 f.

nicht auf die Dauer aufrechterhalten. Es scheint also nichts natürlicher, als daß die Spannung bei der ersten Gelegenheit, wenn auch nicht ausgeglichen, so doch wenigstens gemildert wurde. Andererseits scheint mir die Annahme eines Zwangs den Rest der alten Auffassung des Nationalstaates aus dem 19. Jahrhundert darzustellen. Die Mobilität — darum geht es ja — muß nicht durch Zwang ausgelöst werden. Bessere Verhältnisse (manchmal sogar nur die Hoffnung auf bessere Verhältnisse) und Unternehmungslust lassen Menschen weite Wege wandern.

3.

Der Vorgang und die Ergebnisse der deutschen Ostsiedlung sollen unserem Programm entsprechend zuerst in politischer Hinsicht untersucht werden. Vielleicht dürfen wir schon hier darauf hinweisen, daß die Erforschung dieser Fragen gewisse Schwierigkeiten bietet, weil es nicht immer einfach ist, die Deutschen — oder die deutsche Leistung — aus dem Gesamtvorgang einwandfrei herauszuheben. Deswegen haben wir unser Augenmerk vor allem auf die zwei geschlossenen deutschen Siedlungsgebiete, auf die Gebiete der Siebenbürger und Zipser Sachsen, und auf jene Städte gerichtet, die zweifellos deutsch waren. Es kann auch nicht unser Ziel sein, hier die frühe ungarische Verfassung und deren Wandlungen eingehend zu schildern. Wir möchten aber einige Züge hervorheben, hauptsächlich diejenigen, welche von den europäischen Verhältnissen abweichen und zugleich die Lage der Einwanderer beeinflußten.

Ungarn war zwar ein Königreich, das mehrere Einrichtungen vom karolingischen politischen System übernahm, all das aber — so verwunderlich das auch dem westeuropäischen Historiker erscheinen mag —, ohne das Lehenswesen einzuführen. Der König ist kein primus inter pares, sondern verfügt über eine Macht, die an den zeitgenössischen westlichen Königtümern gemessen fast unbeschränkt zu sein scheint. Für einen Otto von Freising ist die Fülle dieser Macht unverständlich, es geht ihm nicht in den Kopf, daß der König die Mächtigen des Landes durch seinen kleinsten Diener verhaften lassen kann und seine Urteile über sie ohne standesgleiche Schöffen fällt [33]. Otto findet es merkwürdig, daß der ungarische König über ausschließliche Rechte verfügt, daß er allein das Münzrecht besitzt [34]. Fügen wir hinzu, daß die königliche Macht sich praktisch durch verschiedene Einrichtungen durchsetzte, vor allem durch die königliche Komitatsverfassung und durch die alle Untertanen um-

---

33) Gesta Frederici I, 33 (wie Anm. 18) S. 194: ... *quilibet infime conditionis lixa a curia missus eum* (sc. comitem), *licet satellitibus suis stipatum, solus comprehendit, in vinculis ponit ... Nulla sententia a principe ... per pares suos exposcitur, nulla accusato excusandi licentia datur, sed sola principis voluntas aput omnes pro ratione habetur.*
34) Gesta Frederici I, 33 (wie Anm. 18) S. 194: ... *nullusque in tam spatioso ambitu, rege excepto, monetam vel theloneum habere audeat.*

fassende Zuständigkeit der Königsrichter. Die Mächtigen des Landes waren nicht lehensrechtlich, sondern gefolgschaftsrechtlich an den Herrscher gebunden, sie hüteten noch in einer christianisierten Form die Sippenverfassung der Reiternomaden. Sie verfügten zwar über ausgedehnte Güter, doch waren die königlichen Güter noch weitaus die größten. Wir wollen nicht behaupten, daß die königliche Macht immer so stark war; Otto von Freising lernte sie zweifellos auf einem ihrer Höhepunkte kennen. Doch steht es außer Zweifel, daß sie bis zum Anfang des 13. Jahrhunderts immer größer war als im Westen, und diese Tatsache übte ihren Einfluß auch auf die erste Periode der deutschen Ostsiedlung aus.

Die erste deutsche Ansiedlung erfolgte allem Anscheine nach ausschließlich auf den königlichen Gütern, u. zw. in zwei Formen: a.) in großen, mehr oder weniger geschlossenen geographischen Einheiten (Siebenbürger und Zipser Sachsen, die Gespanschaft von Vizsoly); b.) in verstreuten Siedlungen [35]. In beiden Fällen erhielten die Einwanderer Freiheiten. Sie wurden von der Zuständigkeit des Königsrichters in der niederen Gerichtsbarkeit und von der des königlichen Gespans in administrativen Fragen befreit. Dazu gesellte sich noch die freie Pfarrerwahl, die an die Stelle der Präsentation des Patronatsherren (d. h. des Königs) getreten war. Die Siebenbürger und Zipser Sachsen wurden mit freien Märkten und Zollfreiheit und mit einer Organisation ausgestattet, die dann bis zum Ende des Mittelalters aufrecht erhalten blieb [36]. Sie wurden in Siebenbürgen *Saxones* genannt, was die Zugehörigkeit zu einer nach Nationalität und Recht geschlossenen Sozialformation bedeutet, die nach dem Rechtswesen der Hermannstädter Provinz lebt [37]. Die Freiheiten der verstreuten Siedlungen waren weniger umfangreich. Zwar erhielten sie ebenfalls die niedere Gerichtsbarkeit, standen aber in bezug auf das Blutgericht weiterhin unter dem Königsrichter; auch sie durften ihre Pfarrer selbst wählen [38].

---

35) E. Mályusz, A középkori nemzetiségi politika [Die Nationalitätenpolitik im Mittelalter]. In: Századok 73, 1939, S. 264–271. Diese verstreuten Siedlungen führen den Ortsnamen Németi (= Deutsch). Mályusz stellte 35 solche Dorfnamen zusammen (ebd. S. 276–280), von denen aber das im Komitat Abauj liegende abgezogen werden muß, da es zur Vizsolyer Gespanschaft gehörte.

36) Fr. Zimmermann – K. Werner, Urkundenbuch zur Geschichte der Deutschen in Siebenbürgen. Bd. I, Hermannstadt 1892 (künftig: Zimmermann–Werner), S. 34; S. L. Endlicher, Rerum Hungaricarum monumenta Arpadiana, Sangalli 1849 (künftig: Endlicher), S. 522.

37) L. Makkai, Társadalom és nemzetiség a középkori Kolozsváron [Sozialstatus und Nationalität im mittelalterlichen Klausenburg], Kolozsvár 1943, S. 13.

38) Das Kirchensystem der deutschen Einwanderer stellt zwei Fragen: die freie Pfarrerwahl und das Zehntenwesen.
Über die freie Pfarrerwahl behauptete die ältere Forschung besonders in bezug auf die Siebenbürger Sachsen »mit überraschender Einmütigkeit und Selbstverständlichkeit«, daß sie den Kolonisten »von vornherein eigen war, weil die deutschen Einwanderer die kirchenrechtlichen Verhältnisse aus ihrer alten Heimat in die neue übertragen hätten«, D. Kurze, Zur historischen Einordnung der kirchlichen Bestimmungen des Andreanums. In: Zur

Rechts- und Siedlungsgeschichte der Siebenbürger Sachsen (= Siebenbürgisches Archiv 8) 1971, S. 139. KURZE bewies dagegen, daß die Pfarrerwahl »nicht in gemeinschaftlich-eigenkirchlichen, auf Fundation beruhenden Ansprüchen der Siedler und Gäste, sondern in der Freiheit und Selbstbestimmung garantierenden Privilegierung durch den König« zu suchen ist, ebd. S. 157.

Überblickt man die ungarischen städtischen Freiheitsbriefe des 13. Jhs., so kommt man zum Ergebnis, daß die Pfarrerwahl nur dann nicht gewährt wurde, wenn a.) es sich um Bestätigungen von früher erlassenen Privilegien handelt (Désvár 1261, Göllnitz 1276, Ödenburg 1277, Torda 1291, Eperjes 1299; vgl. E. FÜGEDI, Középkori magyar varosprivilégiumok [Ungarische Stadtprivilegien im Mittelalter]. In: Tanulmányok Budapest multjából 14, 1961, S. 72–81), oder b) wenn diesem Sonderrecht die vorangehende kirchenrechtliche Entwicklung im Wege stand. So war in Stuhlweißenburg seit dem Anfang des 12. Jhs. das Nikolai-Stift (unter königlichem Patronat) mit der Seelsorge beauftragt, so daß die *Latini* das Recht der Pfarrerwahl nicht erhielten (E. FÜGEDI, Der Stadtplan von Stuhlweißenburg und die Anfänge des Bürgertums in Ungarn. In: Acta Historica Academiae Scientiarum Hungaricae 15, 1969, S. 120–121, 125). Raab und Neutra waren Bischofsitze, in Preßburg und Eisenburg saßen königliche Pröpste. In keinem Fall war die freie Pfarrerwahl den Bürgern gewährt. Nebenbei sei bemerkt, daß im Laufe des 13. Jhs. auch Privatgrundherren auf ihr Patronatsrecht zu Gunsten der Einwanderer verzichteten, wie dies aus den Freiheitsbriefen von Güssing (FEJÉR, Cod, dipl. Hungariae (wie Anm. 11) Bd. VIII/3, S. 279) und Rimaszombat (G. WENZEL, Árpádkori új okmánytár (Codex diplomaticus Arpadianus continuatus), Pest 1860 – Budapest 1874 (künftig: ÁUO), Bd. VIII, 1870, S. 212) hervorgeht. Der Grund der Gewährung der freien Pfarrerwahl kommt eben in der letztgenannten Urkunde zum Ausdruck, in der es heißt: *Item sacerdotem quem voluerint iuxta suum ydioma honestum ac omni exceptione maiorem invenerint, ius habeant ad suam ecclesiam prestandi.* Der König übertrug seinerseits sein Patronatsrecht *quantum ad nos contingit* (Hazai okmánytar (Codex diplomaticus patrius), hg. I. NAGY, I. PAUR u. a., 8 Bde., Györ 1865–73 u. Budapest 1876–91 (künftig: HO), Bd. VI, 1881, S. 157). Anscheinend haben nicht nur die Siebenbürger Sachsen, (denen das Andreanum die freie Pfarrerwahl gewährte,) sondern auch die Zipser Pfarreien das Vorrecht der libera electio genossen (1273: *preposito de Scepes nomine ipsorum Saxonum presentent,* ENDLICHER (wie Anm. 36) S. 535). Die Lage in den verstreut liegenden deutschen Siedlungen ist leider noch nicht geklärt worden.

Das Zehntenwesen wurde durch zwei Verordnungen geregelt: a) die Zehnten der Landbevölkerung gebührten in Ungarn im allgemeinen dem Bischof, nur ein Viertel derselben fiel den Pfarrern zu. In den deutschen Dörfern besaßen aber die Pfarrer die Zehnteinkünfte und mußten davon nur einen gewissen Anteil (unmittelbar, oder mittelbar als *census synodalis* oder *cathedraticum*) dem Bischof bzw. Archidiakon abliefern. b) Außerdem scheint es ein Sonderrecht gewesen zu sein, daß die Einwanderer ihre Zehnten in besonderer Weise leisten durften. Schon im Freiheitsbrief von Tirnau (1238) ist zu lesen *decimas more Teutonicorum in capeciis persolvent,* A. HUSČAVA, Najstaršie výsady mesta Trnavy [Der älteste Freiheitsbrief der Stadt Tirnau], Bratislava 1939, S. 41. Der Ausdruck kehrt im Privileg von Preßburg (1291) wieder: *Item decimas frugum persolvant more Teutonico prout hospites aliarum civitatum,* ENDLICHER (wie Anm. 36), S. 623. In jenem von Käsmark (1269) wird ein anderer Ausdruck benützt: *Item decimas in campis solvent more Saxonum aliorum* (HO, Bd. VI, S. 157). Es ist nicht klar, ob es sich um dieselbe Weise der Zehntenleistung handelt und ob diese Weise mit den *decimae liberae* (E. FÜGEDI, Kirchliche Topographie und Siedlungsverhältnisse im Mittelalter in der Slowakei. In: Studia Slavica 5, 1959, S. 397–399) identisch ist.

Diese Ansiedler werden *hospites* genannt. Der Ausdruck bedeutet aber etwas ganz anderes als in den deutschen Ländern, vor allem keine Nationalität, sondern einen Rechts- und Sozialstatus [39]. Zwischen den verstreuten deutschen Siedlungen und

39) Dieser lateinische Fachausdruck des frühen ungarischen Verfassungsrechtes ist wirklich geeignet, den Leser irrezuführen. Das Wort bedeutet »Gast« und wurde anfangs in diesem Sinne verwendet, d. h. kennzeichnete jeden Einwanderer ungeachtet seiner Nationalität und seiner sozialen Stellung. In den Gesetzen des 11. Jhs. nennt man die eingewanderten Kleriker und Ritter *hospites*. (Freundlicher Hinweis, für den ich Herrn J. Szücs dankbar bin.) 1156 spricht König Gejza II. von *hospitibus meis, videlicet Gotfrith et Albreth militibus strenuis, qui ad vocacionem meam relicta patria sua et hereditate regnum Hungarie sunt honorifice ingressi;* Urkundenbuch des Burgenlandes, bearb. v. H. WAGNER (künftig: UB Burgenland) Bd. I, 1955, S. 21; (vgl. die Bestätigung Kg. Stephans III. von 1171, ebd. S. 24 f.); Andreas II. nennt *Johann Latinus hospes fidelis noster miles*, ZIMMERMANN-WERNER (wie Anm. 36) Bd. I, S. 8; es handelt sich also in beiden Fällen um deutsche Ritter (Vgl. noch K. K. KLEIN, Latini in Siebenbürgen. In: Siebenbürgisch-sächsischer Hauskalender 1959, S. 63–65). Ebenfalls königlicher Gefolgsmann und Ritter war jener *comes* Symon, der aus Aragon stammte, und da er König Andreas II. *ad beneplacitum nostrum in cunctis servivisset*, den König bat, *ut locum descensionis in regno nostro sibi et cognatis suis, qui cum eo aderant et post ipsum venturi erant, iure hereditario possidendum conferemus eodem titulo et privilegio libertatis, quo ceteri hospitum nobilium ex gratuita donacione predecessorum nostrorum optinuerunt* (1223), UB Burgenland Bd. I, S. 91. Otto von Freising erwähnt ebenfalls die im königlichen Dienste stehenden eingewanderten Ritter: *in ipsa regis acie hospites, quorum ibi magna copia est et qui aput eos principes dicuntur, latus principis ad muniendum ambient*, Gesta Frederici I, 33 (wie Anm. 18), S. 194. In diesem Sinne erwähnt die Goldene Bulle (1222) jene Einwanderer, die »bessere Leute« waren (*Si hospites, videlicet boni homines ad regnum venerint, sine consilio regni ad dignitates non promoveantur*, Monumenta ecclesiae Strigoniensis, hg. F. KNAUZ, Bd. I, Strigonii 1874, (künftig Mon. Strig.) S. 235). Der Ausdruck trägt also von Anfang an einen »negativen« Charakter und bedeutet einen Nicht-Ungarn (d. h. einen, der nicht im Königreich geboren wurde). Als dann auch Bauern als Einwanderer auftauchten, ging das Wort auf sie über, bewahrte aber seinen »negativen« Charakter. Wollte man daher außer der Tatsache, daß die erwähnten Leute Einwanderer waren, auch ihre Nationalität angeben, so fügte man die nationale Bezeichnung hinzu, sprach also von *hospites nostri (regis) Latini* (L. ERDÉLYI, A pannonhalmi föapátság története [Die Geschichte der Hauptabtei Pannonhalma] (= PRT (wie Anm. 24) Bd. 1), Budapest 1902, S. 680), *hospites Teotonici* (Mon. Strig. I, S. 298), *hospites nostri Saxones* (ZIMMERMANN-WERNER (wie Anm. 36), Bd. I, S. 66), *hospites de provincia Novi castri, scilicet Teutonici* (Regestrum Varadiense examinum ferri candentis ordine chronologico digestum, hg. J. KARÁCSONYI u. S. BOROVSZKY, Budapest 1903, S. 116, usw. Meistens werden sie jedoch ohne Nationalitätsbezeichnung erwähnt. Den Einheimischen gegenüber waren die »Gäste« von der Zuständigkeit des königlichen Richters (wenigstens hinsichtlich der niederen Gerichtsbarkeit) und des Gespans befreit, und da man von nun an (Anfang des 13. Jh.) die eingewanderten Kleriker und Ritter meistens nicht mehr *hospites* nannte, so wandelte sich die Bedeutung des Wortes, doch behielt es weiterhin seinen »negativen« Charakter, indem es jetzt schon jene bezeichnete, die nicht unter der Macht des Königsrichters standen. Am besten ist dieser »negative« Charakter aus der schon zitierten Goldene Bulle ersichtlich, wo es heißt: *Similiter et hos-*

den großen Provinzen steht eine kleine Insel, die Gespanschaft Vizsoly genannt, die aus zehn der Königin gehörenden Dörfern bestand und ihr Deutschtum und ihre Sonderstellung bis ins 14. Jahrhundert bewahren konnte [40].

pites cuiuscunque nationis secundum libertatem ab initio eis concessam teneantur, ZIMMER-MANN-WERNER (wie Anm. 36), Bd. I, S. 19. Die Bedeutung ist ganz klar: alle Eingewanderten, welcher Nationalität sie auch immer sind, sollen in jenen Freiheiten erhalten werden, mit welchen sie zur Zeit ihrer Ansiedlung ausgestattet wurden. Die *hospites* sind also untereinander weder in bezug auf Nationalität noch auf Sonderrechte gleich, sie sind aber gleich darin, daß sie privilegierte Einwanderer oder deren Nachkommen sind. Im Gesetzartikel IX. v. J. 1231 wird in Streitfragen der *hospes* dem *domesticus* gegenübergestellt, was am besten beweist, daß hier von privilegierten Leuten die Rede ist.

Im Laufe des 13. Jhs. verlor das Wort sogar seinen Sinn »Einwanderer«. Im Laufe des Landesausbaus bei Erschließung der Wälder und Gründung neuer Dörfer nahmen an der Arbeit auch Ungarn (= Einheimische) teil. Sie erhielten dafür ebenfalls einen besonderen Status, und so mußte der *hospes* jetzt nicht mehr ein Einwanderer sein, sondern war ein Privilegierter, der diesen Rechtsstand durch Ansiedlung erworben hatte. In diesem Sinne spricht der König schon 1240 von *hospites nostri tam Hungari quam Teothonici* (ÁUO (wie Anm. 38) Bd. VII, 1869, S. 103).

Königliche Verordnungen konnten ebenfalls dazu führen, daß Einheimische sogar privilegierte Gäste geworden sind. Die Grenzwächter *(sagitarii)* in der Umgebung von Ödenburg wurden von Béla IV. in die Stadt Ödenburg umgesiedelt *in ipsorum civium numerum augmentationem* und *libertatem ipsorum civium eisdem concedendo (*UB Burgenland Bd. II, S. 95), was von König Ladislaus IV. 1283 so formuliert wird: *sagitarios ... castri nostri Svpvrniensis hospitibus de eodem ... adiunxerimus in eorundem libertate hospitum permansuros* (ebda S. 173).

Die Verschenkung der königlichen Güter und fieberhafter Landesausbau brachten es mit sich, daß nicht nur der König, sondern auch Privatpersonen ihre *hospites* hatten. 1223 erteilt der König Zollfreiheit *omnibus venientibus hospitibus de exteris regnis* (UB Burgenland Bd. I, S. 90). 1146 vermachte eine Frau ihr Gut dem Kloster Pannonhalma, wobei sie feststellte *in suscipiendis etiam aut dimittendis liberis hospitibus, qui volunt terram inhabitare et colere, dominus abbas loci habeat potestatem, qui tamen proficisci debent ad exercitum et regis expeditionem, sicut fecerunt nobis viventibus* (ÁUO (wie Anm. 38), Bd. I, 1860, S. 57). 1158 verschenkte ein privater Grundherr an eine Benediktinerabtei sein Gut Szántó (Komitat Bars) samt seinen *hospites,* doch wissen wir nicht, von wem sie dort angesiedelt wurden und welcher Nationalität sie waren (Mon. Strig. (wie Anm. 38), Bd. I, S. 116). 1217 werden (ohne Angabe der Nationalität) die *hospites* des Propstes von Eisenburg erwähnt (ÁUO Bd. VI, 1867, S. 384). Manchmal wurden sie vom König auf Privatgrundbesitz berufen, so nach Füzegtő *terram monasterii sancti Martini de sacro monte Pannonie ... hospites libere conditionis fecissemus pro nostro seu regni nostri commodo congregari de consensu et beneplacito abbatis monasterii* (ÁUO Bd. III, S. 38).

Die Nationalität von *hospites* kann also nur dann angegeben werden, wenn sie ausdrücklich erwähnt ist. (So schon J. SZALAY, Városaink nemzetiségi viszonyai a XIII. században [Die Nationalitätenverhältnisse unserer Städte im 13. Jh.]. In: Századok 14, 1880, S. 536.).

40) GY. GYÖRFFY, Az Árpád-kori Magyarország történeti földrajza. Geographia historica Hungariae tempore stirpis Arpadianae. Bd. 1, Budapest 1963 (Künftig: GYÖRFFY, Geogr. hist.) S. 156—157.

486

Die Spielregeln der Besiedlung sind aus den Privilegien — von denen das 1224 den Siebenbürger Sachsen erteilte Andreanum das bekannteste ist [41] — ganz klar: der ungarische Herrscher sichert den Einwanderern wirtschaftliche Freiheit, die Ausübung eigenen Gewohnheitsrechtes, die Pflege des Kults in eigener Sprache und fordert auf der anderen Seite Treue zu seiner Person und zur Krone. Letztere ist eine Grundbedingung, die von den deutschen Einwanderern mit einer Ausnahme eingehalten wurde. Die einzige Ausnahme war der Deutschritterorden, der wegen seiner Untreue vom ungarischen König vertrieben wurde [42].

41) ZIMMERMANN-WERNER (wie Anm. 36), Bd. I, S. 34.
42) Die Frage der Vertreibung des Deutschritterordens wurde öfters aufgegriffen, und die Historiker waren in der Beurteilung der Geschehnisse immer schon geteilter Meinung. Einige waren der Ansicht, daß die Ritter des Hochverrates schuldig geworden waren, E. G. MÜLLER, Die Ursachen der Vertreibung des deutschen Ritterordens aus dem Burzenlande und Kumanien. In: Korrespondenzbl. d. Vereins f. Siebenbürg. Landeskde. 48, 1925, S. 41–69; B. HÓMAN, Geschichte des ungarischen Mittelalters. Bd. II. Vom Ende des zwölften Jahrhunderts bis zu den Anfängen des Hauses Anjou, Berlin 1943, S. 29 f.; GY. SZÉKELY, Kapcsolatok a keleteurópai népek harcában a feudális német hódítók ellen a 11–14. században [Zusammenhänge in den Kämpfen der Völker Osteuropas mit den deutschen Eroberern im 11.–14. Jh.]. In: Hadtörténeti Közlemények. Uj Folyam 1, 1954, S. 152–153; andere nahmen eine entgegengesetzte Stellung ein, F. SCHUSTER, Die Ursache der Vertreibung des deutschen Ritterordens aus dem Burzenlande. In: Siebenbürgische Vjschr. 61, 1938, S. 47–51; M. PERLBACH, Der Deutsche Orden in Siebenbürgen. In: MIÖG 26, 1905, S. 415–430. GYÖRFFY, Geogr. hist. (wie Anm. 40), Bd. I, S. 823 — teilweise Schusters Argument folgend — deutet die päpstliche »Exemption« zwar an sich nicht als Erteilung eines tatsächlichen Hoheitsrechtes, behauptet aber, daß die Gefahr der Bildung eines souveränen Ordensstaates bestand und dies den König zum Handeln bewog.
Aus den Quellen läßt sich ein abweichendes Bild zeichnen. Vor allem sei auf die Urkunde des Bischofs von Siebenbürgen hingewiesen, in der der Diözesan 1213 bei höchster Anerkennung der Leistung des Ordens ihm zwar die Zehnten überließ, sich ansonsten jedoch die bischöfliche Jurisdiktion vorbehielt, indem er ausdrücklich auf dem Präsentationszwang und der Durchführung von Disziplinverfahren gegen Kleriker vor dem Bischof bestand, ZIMMERMANN-WERNER (wie Anm. 36), Bd. I, S. 15. Diese Schenkung wurde vom Papst Honorius III. 1218 bestätigt, ebd. Bd. I, S. 16. Fünf Jahre später, 1223, behauptete derselbe Papst, daß das Burzenland *praeter Romanum pontificem non habet episcopum vel praelatum*, und wollte dort ein Archipresbyterat aufstellen, ebd. Bd. I, S. 24. Noch am Ende desselben Jahres richtete Honorius III. an den Bischof von Siebenbürgen ein Schreiben, in dem er den zitierten Rechtssatz wiederholte und dem Bischof vorwarf *in ea* (sc. terra) *tibi iurisdictionem indebitam usurpare contendens presbyteros et clericos terrae ad synodum tuam vocas et tam ab eis quam a laicis decimam et alia episcopalia iura niteris extorquere*, ebd. Bd. I, S. 24. Es ist kaum nötig zu bemerken, daß dieses Verfahren weder mit den Prinzipien, noch mit der traditionellen Praxis Roms im Einklang stand. Der Grund der jähen Wandlung in der päpstlichen Politik kommt erst in einer Bulle des nächsten Jahres zum Vorschein. Es besteht kein Zweifel, daß der Ritterorden das Burzenland dem Papst als Lehen angeboten hat (*petistis siquidem ut terra Boze et ultra montes nivium . . . in ius et proprietatem apostolicae sedis recipere dignaremur*, ebd. Bd. I, S. 29). Können wir den Ausdruck *in ius et proprietatem apostolicae sedis* einwandfrei auslegen, so ist die Frage gelöst.

Tatsächlich – darin haben Schuster und Györffy recht – wurden Klöster *in ius et proprie-tatem apostolicae sedis* übernommen. Es besteht kein Zweifel, daß in Ungarn diese höchste Exemption dem Kapitel von Stuhlweißenburg, der Abtei von Pannonhalma, weiterhin den Johannitern und den Tempelherren erteilt wurde. Doch muß darauf hingewiesen werden, daß dies nur die Befreiung von jeglicher Diözesanjurisdiktion bedeutete, woraus folgt, daß 1.) die Übernahme *in ius et proprietatem apostolicae sedis* in diesen Fällen nur die kirchlichen Verhältnisse betraf. Sie ging deshalb den weltlichen Herrscher nichts an, so daß dessen Zustimmung auch nicht eingeholt werden mußte. 2.) In den weltlichen Fragen, z. B. in besitzrechtlichen Angelegenheiten, änderte sich dadurch nichts. Pannonhalma unterstand in um Güter geführten Prozessen weiterhin den königlichen Richtern. Für den Ritterorden hätte eine solche ausschließlich kirchenorganisatorische Exemption keinen Sinn gehabt, höchstens für den von ihnen vorgeschlagenen Erzpriester. Sie hätte auch den ungarischen König nicht berührt, sondern nur den Bischof von Siebenbürgen, der in seinen Rechten geschmälert wurde. Von einem Protest des Diözesans wissen wir nichts.

Auch das kann kaum geleugnet werden, daß in solchen Fällen die eximierte Institution zu einem gewissen Jahreszins (in Naturalien oder in Geld) verpflichtet wurde.

Daß es aber in diesem Fall nicht um eine kirchliche Angelegenheit ging, beweist ein anderer Satz der Bulle von 1224, daß nämlich das Gebiet viel leichter bevölkert werden könnte, falls die Einwanderer wüßten, daß es *apostolicae sedis dominationis subiectam* sei. Das Wort *dominatio* (das SCHUSTER, S. 49, Anm. 1, übrigens viel Kopfzerbrechen bereitet hat) kann sich nicht auf kirchliche Angelegenheiten beziehen, es bedeutet »weltliche Herrschaft«. Honorius III. erlaubte sich ein böses Spiel, indem er *ius et proprietas* schrieb, doch an *dominatio sedis apostolicae* dachte, besser gesagt durch die rein kirchliche Formel die Oberherrschaft verwirklichen wollte. Es lag nicht an ihm, sondern an König Andreas II. – der übrigens wirklich kein energischer Herrscher war –, daß diese Aktion scheiterte.

Zusammenfassend müssen wir behaupten, daß der Ritterorden nicht die kirchliche Exemption, sondern die weltliche Herrschaft erstrebte. Unter den Hl. Stuhl gestellt – besonders laut Auffassung der Wortführer der Theokratie – hätte er die Landesherrschaft, die Souveränität erlangt. Von ungarischer Seite betrachtet, war das Hochverrat. Das ist kaum bestürzend, denn das Ausgangsgebiet (das Burzenland) wurde vom ungarischen König ohne Verzicht auf seine bestehenden Hoheitsrechte überlassen. In dieser Hinsicht ist es äußerst aufschlußreich – und auch für den Fall der Deutschritter ein bisher unbeachtetes Argument –, daß 1250, als das Gebiet Szörvény den Johannitern übergeben wurde, der ungarische König ausdrücklich darauf bestand, *quod preceptor seu magister, qui pro tempore ad gubernationem domorum in regnis nostris existentium mittetur . . . in introitu suo promittere teneatur . . . omnem fidelitatem regi et regno*, A. THEINER, Vetera monumenta historia Hungariam sacram illustrantia, Bd. I, Romae 1859, S. 210.

Auch das Verhalten der Ritter verwundert nicht. Sie haben von dem Burzenland aus jenseits der Karpaten liegende Gebiete erobert, eine rasche Kolonisation durchgeführt und schöne Ergebnisse erzielt. Es ist ganz verständlich, wenn sie eher auf dem Schlachtfelde fallen wollten, als diese Gebiete aufzugeben, ZIMMERMANN-WERNER (wie Anm. 36), Bd. I, S. 41. In jeder Hinsicht hatten sie einen guten Ausgangspunkt für die Schaffung eines souveränen Ordensstaates.

Es ist noch eine Frage zu klären, und das ist die Erwähnung der vom Bischof von Siebenbürgen beanspruchten Zehnten in der Bulle vom 12. Dez. 1223. Dieser Hinweis scheint nämlich darauf zu zielen, daß der Bischof die von ihm zehn Jahre früher erteilte Freiheit zurückzog. Streit konnte hier rasch und häufig entstehen, da der Bischof 1213 die Zehnten der im Ordensgebiet lebenden Ungarn und Székler für sich behielt. Die jedenfalls verdächtige

Jene politische Struktur, die mit der fast unbeschränkten Macht des Königs gekennzeichnet werden kann und die Otto von Freising noch bewunderte, brach binnen des nächsten halben Jahrhunderts zusammen. Den Wunsch einer Wiederherstellung der Königsmacht vereitelte der Tatareneinfall ein für allemal. Das wesentliche an der neuen politischen Entwicklung war das Entstehen der Stände der Prälaten, dann der Herren, die die königliche Macht einschränkten und am Ende des 13. Jahrhunderts sogar für ein Menschenalter das Land in kleine Oligarchien zerstückelten. Die Prälaten setzten die Vertreibung der Mohammedaner durch; dadurch schufen sie neue Plätze für die westlichen Einwanderer. Dieser Vorgang kann am besten am Beispiel von Pest veranschaulicht werden. Pest war am Donauübergang ein wichtiger Handelsplatz und von Sarazenen bewohnt. Zu einem unbekannten Zeitpunkt, aber sicherlich nach 1216 und wahrscheinlich gegen 1230, wurden die Sarazenen vertrieben, und an ihrer Stelle trafen Deutsche ein, die dann nach dem Tatareneinfall vom König auf den Ofner Berg übersiedelt wurden und mit dem Pester Privileg die spätere Hauptstadt des Landes gründeten [43].

Im Laufe der politischen Wandlung wurden die königlichen Güter größtenteils verschenkt, die Mächtigen des Landes trachteten zusammenhängende Domänen zu schaffen, deren Mittelpunkte neugebaute Burgen bildeten. Zum Burgenbau mußte die ganze Kapazität der Domänen aufgeboten werden, es mußten, wo nur möglich, neue Dörfer ins Leben gerufen werden. Dies zog eine zweite, nach dem Tatareneinfall (1241) einsetzende Welle deutscher Einwanderer ins Land. Spielte ungarischerseits in der ersten Welle der Einwanderung der König die Hauptrolle, so traten jetzt die Mitglieder der regierenden Schicht an seine Seite. So siedelte beispielsweise der Zisterzienser-Abt von Heiligenkreuz im nördlichen Transdanubien auf seinen neu erworbenen Gütern Deutsche an [44]. Gewisse Zeichen deuten darauf hin, daß diese zweite Welle zahlenmäßig schwächer war als die erste [45]. Das Ausschlaggebende

(wenn nicht gefälschte) Urkunde des Königs vom J. 1222 (ZIMMERMANN-WERNER (wie Anm. 36), Bd. I, S. 18; vgl. E. SZENTPÉTERY, Regesta critica regum stirpis Arpadianae critico-diplomatica, Bd. I, Budapest 1923, Nr. 380.) deutet darauf hin, daß die Ritter tatsächlich Siebenbürger übersiedeln ließen. Stimmt diese Nachricht, so ist es sehr wahrscheinlich, daß sich unter ihnen auch Ungarn befanden, die weiterhin dem Bischof ihre Zehnten zu entrichten hatten.

43) FÜGEDI, Entstehung (wie Anm. 6), S. 113—114.

44) Vgl. K. MOLLAY, Zur Chronologie deutscher Ortsnamentypen im mittelalterlichen Ungarn. In: Acta linguistica acad. Sc. Hung. 11, 1961, S. 93; dasselbe wurde in bezug auf die andere Zisterzienserabtei bewiesen, vgl. E. KALÁSZ, A szentgotthárdi apátság birtokviszonyai és a ciszergazdálkodás a középkorban [Die Besitzverhältnisse der St. Gottharder Abtei und die Wirtschaft der Zisterzienser im Mittelalter], Budapest 1932.

45) Es stehen uns leider keine statistischen Auswertungen, sondern nur gewisse Indizien zur Verfügung, die darauf hindeuten, daß die zweite Welle zahlenmäßig schwächer war. In der schon zitierten Urkunde vom J. 1250 (vgl. Anm. 42), in der das Gebiet Szörény den

war allerdings, daß die Bauern der zweiten Welle im Rahmen der privaten Grundherrschaften angesiedelt wurden. Dies bedeutete einerseits, daß die deutschen Dörfer
meistens zwischen Dörfern anderer Nationalität verstreut lagen. Dadurch war die
Bildung so großer geschlossener Inseln, wie die der Sachsen, ausgeschlossen. Selbst
dort, wo die Domäne größtenteils aus Waldungen bestand und die neuen Dörfer
durch Rodung angelegt wurden, wie z. B. im Komitat Neutra, erreichte die Zahl
der deutschen Siedlungen nicht die zehn Dörfer der Vizsolyer Gespanschaft [46].

Johannitern überlassen wurde, finden wir seitens des Königs die Bedingung: *quod curam
et operam dabit ad populandum* ... *et quod rusticos de regno nostro cuiuscungue conditionis et nationis ac Saxones vel Teutonicos de nostro regno non recipiant ad habitandum
terras supradictas nisi de licentia regia speciali,* THEINER (wie Anm. 42), Bd. I, S. 210.
U. E. ist dieser Satz in der Weise auszulegen, daß es schwerer geworden war, ausländische
Siedler zu finden, und so die Gefahr bestand, daß die Johanniter ihren Besitz mit einheimischen (ungeachtet ob eingewanderten oder nicht) Bauern bevölkern und dadurch des
Königs Ziel vereiteln würden.
Es muß auch für kennzeichnend gehalten werden, daß das während des Tatareneinfalls ver-
wüstete Gebiet südlich von Eger mit Franzosen aus Liège besiedelt wurde, die noch im
16. Jh. französisch gesprochen haben. Vgl. G. BÁRCZY, A középkori vallon-magyar érint-
kezésekhez [Beiträge zu den wallonisch-ungarischen Beziehungen im Mittelalter]. In: Századok 71, 1937, S. 399—416.
In dieser Hinsicht müßte man auch die ungarischen Städte des 13. Jhs. in bezug auf die
Bevölkerungszahl untersuchen. Es kann kein Zufall sein, daß nach dem Tatareneinfall hauptsächlich die Städte deutsche Einwanderer aufgenommen haben, während in derselben Zeit
weniger deutsche Dörfer gegründet wurden. Es stellt sich eine Reihe von Fragen, die heute
leider noch nicht beantwortet werden können. War es im Gegensatz zu der Zuwanderung
von Bauern in der ersten Welle ein Unterschied qualitativer Art, daß die Einwanderer der
zweiten Welle größtenteils Bürger waren? Die Bergleute bedeuten allerdings einen quali-
tativen Unterschied. Waren aber die Stadtbewohner auch in ihrer Heimat Bürger, oder sind
sie es erst in Ungarn geworden? Auf ersteres deutet der Aufstieg von Ofen gegenüber dem
alten Handelsmittelpunkt Gran hin, auf letzteres, daß die Landwirtschaft (hauptsächlich der
Weinbau) in den Städten besonders im 13. und am Anfang des 14. Jhs. eine große Rolle
spielte. Von einem zielbewußten Vorstoß deutscher Kaufleute kann kaum gesprochen werden, da z. B. Großwardein, einer der wichtigsten Umschlagplätze zwischen Ofen und Kaschau
bzw. Hermannstadt und Kronstadt keine deutsche Einwohner hatte. Dasselbe gilt für Fünfkirchen und Szegedin. Das weist ebenfalls auf das Versickern der Ostsiedlung (noch vor der
großen Pest) hin.
46) Im Komitat Neutra entfachte die Herrschaft Weinitz eine rege Siedlungstätigkeit, um das
Goldvorkommen im Quellengebiet der Neutra zu erschließen. Um Deutsch-Proben wurde
eine Reihe deutscher Dörfer ins Leben gerufen, der Zahl nach fünf (Andreasdorf, Zeche,
Nickelsdorf, Schmiedshau und Krickerhau). Unmittelbar nebeneinander lagen aber von ihnen
nur vier, nämlich Deutsch-Proben, Zeche, Nickelsdorf und Schmiedshau. Andreasdorf und
Krickerhau lagen weiter nach Süden, zwischen ihnen und der Deutsch-Probener Gruppe befand sich eine Reihe slowakischer Siedlungen. Die Deutsch-Probener Gruppe hatte aber
Anschluß an drei oder vier (allerdings in einer anderen Grundherrschaft liegende) Dörfer
im Komitat Turz; Krickerhau lag an der Insel von Kremnitz. E. FÜGEDI, Nyitra megye

Die Einwanderer standen diesmal nicht dem König, sondern dem Grundherrn gegenüber und waren ihm zur Treue verpflichtet [47]. Der Grundherr konnte aber auch bei bestem Willen nicht mehr Freiheit geben, als er selbst besaß, d. h. er konnte seine Siedler von den grundherrschaftlichen Abgaben teilweise befreien, nicht aber von den Leistungen gegenüber dem König. Er konnte ihnen die freie Pfarrerwahl zusichern, da es in seiner Macht lag, als Patronatsherr auf die Präsentation des Pfarrers zu verzichten, konnte aber keine Freiheiten in bezug auf die Zehnten erteilen, da die Zehnten nicht ihm, sondern dem Bischof gebührten. Gegenüber den Siebenbürger und Zipser Sachsen bedeutet das einen großen, vor allem wirtschaftlichen Nachteil.

Die verstreuten deutschen Siedlungen der ersten Periode, die wir oben erwähnten, sollten die politische Wandlung auch zu spüren bekommen, indem sie durch Verschenkung aus dem königlichen in Privatbesitz geraten waren [48]. Doch — und das soll hier betont werden — behielten sie ihren Sozialstatus als *hospites* und blieben weiterhin im Besitz der niederen Gerichtsbarkeit und Pfarrerwahl und so in einer besseren Lage als die alten einheimischen Dörfer.

Im Laufe des 13. Jahrhunderts kam es nicht mehr zu Gründungen geschlossener deutscher Sprachinseln, desto mehr aber zu Städtegründungen. Die Zeit der großen Sozialwandlungen bedeutet zugleich eine Entwicklungsphase des ungarischen Städtewesens. Einerseits wurden alte, noch nomadischen Charakter tragende Städte umgestaltet, andererseits neue Gründungen unternommen, die manchmal — besonders im Falle der Bergstädte — aus wilder Wurzel erfolgten. Ein Teil der neugegründeten Städte, besonders die Bergstädte, trugen den Charakter einer deutschen Kolonisationsstadt, doch in politischer Hinsicht sind bedeutende Abweichungen festzustellen. Vor allem entstanden diese Städte auf königlichen Gütern; der Herrscher gründete die Stadt und erteilte den Bewohnern der künftigen Siedlung Freiheiten. Es ist hier wieder einmal zu betonen, daß dieser Akt ohne Rücksicht auf die Nationalität der künftigen Bürger vollzogen wurde, obzwar er tatsächlich die Nationalität der Stadt entscheidend beeinflußte. Erfolgte die Gründung aus wilder Wurzel, so kam es

betelepülése. In: Századok 72, 1938, S. 493–494; DERS., Kirchliche Topographie (wie Anm. 38), S. 395–397; zu den übertriebenen Behauptungen von J. HANIKA, Ostmitteldeutschbaierische Volkstumsmischung im westkarpathischen Bergbaugebiet, Münster i. W. 1933, und H. WEINELT, Die mittelalterliche deutsche Kanzleisprache in der Slowakei (= Arbeiten zur sprachlichen Volksforschung in den Sudetenländern 4), Brünn-Leipzig 1938, vgl. E. FÜGEDI, A Felvidék település történetének ujabb német irodalma [Die neuere deutsche Literatur über die Siedlungsgeschichte Oberungarns]. In: Századok 75, 1941, S. 405–421.

47) *...promiserunt dicti Teothonici prestito iuramento, quod nec facto nec consilio venient contra fratres ecclesie memorate, sed ei fideles erunt in omnibus*, Mon. Strig. (wie Anm. 38) Bd. I, S. 298.

48) Es wurden fast alle 35 Németi-Orte verschenkt. Im 14.–15. Jh. befanden sie sich in Privatbesitz; vgl. MÁLYUSZ (wie Anm. 35), S. 276–280.

öfters vor, daß die Gründungseinwohner ausschließlich oder beinahe ausschließlich Deutsche waren und die neue Siedlung auch hinsichtlich der Nationalität ihrer Bewohner eine deutsche Stadt war. Wurde dagegen ein Dorf durch Einschalten deutscher Einwanderer zur Stadt erhoben oder geschah dasselbe im Laufe einer Umgestaltung einer älteren Stadt, so konnte das Deutschtum keine Ausschließlichkeit für sich beanspruchen, da die neue Stadt auch die alten Ortsbewohner in sich schloß [49]. Von einem zwangsmäßigen Übersiedeln der einheimischen Bevölkerung ist bisher keine Angabe bekannt geworden, allein der Fall von Kaschau scheint darauf hinzuweisen [50].

Aus diesen Kennzeichen des Gründungsaktes geht klar hervor, daß die neue Stadt — mit oder ohne fremde Einwohner — den Forderungen der ungarischen politischen Struktur sich fügen mußte. Dies ist auch dadurch ersichtlich, daß trotz aller erteilten Freiheiten der König weiterhin der Stadtherr blieb, und an dieser Tatsache änderte die im 13. Jahrhundert erfolgte Einschränkung der königlichen Macht nichts. Der Herrscher besaß das Recht, die Stadt zu veräußern, zu verpfänden oder zu verschenken, wie dies öfters tatsächlich vorkam [51].

Die Einordnung der Städte in die politische Struktur des Landes wird noch klarer, wenn wir das Gerichtsverfahren in Betracht ziehen. Der König gewährte den Bürgern die freie Richterwahl und die ausschließliche Zuständigkeit des Richters in allen Streitfragen, also auch in Fragen des Blutgerichts. Die deutschen Städte übten diese Sonderrechte auf Grund deutscher Stadtrechte aus, die bekanntesten sind die Rechte von Ofen und Schemnitz [52]. Der Unterschied liegt nicht hier, sondern in dem Appellationsweg. Falls ein Prozeß nicht vor dem Stadtgericht abgeschlossen werden konnte, so war die nächste Instanz der König oder der Tarnakmeister. Dadurch kam im 14. Jahrhundert für die großen Handelsstädte eine spezifisch ungarische Rechtsinstitution zustande, der sog. Tarnakstuhl, wo der Tarnakmeister (meistens ein Aristokrat) den Vorsitz führte und mit den Delegierten der sieben Städte das Urteil fällte [53]. Andere Städte gehörten zum *personalis regie maiestatis*, der

---

49) Fügedi, Entstehung (wie Anm. 6), S. 115.
50) Ebd.
51) E. Fügedi, Városprivilégiumok (wie Anm. 38), S. 42.
52) K. Mollay, Das Ofner Stadtrecht, Budapest 1959; G. Wenzel, Das Stadt- und Bergrecht der k. Frei- und Bergstadt Schemnitz aus dem 13. Jh. In: Anzeigeblatt der Jahrbücher für Literatur 104, Wien 1843, S. 1–21. V. Chaloupecky, Kniha Žilinská. Bratislava 1933.
53) I. Szentpétery iunior, A tárnoki itélőszék kialakulása [Die Entstehung des Tarnakstuhls]. In: Századok 68, 1934, S. 510–590. I. Bertényi, Szepesi Jakab. A magyar királyi kuria biráskodás történetéhez a XIV. században [Jakob von der Zips. Beiträge zur Geschichte der Richter der königlichen Kurie], Budapest o. J. [maschinenschr. vervielf.].

ebenfalls ein Edelmann war [54]. Es führte also kein Appellationsweg in das Ausland.

Diese rechtliche Entwicklung der Städte in Ungarn weicht von den westslawischen Verhältnissen in einem so hohem Maße ab, daß sie einer Erklärung bedarf. Vor allem spielte hier zweifellos die starke Zentralmacht eine entscheidende Rolle. Auch die geschichtliche Entwicklung kam zu Wort. Das erste ungarische Stadtprivileg wurde nicht für Deutsche, sondern für die *Latini* Stuhlweißenburgs ausgestellt [55]. Ihr Privileg bestand aus einer Reihe von Freiheiten, bildete also nur den Rahmen, der mit einem Stadtrecht in jenem Sinne ausgefüllt werden konnte, in dem wir vom Magdeburger Recht sprechen. Zur Entstehung eines spezifisch Stuhlweißenburger Rechtes kam es aber nicht; andererseits erhoben die *Latini* anscheinend keinen Anspruch auf einen Appellationsweg, der in ihre alte Heimat führte. Die *libertas civium Albensium* wurde dann an andere (unter ihnen auch deutsche) Städte verliehen [56]. Da sie aber nur ein Rahmen war, ohne ein besonderes Stadtrecht, entwickelte sich kein Stuhlweißenburger Rechtsfiliationssystem. Starke Königsmacht und Stuhlweißenburgs Freiheitsbrief scheinen aber doch nicht alles vollkommen zu erklären. Sicherlich lag es auch an den deutschen Einwanderern, doch wurde die Frage noch nie unter diesem Gesichtspunkt gestellt.

Freiheiten und Treue waren die Devisen auch der Stadtgründer, und die Treue zum Herrscher fand hier ihren besonderen Niederschlag. Im Ofner Stadtrecht findet man am Anfang nach den Paragraphen über Würde und Ehre des Papstes und Kaisers mehrere Abschnitte *von kunigen des lands zu Vngeren,* dem die Bürger *Stät trew zu halten* haben [57], dessen Krönung sie in Stuhlweißenburg *zirtlich geharnascht ... pey der vorderen thüer* (der Basilika) bewachen [58], den sie nach einer Heerfahrt feierlich empfangen [59]. Man gedenkt auch der Königin; ihre Schwangerschaft oder Entbindung soll der Stadt verkündet werden [60].

Im 12. und 13. Jahrhundert erreichten Ungarn zwei Wellen der deutschen Einwanderer, und interessanterweise entspricht die Chronologie der zwei Wellen den Phasen der ungarischen politischen Entwicklung. Die erste Welle fällt nämlich in den Zeitraum, wo die königliche Macht stark war, die zweite in jenen, in dem die Macht der Herrscher durch die Prälaten und Herren des Landes schon eingeschränkt worden war. Es entspricht dieser Chronologie, daß in der ersten Phase große ge-

54) WERBŐCZY, Tripartitum (Corpus Juris Hungarici, Millenarische Gedenkausgabe, Budapest 1897), Partis III, Tit. 9, S. 390.
55) FÜGEDI, Városprivilégiumok (wie Anm. 38), S. 65—66.
56) FÜGEDI, Stuhlweißenburg (wie Anm. 38), S. 124 ff.
57) MOLLAY, Ofner Stadtrecht (wie Anm. 52), S. 60 f. (5).
58) Ebd., S. 61 (6).
59) Ebd., S. 61 (7).
60) Ebd., S. 61 f. (8).

schlossene deutsche Inseln zustandekamen, die sich nicht nur in sprachlicher, sondern auch in rechtlicher Hinsicht von der Umgebung abhoben. Die zweite Phase war für die einwandernden Bauern weniger günstig, es entstanden keine geschlossenen deutschen Inseln mehr; doch ermöglichte diese zweite Phase die Gründung deutscher Städte. In einer Hinsicht gab es aber keinen Unterschied zwischen den beiden Wellen: die Deutschen — ob massenhaft angesiedelt oder nicht — wurden stets in die politische Struktur Ungarns integriert. Diesbezüglich gibt es keinen Unterschied zwischen den Siebenbürger Sachsen und den Bürgern der deutschen Städte.

In der Lage, die die deutsche Ostsiedlung in Ungarn auslöste, erkannten wir zwei Partner: den König von Ungarn und die deutschen Einwanderer. Das Verhältnis zwischen den Partnern wurde durch Treue zu dem König und durch Erteilung von Freiheiten an die Siedler so geregelt, daß die Einwanderer die Politik des Landes nicht beeinflussen konnten, der ungarische König dagegen in den inneren Angelegenheiten der Einwanderer eine großzügige Autonomie gewährte. Die Deutschen wurden als autonome Einheiten in die politische Struktur des Landes eingefügt. Vom ungarischen Standpunkt aus war das nichts Neues; vor den westlichen Einwanderern wurden östliche in der gleichen Weise in die politische Struktur des Landes eingebaut.

Um die politischen Betrachtungen über die deutsche Ostsiedlung zu Ende führen zu können, sei noch die verfassungsmäßige Entwicklung des Landes im 14. und 15. Jahrhundert kurz geschildert.

Rund hundert Jahre nach dem Tatareneinfall beginnt in Ungarn eine neue politische Wandlung: im Laufe des 14. und 15. Jahrhunderts entstand das politische System des Ständestaates. Die Stände der Prälaten und Herren bildeten sich schon ein Jahrhundert früher aus, seit Ende des 14. Jahrhunderts trug dieser Vorgang seine Früchte. Die Aristokratie behauptete sich, regierte unter schwachen Herrschern tatsächlich das Land, besonders unter Sigismund, und bildete eine geschlossene, durch gegenseitige verwandtschaftliche Bande gestärkte Schicht[61]. Im 15. Jahrhundert begann auch der niedere Adel sich zu organisieren, nach dem Tode von Mathias Corvinus stritten sich die drei Stände — Prälaten, Herren und Adel — um die Teilnahme an der politischen Macht.

Vielleicht ist es unseren Lesern schon aufgefallen, daß wir den Stand der Bürger nicht erwähnt haben. Wir konnten es nicht tun, da er praktisch nicht existierte. Die Verfassung der ungarischen Stände kannte nur die Edelleute und den hohen Klerus, und erstere teilte sie in Herren *(barones regni)* und Adel *(nobiles regni)*. Sie waren

---

61) E. FÜGEDI, A 15. századi magyar arisztrokràcia mobilitása [Die soziale Mobilität der Ungarischen Aristokratie im 15. Jh.] (= Történeti statisztikai füzetek [Historisch-statistische Mitteilungen]), Budapest 1970.

in politischen Entscheidungen zuständig [62]. Die Bürger waren praktisch ebenso frei wie die Edelleute, doch bildeten sie nie einen Stand. In Rechtsangelegenheiten waren nur Städte als Korporationen den Adeligen gleichgesetzt [63]. Städte wurden auch zum Landtag eingeladen, doch bildeten sie auch hier keine besondere Einheit, sondern ergänzten die Zahl der am Landtag teilnehmenden Adeligen. Das Fehlen eines starken Bürgerstandes erklärt auch die politische Schwäche des Landes. Nach Gründen suchend, beruft sich die ungarische Geschichtswissenschaft auf die schwache wirtschaftliche und soziale Entwicklung des Städtewesens [64]. Zweifellos bildet dieser Mangel das schwerste Argument, doch muß hier auch auf eine andere Erscheinung hingewiesen werden, und das ist das Verhalten der Bürger gegenüber politischen Fragen. Liest man die Briefe und Berichte über die Landtage oder jene von städtischen Gesandten an den Hof, so findet man eine verblüffende Kurzsichtigkeit und Gleichgültigkeit, die nur dann einem größeren Interesse weicht, wenn es um die Städte unmittelbar angehende Wirtschaftsfragen geht [65]. Wir beeilen uns hinzuzufügen, daß dieses Verhalten kein Monopol der deutschen Städte war; andere verhielten sich in derselben Weise.

Behaupteten wir, daß Ungarn im Laufe des 12.—13. Jahrhunderts europäisiert wurde, so stellt sich nun zum Schluß unserer politischen Betrachtung die Frage, ob die deutschen Einwanderer oder deren Nachkommen im 14.—15. Jahrhundert eine bedeutende Rolle im politischen Leben Ungarns spielen konnten.

Folgen wir wieder der Hierarchie des Mittelalters, so müssen wir feststellen, daß es unter den politisch bedeutenden Prälaten mit Sicherheit insgesamt nur drei Deutsche gab [66]. Es waren Eberhard, Hermannstädter Probst, dann Bischof von Zag-

---

62) Ebd., S. 8–10.
63) WERBÖCZY, Tripartitum (wie Anm. 54), Partis IV, Tit. 9, S. 390: *Quarumquidem civitatum cives et inhabitatores in eorum homagiis nobilibus regni huius aequiparantur; in aliis tamen libertatibus nobilibus inequales habentur et eorum privilegiis non uiuntur.*
1. Nam et testimonia ipsorum civium extra eorum civitates et territoria penes nobiles non acceptantur; neque pro damnorum aut debitorum recuperatione extra civitatem singillatim ultra unum florenum iuare permittuntur.
64) J. SZÜCS, Das Städtewesen in Ungarn im 15.–17. Jh. In: La Renaissance et la Réformation en Pologne et en Hongrie (= Studia Historica Academiae Scientarum Hungaricae 53), Budapest 1963, S. 102–109.
65) Solche Briefe und Berichte findet der Leser in den Regestenwerken von B. IVÁNYI, Eperjes sz. kir. város levéltára [Das Archiv der königlichen Freistadt Eperjes], Budapest 1931, und DERS., Bártfa sz. kir. város levéltára 1319–1526 [Das Archiv der königlichen Freistadt Bártfa 1319–1526], Bd. I: 1319–1501, Budapest 1912.
66) Über die Identität des Bischofs Hartwick, der am Anfang des 12. Jhs. eine Legende des hl. Stephan verfaßte, wurde im Laufe einer Diskussion behauptet, er sei ein politischer Flüchtling des Investiturstreites gewesen, indem CSÓKA ihn für jenen Hartwig hielt, der 1072–1085 Abt in Hersfeld, dann Erzbischof von Magdeburg war. Vgl. GY. PAULER, Ki volt Hartvik püspök? [Wer war Bischof Hartwick?]. In: Századok 16, 1883, S. 803–804;

reb, ein Berater König Sigismunds [67], und der Breslauer Johann Beckenschloer, ein Günstling von König Mathias [68], während die größte Karriere Berthold von Meranien gegönnt war, der Erzbischof von Kalocsa wurde und zwei Jahre hindurch auch das Amt des Siebenbürger Woiwoden bekleidete (1212–1213), doch eben wegen seiner politischen Tätigkeit aus dem Lande flüchten mußte [69]. Die großen Prälaten des 12.–13. Jahrhunderts, die sich gegenüber der Zentralmacht durchsetzten, waren keine Deutschen, sondern Ungarn und ein Franzose [70]. Die Prälaten stammten übrigens schon im 12. Jahrhundert regelmäßig aus den mächtigen Sippen des Landes, im 14.–15. Jahrhundert blieb diese Praxis aufrechterhalten. Neben ihnen kamen auch königliche Günstlinge auf, die im 14. Jahrhundert meistens Italiener waren, im 15. Jahrhundert dagegen vereinzelt aus den Reihen des niederen Adels, ausnahmsweise von Leibeigenen ungarischer Nationalität stammten [71].

Die Bedeutung der Aristokratie wird bereits aus dem bisher Gesagten klar. Es gab in Ungarn etwa 50 Sippen, die zwischen dem 13. und 15. Jahrhundert die Mehrzahl der politischen Führungspositionen besetzten und manchmal — wenn auch in verschiedenen Zweigen — ihre Rolle drei Jahrhunderte lang beibehielten. Manche waren blutsmäßige Abkommen der heidnischen Stammeshäuptlinge [72], andere wiederum — ihre Zahl belief sich auf 15 — Abkommen eingewanderter Ritter. Hier

Z. Tóth, A Hartwick legenda kritikájához [Zur Kritik der Hartwick-Legende], Budapest 1942, S. 114–116; J. Csóka A latinnyelvü történeti irodalom kialakulása Magyarországon a XI–XIV. században [Die Entstehung der lateinisch-sprachigen Geschichtsliteratur in Ungarn im 11.–14. Jh.], Budapest 1967, S. 154–156.

67) In der ungarischen Literatur wird er als ein Angehöriger der Familie von Alben bezeichnet, doch war er mit dieser Familie nur (über seine Schwester) verschwägert; seine Herkunft ist unbekannt. Vor 1397 Propst von Hermannstadt, 1397–1407 und 1409–1420 Bischof von Agram, 1407–1409 von Großwardein, 1404–1420 Kanzler, seit 1397 vertrauter Berater des Königs Sigismund, spielte er eine große Rolle in dessen gegenpäpstlicher Politik.

68) Vgl. J. Gottschalk, Der Breslauer Johannes Beckenslor († 1489), Erzbischof von Gran und Salzburg. In: Archiv für schlesische Kirchengeschichte 27, 1968, S. 98–129.

69) Sohn des Herzogs von Meranien, Berthold; zunächst Propst in Bamberg, 1205–1218 Erzbischof von Kalocsa (doch durfte er wegen seiner Jugend und seiner mangelnden Bildung sein Amt nicht ausüben), 1212–1213 Woiwode von Siebenbürgen, 1213 auch Banus von Kroatien, Dalmatien und Slavonien, zugleich des Königs Statthalter während seiner Heerfahrt. Flüchtete nach Ermordung seiner Schwester, Königin Gertrud, aus Ungarn; war danach 1218–1251 Patriarch von Aquileja.

70) Lukas stammte aus dem Geschlecht Gutkeled, studierte in Paris und war der erste Vertreter der gregorianischen Auffassung in Ungarn; 1156–1157 Bischof von Erlau, 1158–1181 Erzbischof von Gran. Robert stammte aus Liège und war 1207–1209 Propst von Stuhlweissenburg und Kanzler, 1209–1226 Bischof von Veszprém, 1226–1239 Erzbischof von Gran.

71) E. Fügedi, Hungarian Bishops in the Fifteenth Century. In: Acta Historica Acad. Sc. Hung. 11, 1965, S. 375–383.

72) Gy. Györffy, Tanulmányok a magyar állam eredetéröl [Studien zur Herkunft des ungarischen Staates], Budapest 1959, S. 4–6.

VIII

496

kommt die Erscheinung, daß die Einwanderer aus Europas verschiedensten Völkern stammten, wieder ans Licht. Es waren unter ihnen acht deutschen [73], die übrigen französischen, italienischen, böhmischen, sogar spanischen und russischen Ursprungs [74]. Über die politische Tätigkeit dieser eingewanderten Ritter und ihrer Nachkommen stehen uns scheinbar gegensätzliche Angaben zur Verfügung. Vor allem muß festgestellt werden, daß sie — mit zwei Ausnahmen [75] — in der ersten Generation keine Landeswürde bekleideten, meistens war es erst die dritte, in der ein Mitglied der Familie *baro regni* geworden war [76]. Diese Feststellung ruht aber auf genealogischen Beobachtungen und schließt keineswegs aus, daß die eingewanderten Ritter schon in der ersten Generation der königlichen Gefolgschaft angehörten und dort tätig waren. Allem Anscheine nach wurden nur die Landeswürden für die spätere Generation vorbehalten [77]. Wahrscheinlich ging es hier um eine gewisse politische,

73) Und zwar die Sippen Balog, Gutkeled, Győr, Hahót, Héder, Hermány, Hontpázmány, Ják.

74) Französischer Herkunft: Smaragd, italienischer: Rátót, spanischer: Kökényes-Radnót, böhmischer: Bogát-Radvány und Ludány, russischer: Dobák.

75) Der Urahne des Geschlechts Ják war laut der Bilderchronik *Vencilinus hospes Alamanus* (E. SZENTPÉTERY, Scriptores rerum Hungaricarum tempore ducum regumque stirpis Arpadianae gestarum, Bd. I, Budapest 1937, S. 313), der als Heerführer Stephans I. gegen den aufständischen Koppány eine Rolle spielte (J. KARÁCSONYI, A magyar nemzetségek a XIV. század közepéig [Ungarische Geschlechter bis zur Mitte des 14. Jh.], Budapest 1901, Bd. II, S. 244.). – Die Brüder Hont (Kunz) und Pázmány werden in demselben Fall als die Führer der Leibgarde Stephans erwähnt: *qui sanctum Stephanum regem ... gladio Theutonico more accinxerunt*, SZENTPÉTERY, Bd. I, S. 297. – Ich habe hier den Königinbruder Berthold von Meranien außer Betracht gelassen.

76) Die Ahnen des Geschlechts Hahót kamen unter der Regierung Stephans III. (1162–1172) aus der Steiermark nach Ungarn. In der dritten Generation im Lande befindet sich die Familie des Buzád, der 1222–1223 Gespan des Komitats Preßburg, 1226–1229 Banus von Slavonien war; er trat vor 1233 in den Dominikanerorden ein und wurde 1241 im Pester Kloster von den Tataren getötet, KARÁCSONYI (wie Anm. 75), Bd. II, S. 122–123. – Die Ahnen der Héder waren die Brüder Wolfger und Heidrich, die in der Regierungszeit Gejzas II. (1141–1162) ebenfalls aus der Steiermark einwanderten. Bereits in der vierten Generation im Lande ansässig war die Familie des Heinrich, Gespan des Komitats Eisenburg, 1247–54 des Komitats Somogy; Heinrich bekleidete 1254–1260 die Würde des Landesrichters, 1260–1266 die des Palatins, 1267–1270 und 1273–1274 jene des Banus von Slavonien, doch gab es schon in der dritten Generation (in einem anderen Zweig des Geschlechts) einen königlichen Marschall *(magister agazonum)*, KARÁCSONYI (wie Anm. 75), Bd. II, S. 145–147, 160.

77) Vgl. Anm. 75 über die Brüder Hont und Pázmány. Die Kenntnis der Abstammung ihrer Nachkommen ist insofern lückenhaft, als der Zusammenhang der im 13. Jh. blühenden Zweige dieses Geschlechts weitgehend unbekannt ist, so daß die Abfolge der Generationen nicht im Einzelnen festgestellt werden kann. Gesichert ist immerhin die Abfolge der Agnaten des Hont bis in die vierte Generation. In der dritten Generation heiratete Lampert, der Gründer des Prämonstratenserhauses in Bozók, die Arpaden-Fürstin Sophie, vgl. KARÁCSONYI (wie Anm. 75), Bd. II, S. 184–185.

aber keine nationale Assimilation, denn es gab auch Sippen, deren einer oder anderer Zweig deutsch blieb [78]. Diese waren aber Ausnahmen, und die meisten fremden Familien wurden auch in nationaler Hinsicht assimiliert. Wüßten wir von den Eheverbindungen in der frühen Periode mehr, so könnten wir auch über die Assimilation dieser Sippen mehr sagen.

Prälaten und Ritter waren eine winzige Minderheit gegenüber der Anzahl der deutschen Bürger und Bauern. Diese konnten keine politische Rolle spielen, sie waren keine Edelleute und standen deswegen außerhalb der Körperschaft der politischen Nation.

Vielleicht scheint es ein Widerspruch zu sein, daß wir die Möglichkeit politischer Wirksamkeit und die tatsächliche Rolle in politischen Angelegenheiten an sozialen Kennzeichen gemessen haben, aber es ist eben unsere feste Überzeugung, daß im mittelalterlichen Ungarn der Sozialstatus weitaus entscheidender war als die Nationalität. Der Enkel eines eingewanderten deutschen Ritters durfte nicht deswegen ein Landesamt bekleiden, weil er ein Deutscher war, sondern weil er als Gutsbesitzer und Adeliger dazu berechtigt war, und umgekehrt blieb dem deutschen Bürger die politische Rolle nicht deswegen untersagt, weil er ein Deutscher war, sondern weil er dem Bürgertum angehörte. Daß eine politische Rolle selbst im Rahmen eines Komitats ohne eine Assimilation an den ungarischen Adel undenkbar war, beweist

78) Sicherlich war das der Fall bei den Grafen von Bösing und Sankt Georgen aus der Sippe der Hont-Pázmány, vielleicht auch bei den Güssinger aus der Sippe Héder. — Leider wurden bisher — nicht zuletzt weil das Thema heikel ist und es an Quellen mangelt — keine Forschungen über die Assimilation durchgeführt. Bei den Sippen, welche im 12. Jh. eingewandert waren, kann eine Erscheinung, die allem Anscheine nach mit der Assimilation zusammenhängt, mit Hilfe einer Auswertung der Namen festgestellt werden. Wir geben hier eine kleine Tafel, in der wir das Nachleben der mitgebrachten deutschen Namen bei zwei Geschlechtern schildern.

	1.	2.	3.	4.	5.
			Generation		
HAHÓT					
Zahl der Männer	1	2	12	20	11
Zahl der deutschen Namen	1	2	7	5	1
Zahl der ungarischen Namen	—	—	2	2	1
HÉDER					
Zahl der Männer	2	3	7	12	9
Zahl der deutschen Namen	2	2	3	2	2
Zahl der ungarischen Namen	—	—	3	2	—

Die Tafel weist auf eine Wandlung hin, die darin Ausdruck findet, daß die deutschen Namen schon von der dritten Generation an abnehmen und an ihre Stelle gemeinchristliche (Johannes, Nicolaus, usw.) oder gar in kleiner Zahl ungarische treten (Csák, Ákos).

498

die Geschichte der Greven der Siebenbürger Sachsen, die in dem ungarischen Adel aufgingen und mit dem neuen Sozialstatus ihre ursprüngliche Nationalität aufgaben [79].

Zusammenfassend kann festgestellt werden, daß die deutsche Ostsiedlung die Politik und die Verfassung Ungarns nicht beeinflussen konnte, obwohl die Deutschen ihre Freiheiten erhielten und — wenigstens was die Siebenbürger und Zipser Sachsen und einen Teil der Städte anbelangt — ihre Nationalität zu bewahren vermochten.

4.

Die erste Welle der deutschen Einwanderer bestand — Kleriker und Ritter ausgenommen — ausschließlich aus Bauern, und ein bedeutender Teil der zweiten Welle gehörte ebenfalls zu ihnen. Wenn wir ihre spätere soziale Lage beurteilen wollen, dann ist der entscheidende Punkt nicht der, ob sie zu der ersten oder zweiten Welle, sondern ob sie zu der privilegierten geschlossenen Einheit der Siebenbürger bzw. Zipser Sachsen gehörten oder nicht. Diese beiden Einheiten konnten ihre Sonderstellung bewahren, die übrigen Bauern wurden in die Klasse der Leibeigenen eingereiht, ungeachtet dessen, wann sie angesiedelt wurden.

Stellen wir die Frage nach der sozialen Mobilität der Bauern, so muß vor allem darauf hingewiesen werden, daß sie sich in derselben Lage befanden wie die übrigen Hörigen des Königreichs, d. h. es öffneten sich zwei Wege, um in eine höhere Schicht aufsteigen zu können, und zwar über den Eintritt in den Klerus oder das Bürgertum.

Offensichtlich schickten viele deutsche Bauern ihre Söhne auf die kirchliche Laufbahn; leider kann ihre Menge zahlenmäßig nicht erfaßt werden. Viel Glück haben sie kaum gehabt. Die Prälaten, wie gesagt, gingen aus der Aristokratie oder aus dem Adel hervor. So dürfte die höchste kirchliche Stelle, die ein Deutscher erreicht haben kann, die Propstei von Hermannstadt gewesen sein. Es muß allerdings betont werden, daß hier von den einheimischen Deutschen die Rede ist, denn es gab auch deutsche Prälaten in Ungarn, die aber Ausländer waren, angefangen von dem oben erwähnten Hartwick bis zu den schlesischen Klerikern, die im 15. Jahrhundert in Ungarn die Bischofswürde erreichten [80]. Sicherlich gelang es keinem Deutschen, auf diesem Wege seiner Familie zu einer besseren sozialen Lage zu verhelfen; seine Laufbahn konnte nur gemäßigte materielle Vorteile sichern.

79) MÁLYUSZ (wie Anm. 35), S. 404–408., F. MAKSAY, Die Ansiedlung der Sachsen. In: Siebenbürgen und seine Völker, hg. E. MÁLYUSZ, Budapest 1943, S. 141.
80) Vgl. Anm. 66. Außer Beckenschläger war auch Nikolaus Stoltz, 1470 Bischof von Großwardein, ein Schlesier.

Ein größerer Erfolg erwartete jene, die in die Städte zogen und dort ihre Freiheit erlangten. Die Städte waren in demographischer Hinsicht auch in Ungarn ein Moloch, der die Bevölkerung an sich zog und dann unbarmherzig vernichtete. Nur ein fortwährender Nachschub an Menschen konnte die Bevölkerungszahl der Städte erhalten. Es war nichts natürlicher, als daß man Leute vom Lande in die Reihen der Bürger aufnahm [81]. Auch in Klausenburg — um ein konkretes Beispiel zu bieten — ist vom Ende des 14. Jahrhunderts an eine Einwanderung aus verschiedenen Siebenbürger Dörfern nachweisbar. Ein Geschworener, Jakob Polkyscher — der auch artium liberalium magister war und diesen Grad an der Wiener Universität erlangte — erwarb für seine Stadt ein Privileg von König Sigismund. Er oder seine Familie stammte — wie der Name besagt — aus dem Dorfe Bulkesch und wanderte nach Klausenburg ein. Er starb nach 1423 in hohem Ansehen und reich, seine Familie lebte weiterhin in den Reihen der führenden Kreise Klausenburgs [82]. Seine Lebensgeschichte ist ein schönes Beispiel der Mobilität des deutschen Bauern in Ungarn, der den Status eines Bürgers erreichte.

In der zweiten Welle der deutschen Siedler, aber schon in den dreißiger Jahren des 13. Jahrhunderts, kamen auch solche nach Ungarn, die sich als Bürger auf den Weg machten oder wenigstens, hier in den Städten angesiedelt, Bürger geworden sind. Die Sozialgeschichte dieser Städte zeigt einen Typ, der von dem des traditionellen Bürgers abweicht. Er ist für den Historiker schon deswegen auffallend, weil er trotz seines Bürgerrechts in den zeitgenössischen Quellen den feudalen Titel *comes* trägt. Diese Leute waren vor allem Unternehmer und befaßten sich mit allen möglichen Dingen. Sie besaßen Meierhöfe in der Stadtgegend, oft liegende Güter zum Titel adeligen Rechts, waren Gewölbherren in Ofen und Mitglieder des Gründerkonsortiums in den Bergstädten, Pächter wichtiger und großer königlicher, kirchlicher und städtischer Einnahmen, Stadtrichter oder wenigstens Geschworene, manchmal sogar Heerführer, die auf dem Schlachtfelde ihr Leben beendeten [83]. Es nimmt kaum Wunder, daß sie mit den mächtigen Familien des Landes verschwägert waren [84]. Aus unbekannten Gründen — die demographischen Verhältnisse der Städte begründen es nicht genügend — verschwanden diese mächtigen, auch im politischen Leben tätigen Bürger am Ende des 14. Jahrhunderts. Die letzten von ihnen hatten meist nur Töchter, die, an Aristokraten vermählt, oft das bürgerliche Familienver-

---

81) Über die Neubürger von Kremnitz vgl. HANIKA (wie Anm. 46), S. 62—68, und T. LAMOŠ. Vznik a počiatky mesta Kremnice [Die Entstehung und Anfänge der Stadt Kremnitz], Bratislava 1969, S. 47—50.
82) MAKKAI (wie Anm. 37), S. 41—43; vgl. J. SZŰCS, Városok és kézmüvesseg a XV. századi Magyarországon [Die Städte und das Handwerk in Ungarn im 15. Jh.], Budapest 1955, S. 325—326.
83) FÜGEDI, Entstehung (wie Anm. 6), S. 117—118.
84) Die Hencfis aus Ofen waren mit der Familie Lackfi verschwägert.

mögen der Aristokratie zuführten. Trotz ihrer regen Tätigkeit konnte sich keine dieser führenden bürgerlichen Familien in die Reihen der Aristokratie emporarbeiten.

Die Schicht, die wir hier charakterisiert haben, war die Führungsschicht der Städte und tat alles, um ihre Macht in der Stadt beibehalten zu können. Die Formen waren mannigfaltig. Das Ofner Stadtrecht forderte, daß der neu erwählte Richter vier deutsche Großeltern haben solle [85]. Diese Vorbedingung, die erst nach dem Putsch der ungarischen Zunftmitglieder eingeführt worden war [86], tötete mit einem Schlag zwei Fliegen. Einerseits war sie geeignet, die deutsche Nationalität der Führungsschicht aufrechtzuerhalten, andererseits sicherte sie die Erhaltung der führenden Schicht. Wer konnte sich schon an die vier Großeltern eines kleinen deutschen Flickschusters erinnern? Dagegen waren die Großeltern eines führenden Mannes ebenfalls mächtige und reiche Leute, die im Gedächtnis der Bürger ebenso ihre Spuren hinterließen, wie zwischen den Grabplatten der Kirchen und in den Besitzverhältnissen der Gemarkung. Ofens Kodifikation stellt das eine Extrem dar, jene der Bergstädte das andere. Nach den Forschungen von O. Paulinyi sind in den Bergstädten die Mitglieder des ursprünglichen Gründerkonsortiums Ringbürger geworden, die die wirtschaftliche und politische Macht sich und ihren Nachkommen dadurch sicherten, daß sie die Ausübung gewisser Vorrechte an die Häuser und Grundstücke des Ringes knüpften. Jahrhunderte lang bestand dieser Zustand in den Bergstädten, ohne daß von dem ganzen System auch nur ein Wort kodifiziert worden wäre [87].

Wirtschaftliche Macht und Anzahl der verschiedenen Nationalitäten waren nicht immer im Einklang. Die dünne deutsche Führungsschicht konnte wirtschaftlich mächtig, zahlenmäßig aber klein sein. Die Wahl des Richters und der Geschworenen war auch in Ungarn keine Wahl im späteren demokratischen Sinne des Wortes. So kamen die Mitglieder des Stadtregiments oft aus den Reihen der deutschen Minderheit. Dies war der Fall in Silein, wo König Ludwig 1381 mit einem Freiheitsbrief die Wahl der Geschworenen regelte. Der König stellt fest, daß in Silein und in der Umgebung gegenüber den Deutschen die »slawischen« Bürger die Mehrheit bilden und daß die Bürger der zwei Nationalitäten ihren Verpflichtungen in gleicher Weise nachkommen; deswegen verordnet er, daß die Geschworenen zur Hälfte von den Deutschen, zur anderen Hälfte von den Slawen gewählt werden sollen [88]. Hinter dieser königlichen Verordnung steht scheinbar ein nationaler Gegensatz, doch war dem nicht so. Reiche und Arme standen einander gegenüber, und die widersprechen-

85) Mollay (wie Anm. 52), S. 32.
86) Szücs (wie Anm. 82), S. 282—283.
87) O. Paulinyi, Tulajdon és társadalom a Garamvidéki bányavárosokban [Eigentum und Gesellschaft in den Bergstädten des Grantals]. In: Történelmi Szemle 1962, S. 173—181.
88) V. Chaloupecký, Privilegium pro Slavis. In: Bratislava 10, 1936, S. 349—364.

VIII

de wirtschaftliche und zahlenmäßige Lage führte zur Durchsetzung des Prinzips *non numerantur sed ponderantur*. Daß die Reichen Deutsche, die Armen Slawen waren, war eine Frage zweiten Ranges.

In Silein kam es vor 1381 zu keinen Ausschreitungen, wenigstens werden solche in den Quellen und im Privileg nicht erwähnt. Am Anfang des 15. Jahrhunderts wurde aber Ofen zum Schauplatz eines blutigen Aufstandes, der sich gegen die deutschen Bürger richtete [89]. In diesem Fall nützte eine Gruppe reich gewordener ungarischer Bürger die Wut der armen Bevölkerung aus, um zu einer Teilnahme am Regiment der Stadt zu kommen, was auch tatsächlich gelang, indem der Richter von 1438 an in jedem zweiten Jahr aus den Reihen der Ungarn erwählt wurde [90].

Der Aufstand in Ofen unterschied sich nur in seiner Hitze von den Bewegungen in den übrigen Städten des Landes. In jedem Fall handelte es sich um soziale und wirtschaftliche Fragen, in jedem Fall waren die frühere Stadtentwicklung, die sozialen Gründe und dementsprechend Ziele und Ablauf der Bewegung verschieden. Dort, wo die Bevölkerung national einheitlich war, so z. B. in Szegedin, das ausschließlich von Ungarn bevölkert war, nahm die Bewegung nicht den Charakter des nationalen Gegensatzes an [91]. Überall dort, wo die Bevölkerung national geteilt war, färbte sich die Bewegung auch national, schien sie ein Gegensatz der Deutschen und Ungarn, Deutschen und Slawen zu sein. Ofen ist dafür ein schönes Beispiel, da es allgemein bekannt ist, daß die Stadt weiterhin von Deutschen bewohnt und sogar in jedem zweiten Jahr weiterhin von einem deutschen Richter geführt wurde.

Das wesentliche an diesen Bewegungen war der soziale und wirtschaftliche Gegensatz, und hier kamen die Züge der Rückständigkeit der wirtschaftlichen und sozialen Entwicklung der Städte Ungarns zu Wort. Deswegen soll hier noch kurz darauf aufmerksam gemacht werden, daß diese Bewegungen nicht mit jenen früheren gleichgesetzt werden dürfen, in deren Verlauf die Patrizier in den deutschen Städten des Reichs ihre Macht gegenüber den Zünften eingebüßt haben [92].

Wir möchten auch die Zusammenfassung unserer sozialen Betrachtung mit dieser Feststellung beginnen. Obwohl die Deutschen — und fügen wir hinzu: auch andere Völker Westeuropas — massenhaft eingewandert waren, vermochten sie nicht, die westeuropäischen Sozialverhältnisse zu übertragen. Dies blieb ihnen nicht nur auf dem Lande, sondern auch in den Städten versagt, wo sich der König und die Aristokraten des Landes von den inneren städtischen Angelegenheiten fernhielten. Der Grund lag in der wirtschaftlichen Entwicklung des Landes, das ist unser letzter Gesichtspunkt.

---

89) So schien es sowohl Aeneas Piccolomini als auch dem ungarischen Chronisten Johann Turóci, vgl. Szücs (wie Anm. 82), S. 287–288.
90) Szücs (wie Anm. 82), S. 273–275, 287–290.
91) Ebd., S. 333–335.
92) Ebd., S. 336.

5.

Betrachten wir die wirtschaftlichen Kennzeichen der deutschen Ostsiedlung, so müssen wir drei Leistungen hervorheben: a.) die ländliche Siedlung, b.) den Bergbau und c.) das Städtewesen. Soviel kann schon hier vorausgeschickt werden, daß einerseits die westliche und damit auch die deutsche Siedlung — im Gegensatz zur politischen und sozialen Entwicklung — die höchste Leistung auf diesem Gebiet aufweisen kann, andererseits aber, daß sie dem tragischen wirtschaftlichen Schicksal des Landes ebenso unterlag wie andere Völker des Königreichs.

a.) Wie wir schon öfters erwähnten, waren die Siedler der ersten Welle ausschließlich, jene der zweiten größtenteils Ackerbauer. Das Ungarn des 11.–12. Jahrhunderts benötigte Ackerbauern am meisten und sicherte ihnen durch die politische Organisation und durch die gewährten Freiheiten einen freien Anteil an dem Landesausbau. Es wurden neue Dörfer gegründet, Wälder gerodet, neues Ackerland geschaffen. Die Siedlungen der Siebenbürger Sachsen beliefen sich auf 200, jene der Zipser auf 60–64 Ortschaften, unter denen sich später mehrere zu Städten entwickelten, z. B. Hermannstadt und Kronstadt, Käsmark und Leutschau. Die Ausbreitung der übrigen, kleineren deutschen Siedlungsgebiete, so z. B. jenes um Preßburg oder in der Umgebung der niederungarischen Bergstädte, ist heute nur schwer zu beurteilen. Deutsche Forscher waren — wie wir anderorts gezeigt haben — geneigt, auf Grund deutscher Ortsnamen auf eine deutsche Besiedlung zu schließen. Dieses Verfahren führt zu falschen Ergebnissen, denn ein deutscher Ortsname an sich bedeutet nicht zwangsläufig eine deutsche Einwohnerschaft, sondern nur soviel, daß es in der Nähe der Ortschaft Deutsche gab, die auch deutsche Namen benützten. Allein Personen- und Flurnamen beweisen die Nationalität einer Siedlung [93]. Solange eine solche Untersuchung nicht durchgeführt ist, kann man die genaue Ausbreitung der Deutschen nicht beurteilen.

Wir hoffen unserem gemeinsamen Ziel zu dienen, wenn wir hier noch erwähnen, daß deutsche Wissenschaftler sich viel über die territoriale Logik der deutschen Besiedelung den Kopf zerbrochen haben. Man trachtete z. B. das »Übergreifen« von einem Flußtal ins andere zu begründen. Dabei wurde aber immer nur die deutsche Siedlung in Betracht gezogen [94]. Das ist insoweit falsch, als es immer der Beamte des ungarischen Königs oder der Grundherr (falls sich das Gebiet im Privatbesitz befand) war, der den Ort und die Grenzen der neuen Siedlung festlegte, und das, ohne die Nationalität der Siedler in Betracht zu ziehen. Was danach innerhalb der festgestellten Gemarkung vor sich ging, war die Angelegenheit der Siedler. Soll eine Logik im Landesausbau, in der Erschließung eines Gebietes gefunden werden, so

93) E. Fügedi, A Felvidék településtörténetének ujabb irodalma (wie Anm. 46), S. 421.
94) Ebd., S. 417.

ist es die Logik des Grundherren und nicht die der Siedler, die Logik der wirtschaftlichen Überlegung und nicht die der nationalen. Nur die geschlossenen Einheiten
der Siebenbürger und Zipser Sachsen bildeten mehr oder weniger eine Ausnahme [95].

Im Rahmen des Landesausbaus lernte das Königreich Ungarn zwei Einrichtungen
kennen, die in Ungarn als deutsche Institutionen erschienen, u. zw. den Schult-
heiß und das »deutsche Recht«. Die Institution des Schultheißen drang auf zwei
Wegen in Ungarn ein: der eine führte durch Schlesien in das westliche Oberungarn,
der andere durch Polen in die Zips und in das östliche Oberungarn. Es wurde viel
über sie geschrieben [96]; so können wir uns hier darauf beschränken, nur jenen Zug
hervorzuheben, den wir für den wesentlichsten halten. Nicht die Gründung neuer
Dörfer, nicht die Rodung der Wälder war das wichtigste, sondern die Einschaltung
eines Unternehmers, der einerseits die Unannehmlichkeiten der Besiedlung übernahm,
andererseits — was noch wichtiger zu sein scheint — mit seiner Kapitalkraft und
Organisationsfähigkeit die Besiedlung beschleunigte. Die Institution des *locator* war
eine bequeme und rasche Art, neue Dörfer ins Leben rufen zu lassen. Am Ende des
13. und Anfang des 14. Jahrhunderts war der rasche Landesausbau eine absolute
Notwendigkeit, und die Schultheißen waren in dieser Hinsicht eine große Hilfe. Um
nur ein Beispiel zu nennen, möchte ich hier auf die Dörfer um die Stadt Kremnitz
hinweisen. Als 1328 Kremnitz gegründet und der Goldertrag der *vollen Henne*
abgebaut wurde, waren Rohmaterialien zum Bergbau und zu den Hütten nötig
gewesen. Es wurden binnen einer sehr kurzen Zeit um die Stadt in den Wald neue
Dörfer gesetzt, deren Einwohner sich hauptsächlich mit der Produktion des nötigen
Hilfsmaterials befaßten. Alle waren von einem Schultheißen angesiedelt worden [97].

Das deutsche Recht ist in Ungarn nur im Zusammenhang mit den Dörfern, nicht
aber mit den Städten bekannt. Um die Bedeutung klar zu sehen, müssen wir auf die
älteren Verhältnisse zurückgreifen. Die Hörigen der frühen Periode des Königtums
waren persönlich an ihren Grundherren gebunden, ihre Verpflichtungen waren
verschieden, oft handwerklicher Natur; ihren Anteil an der Gemarkung kennen wir
leider nicht. In der zweiten Hälfte des 13. Jahrhunderts trat ein jäher Wandel ein,
indem die Gemarkungen in Höfe *(sessiones)* aufgeteilt wurden. Jeder Bauernhof
bestand aus einem Grundstück im Inneren des Dorfes, wo das Haus, die Scheune
usw. des Hörigen standen, und aus Ackerfeldern sowie Nutznießungen (Weide,

95) MAKSAY (wie Anm. 79), S. 136 (Karte).
96) Die einschlägige Literatur ist angeführt bei E. FÜGEDI, A »németjogu« falvak települése a szlovák és német nyelvterületen [Die Ansiedlung deutschrechtlicher Dörfer im
slowakischen und deutschen Sprachgebiet]. In: Tanulmányok a parasztság történetéhez
Magyarországon a 14. században [Studien zur Geschichte des Bauerntums in Ungarn im
14. Jh.], hg. GY. SZÉKELY, Budapest 1953, S. 225–239.
97) M. MATUNÁK, Z dejín slobodného a hlavného banského mesta Kremnice [Aus
der Geschichte der freien Hauptbergstadt Kremnitz], Kremnice 1928, S. 128–130.

usw.) in der Gemarkung. Das Wesentliche war aber, daß der Umfang der Höfe einheitlich war und daß von jedem Hof dieselben (meistens Geld-) Abgaben geleistet werden sollten. Dazu gesellte sich logischerweise die Freizügigkeit der Hörigen, und so wurde die personale Abhängigkeit in eine objektive umgestaltet [98]. Es ist dieselbe Wandlung, die etwas früher in Böhmen eintrat und von Šusta so treffend dargestellt wurde [99]. Diese neue objektive Form der Hörigkeit nannte man in Oberungarn »deutsches Recht«. In anderen Teilen des Landes war dieser Ausdruck unbekannt, obzwar der Umgestaltungsvorgang sich ebenso abspielte; hauptsächlich in Transdanubien ist das Fehlen des Ausdrucks auffallend. Um diesbezüglich zu festeren Ergebnissen zu kommen, müßte man die Regelmäßigkeit in der Größe der Bauernhöfe bzw. ihren Zusammenhang mit der Hufe gründlich kennen. Solange diese Fragen unbeantwortet sind, trauen wir uns nicht zu behaupten, daß der ganze Vorgang auf deutschem Muster beruhte.

Die Umgestaltung der Dörfer war vielleicht einer der wichtigsten Schritte am Wege, an dem Ungarn europäisiert wurde, vom Standpunkt des Bauerntums sicher der wichtigste. Dies stellt die Frage, was die einheimische Bevölkerung von den Deutschen gelernt hat? Was die Agrotechnik anbelangt, können wir heute noch keine Antwort geben, gewisse Anzeichen lassen aber einen nicht unbegründeten Zweifel aufkommen. Korn war kein allzu gesuchtes Agrarprodukt, Ungarn war vielleicht das einzige Land Europas, das im Mittelalter nicht von Hungersnöten heimgesucht wurde [100]. Die gesuchten Produkte waren der Wein und das Schlachtvieh. Den Weinbau haben die *Latini* auf einen höheren Stand gebracht [101]; zwar scheint es nach den neuesten archäologischen Feststellungen nicht ganz ausgeschlossen, daß in Transdanubien gewisse Weinanbaugebiete der Römerzeit die Völkerwanderungszeit überlebten [102]. Andererseits sei darauf hingewiesen, daß die Agrotechnik in den verschiedenen Gegenden sehr unterschiedlich war.

b.) Abu Hamid war zu Mitte des 12. Jahrhunderts der erste fremde Reisende, der das Gold- und Silbervorkommen Ungarns erwähnte. Lange konnte diese Tatsache kein Geheimnis bleiben, und im 13. und 14. Jahrhundert wurden im Land eine Reihe von Edelmetallgruben eröffnet und neben ihnen deutsche Bergstädte gegründet. In der ersten Periode, die noch vor dem Tatareneinfall lag, wurde die

98) FÜGEDI (wie Anm. 96), S. 233–234.
99) J. ŠUSTA, Dvě knihy českých dějin. I. Poslední Premyslovci a jejich dědictvi 1300–1308 [Zwei Bücher über böhmische Geschichte. I. Die letzten Premysliden und ihre Erbschaft 1300–1308], Praha 2. Aufl. 1926, bes. S. 1–86.
100) FÜGEDI (wie Anm. 3).
101) Den besten Wein des mittelalterlichen Ungarn – *vina Seremiensia* – produzierten die Bewohner von Francavilla.
102) K. SÁGI – M. FÜZES, Régészeti és archeobotanikai adatok a pannóniai kontinuitás kérdéséhez [Archäologische und archäobotanische Angaben zur Kontinuitätsfrage in Pannonien]. In: Agrártörténeti Szemle 9, 1967, S. 79–98.

Silberproduktion organisiert. Sie begann mit der Gründung von Schemnitz und Radna in den dreißiger Jahren des 13. Jahrhunderts und endete mit der Gründung von Neusohl 1255. Die zweite Periode setzte im zweiten Viertel des 14. Jahrhunderts ein; damals ging es um Gold: Kremnitz (1328), Nagybánya, Offenbánya und Zalatna verdanken ihre Gründung dem Goldvorkommen. Ungarn besaß und produzierte schon früher Gold und Silber, doch wurde jetzt die Produktion durch die Organisation und Erfahrungen der deutschen Bergleute, die sie aus ihrer Heimat mitbrachten, in technischer Hinsicht gefördert. Beide Perioden charakterisiert eine fieberhafte Unternehmungslust. Sie verdankten den raschen Erfolg nicht nur den deutschen Bergleuten, sondern auch den Interessen des westeuropäischen Handelskapitals, das hauptsächlich beim Abwickeln des Levantehandels das Edelmetall Ungarns nicht entbehren konnte. Die Förderung war bedeutend. Nach einer Blüte im 14. Jahrhundert kamen im 15. Jahrhundert im Bergbau die ersten naturbedingten Rückschläge. Die Edelmetallproduktion sank und erreichte nie mehr die Höhe des 14. Jahrhunderts [103].

c.) Nicht nur Bergstädte verdanken ihr Dasein dem Edelmetallschatz des Landes, auch die Blüte des Handels und damit die Entstehung neuer Städte war dadurch begründet. Im 13. Jahrhundert erfolgte auch hier eine fieberhafte Gründungstätigkeit, die eine Reihe von alten Städten umgestalten und eine Reihe neuer Städte entstehen ließ [104]. Nicht alle konnten sich behaupten, aus dem Kampf kam eine Handvoll siegreich hervor. Es ist dennoch nicht leicht zu bestimmen, welche die reichsten und größten Städte Ungarns waren. Bisher bediente sich die ungarische Geschichtswissenschaft des juristischen Merkmals. Einerseits bevorzugte man die sog. königlichen Freistädte, anderseits behauptete man, daß die sieben Städte des zum Tarnakstuhl gehörenden Bundes die größten waren, was auch zweifellos stimmt, doch fehlen dann so bedeutende Handelszentren wie Kronstadt und Hermannstadt, die zum Gebiet der Siebenbürger Sachsen gehörten, oder Szegedin und Großwardein, die keine Freistädte waren bzw. diesen Rang erst spät erreichten. Unlängst versuchten wir mit Hilfe der Zahl der Bettelordensklöster eine neue Rangliste aufzustellen [105]. Das Ergebnis bestritt den Rang Ofens nicht (es blieb weiterhin an der Spitze), doch wurde klar, daß Fünfkirchen und Stuhlweißenburg ebenfalls große Städte waren. Wie dem auch sei, ein Teil der größten Städte war deutsch oder hatte eine bedeutende deutsche Einwohnerschaft (Ofen, Kaschau, Preßburg, Ödenburg,

---

103) Ich danke Herrn O. Paulinyi, daß er das Manuskript seiner Studie mir vor ihrem Erscheinen zur Verfügung gestellt hat: Nemesfémgazdaságunk és országos gazdaságunk alakulása a bontakozó és kifejlett feudalizmus korszakában 1000–1526. Gazdag föld — szegény ország. [Der Edelmetallreichtum und die allgemeine wirtschaftliche Entwicklung Ungarns im Zeitalter des beginnenden und blühenden Feudalismus 1000–1526. Reiche Bodenschätze – rückständige Wirtschaft]. In: Századok 106, 1972, S. 561–605.
104) Fügedi, Entstehung (wie Anm. 6), S. 114–118.
105) Fügedi, La formation des villes (wie Anm. 16).

Hermannstadt, Kronstadt), und diese waren vor allem Handelsstädte. Wir haben schon andernorts betont, daß der entscheidende Faktor in der Entwicklung der Städte in Ungarn — mit Ausnahme der Bergstädte — nicht das Handwerk, sondern der Handel war [106]. Dieser rege Handel wurde nicht nur von den ungarischen Städten, sondern auch von den westlichen Partnern um des aus Ungarn herausgeholten Goldes willen mit allen Mitteln gefördert [107]. Dadurch war die Möglichkeit eines starken Handwerks nicht nur im 13., sondern auch noch im 15. Jahrhundert ausgeschlossen. Man kann sich nicht des Eindrucks erwehren, daß das Bürgertum kein Gefühl für die Entwicklung der Handwerks gehabt hat. Daß es hier nicht um die Nationalität ging, beweist am schönsten das gleichgültige Verhalten Kaschaus gegenüber den durch König Sigismund angesiedelten Barchentwebern. Die Weber waren Deutsche, die Kaschauer Führungsschicht ebenfalls, der Berater des Königs Mark von Nürnberg. Die Einführung des Barchentwebens scheiterte dennoch, und die Kaschauer taten nichts, um diesen Handwerkszweig einzuführen oder zu fördern; für sie war allein der Handel wichtig [108].

Der tragische Schlag kam von den westlichen Handelspartnern eben auf dem Gebiet des Handels. Die Waren des mittelalterlichen Fernhandels kamen tatsächlich aus der Ferne, aus Flandern, dem Rheingebiet, Italien oder aus der Levante. Das größte Stück des Weges lag in den Händen der westlichen (italienischen, deutschen) Kaufleute, den ungarländischen blieb nur die Verteilung der eingeführten und das Sammeln der auszuführenden Ware auf dem Binnenmarkt übrig. Dazu kam noch, daß der westliche Kaufmann im Mittelpunkt eines weitverzweigten Handelsnetzes und im Mittelpunkt eines kapitalkräftigen Kreditsystems saß. Der an die Peripherie gedrängte ungarische Kaufmann mußte früher oder später unterliegen [109]. Am Anfang des 16. Jahrhunderts war Ungarns Handelsbilanz passiv [110], das Handwerk im Lande unbedeutend [111]. Die Folgen waren die Stockung des Städtewesens in wirtschaftlicher und sozialer Hinsicht. Kein Wunder, daß das Bürgertum politisch unbedeutend blieb. Der Anfang war glänzend, eine Reihe von Bergstädten lieferten Gold, Silber und Kupfer, in der Blütezeit der Edelmetallproduktion standen unsere

106) Fügedi, Entstehung (wie Anm. 6), S. 117.

107) Paulinyi (wie Anm. 103).

108) Szücs (wie Anm. 82), S. 212–216; die diesbezüglichen Urkunden bei G. Wenzel, Kassa város parkettkészítése a XV. század elején [Die Barchentweberei der Stadt Kaschau am Anfang des 15. Jhs.], Pest 1871, S. 14–43.

109) Szücs (wie Anm. 64), S. 110–115.

110) Fügedi, Városprivilégiumok (wie Anm. 38), S. 87.

111) Szücs (wie Anm. 64), S. 112.

Städte am nächsten zu den westeuropäischen [112]. Das Ende war aber ein Verfall, und die deutschen Bürger konnten sich aus dieser Lage ebenso wenig retten wie die übrigen Bürger des Landes.

6.

In den vorangehenden Abschnitten haben wir den Versuch unternommen, die mittelalterliche ungarische Entwicklung vom Standpunkt der deutschen Ostsiedlung in großen Zügen darzulegen und den Prozeß samt seinen Folgen unter politischen, sozialen und wirtschaftlichen Gesichtspunkten zu charakterisieren. Die Betonung liegt auf den großen Zügen; denn es ist klar, daß wir gewisse Fragen überhaupt nicht angeschnitten haben und — nicht zuletzt wegen des gegebenen Rahmens eines Aufsatzes — auf Einzelheiten verzichten mußten, die das Bild in vieler Hinsicht hätten feiner gestalten können. Wir haben kein Wort über die Herkunft der deutschen Einwanderer geschrieben, wir haben sie nur schlicht Deutsche genannt und dadurch selbst den falschen Eindruck erweckt, als ob es sich um eine geschlossene Nation gehandelt habe, was offensichtlich nicht der Fall war. Es hätte der historischen Wahrheit näher gestanden, wenn wir wenigstens die Süd- und Norddeutschen — die *Teutonici* und *Saxones* der mittelalterlichen ungarischen Kanzleisprache — unterschieden hätten. Liest man die Werke deutscher Sprachwissenschaftler über die Herkunft der deutschen Einwanderer, so wird es klar, daß selbst die großen geschlossenen deutschen Sprachinseln nicht einheitlich, sondern aus verschiedenen Gruppen von Deutschen zusammengesetzt und zusammengeschmolzen waren. Doch wäre u. E. durch die Berücksichtigung dieses Unterschiedes das Bild vielleicht nur verwirrender geworden. Denn *Teutonici* und *Saxones* sind nur zwei aus den vielen westeuropäischen Völkernamen, deren Träger zum Ausbau und zur Entwicklung des ungarischen Königreiches beigetragen haben. Dadurch, daß wir die anderen fortwährend in Betracht zogen, daß wir außer den Deutschen von der Leistung der Wallonen, Franzosen, Flamen gesprochen haben, hoffen wir, den gesamteuropäischen Charakter der Entwicklung nicht nur schärfer betont, sondern auch bewiesen zu haben. Und wir glauben fest daran, daß es überall so war, daß die deutsche Ostsiedlung — wo immer sie auch stattfand — ein Teil einer Bewegung war, an der nicht nur Deutsche, sondern alle Völker Europas teilgenommen haben. Stellt die deutsche Geschichtswissenschaft die Ostsiedlung in einen europäischen Rahmen, dann wird sie anstatt einer Reihe von regionalgeschichtlichen Tatsachen und Vorgängen einen festen Zusammenhang finden, der der Ostsiedlung ihren Platz und Rang in der Geschichte unseres Kontinents sichert.

---

112) Paulinyi, Nemesfémgazdaságunk (wie Anm. 103).

DIE ENTSTEHUNG DES STÄDTWESENS IN UNGARN

Im Jahre 1961 an einer Konferenz über ungarische Stadt-geschichte habe ich die Entstehung des Städtewesens in Ungarn zusammenfassend geschildert. Das Referat, das damals als Versuch galt, wurde nur in einem kurzen Auszug veröffentlicht.[1] Sieben Jahre können kaum als eine lange Zeit bezeichnet werden, dennoch wurden während dieser Jahre bedeutende Studien geschrieben und ebenso bedeutende Ausgrabungen vorgenommen, die das von mir entworfene Bild teilweise ergänzten, teilweise berichtigten und die ersten zwei Abschnitte der Geschichte des ungarischen Städtewesens in ein schärferes Licht stellten. Ich sah mich in Einzelheiten zu Änderungen gezwungen, doch nicht in der Konzeption, die ich jetzt — dank den Herausgebern dieser Zeitschrift — auch den ausländischen Lesern zugänglich machen kann.

*

Das Karpathenbecken, das die landnehmenden Ungarn am Ende des 9. Jh. eroberten und als einheitlichen Staat bis zur Schalcht bei Mohács (1526) aufrechterhielten, war zwar geographisch eine geschlossene Einheit, zerfiel aber vom Standpunkt der Geschichte in mehrere Teile, die ihre eigene wirtschaftliche und soziale Entwicklung und auch in Bezug auf die Stadtgeschichte besondere Züge aufzuweisen hatten. Der Nordwesten des Landes gehörte zum Grossmährischen Reich, die östlichen und südlichen Teile waren von Bulgarslaven bewohnt, während in Transdanubien neben den Avaren eine äusserst gemischte Bevölkerung teilweise unter fränkisch—slavischer Herrschaft stand. Siebenbürgen und Transdanubien waren ehemalige Römerprovinzen, über die sich die Wellen der Völkerwanderung erschütteten und so lautet auch in der Geschichte des ungarischen Städtewesens die erste Frage: wieweit darf man heute eine Kontinuität des römischen Lebens überhaupt und des römischen Städtewesens inbesonderen annehmen. Noch vor dreissig Jahren glaubte ein ungarische Historiker A. Pleidell, dass die mittelalterlichen Städte Transdanubiens und ihre *latini* genannten Einwohner das Fortleben der römischen *municipia*, bzw. die Nachkommen der romanisierten Stadtbewohner darstellen.[2] Als Reaktion seiner Studie wurde dann durch lange Zeit jegliche Kontinuität abgewiesen, bis archeologische und sprachwissenschaftliche Ergebnisse die Historiker nicht eines besseren belehrten.[3] Es stellte sich heraus, dass römische Siedlungen äusserst zäh, öftere Verstörungen zu überleben und alles von neuem anzufangen fähig waren. Die II. altchristliche Basilika von Fenékpuszta (neben dem Plattensee) wurde öfters zerstört, doch immer wieder aufgebaut, sogar erweitert und stand noch zur Zeit der ungarischen Landnahme.[4] Das benachbarte Keszthely bewahrte in seinem Namen das durch Slaven übernommene lateinische Wort *castellum*.[5] Es kann heute kaum geleugnet werden, dass in gewissen (besonders in den sümpfigen und bewaldeten, also von den Reiternomaden verschonten) Gebieten Transdanubiens zur Zeit der ungarischen Landnahme eine Bevölkerung vorzufinden war, in der die Reste aller hier durchziehenden Völker, darunter auch spärliche Reste der romanisierten Elemente Pannoniens repräsentiert waren.

Während im Lichte dieser archeologischen Ergebnisse die Frage einer gewissen Kontinuität ziemlich einfach erscheint, ist das Fortleben der romanisierten Elemente in den späteren mittelalterlichen Städten viel komplizierter. Vor allem soll darauf hingewiesen werden, dass ein Weiterleben des römischen städtischen Organismus, des *municipium* auch in Ungarn nicht angenommen werden darf.[6] Die Führer-

[1] Sz, 97, 1962, 398—399.

[2] A. PLEIDELL, A magyar várostörténet első fejezete (Der erste Abschnitt der ungarischen Stadtgeschichte), Sz, 68, 1934, 1—44, 158—200, 276—313.
[3] D. DERCSÉNYI, Újabb régészeti kutatások és a pannóniai kontinuitás kérdése (Neuere archeologische Forschungen und die Kontinuitätsfrage in Pannonien), Sz, 81, 1947, 203—211.; A. RADNÓTI, Pannóniai városok élete a korai feudalizmusban (Das Leben in den pannonischen Städten im Frühfeudalismus), MTA 6, 1954 459—508; GY. SZÉKELY, Les sort des agglomérations Pannoniennes au début du Moyen Age et les origines de l'urbanisme en Hongrie., AUSB, I. 3, 1961, 59—96.
[4] K. SÁGI, Die zweite altchristliche Basilika von Fenékpuszta, A. Ant. Hung., 9, 1961, 397—459
[5] D. PAIS, Keszthely (Der Ortsname Keszthely), MNy, 51, 1955, 97—98.
[6] Cf. F. WITTINGHOFF, Zur Verfassung der spätantiken Stadt, Studien zu den Anfängen des europäischen Städtewesens, Landau-Konstanz, 1958, 11—29.; H. v. PETRIKOVITS, Das Fortleben römischer Städte am Rhein und Donau. Ibid, 63—76.; F. VERCAUTEREN; Die europäischen Städte bis zum 11. Jh. Die Städte Mitteleuropas im 12. und 13. Jh. (red. v. W. Rausch), Linz, 1963, 13—18.; E. HERZOG, Die ottonische Stadt, Berlin 1964, 215—218.

schicht dieser Städte hat sich ebenso nach Italienz zürückgezogen wie in den westlichen Provinzen, mit ihrem Abzug ist nicht nur das staatliche, sondern auch das städtische Gebilde verschwunden. Die Frage der Kontinuität lautet also: ob die dort gebliebenen romanisierten Handwerker und Händler und die in die befestigten Zentren geflüchteten Bauern die Völkerwanderungszeit überleben konnten, und ob sie im stande waren die ursprünglichen Römersiedlungen von Zeit zu Zeit mit anderen Völkerresten ergänzt aufrechtzuerhalten. Die Frage wäre am besten mit Hilfe der Ausgrabungen und Analyse der Gräberfelder zu beantworten. Da jedoch die Forschungen heute noch nicht in der Lage sind diese Aufgabe zu lösen, müssen wir uns auch hinsichtlich der Städte an die Sprachwissenschaft wenden. Ausser Steinamanger (lateinisch in der Römerzeit und im Mittelalter Savaria, ungarisch Szombathely) führen unsere Städte in Transdanubien Namen, die von der lateinischen Benennung keineswegs abgeleitet werden können. Scarabantia hiess im Mittelalter ungarisch Sopron, deutsch Ödenburg,[7] Arrabona ungarisch Győr, deutsch Raab, Solva ungarisch Esztergom, lateinisch Strigonium, deutsch Gran, Acquincum ungarisch Buda, deutsch Ofen, Sopianae ungarisch Pécs, lateinisch Quinqueclesie, deutsch Fünfkirchen. Dies beweist hinreichend, dass von einem Fortleben der römischen *municipia*, sogar der eigentlichen römischen Städte als Siedlungen[8] — ausser Steinamanger — keine Rede sein kann. Andere Erscheinungen lassen aber eine kultische Kontinuität erkennen. Es handelt sich um ein Anknüpfen an die spätrömischen (aus der zweiten Hälfte des 4. Jh. stammenden) Siedlungen der mittelalterlichen Städte. In Savaria blieb der Kult des Hl. Martin von Pannonien erhalten.[9] In Fünfkirchen konnten die Ausgrabungen feststellen, dass im römischen Friedhof einige aus dem 4. Jh. stammende altchristliche Grabkammern im 9. Jh. hergestellt und neu bemalt wurden und dass der spätere Schwerpunkt der Stadt in kirchlicher Hinsicht, die Bischofskirche und der Bischofspalast am Ort des Friedhofs entstand.[10]

Diese Ergebnisse untermauern eine ziemlich unsichere Quelle, die *Conversio Bagoariorum et Carantanorum*, die in Fünfkirchen von einer Kirchenweihung im 9. Jh. berichtet.[11] Dabei wird der Ort als *,,ad Quinque Basilicas"* erwähnt. Offensichtlich handelt es sich auch in diesem Falle von einer kultischen Kontinuität, die nicht als *locus ad Quinque Basilicas*, sondern als *quinque martyrum basilica*, d. h. nicht als eine Ortschaft mit fünf Kirchen, sondern als die Kirche der fünf Pannonischen Märtyrer ausgelegt werden sollte.[12]

Die Fälle von Fünfkirchen und Steinamanger weisen schliesslich auch auf eine gewisse ethnische Kontinuität hin. Diese ethnische Kontinuität besteht jedoch nicht zwischen den mittelalterlichen und den blühenden Römerstädten

Pannoniens (wie dies eben der Namenwechsel Sopianae—Quinque Basilicae beweist), sondern mit jene Siedlungen, die am Ort der Römerstädte auch nach der Räumung Pannoniens fortbestanden und eine romanisierte Bevölkerung beherbergten. Dem entsprechend entstanden die Schwerpunkte der mittelalterlichen Städte nicht in den Zentren der ehemaligen *municipia*, sondern zwischen den an den Ausfallstrassen angelegten Gräber der Märtyrer. Diese Erscheinung entspricht der Entwicklung der Römerstädte am Rhein.[13] Die Bedeutung dieser Kontinuität ist teils wirtschaftlicher Natur, sie übermittelte ein stark provinzialisiertes Handwerk[14] und vielleicht auch eine Agrotechnik, vor allem in Weinbau[15], teils politischer Natur, indem sie in den geographischen Räumen den natürlichen Mittelpunkt bewahrte.

Kann eine Kontinuität mit den spätrömischen ,,Städten" in zwei Fällen nachgewiesen werden, so spielte ein anderer Faktor, den ich als ,,römische Erbschaft" bezeichnet habe,[16] eine weitaus grössere Rolle. Unter diesem Begriff sollen jene römische Strassen und Bauten verstanden werden, die zwar in einem verwahrlosten Zustand, ihrer eigentlichen Bestimmung ungeeignet von den landnehmenden Ungarn in Transdanubien vorgefunden wurden. Die Besiedlung der Landnehmen den wurde im allgemeinen, in den späteren mittelalterlichen Städten aber besonders stark von dieser Erbschaft beeinflusst, ohne jedoch dass es eine ethnische Kontinuität gegeben hätte. Die Begriffsgestaltung scheint umso begründeter, als der um 870 schreibende Verfasser der *Conversio Bagoariorum et Carantanorum* noch bemerkte, dass diese Bauten ,,bis jetzt" zu sehen sind.[17] Ein schönes Beispiel liefert uns das Stadtgebiet vom heutigen Budapest (Abb.1.), an dem im Mittelalter drei Städte entstanden sind: Altofen, Ofen und Pest. Obzwar von einer Kontinuität auch hier nicht die Rede sein kann, lag Altofen, auf dem Gebiet des römischen Acquincum, übernahm das Strassensystem des Legionarlagers,[18] wurde nach dem Osten durch die Ruinen der römischen Wasserleitung,[19] nach dem Süden durch einen römischen Meilenstein[20] abgegrenzt. Das südliche Amphiteatrum, in dem schon die Langobarden hausten,[21] wurde zum Sitz des Fürsten der landnehmenden Ungarn, erhielt von ihm den Namen Kursans Burg.[22] Das Strassennetz der kleinen vorstädtischen Siedlung Felhévíz (zwischen Altofen und Ofen) stellt ebenfalls eine Übernahme der römischen Hauptstrasse dar, liegt am Ort eines römischen Kastells.[23] Am linken Ufer der Donau stand zur Bewachung

[7] K. MOLLAY, Scarbantia, Ödenburg, Sopron. Siedlungsgeschichte und Ortsnamenkunde, AECO, 9—10, 1943—44, 225—226.

[8] In Aquincum das mittelalterliche Ofen an dem Ort des Legionslagers und nicht an der der eigentlichen Stadt entstanden. J. SZILÁGYI, Aquincum, Bp., 1956. vol. I. Abb.

[9] I. PAULOVICS, Savaria-Szombathely topográfiája (Die Topographie von Savaria-Szombathely), Szombathely, 1943; A. T. HORVÁTH, A középkori Szombathely topográfiája (Die Topographie des mittelalterlichen Steinamangers), VSz, 1958, 27.

[10] D. DERCSÉNYI—F. POGÁNY, Pécs (Fünfkirchen), Bp., 1956., 32—38, 58.

[11] GY. PAULER—S. SZILÁGYI, A magyar honfoglalás kútfői (Die Quellen der ungarischen Landnahme), Bp., 1900, 311.

[12] D. SIMONYI, Pécs ,,Quinque ecclesiae" nevének eredetéről (Der Ursprung des Namens ,,Quinque ecclesiae" von Fünfkirchen), AntTan, 6, 1959, 101—103,

[13] E. HERZOG, o. c., 218—219.

[14] Á. Cs. SÓS, *Das frühmittelalterliche Gräberfeld von Keszthely-Fenékpuszta*. A. Arch. Hung., 13, 1961, 247—305.

[15] K. SÁGI—F. M. FÜZES, Régészeti és archeolbotanikai adatok a pannóniai kontinuitás kérdéséhez (Archeologische und archeobotanische Angaben zur Frage der kontinuität in Pannonien) Agrártört. Szemle, 9, 1967, 79—98.

[16] E. FÜGEDI, *Topográfia és városi fejlődés a középkori Óbudán* (Topographie und Stadtentwicklung im mittelalterlichen Altofen), TBM, 13, 1959, 9—10. (des weiteren: FÜGEDI, *Altofen*).

[17] GY. PAULER—S. SZILÁGYI, o. c., 306. ,,Antiquis enim temporibus ex meridiana parte Danubii in plagis Pannoniae inferioris et circa confines regiones Romani possederunt, ipsique ibi civitates et munitiones ad defensionem sui fecerunt, aliaque aedificia multa, sicut adhuc apparet."

[18] J. SZILÁGYI, *Kutatások Aquincumból* (Forschungen in Aquincum), AÉrt, 76, 1949, 73—77.

[19] A. GÁRDONYI, *Óbuda és környéke a középkorban* (Altofen und seine Umgebung im Mittelalter), BpR, 14, 1945, 575—576.

[20] GY. SZÉKELY, o. c., 79.

[21] *Budapest az ókorban* (Budapest im Altertum), Budapest története (Die Geschichte von Budapest), (A. ALFÖLDI, L. NAGY, GY. LÁSZLÓ) I., Bp., 1942, 784.

[22] J. BELITZKY, *Észrevételek Budapest koraközépkori helyrajzához* (Bemerkungen über die frühmittelalterliche Topographie von Budapest), Bp., 1941, 11., GY. GYÖRFFY, *Kurszán és Kurszán vára* (Kursan und Kursans Burg), BpR, 16, 1955, 18.

[23] A. KUBINYI, *Budafelhévíz topográfiája és gazdasági fejlődése* (Topographie und Wirtschaftsentwicklung in Budafelhéviz,) TBM, 16, 1964, 86,

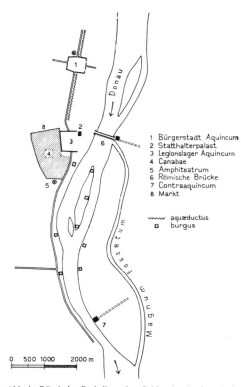

1 Bürgerstadt Aquincum
2 Statthalterpalast
3 Legionslager Aquincum
4 Canabae
5 Amphiteatrum
6 Römische Brücke
7 Contraaquincum
8 Markt

〰〰 aquæductus
▫ burgus

0 500 1000   2000 m

Abb. 1: Römische Besiedlung im Gebiet der Städte Altofen,
Ofen und Pest (nach J. Szilágyi)

Wie die angeführten Beispiele zeigen — ihre Zahl lässt sich
mühelos vermehren[29] — beeinflusste die römische Erbschaft
im weitaus grösseren und bedeutenderen Masse die Besiedlung und auch die Entwicklung der mittelalterlichen Städte,
als die zweifellos bestehende, doch vereinzelte Kontinuität mit den spätrömischen Siedlungen. Dabei möchten wir
nicht verschweigen, dass Savaria keine bedeutende Stadt
während des Mittelalters war, dagegen selbst so bedeutende
Städte wie Stuhlweissenburg überhaupt keine oder nur sehr
bescheidene römische Vorläufer gehabt haben.[30]
    Von einer Kontinuität oder von einer römischen Erb-
schaft kann nur in Transdanubien gesprochen werden, sie
bildeten aber nicht den einzigen Faktor der Stadtentstehung, hier wie in anderen Teilen des Landes waren auch
andere Faktoren tätig. Vor allem muss darauf hingewiesen
werden, dass das Ungarntum trotz der Landnahme und
trotz der damit verbundenen Übersiedlung in das Karpathenbecken weiterhin im Rahmen jenes Wirtschaftskreises
blieb, zu dem es vor der Landnahme angehörte, d. h. zu
jenem ost-, bzw. südosteuropäischen Kreis, dessen Mittelpunkte damals Byzanz und Kiew waren.[31] Dies kam auch
in der Weise zum Ausdruck, in dem das Land gegen den
Westen (selbst nach der Schlacht am Lechfelde, 955) dicht
abgeschlossen wurde.[32] Die Tatsache, dass Ungarn zum
osteuropäischen Wirtschaftskreis angehörte, hatte hinsichtlich des Handels ihre Folgen. Vor fünfzig Jahren wurde vor
von einem regen Transithandel durch Ungarn am Landwege gesprochen, bis dann die Forschungen Domanovszkys
und F. Bastians[33] bewiesen, dass von einem bedeutenden
Transithandel keine Rede sein kann, wenn es überhaupt zur
Weitergabe einiger Handelswaren kam, so erreichte der

der Flussüberfahrt ein römisches Kastell, in das im Laufe
des 9. Jh. mohammedanische Bulgaren angesiedelt wurden,
die erste Kirche entstand im Kastell.[24] Der Archeologe dieser Ausgrabungen nannte es mit Recht den ,,Vorläufer"
der Stadt Pest. Die Beispiele begrenzen sich nicht auf Budapest. Im mittelalterlichen Ödenburg wurden die ursprünglich im 4. Jh. errichteten spätrömischen Mauern als Stadtmauer hergestellt und behalten[25], beeinflussten somit die
topographische Entwicklung der Stadt.[26] Fügen wir hinzu,
dass römische Bauten und Grabsteine willkommenes Rohmaterial lieferten, sie sind in Mengen in den Mauern der
frühen kirchlichten Bauten zu finden[27], ja als der erste König Stephan bestattet wurde, wählte man für ihn einen römisches Sarkophag, das in aller Eile ,,christianisiert" wurde.[28]

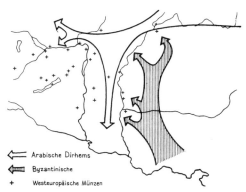

⬅ Arabische Dirhems

⬅ Byzantinische

+ Westeuropäische Münzen

Abb. 2: Fremde Münzfunde aus den 10. Jh. (nach A. Kralovánszky)

[24] L. NAGY, Az Eskü-téri római erőd, Pest város öse (Das Römerkastell am
Eskü Platz, Vorläufer der Stadt Pest), Bp., 1946.
[25] I. HOLL—GY. NOVÁKI—K. Sz. PÓCZY, Városfalmaradványok a
soproni Fabriciusház alatt (Stadtmauerresten unter dem Fabriciushaus in
Ödenburg), AÉrt, 89, 1962, 47—66.; K. Sz. PÓCZY, Sopron rómaikori
emlékei (Die Römerdenkmäler der Stadt Ödenburg), Bp., 1965.
[26] J. MAJOR, A városalapraiz mint a korai magyar városépitéstörténet forrása.
A soproni Belváros kialakulása (Der Stadtgrundriss als Quelle der Stadtgeschichte. Die Entstehung der Ödenburger Innerstadt), Épités- és közleke-
déstudományi közlemények, 1965, 153—174. (des weiteren: MAJOR,
Ödenburger Innerstadt).
[27] I. GENTHON, Magyarország művészeti emlékei (Die Denkmäler Ungarns)
Bp., 1959., 352, 252, 254, usw.
[28] E. NAGY, A székesfehérvári István koporsó keletkezése. (Der Ursprung
des Stuhlweissenburger Stephan-Sarkophages) MüvÉrt, 1954, 101—106.

[29] GY. SZÉKELY, o. c.
[30] A. MAROSI, Volt-e Székesfehérvárott római telep? (Gab es in Stuhlweissenburg eine Römersiedlung?), Sz, 69, 1935, 266—269.; A. KRALO-
VÁNSZKY, Die Entstehung von Stuhlweissenburg auf Grund archeologischer
Angaben, Székesfehérvár évszázadai, 1, 1967, 9.
[31] S. DOMANOVSZKY, A harmincadvám eredete (Der Ursprung des Dreis-
sigstzolls), Ért. a törttud. köréből, XXIV/4, 1916.; N. FETTICH, A levédiai
magyarság a régészet megvilágitásában (Das Ungartum vor der Landnahme
im Lichte der Archeologie), Sz, 67, 1933, 250—276, 369—399.; GY.
LÁSZLÓ, Budapest a népvándorlás korában (Budapest in der Völkerwanderungszeit), Budapest története I., Bp., 1942. 781.
[32] S. DOMANOVSZKY, o. c., 7.
[33] S. DOMANOVSZKY, Die Vergangenheit des ungarischen Donauhandels,
Ungarische Jahrbücher, 2, 1922, 161—187. F. BASTIAN, Die Legende vom
Donauhandel im Frühmittelalter, Vierteljahrschrift f. Soz. u. Wirtschaftsg.
22, 1929, 289.

ungarische Handel mit byzantinischen Waren höchstens Böhmen.[34]

Der Begriff der Stadt war in diesem osteuropäischen Wirtschaftskreis und so dem Ungarntum schon vor der Landnahme bekannt. Im 8—9. Jh. lebten die Ungarn im Rahmen des Kazarenreichs. Aus östlichen (vor allem arabischen) Quellen kennen wir die Hauptstadt des Reiches, das an der Wolga liegende Itil ziemlich gut. Sie stand an den beiden Ufern des Flusses, zerfiel in mehrere Stadtteile, von denen einer den Sitz des Kaganen bildete, war mit einer Mauer umgeben. In der Stadt (die arabischen Quellen bedienen sich dieses Wortes) waren Märkte, Moschees und Bäder zu finden. Die Bevölkerung war nicht nur hinsichtlich ihrer Religion, sondern auch ihrer Beschäftigung nach geteilt. Vom wirtschaftlichen Standpunkt war Itil zweifellos eine Stadt, doch als Sozialgebilde ein nomadischer (asiatischer) Typ derselben, in der die Einwohner den selben Sozialstatus einnahmen wie diejenigen, die nicht Stadtbewohner waren und ein Teil der Einwohner verliess die Stadt im Frühling und kehrte nur im Herbst zurück.[35]

Das landnehmende Ungarntum bestand nicht ausschliesslich aus Reiternomaden, ja ihr Anteil an der gesammten Bevölkerung verminderte sich durch die Landnahme und durch das Unterwerfen der hier lebenden Bevölkerung noch weiter. Die Tendenz wurde immer stärker das westeuropäische, auf Ackerbau fundierte, wir möchten sagen slatische Siedlungsart zu übernehmen. So nimmt es kein Wunder, dass die jüngsten Forschungen schon im 10. Jh. ptanmässige Übersiedlung einiger Volkselemente[36], oder ein Siedlungssystem nachweisen konnten, die auch auf die Entstehung des ungarischen Städtewesens einen Einfluss ausübten.

Es war schon seit geraumer zeit bekannt, dass im 10-12. Jh. die Tätigkeit der Handwerker auch geographisch gebunden war, d. h. dass Hintersassen oder Sklaven die dasselbe Handwerk ausübten in einem Dorf ansässig waren, so z. B. Schmiede, Töpfer, usw. und das Dorf dem entsprechend den Namen des Handwerks führte, z. B. Ács (= Zimmermann), Gerencsér (= Töpfer), usw.[37] Der Zusammenhang zwischen solchen Handwerkersiedlungen und Marktorten rief eine besondere Siedlungsordnung ins Leben. Ein Teil der Marktorte wurde mit dem Namen jenes Wochentages bezeichnet, an dem der Markt stattfand, z. B. Csütörtökhely (= Donnersmarkt). J. Major ist es gelungen festzustellen, dass solche Marktsiedlungen hauptsächlich an der ungarisch-slavischen ethnischen Grenze entstanden, weiterhin, dass in deren unmittelbarer Umgebung immer Handwerkerdörfer und Dörfer die auf mohammedanische oder jüdische Kaufleute hinweisen, gefunden werden können.[38] Als Beispiel soll hier (Abb. 3) ein Gebiet am Rande des Bakony—Gebirges angeführt werden, wo in der Nähe von Szerdahely (=Mittwochmarkt) zwischen Agrarsiedlungen

(Dém, Tamási, Ság) die Handwerkerdörfer Teszér (=Zimmermann), Szücs (=Kürschner), Takácsi (=Weber) und Vaszar (das Wort deutet auf Eisenverarbeitung hin) und ein Szerecseny (d. h. Sarazener) genanntes Dorf zu finden ist. Es handelt sich also um eine Siedlungsgruppe, deren einzelne, ihrem Charakter nach übereinstimmende, jedoch im Aufbau unterschiedliche Elemente sich gegenseitig organisch ergänzten eine lose, doch gewissermassen geschlossene Einheit bildeten.[39] Es ist klar, dass die Bände zwischen Handwerk und Handel schon im 10. Jh. einen tatsächlichen Wirtschaftsfaktor darstellten.

Zu diesen nomadischen Elementen gesellten sich an der Wende des 10/11. Jh. auch neue byzantinische und westeuropäische Faktoren, als das Ungarntum zum Christentum bekehrt, und das Land in ein christlich feudales Königstum umgestaltet wurde.[40] Bischofsitze wurden eingerichtet, Kirchen, Schulen und andere kirchliche Gebäude gebaut, mit den nötigen ausgestattet, eine neue Gruppe, die Kleriker erschienen und all dies bedeutete eine Steigerung des Bedarfs an Agrar- und Handwerksprodukten. Die weltliche Organisation ging Hand in Hand mit der kirchlichen. Es entstanden Komitatszentren, in denen der Gespann mit seiner Gefolgschaft residierte, wo Vorräte an Agrarprodukten angehäuft wurden. Kirchliche und weltliche Organisation wählten regelmässig denselben Ort zu ihrem Sitz, dadurch wurde die Wirkung noch gesteigert.

Die ungarischen Wörter, mit denen diese den Landnehmenden vollkommen fremde Institutionen bezeichnet wurden, sind grösstenteils slavische Lehnwörter, woraus eine

[34] B. HÓMAN, Adalék X—XI. századi pénztörténetünkhöz (Ein Beitrag zur Gelegeschichte des 11—12. Jh.), Sz, 52, 1918, 161—167. Ibrahim ibn Jakub traf in Prag Mohammedaner, Juden und Ungarn aus Ungarn.
[35] Auf Grund der Berichte von Ibn Rosteh (GY. PAULER—S. SZILÁGYI, o. c., 154—155.) und Ibn Fadhlan (ibid. 212—219.) über die Entwicklung der Stadt schrieb Hóman ausführlich, cf. B. HÓMAN—GY. SZEKFÜ, Magyar történet, Bp., 1939[6], I, 62—64.
[36] GY. GYÖRFFY, Tanulmányok a magyar állam eredetéről (Studien über die Enstehung des ungarischen Staates), Bp., 1959. 27.
[37] Die neueste Zusammenfassung gab G. Heckenast in seinem Referat an der 1968. agbehaltenen ungarisch-französischen wirtschaftsgeschichtlichen Konferenz.
[38] J. MAJOR, A magyar városok és városhálózat kialakulásának kezdetei (Die Städte Ungarns und die Anfänge des Stadtnetzes), Településtud. Közl., 18, 1966, 48—69. (des weiteren: MAJOR, Anfänge)

[39] Ibid., 48.
[40] Obzwar sich Stephan I. an Rom anschloss hatte er auch byzantinische Elemente in der kirchlichen Organisation aufgenommen ganz abgesehen von der früheren byzantinischen Missionstätigkeit und ihren Folgen. Vgl. GY. MORAVCSIK, Görögnyelvü kolostorok Szt. István korában (Griechische Kloster zur Zeit des Hl. Stephans), Szt. István Emlékkönyv, Bp, 1938, I., 390—422.

o Agrarsiedlungen
● Handwerkersiedlungen
◼ Marktort
◻ Dorf der Sarazener

Abb. 3: Siedlungen um einen Marktort (nach J. Major).

Gruppe der ungarischen Historiker[41] auf einen starken slavischen Einfluss schloss. Auch die Ortsnamen einiger frühen Städte sind slavischen Ursprungs (vielleicht auch Pécs[42]). Wahrscheinlich war dies der Grund, der E. Molnár dazu bewog die Entstehung des Städtewesens in Ungarn auf ein slavisches Städtewesen zurückzuführen.[43] Die archeologischen Ausgrabungen konnten jedoch nirgends slavische Funde ans Tageslicht fördern, die ungarische Bezeichnungen für Stadt (város), Markt (vásár) und Bürger (polgár) sind keine slavischen Lehnwörter. Unsere schriftlichen Quellen schweigen ebenfalls über slavische Siedlungen, die einen städtischen Charakter haben konnten. In der Sowjetunion, in Polen und auch in Mähren wurden mit dem Spaten frühmittelalterliche Städte freigelegt, doch in der heutigen Slovakei kam nichts ähnliches zum Vorschein. Wir wissen zwar, dass in Svatopluks Hauptstadt monatlich dreitägige Märkte abgehalten wurden,[44] wissen aber nicht wo dieser Sitz zu suchen ist. Eine Übernahme des Städtewesens von den Slaven ist vollkommen unbegründet. Der slavische Beitrag zur Entstehung des Städtewesens in Ungarn muss in der Förderung des Warenaustausches zwischen Slaven und Ungarn, im Aufrechterhalten römischer Siedlungselemente, nicht aber in einem bestehenden Städtewesen zur Zeit der ungarischen Landnahme gesucht werden.

Die hier angeführten Faktoren, einerseits das nomadische Städtewesen und der damit verbundene Handel und Handwerk, die im Lande vorgefundene römische Erbschaft, andererseits die neue weltliche und kirchliche Organisation liessen in Ungarn im 11—12. Jh. Siedlungen entstehen, die wir für Städte asiatischen (nomadischen) Typs halten.[45] Unsere ersten Zeugen sind arabische Schriftsteller. Idrisi, der seine Geographie über Ungarn auf Grund von Fernhändlern erhaltenen Informationen verfasste, schrieb über mehrere Städte Ungarns, rühmte deren Märkte, an denen besonders grosse Mengen von Agrarprodukten zu einem billigen Preis feilgeboten wurden.[46] Sein Zeitgenosse, Abu Hamid, der zwischen 1150—1153 in Ungarn weilte, verglich mit offensichtlich übertriebenen Enthusiasmus die ungarischen Städte mit Bagdad und Isfahan.[47] Diese Quellen wären schon an sich genügend um die Existenz der Städte in diesem Zeitalter als bewiesen hinzunehmen, wenn wir aber diese Informationen mit den einheimischen Quellen ergänzen, können wir die ersten Städte des Landes etwas eingehender kennen lernen.

Die erste Tatsache, auf welche wir hinweisen wollen ist der Wortgebrauch unserer einheimischen Quellen. Sie nennen diese Siedlungen im 11. Jh. urbs oder civitas, im 12.

Jh. civitas oder castrum.[48] Man könnte dagegen einwenden, dass diese Bezeichnungen auch den Sinn 'Burg', in der frühen ungarischen Terminologie sogar den Sinn ‚Komitat' (von der Burg als Zentrum abgeleitet) haben. Dagegen spricht aber, dass das ungarische Wort Stadt (= város) ebenfalls von dem Ausdruck ‚Burg' (= vár) stammt. Und wenn Stuhlweissenburg in der von Bischof Hartwick geschriebenen Legende des Hl. Stephans[49] und ebenso auf dem Krönungsmantel[50] civitas genannt wird, so dann schliesst Hartwicks Herkunft[51] und die Tatsache, dass der Krönungsmantel ein Geschenk der Königin Gisella für die Basilika, Stuhlweissenburg aber kein Bischofsitz war, jeden Zweifel aus. Die Königin und der deutsche Hartwick meinten Stadt und schrieben den im lateinischen korrekter Weise civitas.

Aus der Natur unserer spärlichen und wortkargen Quellen folgt, dass wir hinsichtlich der Wirtschaft am besten über den Handel unterrichtet sind. Aussen- und Binnenhandel können zwar in diesem Zeitalter nicht von einander getrennt werden, jedoch steht es fest, dass zu dieser Zeit der Warenaustausch an den Wochenmärkten abgewickelt wurde. Aus den aus neu gegründeten kirchlichen Institutionen erlassenen königlichen Urkunden und aus den frühen Gesetzen ist es klar, dass das Marktrecht auch in Ungarn ein Regalerecht war[52] und dass schon in der ersten Hälfte des 11. Jh. Marktzinse (meistens nur teilweise) den Abteien überlassen wurden, so z. B. in Neutra (Nitra, Nyitra)[53] oder in Somogyvár.[54] Die Analyse dieser Urkunden wies auch darauf hin, dass in allen Komitatszentren regelmässig Wochenmärkte abgehalten wurden.[55] Binnenhandel mit Agrar- und Handwerksprodukten und Aussenhandel mit orientalischen und byzantinischen Luxuswaren wurden an ein und demselben Markt abgewickelt. Wir besitzen Angaben über russische Händler die mit ihren Rauchwaren in Gran erschienen,[56] über jüdische Kaufleute, die von Russland nach Regensburg fuhren,[57] über byzantinische Kaufleute[58] und über Münzfunde, die nur im Aussenhandel angehäuft werden konnten.[59] Die Träger des Handels waren grösstenteils Mohammedaner, Juden und Griechen. In Pest, dessen Marktzins schon 1055 erwähnt wird,[60] sassen bis zum Anfang des 13. Jh. Sarazener,[61] Abu Hamid be-

[41] E. MOLNÁR, A magyar társadalom története az őskortól az Árpádkorig Die Geschichte der ungarischen Gesellschaft von der Urzeit bis zu den Zeiten der Arpaden), Bp., 1949, 170—174.; Cf. J. KNIEZSA, A magyar állami és jogi terminologia eredete (Der Ursprung der ungarischen staatlichen und rechtlichen Terminologie), MTA nyelv- és irodalomtudományi osztályának közleményei, 1955, 237—266.
[42] J. MELICH, A honfoglaláskori Magyarország (Ungarn zur Zeit der Landnahme), Bp., 1925—1929, 413.
[43] MOLNÁR, o. c., 242.; Cf. E. FÜGEDI, Középkori magyar városprivilégiumok (Ungarische Stadt privilegien des Mittelalters), TBM, 14, 1961, Anm. 20. (des weiteren: FÜGEDI, Stadtprivilegien)
[44] GY. PAULER—S. SZILÁGYI, o. c. 179.
[45] Molnár sah im Székely namens diese Siedlungen „Marktflecken". Cf. FÜGEDI, Stadtprivilegien, Anm. 39. Diese Terminologie ist irreführend, da in Ungarn üblicherweise die jetzigen Siedlungen als Marktflecken bezeichnet werden die vom 14. Jh. an entstanden.
[46] T. LEWICKI, Polska i kraje sąsednie w świetle „Księgi Rogera" geographa arabskiego z XII w. Al Idrisiego (Polen und seine Nachbarländer in dem „Buch des Rogers" vom arabischen Geographen Al Idrisi aus dem XII. Jh.), Prace Komisji Orientalistycznej 34., Kraków, 1945, 219. Es wird über folgende Städte berichtet: Bács, Ödenburg, Keve, Barancs und Neutra, andere werden nur erwänt, z. B. Francavilla, usw.
[47] J. HRBEK, Ein arabischer Bericht über Ungarn, Acta Orientalia, 5, 1955, 20.

[48] F. A. GOMBOS, Catalogus fontium historiae Hungariae aevo ducum et regum ex stirpe Arpad descendentium, Budapestini, 1937, 2433, 2424, 2431, 2587. 2593, 2604.
[49] „in ipsa regalis sedis civitate Alba" Scriptores Rerum Hungaricarum (ed. E. Szentpétery) Bp., 1938, 417. (des weiteren: SRH)
[50] Die Anschrift lautet: „Anno Incarnationis Christi MXXXI Indictione XIII a Stephano rege et Gisla regina casula haec operata et data ecclesiae sanctae Mariae sitae in civitate Alba"
[51] Abt von Hersfeld (1072), später im Investitursreit Erzbischof von Magdeburg, da er dieser Würde nach drei Jahren ablegen musste, kam er nach Ungarn, wo er Bischof von Raab wurde. Als solcher schenkte er den neuem Bistum in Agram der Agenda pontificalis, in der er auch das „civitas" nennt. Vgl. Z. TÓTH, A Hartvik legenda kritikájához (Zur Kritik der Hartwick Legende), Bp. 1942. 114-122.; L. CSÓKA, Arrabona, 6, 1964, 266—268.
[52] FÜGEDI, Stadtprivilegien, 29.
[53] Ibid. 30.
[54] A pannonhalmi Szt. Benedek rend története (Geschichte der Benediktinerordens von Pannonhalma). Des weiteren: PRT) X. 493.
[55] FÜGEDI, Stadtprivilegien, 31—32.
[56] DOMANOVSZKY, A harmincadvám ..., 33.
[57] S. KOHN, A zsidók története Magyarországon (Die Geschichte der Juden in Ungarn), Bp., 1884, 59—60, 406—407.
[58] GY. PAULER, A magyar nemzet története az Árpád házi királyok korában (Die Geschichte der ungarischen Nation unter der Regierungszeit der Arpaden), Bp., 1900², I, 235.; Ungarische Kaufleute in Byzanz werden von Benjamin von Tudela erwähnt vgl. W. HEYD, Geschichte des Levantehandels im Mittelalter, Stuttgart, 1879, I, 274.
[59] A. KERÉNYI, Egy XII, századi óbudai bizánci pénzlelet (Ein byzantinischer Münzfund aus Altofen aus dem 12. Jh.), BpR, 15, 1930, 541—548.; F. KIRÁLY, XII. századi pénzek Magyarországon (Münzen aus dem 12. Jh. in Ungarn), Fol. Arch. 7, 1955, 127—140.; I. MÉRI, Árpádkori pénzváltómérleg (Eine Geldwage aus der Arpadenzeit), Fol. Arch, 6, 1954, 106, 210.
[60] PRT X, 429—430.
[61] L. NAGY, Pest város eredete (TBM, 3, 1934, 1—12.)

richtet über eine zahlreiche mohammedanische Bevölkerung.[62] Die Gesetze König Ladislaus I. (1077—1095) und Kolomanns (1095—1116) befassten sich öfters mit den Märkten. Die Gesetze Ladislaus erwähnen den Händler, der mit seinen Waren von einer Stadt zur anderen, oder von einem Komitat ins andere wandert.[63] Kolomann schuf Regeln für die Abschliessung der Geschäfte, die — hauptsächlich zwischen christlichen und jüdischen Kaufleuten — mit Hilfe der sog. *chartula sigillata* stattfinden sollten.[64]

Über das Handwerk in den Städten besitzen wir nur spärliche Angaben. Dennoch wissen wir, dass in Gran Münzen geprägt wurden[65], und dass ein Teil der späteren Stadt die Siedlung der Schmiede war,[66] deren Schmelzofen durch Ausgrabungen festgestellt wurde.[67] Es ist sicher, dass nach der Schlacht am Lechfelde (955) das ungarische Handwerk, vor allem die Silberschmiede nach Südrussland und vielleicht auch nach Böhmen Schmuckstücke exportierten.[58] Bis die archeologische Forschung diese Frage nicht eingehender untersucht und dadurch unsere Kenntnisse nicht erweitert, sind wir geneigt anzunehmen, dass in den frühen Städten nomadischen Typs der Handel im Vordergrund stand, während das Handwerk am Lande verteilt und nur über den Markt unmittelbar mit der Stadt verbunden war.

Die wirtschaftlichen Merkmale bestimmten gewissermassen die Sozialstruktur der Städte. Auf der einen Seite mohammedanische, (seit der Regierung Kolomans auf die Bischofsitze beschränkte[69]) jüdische Kaufleute, Wandlerhändler, Handwerker, auf der anderen Seite der Gespan und seine Gefolgschaft, der Bischof mit seinen Klerikern und Hörigen. Ein buntes Durcheinander von Einwohnern, die in der Hierarchie der mittelalterlichen Gesellschaft die entgegengesetzte Polen einnahmen, von mächtigen Herren und armen Leuten, sogar Sklaven und zwischen ihnen alles mögliche.

Haben Wirtschaft und weltliche, bzw. kirchliche Organisation den Stadtcharakter bestimmt, so hatte hier auch die Siedlungsart ihr Wort zu sprechen. Auf Grund der wenigen Stadtpläne, die wir aus dieser Zeit kennen, treten zwei Grundtypen vor: 1. eine Burg mit einer Vorstadt, 2. eine auf grösserem Gebiet entstandene Gruppe von Ortschaften. Zum ersten Typ gehören Raab, Neutra[70] und Waitzen (Vác)[71], die eigentlich auf kleineren Hügeln gebaute Fluchtburgen waren. In der Burg selbst — je nach dem Ausmass der ummauerten Fläche — wurden die Kathedrale, der Bischofspalast und das Haus der Domherren untergebracht (Waitzen, Neutra), während der übrige Teil der Bevölkerung unter dieser Burg in einer kleinen Vorstadt sich ansiedelte. War die ummauerte Fläche grösser,

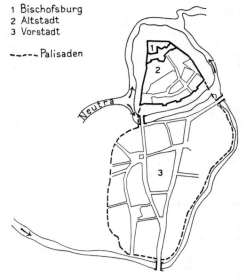

1 Bischofsburg
2 Altstadt
3 Vorstadt

----- Palisaden

Abb. 4: Neutra (nach V. Mencl)

wie z. B. in Raab[72], dann wohnten auch die „zivilen" Einwohner dort. Der Markt nahm in diesen Fällen den Platz vor dem Burgtor ein.[73] Der Grund dafür war, dass einerseits der Markt schon aus Sicherheitsgründen nicht in der Burg abgehalten werden konnte, andererseits konnte vor dem Burgtor noch hinreichender Schutz gewährt werden.

Zwei Städte bilden einen Übergang zwischen diesen ersten und zweiten Typ, u. zw. Stuhlweissenburg und Gran. In Stuhlweissenburg war die Lage am Anfang des 11. Jh. wahrscheinlich dieselbe wie in den Städten, die zum ersten Typ gehören. Es ist anzunehmen, dass die erste kleine Festung, also der Fürstensitz sich auf den kleinen Hügel erstreckte, an dem die Petrikirche (in der Fürst Géza begraben war) stand.[74] Den Markplatz finden wir vor diesem Hügel. Als aber an der Wende des 10/11. Jh. auf der Westseite des Marktplatzes der Königspalast, später zwischen 1011—1038 an der Ostseite die Basilika erbaut wurde, musste die ursprungliche Vorstadt mit einer Mauer umzingelt werden, wodurch der Marktplatz zum Mittelpunkt der späteren, „Burg" genannten Inneren Stadt geworden ist. Die Tatsache, dass die Basilika und der Königspalast ein Areal von ungefähr gleicher Grösse einnahmen[75] und dass der Markplatz aus in der N-S Achse der Stadt im Mittelpunkt steht,[76] beweist eine planmässige Erweiterung.

Einen anderen Übergang zwischen den zwei Typen stellt

[62] E. HRBEK, *o. c.*, 20.
[63] „De negotiatoribus euntibus de civitate in civitatem". Da das Wort civitas sogleich Burg (Stadt), als auch Komitat bezeichnet, ist eine zweifache Übersetzung möglich.
[64] B. L. KUMOROVITZ, *A Kálmán kori „chartula sigillata"* (Die „chartula sigillata" aus Kolomans Regierungszeit), Turul, 57—60, 1944—46, 29—33.
[65] B. HÓMAN, *Magyar pénztörténet* (Ungarische Münzengeschichte), Bp., 1916, 547.
[66] L. ZOLNAY, *Pénzverők és ötvösök a románkori Esztergomban* (Münzer und Schieden im frühmittelalterlichen Gran), AÉrt, 92, 1965, 148—161.
[67] *Ibid.*, 156—159.
[68] B. SZŐKE, *A bjelobrdoi kultúráról* (Über die Kultur von Bjelobrdo), AÉrt, 87, 1960, 44—45.; I. ERDÉLYI, *A honfoglaló magyarság régészeti emlékanyaga keleteurópai kapcsolatainak néhány kérdéséről* (Über einige Fragen des Verhältnisses zwischen den archeologischen Denkmälern der landnehmenden Ungarn und Osteuropa), AÉrt, 87, 1960, 172—173.
[69] Kolomans 75. Gesetzartikel.
[70] V. MENCL, *Stredoveké mestá na Slovensku* (Mittelalterliche Städte in der Slovakei), Bratislava, 1938, 57—60.
[71] D. DERCSÉNYI, *Vác*, Bp. 1960, 20—21.

[72] V. BORBIRÓ—I. VALLÓ, *Györ városépítéstörténete* (Die Stadtbaugeschichte von Raab), Bp, 1956, 42—43.
[73] *Ibid.*, 74—76.; Dass der Marktplatz auch in Neutra ausser der Burg lag geht daraus hervor, dass 1248 König Béla IV. die Genehmigung erteilte den Markt in „ipso casto" abzuhalten. G. FEJÉR, *Codex diplomaticus Hungariae ecclesiasticus ac civilis*, IV/2.455, irrtümlich unter dem Datum 1258! (die unten) CD.)
[74] E. FÜGEDI, *Der Standtplan von Stuhlweissenburg und die Anfänge des Bürgertums in Ungarn*, A. Hist. Hung., 15, 1968, 114.
[75] A. KRALOVÁNSZKY, *Székesfehérvár X—XI. századi településtörténeti kérdése* (Siedlungsgeschichtliche Fragen der Stadtweissenburg aus den 10—11. Jahrhundert), Székesfehérvár évszázadai, 1, 1967, 60. und Abb. 5.
[76] Für diese Angabe bin ich Herren J. M a j o r zum Dank verpflichtet.

1 Wiener Tor
2 Hatvaner Tor
3 Michaeliskirche
4 Hafentor
5 Jakobikirche

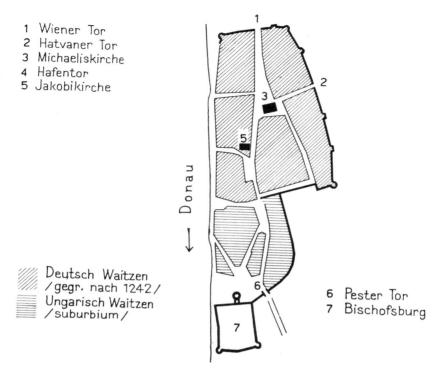

Deutsch Waitzen
/gegr. nach 1242/
Ungarisch Waitzen
/suburbium/

6 Pester Tor
7 Bischofsburg

Abb. 5: Waitzen (nach D. Dercsényi)

Gran dar. An einem hochragenden Hügel an der Donau stand hier das von Slaven benützte Römerkastell Selva, das am Ende des 10. Jh. zum Sitz des Landesfürsten und einige Jahre später auch zum Sitz des Primas von Ungarn, des Erzbischofs von Gran wurde.[77] Südlich von der Burg durch Warmbäder getrennt, neben einer bedeutenden Donauüberfahrt befand sich ein königlicher Wohnturm zur Überwachung der Überfahrt.[78] Neben diesem Turm entwickelte sich der Marktplatz, der — der oben beschriebenen Siedlungsordnung entsprechend — von verschiedenen kleinen Siedlungen umgeben war. Die königlichen Hintersassen, die Hörige des Domkapitels, die Schmiede und die Münzer hatten alle ihre besondere Siedlungen. Die Tatsache, dass ausser der mittelalterlichen Stadtmauern ein jüdischer Friedhof entdeckt wurde[79] und der Ortsname örmény (= Armenier) deuten auf orientalische Kauf- und Finanzleute hin. Im 12. Jh. gesellten sich zu diesen Elementen die *latini* genannte Kaufleute, die ebenfalls abgesondert angesiedelt wurden und eine Kaufmannskolonie mit einer selbständigen Nikolaikirche bildeten. Der Schwerpunkt

dieser Siedlungen lag vom Anfang an am Marktplatz, Wenn wir von der Graner Burg absehen, so erscheint Gran als eine Gruppe kleiner Ortschaften um einen Marktplatz, stellt also dieselbe Siedlungsordnung dar, die von J. Major bestimmt wurde.[80]

Den zweiten Typ bilden jene Städte, wo ähnliche Verhältnisse ohne einer Burg nachweisbar sind. Soweit wir heute wissen, gehörte Altofen mit der Siedlung der Schmiede und einer Agrarsiedlung bis zur Mitte des 12. Jh. zu diesem zweiten Typ.[81] In Fünfkirchen können ähnliche Verhältnisse festgestellt werden. Während im NW, an der Stelle des römischen Gräberfeldes die Kathedrale mit dem Bischofspalast entstand, entwickelte sich eine andere Ortschaft im NO, an den Abhängen des Berge (im Rebenland?) um die Allerheiligenkirche. Nicht weit davon entfernt stand neben einem Bach eine Hadwerkersiedlung, die auch noch später den Namen Malomszeg (= Mühlen [Wasserrad] weiler) führte. Den Mittelpunkt dieser mit einander nicht zusammenhängenden Ortschaften bildete (wenigstens topographisch) auch hier der Marktplatz, der sich um eine Bartholomaeikirche festsetzte. Im Laufe des 12. Jh. wurde dann die Kathedrale und der Bischofspalast mit einer eigenen Mauer umgeben, schied dadurch aus der losen Gruppe

[77] Auch Grans ungarischer, bzw. lateinischer Namen wurde von E. MOLNÁR (*o. c.*, 242.) aus dem slavischen abgeleitet. Nach den sprachwissenschaftlichen Forschungen (E. MELICH, *o. c.*, 413.) stammt der Namen tatsächlich aus einem slavischen Persönnamen Strigon, jedoch — da er ohne jedglichhem Suffix angewendet wurde — entspricht die Bildung den Regeln der ungarischen Sprache. Bis jetzt konnten auch keine slavischen archeologischen Belege gefunden werden.
[78] D. DERCSÉNYI—L. ZOLNAY, *Esztergom*, Bp., 1956, 10—12.
[79] *Ibid.*, 13—14.; K. SCHÜNEMANN, *o. c.*, 63—64.

[80] MAJOR, *Anfänge*, 78.
[81] *Ibid.* 76.

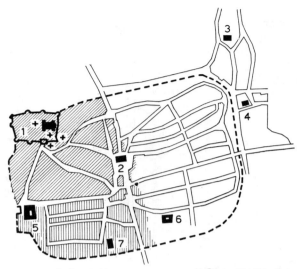

1 Bischofsburg   4 Augustiner   7 Benediktikirche
2 Bartholomaeikirche   5 Franziskaner
3 Allerheiligenkirche   6 Dominikaner   + Altchristliche Grüfte

‖‖‖‖‖‖ Gebiet der Römerstadt   ▨▨▨▨ Gebiet des römischen Friedhofs

Abb. 6: Fünfkirchen (nach Gy. Györffy und F. Fülep)

der Siedlungen aus und wandelte die Stadt in ein Gebilde um, das jenem in Gran ähnlich war.[82]

Zwei Entwicklungszüge sind aus diesen Stadtplänen klar. Der erste, dass durch die kirchliche Organisation in diesem ursprünglichen Nomadenstädten jenes Element erschien, dass seit Rietschel als *civitas* bezeichnet, den kirchlichen und weltlichen Regierungszentrum repräsentierte und ein Mitglied des Dualismus im Stadtwerden darstellte.[83] Soweit wäre die ungarische Entwicklung der westeuropäischen ähnlich, doch fehlt es nicht an abweichenden Zügen. Die *civitas* wurde in Ungarn nur dort topographisch von den übrigen Siedlungselementen abgesondert, wo dazu die geographischen Vorbedingungen gegeben waren (Gran, Neutra, Waitzen und Stuhlweissenburg), obzwar später (wie es der Fall von Fünfkirchen und Grosswardein (Oradea Mare, Nagyvárad) zeigen[84]) die kirchlichen Behörden dazu neigten ihre Immunität durch eine besondere Mauer zu betonen. Die zweite ungarische Besonderheit besteht darin, dass nur Bischofsitze und königliche Stifte in einer Stadt die *civitas* bildeten, monastische Abteien wurden nie zum Zentrum des Stadtwerdens, spielten auch in der Entwicklung des Städtewesens keine Rolle. Bei den grossen und sehr früh gegründeten Benediktinerabteien (z. B. Pannonhalma, Tihany, usw.) entstanden keine Städte. Hingegen

spielten in Altofen, in Grosswardein, Neutra und später in Stuhlweissenburg die Stifte als Stadtzentren eine bedeutende Rolle. Eine andere, ausschliesslich topographische Charakteristik besteht darin, dass in den Städten zweiten Typs nicht eine, fest abgegrenzte, zusammenhängende Vorstadt, sondern mehrere kleine, voneinander getrennte Ortschaften vorhanden waren, die sich später — je nach den geographischen und rechtlichen Verhältnissen — zu einer einzigen Vorstadt oder zu mehreren Vorstädten zusammenballten, u. zw. meistens um den Marktplatz, der den Mittelpunkt der so entstandenen Stadt bildete.[85]

Wenn wir nun die vorangehend geschilderten Merkmale ins Auge fassen, wird es uns klar, dass die durch die arabischen und einheimischen Quellen als Städte bezeichnete Siedlungen in wirtschaftlicher und topographischer Hinsicht tatsächlich als Städte angesehen werden dürfen. Wir sprachen von einem nomadischen Typ der Städte und diese Charakteristik kam teilweise im topographischen Aufbau der Städte zum Ausdruck. Es gibt aber noch ein negatives Merkmal, das den nomadischen Charakter vielleicht noch besser erkennen lässt und das sind die Rechts- und Eigentumsverhältnisse. Alle diese Städte waren im königlichen Besitz und dem königlichen Beamten, dem Komitatsgespan unterworfen. Im 11. Jh. besass die Kirche nur diejeni-

[82] D. DERCSÉNYI – F. POGÁNY, *o. c.*, 33–36.
[83] S. RIETSCHEL, *Markt und Stadt in ihrem rechtlichen Verhältnis*, Leipzig, 1897.
[84] D. DERCSÉNYI – F. POGÁNY – Z. SZENTKIRÁLYI Pécs [Fünfkirchen] Bp. 1966. 28.; GY. GYÖRFFY, *Az Árpád-kori Magyarország történeti földrajza.* (Die historische Geographie Ungarn während der Zeit der Arpaden), Bp, 1963, 687. (des weiteren: GYÖRFFY).

[85] Eine einzige Vorstadt bildeten die 1271 verschmolzenen Ortschaften in Raab (V. BORBIRÓ – I. VALLÓ, *o. c.*, 42–43.), Neutra (V. MENCL, *o. c.*, 57–60.), mehrere Vorstädten entwickelten sich in Stuhlweissenburg (FÜGEDI, *Stuhlweissenburg*), Grosswardein (GYÖRFFY, 687.) Fünfkirchen (*ibid.*, 361.)

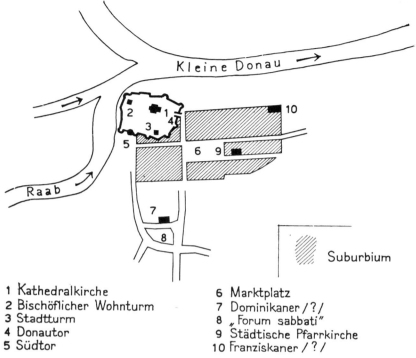

Suburbium

1 Kathedralkirche
2 Bischöflicher Wohnturm
3 Stadtturm
4 Donautor
5 Südtor

6 Marktplatz
7 Dominikaner / ? /
8 „Forum sabbati"
9 Städtische Pfarrkirche
10 Franziskaner / ? /

Abb. 7: Raab (nach V. Borbíró und I. Valló)

gen Grundstücke in den Städten, an denen ihre eigene Gebäuden standen und hatte einen Anteil am Marktzinse, das ebenso zehntenpflichtig war, wie alle übrigen Einnahmen. Aber am Markt walteten Königsrichter und königliche Beamten, sie trieben auch die Marktzins ein.[86] Nirgends sind auch nur die leisesten Spuren irgendeiner Autonomie der Stadtbewohner zu entdecken. Welchen Sozialstatus sie auch eingenommen haben, sie waren königliche Untertanen. Das Fehlen jeglicher Keime einer städtischen Selbstverwaltung gehörte ebenfalls zur nomadischen Charakteristik der Städte.

Überblicken wir jetzt noch zum Abschluss des ersten Abschnittes in der ungarischen Stadtgeschichte die geographische Verteilung dieser Städte nomadischen Typs, so ist es äusserst auffallend, dass sie in überwiegender Mehrheit in Transdanubien zu finden sind. Diese Tatsache kommt schon bei der Verteilung der Bischofsitze zum Ausdruck. Im ganzen Lande wurden von König Stephan I. ingesamt zehn Diözesen gegründet, seine Nachfolger erweiterten ihre Zahl auf elf. Von diesen befinden sich vier in Transdanubien. Dazu kommt noch Stuhlweissenburg und Altofen damit ergeben sich sechs Städte in diesem kleineren Teil des Landes, während im weitaus grösseren Teil nur sechs Bischofsitze, eine Stadt mit einem griechischen Metropolitensitz (Bács) und eine Stadt ohne jeglicher höheren

⁶ FÜGEDI, *Stadtprivilegien*, 29–30.

kirchlichen Institution (Pest) zu finden sind. Dabei lagen sechs dieser Städte an der Donau und zwei von ihnen (Altofen und Pest) von einander kaum entfernt, eher durch den Fluss getrennt dort, wo sich der wichtigste Übergang der Donau befand. Unsere historisch-demographische Forschungen sind heute noch nicht soweit, dass wir diese Verteilung mit der Verteilung der Bevölkerungsdichte erklären könnten, so müssen wir uns damit begnügen zu behaupten, dass diese Verteilung der wirtschaftlichen Bedeutung und Tragfähigkeit Transdanubiens entsprach.

*

In der zweiten Hälfte des 12. Jh. kam es in Ungarn zu grundlegenden Wandlungen sowohl im sozialen, als auch im Wirtschaftsleben, in deren Laufe sich das Land vom osteuropäischen Wirtschaftskreis loslöste und sich dem westeuropäischen anschloss. Noch vor einer Generation vertrat die ungarische Geschichtswissenschaft den Standpunkt, dass diese Wandlungen in erster Reihe durch die Eroberung von Byzanz im vierten Kreuzzug (1204) und durch Kiews Zerstörung durch die Mongolen (1240) eingetreten waren. Heute sind wir der Ansicht, dass die Ursachen vor allem in der inneren Entwicklung des Landes zu suchen sind und eben deswegen muss der Anfang der Wandlungen auf einen früheren Zeitpunkt gesetzt werden. Ungarn war schon

von Raab und Gran

von Ofen

von Veszprém

von Fünfkirchen und Keszthely

1 Basilika
2 Petri - Kirche
3 Marktplatz
4 Königlicher Palast
5 Palotaer Tor
6 Ofner Tor
7 Nikolai - Kirche in der Ofner Vorstadt
8 Johanniter

Abb. 8: Székesfehérvár (nach A. Kralovánszky)

immer ein an Edelmetallen reiches Land, im 9. Jh. wurden in Südrussland ausser Pferden Silber von Ungarn angeboten.[87] Im Laufe des 12. Jh. — so berichtet uns wieder einmal Abu Hamid — wurde auch Gold entdeckt. Das Land war — den damaligen westeuropäischen Verhältnissen gemessen — dünn besiedelt, weite Gebiete fruchtbaren Bodens waren Mangels an Arbeitskraft unbebaut geblieben. Das Gold lockte die Kaufleute, der Boden die Bauern Westeuropas. In den Kreuzzügen bot sich die Gelegenheit das Land kennen zu lernen, zur selben Zeit öffnete der ungarische König die Landesgrenzen und nahm Siedler in das Land auf.

Indessen haben sich auch die inneren Verhältnisse völlig geändert. Die Hauptbeschäftigung der Bevölkerung ist der Ackerbau geworden, der dem Nomadisieren ein Ende bereitete. Das Siedlungswesen näherte sich dem statischen westeuropäischen an.[88] Die königlichen Schenkungen riefen kirchlichen Grossgrundbesitz ins Leben. Die Handwerkersiedlungen begannen sich aufzulösen. Dieser Wandel machte sich auch im Finanzleben des Landes fühlbar. Der ungeheure Grundbesitz des Königs war zusammengeschmolzen, die Einnahmen mussten auf die Steuer und Ausnützung der Regalerechte umgestellt werden, wodurch wieder der Geldverkehr gefördert wurde. Die Pächter der königlichen Einnahmen praktizierten aber eine Geldverschlechterung und so wurden einerseits Friesacher Denare in grossen Mengen ins Land gebracht und später hier nach-

geprägt.[89] Die an Macht zunehmenden und mit dem neuen Wirtschaftssystem unzufriedenen geistlichen Grossgrundbesitzer setzten die Ausschaltung der mohammedanischen und jüdischen Finanzleute, an denen die königliche Einnahmen verpachtet waren, durch. Die Reformern König Andreas II. (1205—1235) wurden zwar von seinem Sohn Béla IV. (1235—1270) zeitweilig rückgängig gemacht, doch der Einfall der Tataren (1241) zwang ihn einen neuen politischen Kurs einzuschlagen. Er förderte die Entstehung des weltlichen Grossgrundbesitzes, liess Burgen bauen, rief erneut ausländische Siedler ins Land um die Lücke, die in der Bevölkerung von den Tataren gerissen wurde, auszufüllen und gewährte eine Reihe von Stadtprivilegien. Unter solchen Umständen konnten die Städte nicht mehr ihre Funktion erfüllen. Der zweite Abschnitt in der Geschichte des ungarischen Städtewesens besteht in der Umgestaltung, bzw. in dem Verfall der alten und in der Gründung neuer Städte. Beide, die umgestalteten alten und die neugegründeten gehörten den Städten westeuropäischen Typs an.

Die ersten bäuerlichen Ansiedler, die in grösseren Massen in das Land kamen waren die Zipser und Siebenbürger Sachsen, die ersten Stadtbewohner die latini, die sich in beiden Hauptstädten des Landes, in Gran und Stuhlweissenburg ausserdem in Agram (Zagreb) und Grosswardein (Oradea Mare, Nagyvárad) niedergelassen haben. Der Namen latinus bedeutete ursprünglich diejenigen, die sich zu dem lateinischen (römischen) Ritus bekannten, war also eine Bezeichnung, die den Gegensatz zum griechischen (orthodoxen) Ritus betonte.[90] Unsere latini waren vor allem Flandrer, Franzosen und Italiener, und der Ausdruck Lateiner war also ein Sammelname, denn dieselbe Nationalitäten wurden auch als Gallicus, Francigena, Italicus (Lombardus) bezeichnet.[91] K. Schünemann untersuchte die Herkunft der Graner Lateiner kam zum Ergebniss, dass sie hauptsächlich aus Nordfrankreich, Lotharigien und Flandern stammten.[92] Wir besitzen einige Angaben, die ebenfalls auf das Zentrum der Wallonen, auf Liège hinweisen,[93] andere deuten auf die Diözese von Vienne[94] und auf die Umgebung von Toulouse und St. Gilles hin.[95] Nach der Studie von H. Ammann ist es klar, dass wir hier mit einer grösseren Ostwanderung der Franzosen zu tun haben.[96]

Während die Herkunft der Lateiner somit gewissermassen gelöst zu sein scheint, ist es schwerer den Zeitpunkt ihrer Einwanderung festzustellen. Aus unseren dürftigen, einander manchmal widersprechenden Quellen gewinnt man den Eindruck, dass die Einwanderung stufenweise, u. zw. in Stufen, die der mittelalterlichen Hierarchie entsprachen, vor sich ging. Den ersten dauernden Kontakt mit dem fran-

[87] GY. PAULER—S. SZILÁGYI, o. c. 375.
[88] I. SZABÓ, A falurendszer kialakulása Magyarországon (Die Entstehung der Dorfverfassung in Ungarn Bp., 1966, 24—35.

[89] J. LÁSZLÓ, Nyugati pénznemek Magyarországon, Tört. Szle, 1915, 229.; I. GEDAI, (Fremde Münzen im Karpaten becken aus den 11-13. Jahrhunderten. Acta Archeol. Acad. Sz. Hung. 21, 1969. 111-131, 145.)
[90] M. AUNER, Latinus, Sz, 50 1916, 28—32.
[91] B. SURÁNYI—G. BÁRCZI, —D. PAIS, Adalékok a ,,Gallicus"-ok nemzeti horvátartozásának kérdéséhez (Beiträge zur Nationalzugehörigkeit der Gallici), MNy, 53, 1957, 450—454.; GY. SZÉKELY: Középkori idegen eredetű plgárságunk elnevezéséhez (Zur Bezeichnung der mittelalterlichen Bürgertums von ausländischen Ursprung), MNy, 54, 1958, 100—103,
[92] K. SCHÜNEMANN, Die Entstehung der Städtewesens in Südosteuropa, Breslau-Oppeln, 1929, 109—110, 115—116.
[93] Z. B. war Erzbischof Robert von Gran ein Liège-er vgl. F. KNAUZ Monumenta ecclesiae Strigoniensis, I, 257—258. (des weiteren: Mon. eccl. Strig.)
[94] Die Kirche deu Latenier von Agram (Zagreb) war dem Hl. Antonius von Egypten geweiht, der Kult dieses Heiligen hatte seinen Mittelpunkt in St. Didier de la Mothe in der Diözese Vienne, M. AUNER. o. c. 37.
[95] Ibid., 38.
[96] H. AMMANN, Die französische Südostwanderung im Rahmen der mittelalterlichen französischen Wanderungen, SüOF, 14, 1955, 406—428.

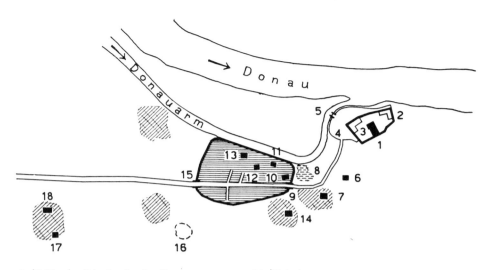

1 Kathedralkirche in der Burg
2 Erzbischöflicher Palast
3 Königspalast
4 Erzbischöfliche Stadt
5 Donautor
6 Thomasstift
7 Augustiner im Dorf der Armenier
8 Warmbäder
9 Laurenzertor
10 Laurenzkirche

11 Wohnturm
12 Nikolaikirche
13 Franziskaner
14 Dominikaner
15 Südtor
16 Judenfriedhof
17-18 Die Kirchen von Kovácsi

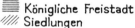 Königliche Freistadt
Siedlungen

Abb. 9: Gran (nach L. Zolnay)

zösischen Sprachgebiet stellten jene französische Benediktiner her, die aus St. Gilles in das 1091 gegründete Kloster von Somogyvár kamen, und mit ihrer Mutterabtei bis ins 13. Jh. in Verbindung blieben.[97] Dem Vorstoss der französischen Mönche folgten dann — aber scheinbar noch vereinzelt — die Ritter. Wir kennen einen Ministerialen, der in den Ardennen 1103 alles verkaufte um mit seinen Söhnen nach Ungarn ziehen zu können.[98] Trotz dieser frühen vereinzelten Einwanderer dauerte es noch eine geraume Zeit, bis grössere Mengen den Weg nach Ungarn fanden. Es scheint, dass sich zwischen den Zipser und Siebenbürger Sachsen auch latini befanden, die villa Latinorum in der Zips und einige Siebenburgische Angaben deuten darauf hin.[99] Die massenweise Einwanderung erfolgte aber nur gegen 1160—1170 nachdem der französische König im dritten Kreuzzug Ungarn überquerte. In dieser Zeit entstanden in den Vorstädten von Gran und Stuhlweissenburg abgesonderte Lateinerviertel. Obzwar vom wirtschaftlichen

Standpunkt die Graner eine grössere Bedeutung besassen, interressieren uns vom Standpunkt der Stadtgeschichte die Stuhlweissenburger mehr. Leider wissen wir von ihrer Siedlung nur soviel, dass sie in der Ofner Vorstadt wohnten, wahrscheinlich also mit ungarischen Hörigen vermengt waren wie in Gran. Wir wissen aber, dass sie vermutlich von König Stephan III. (1162—1172) einen Freiheitsbrief erhielten, den ersten der in Ungarn Bürgern gewährt wurde.[100] Leider ist dieser Freiheitsbrief nur aus einer von Béla IV. 1237 erlassenen Bestätigung und auch diese nur aus Auszügen bekannt, doch steht es fest, dass sie die Freiheit gehabt haben: (1) den Richter und die zwölf Geschworenen frei zu wählen, (2) der Richter und die Geschworenen waren berechtigt in allen Streitfragen ein Urteil zu sprechen, (3) die latini besassen das Recht andere Ansiedler in ihre Gemeinschaft aufzunehmen, und (4) waren im ganzen Lande und an der Landesgrenze von jeglichem Zoll befreit.[101] Die angeführten Rechte bildeten die libertas civium Albensium, die am Anfang des 13. Jh. auch anderen-

[97] S. ECKHARDT, András király francia zarándokai, MNy 32, 1936, 38—40
[98] K. K. KLEIN, Latini in siebenbürgen, Siebenbürgisch - sächsischer Hauskalender 1959. 76.
[99] M. AUNER, c.c., 33.

[100] FÜGEDI, Stuhlweissenburg, 123-124.
[101] Ibid. 124.

Abb. 10: Stadtnetz am Ausgang des 12. Jh.

Städten gewährt wurden und ein Jahrhundert lang die grundlegenden Freiheiten der Bürger bedeuteten. Der Freiheitsbrief hatte auch andere Folgen für die Entwicklung des Städtewesens in Ungarn. Die Lateiner waren nicht Deutsche, sie hielten keine rechtliche Kontakte mit ihrer Heimat auf. Ein rechtliches Affiliationssystem entstand weder zwischen Stuhlweissenburg und dem Mutterland, noch zwischen Stuhlweissenburg und jenen ungarischen Städten, die mit den Freiheiten der *cives Albenses* ausgestattet wurden. Dass sie überhaupt keine Absicht hatten sich gegen die einheimische Bevölkerung hermetisch abzuschiessen beweist der 3. Punkt des Privilegs. Im Gegenteil, sie sicherten freien Zutritt für fremde Elemente, die mit ihnen zusammenleben und wirken wollten. Sie waren westliche Einwanderer, aber keine Kolonisatoren, brachten bürgerliche Vorrechte mit sich, sicherten diese für sich und zugleich für andere Städte des Landes. Der Weg zur Schaffung eines westeuropäischen Städtewesens war damit geöffnet.

Der Werdegang des zweiten Abschnittes in der Geschichte der ungarischen Städtewesens bildet vor allem die Umgestaltung der alten Städte nomadischen Typs. Wie wir darauf bereits hingewiesen haben waren die Städte im königlichen Besitz, doch kam es eben in dieser Hinsicht im 12. Jh. zu Wandlungen, die bei der Umgestaltung im 12/13. Jh. ihre schwere, manchmal sogar verheerende Folgen hatten. Es war der kirchliche Besitz, der sich hier, wie auch anderswo im Lande als erster durchsetzte. Bistümer und Stifte erwarben Liegenschaften[102] und Nutzniessungen in den Städten, sie kamen in den Besitz von Marktzinsen[103], Zolstätten[104] und anderer wirtschaftlichen Einnamen, die bishin von königlichen Beamten verwaltet wurden. Bis zur Mitte des 12. Jh. wurden die kirchlichen Institutionen noch hauptsächlich mit Geldsummen beschenkt, die an gewissen Einnahmequellen gebunden waren.[105] So enthielt das Spital von Neutra von König Géza II. 200 „*pensas auri*", aus dem Neutraer Marktzinse. Doch in der zweiten Hälfte änderte sich die Lage. Gézas Sohn, Béla III. verschenkte 1183 einen Drittel des Neutraer Marktzinses dem Bistum, folglich erschienen nun neben den königlichen, bzw. Komitatsbeamten auch die bischöflichen auf dem Markt.[106] In Stuhlweissenburg erhielt der Probst der Basilika eine Reihe von Gründstücken, praktisch wahrscheinlich die ganze Innerstadt, die Johanniter erwarben die *insula* genannte Vorstadt, die Nikolaikirche bekam Grundstücke in der Ofner Vorstadt.[107] Als die Stuhlweissenburger Lateiner ihre Freiheiten erhielten, gab es ausser dem König drei kirchliche Grundherren. Beabsichtigten die Lateiner nicht nur ihre eigene Freiheiten aufrechtzuerhalten, sondern auch eine Stadt im damaligen westeuropäischen Sinne des Wortes zu entwicklen, so hatten sie den Kampf mit diesen drei kirchlichen Würdenträgern aufzunehmen. Es ist klar, dass sie in so

[102] Z. B. der Bischof von Veszprém ein Haus in Stuhlweissenburg (FÜGEDI, *Stuhlweissenburg*, 117.)

[103] Z. B. der Probst der Basilika in Stuhlweissenburg *(Ibid,*) der Abt von Zobor in Neutra (L. FEJÉRPATAKY: *Kálmán király oklevelei* (Die Urkunden König Kolomans), *Értekezések a törttud. köréből*, XV/5. 1892, 44.
[104] Der Abt von Pannonhalma die Maut in Pressburg, Th. ORTVAY: *Die, Geschichte der Stadt Pressburg*, Pressburg, 1898, II/2, 401—407.
[105] FÜGEDI, *Altofen*, 29—30.
[106] FÜGEDI, *Stadtprivilegien*, 30.
[107] FÜGEDI, *Stuhlweissenburg*, 121.

einem Kampf nicht viel Aussicht auf einen Sieg hatten, denn — wie es König Béla IV. in einer Urkunde betonte — *„quod semel Deo dedicatum est, amplius ad prophanos usus non debet revocari."*[108] Überblicken wir die Geschichte der schon im 11—12. Jh. bestehenden Städte im 13. Jh., so können wir in der Entwicklung einige Typen unterscheiden. Ein Teil der Städte — diese bilden den ersten Typ — war von Anfang an im kirchlichen Besitz. Als König Ladislaus I. ein Stift in späteren Grosswardein gründete, überliess er den Boden dem Stift. Die Folge war, dass als das Bistum von Bihar nach Grosswardein versetzt wurde und um den Bischofsitz — an einem geographisch ausgezeichneten Punkt — sich eine Stadt entwickelte, entstand sie auf dem Grundbesitz des Stiftes, selbst der Bischof war kein Grundherr in dem Stadtgebiet.[109] Scheinbar spielte sich dasselbe in Waitzen ab, wo der Bischof ebenfalls den Boden besass,[110] dagegen scheint Veszprém und Eger in einem frühen Zeitpunkt an die Bischöfe veräussert worden zu sein.[111] Die königlichen Schenkungen wurden im 13. Jh. fortgesetzt. Am tragischsten gestaltete sich die Lage in Altofen, wo 1212 König Andreas II. nicht nur die Stadt und ihre Gemarkung, sondern alle wesentlichen Nutzniessungen (Marktzins, Weinsteuer, usw.) und die Gerichtsbarkeit dem Probst schenkte.[112] Eine 1213 erlassene königliche Urkunde weist darauf hin, dass hier die Einwohner schon gewisse Freiheiten besassen, die hauptsächlich die Gerichtsbarkeit betrafen, deswegen musste ein Kompromiss abgeschlossen werden, demnach der Probst von den *cives* vorgeschlagenen sechs glaubwürdigen Männern der Richter ernennen sollte.[113] Neutra wurde 1288 von König Ladislaus IV. dem Bischof überlassen.[114] In allen diesen Fällen konnte keine Rede von einer weiteren Stadtentwicklung sein. Die Bürger konnten eine vollkommene Freiheit in der Erledigung ihrer Angelegenheiten nicht erreichen, sie blieben zwar persönlich frei, waren aber durch ihre Liegenschaften und durch die Gerichtsbarkeit an ihre Grundherren gebunden.

In drei Fällen — sie repräsentieren den zweiten Typ — war die Entwicklung komplizierter, u. zw. in Stuhlweissenburg konnten zwar die Lateiner nicht ausschliessliche Herren der Stadt werden, da sie aber nach dem Tatareneinfall 1249 vom König in die Innerstadt übersiedelt wurden, kamen sie in den Besitz eines Teiles der Innerstadt, sowie des Marktrechtes und des Marktzinses, auch behielten sie weiterhin ihre Vorrechte. Einen vollkommenen Sieg bedeutete diese Lösung keineswegs, doch auch keine vollkommene Niederlage, die Regelung war ein Kompromiss, der den städtische Autonomie in den Angelegenheiten der Bürger walten liess und die Vorrechte der kirchlichen Grundherren aufrechterhielt.[115] In Raab war das Domstift im Besitz eines Stadtteiles und als 1271 die Einwohner ihren städtischen Freiheitsbrief erlangten, blieb dieser Stadtteil weiterhin im Besitz des Domstiftes.[116] So entstand eine verwickelte Lage, denn die Stadt besass zwar ihre Autonomie, von der aber die Hörigen des Domstiftes ausgenommen wurden, sie blie-

ben weiterhin unter der Gerichtsbarkeit ihres vom Stift ernannten Richters, zahlten weiterhin die Steuern dem Stift, usw. Das Schicksal von Gran bestimmten zwei Tatsachen: 1. der Abzug des königlichen Hofes aus der Burg und Stadt, 2. die Autonomie der Lateiner. Diese zwei Tatsachen verhinderten einerseits die Vereinigung aller kleinen Ortschaften in der Umgebung des Marktplatzes zu einer einzigen Stadt, ermöglichten andererseits auf einem kleineren Gebiet die Entstehung einer königlichen Freistadt[117], die ihre Vorrechte im schweren Kampf mit dem Erzbischof und seinem Domkapitel schützen mussten.

Die Umgestaltung der alten Städte zeigt ein mannigfaltiges Bild, dem entsprechend war auch das Ergebnis der Umgestaltung sehr verschieden. Vom wirtschaftlichen Standpunkt sind Stuhlweissenburg und Grosswardein, Raab und Gran sehr wichtige Handelsplätze geworden, sie wurden auch topographisch entwickelte Städte mit geordneten Marktplätzen, Gassen, Mauern, usw. Vom rechtlichen Standpunkt aus war aber ihre Entwicklung vom Ausgang des Kampfes mit dem kirchlichen Grundherren abhängig. Die Macht der mittelalterlichen Kirche vor Auge haltend ist es kein Wunder, dass nur drei von ihnen (Gran, Raab und Stuhlweissenburg) den Status einer königlichen Freistadt erworben haben, jedoch ohne — mit Ausname von Gran — in vollem Besitz der städtischen Vorrechte zu kommen. Die übrigen waren dem Verfall preisgegeben, sie kamen nie über das Niveau einer Provinzstadt, oder sind so unbedeutende Marktflecken geworden wie Altofen.

Die Umgestaltung von Pest war ebenfalls den geistlichen Grossgrundbesitzer zu verdanken, obzwar — wie schon erwähnt — diese Stadt die einzige frühe Stadt war, in der keine höhere kirchliche Institution gegründet wurde. Der Grund dafür liegt wahrscheinlich darin, dass die Einwohner Sarazenen waren, die noch 1241 erwähnt werden.[118] Als dann der zunehmende Druck der geistlichen Grossgrundbesitzer 1232 einen vollkommenen Sieg über den König errang, wurden die Mohammedaner zum Abzug gezwungen. Obzwar wir den genauen Zeitpunkt nicht feststellen können, ist es sicher, dass auch die Pester Sarazenen ihre Stadt verliessen und dass die Lücke, die nach ihnen blieb, noch in den dreissiger Jahren des 13. Jh. mit Deutschen ausgefüllt wurde.[119] Die Deutschen kamen ohne Mühe in den Besitz des wichtigsten Handelsplatzes im Lande und erwarben sich einen städtischen Freiheitsbrief, der zwar während des Tatareneinfalls verloren ging, doch 1244 von König Béla IV. erneut wurde.[120] Der Tatareneinfall beeinflusste aber das Leben der Pester nur durch die Zerstörung der Stadt. Als 1246 Gerüchte umhergingen, dass die Tataren einen neuen Angriff auf Ungarn vorbereiten, übersiedelte der König die Bürger auf dem heutigen Burgberg von Ofen[121], der vielleicht damals in aller Eile befestigt wurde.[122] Ofens Bürger waren Pester, Ofens Stadtprivileg der Freihetsbrief von Pest aus 1244. Damit war

[108] E. SZENTPÉTERY, *Az Árpád-házi királyok okleveleinek kritikai jegyzéke* (Kritische Regesten der königlichen Urkunden aus der Arpadenzeit), No. 2123.

[109] GYÖRFFY, I, 684.

[110] D. DERCSÉNYI, *Vác*, 16—17.

[111] E. SZENTPÉTERY, *o. c.*, No. 2123.

[112] FÜGEDI, *Altofen*, 31—33.

[113] *Ibid.*, 33.

[114] FEJÉR, CD., V/3. 417.

[115] FÜGEDI, *Stuhlweissenburg*, 130—131.

[116] V. BORBÍRO—I. VALLO, *o. c.*, 42—43.

[117] K. SCHÜNEMANN, *o. c.*, 48—50.

[118] *Budapest történetének okleveles emlékei* (Urkundenbuch der Stadt Budapest), Bp., 1936, 16. (des weiteren: *Bp.O.*)

[119] Aus den Memoiren des Grosswardeiner Domherren Rogerius wissen wir, dass Pest schon 1241 ein villa Theutonica war (F. A. GOMBOS, *o. c.*, 2072.), der Siegel der Stadt weist auf die ersten Jahren König Andreas II. (+1235) hin. A. KUBINYI, *Buda város pecséthasználatának kialakulása* (Der Siegel der Stadt Ofen), TBM, 14, 1961, 114.

[120] *Bp.O.*, I, 37.

[121] L. ZOLNAY, *Opus castri Budensis*. A XIII. századi budai vár kialakulása (Opus castri Budensis. Die Entstehung der Ofner Burg im XIII. Jh.), TBM, 15, 1963, 54—56.

[122] J. GERÉVICH, *A budai vár feltárása* (Die Erforschung der Ofner Burg), Bp., 1966, 261—262.; Mit der Behauptung, dass Ofen in den Typ der „Vorburgstadt" gehört kann ich mich nicht einverstanden sein.

Ofen, das bishin nur eine kleine ungarische Siedlung im Norden des Burgberges um eine königliche *curia* mit einem Wochenmarkt war,[123] neugegründet und die Vorbedingungen für die Entwicklung der bedeutendsten Stadt und späteren Hauptstadt des Landes geschaffen. Keine der alten Städte hatte ein so glückliches Schicksal in ihrer Umgestaltung wie das aus dem sarazenischen Pest entstandene Ofen.

Während alte Städte an Bedeutung verloren, entstanden neue nicht nur am Ofner Burgberg, sondern in allen Teilen des Landes an der Stelle älterer Verwaltungszentren oder Marktorte, bzw. „an grüner Wurzel". Leider sind bis jetzt

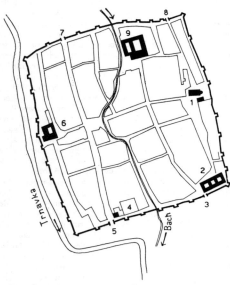

1 Pfarrkirche　　　　6 Franziskaner
2 Klarisser　　　　　7 Obertor
3 Tor　　　　　　　　8 Tor
4 Spital　　　　　　　9 Dominikaner
5 Pressburger Tor

Abb. 11: Tyrnau (nach V. Mencl).

nur wenige von diesen gründlich untersucht worden, doch geben uns auch diese wenigen Beispiele hinreichende Informationen darüber, was vor sich ging. Eine der frühesten städtischen Freiheitsbriefe wurde an Tyrnau (Trnava, Nagyszombat) 1238 erlassen.[124] In diesem, wie auch in anderen Fällen handelt es sich um eine Verschelzung mehrerer Ortschaften zu einer einzigen Stadt. Tyrnau war – wie das der ungarische Ortsname Nagyszombat (= Samstagmarkt) beweist – ein Marktort ebenfalls in dem ungarischslavischen ethnischen Grenzgebiet, der schon 1211 von Bedeutung war und reich sein musste, da die Zehnten der hiesigen Kirche an die Graner Domherren geschenkt wurden.[125] Neben diesem ursprünglichen Marktort mit gemisch-

ter ungarisch-slowakischer Bevölkerung wurden gegen 1220—1230 von Königin Konstanzia deutsche Kaufleute angesiedelt, ihre Siedlung mit der alten Ortschaft vereinigt und mit einer gemeinsamen Mauer umgeben.[126]

Etwas ähnliches kann in Ödenburg beobachtet werden. In der von den ursprünglichen spätrömischen Mauern umgebenen „Burg" residierte der Komitatsgespan von Ödenqurg mit seiner Gefolgschaft, er fand sogar Gelegenheit in der teilweise öden Stadt seine Pferde in einem Marstall zu unterbringen. Im Süden, dem Gespansitz gegenüber liegenden Ende stand ein Marktplatz, dessen Namen Salzmarkt war, der auch annehmen lässt, dass sich in der Stadt ein königliches Salzdepot befand.[127] Unweit von der Stadt stand die Ortschaft der ungarischen Grenzwächter Lövö *(sagittarii)* genannt. Eine Tatsache scheint darauf hinzuweisen, dass ausser diesen königlichen Elementen noch eine weitere Ortschaft berücksichtigt werden muss. Die Stadtpfarre von Ödenburg befindet sich ausser den Mauern und es scheint wahrscheinlich, dass dies die Pfarre einer vielleicht am meisten bevölkerten Siedlung war. Zu den angeführten Elementen gesellten sich im 13. Jh. noch deutsche Einwanderer. Als dann Ödenburg zwischen 1240—1254 ihre städtischen Freiheiten erhielt, wurden diese Elemente zu einer einzigen Stadt hinter den spätrömischen Mauern verschmolzen mit Ausnahme der Grenzwächter, die um 1277 der Stadt angeschlossen und somit ödenburger Bürger geworden sind.[128]

Aus den Beispielen von Pest, Tyrnau und Ödenburg geht eine neue Tatsache klar hervor, u. zw. das Erscheinen deutscher Einwanderer, die Städtebewohner waren, oder wenigstens in Ungarn Städtebewohner geworden sind. Wie bei den Einwanderer aus dem französischen Sprachgebiet, konnte nicht nur die deutsche Ostwanderung, sondern auch die Einwanderung von Geistlichen, Rittern und Bauern nach Ungarn schon auf eine ziemlich lange Vergangenheit zurückblicken, als am Anfang des 13. Jh. die deutschen Städtebewohner erschienen sind. Ihre Rolle in der Entstehung des ungarischen Städtewesens hatte keinen so einschlägigen Charakter als der der Lateiner, die sich in den bestehenden grössten Städten des Landes angesiedelt haben. Bei den ersten deutschen Bürgern kann insofern eine Ähnlichkeit mit den Lateinern festgestellt werden, dass sie ebenfalls zwischen anderen Volkselementen vermengt waren. In Pest lebten nicht nur Sarazenen, und als die Pester Deutschen nach Ofen übersiedelt wurden, sind sie auch nicht ausschliessliche Bewohner der Stadt geworden, denn an dem Burgberg stand schon damals ein ungarischer Marktorr, dessen Bevölkerung mit den Deutschen zusammen das Bürgertum von Ofen bildeten. Dass in Tyrnau, bzw. Ödenburg ebenfalls deutsche, ungarische, bzw. slowakische Elemente in Erwägung gezogen werden müssen, steht fest.[129] Ausser diesen ergänzenden deutschen Ansiedlungen, die deutsche und nicht-deutsche Elemente vereinigten, war auch eine andere deutsche Einwanderung im Gange, welche die schon bestehenden Städte berührte. In Stuhlweissenburg finden wir eine,, Deutsche Gasse" *(vicus Teutonicalis)*, in Gran hat Schünemann ihre Anwesenheit bewiesen.[130]

[123] FÜGEDI, *Stadtprivilegien*, 78—80.; L. ZOLNAY, Opus castri Budensis' 43—81.
[124] A. HUŠČAVA, *Najstaršie výsady mesta Trnavy* (Der älteste Freiheitsbrief von Tyrnau), Bratislava 1939.; B. VARSIK: *Vznik a počiatky mesta Trnavy* (Ursprung und Anfänge der Stadt Tyrnau), Historické štúdie, 3, 1957, 228—274.
[125] *Mon. eccl. Strig.*, I. 197.

[126] VARSIK, *o. c.*
[127] MAJOR, *Innerstadt*, 165—166.
[128] MOLLAY, *o. c.*
[129] B. SURÁNYI, *Kereskedögilde Nagyszombaton a Visegrádi Kongresszus évében* (Eine Kaufmannsgilde in Tyrnau im Jahre des Kongresses von Visegrád), Tört. Sz, 1959 259.
[130] FÜGEDI, *Stuhlweissenburg.*; K. SCHÜNEMANN, *o. c.*, 110—110, 115.

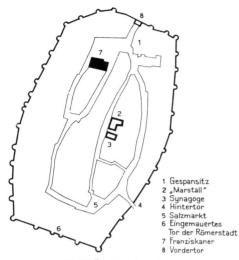

1 Gespansitz
2 „Marstall"
3 Synagoge
4 Hintertor
5 Salzmarkt
6 Eingemauertes
  Tor der Römerstadt
7 Franziskaner
8 Vordertor

Abb. 12: Ödenburg (nach J. Major)

In diesem Fall musste aber ihre Anzahl so gering gewesen sein, dass sie weder eine abgesonderte Siedlung gründen, noch eine grössere Rolle in der Stadführung spielen konnten. Die so angesiedelten Deutschen verloren ihre Nationalität rasch und gingen in der einheimischen Bevölkerung auf. In einigen Städten hingegen, wo es zu einer Verschmelzung mehrerer Ortschaften kam, gewann die deutsche Bürgerschaft mehr oder weniger die Oberhand und konnte ihre Vorherrschaft für die kommenden Jahrhunderte sichern. Das kam am schärfsten in Ofen zum Ausdruck, wo laut des Stadtrechts der Richter von deutschen Eltern, ja sogar deutschen Grosseltern stammen sollte,[131] bis dann am Anfang des 15. Jh. in der Stadführung ein grundlegender Wandel eintrat.[132]

Das Beispiel von Ofen scheint deswegen so wichtig zu sein, weil verschiedene Merkmale des Beitrages zur ungarischen Standtenwicklung beobachtet werden können. Die Einwanderung der deutschen Siedler erfolgte nicht auf jenem Wege, in dem es in den westslavischen Gebieten gewohnheitsmässig vor sich ging, d. h. eine feste Abschliessung der Deutschen erfolgte nicht durch Vertreibung der einheimischen Elemente. Im Gegenteil, die Deutschen bildeten mit ihnen ein gemeinsames Burgertum. Dass die Deutschen die Oberhand gewannen, war nicht die Folge einer planmässigen Politik, sie hatte eher wirtschaftliche Ursachen, auf die wir noch zurückkehren. In den übrigen Orten (Tyrnau[133], Ödenburg[134]) waren in der Führerschicht nicht nur die Deutschen allein, sondern verschiedene Nationalitäten vertreten.

Trotzdem war Ofen nur ein Übergang zwischen den Städten mit einer gemischten Führerschicht und den wahr-

haftigen Kolonisationsstädten, die im Norden des Landes entstanden sind. Vor allem soll hier Kaschau (Košice, Kassa), als ein problematischer Fall erwähnt werden, wo die Bevölkerung zwischen 1230–1249 ethnisch vollkommen ausgetauscht wurde und an der Stelle der Ungarn Deutsche erschienen. Die Ursachen können leider nicht festgestellt werden, allerdings darf die Möglichkeit nicht ausgeschlossen werden, dass die Ungarn während des Tatareneinfalls niedergemetzelt, vertrieben wurden oder aus einigem Willen die Ortschaft verliessen. Wie dem auch sei, Kaschau ist der einzige Ort im Lande, wo binnen zwei Jahrzehnten anstatt dem Ungartum Deutsche erschienen sind und eine Stadt planmässig angelegt haben.[135]

Einen anderen Typ der deutschen Kolonisationsstadt repräsentieren die „auf grüner Wurzel" gegründeten Bergstädte, am schönsten die Bergstadt des ungarischen Kupfers, Neusohl (Banska Bystrica, Besztercebánya). Hier legte das deutsche Bürgertum planmässig eine Stadt an und konnte seine ausschliessliche Herrschaft über die Stadt bis in die Neuzeit erfolgreich bewahren. O. Paulinyi ist nach Erforschung der Eigentums- und Rechtverhältnisse, sowie der Stadttopographie zum Ergebnis gekommen, dass die Grundlage sowohl für die Mitgliedschaft in der Führerschicht, als auch für die Ausübung wirtschaftlicher und politischer Vorrechte von dem Besitz eines Hauses am Ring Abhängig war. Es stellte sich heraus, dass die Stadt von einer Unternehmergesellschaft gegründet wurde, die Unternehmer sind Ringbürger geworden und regierten die Stadt auf diesem Grund.[136] Neusohl erhielt das Stadtprivileg 1255, Schemnitz (Banská Stiavnica, Selmecbánya) dürfte ein halbes Jahrhundert älter gewesen sein, Kremnitz (Kremnica, Körmöcbánya) wurde 1328 gegründet.[137]

Die Untersuchungen Paulinyis wiesen auf die Bedeutung des in der Handelstätigkeit angehäuften Kapitals hin und es ist wirklich nicht schwer die Tatsache zu erkennen, dass die deutschen Kolonisationsstädte eben dort — und wahr-

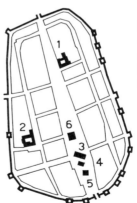

1 Franziskaner
2 Dominikaner
3 Pfarrkirche
4 Michaeliskirche
5 Spital
6 Rathaus

Abb. 13: Kaschau (nach V. Mencl)

[131] „der sol ein deutscher man von allen seinen vier annen" K. MOLLAY, Das Ofner Stadtrecht Bp., 1959, 70.
[132] J. SZŰCS, Városok és kézművesség a XV. századi Magyarországon. (Städte und Handwerk in Ungarn im 15. Jh.), Bp., 1955, 278–294.
[133] B. SURÁNYI, o. c., 260.
[134] K. MOLLAY

[135] GYŐRFFY, I. 105.
[136] O. PAULINYI, Tulajdon és társadalom a Garamvidéki bányavárosokban (Eigentum und Gesellschaft in den Bergstädten des Grantals), TörtSz., 1962, 173–181.
[137] MENCL, o. c., 49–53.; J. HANIKA, Die Entstehung der Berg und Münzstadt Kremnitz, Karpathenland 6, 1933, 33.

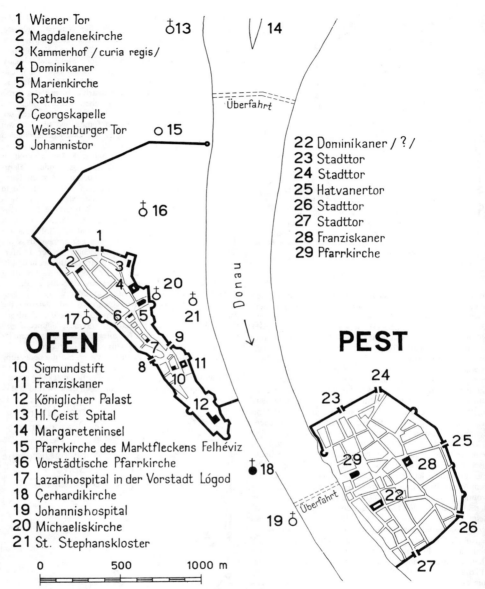

1 Wiener Tor
2 Magdalenekirche
3 Kammerhof / curia regis /
4 Dominikaner
5 Marienkirche
6 Rathaus
7 Georgskapelle
8 Weissenburger Tor
9 Johannistor

22 Dominikaner / ? /
23 Stadttor
24 Stadttor
25 Hatvanertor
26 Stadttor
27 Stadttor
28 Franziskaner
29 Pfarrkirche

OFEN

10 Sigmundstift
11 Franziskaner
12 Königlicher Palast
13 Hl. Geist Spital
14 Margareteninsel
15 Pfarrkirche des Marktfleckens Felhéviz
16 Vorstädtische Pfarrkirche
17 Lazarihospital in der Vorstadt Lógod
18 Gerhardikirche
19 Johannishospital
20 Michaeliskirche
21 St. Stephanskloster

PEST

0   500   1000 m

Abb. 15: Pest und Ofen am Ende des Mittelalters (nach A Kubinyi und L. Nagy)

116

scheinlich hauptsächlich nur dort — erschienen sind, wo der Bergbau eine ansehnliche Investition erforderte. Diese Tatsache führt uns zu Ofen und zu den anderen neugegründeten Städten des Landes zurück, wo sich die Frage ergibt, warum es den Deutschen gelungen ist ihre Herrschaft über die Stadt so lange zu erhalten. Dass die Ursache — ebenso wie in den Bergstädten — letzten Endes eine wirtschaftliche Tatsache oder Entwicklung sein muss, liegt an der Hand. Deswegen, bevor wir noch die gestellte Frage beantworten, müssen wir uns mit der Umgestaltung, bzw. Neugründung der Städte vom wirtschaftlichen Standpunkt befassen.

Der erste ungarische städtische Freiheitsbrief, der für die Stuhlweissenburger Lateiner erlassen wurde, enthält lediglich einen einzigen Punkt in Bezug auf die Wirtschaft, u. zw. die Zollfreiheit im ganzen Lande und an den Landesgrenzen, also sowohl im Binnen als auch im Aussenhandel. Die ersten Urkunden, die diese Lateiner erwähnen stammen aus einem Prozess, der gegen sie wegen ihren Weinhandel vom Abt von Pannonhalma geführt wurde.[138] Auch die Graner Lateiner bildeten eine Kaufmannskolonie.[139] Im 13. Jh. kam in Stuhlweissenburg eine neue Marktform auf, der zwei Wochen lang dauernde Jahrmarkt. Wir wissen nicht genau wann diese neue Form gewährt wurde, wir wissen nicht einmal ob die Stuhlweissenburger über ein Jahrmaktsprivileg verfügten, fest steht nur, dass der Jahrmarkt vor 1275 regelmässig abgehalten wurde, weiterhin dass Ofen 1287 ein solches Privileg erwarb. Andere Städte folgten zur Mitte des 14. Jh. (Ödenburg und Pressburg 1344, Kaschau 1347).[140] Die Daten, an denen der Jahrmarkt abgehalten wurde beweisen, dass es sich hier um ein System handelt, in Stuhlweissenburg war es der 14—28. August, in Ofen der 1—15 September, Pressburg setzte den Jahrmarkt auf den 3—17 August. Der aus dem Westen kommende Kaufmann hatte also die Gelegenheit nach der Ernte seine Waren in drei Städten in einem Zug zu verkaufen und entsprechende Waren einzukaufen. Wie wir schon dargelegt haben, hat sich in der zweiten Hälfte des 12. Jh. die Richtung des Aussenhandels geändert. Aber es ging nicht allein um eine Änderung in der Richtung, sondern um einen Strukturwandel im Handel. Während bis zur Mitte des 12. Jh. orientalische und byzantinische Luxuswaren eingeführt wurden, kamen jetzt aus dem Westen ausser Luxuswaren (vor allem Tuche) auch Massenwaren des Handwerks nach Ungarn. Ausgrabungen beweisen uns, dass selbst so einfache und auch im Land überall herstellbare Waren, wie Töpfe massenhaft aus Österreich importiert wurden.

Suchen wir also nach wirtschaftlichen Faktoren, die die Stadtenstehung förderten, so müssen wir als den bedeutendsten den Handel bezeichnen. Die Stadtprivilegien und andere Dokumente bestätigen diesen Schluss, indem sie beinahe in jedem Fall über Marktrecht und Zollfreiheit sprechen, oft auch andere, den Handel betreffende Punkte erhalten, aber nur in einem einzigen Fall das Meilenrecht des Handwerks erwähnen.[141] Überblicken wir die detaillierten Vorschriften über den Marktzins in Ofen aus dem Jahre 1255, so finden wir darin vierzehn Waren vorgezählt, die

nach der Wagenlast den Zoll entrichten, von denen aber nur drei Handwerksprodukte (Tuch, Eisen, Blei), alle übrigen Agrarprodukte (Obst, Wein, Salz, Häuter, Honig, usw.) waren.[142] In den Privilegien, die einen Brückenzoll genehmigen, werden immer nur die „mázsa" genannten grossen Wagen der Kaufleute und jene Wagen, die einheimischen Wein und Salz führen, von einander unterschieden und falls die Vorschrift über die grossen Wagen der Kaufleute detailliert wird, so werden wieder die Tuche hervorgehoben.[143]

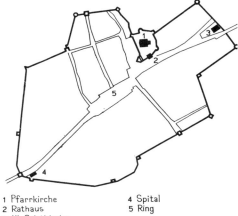

1 Pfarrkirche   4 Spital
2 Rathaus   5 Ring
3 Hl. Geistkirche
Stadtmauern im 16. Jh. erbaut, Kirche im 15. Jh. befestigt

Abb. 14: Neusohl (nach V. Mencl)

Allem Anscheine nach war das einheimische Handwerk zu schwach entwickelt um den Konkurrenzkapf mit den Importwaren aufzunehmen. Es muss also als charakteristisch angesehen werden, dass von den Handwerkern am besten und als erste die Münzer (heute möchten wir sagen ein staatlich subventionierter Industriezweig) und die Schiffer an den Flussübergängen organisiert waren.[144] Wir haben nicht die Absicht die Existenz des Handwerks in den Städten zu leugnen, doch war sie u. E. in den Hintergrund gedrängt, Handwerker konnten sich kaum in Einfluss mit den Lateinern oder deutschen Kaufleuten messen. Es ist äusserst kennzeichnend, dass in Gran 1288 die Handwerker von ihren Werkstätten wöchentlich einen halben, die Kaufleuten am Markt dagegen von ihren Geschäften einen ganzen Friesacher zu zahlen hatten.[145] Die Tatsache, dass die Handwerker arm waren, oder wenigstens viel ärmer als die Kaufleute, war allgemein bekannt.

Ist die Auffassung der ungarischen Geschichtswissenschaft stichhaltig, wonach unsere städtischen Handwerker — wenigstens teilweise — aus den Handwerkerdörfern kamen, die wir oben geschildert haben, dann muss ihnen der Lateiner und der Deutscher vor allem als Unternehmer gegenübergestellt werden. Nicht nur die Vorfahren der

[138] PRT. I, 650—652.
[139] K. SCHÜNEMANN, o. c., 48—50.
[140] FÜGEDI, Stadtprivilegien, 34—36.
[141] Ibid., 57—58.
[142] Ibid., Anm. 160.

[143] Ibid., 37.
[144] E. LÉDERER, A legrégibb magyar iparososztály kialakulása (Die Entstehung der ältesten ungarischen Handwerkerklasse), Sz, 62, 1928, 639—645.
[145] Mon. eccl. Strig., II, 23.

Ringbürger in den Bergstädten waren Unternehmer, wir finden sie auch in den Reihen der Graner und Ofner Bürger. Sie bekleideten bedeutende Wirtschaftsposten im Lande, traten an die Stelle der vertriebenen mohammedanischen und jüdischen Finanzleute als Pächter der königlichen Einnahmen oder Grafen der Münzstätte[146] sind Pächter der kirchlichen Zehnten[147] und schliesslich Gewölbherren in Ofen geworden,[148] nebenbei nahmen sie oft als Feudalherren an der Politik teil.[149] Kein Wunder, dass Pest nach einigen Jahren der deutschen Einwanderung als *magna et ditissima Theutonica villa*[150] bezeichnet wird. Zahlenmässige Angaben beweisen, dass der Reichtum auch hier aus dem Handel stammte[151]

Die Verschmelzung verschiedener Ortschaften in eine Stadt hat noch eine wirschaftliche Folge gehabt, dass nähmlich unsere Städte grösstenteils einen mehr oder weniger starken Agrarcharakter bewahrten. Selbst die Kaufmannsstädten konnten sich vom der Landwirtschaft nicht loslösen. Die Ofner Bürger beschäftigten sich ebenso mit Weinbau wie die Pressburger, Ödenburger oder Tyrnauer. Der Bodenbesitz und hauptsächlich der Weingarten war immer eine unentbehrliche bürgerliche Charakteristik geblieben.

Obzwar die Bergstädte unter allen Umständen als Kolonisationsstädte zu bezeichnen sind, sind sie in einer Hinsicht, nämlich in der Rechtspflege nie Kolonisationsstädte in dem Sinne des Wortes geworden, wie jene in den westslavischen Gebieten. Seit dem Freiheitsbrief der Stuhlweissenburger Lateiner war es eine grundlegende Notwendigkeit, dass die Bürger ihren Richter und ihre Geschworenen frei wählen konnten und diese in allen Streitfragen der Bürger — in kleinen sowohl, wie in den Kapitalverbrechen — ein Urteil sprechen dürften. In den westslavischen Gebieten folgte daraus, dass die Bürger das Stadtrecht einer deutschen Stadt übernahmen und der Appellationsweg führte ausser den Landesgrenzen zur Mutterstadt, meistens nach Magdeburg. In den ungarischen Stadtprivilegien finden wir nur ein einziges Mal eine derartige Erscheinung, es war das unbedeutende Sillein (Žilina, Zsolna), das an Teschen appellieren durfte. In allen übrigen Fällen führte der Appellationsweg zum König oder zum Tarnakmeister. Als im Laufe des 14. Jh. sich die teilweise nach deutschen Vorlagen entwickelten Stadtrechte von Ofen, Karpfen (Krupina, Korpona) und Schemnitz durchsetzten, ist aus ihnen ebenfalls kein Affiliationssystem der grossen Städte entstanden, diese Stadtrechte wurden eher von kleineren Marktflecken, ja sogar von Dörfern übernommen.[152] Hingegen kam eine spezifisch ungarische Rechtsinstitution ins Leben, der sog. Tarnakstuhl, an dem die Delegierten der grossen Städte des Landes unter dem Vorsitz des Tarnakmeisters das Recht sprachen.[153] Den Grund dieser Entwicklung bildete die Tatsache, dass die Zentralmacht in Ungarn verhältnismässig stark war. Es muss als äusserst kennzeichnend angesehen werden, dass der einzige nach dem Ausland führende Appellationsweg von Matheus Csák, also einem Olygarchen zu jener Zeit gewährt wurde, als nach dem Aussterben der

Arpaden die Zentralmacht praktisch ausgeschaltet war.

Ausser der Stärke der Zentralmacht spielte hier auch die oben angedeutete Charakteristik der Lateiner eine bedeutende Rolle, indem sie ein Affiliationssystem nicht bevorzugten.

Vergleichen wir das Städtewesen in Ungarn im 11. und 13. Jh. so ist nicht nur die zahlenmässige Zunahme der Städte auffallend, sondern noch viel mehr, dass aus den Städten nomadischen Typs regelrechte mittelalterliche Städte geworden sind, die mit allen topographischen, wirtschaftlichen und rechtlichen Kennzeichen des westeuropäischen Typs ausgestattet waren. Verschiedene Faktoren wirkten in der Umgestaltung und Gründung neuer Städte, es entwickelten sich verschiedene Typen sowohl in wirtschaftlicher als auch rechtlicher Hinsicht. Wie die mittelalterliche geographische Lage Ungarns, war auch das Städtewesen ein Ergebnis der einheimischen Grundlagen und verschiedenen ausländischen Beiträge, die von den romanischen Völkern ebenso geleistet wurden wie von den Deutschen. Als ganzes betrachtet war aber der Wandel des Städtewesens eigentlich ein Teil jener Wandlungen, die im ganzen Lande und im gesammten Wirtschaft Ungarns stattfanden und so eine organische Entwicklung.

Der zweite Abschnitt in der Geschichte des ungarischen Städtewesens ging zur Mitte des 14. Jh. in Begleitung von der bisherigen Entwicklung gegengesetzten Erscheinungen zu Ende. Es kam anstatt der Einheit der königlichen Freistädte zu einer Differenzierung derselben in Handels- und Bergstädten, das auch im Ofner, Karpfener, bzw. Schemnitzer Stadtrecht zum Ausdruck kam. In den Städten verschwanden diejenigen Typen des Unternehmers, die am Anfang der Umgestaltung, bzw. Gründung so eine grosse Rolle spielten. Die Stadtgründungen wurden fortgesetzt, aber die neuen Städte waren keine königlichen Freistädte mehr, sondern grössere Dörfer, die durch königliche oder grundherrschaftlichen Privilegien zu Marktflecken erhoben wurden, doch weiterhin unter grundherrschaftlicher Gerichtsbarkeit und Verwaltung blieben und wirtschaftlich sich zwischen Dörfern und königlichen Freistädten eingeschoben haben.

Das Stadtnetz hat sich auch hinsichtlich seiner geographischen Verteilung stark verändert. Dem Erzvorkommen entsprechend entstanden drei Bergstadtgruppen, die sog. niederungarischen um Schemnitz, die oberungarischen um Gölnitz (Gelnica, Gölnicbánya) und Nagybánya. Die Handelsstädte gruppierten sich dagegen an der Landesgrenze. Im Westen Güns (Kőszeg), Ödenburg, Pressburg und Tyrnau, im Norden Kaschau, Kesmark (Kezmarok, Késmárk), Leutschau (Levoča, Lőcse), Eperjes (Prešov) und Bartfeld (Bardejov, Bártfa) im Süden Hermannstadt (Sibiu, Nagyszeben) und Kronstadt (Brasov, Brassó). Die Länder selbst haben an den geographisch vorteilhaften Plätze eingenommen, Rab, Stuhlweissenburg Szeged und Grosswardein waren die reichsten von ihnen. In der Mitte des Landes um Ofen entwickelte sich später ebenfalls eine Stadtlandschaft. Mit den Verhältnissen des 12. Jh. verglichen muss festgestellt werden, dass Transdanubien die Führung verloren hat und das sich die Städte — mit Ausnahme der grossen Tiefebene — jetzt mit Ausnahme der Bergstädte an der Landesgrenze festgesetzt haben.

---

[146] T. A. HORVÁTH–L. HUSZÁR, *Kamaragrófok a középkorban* (Kammergrafen im Mittelalter), NK, 54/55, 1955—1956, 22—24.
[147] *Bp.O.* I, 290, 308, 353.
[148] K. MOLLAY, *Ofner Stadtrecht*, 88.
[149] L. ZOLNAY, *Opus castri Budensis*, o. c., 65—67.
[150] F. A. GOMBOS, *o. c.*, 2072.
[151] Bp. 0. I. 14, 295.
[152] FÜGEDI, *Stadtprivilegien*, 67—71.
[153] I. um. SZENTPÉTERY, *A tárnoki ítélőszék kialakulása* (Die Entstehung des Tarnakstuhls), Sz, 68, 1934, 510. 591.

X

Der Stadtplan von Stuhlweissenburg und die Anfänge des Bürgertums in Ungarn

1. In dem folgenden Aufsatz soll der Versuch unternommen werden einen mittelalterlichen Stadtplan und durch denselben die Entwicklung einer Stadt darzulegen.[1] Stuhlweißenburg (ungarisch im MA Fehérvár, heute Székesfehérvár, deutsch im MA Weißenburg, im slavischen Belgrad, lateinisch Alba oder Alba Regia) war eine der bedeutendsten Städte des mittelalterlichen Ungarns. Sie verdankte ihre Bedeutung teils ihren angesehenen Kirchen und kirchlichen Körperschaften, teils ihrem regen Handel. In der vom König Stephan I. gegründeten Basilika wurden die Könige des Landes gekrönt und zu letzte Ruhe gesetzt. Der Handel war schon im XII. Jh. bedeutend und blieb es auch bis zum XVI. Jh.

Trotz aller Bedeutung ist Stuhlweißenburgs Vergangenheit fast undurchdringlich, die Rekonstruktion des mittelalterlichen Stadtplans stößt auf fast unüberwindbare Schwierigkeiten. Infolge der Türkenherrschaft (1543—1601, dann 1602—1689) ging nicht nur das Archiv der Stadt, sondern auch jene der großen kirchlichen Institutionen verloren, allein den Johannitern gelang es einen Bruchteil ihrer Urkunden zu retten.[2] Die uns heute zur Verfügung stehenden Quellen sind zufällig erhaltene Bruchstücke, aus denen nur vorsichtig Schlüsse über die mittelalterlichen Verhältnisse gezogen werden dürfen. Als Folge der Türkenherrschaft verlor die Stadt auch ihre topographische Tradition. Von den einst prachtvollen großen Bauten sind heute kaum zwei-drei lokalisierbar, 1691 übergab man den ehemaligen Königspalast als »türkisches Arsenal« den Franziskanern.[3] Urkundlich belegte Straßennamen können mit

---

[1] Die Originalfassung des vorliegendes Aufsatzes ist 1964 entstanden und in ungarischer Sprache in der Zeitschrift »Településtudományi Közlemények« 20/1967. S. 31—45. erschienen. Seitdem wurden aber teilweise historische, teilweise archeologische Forschungen durchgeführt, die uns manche Fragen in ein neues Licht stellten. Deswegen sahen wir uns gezwungen in dieser deutschsprachigen Ausgabe auf die neuesten Forschungsergebnisse Rücksicht zu nehmen.

[2] Diese werden heute im Archiv des Kapitels in Preßburg (Pozsony, Bratislava) unter dem Titel »Capsa Cruciferorum Albensium« aufbewahrt und standen uns verfilmt im Országos Levéltár [Ungarisches Staatsarchiv, Budapest] zur Verfügung. Die aus dem XVIII. Jh. stammenden Abschriften der Urkunden sind in der Universitätsbibliothek in Budapest (Handschriftensammlung AB 72/1—3.) zu finden.

[3] J. Károly: *Fejér vármegye története* [Geschichte des Komitats Fejér] Székesfehérvár 1896—1904. II. 179.

X

104

dem erhaltenen Grundriß nur ausnahmsweise identifiziert werden. Was rechtfertigt aber den mühsamen Versuch den Stadplan trotz den genannten Schwierigkeiten auszuarbeiten? Vor allem die Tatsache, daß Stuhlweißenburg in einem frühen — und sehr bedeutenden — Zeitraum eine hervorragende Rolle einnahm. Deswegen wollen wir hier zuerst die erste Phase der Geschichte des ungarischen Städtewesens zusammenfassen, um die Entwicklung der Stadt eingliedern zu können und sodann die Schlüsse aus der Entwicklung des Stadtplans ziehen.

2. Ungarische und ausländische Forscher beurteilten die Frage der Stadtentstehung in Ungarn seit dem Anfang unseres Jahrhunderts übereinstimmend. Sie behaupteten, daß das nomadische Ungarntum die Städte scheute, deutsche Einwanderer führten die Stadt als Siedlungsform ins Land ein. Diesen Standpunkt vertrat nicht nur Kaindl und Schünemann, sondern auch Hóman.[4] In gewissem Sinne folgten ihnen auch Planitz und Ennen, wobei Ennen auch noch die Verbreitung eines asiatischen Stadttyps erneut aufgriff.[5] In den letzten dreißig Jahren erzielte aber auch die ungarische Wirtschafts- und Sozialgeschichte einige Ergebnisse, auf Grund deren wir heute schon in der Lage sind die Anfänge des ungarischen Städtewesens etwas eingehender zu schildern.

Die Entwicklung des Städtewesens in Ungarn kann in zwei Abschnitte zusammengefaßt werden. Der zwischen 1100 und 1150 beendete erste Abschnitt deckt sich im großen und ganzen mit einer Phase der allgemeinen Wirtschaftsgeschichte des Landes. Diese Phase beurteilte man eine Zeit lang vollkommen negativ, als eine Phase der Auflösung der Nomadenwirtschaft und der Abschließung des Landes von den westlichen Nachbarn. Die Forschungen A. Domanovszkys brachten die positiven Züge dieser Entwicklungsphase zu Tage,[6] die archeologischen Ergebnisse bereicherten das von ihm entworfene Bild mit wertvollen Einzelheiten.[7] Laut diesen Ergebnissen kann heute festgestellt werden, daß das Ungarntum nach der Landnahme (896) bis zum Anfang des XII. Jh. weiterhin im Ramen jenes Wirtschaftsgebietes

---

[4] F. Kaindl: *Geschichte des Deutschtums in den Karpathenländern.* Gotha 1907, Ders. *Studien zur Geschichte des deutschen Rechtes in Ungarn.* Arch. f. österr. Gesch. 1909., K. Schünemann: *Die Entstehung des Städtewesens in Südosteuropa* [Südosteuropäische Bibliothek 1.] Breslau [1929]. B. Hóman: *A magyar városok az Árpádok korában* [Die ungarischen Städte im Zeitalter der Árpáden] Bp. 1908.

[5] H. Planitz: *Die deutsche Stadt im Mittelalter. Von der Römerzeit bis zu den Zunftskämpfen.* Graz—Köln 1954, 158. E. Ennen: *Frühgeschichte der europäischen Stadt.* Bonn 1953, 303.

[6] S. Domanovszky: *A harmincadvám eredete* (Értekezések a történettudományok köréből) [Der Ursprung des Dreißigstzolles] Bp. 1916., Ders.: *Die Vergangenheit des ungarischen Donauhandels.* Ungarische Jahrbücher II (1922) 161—187.

[7] N. Fettich: *A levédiai magyarság a régészet megvilágításában* [Das Ungarntum vor der Landnahme im Lichte der Archeologie] Századok LXVII (1933) 250—276, 369—399., Gy. László: *Budapest a népvándorlás korában* [Budapest in der Völkerwanderungszeit] Budapest története [Die Geschichte von Budapest] I. Bp. 1942, 781 ff.

blieb, dem es vor der Landnahme angehörte, d. h. Handelsbeziehungen wurden in erster Reihe mit Byzanz und Kiew aufrechterhalten, und obzwar durch den Prager Markt ungarische Handelsgüter — vor allem Sklaven — auch Nordeuropa erreichten, wurde der große Transitohandel zwischen Ost und West auch zu dieser Zeit nicht auf dem Landwege über Ungarn abgewickelt. Die Träger des Handels waren mohammedanische Donau-Bulgaren, Russen und Juden. In Pest ist uns auch eine frühe sarazenische Siedlung bekannt.[8] Eine, vor einigen Jahren entdeckte mohammedanische Quelle bestätigte vollkommen das auf Grund historischer und archeologischer Forschungen entworfene Bild.

Vor dreißig Jahren suchte ein ungarischer Forscher, A. Pleidell die Anfänge des ungarischen Städtewesens im Fortleben der römischen Städte Pannoniens.[9] Seine Ansichten fanden keine allgemeine Annahme, doch konnte die Frage der römischen Kontinuität nicht einfach abgelehnt werden. In zwei Fällen (Sabaria-Steinamanger (Szombathely) und Sopianae — Quinque Basilicae — Fünfkirchen (Pécs))[10] blieb irgendeine Siedlungskontinuität, die in der Form von religiöser Tradition auftrat, aufrechterhalten. Dennoch darf eine allgemeine Siedlungskontinuität nicht, eine Kontinuität des römischen Munizipiums noch weniger vorausgesetzt werden. Eine viel bedeutendere Rolle spielte die sog. »römische Erbschaft«. Unter diesem Ausdruck sind diejenigen Siedlungselemente (Strassen, Wasserleitungen, Amphiteatren, usw.) zu verstehen, die nach dem Untergang der Römerherrschaft in einem verwahrlosten Zustand weiterlebten und in hohem Maße die Besiedlung der Völkerwanderungszeit, den Ort der mittelalterlichen Städte, in manchen Fällen sogar den Stadtgrundriß bestimmten. Langobarden wählten das Amphiteatrum von Acquincum,[11] die Awaren das verheerte Arrabona zum Sitz ihrer Fürsten, letztere erbauten dort ihre erste Kirche.[12]

---

[8] L. Nagy: *Pest város eredete* [Der Ursprung der Stadt Pest] Tanulmányok Budapest múltjából III. (1934), Ders.: *Az Eskü-téri római erőd, Pest város őse* [Das Römerkastell am Eskü-tér, der Vorgänger der Stadt Pest] Bp. 1946.

[9] A. Pleidell: *A magyar várostörténet első fejezete* [Der erste Abschnitt der Geschichte des ungarischen Städtewesens] Századok LXVIII (1934) 1—44, 158—200, 276—313.

[10] D. Dercsényi: *Újabb régészeti kutatások és a pannóniai kontinuitás kérdése* [Neue archeologische Forschungen und die Kontinuitätsfrage in Pannonien] Századok LXXXI (1947) 203—211. A. Radnóti: *Pannóniai városok élete a korai feudalizmusban* [Das Leben in den Städten Pannoniens im Zeitalter des Frühfeudalismus] MTA történeti-társadalmi osztályának közleményei V. (1954) 489—508. E. Fügedi: *Topográfia és városi fejlődés a középkori Óbudán* [Topographie und Stadtentwicklung im mittelalterlichen Altofen] (des weiteren: Fügedi, *Altofen*) Tanulmányok Budapest múltjából XIII (1959) 9—10., G. Székely: *Le sort des agglomérations pannoniennes au début du moyen âge et les origines de l'urbanisme en Hongrie.* Annales Universitatis Scientiarum Budapestiensis de R. Eötvös nominatae. Sectio Historica III. (1961) 59—96., K. Sági: *Die zweite altchristliche Basilika von Fenékpuszta.* Acta Antiqua IX (1961) 397—440.

[11] Fügedi, *Altofen* 14, Budapest története I. 784., ein ähnlicher Fall ist uns von Nîmes in Frankreich bekannt. L. Mumford: *The City in History*, New York 1961. 248.

[12] Leider ist der Vortrag von P. Váczy noch nicht erschienen. Ein Auszug in Arrabona 6 (1964) 265—266.

Der arabische Geograph Idrisi schrieb in seinem, zu Mitte des XII. Jh. verfaßten Werk über mehrere Städte Ungarns, rühmte deren Märkte, an denen billige Agrarprodukte in Fülle und Hülle feilgeboten wurden.[13] Idrisis Zeitgenosse, Abu Hamid, der zwischen 1150—1153 in Ungarn weilte, verglich die ungarischen Städte mit Bagdad und Isfahan.[14] Diese beiden Quellen wären schon an sich genügend um behaupten zu dürfen, daß es in Ungarn schon zur Mitte des XII. Jh., also noch vor dem Eintreffen der ersten größeren westlichen Einwanderergruppe Siedlungen gab, die städtische Funktionen erfüllten und einen städtischen Charakter trugen. Ergänzen wir die Feststellungen der beiden Araber mit Angaben aus anderen Quellen, so gewinnt unsere Behauptung einen noch klareren und festeren Umriß.

In den letzten Dekaden des heidnischen Fürstentums und in den ersten Jahrzehnten des christlichen und feudalen Königstums entstanden an den Sitzen des Königs (bzw. Fürsten und des heidnischen Würdenträgers *gyula*) in den verheerten und verlassenen Römerstädten in den durch Slaven erhaltenen Festungen[15] (vor allem in Gran (Esztergom), Veszprém, Altofen (Óbuda), Csanád, Raab (Győr), Fünfkirchen, Neutra (Nyitra) und Pest) Siedlungen, die als Mittelpunkt dienten, in denen die Einwohner mit aus dem Süden und Osten importierten Luxuswaren und einheimischen Agrarprodukten (zur Kriegszeit auch mit Sklaven) Handel trieben oder Handwerker waren. Die Einrichtung der christlichen Kirche trug dazu bei diese Siedlungen als Mittelpunkte weiter zu entwickeln. Gran wurde zum Sitz eines Erzbischofs, Csanád, Fünfkirchen, Veszprém und Raab eines Bischofs, in Neutra und Altofen wurden bedeutende Stifte gegründet. Die wirtschaftliche Ansprüche der kirchlichen und weltlichen Würdenträger förderten sicherlich den nicht allzu lebendigen Warenaustauseh. Der Bischofsitz, der Sitz eines Komitatsgespans *(comes parochialis)* und die damit verbundenen Funktionen (Rechtssprechen, Schule, usw.) zogen einen Teil der Bevölkerung aus der Umgebung in diese Mittelpunkte, im Falle von Altofen konnte eine Konzentration der Agrarbevölkerung festgestellt werden.[16]

Ein Teil der Bevölkerung beschäftigte sich schon zu dieser Zeit zweifellos hauptsächlich mit Handel und Handwerk. Es liegt in der Natur unserer Quellen, daß wir mehr Angaben über den Handel als über das Handwerk besitzen. Unsere Quellen sprechen von Sarazenen in Pest,[17] von einer zahl-

---

[13] T. Lewicki: *Polska i kraje sąsednie w świetle »ksiegi Rogera« geografa arabskiego z XII w. Al-Idrisiego* [Polen und seine Nachbarstaaten im Lichte des »Buches von Roger« vom arabischen Geograph Al-Idrisi aus dem XII. Jh.](Prace Komisji Orientalistycznej 34.) Kraków 1945. Vgl. Gy. Györffy: *Das Güterverzeichnis des griechischen Klosters zu Szávaszentdemeter (Sremska Mitrovica) aus dem XII. Jh.* Studia Slavica V (1959) 26.

[14] I. Hrbek: *Ein arabischer Bericht über Ungarn.* Acta Orientalia V (1955) 21.

[15] Vgl. E. Fügedi: *Középkori magyar városprivilégiumok* [Ungarische Stadtprivilegien des Mittelalters] (die weiteren: Fügedi, *Stadtprivilegien)* Tanulmányok Budapest múltjából XIV (1961) 83. Anm. 20.

[16] Fügedi, *Altofen* 27.

[17] *Budapest történetének okleveles emlékei* (Budapester Urkundenbuch) I. 16.

reichen mohammedanischen Bevölkerung,[18] erwähnen russische Pelzhändler die auf dem Graner Markt erscheinen,[19] Juden, die mit ihren Waren von Russland nach Regensburg fuhren.[20] König Kolomann regelte in seinen Gesetzen (1097—1116) die Handelstätigkeit der einheimischen Juden, die nur in den Bischofsitzen wohnen durften.[21] Wir besitzen Angaben über ungarisch— byzantinische Handelsbeziehungen[22] und Münzfunde, die ausschließlich im Rahmen des Handelsverkehrs angehäuft werden konnten.[23] Endlich kennen wir auch den Warenhändler, der laut König Ladislaus' I. Gesetz von Stadt zu Stadt oder von Komitat zu Komitat zog.[24] Alle diese Angaben bestätigen die Behauptungen Idrisis und Abu Hamids, daß es in Ungarn Siedlungen gab, in denen Warenaustausch stattfand, wo man Wochenmärkte hielt und Kaufleute sich angesiedelt haben.

Bescheidener sind unsere Kenntnisse über die Handwerker, und mehr werden wir auch nicht wissen, solange die Archeologie diese Frage nicht ergründet. Abgesehen von solchen Siedlungen, wie die der Münzpräger in Gran, scheint es aus Idrisis und Abu Hamids Ausführungen eher wahrscheinlich, daß das Handwerk in den Hintergrund gedrängt war, an dem Markt spielten wegen des großen Angebots billige Agrarprodukte die Hauptrolle.[25] Das soziale Bild dieser Siedlungen ist klar erfaßbar: das königliche und bischöfliche Gefolge, mohammedanische und jüdische Kaufleute und ungarische Bauern lebten in buntem Durcheinander auf einem kleinen Platz zusammengepfercht. Spuren eines Bürgertums im Sinne der späteren Zeit fehlten. Der Marktzins wurde von königlichen und Komitatsbeamten eingehoben,[26] Streitfragen vom Königsrichter entschieden.[27] Auch die Steuer der Kaufleute wurde von königlichen Beamten eingetrieben.[28] Nicht einmal die Keime einer städtischen Autonomie waren vorhanden.

---

[18] HRBEK, a. a. O. 20.
[19] DOMANOVSZKY, a. a. O. 33.
[20] S. KOHN: *A zsidók története Magyarországon* [Die Geschichte der Juden in Ungarn] Bp. 1884. 59—60, 406—407
[21] Gesetzartikel 75. L. ZÁVODSZKY: *A Szt. István, László és Kálmán korabeli törvények és zsinati határozatok* [Gesetze und Synodalbeschlüsse aus der Zeit des Hl. Stephans, Ladislaus und Kolomanns] Bp. 1904.
[22] FÜGEDI, Altofen 28—29.
[23] A. KERÉNYI: *Egy XII. századi óbudai bizánci pénzlelet* [Ein byzantinischer Münzfund in Altofen aus dem XII. Jh.] Budapest Régiségei XV (1950) 524., KIRÁLY F.: *XII. századi pénzek Magyarországon* [Az esztergomi lelet összefoglaló feldolgozása] (Münzen aus dem XII. Jh. [Zusammenfassende Darstellung des Graner Münzfundes]). Folia Archeologica VII (1955) 127—140., I. MÉRI: *Árpádkori pénzváltó mérleg* [Eine Geldwage aus der Arpadenzeit] Folia Archeologica IV (1954) 106.
[24] Gesetz III. Art. 11. »De negotiatoribus euntibus de civitate in civitatem« Da das Wort civitas nicht nur Stadt sondern (in dieser Zeit) auch Komitat bedeutete, kann der Satz auf zwei Arten übersetzt werden.
[25] LEWICKI, op. cit. 129., HRBEK, a. a. O. passim.
[26] DOMANOVSZKY, a. a. O. 27—29.
[27] FÜGEDI, *Stadtprivilegien* 87, Anm. 100.
[28] Ebda.

In bezug auf die Siedlung sind zwei Typen zu unterscheiden. Den einen vertraten die Burgen (Veszprém, Raab, Neutra, Pest und wahrscheinlich auch Csanád), die man in den lateinischen Quellen im XI. Jh. *urbs*, im XII. Jh. *castrum* oder *civitas* nannte.[29] Diese Siedlungen waren den Rettungsburgen ähnlich, boten in der Not der Bevölkerung der benachbarten Dörfer Schutz. Den anderen Typ repräsentierten Altofen und Gran (bis Ende des XII. Jh.), wo keine Wehranlagen zu finden waren. Den Mittelpunkt der ummauerten oder offenen Siedlung nahm die verhältnismäßig überdimensionierte Kathedrale ein. Außer der Kathedrale durften nur wenige Ziegel- oder Steinbauten vorhanden sein, obwohl die Steine der verheerten Römerstädte als Baumaterial eine große Rolle spielten.[30] Im Schatten der Kathedrale wurden aus Lehm oder Holz kleine Häuser gebaut, die sich unregelmäßig aneinander drängten. In den dicht bebauten Siedlungen blieb kein Platz für den Markt übrig, dies verboten auch die Sicherheitsmaßnahmen, der Wochenmarkt wurde außerhalb der Mauern, doch in der Schutz bietenden Nähe derselben abgehalten.[31]

Die hier beschriebenen Siedlungen dürfen wohl als Städte angesehen werden, die Zeitgenossen nannten sie ebenfalls *civitates*. Otto von Freisingen, der zur Mitte des XII. Jh. durch Ungarn zog, fand keine Städte im Land.[32] Er hatte in jenem Sinne Recht, daß die ungarischen Städte in ihrer Erscheinung den deutschen kaum ähnlich gewesen sein konnten, auch das Bürgertum fehlte in ihnen. Schon dies weist darauf hin, daß der Widerspruch zwischen Otto von Freisingens und Abu Hamids Behauptungen am einfachsten dadurch gelöst werden kann, daß die ungarischen Städte ihrem Charakter nach dem asiatischen Stadttyp angehörten. Die angeführten Merkmale, daß diese Siedlungen Mittelpunkte des Warenaustausches waren, daß in ihnen Händler und Handwerker lebten, und daß sie doch keine Autonomie besaßen, gehören ebenfalls zu diesem Stadttyp.

Den wirtschaftlichen Boden, auf dem dieser asiatische Stadttyp sich entwickeln konnte, gewährte der Handel mit Byzanz und Kiew und die wirtschaftliche Unterentwickeltheit des Landes. Zur Mitte des XII. Jh. trat in dieser Hinsicht eine jähe Wandlung ein.

Die Wandlung kann am besten durch die Tatsache charakterisiert werden, daß Ungarn — das sich im Laufe des XI. Jh. von dem Westen her-

---

[29] A. F. GOMBOS: *Catalogus fontium historiae Hungaricae aevo ducum et regum ex stirpe Arpad descendentium*. Bp. 1938 (des weiteren: GOMBOS: *Catalogus*) 2413, 2424, 2584, 2587, 2593, 2604.
[30] SZÉKELY, a. a. O.
[31] Über Raab vgl. V. BORBIRÓ—I. VALLÓ: *Győr városépítéstörténete* [Die Baugeschichte der Stadt Raab] Bp. 1956, 73—74., über Veszprém GY. KOROMPAY: *Veszprém* Bp. 1957² 21—22. Auch in Neutra hielt man die Märkte vor 1248 außer der Burg, vgl. FEJÉR G.: *Codex diplomaticus Hungariae ecclesiasticus et civilis* (des weiteren: FEJÉR, *CD.*) IV/2. 455. (mit dem irrtümlichen Datum 1258!) I. SZENTPÉTERY: *Regesta regum stirpis Arpadianae critico-diplomatica* (des weiteren: SZP.) 885.
[32] GOMBOS, *Catalogus* 1767.

metisch abgeriegelt hat — jetzt sich der Wirtschaft Europas anschloß. Die Ursache dieser Erscheinung ist nicht nur darin zu suchen, daß 1096 bzw. 1147 die Kreuzfahrer das Land durchquerten und kennenlernten, sondern daß man in Ungarn — dafür ist wieder einmal Abu Hamid Zeuge[33] — Gold fand, das das Interesse der Kaufleute im goldarmen Europa erweckte. Von der verhältnismäßig dünnen Besiedlung und vom Reichtum des Landes angelockt kamen fremde Einwanderer ins Land. Die im Laufe des XII. Jh. erscheinenden westlichen Einwanderer waren überwiegend Bauern, doch die aus dem romanischen Sprachgebiet stammenden *latini* waren Städtebewohner.[34] Sie ließen sich in den zwei Hauptstädten des Landes, in Gran und Stuhlweißenburg nieder. Die Privilegien der Stuhlweißenburger wurden im Laufe des XIII. Jh. an andere ungarische Städte verliehen.[35] Unsere Stadt und ihre Bürger spielten also eine wichtige Rolle in der Eröffnung des zweiten Abschnittes in der Geschichte des ungarischen Städtewesens, im Laufe dessen der asiatische Stadttyp verschwand und durch einen westeuropäisch geprägten Typ ersetzt wurde. Deswegen müssen wir uns mit dem Stadtplan Stuhlweißenburgs befassen und die daraus gezogenen Schlüsse für die Geschichte des ungarischen Städtewesens verwerten.

3. Aus dem XVI. Jh. besitzen wir zwei Beschreibungen Stuhlweißenburgs, die eine von dem späteren Erzbischof von Gran, Nikolaus Oláh und die zweite vom Historiker Nikolaus Istvánffy.[36] Die zwei Autoren brachten abweichende Gesichtspunkte zur Geltung. Oláh erwähnte die geographische Lage, die Sehenswürdigkeiten und Märkte der Stadt, Istvánffy schrieb über die wehrgeographische Lage derselben. Das unmittelbar an die Stadtmauer grenzende Moor gewährte nicht nur Schutz, sondern auch wirtschaftliche Vorteile. Am Ende des XIV. Jh. zählte man im Moorland 18 Fischteiche, 38 Joch Wiesen und schätzte den Moor auf 2 *aratra*, deren Schilf großen Wert repräsentierte.[37] Im von der Stadt nördlich gelegenen Tal trieben zwei Bäche Mühlen,[38] auf dem östlich gelegenen, sanften Hügel breiteten sich

---

[33] HRBEK, a. a. O.

[34] M. AUNER: *Latinus.* Századok L (1916) 28—32., über die französische Wanderung vgl. H. AMMANN: *Die französische Südostwanderung im Rahmen der mittelalterlichen französischen Wanderungen.* Südostforschungen XIV (1955) 406—428.

[35] An Tyrnau (Trnava, Nagyszombat) 1238: A. HUŠČAVA: *Najstaršie výsady mesta Trnavy* [Die ältesten Freiheiten der Stadt Tyrnau] Bratislava 1939., Szp. 647. — an Neutra 1248: FEJÉR, CD. IV/2. 455. SZP. 885. — an Raab 1271 S. L. ENDLICHER: *Monumenta Arpadiana,* Sangalli 1849, 526., SZP. 2132. — an Szatmár 1271: ENDLICHER, op. cit. 505 (mit dem irrtümlichen Datum 1264!) SZP. 2133. — an Ödenburg (Sopron) 1277 FEJÉR CD. V/2. 397, vgl. J HÁZI: *Sopron város története* I/1. 7—8., SZP. 2809. — und Vasvár (Eisenburg) 1279 ENDLICHER, op. cit. 551, SZP. 2973.

[36] M. ISTHVÁNFI: *Historiarum de rebus Ungaricis libri XXXIV.* Viennae 1718, 314.; N. OLÁH: *Hungaria-Athila* (ed. C. Eperjessy et L. Juhász) Bp. 1938, 10.

[37] »decem et octo piscinas . . . reperissent, prata vero ad trigintaocto iugera terrarum. se extendentia conspexissent, paludmentum autem cum arundineto inter ipsas piscinas et prata existens ad duo aratra sufficiens estimassent . . .« Ung. Staatsarchiv, Mittelalterliche Urkundensammlung (des weiteren: Dl.) 23.113.

[38] Universitätsbibliothek Bp. Handschriftensammlung Ab 71/2. p. 233.

Wiesen, Acker und Rebenland aus.[39] Die Stadt bestand zu dieser Zeit aus der Burg *(castrum)* genannten Inneren Stadt, aus der nordöstlichen Ofner Vorstadt *(suburbium* oder *civitas exterior)*, aus den westlichen Vorstädten Sziget *(insula)* und Ingovány und aus einer südlichen kleinen Siedlung Újfalu *(nova villa)*. Ein tiefer Wassergraben teilte die Burg von den Vorstädten, vom Osten schützte sie der Sumpf Sóstó. Sziget und Ingovány standen an kleinen Inseln des westlichen Moorlandes. Die Ofner Vorstadt war ebenfalls von einem Wassergraben umgeben, hier aber fehlte ein Schutz gewährender Sumpf, die Stadt konnte von hieraus am besten belagert werden.[40]

Ein Knotenpunkt der Landstraßen befand sich am Marktplatz der Burg, wo auch die beiden wichtigsten Gebäude, der Königspalast und die Basilika standen.[41] Die Domherren des Marienstiftes betreuten die Krönungszeichen, die Königsgräber, die Schatzkammer und bis zum XIV. Jh. auch das Archiv. Außer diesem Stift waren in der Burg noch zwei Pfarren zu finden, eine Petri und eine Kreuzpfarre. Eine Emerichkapelle wies auf den Geburtsort des Prinzen (Sohn König Stephans I.) hin. In der Ofner Vorstadt stand das Nikolai-Stift und die Dominik-Pfarre, ein Dominikaner- und ein Franziskanerkloster. In Sziget waren die Johanniter, in Újfalu eine Martini-Pfarre tätig. Die Pfarre von Ingovány war wahrscheinlich der Hl. Elisabeth geweiht. Mit Ausnahme des Marienstiftes und der Johanniter waren alle Kirchen der Amtsgewalt des Bischofs von Veszprém unterstellt.

Die Amtsgewalt des Stadtrates erstreckte sich nicht auf alle Stadtteile. Sziget war das Gut der Johanniter, Ingovány das Gut des Marienstiftes, unterstanden also anderen Dörfern ähnlich der Befugniß des Grundherren, ihre Einwohner waren Hörige. Die in der Burg und in der Ofner Vorstadt ansässigen Bürger waren am Anfang des XVI. Jh. ungarischer Nationalität, einige Straßennamen bewahrten aber noch die Erinnerung an die französischen und deutschen Vorfahren.[42] Die Bürger waren meistens Kaufleute, einige der erhaltenen Personennamen deuten Handwerk und Agrarbeschäftigung an.[43]

---

[39] Vgl. unten Anm. 134.

[40] Aus dieser Richtung wurde die Stadt 1490 von Kaiser Maximilian belagert.

[41] KÁROLY, a. a. O. II. 234—241.

[42] Angeblich gab es eine »Olasz utca« (= Welschgasse) in der Burg (KÁROLY, a. a. O. II. 50.), wir konnten aber keine Belege dafür finden. Die Existenz einer Német utca (= vicus Teutonicalis) ist bewiesen (vgl. unten Anm. 136).

[43] Für die frühere Periode beweisen uns die Prozesse mit der Abtei von Pannonhalma die Handelstätigkeit (*Pannonhalmi Szt. Benedek rend törtéte* [Die Geschichte des Benediktinerordens von Pannonhalma] (des weiteren: PRT) I. 650—652, 680), für die spätere sind uns Urkunden über die Handelstätigkeit der Stuhlweißenburger in anderen Städten erhalten. Vgl. E. MÁLYUSZ: *Zsigmondkori Okmánytár* [Urkundenbuch aus der Regierungszeit des Königs Sigismund] I. 126, Dl. 14. 151., 16.939., 25.361., 18.091., 55.249. — Bürgernamen wie Kalmár (= Kaufmann) weisen ebenfalls auf den Handel hin (Kapitelarchiv Preßburg, Protocollum Budense f° 62, 127). Auf Handwerk weisen die Namen Aurifaber, Carnifex, Sartor, Nyerges (= Sattler), Kővágó (= Steinmetz) und Fazekas (= Töpfer) hin (Dl. 17.267., 18.022., 42.874.).

4. Die hier geschilderten verwickelten Verhältnisse waren das Ergebnis einer rund fünf Jahrhunderte lang dauernden Entwicklung, deren Anfang noch vor der Gründung des Königtums (1001) gesetzt werden muß und teilweise den geographischen Gegebenheiten der Stadt zu verdanken war.

Östlich von Stuhlweißenburg erstreckt sich in NW—SO Richtung ein fruchtbares Lößplateau, welches nach W durch den Bach Gaja abgegrenzt wird. Westlich der Stadt, wo sich die Gaja mit der Sárvíz vereinigt, lag noch im XVIII. Jh. ein ausgedehntes Moorland. Die südliche Grenze dieses Moor-

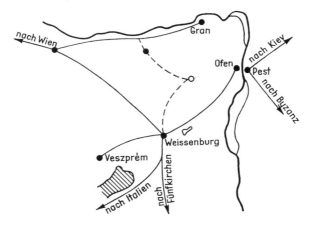

Abb. 1. Straßennetz von Stuhlweißenburg

landes bildete zwischen Sárpentele, Stuhlweißenburg und Battyány eine ungefähr dreieckige Kieselinsel. Die Stadt entstand an den westlichen Ausläufern des Lößplateaus dort, wo die Entfernung zwischen dem Lößplateau und der Kieselinsel am geringsten war, wo sich also eine bequeme Überfahrt bot. Die Entstehung der Stadt erklärt eben dieser Übergang und die damit verbundene Straßenkreuzung, die in den Zeiten der Römerherrschaft noch nicht vorhanden war. Der Schwerpunkt des Verkehrs lag damals nicht in Stuhlweißenburg, sondern südlicher in der Stadt Gorsium (beim heutigen Dorfe Tác), in Stuhlweißenburg dürfte nach Ansicht der Archeologen nur eine unbedeutende Poststation oder Siedlung gewesen sein.[44] Die Wandlung

[44] A. MAROSI: *Volt-e Székesfehérvárott római telep?* [Gab es eine Römersiedlung in Stuhlweißenburg?] Századok LXIX (1935) 266—269., J. FITZ: *Adatok Fejér megye római úthálózatához* [Beiträge zum römischen Straßennetz im Komitat Fejér] Alba Regia (im Druck). A. KRALOVÁNSZKY: *Székesfehérvár kialakulása régészeti adatok alapján* [Die Entstehung Stuhlweißenburgs auf Grund archeologischer Angaben] *Székesfehérvár évszázadai* [Die Jahrhunderte Stuhlweißenburgs] I. Székesfehérvár 1967. 9, 15.

X

112

trat allem Anscheine nach im X. Jh. und in mehreren Etappen ein. Am Anfang des X. Jh. entstand ein Knotenpunkt derselben Straßen südlich der heutigen Stadt[45] und dann im letzten Drittel des X. Jh. erscheinen an den sich in Stuhlweißenburg kreuzenden Straßen die Gräberfelder der landnehmenden Ungarn.[46] Wir sind leider nicht in der Lage die Wandlung zu ergründen, vermuten aber, daß sie das Ergebnis einer planmäßigen Neuordnung war[47] und kennen die durch ihr geschaffene neue Lage, für die wir natürlich nur aus dem XI. Jh. zuverlässige schriftliche Quellen besitzen.

Die größte Bedeutung besaß die alte Römerstraße, die vom Westen der Donau entlang nach Raab, von dort nach Stuhlweißenburg,[48] dann über Tolna und Baranyavár nach Belgrad und als Endziel in das Hl. Land führte. Eine nach Györffy aus 1030—1043 stammende »Descriptio itineris in terram sanctam« gibt eine detaillierte Beschreibung dieser Route.[49] Demnach legten die Pilger den Weg von Raab nach Stuhlweißenburg und von dort nach Tolna in je drei Tagen zurück. Eine in der ersten Hälfte des XI. Jh. noch weniger wichtige, aber am Ende des Jahrhunderts schon bedeutende Landstraße erreichte Stuhlweißenburg von Gran aus über Totis (Tata).[50] Diese in N—S Richtung laufende Straßen kreuzten in Stuhlweißenburg eine ebenfalls römische Straße, die von der Donauüberfahrt in Pest an dem Nordufer des Velence-Sees Stuhlweißenburg erreichte und von dort in zwei Richtungen nach dem Westen weiterführte. Die eine ging nach Veszprém, die andere zum Plattensee.[51] Den tatsächlichen Gebrauch beider Straßen beweisen uns Quellenangaben aus dem XI. Jh.[52]

Die Straßenführung kann auch in dem Stadtplan verfolgt werden. Die aus Raab und Pest kommenden Straßen vereinigten sich vor der Burg in der (späteren) Ofner Vorstadt und traten als ein einziger Weg durch das Ofner Tor in die Burg. Diese Hauptstraße (vicus magnus) bog vor der Basilika nach dem Westen ab, verließ die Burg durch das Palotaer Tor und zweigte in der Vorstadt Sziget nach Veszprém bzw. nach dem Süden ab. Nachdem der südliche Zweig die Sárvíz übertrat, spaltete er sich nach Tolna bzw.

---

[45] KRALOVÁNSZKY, a. a. O. 15.
[46] K. BAKAY: Székesfehérvár környékének X—XI. századi temetői és a fejedelmi székhely kérdése [Die Gräberfelder aus dem X—XI. Jh. in der Umgebung von Stuhlweißenburg und die Frage des Fürstensitzes] Alba Regia (im Druck).
[47] KRALOVÁNSZKY, a. a. O. 15.
[48] L. GLASER: A Dunántúl középkori úthálózata [Das mittelalterliche Straßennetz Transdanubiens] Századok LXIII (1929) 144—145.
[49] GOMBOS: Catalogus. 844—845. GYÖRFFY GY.: Az Árpádkori Magyarország történeti földrajza [Die historische Geographie Ungarns in der Zeit der Arpaden] Bp. 1963. I. 279—280.
[50] GLASER, a. a. O. 144. Das türkische Heer benutzte noch im XVI. Jh. diese Straße, vgl. G. BÁLINTH: A magyarországi török hódoltságról [Von der Türkenherrschaft in Ungarn] Századok IV (1870) 240—241.
[51] GLASER, a. a. O. 143—145.
[52] Als Pilger kamen an der Straße Raab-Stuhlweißenburg 1065 Altman (GOMBOS, Catalogus 2310—2311.) vgl. S. ECKHARDT: András király francia zarándokai [Die französischen Pilger unter Andreas I.] Magyar Nyelv 1935. 38—40. Bischof Gerhard benützte die Straße von Stuhlweißenburg nach Ofen (GOMBOS: Catalogus 2431).

nach dem Plattensee. In dem Mittelpunkt der Burg, wo der Weg nach dem Westen abbog, befand sich einer der wichtigsten Handelsplätze des frühmittelalterlichen Ungarns.

Die früheste Erwähnung Stuhlweißenburgs finden wir in der Gründungsurkunde des Bistums von Veszprém. Die Urkunde stammt — wie es neuestens Györffy bewiesen hat[53] — aus dem Jahre 1009 und aus ihr geht klar hervor, daß Stuhlweißenburg zu dieser Zeit schon der Sitz eines Komitatsgespans war. Die Legenden des Hl. Stephans und die ungarischen Chroniken erwähnen

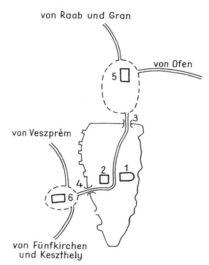

Abb. 2. Die Straßenverzweigung in Stuhlweißenburg

Stuhlweißenburg im Zusammenhang mit der Gründung der Basilika.[54] Sie berichten, daß Stephan die Kirche aus dem im gegen die Bulgaren geführten siegreichen Krieg erbeuteten Schatz erbauen ließ. Györffy kam nach Konfrontierung der Quellen zu dem Schluß, daß dieses Ereignis auf 1015 zu setzen ist.[55] Die Behauptung, daß die Kirche tatsächlich von Stephan gegründet wurde, wird auch dadurch unterstützt, daß der spätere ungarische Krönungsmantel ursprünglich ein Geschenk Stephans und seiner Gemahlin Gisela für die Basilika war, wie dies die Anschrift des Mantels beweist.[56] Die Lokalisierung der Kirche verursacht keine Schwierigkeiten, da die Grundmauern

[53] GY. GYÖRFFY: *Székesfehérvár feltűnése a történeti forrásokban* [Das Erscheinen Stuhlweißenburgs in den Geschichtsquellen] Székesfehérvár évszázadai I. 19—24.
[54] GOMBOS: *Catalogus.* 2587, 2593, 2610.
[55] GYÖRFFY: *Studia Slavica.* V (1959) 21.
[56] Sie lautet: »Anno Incarnationis Christi MXXXI Indictione XIII a Stephano Rege et Gisela Regina Casula haec operata et data ecclesiae Sanctae Mariae sitae in Civitate Alba«. A. IPOLYI: *A magyar szentkorona és koronázási jelvények* [Die ungarische Krone und die Krönungszeichen] Bp. 1886.

X

114

größtenteils ausgegraben und zur Besichtigung freigelegt sind. Doch eben die Lage der Kirche und die Überlieferung über ihre Gründung stellt uns einige nicht ganz leicht lösbare Fragen.

Unsere Quellen erzählen die Gründung der Basilika beinahe Wort für Wort einstimmig, da wahrscheinlich alle aus einer in der Regierungszeit Ladislaus I. (1077—1095) verfaßten und verschollenen *Gesta Ungarorum* schöpften. Der Bericht lautet, daß Stephan die Gründung »*in ipsa regalis sedis civitate, quae dicitur Alba*«[57] vornahm, daraus folgt, daß die Siedlung zur Zeit der Gründung schon bestand und den Namen »Weißenburg« führte. Außer einem[58] nennt kein einziger Variant Stephan den Gründer der Stadt, obwohl — wenn er es gewesen wäre — dies von den Chroniken, noch mehr aber von den Legenden zu erwarten wäre. Scheinbar war Stephan nicht der Gründer der Stadt und diese Tatsache wird auch von anderen Überlegungen unterstützt. Laut Tradition wurde Stephans Sohn, Emerich in Stuhlweißenburg geboren. Am Anfang des XV. Jh. ließ der Probst Kálmáncsehi am angeblichen Geburtsort eine Gedenktafel errichten.[59] Emerich wurde 1007 geboren, wenn er also das Tageslicht in der Burg erblickte, dann mußte der Königspalast schon 1007 stehen, was übrigens mit der Stiftsurkunde des Veszprémer Bistums im Einklang steht. Unser zweites Argument hängt mit der Petrikirche zusammen. Die sog. Wiener Bilderchronik erwähnt, daß Béla IV. noch als *rex iunior* — also 1220—1235 — diese Kirche weihen ließ.[60] Die Chronik nennt die Kirche in auffallender Weise *cathedralis*, obwohl — wie das schon der Herausgeber Domanovszky feststellte — sie keine Bischofskirche war und neben der Basilika nicht einmal als vornehm bezeichnet werden konnte. Ohne Grund verwendete aber der Chronist das ehrenvolle Attribut doch nicht, da die Kirche im Krönungszeremoniell eine wichtige Rolle spielte. Der König wurde in der Basilika gekrönt, danach ging er im feierlichen Zug zur Petrikirche hinüber, wo er seine erste Regierungshandlungen vornahm: er sprach einige Urteile und schlug Auserwählte zu Rittern.[61] Die Eingliederung der Kirche in das Zeremoniell kann keinesfalls mit der Vorliebe Bélas für die Kirche erklärt werden. Beide Erscheinungen — das Attribut *cathedralis* und die Rolle im Krönungszeremoniell — erklärt uns der polnische Historiker Johann Dlugosz, der in seinem Werke die Krönung seines Herrn, Wladyslaw Jagiello darstellend bemerkt, daß Fürst Géza (Stephans Vater) und seine Gemahlin hier begraben waren.[62]

---

[57] GOMBOS, *Catalogus*. 2587. In der sog. kleinen Legende »in Alba civitate . . . templum instauravit« (ebda 2610.).
[58] *Scriptores Rerum Hungaricarum* (ed. E. SZENTPÉTERY) (des weiteren: *SRH*) I. 102. GYÖRFFY: *Székesfehérvár évszázadai*. I. 20. Diese Version ist aber eine spätere Interpolation.
[59] E. PRAY: *Dissertatio historico-critica de S. Emerico duce*. Posonii, 1774.
[60] SRH I. 467.
[61] J. FITZ: *Adatok Székesfehérvár középkorához* [Beiträge zur mittelalterlichen Geschichte Stuhlweißenburgs] Fehérvár I. (1955) 66. u. ff.
[62] J. DLUGOSZ: *Historiae Polonicae libri XII*. Lipsiae 1711. I. 742—743.

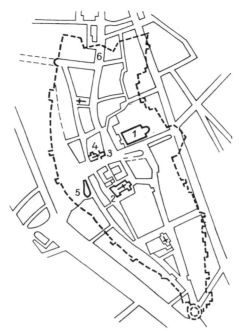

Abb. 3. Der Grundriß der Innenstadt. 1 = Die Basilika, 2 = Die Petrikirche, 3 = Marktplatz, 4 = Königspalast, 5 = Das Palotaer Tor, 6 = Das Ofner Tor

Zu den Argumenten aus den Quellen gesellen sich noch solche aus dem Stadtplan. Die Petrikirche steht heute am höchsten Punkt der Stadt, ungefähr 6 m. höher als die Basilika. Da zu jener Zeit der Wehrcharakter der Burg stark in den Vordergrund trat, ist es kaum vorstellbar, daß man die Familienkirche des Königs, die Basilika nicht auf dem höchsten, am besten schützbaren Punkt aufgebaut hätte. War sie also nicht dort erbaut, kann das nur dadurch begründet werden, daß am höchst gelegenen Punkt für sie kein Platz mehr da war, da zu dieser Zeit schon die Petrikirche den kleinen Hügel einnahm. Fürst Géza starb 997 als ein aus politischen Gründen getaufter, aber keineswegs überzeugter christlicher Herrscher. Sein Sohn Stephan I., der schon ein Gläubiger war, ließ ihn in einer Kirche zu letzte Ruhe setzen, was dem Fürsten des Landes sicherlich gebührte. Diese Kirche mußte also schon 997 eingeweiht gewesen sein. Daraus folgt aber, daß Stuhlweißenburg nicht unter Stephan I., sondern unter einem seiner Vorfahren entstand. Der Name Weißenburg befürwortet in mehreren Hinsichten Gézas Regierungszeit.[63]

[63] Der Namen Stuhlweißenburgs stellt ein Problem dar, daß von der ungarischen Geschichts- und Sprachwissenschaft seit längerer Zeit diskutiert wurde. Der Slavist J. MELICH wies darauf hin, daß der Name Gézas Gemahlin Sarolt dieselbe Zusammensetzung aus *šary (= weiß) + *aldy (= Hermelin) ist, wie das von Konstantinos Porphyrogenitos erhaltene Sarkel aus *šary + käl (= Haus), das russisch Běla Veža genannt wurde. (J. MELICH: *A honfoglaláskori Magyarország* [Ungarn zur Zeit der Landnahme] Bp. 1925—1929. 45—46.) Die

Die aus den Quellen und aus dem Stadtplan geschöpften Argumente weisen also auf die Entstehung Stuhlweißenburgs im X. Jh. hin, weisen aber keineswegs auf die Ausdehnung der ersten Siedlung. Es wäre am einfachsten anzunehmen, daß diese erste Siedlung sich auf dem kleinen Hügel um die Petrikirche erstreckte. Dies könnte einerseits durch die Tatsache unterstützt werden, daß der Marktplatz sich in diesem Falle vor der Burg befände (was der üblichen Praxis durchaus entspräche)[64] weiterhin durch die Tatsache, daß man am Fuße des kleinen Hügels (unter dem heutigen Rathaus) mittelalterliche Mauern (mit einem Wassergraben) und Brunnen bzw. Zisternen fand.[65] Leider aber können wir heute weder beweisen, daß der Markt schon vor der Erbauung der Basilika an seinem späteren Platz abgehalten wurde, noch eine beiläufige Chronologie für die Erbauung der erwähnten Mauern feststellen. Außerdem würde eine solche Lösung noch bedeuten, daß die Basilika außer dem Bereich der Festung stand, was nicht sehr wahrscheinlich ist, oder eine Erweiterung der Burg in der Regierungszeit Stephans I., des Näheren im Zeitraum 1015—1038 voraussetzen würde. Die erste schriftliche Angabe über die Wehrbauten stammt aus 1063, als im letzten Heidenaufstand der König und seine Gefolgschaft gezwungen waren sich in die Burg zurückzuziehen.[66] Leider spricht aber diese Angabe kein einziges Wort über die Art und Ausdehnung der Festung, letzten Endes konnte hier auch nur vom Königspalast (der zwei Türme hatte)[67] die Rede sein. Die Forschungen über die historische Topographie der Stadt ergaben bis jetzt soviel, daß das Areal des Marienstiftes und des königlichen Palastes zwei Komplexe von ungefähr gleicher Größe (11.500 bzw. 11.300 m²) darstellen und eine planmäßige Ausdehnung oder wenigstens eine planmäßige Gestaltung des Terrains anzunehmen ist.[68] In allen diesen Fragen sollen künftig methodisch durchgeführte Grabungen entscheiden, bishin müssen wir uns mit der Feststellung zufrieden stellen,

sog. kleine Legende des Hl. Stephans behauptet, daß die Stadt Alba »ob specialitatem nobilitatis sue nomen accepit«. GYÖRFFY (*Székesfehérvár évszázadai.* I. 20.) vertrat den Standpunkt, daß die Benennung von der Farbe der Gebäuden stammt. J. HORVÁTH sieht in den Namen Weißenburg einen Beweis dafür, daß die Siedlung der Mittelpunkt der unter der Regierung Fürst Gézas lebenden »weißen Ungarn« war und weist darauf hin, daß in der Namensgebung der Nomaden die Farben eine wichtige Rolle spielen (*Székesfehérvár évszázadai.* I. 107—108). Wie immer dem auch sei, es besteht kein Grund den Namen aus dem slavischen (Belgrad) abzuleiten, wie dies E. MOLNÁR *(A magyar társadalom története az őskortól az Árpádkorig)* [Die Geschichte des ungarischen Volkes von der Urzeit bis zur Zeit der Arpaden] Bp. 1949² 242.) tut, ohne aber seinen Standpunkt zu begründen.

[64] Vgl. Anm. 31.

[65] Á. DORTMUTH: *Adatok a városháza múltjához* [Beiträge zur Vergangenheit des Rathauses] Székesfehérvári Szemle 1937. 18—23. Der Verfasser vertritt die Ansicht, daß die Mauer und der Graben zur Befestigung der Petrikirche gehörten ohne aber eine Chronologie zu erwähnen.

[66] *SRH.* I. 359. »Rex autem et episcopi cunctique proceres videntes immensam multitudinem timuerunt, ne forte irruerunt in eos. Et intrantes civitatem observaverunt eam.«

[67] KÁROLY, a. a. O. II. 234—241.

[68] A. KRALOVÁNSZKY: *Székesfehérvár X—XI. századi településtörténeti kérdései* [Siedlungsgeschichtliche Probleme Stuhlweißenburgs in den X—XI. Jh.] Székesfehérvár évszázadai I. 39—40.

daß Stuhlweißenburg im X. Jh. (wahrscheinlich unter Fürst Gézas Regierungs-
zeit) entstand. Eine großzügige Entwicklung erlebte Stuhlweißenburg zwischen dem
Tode Stephans (1038) und dem Anfang des XII. Jh. kaum. Die politischen
Ereignisse des XI. Jh. (Heidenaufstände, Kämpfe mit dem Kaiser um die
Unabhängigkeit) waren für eine friedliche Entwicklung vollkommen ungünstig.
Die Bedeutung dieses Zeitalters lag eher darin, daß die Funktionen Stuhlweißenburgs als der Hauptstadt des Landes sich festigten. Diese Funktionen
sind trotz den spärlichen Angaben klar zu erkennen. Die größte Rolle spielte
die Stadt als religiöser Mittelpunkt. Stephan — das betonen unsere Quellen
einstimmig — gründete die Basilika als Eigenkirche *(ecclesiam in propriam
capellam rex sibi retinens),*[69] enthob sie deswegen von der bischöflichen Amtsgewalt und unterstellte sie unmittelbar dem Hl. Stuhl.[70] Eine Analyse der
Quellen ließ vermuten, daß die Basilika an eine früher bestehende Kirche
anknüpfte,[71] eine Grabung im Jahre 1965 bewies, daß die Basilika tatsächlich
an der Stelle eines früheren christlichen Friedhofs steht.[72] Die zunehmende
Kraft des Christentums zog — besonders nach der Kanonisierung Stephans
und Emerichs (1083) — scharenweise Pilger in die Kirche und es entwickelte
sich rasch der Gebrauch Maria Himmelfahrt (15. August) in Stuhlweißenburg
zu feiern.[73] Seit Kolomann (†1116) setzte man die Herrscher des Landes
regelmäßig hier zur letzten Ruhe.[74] Man nahm Staatsakte in Stuhlweißenburg
vor, hier setzte der Kaiser seinen Schützling, Peter Orseolo auf den Thron
des Landes zurück (1045), hier empfing König Salomon den Kaiser (1063).[75]
Religiöse Tradition und Staatsakte zogen andere Institutionen mit sich, über
eine Schule sind uns schon aus Stephans Regierungszeit Angaben erhalten
geblieben.[76] Auch hohe kirchliche Würdenträger, z. B. der Bischof von Veszprém
erwarben sich hier Haus und Liegenschaften.[77]

Von den städtischen wirtschaftlichen Funktionen finden wir vor dem
XII. Jh. die Funktion des Warenaustausches. Obzwar unmittelbare Angaben
über den Marktzins nur aus der Mitte des XIII. Jh. uns zur Verfügung

[69] GOMBOS: *Catalogus* 615.
[70] J. SEBESTYÉN: *A székesfehérvári prépostság és káptalan egyházi kiváltságai* [Die kirchlichen Freiheiten der Stuhlweißenburger Propstei und Kapitel] Századok LIX—LX (1925—1926)
376—395, 462—477.
[71] J. HORVÁTH: *Székesfehérvár korai történetének néhány kérdése az írásos források alapján*
[Einige probleme der Frühgeschichte von Stuhlweißenburg auf Grund schriftlichen Quellen]
Székesfehérvár évszázadai I. 111—112.
[72] KRALOVÁNSZKY: *Székesfehérvár évszázadai.* I. 41—42.
[73] GOMBOS: *Catalogus* 2587.
[74] DERCSÉNYI: *A székesfehérvári királyi bazilika* [Die königliche Basilika in Stuhl-
weißenburg] Bp. 1943. 37.
[75] GOMBOS: *Catalogus.* 98, 103.
[76] Ebda 2428.
[77] »pallatium ecclesia episcopatus Vesprimiensis a tempore fundationis eiusdem ecclesie
in castro Albensi habitum« KÁROLYI, a. a. O. II. 690.

stehen,[78] haben wir bei einer anderen Gelegenheit bewiesen, daß man in den Komitatszentren schon in der zweiten Hälfte des XI. Jh. regelmäßig Wochenmärkte hielt und daß sich mit ihnen die Gesetzgebung seit König Ladislaus I. öfter befaßte.[79] Diese Gesetze bezogen sich in erster Reihe auf die Märkte der zwei Hauptstädte Stuhlweißenburg und Gran.[80] In Stuhlweißenburg besassen das Marienstift und der Bischof von Veszprém den Marktzins.

Archeologische Forschungen weisen auf eine Bevölkerungskonzentration hin, indem sich die Friedhöfe des X—XII. Jh. allmählich der Stadt näherten.[81] Eine Schätzung ergab für die Stadt eine Bevölkerung zwischen 2300—2700 Seelen am Anfang, 3200—3800 Seelen am Ausgang des XI. Jh., für die nähere Umgebung 200—1000 Seelen am Anfang, 300—1300 am Ausgang des XI. Jh.[82]

Trotz der hier erwähnten Funktionen dürfen wir Stuhlweißenburg nicht als eine Stadt im europäischen Sinne des Wortes ansehen. Die Stuhlweißenburger waren nämlich keine Bürger, sondern Kleriker, königliche Hof- und Kriegsleute, königliche oder kirchliche Hintersassen oder Sklaven. Eine Selbstverwaltung im späteren Sinne des Wortes darf ebenfalls nicht vorausgesetzt werden. Deswegen halten wir Stuhlweißenburg samt anderen Städten Ungarns im XI—XII. Jh. für Städte asiatischen Typs, welche zwar ebenso Mittelpunkte des Warenaustausches waren, ebenso Händler und Handwerker in sich schlossen wie die europäischen, ebenso befestigte und dicht bevölkerte Siedlungen waren, wie diese, also in bezug auf die wirtschaftlichen Funktionen und auf die Siedlungsform tatsächliche Städte waren, in welchen aber das rechtlich abgesonderte Bürgertum fehlte, eine bürgerliche Selbstverwaltung unbekannt und der König bzw. seine Beamten die einzigen Machtinhaber und Gebieter waren.

5. Die genannten Funktionen ließen bis zur Mitte des XII. Jh. rund um die Burg die schon erwähnten vorstädtischen Siedlungen entstehen. Von der Pfarrkirche der südlichen kleinen Siedlung Újfalu (nova villa) konnte J. Fitz feststellen, daß sie zur Mitte des XII. Jh. erbaut wurde.[83] Darf man die Verhältnisse, die auf den Karten des XVIII. Jh. festgehalten sind, auf das Mittelalter zurückprojizieren, so bestand Újfalu aus einer einzigen Gasse, die auf einer kleinen Insel entlangführte.[84] Diese Gasse war aber kein Teil einer Landstraße, ebendeswegen müssen wir Újfalu für die jüngste Vorstadt

[78] *Monumenta Romana episcopatus Vesprimensis* (des weiteren: *Mon. Rom. Vespr.*) I. 228

[79] FÜGEDI: *Stadtprivilegien.* 28—30.
[80] DOMANOVSZKY, a. a. O. 33.
[81] BAKAY, a. a. O.
[82] J. NEMESKÉRI—A. KRALOVÁNSZKY: *Székesfehérvár becsült népessége a X—XI. századokban* [Die geschätzte Bevölkerungszahl Stuhlweißenburgs in den X—XI. Jh.] *Székesfehérvár évszázadai.* I. 125—138
[83] J. FITZ: *A középkori Szt. Márton templom Székesfehérvárott* [Die mittelalterliche Martinikirche in Stuhlweißenburg] *Művészettörténeti értesítő* V. (1956) 26—31.
[84] Die Karte wurde in der Zeitschrift *Műemlékvédelem* VIII (1964) 35. veröffentlicht.

halten, jünger als Sziget und die Ofner Vorstadt waren, die beide an der Landstraße entstanden. Noch eine Erscheinung deutet darauf hin, daß Újfalu unbedeutend gewesen war und blieb. Im XV. Jh. hat man die zwölf Geschworenen aus den verschiedenen Stadtteilen gewählt und sie dementsprechend in den Urkunden angeführt. Die beiden Geschworenen aus der *nova villa* erwähnte man als letzte.[85]

Sziget *(insula)*, wie schon der Name besagt,[86] befand sich ebenfalls auf einer kleinen Insel. Über die Entstehung dieser Siedlung gibt uns die Gründungsurkunde des hier erbauten Johanniter Klosters einige Hinweise. Laut dieser, 1193 ausgestellten Urkunde legte der Graner Erzbischof Martirius den Grundstein der Kirche zu ehren des heiligen Königs Stephan, die Kirche war aber nur halbwegs erbaut, als Martirius starb. Königin Euphrosine ließ nicht nur den Bau der Kirche vollenden, sondern errichtete auch ein Kloster daneben, das sie den Johannitern übergab.[87] Diese setzten ihre Tätigkeit im *domus hospitalis S. Stephani regis* bis zur Türkenherrschaft (1543) fort. Um die Chronologie dieser Geschehnisse darzustellen, soll hier erwähnt werden, daß Martirius 1150—1158 Erzbischof von Gran war,[88] d. h. die Kirche war 1158 nur halbwegs erbaut. Königin Euphrosine genoß hauptsächlich in der Regierungszeit ihres ersten Sohnes Stephans III. (1162—1172) großen Einfluß, da sie aber nach 1172 gegen ihren Sohn Béla III. auftrat, wurde sie 1186 in ein Kloster gesperrt und noch im selben Jahr verbrannt.[89] Demnach fällt ihre Tätigkeit als Gründerin vermutlich zwischen 1162 und 1172. Den Grundstein legte also Martirius frühestens 1150, die Johanniter konnten spätestens 1172 in das neue Ordenshaus einziehen. Die Siedlung, die als Rahmen der Kirchengründung diente, dürfte demnach spätestens in der ersten Hälfte des XII. Jh. entstanden sein.

Die Vorstadt Sziget hatte anfangs zwei Funktionen. Die eine erfüllte das Kloster, indem es den Pilgern Schutz und Verpflegung bot, doch diese Funktion bestand nur bis zum Ausgang des XII. Jh., vom XIII. Jh. an war das Ordenshaus als glaubwürdiger Ort tätig. Die Funktion der Siedlung war eine ganz andere. Aus der Gründungsurkunde geht es klar hervor, daß das Ordenshaus keine Liegenschaften (außer dem Grundstück an dem es stand) in Stuhlweißenburg besaß, diese lagen außer der Gemarkung der Stadt. Sziget war aber der Mittelpunkt und die Verwaltungszentrale ihrer Güter, der Wein aus den im Komitat Somogy liegenden Weingärten wurde hierher transportiert, das Korn zu Mehl gemahlen, usw.[90] Die Einwohner Szigets waren Hand-

---

[85] B. Z. Dl. 42.874., 18.022., 18.023., 18.085. usw.
[86] Das ungarische Wort »sziget« bedeutet Insel.
[87] *Monumenta ecclesiae Strigoniensis* (ed. F. KNAUZ) I. 142—146., Szp. 155.
[88] Ebda I. 105—106.
[89] GYÖRFFY: *Studia Slavica.* V (1959) 35—37.
[90] J. MIKOS: *A fehérvári keresztesek 1193. évi oklevele mint magyar nyelvemlék* [Die Urkunde der Stuhlweißenburger Johanniter aus d. J. 1193 als ungarisches Sprachdenkmal] Magyar Nyelv XXX (1935) 300. u. Karte.

werker (Bäcker, Weber, Fleischhacker) und Kaufleute. Agrarbevölkerung wohnte in dieser Vorstadt kaum, da zu den Grundstücken keine Ackerfelder gehörten,[91] in diesem Sinne war Sziget eher ein städtisches als ein vorstädtisches Gebilde. In bezug auf die Amtsgewalt und Rechtspflege trug die Siedlung den Charakter eines Privatgutes, das der Richter der Johanniter verwaltete,[92] und in dem die Bürger der Stadt keine Rechte besaßen.

Die älteste Vorstadt war zweifellos die spätere Ofner Vorstadt *(suburbium* oder *civitas exterior)*, für deren Entstehung wir in der Geschichte des Nikolaistiftes und der Siedlung der *latini* Hinweise finden.

Wie schon erwähnt stand in der Ofner Vorstadt ein dem Hl. Nikolaus geweihtes Chorherrenstift *(extra muros)*, über das wir nur spärliche Angaben besitzen. Die Nikolaikirche taucht zum erstenmal 1215 auf, doch aus der Urkunde kann nur soviel festgestellt werden, daß der König die Kirche *(ecclesia s. Nicolai)* im Komitat Somogy mit einem Gut belehnte.[93] Einige Jahre später wird die Kirche öfters erwähnt und wir erfahren, daß sie eine *ecclesia hospitalis* war.[94] Nach dem Tatareneinfall, 1244 hören wir von dem Probst der Nikolaikirche[95] und damit ist scheinbar alles wissenswerte abgeschlossen, da die Probstei und das Chorherrenstift bis zur Türkenherrschaft erhalten blieb. Doch am Ende des XIV. Jh. treten uns in einer päpstlichen Urkunde neue Titel entgegen. 1392 erwähnt der Papst *prepositura, magistratus nuncupata s. Nicolai extra muros Albensis.*[96] Diese Angabe scheint dadurch vollkommen berechtigt zu sein, daß — wie wir es 1447 in einer ebenfalls päpstlichen Supplication lesen — die Kirche auch mit Seelsorge beauftragt war *(cui cura imminet animarum)*[97] und in diesem Fall auch als *magistratus*

---

[91] 1272 befreite König Stephan V. die Bewohner von der Pflicht den Magnaten des Landes Unterkunft zu bieten »cum dicti populi terras arabiles aut silvas aut alias aliquas utilitates preter areas et fundos domorum suarum non [habent] unde se commode possent sustentare« FEJÉR *CD* V/1.211. Szp. 2182.

[92] »iudex, iurati, ceterique cives et iobagiones ... fratris preceptoris ac conventus ecclesie Cruciferorum S. Regis Stephani de Alba, in eadem civitate Alba constituti« Universitätsbibliothek. Handschriftensammlung Ab. 71/2 38.

[93] Dl. 44.118.

[94] *Mon. Rom. Vespr.* I. 80. ((1229) und »sancti Nicolai hospitalis Albensis« ebda I. 95 (1234).

[95] »prepositus ecclesie sancti Nicolai Albensis« ebda I. 119.

[96] Ebda II. 283.

[97] Ebda IV. 129. Außerdem gibt es zwei Angaben, die geeignet sind, die Frage der Nikolaikirche noch verwickelter zu gestalten. 1395 lesen wir in einer päpstlichen Bulle (ebda II. 297) »super perpetuum prioratum sive magistratum nuncupatum ecclesie sancti Nicolai extra muros Alberegalis«. Im Westen könnte der Ausdruck »prioratus« als ein Benediktinerkloster oder als irgendeine Filiation eines Benediktinerklosters gedeutet werden. In Ungarn aber war die Bezeichnung »prior« bei den Benediktinern nicht üblich, die dem Abt zunächst folgende Würde war der »decanus«. (Für diese freundliche Mitteilung bin ich Herrn L. Mezey zum Dank verpflichtet.) Außerdem lag in der Nähe kein Kloster, das in Frage käme. Pannonhalma hat ein viel besser erhaltenes Archiv als daß man voraussetzen könnte, daß die diesbezüglichen Angaben verloren gegangen wären. Das nächste Kloster, Totis, war demgegenüber eine private Gründung, was sich wieder mit dem königlichen Patronatsrecht des Nikolaistiftes nicht in Einklang bringen läßt. (M. KOMJÁTHY: *Tata és a tatai bencés apátság az Árpádok korában.* [Totis und die Benediktinerabtei in der Zeit der Arpaden] Regnum 1944—1946. 232—235).

(rectoratus) angesehen werden dürfte. Die vom König gegründete Nikolai-kirche stand allem Anscheine nach mit den Pilgerfahrten im engsten Zusammenhang, wurde aus einer bedeutenden Hospitalkirche in ein Stift umwandelt, oder schon als solches gegründet. Aus der Feststellung, daß die Kirche vor allem als Hospitalkirche fungierte, können wir auf ihre Gründungszeit schliessen. Vor 1087, also die Übertragung der Nikolaireliquien nach Bari und somit vor dem Beginn des Kultes des Hl. Nikolaus ist die Gründung der Kirche unwahrscheinlich. Vor 1095 dürften die Pilger kaum eine große Zahl erreicht haben, nach 1097 aber mußte ihre Zahl rapid zunehmen. Diesmal waren es nicht nur Ausländer, sondern auch Ungarn, für die 1135 eine Ungarin in Jerusalem ein Hospiz gründete.[98] Der zweite Kreuzzug, der 1147 das Land durchquerte, förderte diese Bewegung noch. Als wahrscheinlichstes Datum für die Gründung der Nikolaikirche erscheint die erste Hälfte des XII. Jh. Sicher ist es, daß sie vor der Ankunft der Lateiner gegründet wurde, da das Stift in der Ofner Vorstadt seine eigene Hörigen hatte und über ihnen volle grundherrschaftliche Rechtsgewalt besaß.[99]

In der Ofner Vorstadt hat sich auch die von unserem Standpunkt aus bedeutendste Volksschicht, die *latini* niedergelassen.

Mit diesen Lateinern befaßte sich die ungarische und ausländische Literatur schon seit längerer Zeit und diese Tatsache entledigt uns einer eingehenden Untersuchung ihrer Nationalität. Es genügt vollkommen darauf hinzuweisen, daß sie hauptsächlich Franzosen und Flanderer waren, die Italiener bildeten eine Minderheit. Der Stammort der Stuhlweißenburger *Latini* kann wegen Mangel an Quellenmaterial nicht näher bestimmt werden. Von unserem Standpunkt bildet die Zeit ihrer Einwanderung die wichtigste Frage. Es ist sicher, daß sie 1221 schon seit längerer Zeit hier wohnten, da gegen sie seitens der Benediktinerabtei Pannonhalma ein Prozeß geführt wurde.[100] Um ihre Einwanderungszeit festzustellen müssen wir die ungarisch—französischen Beziehungen im allgemeinen überblicken. Vereinzelte Beziehungen bestanden schon seit dem Anfang des XI. Jh. (z. B. mit Cluny),[101] doch waren sie eher persönlicher Natur und hörten während der Heidenaufstände auf.[102] Die ersten engeren Beziehungen entstanden — im Mittelalter kaum anders zu erwarten — auf dem Gebiet der kirchlichen Organisation.

Die andere Angabe stammt aus einer Supplication. 1436 ersuchte der Propst des Nikolaistiftes den Papst »ut parochialis ecclesia s. Nicolai praepositurae suae incorporetur« (P. LUKCSICS: *Diplomata pontificum saec.* XV. Budapestini 1931. II. 408.). Als Grund gab er an »dicta ecclesia parochialis duodecim annos vacat eiusque domus et mansiones sunt in totum destructae«. Wir glauben, daß es sich hier eigentlich von einer Kirche, aber von zwei Benefizien handelt, indem außer dem Propst auch ein »rector« fungierte, bzw. separate Pfründe zog.

[98] B. HÓMAN—GY. SZEKFÜ: *Magyar történet* [Ungarische Geschichte] I. Bp. 1937. 6.
[99] KÁROLY, a. a. O. II. 107.
[100] PRT. I. 650—652.
[101] AMMANN, a. a. O.
[102] ECKHARDT, a. a. O.

1091 kamen französische Mönche aus St. Gilles in das von Ladislaus I. gegründete Kloster von Somogyvár, die Verbindung zwischen den beiden Abteien bestand sicherlich bis zum Ausgang des XIII. Jh.[103] Als 1096 und 1147 die Kreuzfahrer durch Ungarn zogen, nahmen daran auch Franzosen teil und Odo de Deogilo erwähnte in seinem über den zweiten Kreuzzug verfaßten Bericht auch Stuhlweißenburg.[104] Aus diesem Bericht kann ein *argumentum ex silentio* geschöpft werden. Da er nämlich weder in Gran (das er persönlich besuchte), noch in Stuhlweißenburg französische Einwanderer erwähnte, dürfen wir daraus folgern, daß solche sich hier noch nicht befanden. Damit wäre ein *terminus post quem* in dem Jahre 1147 gegeben.

Um den *terminus ante quem* zu bestimmen, wollen wir den 1237 erlassenen Freiheitsbrief der Stuhlweißenburger Lateiner eingehender untersuchen. Leider ist diese Urkunde weder im Original noch in einer Abschrift in ihrem vollen Wortlaut erhalten geblieben, wir besitzen nur zwei Auszüge[105] derselben. Der eine, ausführlichere stammt aus 1496, als die Stuhlweißenburger den Freiheitsbrief in einem Prozeß als Beweismaterial vorlegten. Laut diesem Auszug ersuchten die Bürger König Béla IV. ihre Sonderrechte zu beurkunden, da ihr ursprünglicher Freiheitsbrief, der von Stephan I. stammte, verbrannt war.[106] Béla IV. ließ ihre Freiheiten in eine neue Urkunde fassen, da die Sonderrechte allgemein bekannt waren, keinem Zweifel unterlagen und die Bürger ununterbrochen im Besitz derselben waren.[107] Danach folgten die Punkte, von denen der eine Auszug drei über die Zollfreiheit und über den Zuzug anderer »Gäste« *(hospites)*, der andere nur einen Punkt über die Zoll‑ freiheit anführt. Wir möchten hier sofort auf die allgemeine Praxis der unga‑ rischen königlichen Kanzlei aufmerksam machen. In solchen Auszügen führte man den Urkundengeber und das pünktliche Datum der Urkunde an, gab einen Auszug aus der Einleitung und schrieb dann Wort für Wort die in Frage kommende Verfügung *(dispositio)* aus der Urkunde ab. So ist es auch in unserem Fall geschehen. Dies erklärt, daß die Verfügung über die Zollfreiheit in beiden Auszügen vollkommen übereinstimmend lautet. Es entspricht auch dieser Praxis, daß diese drei Punkte der Verfügung Ausdrücke erhalten, die

---

[103] PRT. XII/B. 151.

[104] GOMBOS: *Catalogus* 1720. »castrum . . . quod Bellagrava dicitur Bogarensis respectu eiusdem, quae in Hungaria est eiusdem nominis civitas«.

[105] Die beiden Auszüge: A = 1496. Stadtarchiv Preßburg no. 2713., FEJÉR: *CD.* IV/1. 73. — B = Dl. 9713.

[106] Auszug A.: »In principio eedem littere exprimebant, quod cum privilegium sancti regis Stephani pariter et legati tunc sedis apostolice hospitibus Albensibus concessum infausto casu incendii fuisset conversum in cinerem, ydem cives Albenses libertatis sue statum timentes tractu temporum in dubium revocari seu aliquatenus aggravari eidem domino Bele regi humi‑ liter supplicassent, ut concessam ipsis a memorato sanctissimo rege libertatem ipse dominus Bela rex suo dignetur privilegio communiri.«

[107] Auszug A: »Idem igitur dominus rex Bela ipsorum civium preces favorabiliter ad‑ mittendo cum esset notorium et nullatenus veniret in dubium ipsos privilegiatos extitisse, absque ulla interruptione libertate inferius in dictis litteris suis annotata usos continue fuisse. benigne concessisset, quod petebant . . .«

zu Béla IV. Regierungszeit schon veraltet waren. Am auffallendsten ist die Formel »*iram regie maiestatis et rerum suarum dispendium merito sustinebit*«, die auf einen viel früheren Zeitpunkt (bis zur Mitte des XII. Jh.) weist.[108] An Hand dieser Formel können wir feststellen, daß dem Aussteller des Freiheitsbriefes von 1237 eine frühere Urkunde als Unterlage dienen mußte.

Diese Feststellung steht aber im schroffen Gegensatz zu dem, was wir von der Einleitung der Urkunde wissen. Nach all dem, was wir im vorangehenden Abschnitt über die Entwicklung Stuhlweißenburgs darstellten, ist es klar, daß die Lateiner keinesfalls von Stephan I. ihre Sonderrechte erhalten haben konnten. Dies erschien auch Béla IV. unwahrscheinlich. Aus anderen Fällen wissen wir, daß Stephans I. Verfügungen in einem Buch, das auch seine Legende enthielt abgeschrieben und bis ins XIV. Jh. im Stuhlweißenburger Marienstift aufbewahrt waren.[109] Die Bürger hätten also Gelegenheit gehabt ihre Behauptungen zu beweisen. In diesem Buch konnte aber nichts über die Bürger oder ihre Freiheiten gefunden werden. Deswegen sprach der König von erworbenen Rechten, im mittelalterlichen Sinne von einer schon längst bestehenden *consuetudo*, stimmte aber — soweit man dies aus dem Auszug beurteilen kann — keineswegs den Behauptungen der Bürger, einen Freiheitsbrief von Stephan I. bekommen zu haben, bei.

Wie kann der Widerspruch zwischen der Feststellung, daß die Verfügungen auf einen älteren Text hinweisen und der anderen Feststellung, daß der König den Bürgern keinen Glauben schenkte, beseitigt werden? Unseres Erachtens nach nur auf eine Weise. Die Bürger verfügten tatsächlich über eine Abschrift, die sie von einer Urkunde eines Königs Stephans verfertigten, die aber — da das Original einem Brand zu Opfer fiel — ohne Siegel keine Beweiskraft besaß. Sie behaupteten, daß die Urkunde von Stephan I. ausgestellt worden sei. Dazu soll noch bemerkt werden, daß es in Ungarn schon im XIII. Jh. allgemeine Sitte war bei älteren Institutionen sich auf die »heiligen Könige« zu berufen, unter denen man in erster Reihe Stephan I. verstand. Konnte es aber nicht ein anderer Stephan gewesen sein? Aus anderen Fällen wissen wir, daß man sich zur Zeit Bélas IV. noch auf die Regierung Bélas III. (1172—1196) gut erinnerte,[110] obwohl sie schon mehr als eine Generation zurücklag. Vor Béla III. regierte Stephan III. (1162—1172) und wir glauben, daß die Stuhlweißenburger tatsächlich im Besitz eines Privilegs von Stephan, doch nicht Stephan I., sondern Stephan III. waren. Mit den allgemeinen politischen Verhältnissen ließe sich dies gut in Einklang bringen. Nach den zunehmenden kirchlichen und politischen Beziehungen mit Frankreich sandte man in der ersten Hälfte des XII. Jh. junge ungarische Kleriker

---

[108] In den Urkunden Andreas II. von 1214—1224 (Szp. 289—414) ist diese Formel nicht mehr zu finden.
[109] PRT. II. 402—403.
[110] R. Békefi: *A pilisi apátság története* [Die Geschichte der Abtei von Pilis] I. 316.

auf die Universität von Paris.[111] Einer von ihnen, Lukas wurde Erzbischof von Gran (1158—1181) und zugleich ein intransigenter Vorkämpfer der Machtstellung der Kirche und der Prälaten. Sein Einfluß erreichte seinen Höhepunkt unter Stephan III.[112] Diese Zusammenhänge vor Auge haltend möchten wir den *terminus ante quem* auf das Jahr 1172 und als wahrscheinlichsten Zeitpunkt für die Einwanderung der *latini* den Zeitraum 1162—1172 angeben.

Die von dem Freiheitsbrief verfertigten Auszüge zählten nur jene Punkte auf, die hinsichtlich des Prozesses über eine Beweiskraft verfügten. Andere Punkte kennen wir aus den Stadtprivilegien, die der König auf Grund der Stuhlweißenburger Sonderrechte erteilte. Die Auszüge und andere Stadtprivilegien lassen uns folgende Punkte der Stuhlweißenburger Freiheiten erkennen: (1) freie Wahl des Richters und der zwölf Geschworenen,[113] die (2) berechtigt waren in allen Streitfragen ein Urteil zu sprechen,[114] (3) der freie Zuzug anderer Siedler,[115] (4) die allgemeine Zollfreiheit im ganzen Lande und an der Landesgrenze.[116]

Alle diese Sonderrechte tragen einen städtischen Charakter, nur die freie Richterwahl ist anscheinend eine Ausnahme. Die Wahl eines Richters wurde nämlich auch anderen, nicht städtischen Siedlern aus dem Ausland *(hospites)* zugesprochen.[117] Der Unterschied zwischen ihren und den Stuhlweißenburger Freiheiten bestand darin, daß während die übrigen erwählten Richter nur die niedere Gerichtsbarkeit besassen (die höhere blieb den Königs-

---

[111] A. GÁBRIEL: *Magyar diákok és tanárok a középkori Párizsban* [Ungarische Studenten und Professoren im mittelalterlichen Paris] Egyetemi Philologiai Közlöny LXII (1938) 182.
[112] *Monumenta ecclesie Strigoniensis* I. 114.
[113] In den folgenden bringen wir den Wortlaut der Auszüge (Quellenangaben unter Anm. 105) und der verschiedenen Stadtprivilegien (Quellenangaben s. unter Anm. 35).
Szatmár 1271:»ut dicti oppidani iisdem libertatibus quibus Albenses perfruere dinoscuntur . . . uti et frui possent, ita ut villicum quem voluerint inter se eligent«.
[114] Neutra 1248:»ipsis et ipsorum successoribus perpetuo Albensium civium dedimus libertatem, ut villicus ex se ipsis, qui pro tempore fuerit constitutus omnes causas pecuniarias civiles et criminales ad instar civium Albensium cum duodecim iuratis debeat fine debito terminare . . .«
Szatmár 1271:»qui [villicus] omnes causas maiores et minores inter se exortas iudicare possit . . .«
Ödenburg 1277:»Ita, quod omnes causas tam maiores quam minores quoque super effusione sanguinum vel homicidii inter ipsos emergente villicus ipsorum pro tempore constitutus, . . . iudicet et decernat more civium Albensium . . .«
[115] Auszug A 1237:»Preterea quicunque ad eos transire et cum eos conversari voluerint, ea libertate qua ipsi fruuntur similiter in perpetuum potiantur«.
[116] Auszug A 1237:»quod in toto regno suo, nec in aliqua porta confinii tributum alicui solvere teneantur . . . quod siquis tributum violenter ab ipsis extorserit, iram regie maiestatis et rerum suarum dispendium merito sustinebit.«
Auszug B 1237:»quod prefatus rex Bela ipsis civibus et hospitibus civitatis Albensis inter cetera hanc libertatem gratiose concessisset, quod ipsi nec in toto regno, nec in aliqua porta confinii tributum alicui solvere teneantur.«
Tyrnau 1238:»Super solutione vero tributi eodem iure censeantur, quo cives Albenses.«
[117] FÜGEDI: *Stadtprivilegien* 26.

richtern vorbehalten), war der Stuhlweißenburger Richter in allen Prozessen zuständig.

Die allgemeine Zollfreiheit begünstigte die Hauptbeschäftigung der Lateiner, die in erster Linie Kaufleute waren. Der Mangel an Quellen ermöglicht uns nicht die Bestimmung aller Waren, mit denen sie handelten, wir wissen nur soviel, daß sie schon am Anfang des XIII. Jh. mit dem im Komitat Somogy gekauften und auch selbst erzeugten Wein Handel trieben.[118] Wir vermuten aber, daß sie schon damals mit allen möglichen Waren vor allem mit Tuch aus dem Westen und mit Gewürzen aus dem Osten handelten und daß schon damals Kaufleute aus allen Teilen des Landes ihr Quartier aufsuchten.[119]

Die Vorrechte der Lateiner schufen die erste bürgerliche Siedlung, die nicht nur in rechtlicher Hinsicht städtischen Charakter trug. Jedoch ist es schwer ihr Quartier innerhalb der Ofner Vorstadt zu bestimmen. Hier helfen uns auch die kirchlichen Verhältnisse nicht. In Gran besaßen die Lateiner eine eigene Pfarrkirche zu Ehren des Hl. Nikolaus. In der Ofner Vorstadt kann aber eine besondere *latini*-Pfarre nicht nachgewiesen werden. Die Stuhlweißenburger Nikolaikirche bestand schon vor der Einwanderung der Lateiner. In der Ofner Vorstadt stand noch eine Dominicikirche, doch kann auch diese nicht mit den Lateinern in Zusammenhang gebracht werden.[120] Dabei wollen wir auf einen auffallenden Zug des Freiheitsbriefs aufmerksam machen. Weder die Auszüge, noch die anderen Städten erlassenen Privilegien erwähnen die freie Wahl des Pfarrers. Dies ist umso auffallender, da auch die viel einfacheren Agrarsiedlungen fremder »Gäste« das Recht besassen ihren Pfarrer zu wählen. In Stuhlweißenburg gibt es scheinbar zwei Lösungen: (1) entweder bestand zu dieser Zeit die Nikolaikirche noch allein in der Ofner Vorstadt, über sie verfügte der König auf Grund seines Patronatsrechtes und übergab die Kirche den Lateinern nicht, oder (2) wirkte zu dieser Zeit auch schon die Dominicikirche als eine Pfarrkirche der Vorstadt, wurde aber den Lateinern nicht überlassen.

Das Fehlen der selbständigen Pfarrkirche wird noch auffallender, wenn wir die Tatsache vor Augen halten, daß der durch die Lateiner hervorgerufene wirtschaftliche Aufschwung am Anfang des XIII. Jh. die Gründung zweier Kloster in der Vorstadt ermöglichte: eines mit dem königlichen Hof eng verbundenen Dominikaner- und eines Franziskanerklosters.[121]

---

[118] PRT. I. 680.

[119] Im 15. Jh. kamen Kaufleute aus Siebenbürgen und Bartfeld (Bardejov, Bártfa) nach Stuhlweißenburg um dort am Jahrmarkt Geschäfte zu schließen. ZIMMERMANN—WERNER: *Urkundenbuch zur Geschichte der Deutschen in Siebenbürgen.* Hermannstadt 1897. II. 401., 403. — L. FEJÉRPATAKY: *Magyarországi városok régi számadáskönyvei* [Alte Rechnungsbücher der Städte Ungarns] Bp. 1885. 197, 201, 204.

[120] Sie wird zum erstenmal 1331 erwähnt (Archiv des Bistums von Veszprém, Alba 7). Über ihre Lage vgl. FITZ: *Székesfehérvár* 11.

[121] KÁROLY, a. a. O. II. 170, 174—181.

Nach der Feststellung A. Kubinyis ließ sich die Bürgerschaft noch vor dem Tatareneinfall auch das Stadtsiegel verfertigen. Seine Anschrift brachte die Vorherrschaft der *latini* zum Ausdruck.[122]

6. Eine Stuhlweißenburger Handelsstelle des königlichen Schatzamtes wurde mit Hilfe einer eingehenden Analyse des Textes der sog. »Goldenen Bulle« (1222) von L. Kumorovitz bewiesen. Laut des XXV. Artikels der Goldenen Bulle durfte im Inneren des Landes kein Salz deponiert werden *(sales in medio regni non teneantur)*.[123] Die Goldene Bulle war das Ergebnis eines bitteren Kampfes zwischen den kirchlichen Großgrundbesitzern einerseits und der königlichen Kammer bzw. ihren jüdischen und mohammedanischen Pächtern andererseits. Der XXV. Artikel war keineswegs eine Ausnahme. Es standen kirchliche Großgrundbesitzer die von der königlichen Kammer jährlich große Mengen von Salz erhielten und die Pächter einander gegenüber, die wiederum das Salz aus ihren eigenen Salzämtern verteilten und dadurch den Verkauf des den kirchlichen Würdenträgern angewiesenen Salzes vereitelten. Unter dem Ausdruck *medium regni* soll — wie es Kumorovitz bewies — Stuhlweißenburg verstanden werden, da König Andreas II. 1233 in einer Urkunde in bezug auf das dem Kloster von Tihany gebührende königliche Salz verfügte, daß es am Tag des Hl. Stephans (20. August) in Stuhlweißenburg, das in der Mitte des Landes liegt *(in Albensi castro, quod est in medio Hungarie)* übergeben werden soll.[124] Bestehen wir auf eine wortwörtliche Übersetzung dieser Verfügung, so müssen wir behaupten, daß das Salzdepot in der Burg stand. Dies scheint umso natürlicher als die Burg den am meisten befestigten Teil der Stadt bildete und hier das Depot in der Nähe des Marktplatzes untergebracht werden konnte. Leider besitzen wir keine weitere Angaben über das Salzdepot und so kann sein Platz in der Stadt nicht näher bestimmt werden.

Trotzdem, daß wir den genaueren Ort des Salzdepots in der Stadttopographie nicht bestimmen können, stehen zwei Tatsachen außer Zweifel. Die eine Tatsache ist die Existenz des Depots, die zweite, daß dieses Depot den Interessen eines kirchlichen Großgrundbesitzers entgegengesetzt war. Vier solche Großgrundbesitzer können in der weiteren Umgebung der Stadt genannt werden: der Bischof von Veszprém, die Äbte von Pannonhalma, Tihany und Szekszárd. Der Handelsbereich des Salzamtes erstreckte sich also wahrscheinlich bis zu diesen Punkten, sicher aber bis zum Sitz des Abtes von Tihany,

---

[122] A. KUBINYI: *Buda város pecséthasználatának kialakulása* [Die Entwicklung der Siegelbenutzung der Stadt Ofen] Tanulmányok Budapest múltjából XIV (1961) 119. Die Anschrift: »S[igillum] Latinorum Civium Albensium«.
[123] Ich möchte auch hier meinen aufrichtigen Dank Herrn Prof. L. Kumorovitz aussprechen, der das Manuskript seiner Studie »Újabb adatok Óbuda koraközépkori történetéhez« [Neue Beiträge zur frühmittelalterlichen Geschichte Altofens] mir zur Verfügung stellte und die Verwendung der Stuhlweißenburger Angaben erlaubte.
[124] *Monumenta ecclesiae Strigoniensis* I. 235.

sonst hätte er das Salz nicht von Stuhlweißenburg bekommen. Holte aber der Abt von Tihany das Salz von Stuhlweißenburg, dann reichte der Wirkungskreis der Stadt weit über die Grenzen eines Tagesmarsches (25 — 30 km). Diese Tatsache erklärt auch die Notwendigkeit zwei Hospitzen in der Stadt aufrecht zu erhalten, da auch die Hörigen des Abtes von Tihany gezwungen waren in der Stadt zu übernachten.

Die Behauptung des Königs Stuhlweißenburg liege in der Mitte des Landes ist allerdings überraschend. Für den mittelalterlichen Mensch, der große Entfernungen zu Fuß oder am Pferd überqueren gewohnt war, konnte es kein Geheimnis sein, daß Stuhlweißenburg nicht in der Mitte des Landes liegt. Verstehen wir aber den Ausdruck, als »Mittelpunkt« und nicht als die geographische Mitte des Landes, so kommt die Bedeutung der Stadt klar zu Tage.

Kein anderer Satz eignet sich besser die Entwicklung Stuhlweißenburgs zusammenzufassen als der der königlichen Urkunde von 1233 »*Albense castrum, quod est in medio Hungarie*«. Aus den vorangehenden Erwägungen ist es klar, daß Stuhlweißenburg als Hauptstadt des Landes zunehmendes Ansehen genoß, daß infolgedessen im Laufe des XII. Jh. auf dem Gebiet neben der Burg neue Siedlungen entstanden, die verschiedenen wirtschaftlichen Charakter trugen und dementsprechend auch in verschiedener sozialer und rechtlicher Lage waren. Diese neue Siedlungen können als Vorstädte angesehen werden. Die größte Bedeutung erreichte unter ihnen die Ofner Vorstadt, in der sich mit Sonderrechten ausgestattete ausländische »Gäste« angesiedelt haben. Durch ihre Anwesenheit und durch ihre Freiheiten entstand jener topographische Pluralismus, der die europäische Stadt in ihrer Frühgeschichte charakterisierte. Es entwickelte sich einerseits die *civitas* (hier *castrum* genannt), welche den Mittelpunkt der weltlichen und kirchlichen Regierung bildete, andererseits die ihr entgegengesetzte, mit Sonderrechten ausgestattete Marktsiedlung, das *suburbium*. Stuhlweißenburg verließ den Entwicklungsweg des asiatischen Stadttyps und betrat den Weg des europäischen. Diese Wandlung ging nicht nur in Stuhlweißenburg, sondern auch in den übrigen Städten des Landes vor sich. Von der allgemeinen wirtschaftlichen Entwicklung des Landes gezwungen mußten die bestehenden Städte asiatischen Typs entweder umgestaltet werden, oder verloren sie ihre Bedeutung. Den neu gegründeten Städten gewährte der König die Freiheiten der Stuhlweißenburger. Aber noch bevor sich diese Entwicklungstendenz voll entfaltet hätte, kam es in Land und Stadt, so auch in Stuhlweißenburg zu einer mächtigen Erschütterung.

7. 1241 fielen die Tataren ins Land ein. König und Heer erlitten eine katastrophale Niederlage, das ganze Land östlich der Donau wurde geplündert, Städte zerstört, Dörfer verwüstet. Im Winter, als die Donau fest zugefroren war, brachen die Tataren in Transdanubien ein. Sie jagten nach dem König,

hatten also für langwierige Belagerungen keine Zeit. Stuhlweißenburg konnten sie nicht einnehmen. Der Wardeiner Domherr, Rogerius, der einen ausführlichen Bericht über den Tatareneinfall hinterließ, schrieb dies der Lage der Stadt zu. Er erklärt, daß die Sümpfe, die die Stadt umgaben, schon auftauten, deswegen konnten die Tataren die Stadt nicht einnehmen.[125] Wahrscheinlich steht sein Zeitgenosse, Thomas, Archidiakon von Spalato (Split) der Wahrheit näher, indem er außer den auftauenden Sümpfen auch die Wehranlagen und die Kampfbereitschaft der Lateiner als Ursache des Scheiterns anführt.[126] Aus seiner Chronik erfahren wir noch ein wichtiges Moment: die Häuser der Vorstadt brannten ab. Dieser Bericht wird auch durch den Stadtplan bestätigt. Die Innere Stadt und zwei Vorstädte (Sziget und Újfalu) waren vom Moorland umgeben, die Stadt konnte also nur von NO aus, wo die Ofner Vorstadt lag, belagert werden. Hier gab es keine Sümpfe, hier mußten die Einwohner der Vorstadt (also hauptsächlich die Lateiner) den Kampf aufnehmen. Diesem Bericht können wir mit Gewissheit entnehmen, daß die Ofner Vorstadt schon 1242 Mauern besaß.

Das Schicksal, das der Ofner Vorstadt zu Teil wurde, war im Mittelalter nichts außerordentliches. Brände konnten Stadtteile, manchmal ganze Städte verwüsten, ohne daß sie belagert gewesen wären. Die Ofner Vorstadt erholte sich vermutlich ebenso rasch, wenn nicht rascher als Gran, in dem schon 1243 rege Handelstätigkeit zu beobachten war.[127] Die Wandlung, die in einigen Jahren eintrat, war nicht im Schicksal der Stadt, sondern in der Persönlichkeit König Bélas IV. begründet.

Béla betrat den Thron 1235 fest entschlossen, die frühere Machtstellung des Königs, die während der Regierung seines Vaters geschwächt war, herzustellen. Sechs Jahre später, als die Tataren das Land angriffen, erlitt Bélas Politik einen jammervollen Zusammenbruch. Als er nach dem Abzug der Tataren aus Dalmatien zurückkehrte, inaugurierte er — ein Beweis seiner außerordentlichen Willenskraft und seiner menschlichen Größe — einen neuen, seiner alten Politik schroff entgegengesetzten Kurs. Den Schock des Tatareneinfalls hat er aber nie überwunden. 1246 gingen Gerüchte umher, daß der Papst von dem Mongolenherrscher einen Brief enthielt, in dem der Plan eines neuen Einbruchs in Europa dargestellt wurde.[128] Béla entfaltete 1247—1249 eine fieberhafte Tätigkeit um das Land für die Abwehr eines neuen Einbruchs

[125] »Et cum ad Albam regiam civitatem accederent [Tartari], que est paludibus circumsepta, cum esset in dissolutione nivis et glaciei, nequierunt eam occupare«. GOMBOS: *Catalogus* 2085.
[126] »Inde discedens [dux Caydanus] recto cursu devenit ad urbem Albensem et continuo cuncta suburbanae habitationis domicilia concremavit, civitatem vero aliquot diebus obsessam factis insultibus invadere satagebant; sed quia locus circumfusa palustrium aquarum copia satis erat munitus, quem optima Latinorum presidia erectis undique machinis tuebantur, dux impius, vano frustratus labore discessit.« Ebda 2241.
[127] L. ZOLNAY: *Opus castri Budensis.* Tanulmányok Budapest múltjából XV (1963) 52.
[128] Ebda 52—57.

vorzubereiten. Wo es nur möglich war, ließ er die Bürger aus den Städten und Vorstädten in die Burgen übersiedeln. Auch Stuhlweißenburg kam an die Reihe.[129]

Was eigentlich in Stuhlweißenburg vor sich ging, ist uns in zwei Urkunden erhalten. Der 1250 geschriebene Brief des Papstes erhielt uns die Beschwerden des Propstes vom Marienstift. Das Stift verfügte in der Inneren Stadt und auch der Ofner Vorstadt über ausgedehnten Grundbesitz, der außer den Häusern der Stiftsherren auch Grundstücke der Hörigen umfaßte.[130] Das Stift besaß auch einen Teil des Marktzinses. Der König ließ die Bürger in die Innere Stadt übersiedeln, sie nahmen den Grundbesitz des Stiftes und auch den Marktzins in Anspruch.[131] Der Propst leistete Widerstand, rief dadurch den Zorn des Königs auf sich, war aber schließlich gezwungen nachzugeben und auch die entsprechende Urkunde mit seinem Siegel zu versehen.[132] Als Grund für die Handlung des Königs gab der Propst an, daß der König durch Zunahme der Bevölkerung die Sicherheit des Landes steigern wollte.[133]

Die andere Urkunde blieb nur in Auszügen erhalten. Laut dieser legten die Bürger am Ende des XIV. Jh. in einem Prozeß eine Urkunde vor, die 1249 vom Propst und Stift und den Bürgern gemeinsam ausgestellt war und die eine undatierte Urkunde König Bélas Wort für Wort enthielt. Der Inhalt der königlichen Urkunde sprach von Übersiedlung der Bürger in die Burg *(translatio eorundem civium in dictum castrum Albense facta)* und über eine Teilung der Felder zwischen dem Stift und den Bürgern.[134] Bei dieser Gelegenheit übernahm man die Grenzbegehung jener Felder, die den Bürgern zugeteilt worden waren. Ein anderer Auszug erhielt uns die Grenzbegehung des Stiftbesitzes.[135] Aus diesen Auszügen geht es klar hervor, daß hier eine grundlegende Regelung stattfand. Die *latini* der Vorstadt wurden in die Burg über-

---

[129] Ebda 52—57.

[130] »prepositi et sancti Henrici [= Emerichkapelle] necnon canonicorum palatia cum curiis eorundem ac terram arabilem et etiam que est in eodem suburbio in qua multi conditionales ac hospites vestre ecclesie morabantur.« *Mon. Rom. Vespr.* I. 128.

[131] »sibi conferri ab eodem rege ac remitti omnino tributum fori, quod eadem habebat ecclesia« Ebda.

[132] »Et licet predictis regi et habitatoribus aliquamdiu super hiis duxeritis resistendum, propter indignationem tamen ipsius regis oportuit vos tandem vestrum in hoc prebere assensum et etiam concedere inde litteras quammodo violenter.« Ebda.

[133] »cum . . . rex Ungarie . . . post recessum Tartarorum de partibus vestris, habitatores suburbii castri Albensis in idem castrum transferri fecisset, ut tutius et fortius propter multitudinem populi reddetur . . .« Ebda.

[134] »unam [litteram] magistri Achilli prepositi et capituli Albensis ac universorium civium eiusdem loci alphabeto intercisam sub quatuor sigillis eorum anno Domini millesimo ducentesimo quadragesimo nono, quarto Kalendas Decembris privilegialiter editam in se transumptive de verbo ad verbum tenorem litterarum domini Bele dei gratia regis sine anno confirmatarum, translationem eorundem civium in dictum castrum Albense factam ac divisionem terrarum dicti castri et aliarum terrarum modo et ordine litteris in eisdem denotato inter eosdem dominum prepositum et capitulum ac cives Albenses factam denotantium« Szp. 919.

[135] Dl. 23.112.

siedelt, sie erhielten einen Teil des Stiftbesitzes.[136] Die Gemarkung der Stadt wurde zwischen dem Probst bzw. Stift und den Bürgern geteilt. Leider sprechen weder die erwähnten Auszüge, noch die päpstliche Urkunde davon, wie der König die Innere Stadt teilte, und hier helfen uns auch die Kenntnisse der kirchlichen Verhältnisse wenig.

Aus den späteren Verhältnissen ist es klar, daß die Bürger bei dieser Regelung die Petrikirche als Pfarrkirche bekamen.[137] Doch befand sich außer der Petrikirche noch eine andere Pfarre in der Burg, eine Kreuzkirche, die in dem Friedhof der Basilika stand.[138] Wir wissen außerdem, daß nicht alle Besitzungen des Marienstiftes den Bürgern zufielen, einige blieben weiterhin im Besitz des Stiftes. War die Kreuzkirche den Stiftshörigen zuständig? Und wenn ja, wie wurde dann die Innere Stadt zwischen den beiden Pfarren geteilt? Auf Grund eines territorialen oder eines persönlichen Prinzips? Wenn wir hier an Ofen denken, wo die Stadt ebenfalls zwischen zwei Pfarrkirchen geteilt war, dann müssen wir das territoriale Prinzip befürworten. Grundsätzlich war ja das Pfarrsystem überhaupt ein Territorialsystem. Wie dem auch sei,

[136] Leider kann die Teilung der Inneren Stadt auf Grund der erhaltenen Liegenschaftsübertragungen nicht bestimmt werden. Wir kennen folgende Gassen bzw. Grundstücke: *A. vicus S. Petri. a)* 1381 (Hazai Okmánytár [Vaterländisches Urkundebuch] III. 215).— *b)* 1446 (Dl. 42.874). In beiden Fällen waren die übertragene Grundstücke und ihre beiden Nachbaren Bürger. — *c)* 1471 (KÁROLY, a. a. O. II. 630. Dl. 17.267), 1477 (KÁROLY, a. a. O. II. 632., Dl. 18.022). Hier gehörte ein Haus dem Nikolaistift, u. zw. schon seit alten Zeiten. — *d)* 1511 (Kapitelarchiv Preßburg. Protocollum Budense, f° 62—63.) zwei bürgerliche Grundstücke. — Diese Gasse ist mit der heutigen Arany J.-Gasse identisch, hier stand von einem Friedhof umgeben die Petrikirche, daneben hat ein Bürger Namens Hensel das noch heute bestehende einzige mittelalterliche Gebäude, die Annakapelle gegründet.
B. vicus magnus. a) 1387 (Zsk. O. I. 126.), 1406 (Zsk. O. II. 4902.), 1489 (Zipser Kapitelarchiv Scrin. XIV. fasc. 7. no. 18.) ein bürgerlicher Grundbesitz, der sich unmittelbar an die Kapelle der Basilika anschloß. — *b)* 1470 (Mon. Rom. Vespr. IV. 199.) mehrere Grundstücke des Propstes auf der westlichen Seite der Gasse. — *c)* 1489 (Zipser Kapitelarchiv Scrin. XIV. fasc. 7. no. 18.) bürgerlicher Grundbesitz. — Die Gasse ist mit der heutigen Március 15-Gasse identisch.
C. teatrum civitatis. Ein Haus 1512 genannt »Rostásház« (Kapitelarchiv in Preßburg Protocollum Budense f° 127—128). Das Grundstück gehörte der Emerichkapelle. Der Platz ist der heutige Szabadság-Platz.
D. Vicus s. Bartholomaei. a) 1478 (Dl.18.085) bürgerliches Haus mit bürgerlichen Nachbaren. — *b)* 1488 (Dl. 18.252) einer der 1478 erwähnten Grundstücke in dessen Nachbarschaft ein alter Turm stand. — Die Gasse ist leider nicht identifizierbar, den einzigen Hinweis gibt uns ein türkischer Defter aus 1544, der in der »Kapitelgasse« von einer verfallenen Bartholomaeikirche spricht. Dürfte demnach in der Nähe der nächsten Gasse liegen?
E. vicus canonicalis. Ein einziges Haus wird 1474 erwähnt (Dl. 17.592). Aus der Urkunde geht es klar hervor, daß nicht nur das betreffende Haus, sondern die Ganze Gasse (vicus noster) dem Marienstift gehörte. Leider besitzen wir keine Hinweise die Gasse identifizieren zu können.
F. vicus Teutonicalis. 1446 (Dl. 42.874) bürgerliches Haus mit bürgerlichen Nachbaren. Hier standen die Fleischhackerbänke der Stadt.
Die Aufzählung gibt ein Bild von der verworrenen Lage, die wir den Urkunden entnehmen können. Die Liegenschaften der Stifter waren demnach — mit Ausnahme des vicus canonicalis — zwischen bürgerlichen Grundstücken eingekeilt. Ein System läßt sich nicht ergründen.
[137] Dies ist am klarsten aus der Urkunde von 1478 (KÁROLY, a. a. O. II. 671., Dl. 18.023) ersichtlich, in welcher die Bürger von dem Umbau der Kirche und der Erweiterung des Friedhofs sprechen.
[138] 1418 (LUKCSICS, op. cit. I. 120.) — 1439: rector ecclesiae parochialis s. Crucis in cimiterio dictae ecclesiae [B. Mariae Alberegalis] (ebda. II. 605).

das wichtigste für uns ist die Feststellung: die Übersiedlung der Bürger bedeutete nicht, daß sie die Patronatsrechte beider Pfarren erhielten. Die Regelung von 1249 war offensichtlich auch auf dem Gebiet der kirchlichen Organisation ein Kompromiß.

Infolge der Regelung verteilte man die den Bürgern zugeteilten Felder zwischen den Einwohnern der Inneren Stadt.[139] Zu den Grundstücken der Vorstadt gehörten (von da an?) keine Felder bzw. keine Weingärten und Wiesen.

8. Die Verhältnisse, die die Regelung von 1249 geschaffen hatten, blieben wesentlich bis zur Türkenherrschaft unverändert, die Stadtentwicklung blieb an dieser Stufe stecken. Um die Bedeutung dieser Tatsache voll begreifen zu können, müssen wir die Folgen der Regelung im Zusammenhang mit der späteren Entwicklung des ungarischen Städtewesens ins Auge fassen.

Im wirtschaftlichen Leben der Stadt war unzweifelhaft die Regelung der Marktverhältnisse von größter Bedeutung. Bis 1249 waren die Wochenmärkte von Stuhlweißenburg königliche Märkte, deren Zins dem Marienstift und dem Bischof von Veszprém gebührten.[140] Wie wir bei einer anderen Gelegenheit beweisen konnten, war das Marktrecht in Ungarn schon im XI. Jh. ein Regalerecht und bis zur Mitte der XII. Jh. blieben alle Märkte im königlichen Besitz. Die grundlegende wirtschaftliche Freiheit der Städte bestand aus dem sog. »befreiten Markt« *(forum liberum).* Unter diesem im Laufe des XII. Jh. entstandenen Begriff soll ein Markt verstanden werden, der vom Einheben des königlichen Marktzinses, vom Eingreifen der königlichen Beamten und der Amtsgewalt des königlichen Richters befreit war.[141] Obzwar am Anfang des XIII. Jh. dieser »befreite Markt« nicht nur in den Städten, sondern auch auf Privatgütern gewährt wurde, besaßen die Stuhlweißenburger dieses Vorrecht nicht. 1249 ist es den Bürgern gelungen die Marktrechte dem Marienstift und dem Bischof von Veszprém zu entreißen.

Der befreite Markt und der am Anfang des XIII. Jh. eintretende wirtschaftliche Aufschwung des Landes ermöglichten den Stuhlweißenburgern die Form des Jahrmarktes zu entwickeln. Die Grundlagen waren dafür in der Entwicklung des XI—XII. Jh. gegeben. Die Sitte Mariä Himmelfahrt und Stephanstag (15. bzw. 20. August) in Stuhlweißenburg zu feiern bot eine günstige Gelegenheit zur Abhaltung eines Jahrmarktes zwischen dem 14. und

---

[139] 1388 (Zsk. O. I. 448.) eine Bürgerin verkauft »totalem portionem suam in quodam fundo curie castri Albensi . . . cum quibuslibet suis utilitatibus et pertinentiis universis, necnon terris arabilibus intra ambitum metalem dicte civitatis nostre Albensis adiacentibus ad ipsam portionem suam spectantibus«. Ähnlich 1446 (Dl. 42.874), 1477 (KÁROLY, a. a. O. II. 632., Dl. 18.022).

[140] 1279 verschenkt der Bischof von Veszprém »palatium nostrum episcopale in castro Albensi existens . . . cum omnibus utilitatibus et pertinentiis . . . tributo in festo sancti regis« (KÁROLY, a. a. O. II. 688).

[141] F. ECKHARDT: *Magyar jog és alkotmánytörténet* [Ungarische Rechts- und Verfassungsgeschichte] Bp. 1946. 71., FÜGEDI: *Stadtprivilegien.* 28—31.

X

28. August. Die Anfänge des Stuhlweißenburger Jahrmarktes können nicht genau bestimmt werden, ein diesbezügliches Priviteg fehlt, war vielleicht überhaupt nicht vorhanden. Sicher ist es dagegen, daß man schon vor 1279 die Jahrmärkte hielt.[142] Als Ofen 1287 ein Jahrmarktsprivileg bekam, richteten sie sich nicht nur nach den Stuhlweißenburger Gewohnheiten, sondern bestimmten auch den Zeitpunkt so, daß der vom 1. bis 15. September in Ofen abgehaltene Jahrmarkt zeitlich eine Fortsetzung des Stuhlweißenburgers bildete.[143] Stuhlweißenburg wurde einer der wichtigsten Umschlagplätze des Landes für in- und ausländischen Waren.

Hinsichtlich des Marktrechtes wurde also ein durchschlagender Erfolg erzielt. Von anderen wirtschaftlichen Freiheiten kann dasselbe nicht behauptet werden. Am Ausgang des Mittelalters waren die meisten ungarischen Städte schon im Besitz der früheren grundherrschaftlichen Nutznießungen.[144] In Stuhlweißenburg besaß die Bürgerschaft die Nutznießungen nur auf jenen Grundstücken bzw. auf jenem Teil der Gemarkung, welche ihnen 1249 zugeteilt waren. Die Regelung war eben auch in dieser Hinsicht ein Kompromiß.

Es scheint, daß die Stadt sich auch des Heimfallsrechts *(ius spolii)* des ehemaligen Grundherrn, des Königs nicht entledigen konnte, zumindest nicht im Laufe des XIII. Jh. Starb ein Bürger ohne Testament hinterzulassen, so fiel sein Gut und Habe an dem König.[145]

Infolge der Teilung des Stadtbodens konnte sich auch ein bürgerliches Liegenschaftsrecht nicht voll entwickeln. Man veräußerte die bürgerlichen Grundstücke vor dem Stadtrat, andere aber vor dem Kapitel des Marienstiftes, als glaubwürdigen Ort.[146] Der Stadtrat konnte seine Entscheidungen über die bürgerlichen Grundstücke nach Belieben treffen,[147] war aber für jene Teile des Stadtgebietes, die 1249 nicht den Bürgern zugeteilt wurden, nicht zuständig. Aus demselben Grund hatte der Stadtrat keine vollkommen freie Hand in wirtschaftlichen Angelegenheiten. Entscheidungen, die nur den bürgerlichen Teil der Stadt trafen, konnten unbehindert durchgeführt werden, so z. B. über den Ort und die Steuer der Fleischhackerbänke, weil dieselben sich offenbar in dem bürgerlichen Stadtteil befanden.[148] Als aber die Weineinfuhr in die Stadt 1485 geregelt werden sollte, mußte der Rat mit dem Marien-

[142] Vgl. Anm. 140.
[143] FÜGEDI: *Stadtprivilegien.* 34—35.
[144] Ebda 46—49.
[145] *Hazai Okmánytár* VIII. 239.
[146] Über Veräußerungen bürgerlicher Liegenschaften stellte regelmäßig der Stadtrat die Urkunde aus. Eine Ausnahme bilden jene Fälle, in welchen außer städtischem auch Landbesitz verkauft wurde (1381: *Hazai Okmánytár* III. 215.). Demgegenüber wurden kirchliche Grundstücke immer vor dem Kapitel veräußert (1474:Dl. 17.592., 1512: Kapitelarchiv in Preßburg, Protocollum Budense f° 127—128.).
[147] So entschied der Stadtrat über Erweiterung (1479: Dl. 18.252.), Teilung (1347: Zipser Kapitelarchiv Scrin. XII. fasc. 5. no. 10.) und über Steuerbefreiung (1478: KÁROLY, a. a. O. II. 671., Dl. 18.023.) eines Grundstückes.
[148] Zsk. O. I. 3762.

und Nikolaistift und mit den Johannitern verhandeln und auch die diesbezügliche Verordnung mit ihnen gemeinsam erlassen.

In bezug auf die rechtliche Stellung befanden sich die Bürger in einer
etwas besseren Lage. Sie durften ihren Richter und ihre Geschworenen selbst
wählen und diese waren in allen Streitfragen zuständig, soweit diese zwischen
Bürgern entstanden. Freie Richterwahl und Zuständigkeit in allen Streitfragen waren die grundlegenden Freiheiten der Stuhlweißenburger, die der
König dann auch anderen Städten verlieh. Die ältere ungarische Geschichtsschreibung sprach auf Grund dieser Tatsache von einem »Stuhlweißenburger
Recht« in jenem Sinne des Wortes, wie wir z. B. vom Magdeburger Recht
sprechen. Wie wir es bewiesen haben, kann in diesem Sinne keineswegs von
einem »Stuhlweißenburger Recht«, sondern nur von Stuhlweißenburger Freiheiten die Rede sein.[149] Die in den Privilegien anderer Städte erwähnten
Sonderrechte bildeten keinesfalls ein geschlossenes Rechtssystem, Stuhlweißenburg war auch kein Appellationsgericht für diese Städte geworden. Es ist
für die Entwicklung des ungarischen Städtewesens kennzeichnend, daß sich
das Appellationsverfahren in zwei — von einander gut trennbaren — Phasen
entwickelte. In der ersten Phase verlieh der König die Stuhlweißenburger
Freiheiten oder jene anderer schon bestehender Städte, behielt aber das Urteil
über appellierte Prozesse für sich bzw. für die sog. *presentia regia*.[150] Bis zum
Ausgang des XIII. Jh. kann weder ein einheimisches, noch ein ausländisches
Stadtrecht in Ungarn nachgewiesen werden. In dieser Phase spielten die
Freiheiten Stuhlweißenburgs die führende Rolle.

In der darauf folgenden Phase nahm der Appellationsweg der ungarischen
Städte seine endgültige Form an. In Ofen, Schemnitz (Selmecbánya, Banská
Štavnica) und Karpfen (Korpona, Krupina) entwickelte sich ein selbständiges Stadtrecht. In der Mitte des XIV. Jh. hören wir kaum mehr von den
Stuhlweißenburger Freiheiten, es können aber Stadtrechtsübertragungen
beobachtet werden. Die großen Städte des Landes waren jedoch — und das
ist für die ungarische Entwicklung äußerst kennzeichnend — nicht geneigt
andere Stadtrechte zu übernehmen. Dagegen übernahmen die kleinen Marktflecken (und sogar Dörfer) mit Vorliebe das Rechtssystem führender Städte.
Es ist kaum ein Zufall, daß mit einer einzigen Ausnahme kein Appellationsweg nach dem Ausland führte. Zur Mitte des XIV. Jh. war die Lage schon
ziemlich verwickelt. Die großen Städte besaßen das Recht zur *presentia regia*,
oder zum Tarnakmeister *(magister tavarnicorum)* zu appellieren, die kleineren
wendeten sich an Ofen, Karpfen oder Schemnitz. König Ludwig I. (1342—1382)
löste die verworrene Lage, indem er für die großen Städte ein Sondergericht
den sog. Tarnakstuhl *(sedis tavernicalis)* schuf, wo die Beisitzer die Gesandten

[149] FÜGEDI: *Stadtprivilegien.* 65—66.
[150] Tyrnau 1238: »ad regis iudicium«, Neutra 1248: »ad nostram presentiam vel magistri
Tauarnicorum«, Raab und Szatmár 1271, bzw. Ödenburg 1277: »ad nostram presentiam«.

X

des städtischen Bürgertums waren. Von da an waren nur jene Städte als vollberechtigte königliche Freistädte anerkannt, die diesem Gericht unterstanden.[151]

Stuhlweißenburg spielte in der ersten Phase eine große Rolle, nahm aber an der weiteren Entwicklung nicht mehr Teil, ist auch kein Mitglied des Tarnakstuhls geworden. Auch dies war eine Folge der Regelung von 1249. Wenn es auch nicht die Aufgabe der Geschichtswissenschaft ist sich mit verlorengegangenen Chancen zu befassen, muß doch die Frage gestellt werden, was aus den *latini* geworden wäre, wenn der König Sie 1249 nicht in die Burg übersiedelt hätte. Die Schicksale anderer Städte bieten eine reiche Auswahl. Im besten Fall hätten sie in der Vorstadt den Sieg über das Nikolaistift errungen, wie es in Preßburg (Pozsony, Bratislava) geschah, wo das Stift zu einen Kompromiß gezwungen war. Was aber dem Nikolaistift gegenüber gelungen sein könnte, war einem der vornehmsten kirchlichen Körperschaften, dem Marienstift gegenüber aussichtslos. Im schlimmsten Fall wären die Lateiner ebenso in kirchlichen Besitz geraten wie es den *latini* in Gran geschah, wo der Jahrhunderte lang dauernde zähe Kampf der Bürgerschaft gegen den Erzbischof und gegen das Domstift mit einer vollkommenen Niederlage endete. Stuhlweißenburg ging aber den Mittelweg, blieb ein blühender Handelsplatz in wirtschaftlicher, eine unvollkommen entwickelte Freistadt in rechtlicher Hinsicht.

Trotz alldem drückte Stuhlweißenburg ihren Stempel der Entwicklung des ungarischen Städtewesens auf. Besonders auffallend ist diese Tatsache, wenn wir die ungarische Entwicklung mit jener anderer osteuropäischer Länder vergleichen. Die *latini* waren Kaufleute, der Nationalität nach vielleicht auch nicht vollkommen einheitlich, aber sicherlich waren die Franzosen die Tonangebenden unter ihnen. Sie bestanden auf Gewährung jener Freiheiten, die ihren Handel förderten, nicht aber auf die Gewährung eines kodifizierten Stadtrechtes, wie die Deutschen. Als ihre Freiheiten an andere Städte verliehen wurden, waren sie nicht bestrebt auf diesem Grund ein stadtrechtliches Filiationsverhältnis auszubauen. Die relativ starke zentrale Macht des ungarischen Königstums allein kann es nicht erklären, daß sich die *presentia regia* so leicht durchsetzte. Dazu war auch die Politik der *latini* unerläßlich, die sich zwar ebenso unter königliche Obhut stellten, wie die Deutschen, aber keine rechtliche Bande mit ihrer alten Heimat aufrechterhielten. Auch die Regelung von 1249 hatte hier ihr Wort zu sprechen. Wenn die *latini* bis 1249 kein den osteuropäischen deutschen Bürgern ähnliches Bestreben hegten, dann bot sich nach 1249 auch keine Gelegenheit mehr dazu sie durchzuführen. Einige Züge in der Entwicklung des ungarischen Städtewesens sind somit Stuhlweißenburg zu verdanken.

---

[151] FÜGEDI: *Stadtprivilegien*, 66—71., I. SZENTPÉTERY: *A tárnoki itélőszék kialakulása* [Die Entstehung des Tarnakstuhles] Századok LXVIII (1934), E. BORECZKY: *A királyi tárnokmester hivatala* [Das Amt des königlichen Tarnakmeisters] Bp. 1905.

XI

Kaschau, eine osteuropäische Handelsstadt am Ende des 15. Jahrhunderts

Einige Jahrzente nach der Schlacht bei Mohács, als das mittelalterliche Ungarn schon unter den Trümmern der verheerenden Türkenherrschaft verschwand, verfaßte der Graner Erzbischof und Humanist, Nikolaus Oláh ein Werk über das alte Ungarn. In seinem Buch erwähnte er auch in einem kurzen Satz die oberungarische Stadt Kaschau, wobei er mit besonderem Nachdruck hervorhob, daß die hübsche und gut befestigte Stadt ein belebter Handelsplatz war, wo sich nicht nur Ungarn, sondern auch Polen und andere Völker des Nordens trafen.[1]

Kaschaus Lage war ganz dazu geeignet, die Stadt zu einem Treffpunkt zu entwickeln. Sie lag nahe der ungarisch-slowakischen ethnischen Grenze, war von Polens größter Handelsstadt, Krakau nicht weit entfernt und lag an dem Übergangspunkt von zwei geographisch voneinander scharf abgesonderten Gebieten, der Ungarischen Tiefebene und den Bergen der heutigen Slowakei. Wenn wir also einen Typ der mittelalterlichen ungarischen Handelsstadt suchen, so ist geradezu Kaschau durch seine geographische Lage und durch seinen Handelscharakter dazu geeignet, Gegenstand einer solchen Untersuchung zu werden. In der folgenden Untersuchung wollen wir ebendeswegen an Kaschaus Geschichte einerseits neues Material zur Kenntnis der ungarischen und slowakischen Wirtschaftsgeschichte gewinnen, anderseits hoffen wir mit Hilfe der vergleichenden Methode die Stellung der Stadt nicht nur in der ungarischen und slowakischen, sondern auch in der osteuropäischen Geschichte näher bestimmen zu können. Dabei geht es in erster Linie um die Frage der Kapitalbildung, nach der Frage der wichtigsten wirtschaftlichen Erscheinung in allen mittelalterlichen Städten.

Die Schwierigkeit dieser Aufgabe ergibt sich durch das lückenhafte Quellenmaterial, das uns zur Verfügung steht. Die verschiedenen Aufzeichnungen über Stadtverfassung, Rechtspflege, über Steuern, städtische und

---

[1] Nicolai Olah Hungariae Lib. I. cap. X. § VII. : »Haec civitas, non minus pulchra quam munita est, civitate et incolarum comitate inclyta, olim frequens emporium, quo non modo Hungari, sed etiam Poloni et pleraeque aliae Septentrionis nationes confluebant.«

private Wirtschaft sind nur teilweise überliefert worden. Wir besitzen zwar
aus unserer Periode ein Stadtbuch, in dem die wichtigsten Immobilienübertragungen aufgezeichnet worden sind, doch an Rechnungsbüchern fehlt es
ganz und gar. Statt einer vollständigen Reihe der Steuerbücher finden wir
nur einige Bruchstücke derselben.[2] Diese Schwierigkeit wird noch dadurch
vergrößert, daß die von der Stadt geführten Bücher manchmal nur ihrem
Titel nach mit den ähnlichen westeuropäischen Aufzeichnungen identisch
sind, ihr Inhalt deckt sich nur teilweise mit den westlichen, die Eintragungen
sind meistens kürzer — und ebendeswegen — meist auch weniger instruktiv.
Doch ist es nicht für beinahe alle osteuropäischen Städte kennzeichnend, daß
das geschichtliche Quellenmaterial teilweise vernichtet wurde, teilweise
verloren ging, oder wegen Ungenauigkeit der Aufzeichnung nicht in demselben
Maße ausgewertet werden kann, wie die der westeuropäischen Städte? Gab
es nicht immer diese Schwierigkeit, mit der die osteuropäischen Wissenschaftler
zu kämpfen hatten? Und wenn es wirklich so ist, so müssen wir es doch versuchen auf Grund der lückenhaften und mageren Quellen die Größe der Stadt,
die Vermögensverhältnisse der Einwohner, die wirtschaftliche Tätigkeit der
Bevölkerung und die wirtschaftliche Struktur der Stadt ergründen zu können.
Obwohl das so gewonnene Bild nicht die klaren Züge der westeuropäischen
Stadtgeschichte aufweisen kann, die Züge selbst werden sicherlich sichtbar
und die Proportion der ermittelten Vorgänge wird im Grunde genommen
sicherlich nicht täuschend wirken.

*

Wie groß war Kaschaus Bevölkerung im Mittelalter? Dies ist die erste
Frage, die wir zu beantworten haben.

Volkszählungen sind selbst noch in den späteren Jahrhunderten Ausnahmen im ungarischen Quellenmaterial, wir dürfen nicht einmal hoffen, daß
solche noch zum Vorschein kommen werden. Ebendeswegen ist es Sitte geworden, bei der Feststellung der Bevölkerungszahl, die Steuerbücher als
Unterlagen zu wählen.[3] Bei Kaschau steht aber nicht enmal eine vollständige
Steuerliste zur Verfügung, nur Bruchstücke wurden aus dem 15. Jahrhundert
gefunden. Aus diesen Fragmenten geht es klar hervor, daß die Stadt im 15.
Jh. auf die vier Vierteln der inneren, mit Mauer umgebenen Stadt und auf die
Vorstadt aufgeteilt war. Die Steuerbezirke der inneren Stadt richteten sich
nach dem Ring, der eigentlich eine lange und breite Straße war, und die heu-
tige Hauptsraße der Stadt bildet. Durch diese, von Norden gegen Süden

---

[2] KEMÉNY L., Kassa város régi számadáskönyvei 1431—1553. [Die alten Rechnungsbücher der Stadt Kaschau 1431—1553.] Kassa 1892, 45—56.
[3] Dieselbe Methode wurde von F. KOVÁTS bei Preßburg (Magyar—zsidó oklevéltár. IV. Bev. [Ungarisch—jüdisches Urkundenbuch. IV. Einl.]) und von J. HÁZI bei
Ödenburg (HÁZI J., Sopron város története. [Urkundenbuch von Ödenburg.] 2/2, 3.
Einleitungen) angewendet.

führende Straße wurde die Stadt in einen westlichen und östlichen Teil zergliedert und jeder Teil wurde noch einmal geteilt. So entstanden vier Bezirke, die mit dem lateinischen Wort *quartale* bezeichnet, den Rahmen der Steueradministration bildeten. Das erste und letzte Viertel *(quartale primum und quartale ultimum)* lag im östlichen Teil der Inneren Stadt, das zweite und dritte Viertel dagegen im westlichen. Die Vorstadt war von der Administration des Steuerwesens als eine besondere Einheit behandelt. Aus dem 15. Jh. sind uns folgende Steuerrollen erhalten geblieben :

Quartale	primum aus den Jahren			1483, 1487[4]
«	secundum «	«	«	1475[5]
«	tertium «	«	«	1484[6]
«	ultimum «	«	«	1480[7]

Für die Vorstadt aus dem Jahre 1480.

Einige Zeichen deuten darauf hin, daß die bezüglich des Quartale primum, ultimum und der Vorstadt erhalten gebliebenen Steuerrollen vollständig sind, dagegen bezüglich der anderen zwei Viertel nur Bruchstücke erhalten blieben.[8] Das heißt, daß wir auf Grund der Steuerrollen nur die halbe Stadt und die Vorstadt kennenlernen können, und alle unsere Berechnungen und Schätzungen demgemäß durchführen müssen.

Aus den Steuerrollen ergibt sich von den Steuerpflichtigen folgendes Bild :

Quartale	primum, 1487 enthält	196 Steuerpflichtige in	137 Häusern
«	ultimum, 1480 «	118 « «	71 «
Insgesamt :		314 « «	208 «

Die Zahlen beziehen sich auf die Hälfte der Stadt, so müssen wir sie schätzungsweise verdoppeln, um ein beiläufiges Resultat zu bekommen. Demnach dürfen wir voraussetzen, daß in der mit Mauer umgebenen Stadt

---

[4] KEMÉNY a. a. O. »Anno 83 quartale primum gelehen« und ebenda »Anno Domini MCCCCLXXX septimo media taxa cum marcellis exigi inchoata feria secunda post Martini . . . Quartale primum.«
[5] Ebenda 45 : »Integra taxa quartalis secundi exacta feria secunda proxima post Martini Anno Domini 1475.«
[6] Ebenda : »Anno 1484 ad taxam integram per regiam Maiestatem exhibitam feria secunda post Assumptionis Marie accommodata, quartale tertium.«
[7] Ebenda : »Taxa media exacta in quartali ultimo feria secunda post Conceptionis Marie Anno Domini MCCCCLXXX.«
[8] Für die Vollständigkeit der Steuerrollen des ersten Bezirkes sprechen, daß a) beide mit denselben Steuerpflichtigen enden ; b) die Steuerpflichtigen der beiden Steuer- rollen stimmen mit einigen Ausnahmen überein. — Die Steuerrolle der Vorstadt enthält eine »Summa« als Resultat.

insgesamt 628 Steuerpflichtige lebten, und 416 Häuser waren. Wenn wir diese Zahlen mit der Nürnberger Umrechnungszahl 4,68 Personen auf einen Steuerpflichtigen multiplizieren, dann wird unser Verfahren 2939 Personen ergeben. Dazu kommen noch die Mönche der zwei Klöster[9] (Franziskaner und Dominikaner), das Personal der Pfarrkirche (insgesamt 60 Personen) und so werden wir für die Stadt 3000 Einwohner annehmen können.

Die Steuerrolle der Vorstadt enthält 262 Steuerpflichtige, doch darunter 16 solche steuerpflichtige Personen, die in der Stadt wohnten und nur wegen ihren vorstädtischen Häusern hier wieder aufgenommen wurden. Wenn wir diese 16 Personen abrechnen, so bleiben 246 Steuerpflichtige, oder — mit der Nürnberger Umrechnungszahl multipliziert — 1151 Personen. Dazu kommen noch die Einwohner des städtischen Spitals, das ebenfalls außer der Stadtmauer lag, doch in der Steuerrolle nicht erwähnt ist, dann die Pfarrer der St. Leonhardtkirche, insgesamt 20 Personen — und so ergibt sich für die Vorstadt eine Einwohnerzahl von 1171 Personen. Die Zahl der Häuser war in der Vorstadt 202, dazu kamen noch 17 Meierhöfe, also insgesamt 219 Gebäude.

Als Endresultat können wir also behaupten, daß Kaschau am Ende 15. Jadrhunderts beiläufig 4170, rund 4200 Einwohner hatte, die in 635 Häusern verteilt waren.

Eine gewisse Kontrolle unserer Schätzung ergibt sich aus der Angabe, daß in Kaschau im Jahre 1667 500 Häuser waren. Nehmen wir in Betracht, daß im Zeitraum 1480—1667 der Umbau der Stadt vor sich ging, der ihr den noch heute fühlbaren barocken Charakter gab. Der Umbau der kleineren Bürgerhäuser in größere Barockhäuser war von einer wesentlichen Verminderung der Zahl der Häuser begleitet und so können wir unsere Schätzung, die 635 Häuser ergab, als annehmbar beurteilen.

Kaschau war also — nach der Einwohnerzahl gemessen — eine Mittelstadt. Weit entfernt davon, eine mittelalterliche Großstadt zu sein, doch ebenfalls weit davon entfernt, eine der Kleinstädte zu sein, hatte sie eine Einwohnerzahl, die die von Preßburg in Ungarn,[10] oder Heidelberg in Deutschland erreichte.[11] Unser Urteil wird auch durch die Durchschnittszahl der Steuerpflichtigen und Einwohner je eines Hauses bestätigt. In Augsburg fielen in 1498 auf ein Haus 2,23 Steuerpflichtige, dieselbe Zahl ist in Kaschau in dem ersten Bezirk 1,43, im letzten Bezirk 1,68, in der Stadt durchschnittlich 1,51. Natürlich waren die inneren Bezirke im Vergleich mit der Vor-

---

[9] Die Vorstellung, daß im Dominikanerkloster im Mittelalter rund 300 Mönche Unterkunft fanden, ist ins das Reich der Legenden zu verweisen. Vgl. : WICK, Adatok a kassai domonkosok történetéhez. [Angaben zur Geschichte der Dominikaner in Kaschau.] Kassa 1936, 6.

[10] Die Einwohnerzahl der Stadt wurde von Kováts für 1503 auf 4200—4700 Personen geschätzt (a. a. O. LIII.).

[11] EULENBURG, Zur Bevölkerungs- und Vermögensstatitik des 15. Jahrhunderts. — Ztschr. f. Sozial- u. Wirtschaftsgesch. 3 (1895) 434.

stadt überfüllt, da in der Vorstadt 1,22 Steuerpflichtige in einem Hause lebten. Wenn wir diese Ziffern mit der Umrechnungszahl 4,68 multiplizieren, dann ergibt sich folgendes : in der Stadt 7,07 Personen auf ein Haus, was mit den Dresdener Resultat auffallend übereinstimmt,[12] dagegen wird in der Vorstadt, wo nur 5,71 Personen auf ein Haus kommen, unsere Zahl höher sein, als die Dresdener (5,1). Das Bild ist jedem, der sich mit mittelalterlicher Stadtgeschichte befaßte, vertraut, in der Stadt sind die Einwohner in kleinen Häusern zusammengepfercht, dagegen gibt es mehr Luft in der Vorstadt die Häuser sind zwar noch kleiner und auch materiell schlechter ausgestattet, doch es leben nicht so viel Mieter in einem Gebäude. Die Kaschauer Zahlen bestätigen uns das Ergebnis, daß wir aus der Gesamtzahl der Einwohner gewonnen haben : Kaschau war eine Mittelstadt, gemäß ihrer Größe und auch der Unterkunft der Einwohner.

*

Wenn wir uns jetzt nach Feststellung der Einwohner- und Häuserzahl zur Frage der Vermögensverteilung wenden, so erwachsen uns neue Schwierigkeiten. Die Steuerrollen sind nicht nur lückenhaft, sie sind auch nach verschiedenen Prinzipien zusammengestellt worden. Die meisten Einzelheiten sind in der Steuerrolle des ersten Bezirks aus dem Jahre 1487 zu finden. Hier wurden die Steuerpflichtigen nicht nur nach ihrem Wohnsitz aufgezählt und nicht nur die gesamte Steuerpflicht angegeben, sondern bei jedem Steuerpflichtigen wurde der Wert des Hauses, der Wert des Malzhauses, des Meierhofs und die Größe der Äcker beigefügt.[13] Die Schätzung der Häuser und anderer Immobilien wurde in Silbermark vorgenommen, die nach einigen Angaben mit 4 fl. pro Mark übereinstimmt.[14] Aber selbst in dieser detaillierten Steuerrolle fehlen die Angaben über dem Steuerfuß, und so ist es unmöglich zu beurteilen, in welchem Maße die fahrende Habe und Immobilienbesitze bei der Steuerfestsetzung berücksichtigt wurden. Aus den Ziffern dieser Steuerrolle geht es aber ganz klar hervor, daß nicht der immobile Besitz, oder wenigstens nicht nur die Immobilien die Grundlage der Steuerfestsetzung bildeten, da die Inhaber der gleich geschätzten Häuser nie dieselbe Steuer zu zahlen hatten.[15]

[12] JASTROW, Die Volkszahl deutscher Städte zu Ende des Mittelalters und zu Beginn der Neuzeit. Berlin 1886, 61.
[13] Z. B. »Michel Hynterlewter fl. 2 dedit,
    marcas 17
    allodium 29
    agros sel 5
    brasiatorium 6.«
[14] Die Preise der Häuser scheinen den Wert einer Mark Silber = 4 fl. zu bestätigen. Z. B. Peter Bartoks Haus wurde in der Steuerrolle 1487 auf 29 Mark geschätzt, er kaufte es um 118 fl. von Jakob Kraus (Vorborsbuch, p. 74 v.). — Hans Rußdorfers Haus wurde auf 49 Mark geschätzt und um 200 fl. verkauft (a. a. O. 36 v.).
[15] W. Satler, H. Tetczel, H. Gürtler und M. Gasser verfügten z. B. über Häuser, deren Wert je 10 Silbermark war, doch zahlten sie die Steuer von 0,50, 1, —, 0,25, 0,50 fl.

Wenn aber außer Immobilien auch die fahrende Habe in die Schätzung einbezogen war, so ist es wahrscheinlich, daß die Steuerrollen ein ungefähres Bild der Vermögensverteilung geben können.

All das bezieht sich aber nur auf die Steuerrolle des ersten Bezirkes, die anderen Steuerrollen sind — was die detaillierte Aufzeichnung des Vermögens betrifft — weitaus einfacher, und ebendeswegen viel weniger ausführlich. Meistens werden nur die Namen der Steuerpflichtigen und die Festsetzung der jährlichen oder halbjährlichen Steuern angegeben. Die Häuser, ihre Besitzer und die Mieter werden aber auch in diesen kurzen Steuerrollen immer hervorgehoben.

Ein gemeinsamer Fehler der Steuerlisten ist, daß sie die Weingärten der Kaschauer außer acht lassen. Dies ist ein um so größerer Fehler, da die Kaschauer Bürger zur Zeit nicht nur im Stadtgebiet, sondern auch in dem weiter entfernten Tokajer Weingebirg große Besitze hatten. Einen beträchtiglichen Teil des Immobiliarbesitzes bildeten eben diese, in den Markten Szikszó, Tállya, Tolcsva und anderen Dörfern liegenden Weingärten.

Die Ungleichheit der knappen und detaillierten Steuerrollen, das Fehlen der Angaben über die Weingärten ermöglichen uns keine ausführliche Untersuchung des Immobiliarbesitzes, sie beschränken unsere Tätigkeit auf die Häuser, deren Besitzer aus den Steuerrollen immer bekannt sind ; und so können wir nur die Frage der Verteilung der Häuser in der Stadt und die Verteilung der Bevölkerung nach den festgestellten Steuern erörtern. Wir hoffen durch eine doppelte Untersuchung dem Tatbestand näher kommen zu können.

In der erhaltenen Steuerrollen, also in den achtziger Jahren des 15. Jhs. waren die Kaschauer Steuerpflichtigen am Besitz der Häuser in der Stadt folgendermassen beteiligt :

	Steuerpflichtige		Häuser	
	insgesamt	%	insgesamt	%
Hausbesitzer mit je 3 Häusern	4	1,28	12	5,77
,, ,, ,, 2 ,,	14	4,46	28	13,46
,, ,, ,, 1 Haus	161	51,27	161	77,40
Innleute	135	42,99	—	—
Steuerfreie Häuser	—	—	7	3,37
Insgesamt	314	100,00	208	100,00

Wenn wir auch die Vorstadt in Betracht ziehen, dann ändert sich unser Resultat folgendermaßen :

	Steuerpflichtige		Häuser	
	insgesamt	%	insgesamt	%
Hausbesitzer mit je 4 Häusern	1	0,17	4	0,98
,, ,, ,, 3 ,,	5	0,87	15	3,66
,, ,, ,, 2 ,,	13	2,27	26	6,34
,, ,, ,, 1 Haus	357	62,42	357	87,07
Innleute	196	34,27	—	—
Steuerfreie Häuser	—	—	8	1,95
Insgesamt	572	100,00	410	100,00

In groben Zügen zusammengefaßt heißt das, daß 34% der Steuerpflichtigen Mieter waren und keine eigenen Häuser hatten, während 66% derselben
in eigenen Häusern wohnten und noch über Miethäuser verfügten. Die Auffassung, daß im Mittelalter die ganze städtische Bevölkerung, oder wenigstens
ein überwiegender Teil derselben im eigenen Hause wohnte, ist schon lang
überholt. Die Kaschauer Angaben sind von diesem Standpunkt aus gesehen,
uninteressant. Doch die Proportionem die sich aus den zwei Tabellen ergeben,
sind von gewissem Interesse. Wir wissen, daß in Breslau im Jahre 1403 55%
der Steuerpflichtigen Mieter waren,[16] in Brünn ist im Jahre 1365 der Prozentsatz der Inleute 47, in der Prager Altstadt (1429) auch 46%.[17] Wenn wir diese
Zahlen mit den Kaschauern vergleichen, so dürfen wir behaupten, daß die
Wohnungsverhältnisse in Kaschau besser waren, als in den drei erwähnten
Städten, und zwar nicht nur in ihrer Gesamtheit, sondern auch in den einzelnen
Stadtteilen. Selbst die überfüllte innere Stadt weist nur 47% der Mieter auf,
das heißt, einen besseren Prozentsatz, als die um rund hundert Jahre älteren
Verhältnisse Brünns oder Breslaus. Umso auffallender ist die große Zahl
der Mieter in der Vorstadt, die sich nur durch eine Konzentration erklären
ließe, die in der inneren Stadt zu fehlen scheint. Doch wenn wir die innere
Stadt besser ins Auge fassen, so läßt sich die verhältnismäßig niedere Zahl
der Mieter durch den Bau der am Ring stehenden Häuser erklären. In der
Stadt waren in den kleinen Gassen die Häuser auf einem Grundstück aufgebaut, so stand an jedem einzelnen Grundstück nur ein Haus. Am Ring
war es ganz anders. Die Grundstücke am Ring liefen bis zur nächsten parallelen
Gasse und vereinigten so meistens zwei Häuser, das größere Haus, das am
Ring stand und von dem Inhaber selbst bewohnt wurde, und ein »domus

---

[16] F. MENDL, Breslau zu Beginn des 15. Jh.-s. Ztschr. f. Gesch. Schlesiens 36
(1929) 177.
[17] Ebenda.

posterior«, das auf die hintere Gasse einen Ausgang hatte. Diese kleineren Häuser waren vermietet. Damit soll natürlich nicht gesagt sein, daß andere Häuser keine Mieter beherbergten ; doch der überwiegende Teil der Mieter lebte in solchen Häusern, deren Besitzer am Ring wohnten.[18] Die Zahl der von Mietern bewohnten Häuser konnte in zwei Bezirken ermittelt werden :

	Häuser insgesamt	Häuser mit Inleuten		Inleute	
		insgesamt	%	insgesamt	pro Haus
Quartale primum	137	45	32,84	79	1,76
Quartale ultimum	71	24	33,80	56	2,33
Zusammen	208	69	33,17	135	1,96
Vorstadt (ohne Meierhöfe)	202	30	14,85	48	1,60
Zusammen	410	99	24,15	183	1,85

Wenn wir in der Vorstadt die Meierhöfe mit ihren Inleuten mitberücksichtigen, so ändert sich das Endresultat der Tabelle folgend :

Vorstadt (mit Meierhöfen)	219	47	21,46	61	1,30
Zusammen	427	116	27,17	196	1,69

Rund ein Drittel der Häuser in der Stadt hatten Mieter und nicht ganz ein Fünftel der Häuser in der Vorstadt war ebenfalls von Mietern besetzt. 34% der Mieter stehen den 66% Hausbesitzern entgegen. Die stärkste Gruppe der Hausbesitzer verfügte über ein Haus, sie macht rund 62% aus. Diese Zahl ist aber eben wegen des lückenhaften Quellenmaterials zu hoch und zeigt nicht den wirklichen Tatbestand. Es gibt mehrere Namen in den Steuerrollen, die ohne Steuerfestsetzung nur mit der Angabe, daß sie ein Haus besitzen, erwähnt werden. »Domus domini Jacobi Gwam« sagt die Aufzählung und danach folgt eine neue Reihe und in dieser wird mit dem Wörtchen »ibidem« ein Mieter eingeführt. In einigen Fällen konnten wir feststellen, daß es sich um solche Steuerpflichtige handelt, die mehrerer Häuser besassen, und natürlich ihre Steuer wurde nur einmal festgesetzt.[19] Da wir aber bezüglich zwei Bezirke nur Bruchstücke und keine vollständigen Steuerrollen besitzen, so kommt es öfters vor, daß die zwei Erwähnungen desselben Steuerpflichtigen fehlen. Wir müssen sie aber doch als Besitzer von zwei Häusern

[18] B. Roth, A. Rothel, N. Tierbach, B. Apotheker und H. Brechtel wohnten z. B. in der secunda acies circuli und ihre »domus posterior« sind »Hinter dem Kloster« zu finden.
[19] Jacob Gwman hatte z. B. Häuser im ersten, in letzten Bezirk und in der Vorstadt, zahlte aber nur im letzten Bezirk Steuer, wo er selbst wohnte.

betrachten, und mit ihnen die Zahl der über ein Haus verfügenden korrigieren. Wenn wir diese Korrektur durchführen, so stellt es sich heraus, daß nicht nur 13, sondern 37 Personen je zwei Häuser hatten, und die Zahl der mittleren Gruppe, also der Hausbesitzer mit je einem eigenen Haus von 357 auf 333 herabfällt und das sind nur 52% der vorausgesetzten Zahl der Steuerpflichtigen. Doch selbst mit dieser Korrektur bleibt die mittlere Gruppe ziemlich stark, und es hat den Anschein, daß in Kaschau ein wirtschaftlich starker und breiter Mittelstand lebte.

Der Prozentsatz der obersten Gruppen der Hausbesitzer scheint damit im Einklang zu stehen. Die erwähnte Korrektur kann die grundlegenden Züge dieser Gruppen nicht wesentlich ändern, die Zahl der über drei und vier Häuser verfügenden Besitzer bleibt umverändert, sie bilden rund 1% der Steuerpflichtigen und verfügen über 5% der Häuser in der Stadt.

Zusammenfassend können wir behaupten, daß die Verteilung des Hausbesitzes in Kaschau günstig war, wenigstens günstiger, als in den anderen osteuropäischen Städten. Die Zahl der Mieter ist gering, sie erreicht nicht den Prozentsatz der Mieter im Vergleich zu den um hundert Jahre älteren Verhältnissen in Breslau und Brünn. Die Gruppen der Besitzer zeigen einen starken Mittelstand, und selbst die Bürger, die mit drei oder vier Häusern die oberste Gruppe bilden, sind nicht zahlreich. Die oberste Schichte besteht eigentlich aus den Ringbürgern, die meistens am selben Grundstück über zwei Häuser verfügen, so eine Konzentration durchsetzen, und ihre Häuser durch Vermieten verwerten. Wenn wir nach der Besitzverteilung der Häuser zu urteilen haben, so sind die Ringbürger der Stadt — obwohl dieser Ausdruck in Kaschau im Mittelalter niemals geläufig war[20] — die oberste Schicht, trotzdem daß die Stadt hinter den osteruopäischen Mitterlstädten zurückgeblieben war, dennoch eine gewisse Konzentration des Grundeigentums durchzusetzen vermochte.

Das hier entworfene Bild wurde durch die Untersuchung des Hausbesitzes und allein nur des Hausbesitzes aus den kärglichen Aufzeichnungen der Steuerrollen gewonnen, und es bleibt eine offene Frage, ob die Vermögensverteilung einer mittelalterlichen Stadt wirklich auf Grund des Hausbesitzes beurteilt werden kann. Ebendeswegen fühlen wir uns verpflichtet, auch die Steuerverteilung zu untersuchen. Die Lücken des Quellenmaterials verursachen hier keine große Schwierigkeiten. Wie schon erwähnt wurde, erfolgte in allen Steuerrollen, selbst in den wortkargesten, die Festsetzung der Steuerpflicht in ungarischen Goldgulden. Außer dem ungarischen Gulden und seinen Teilen, den sog. »denarii«, begegnen wir nur dem »Ort«, der den Viertel des Guldens ausmacht. Es ist also nicht schwierig, für alle in den Steuerrollen auf-

---

[20] Dagegen wurden die vornehmen Kaschauer Bürger in den Aufzeichnungen der Stadt immer als »Herr«-en betitelt.

	Steuer-pflicht Personen	Es zahlen keine St.		Von Steuerzahlenden									
				—1 fl.		1—3 fl.		4—5 fl.		6—10 fl.		10— fl.	
		P.	%	P.	%	P.	%	P.	%	P.	%	P.	%
Quartale primum	196	33	16,84	99	50,51	52	26,53	9	4,59	2	1,02	2	0,51
Quartale ultimum	118	21	17,80	57	48,31	24	20,34	10	8,47	3	2,54	3	2,54
Insgesamt	314	54	17,20	156	49,68	76	24,20	19	6,66	5	1,59	4	1,27
Vorstadt	246	35	14,23	208	84,55	3	15,45	—	—	—	—	—	—
Insgesamt	560	89	15,89	364	65,00	79	14,11	19	3,39	5	0,89	4	0,72

gezeichneten Personen die Steuerlast zu bestimmen. Wir haben hier die zwei Stadtbezirke und die Vorstadt ebenfalls gesondert gezählt und die Ergebnisse in einer Tabelle zusammengefasst.

Diese Zusammenstellung über ide festgesetzte Steuer der Steuerpflichtigen zeigt uns ein Bild das einen scharfen Gegensatz zu unseren Ergebnissen über die Verteilung des Hausbesitzes aufweist. Die Steuerpflichtigen teilen sich hier in zwei, voneinander stark abgegrenzte Gruppen, in die der wohlhabenden und die der Armen ; der Mittelstand, den wir bei der Untersuchung des Hausbesitzes so hoch schätzten, ist beinahe spurlos verschwunden. Im allgemeinen sehen wir, daß 16% der Steuerpflichtigen über kein Vermögen verfügten und so arm sind, daß sie überhaupt keine Steuer zahlen. Die zweite Gruppe schließt sich eng an die der Unvermögenden an, Steuerpflichtige deren Steuer unter 1 fl. blieb, bilden diese Gruppe und diese is so groß, daß ihr in der Vorstadt nur 3 Bürger nicht angehören. Selbst in der Stadt hat diese zweite Gruppe die Oberhand und im Durchschnitt bildet sie 65% der Steuerpflichtigen. Die mittlere Gruppe weist in der Stadt zwar noch 24% auf, aber wenn wir die ganze Stadt samt der Vorstadt ins Auge fassen, so fällt der Prozentsatz auf 14% herab. Dementsprechend wird auch die Gruppe der höchst besteuerten stark abgesondert und zahlt der großen Massen gegenüber die mehr als zehnfache Steuer von 10 fl.

Außer den scharfen Gegensätzen zwischen den Steuerpflichtigen fällt die Armut der Vorstädter auf. Abgesehen von den 3 Personen, deren Steuer mit je 1 fl. festgesetzt wurde, zahlen alle vorstädtische Steuerpflichtigen den niedersten Steuerertrag oder überhaupt keine Steuer.

Auf Grund der Steuersumme müssen wir also feststellen, daß Kaschau tatsächlich eine Mittelstadt war, wo die Vermögensverhältnisse durch eine entgegengesetzte Tendenz des sich zuspitzenden Reichtums und der Armut gekennzeichnet war. Die Verhältniszahl der niedersten Gruppe ist aber schlechter, als in Heidelberg und anderen Städten der Pfalz, die über mehr als eintausend Einwohner verfügten, und erreichte beinahe die um ein halbes Jahrhundert jüngeren Verhältnisszahl Basels und Freiburgs.[21]

Die Tabelle der Hausbesitzer und die der Steuerpflichtigen führten zur entgegengesetzten Ergebnissen. Welches von den beiden sind richtig, den tatsächlichen Verhältnissen am nächsten? Wenn wir die über die meisten Häuser verfügenden Steuerpflichtigen und ihre Steuer einander gegenüberstellen, so werden wir eine einschlägige Antwort auf unsere Frage erhalten.

Name	Steuer fl.	Anmerkung
Bartholm Apotheker	5	2 Häuser, Garten, Felder, Meierhof
Peter Bartok	3	Haus Garten, Felder, Malzhaus
Peter Brechtel	2	—
Georg Gabriel	18	2 Häuser
Vince Kis	2	2 Häuser
Hans Opitzer	3,50	Haus
Bartholomeus Roth	6	2 Häuser, Felder, Meierhof
Klemens Zipser	12	Haus
Simon Zengel	6	2 Häuser
Hans Szobránci	4	Haus
Jacob Scholtis	1,50	Haus, Meierhof
Hieron. Trinkaus	2	Haus
Hans Russdorfer	4	2 Häuser, Malzhaus, Felder, Meierhof
Frau Toth Mihalin	3	Haus

Aus der Tabelle geht es klar hervor, daß die höchstbesteuerten und die über die meisten Häuser verfügenden Personen nicht identisch waren. Obzwar der höchstbesteuerte Bürger der Stadt, Franz Szatmáry selbst über zwei Häuser verfügte und zweifellos der reichste Mann der Stadt war, können wir ihn keinesfalls mit Peter Brechtel in eine Gruppe stellen, dessen Steuer trotz seiner 3 Häuser nur 1 fl. war. Noch weniger sind Szatmárys 2 Häuser und 35 fl. Steuer den zwei Häusern des Johann Ambrosy und seiner Steuer von 0,75 fl. gleichzustellen. Diese Tabelle beweist, daß wir die Vermögensunterschiede der Kaschauer Bürger keineswegs auf Grund des Immobiliarbesitzes beurteilen dürfen. Ein dem Tatbestand annäherndes Bild kann nur durch die Untersuchung der festgesetzten Steuern gegeben werden ; ein dem Tatbestand vollkommen entsprechendes Bild kann ohnehin nicht entworfen werden. Nicht nur wegen der Lücken in den Steuerrollen, sondern auch wegen

---

[21] F. BUOMBERGER, Bevölkerungs- und Vermögensstatistik in der Stadt und Landschaft Freiburg i. Ü. um die Mitte des 15. Jh.-s. Bern 1900, 135.

der Art der mittelalterlichen städtischen Steuerverteilung. Wir dürfen ruhig behaupten, daß die Vermögenden in Kaschau ebenso Gelegenheit hatten, ihr Vermögen von den Steuern teilweise zu entlasten, als es die Reichen in Augsburg taten. Die gesetzte Steuer Szatmárys war in Verhältnis seines tatsächlichen Vermögens keinesfalls so hoch, wie der kleine Besitz der Steuerpflichtigen, die 1 fl. zu zahlen hatten. Da aber keine Quellen zu Verfügung stehen, die eine Korrektur der Steuerrollen ermöglichen, so sind wir gezwungen in unseren weiteren Untersuchungen die Vermögensunterschiede der Kaschauer Bürger auf Grund der in den Steuerrollen aufgezeichneten Steuer festzustellen. Wenden wir uns jetzt von unten nach oben fortschreitend den einzelnen Steuerklassen zu, wie sie in der Tabelle festgehalten sind.

Verhältnismäßig wissen wir das wenigste — oder vielleicht das meiste — über die unterste Klasse, deren Mitglieder überhaupt keine Steuer zahlten. Sie waren Bettler, Witwen, Taglöhner, Lohnarbeiter, manchmal auch Anfänger, die vom Lande oder aus anderen Städten kommend ihr Glück vom neuen versuchten. Ihre materielle Lage ist schon dadurch genügend gekennzeichnet, daß selbst das erbarmungslose städtische Steuerwesen keinen Heller ihnen erpressen konnte. In der Vorstadt lebend oder in gemieteten Wohnungen der ummauerten inneren Stadt zusammengepfercht, führten sie ein karges Dasein, kämpften mit Schulden, Arbeitslosigkeit und mit der Stadt selbst. Es lohnt sich nicht, hier Einzelheiten zu erwähnen, die Kaschauer Geschichte kann nichts Neues bieten, das aus dem Quellenmaterial anderer Städte nicht genügend bekannt wäre.[22]

Von der ersten Klasse nicht weit entfernt steht unsere zweite Klasse, die der unter 1 fl. besteuerten Einwohner. Die Mitglieder dieser Gruppe waren ebenfalls meist Mieter oder Vorstädtler. Wir finden unter ihnen Handwerker, und sind geneigt zu behaupten, daß das Übergewicht dieser Klasse eben von Handwerkern gebildet wurde. Leider stehen uns keine Zunftrollen zur Verfügung und die zweite allgemein übliche Methode, die Handwerker mit Hilfe ihrer Familiennamen zu bestimmen, kann auch nicht angewendet werden. In Kaschau des ausgehenden 15. Jhs waren die Familiennamen schon zu sehr entwickelt, um sie als eine sichere Grundlage der Beschäftigung beurteilen zu können. Nicht alle »Cromer« (Krämer) waren Kaufleute und solche Namen wie Wasserbauch, Trinkaus usw. würden uns keine nähere Aufklärung geben. So bleibt uns nichts anderes übrig, als die in anderen Quellen erhaltenen Angaben zu verwerten und jene Handwerker, die in Urkunden, oder in dem »vorpotsbuch« der Stadt als Handwerker bezeichnet werden, in eine Tabelle zusammenzufassen :

---

[22] Graus, Městská chudina v dobe předhusitské. [Die Armen in den Städten der vorhussitischen Zeit.] Praha 1949.

Name	Beruf	Steuer	Immobilien
Niclos Birger	Schneider	1,50	Haus, Weingarten in Tarcal
Peter Czöff	,,	1,—	Haus, Malzhaus
Christian Mangler	Zwilcher	1,50	Haus
Jurg Kresner	,,	1,—	Haus
Oswald	,,	1,—	Haus
Demeter Hutter	Hutter	1,—	Haus
Michael Hutter	,,	0,25	—
Hans Kolbil	Fleischer	0,75	Haus
Cosmas Goldschmiedt	Goldschmied	0,12	—

Zwar sind diese Namen nur zufälligerweise erhalten geblieben, stellen sie doch ein dem Durchschnitt nahe stehendes Bild der Handwerker dar. Es handelt sich nicht um den untersten und am wenigsten vermögenden Teil der Handwerker. Oswald Zwilcher erscheint 1489 als Vetreter der Zwilcher,[23] Demetrius und Michael Hutter waren Vorstände der Hutmacherzech gewesen, sie verhandelten über die Geldangelenheiten der Hutmacher.[24] Sie gehörten auch keinesfalls zur ärmsten Gruppe der Stadtbewohner. Abgesehen von den zwei Personen, deren Steuer am niedrigsten festgestellt worden war, hatten sie alle ihr eigenes Haus. Brieger besaß sogar einen Weingarten in dem Dorfe Tarcal,[25] Peter Czöff, der mit dem Stadtpfarrer verwandt war, verfügte über ein Malzhaus. Mit Ausnahme der drei letzten Meister, hatten sie 1 fl. oder einen etwas höheren Steuerbetrag zu zahlen. Das alles bedeutet, daß ein Teil der weniger als 1 fl. zahlenden Steuerträger und ein Teil der dritten Steuerklasse (1—3 fl.) sich aus den Handwerkern der Stadt rekrutierte.

Den anderen Teil der dritten Steuerklasse bildeten hauptsächlich die Krämer und Kaufleute. Wenn wir die Mitglieder der Bruderschaft der Krämer in eine Tabelle zusammenfassen, so werden wir nicht nur die Mitglieder der dritten, sondern auch der zwei oberen Steuerklassen unter ihnen finden.

Die Tabelle ist leider unvollständig, da von den Steuerrollen die der halben ummauerten Stadt fehlen ; doch wird es sofort auffallen, daß unter diesen Steuerträgern der niedrigste Steuerbetrag 1,50 fl. ausmacht, und mit Ausnahme Peter Brechtels alle wenigstens ein Haus hatten. Sie wurden nicht nur von den städtischen Steuerbehörden und von der öffentlichen Meinung als wohlhabende Leute gehalten, sie bezeichneten sich selbst auch als die »reichen Cromer«.[26]

[23] Vorbotsbuch 178 r.
[24] Ebenda 62 v., 88 r.
[25] Ebenda 92 r.
[26] Magyar Gazdaságtörténeti Szemle 5 (1898) 31.

Die »Reychcromern« führen uns zur letzten Klasse unseren Tabelle, zur Klasse der Höchstbesteuerten. Versuchsweise stellten wir zwei Tabellen zusammen. In der ersten treten uns die Ringbürger, in der zweiten die Virilisten entgegen.

Namen der Ringbürger	Steuer	Namen der Höchstbesteuerten		Steuer
Prima acıes circuli				
Mich. Goldschmied	4,—	Franz Szatmári	x	35,—
Hermann Tetzel	1,—	Hans Schurger		22,—
Gallus Setz[1]	—	Georg Gabriel	x	18,—
Mich. Schwertfeger	2,50	Marta Skopyn	x	14,—
Lorenz Goldschmidt	2,—	Georg Schwarcz	x	10,—
Gabriel Goldmutz	2,—	Niklas Tropper		8,—
Hans Russdorfer	4,—	Hans Colmaryn	x	7,—
Gilg Hausenstetter	1,—	Simon Zengel		6,—
Niklas Barbierer	1,—	Balth. Roth	x	6,—
Hieron. Stenczel	2,—	Barth. Apotheker	x	5,—
Secunda acies circuli		Hans Waickhart	x	5,—
Stephan Reich	2,—	Mich. Reuter		5,—
Silvester Panczermacher	5,—	János Pathaky	x	5,—
Jurg Sauermann	3,—	Martin Wagmeister	x	5,—
Vince Kis	2,—	Silvester Panczermacher	x	5,—
Barth. Apotheker	5,—	Durchschnittlich		10,40
Hans Brechtel	1,—			
Mich. Schwarcz	4,—			
Balth. Roth	6,—			
Andreas Rothel	—			
Durchschnittlich	2,91			

Die zwei Tabellen geben uns einigen Bescheid über die Zusammenstellung der obersten Steuerklassen. Die Ringbürger stehen zwar unter den Reichkrämern, erreichen zwar die Höchstbesteuerten nicht, doch sind die Höchstbesteuerten meistens auch Ringbürger. Diese Klassen der Wohlhabenden verfügten über die meisten Häuser, zahlten die größte Steuer und befaßten sich mit Handel, Bergwerksunternehmungen und Geldgeschäften.

Wir haben Kaschaus Einwohnerschaft in bezug auf den Hausbesitzes und die Steuer überblickt. Die Ergebnisse der zwei Untersuchungen gingen in gewissen Punkten zwar stark auseinander, doch bezeugten sie eine Oberschicht, die nach dem Hausbesitz zu beurteilen schwach, nach der Steuerpflicht

zu beurteilen stark war und den Durchschnitt weit übertraf. Da wir die Steuerpflicht als den entscheidenden Maßstab der Vermögensverhältnisse anzu-
erkennen gezwungen waren, müssen wir jetzt feststellen, daß Kaschau ihrer
Grösse nach eine Mittelstadt war, in der die Vermögensverhältnisse sich
schlechter gestalten, als es nach der Geschichte anderer Städte zu erwarten
wäre. Den mächtigen und materiell sehr starken Wohlhabenden steht eine
breite Masse der Habenichtse gegenüber ein Mittelstand fehlt beinahe vollkommen. Schon bei der Analyse der einzelnen Steuerklassen versuchten wir
das wirtschaftliche Betätigungsfeld der Klassen zu bezeichnen. Wir sind
überzeugt davon, daß die Entwicklung der Kaschauer Vermögensverhältnisse nur durch die Entwicklung der einzelnen Wirtschaftszweige zu erklären
ist. Nur der Überblick der Entwicklung des Weinbaues, des Handels und der
Bergwerksunternehmungen kann uns eine annehmbare Antwort auf die
Frage geben : warum eben die Krämer und Handelsleute und die Unternehmer in den Bergwerken die reichsten waren, oder umgekehrt, warum die
Handwerker in ihren Vermögensverhältnissen den Krämern gegenüber so
weit zurückgeblieben sind? Diese Antwort wird zur selben Zeit auch die
Frage der Kapitalsbildung in Kaschau beantworten. Bevor wir aber noch die
einzelnen Wirtschaftszweige in ihrer Entwicklung untersuchen, müssen wir
ein allgemeines Bild von den wirtschaftlichen Grundlagen der Stadt haben.

Die spärlichen Angaben des 13. Jh.-s lassen uns Kaschau als eine kleine
deutsche Siedlung erscheinen, die im raschen Takt sich zur einer kleinen Stadt
entwickelt. Das erste Privileg wurde vor 1249 ausgefertigt und noch im 13.
Jh. wurden die Stadtkirche, die an der Stelle des heutigen Domes stand, das
Dominikanerkloster und die Stadtmauer gebaut.[27] Es gelang der Stadt die
Patronatsrechte der Stadtkirche zu erwerben und eine Freiheit zu erlangen,
nach der die Stadt den Weinzehnt in Geld begleichen konnte. An der Wende
des 13. und 14. Jh.-s entfaltet die junge Stadt eine starke wirtschaftliche
Expansion, es werden in der Nachbarschaft Wälder erworben und in Weingärten umgewandelt.[28] Der Weinbau war in diesen Jahrzehnten von grundlegender Bedeutung. 1347 erwähnt eine königliche Urkunde, die Stadt habe
überhaupt keinen Ackerbau[29] und 1411 war die Weinlese so reichlich, daß
sie nicht nur die Stadt, sondern auch ganze Landesteile versehen konnte.[30]
In der kleinen Stadt finden wir auch Handwerker, die die Umgebung mit
ihren Produkten versehen. Zur selben Zeit melden sich die anderen zwei

---

[27] MENCL, Stredoveké mesta na Slovensku 179—182, und B. VARSIK, Slovenská
ulica v Košiciach a vznik mesta Košice. [Die Windische Gasse in Kaschau und die
Entstehung der Stadt Kaschau.] Historica Slovaca 6—7 (1948) 83—94.
[28] OSVÁTH GY., Adatok Kassa közjogi helyzetéhez és közigazgatási szervezeté-
hez 1657 előtt. [Beiträge zur Kaschaus verfassungsrechtliche Lage und Behörden-
organisation vor 1657.] Kassa 1918.
[29] »cum iidem (nämlich die Kaschauer) nec aratrum nec alios proventus habeant
preter vineas et vina eorundem.« Ebenda 86.
[30] Ebenda 124.

Wirtschaftszweige : das Bergwerk und der Handel. Kaschau war ein natürlicher Mittelpunkt der in der Umgebung liegenden Bergwerke. Die Produkte der verschiedenen Metallbergwerke wurden durch Kaschau verwertet, die Bergstädte wurden durch Kaschau mit Lebensmitteln versorgt. Diese zwei Bedürfnisse hoben Kaschau aus der Reihe der kleinen Marktflecken heraus und die Stadt begann sich wirtschaftlich rasch zu entwickeln. Die erste Periode der Stadtgeschichte endet mit einem symbolischen Ereignis : der Oligarch Omode ließ vier Stück Tuch und zwei Pferde von einem Kaschauer Bürger beschlagnahmen.[31] Zwischen Omode und der Stadt entsteht ein Streit, in welchem Omode von den Bürgern erschlagen wird. In der Versöhnungsurkunde, die die Stadt zusammen mit Omodes Nachfolgern ausstellt, bringt die Stadt ihre wirtschaftlichen Forderungen zur Geltung : Kaschau übernimmt den großen Wald, der zwischen der Stadt und der Zips liegt, Omodes Nachfolger versprechen feierlich, daß sie den Stadtmarkt und seine Besucher nie mehr stören werden.[32]

Die zweite Periode der Stadtgeschichte baute auf diesen Grundlagen weiter. Die Stadt stellt sich auf die Seite des Königs Karl Robert, sichert sich damit den mächtigsten ihrer Patrone. In langer Reihe folgen nun königliche Privilegien, die die errungene wirtschaftliche Stellung der Stadt bekräftigen. 1347 wird die Stadt mit dem Ofner Recht ausgestattet, erhält das Stapelrecht. Im selben Jahre sichert ein anderes Privileg den Stadtmarkt für die Kaschauer Weine: König Ludwig verordnet, daß niemand bis Pfingsten Landwein in die Stadt bringen darf, das heißt, bis die Kaschauer ihren Bauwein nicht ausgeschenkt haben.[33] Die königlichen Freiheitsbriefe werden durch einen Handelskontrakt ergänzt, den Kaschau 1324 mit Krakau geschlossen hat.[34] Zu Beginn des 14. Jh.-s wurde Krakau mit dem Stapelrecht ausgestattet und entwickelte sich infolgedessen zu einer bedeutenden Handelsstadt, die hauptsächlich die von der Ostsee und von dem Westen nach Südosten gerichteten Waren für Krakau sicherte. Für diesen Handel konnte Kaschau das ungarische Kupfer liefern, das den Krakauern am meisten fehlte, und konnte dafür Industrieprodukte bekommen, die wiederum Kaschau am meisten benötigte. Der Kontrakt brachte für Kaschau weiteres Aufblühen. 1404 erläßt König Sigmund eine bedeutungsvolle Verordnung, in der die Freiheiten der Stadt bestätigt, das Stapelrecht mit besonderem Nachdruck hervorgehoben und die bisherigen Freiheiten dadurch erweitert werden, daß außer Wochen- und Jahrmärkten Fremde mit gewissen Waren nur en gros Geschäfte schließen dürfen.[35] Diese Verordnung ist die letzte in der Reihe

---

[31] FEJÉR, CD. 6/2 : 339.
[32] TUTKO J., Sz. kir. Kassa városának történeti évkönyve. [Historische Annalen der kön. Freistadt Kaschau.] 207.
[33] OSVÁTH a. a. O. 82.
[34] Cod. dipl. Cracov. 1 : 17.
[35] Századok 2 (1868) 158, 1. Anmerkung.

der Freiheiten und Verordnungen, die Kaschau zu einer Stadt in europäischem Sinne erhoben haben. Unabhängiges Stadtregiment, das nicht einmal von der kirchlichen Hierachie durchbrochen wurde, eigenes Rechtwesen und alle wirtschaftliche Maßnahmen, die in der Geschichtswissenschaft unter dem Schlagwort Stadtwirtschaft bekannt sind : Straßenzwang, Stapelrecht, der erzwungene Großhandel der fremden Kaufleute, Zunftwesen, eigenes Maß, sind hier alle zu finden. In kaum 200 Jahren ist aus der kleinen Siedlung der wirtschaftliche Mittelpunkt Oberungarns geworden.

Theoretisch konnte jeder Wirtschaftszweig, der in Kaschau vertreten war, seine Rechnung finden. Jeder Wirtschaftszweig hatte genügend Gelegenheit, sich frei zu entwickeln und eine Gruppe kapitalstarker Elemente ins Leben zu rufen. Doch es geschach nicht so, denn die wirtschaftliche Entwicklung der Stadt begünstigte nicht alle Zweige gleich.

Der Weinbau blieb in Kaschau durch das ganze Mittelalter und auch durch das ganze 16. Jh. von fundamentaler Bedeutung. In den ersten Perioden der Stadtgeschichte wurden ausgedehnte Wälder in Weingärten umwandelt, es wurde viel mehr Wein produziert, als es nötig war. Der überflüssige Wein wurde in zwei Richtungen abgesetzt. Einesteils wurde damit die Gegend der Gruben versehen, anderenteils wurde er in der Stadt selbst verbraucht. Hier wirkte auch Kaschaus glückliche geographische Lage günstig mit. Nördlich von der Stadt konnte keine größere Weinkultur angebaut werden, die Zipser Städte, die Bergstädte waren auf Kaschaus Wein angewiesen. Als sich der Handelsbereich der Stadt gegen Polen erweiterte, konnte auch nach Polen eine große Menge von Wein geliefert werden. Doch wenn wir auch Kaschaus Weinbau als ausgedehnt bezeichneten, er konnte keinesfalls so ausgedehnt sein, daß er die enormen polnischen Bedürfnisse selbst befriedigen konnte. Eben der gesteigerte Bedarf, der sich nach dem Handelsabkommen mit Krakau fühlen ließ, zwang die Kaschauer dazu, ihren Weinbau indirekt auszudehnen. Südöstlich von Kaschau gaben die Tokajer Weingebiete eine gute Gelegenheit dazu, Weingärten zu erwerben, und sie durch billige Arbeitskraft anbauen zu lassen. Tatsächlich drangen die Kaschauer im Tokajer Weingebiet vor und erlangten an gewissen Orten die Mehrheit an Grundeigentum.[36] Es scheint uns, daß die im Stadtgebiet angebaute Weinkultur dieser Konkurrenz noch gewachsen war, Kaschauer Wein und Landwein (d. h. Tokajer) wurden als ebenbürtig angesehen.[37] Vielleicht noch im 14. Jh. erschien aber auch hier der beste ungarische Wein, der in der südlichen Pro-

[36] Es handelt sich hauptsächlich um die Marktflecken Szikszó, Szerencs, Tállya, Mád, Tolcsva und die anschließenden kleineren Dörfer. Wie weit hier die Kaschauer die Oberhand gewonnen haben, zeigt uns eine Eintragung im Verbotsbuch der Stadt, nach der die Geschworenen des Dorfes Tarcal nach Kaschau kamen, um dort eine Teilzahlung für den Ankauf eines Weingartens durch einen Kaschauer Bürger der Stadt anzumelden. (Verbotsbuch p. 60. r.)

[37] Kaschauer und Landwein ist gemeinsam in Jakob Kraus' Testament erwähnt. (Ebenda 74 r.)

XI

vinz Sirmium (heute Novi Sad in Jugoslawien) angebaut und durch die Bürger
der Stadt Szeged verkauft wurde. Leider stehen uns zu wenig Angaben zur
Verfügung, um die Konkurrenz dieses Weines zu beurteilen ; es ist aber sicher,
das er in nicht unterschätzenden Mengen eben durch Kaschau nach Polen
weitergefördert wurde und eine erstklassige Qualität besaß.[38] Die Kaschauer
und Tokajer Weine waren von unmittelbaren Nutzen für beinahe alle Kaschauer Bürger, aber der südliche Wein brachte nur den Kaufleute Nutzen, die
ihn kauften, und gegen Krakau weiterkauften. Die im Handel tätigen Personen
erlangten also hier den maximalen Profit und damit auch die Gelegenheit,
aus dem Weinhandel Kapitalien herauszuschlagen.

Trotz der Konkurrenz des Südweines blieb in Kaschau der Weinbau
und der Besitz der Weingärten auch weiterhin von höchster Bedeutung.
Wenn wir die Jahrgänge 1489—1492 des Vorpotsbuchs durchblättern, finden
wir in den Kreditgeschäften überall Weingärten verzeichnet. Es ist durchaus
bezeichnend, daß in diesen Jahren 19 Weingärten im Werte von 1425 fl. ver-
pfändet wurden und dagegen in demselben Zeitraum nur 14 Häuser in einem
Wert von 736 fl. Und der Unterschied wird noch stärker, wenn wir uns die
einzelnen Fälle näher betrachten. Häuser wurden meistens in der Vorstadt
versetzt, die Geldsummen sind niedrig, die Besitzer hatten eben keinen Weingarten zu verpfänden.[39] Einwohner der inneren Stadt kommen nur zweimal
vor, in beiden Fällen versetzten sie alles, was sie hatten, so auch ihre Häuser.[40]
Die Besitzer der Weingärten sind keine Vorstädtler. Es gibt unter ihnen
Höchtsbesteuerte, »Reychcromer« und besser situierte Handwerker. Sie
verpfänden nicht nur solche Weingärten, die im Stadtgebiet liegen, im Gegenteil, von den 19 Weingärten sind nur 12 Kaschauer, die anderen 7 fallen in
das Tokajer Weingebiet.[41]

Eben das »vorpotsbuch« macht uns darauf aufmerksam, daß der Besitz
eines Weingartens für den Kaschauer Bürger beinahe unerläßlich war, den
er bildete die Grundlage für die Kreditfähigkeit.

Doch Reichtum wurde dennoch nicht aus den Weingärten erworben.
Wir kennen zwar keine einzige Angabe über die Anbauungskosten und den
erzielten Gewinn, sehen aber (wenn auch alle wohlhabenden Kaschauer
Bürger über Weingärten verfügten), daß der, der sich zu einem höheren Ver-
mögungsniveau emporgearbeitet hat, sein eigentliches Vermögen sich aus
anderen Quellen erwarb. In allen Fällen, wo größeres Vermögen zusammen-
gebracht wurde, war Handel, Bergwerk oder Geldgeschäft anwesend, der
Weingarten diente nur als Hintergrund, als ein verpfändbares Objekt. Kapital

[38] Reizner S., Szeged város története. [Die Geschichte der Stadt Szeged.] 4 ; 83.
[39] Z. B. zwei Häuser in Ludmannsdorf, das eine um 21 fl., das andere um 4 fl.
(Verbotsbuch p. 24 r. und 35 r.)
[40] Z. B. Hans Rußdorfer, der gegen 1070 fl. Schuld alle seine Weingärten, sein
Haus und seinen Laden versetzte. (Ebenda 52 v.)
[41] In Tállya, Liszka, Szikszó, Tölcsvár und Szántó. (Ebenda p. 33 v., 40 v., 64 r.
69 r.)

konnte höchstens aus dem Weinhandel gesammelt werden, aber aus dem Weinbau nicht. Wenn wir uns der zweiten Gruppe der Steuerzahlenden zu wenden und die Entwicklung des Zunftwesens näher ins Auge fassen, so muß daran erinnert werden, daß die wirtschaftliche Lage der Stadt in den ersten zwei Perioden der Stadtgeschichte günstig war. Zwar war zu dieser Zeit das Handwerk noch schwach vertreten, aber die Möglichkeiten waren glänzend. Die in der Nachbarschaft liegenden Gruben konnten Edelmetalle und Eisen bieten, Produkte konnten im Handelsbereich der Stadt abgesetzt werden. Und fügen wir hinzu, daß das Gewerbe der ungarischen Städte zur selben Zeit noch so wenig entwickelt war, daß jede Stadt, die die notwendigen Vorbedingungen dazu besaß — und die Handwerker von Kaschau besaßen sie in vollen Umfang — sich zu einer Industriestadt im mittelalterlichen Sinne des Wortes entwickeln konnte.[42]

Die Geschichtsquellen der Stadt lassen uns das Zunftwesen in ihrer Entwicklung erblicken. Im Laufe des 15. Jh.-s wird ein Zunftbrief nach dem anderen ausgegeben. Wenn wir die Zunftbriefe mit einer Liste von 1514 vergleichen, die die Zünfte gelegentlich einer Waffenausteilung anführt,[43] so können wir die Entwicklung des 15. Jh.-s in ihrer Grundlage erkennen. Als Schema verwenden wir die von Bücher aufgestellte Reihenfolge.

Gewerbe	Zunftbrief	Erwähnt 1514
I. Metall	1461 : Spohrer, Schlosser, Panzermacher und Schwertfeger	Schmiede, Schlosser
II. Heiz- und Leuchtstoff	—	Ölschleger
III. Textil	1411 : Barchentweber 1429 : Weber	Tuchmacher Zwilcher
IV. Leder	1467 : Gerber 1461 : Sattler	Gerber Sattler Riemer
V. Holz- und Schnittzstoffe	1459 : Wagner, Dressler, Tischler	Wagner Binder
VI. Lebensmittel	—	Fleischer
VII. Bekleidung und Reinigung	— : Schuster 1480 : Schuhmacher 1439 : Gürtler und Taschner 1461 : Schneider	Schuster Gürtler Schneider Kürschner
VIII. Baugewerbe	—	Töpfer

[42] Szűcs J., A városok és kézművesség a XV. századi Magyarországon. [Städte und das Handwerk in Ungarn im 15. Jh.] Budapest 1955, 53—122.
[43] Történeti Tár 1887, 785.

Diese Zusammenstellung unterrichtet uns von der Zunftentwicklung im mittelalterlichen Kaschau. Vor allem zeigt es ein sehr schwach entwickeltes Zunftwesen. Das ganze Metallgewerbe ist im Rahmen einer Zunft zusammengepreßt und spaltet sich auch nach 50 Jahren nur in zwei Zünfte, die wahrscheinlich ebenfalls mehrere Zweige zusammenfassen. Dasselbe kann beim Holzgewerbe beobachtet werden. Bei zwei Gewerben, beim Heiz- und Lichtstoff- und beim Lebensmittelgewerbe ist uns überhaupt kein Zunftbrief erhalten geblieben und beide Gewerbe sind auch noch 1513 durch je eine Zunft repräsentiert. Die größte Zergliederung weisen die Handwerker auf, die sich mit Lederbearbeitung und mit Herstellung von Bekleidung befassen. Im Jahre 1513 ist am stärksten das Bekleidungsgewerbe vertreten, und danach folgt sofort das Ledergewerbe. Diese Angaben deuten auf ein schwaches Zunftwesen und auf eine noch schwächere Entwicklung der Handwerker hin. Dieses Ergebnis wird auch durch das Bürgerbuch aus der Zeit 1489—1526 bestätigt.

Die neuen Bürger wurden in Kaschau in gleicher Weise matrikuliert wie in den Großstädten des Westens und zufälligerweise ist uns dieses Buch überliefert wurden. Natürlich sind die Eintragungen weitaus nicht so genau, wie in den westeuropäischen Städten. So können wir z. B. nicht immer zweifellos bestimmen, ob es sich um einem Kaschauer Bürgersohn oder um einen Einwanderer handelt. In einem ziemlich hohen Prozentsatz ist jedoch der Beruf des betreffenden Neubürgers bestimmbar[44] und die Angaben über bestimmte Berufe können in einer Tabelle zusammengestellt werden.

	Zahl der Berufe	Zahl der Neubürger	Neubürger mit Beruf	
			Zunftzwang	ohne Zunftzwang
I. Metallgewerbe	9	28	16	12
II. Holz- und Leichstoff	1	1	1	—
III. Textilgewerbe	4	16	11	5
IV. Ledergewerbe...........................	3	17	17	—
V. Holz- und Schnitzstoffe	5	19	19	—
VI. Lebensmittel	1	23	23	—
VII. Bekleidung und Reinigung	8	40	35	5
VIII. Baugewerbe	3	9	—	9
Insgesamt	34	153	122	31

Es könnte tatsächlich nicht schwer sein, eine Zunftmitgliederschaft zu erwerben, wo rund 80% der neuen Handwerker Berufe hatten die unter

[44] Rund 23% der Neubürger hatten einen bestimmten Beruf, der eingetragen wurde.

Zunftzwang standen. Nicht nur das Zunftwesen, sondern auch das Gewerbe im allgemeinen wird ziemlich schwach gewesen sein. Doch bietet diese Tabelle noch andere, verwendbare Angaben. Auf der ersten Stelle steht wieder das Bekleidungsgewerbe. Die 9 Berufe des Metallgewerbes überflügeln zwar die 8 Berufe des Bekleidungsgewerbes, doch ist das Bekleidungsgewerbe an Zahl der beschäftigten Personen weitaus überlegen. Von den 8 Berufen gehören nur zwei den Gewerben für Reinigung (Bäder und Barbier), die Beutler, Schneider, Kürschner, Schuster, Gürtler, Taschner, mit Ausnahme der Beutler stehen alle unter Zunftzwang. Das Metallgewerbe ist das zweite Gewerbe, das verhältnissmässig große Mengen aufnehmen kann, doch gehört beinahe die Hälfte der Neubürger zu solchen Berufen, für die in Kaschau warscheinlich noch kein Zunftzwang bestand. Es gaben Goldschmiede, Büchsen-, Kanne- und Rotgießer und einen Nagler. Es ist beinahe unverständlich, daß es in Kaschau keine Zunft für die Rotgießer gab, in der Stadt die im Laufe des 15. Jh.-s grosse Mengen ungarischen Kupfers exportierte!

Doch eben das Verhältnis zwischen Handel und Gewerbe erklärt in Kaschau das Fehlen eines starken Metallgewerbes und eines starken Gewerbes überhaupt. Als König Sigmund 1411 die Übersiedlung aller in Ungarn arbei- tender Barchentweber nach Kaschau verordnete und ein starkes Barchent- gewerbe gründen wollte, blieben alle seine Bemühung erfolglos, weil er dem Barchentimport keinen Einhalt bieten konnte.[45] Die kleine Kaschauer Kolonie der Barchentweber ist im Laufe einiger Jahrzehnten spurlos verschwunden, die Meister, die in der Stadt blieben, schlossen sich der Zwilcherzunft an.[46] Zwar wurden 1508 wieder sechs Tuchmacher aus den umgebenden Markt- flecken nach Kaschau berufen,[47] doch produzierten sie wahrscheinlich nur die minderste Qualität des sog. »pannus griseus«.

Der Mißerfolg der königlichen Bemühungen ist im Textilgewerbe nicht überraschend. Das Textilgewerbe wurde im Laufe des 15. Jahrhunderts nicht nur in Kaschau, sondern in ganz Ungarn vom Wettbewerb der schlesischen, böhmischen und polnischen Tücher, besser gesagt, vom Wettbewerb des Handels, der diese Tücher billig importieren konnte, ruiniert.[48] Es ist um so mehr auffallend, daß in Kaschau das Metallgewerbe sich nicht besser ent- wickeln konnte, wo doch kein so großer Wettbewerb bestand.

Das Übergewicht des Handels erklärt uns die Lage der Handwerker in Kaschau. Reiche Leute wurden aus den Handwerkern nicht, sie litten eher an Mangel der Kapitalien und waren den Handelsleuten ausgeliefert.

---

[45] Szűcs a. a. O. 217—220. ; die Verordnungen König Sigmunds sind von Wenzel herausgegeben worden (WENZEL G., Kassa város parkettkészítése a XV. sz. kezdetén. [Die Barchentweberei der Stadt Kaschau am Anfang des 15. Jh.] Pest 1871.)
[46] »dy erbaren meister des ganzen czwilcher czech vnd parchyntter.« (1499 : Verbotsbuch 175. r.)
[47] Aus Kapos und Nagymihály. (Bürgerbuch, 1508.)
[48] Szűcs a. a. O. 123—131.

Und das Kapital beutete sie erstens durch das Vorstreckung des Rohmaterials aus. Aus dem Verbotsbuch der Stadt scheinen am meisten die Hutmacher zu leiden. Im Jahre 1492 war die Zunft einem Krakauer Kaufmann für »Scherwolle« 60 fl. schuldig. Im nächsten Jahre sind die zwei Zechmeister Wilhelm und Demetrius Hutter einer gewissen Frau Dorothea schuldig, die Summe betrug in einem Fall 23,25 fl., in dem anderen 16,27 fl., da Frau Dorothea sie »vorlegt hot mit woll«. Beide versprachen feierlich aus dem Nutzen, den sie aus der Wolle durch die daraus gemachten Hüte einbringen würden, erstens die genannte Frau Dorothea zu befriedigen.[49] In diesen Fällen wurde die Ursache des Kredits genau angegeben, doch wir hoffen uns nicht sehr zu irren, wenn wir behaupten, daß die ziemlich hohe Schuld von 575 fl., die die Zwilcherzunft einer Krakauer Handelsgesellschaft schuldete, und in 14 Tagen zu bezahlen hatte, oder die 90 fl., mit der die dieselbe Zunft einem wohlhabenden Kaschauer Bürger im nächsten Jahr schuldig ist (und ebenfalls in 14 Tagen zu bezahlen hat) — auch durch Vorstreckung des Rohmaterials entstand.[50] Das Verbotsbuch enthielt auch die andere Form der Ausbeutung, nämlich den Lohnvorschuß. Auf Gregor Brückner wurde wegen 2 fl. ein Verbot verlegt, das er durch Arbeit abzulösen hatte.[51]

Einige Meister konnten aus diesen schweren Verhältnissen doch einen Ausweg finden, hauptsächlich die, die über ein Betriebskapital verfügten, oder mit fremden Betriebskapital arbeiten konnten. Eines dieser Meister war Nikolaus Krompholz, der aus der schlesischen Stadt Neisse stammte und als Baumeister 1492 in den Bürgerstand aufgenommen wurde. Er hatte zwei größere Aufgaben. Die eine war die Wiederherstellung des bei der Beschießung der Stadt beschädigten Domes, die andere die Entwässerung des Stadtkellers. Beide wurden mit Erfolg durchgeführt und Krompholz kaufte sich ein Haus und trat 1498 in die Bruderschaftzunft der »Reychcromern«. Er mußte zwar die Ausübung seines Berufes aufgeben, hat aber später als Kaufmann ein beträchtliches Vermögen erworben.[52] Sein Fall schildert lebhaft den Weg, den jeder, der sich nach einem größeren Vermögen sehnte, in Kaschau zu betreten hatte. Gewerbe und besonders Handwerk waren nicht dazu geeignet. Trotz der günstigen Lage der Stadt, trotz der günstigen wirtschaftlichen Verhältnisse ist das Gewerbe nie zu einem leitenden Wirtschaftszweig der Stadt geworden. Im Gegenteil, die »ehrbaren« Meister werden immer mehr von den Kaufleuten abhängig, sie sind immer mehr auf das Kapital angewiesen, das sie nicht besaßen, sondern bei den reichen Kaufleuten zu suchen hatten. Deswegen finden wir sie weit von den Wohlhabenden, in den unteren Steuerklassen.

[49] Verbotsbuch p. 88 r.
[50] Ebenda 28 v., 39 v.
[51] Ebenda.
[52] MIHALIK J., A kassai Szt. Erzsébet templom. [Die Kaschauer Elisabeth-Kirche.] Budapest 1912.

Ein Aufblühen des Gewerbes wurde also durch die Handelstätigkeit verhindert, der Nutzen am Wein und damit der Weinhandel wuchs an. Es scheint, daß der Handel der stärkste, und am besten entfaltete Wirtschaftszweig der Stadt war. Und in der Tat war es auch so.

Die Grundlage für eine rasche und ergebnisvolle Entwicklung des Kaschauer Handels war das Abkommen, das zwischen Kaschau und Krakau 1324 geschlossen wurde. Bis 1324 wickelten die Kaschauer ihre Geschäfte im natürlichen geographischen Bereich der Stadt ab, der das mittelalterliche Ungarn bis zur Theiß und den Karpaten umfaßte. Doch die Hilfe, die Krakau der Stadt im Handel leistete, ließ Kaschau jetzt schnell weiter vordringen. Das Gebiet jenseits der Theiß wurde rasch erobert, Debrecen und Großwardein wurden Hauptabsätzplätze für Kaschauer Waren. Es gelang zwar den Kaschauern nicht, die Ofner Kaufleute völlig zu verdrängen, doch wurden die zwei erwähnten Städte von den Kaschauern beherrscht. Noch vor der Mitte des 14. Jh.-s wagten die Kaschauer einen weiteren Schritt, sie versuchten ihren Handel nach Siebenbürgen und von da in die rumänischen Herzogtümer zu erweitern. Als 1369 König Ludwig Kronstadt das Stapelrecht verlieh, verbot er den Kaufleuten mit Waren nach Rumänien weiterzuziehen. Das Verbot erstreckte sich auf alle fremde, deutsche und böhmische Kaufleute und Gewandschneider, ausgenommen die ungarischen »und besonders die Kaschauer«.[53] Diese, für die Kaschauer so vorteilhafte Verordnung konnte aber nicht lange auferhalten bleiben. Die Siebenbürger Städte führten wahrscheinlich einen bitteren Kampf gegen die Kaschauer Konkurrenz. Ihr Kampf endete bald erfolgreich. Im Jahre 1378 wurde der aufgezwungene Großhandel der fremden — und hauptsächlich der Kaschauer Kaufleute in einer königlichen Urkunde bestätigt. Vier Jahre später wurde ihnen auch der Weg nach Rumänien versperrt.[54] Der Kaschauer Handel wurde zugunsten des siebenbürgischen auf die Tiefebene diesseits Siebenbürgens zurückgewiesen. Im Jahre 1413 war das Verbot des siebenbürgischen Handels zum letzten Male wiederholt,[55] aber in diesem Jahre hatten sich die Kaschauer schon bis Großwardein zurückgezogen. Siebenbürgen ging für den Kaschauer Handel verloren. Im Laufe des Jahrhunderts ändert sich diese Lage nicht mehr, das Handelsbereich der Stadt wurde nicht mehr erweitert. Die Kaschauer übernahmen die Ware in Krakau, und fuhren damit bis Debrecen, Großwardein und Nagybánya. Hier im Osten des Landes wurde die Ware auf den großen Jahrmärkten abgesetzt. Zu größter Bedeutung gelangten ide Jahrmärkte in Großwardein, wo sich Kaschauer und Siebenbürger trafen und ihre Waren austauschten.[56] Krakau und Großwardein waren die Endstationen einer

[53] ZIMMERMANN—WERNER, Urkundenbuch 2 : 336.
[54] Ebenda. 2: 410.
[55] Ebenda. 2: 463.
[56] Die Zeit in der die Kaschauer Kaufleute aus Großwardein ankamen, war ein Zahlungstermin. (Verbotsbuch 23 r.)

regelrechten Geschäftsreise im 15. Jh. geworden. In Krakau wurden Produkte
der westlichen Gewerbe, Blei und Seefische übernommen. Von den Gewerbe-
artikeln spielten Textilien die größte Rolle. Flämische und westdeutsche
Tücher von hoher Qualität und hohem Preis, süddeutsche, schlesische und
polnische Tücher für den Alltagsgebrauch und Schnittware, Gürtel, Hüte,
Beutel, Hosen, usw. Letztere waren — wenigstens teilweise — Krakauer
Produkte. Nach Krakau wurden in erster Reihe Kupfer geliefert, dann Wein,
Gewürze und Wachs.[57] Gewürze und Wachs wurden am Großwardeiner Markt
eingekauft, wohin sie von den Siebenbürger Kaufleuten gebracht wurden.[58]

Im Rahmen der Stadtwirtschaft rief der lebhafte Handel neue Institution ins Leben. Wir sahen, daß in Kaschau das Zunftwesen der Gewerbe
immer schwach blieb, die Zünfte der Kaufleute entfalteten sich dagegen besser
und ihre Organisation weist eine besser detaillierte Arbeitsteilung auf. 1446
traten die reichen Krämer zu einer Bruderschaft zusammen.[59] Die neue
Organisation war keine Zunft im juristischen Sinne des Wortes, doch war sie
eine Interessengemeinschaft, deren Mitglieder die Inhaber des städtischen
»Steincromes« waren. Die Vorbedingung der Mitgliedschaft war der Besitz
eines Krämerladens in der städtischen Kaufhalle und die Bezahlung eines
Eintrittsgeldes von 2 fl. 1461 wurde eine Zunft der Gewandschneider ver-
brieft,[60] und 1475 die Bruderschaft der Reichkrämer ebenfalls zur einer regelrechten Zunft erhoben.[61] Wenn wir nun daran denken, daß außer diesen
beiden Zünften auch noch »Armenkremler« existierten,[62] so ist es nicht schwer
zu behaupten, daß der Handel eine weitaus besser gegliederte Arbeitsteilung
in Kaschau erreichen konnte, als das Gewerbe. Großhandel und Kleinhandel
wurden geteilt, der Großhandel wurde jedem Fremden aufgezwungen, und
jedem Kaschauer Bürger frei zugelassen. Der Kleinhandel wurde dagegen
geteilt zwischen den Krämern, die Gewürze und Schnittware verkauften
und den Gewandschneidern, die Tücher ausschnitten. Diese Entwicklung
hat auch die Vermöglensunterschiede unter den Bürgern verstärkt; die
Unterschiede wurden durch die Gründung von Handelsgesellschaften noch
mehr verschärft. Reiche Kaufleute gründen erst in Jahre 1502 eine größere
Gesellschaft, später erlebt diese Gesellschaft einen Aufschwung, den auch die
Stadt fördert, um Kapital in den Handel zu stecken. Die Gesellschaft beginnt
ihre Tätigkeit mit einem Kapital von 5000 fl. und zahlt in erstem Jahre 20%
Gewinn aus.[63] Dieser Prozentsatz ist leider der einziger, den wir aus unserem
Quellenmaterial über den Gewinn aufweisen können.

[57] KUTRZEBA S., Handel Krakowa w wiekach średních 24.
[58] Vgl. die Zwanzigstrechnungen (eine art Zoll). — Quellen zur Geschichte der
Stadt Kronstadt 1 : 1.
[59] Vgl. Anmerkung 26.
[60] Magyar Gazdaságtörténeti Szemle 10 (1903) 428.
[61] Stadtarchiv Kaschau 433.
[62] Magyar Gazdaságtörténeti Szemle 9 (1902) 139.
[63] Ebenda 5 (1898) 31.

Die große »städtische Gesellschaft« war vielleicht die einzige im Kaschauer Handel, die nicht an Kapitalmangel zu leiden hatte und die sich von Krakau unabhängig machen konnte. Den trotz des lebhaften Verkehrs, des großen Umsatzes und den Wert der abgesetzten Ware, blieb der ganze Kaschauer Handel von dem Kredit der Krakauer Handelsleute abhängig.[64] 1489 sind im Verbotsbuch der Stadt insgesamt 8129 fl. Schuld ziffernmäßig eingetragen worden (in manchen Fällen fehlt die Angabe der Schuld in fl.),[65] und aus diesen waren die Kaschauer mit 3909 fl., also rund 48% der ganzen Summe einigen Krakauern schuldig. Franz Bank, Hans Thurzó, Hans Gafram, Jurg Bloe und seine Gesellschaft hatten in Waren den Kaschauern Kredit geöffnet. Sie gaben den Kredit meistens in Waren und forderten dagegen ebenfalls Waren, so Hans Gafram, der für seine 316 fl., die ihm der Kaschauer Georg Schwarz schuldete, um einen im voraus festgesetzten Preis »geschlagenes Kupfer« beanspruchte.[66] Franz Bank legte wegen einen Ballen Gewand ein Verbot auf Bartholomei Zothmans Geld.[67] Das Rechnungsbuch von 1502/03 der Kaufgesellschaft zeigt klar, in welchem Maße sie von dem Krakauer Hans Thurzó abhängig war.[68] Es hat den Anschein, als wenn die ganze Gesellschaft eigentlich nur eine Faktorei Thurzós wäre, da sie ausschließlich nur Thurzós Waren absetzt.

Wollen wir die Lage des Kaschauer Handels zusammenfassen, so müssen wir behaupten, daß der Handel der bedeutendste Wirtschaftszweig war. Von allen Wirtschaftszweigen ist es dem Handel am meisten gelungen, Kapitalien anzuhäufen, deswegen übte er eine große Anziehungskraft auf alle aus, die reich werden wollten und auf alles, das in der Stadt geschah. Der Handel verhinderte die Entwicklung eines starken Gewerbes, er beherrschte den Weinbau. Doch litt er selber an Kapitalmangel, weswegen er von dem Krakauer Handel und Kredit abhängig blieb.

*

Der Mangel an Kapital ist im mittelalterlichen Ungarn im allgemeinen zu beobachten. Auch in Kaschau wird er überall fühlbar, wo sich Geld zum Kapital anhäufte.

Auch in Ungarn war am Lande der Klerus einer der mächtigsten Kapitalanhäufer. Was an Geldmitteln in den Dörfern und Marcktflecken erspart werden konnte, sammelte sich in den Pfarrkirchen in der Form frommer Stiftungen. Die Pfarre verfügte meistens über mehrere Weingärten, erhielt

---

[64] KUTRZEBA a. a. O.
[65] In vielen Fällen wurde das Verbot »of alle gutter« des Betreffenden gelegt, aber ohne die ziffernmäßige Angabe der Schuld. (1489 wurden 152 Schulden eingetragen, von denen in 10 Fällen die Schuldsumme unbekannt ist.)
[66] Verbotsbuch 25 r.
[67] Ebenda 42 r.
[68] Magyar Gazdaságtörténeti Szemle 9 (1902) 106.

kleine Summen baren Geldes aus den Testamenten der Bauern und Bürger. Die Pfarrer spielen in Kaschaus Geldgeschäften eine nicht zu unterschätzende Rolle. Georg, ein Prediger von Gönc hat im Jahre 1490 im Werte von 93 fl., 1492 im Werte von 157 fl. einen Verbot eingelegt gegen verschiedene Kaschauer Bürger.[69] 1468 war die Stadt einem gewissen Urban Pfarrer nicht weniger als 754,50 fl. schuldig.[70] Doch ist es kennzeichnend, daß im Testament des Pfarrers von Szikszó aus 1517 insgesamt über 401 fl. verfügt, dann folgt der Satz : »Nemo credat tantas me habere pecunias in promptu, sed in debito.« Nachher werden die Schuldner aufgezählt, vom Pfarrer des benachbarten Ortes Szántó (20 fl. Schuld) bis zu seinem eigenen Bauer (1 fl. Schuld) die verschiedensten Personen.[71] Der Klerus verfügte zwar über ein Vermögen, aber meistens nicht in mobilen Münzen, sondern in Forderungen.

In Kaschau selbst wurden die Geldangelegenheiten der Kirchen von der Stadt selbst übernommen. Der Magistrat verwaltete das Vermögen der Stadtkirche und anderer geistlicher Institutionen der Stadt, mit Ausnahme der Klöster. Dieses Vermögen bestand ebenfalls aus Grundstücken (hauptsächlich Weingärten im Tokajer Weingebirg),[72] aus Renten[73] und Legaten in barem Gelde. Letztere waren aber keine großen Summen und die Stadt war sicherlich nur durch große, teils bar bezahlte Stiftungen in der Lage, Kapital in ein Handelsgeschäft zu stecken. Die Gelder, die bei der Stadtpfarre sich sammelten, waren ebenfalls kleine Summen, abgesehen von den Indulgenzsammlungen, die im Jahre 1470 590 fl. ergaben.[74]

Die Stadt selbst hatte auch mit dem Mangel an barem Gelde zu kämpfen. Charakteristisch für diese Zeit ist es, daß die Stadt im Juli 1481 von 6 Kaufleuten zehn Ballen Gewand übernahm, um damit die Laurenztagssteuer zu begleichen. Der Wert der Tücher betrug insgesamt 731 fl., die Stadt bezahlte diese Summe nur im Jahre 1482 in folgenden Raten : am 9. Feber 73, fl., am 23. Feber 100 fl., am 9. März 73 fl., am 23. März 122 fl. ; 147 fl. derselben Schuld wurde aus den Steuern bezahlt und 186 fl. blieben noch am 11. Mai zu begleichen.[75] Die Rechnung über den Verkauf des Hauses der Nonnen und der Kauf eines anderen Hauses dafür zeigt ein verworrenes Bild, ohne daß der Gewinn der Stadt bemerkbar wäre.[76]

Doch wenn die Stadt über Mitteln verfügte, wurden sie ohne Bedenken den vornehmen Bürgern zur Verfügung gestellt.[77] So geschah es im Falle der

[69] Verbotsbuch 40 v., 64 v.
[70] L. KEMÉNY a. a. O. 13.
[71] Stadtarchiv Kaschau 978.
[72] Stadtarchiv Kaschau. Geheimarchiv C.
[73] Ebenda.
[74] Ebenda 18.098.
[75] L. KEMÉNY a. a. O. 16.
[76] Ebenda 20.
[77] Im Jahre 1464 wurde z. B. die Schuld des A. Cromere und B. Schneidere, insgesamt 100 fl. durch die Stadt beglichen (Stadtarchiv Kaschau 18.095).

Handelsgesellschaft, als die Stadt der größte Teilnehmer mit 1500 fl. war, die anderen Mitglieder steuerten je 100—500 fl. bei. Die Handelsgesellschaft übernahm die Stadtgelder auch in Form von Zinsdarlehen, so die 2000 fl., die aus M. Günters Stiftung in den Besitz der Stadt kamen ; sie wurden der Gesellschaft gegen einen Zins von 60 fl. (3%) geliehen,[78] was unter mittelalterlichen Verhältnissen ein außerordentlich niedriger Zinsfuß war. Dies geschah im Jahre 1518, doch zwanzig Jahre früher war die Stadt noch selbst auf der Suche nach einem Zinsdarlehen und fand es — charakteristisch — in einem Kloster, das 2000 fl. für einen Zins von 90 fl. (4,5%) ein Darlehen anbot.[79] Zu dieser Zeit litt aber nicht nur die Stadt, sondern auch die wohlhabende Bürgerschaft unter schwerem Geldmangel. Wenn wir das Verbotsbuch durchblättern, fällt es sofort auf, daß selbst kleine Schulden nur durch langwierige Teilzahlungen getilgt werden können. Hans Opyczer, dessen Steuer auf 2 fl. festgesetzt war, versprach seine Schuld von 128 fl. dem Krakauer Gaspar Beer in 4 Jahren, in 4 Teilzahlungen zu tilgen.[80] Und noch andere höher besteuerte Personen müssen ihre Schuld in Raten abzahlen, da es ihnen an barem Gelde fehlte. Immobilienübertragungen finden nur ausnahmsweise gegen Barzahlung statt, die Schulden werden meist in jährlichen Raten bezahlt. Die Regel heißt : kleiner Vorschuß und noch kleinere Teilzahlungen.[81]

Wie wenig bei den Kaufleuten bares Geld zur Hand war, geht auch daraus hervor, daß zur Gründung der städtischen Handelsgesellschaft, abgesehen von den 1500 fl. der Stadt, noch elf Kaufleute nötig waren, um ein Gründungskapital von 3200 fl. zusammenzubringen. Von den elf Mitgliedern haben 2 Personen je 500 fl., vier je 400 fl., eine Person 200 fl., und drei Personen je 100 fl. beigesteuert. Nicht alle elf waren ausgesprochen Kaufleute, einige von ihnen befaßten sich zur Zeit auch mit anderen Geldgeschäften.[82] Diese Bürger, die sich mit Geldgeschäften befaßten, haben möglicherweise über größere Kapitalien verfügt. Eine kleine Gruppe befaßte sich mit Vorliebe mit der Einhebung von weltlichen Steuern oder mit dem Pacht kirchlicher Zehnten. Hans Tocklar war 1467 mit dem Steuereinnehmen in dem Komitate Sáros beauftragt. Er übernahm das Geschäft gemeinsam mit einem Ofner Bürger.[83] Leider sind Einzelheiten über dieses Geschäft nicht bekannt, doch wissen wir, daß im Jahre 1476 — als ein anderer Kaschauer Steuereinnehmer erkrankte, er mit der Einhebung der Steuer in den Komitaten Abaúj und Sáros beauftragt wurde. Diesmal hatte er in zwei Teilzahlungen ins-

---

[78] KEREKES GY., Kassa polgársága, ipara és kereskedése a középkor végén. [Kaschaus Bürgertum, Gewerbe und Handel am Ende des Mittelalters.] Budapest 1913, 101, 102.
[79] Stadtarchiv Kaschau 696. (1942.)
[80] Verbotsbuch 47 v.
[81] Diese Regel wurde selbst bei kleinen Kaufpreisen befolgt.
[82] KEREKES GY. a. a. O. 100 und nennt die Teilnehmer bei ihren Namen im ersten Teil (34—55).
[83] Stadtarchiv Kaschau 366.

gesamt 5934 fl. der königlichen Schatzkammer übergeben.[84] Drei Jahre später pachtete er mit einem Szikszóer Bürger zusammen die Zehnten des Dekanats Szerencs und beide zahlten dem Erlauer Kapitel 350 fl.[85] Die erste Summe ist in Kaschau gewiße als hoch zu bezeichnen. Doch der Gewinn konnte nicht besonders groß sein. Toklar hat seine 6 Weingärten in Szikszó im Jahre 1467 um 270 fl. verkauft,[86] und zahlte am Ende des Jhs. nur 2 fl. Steuer.[87] Selbst wenn wir annehmen, daß er bei der Festsetzung der Steuer in irgendeiner Weise begünstigt wurde, oder einen Teil seines Vermögens der Besteuerung entziehen konnte, können wir ihn höchstens als einen wohlhabenden, aber keinesfalls als einen reichen Mann bezeichnen. Die Summen, die wir in anderen Fällen kennen, sind auch nicht besonders hoch.[88] Die Kredite, die den Bergwerken gewährt wurden, sind verhältnismäßig die höchsten. Mathias Goldemütz's Forderung in Nagybánya lief auf 2741 fl.,[99] die Forderung einer Kaschauer Gesellschaft, die in Rosenau (Rozsnyó) bei den Gruben interessiert war, machte 1772 fl. aus.[90] Das größte Kaschauer Vermögen des 15. Jh.-s wurde ebenfalls durch Handel und Bergwerksunternehmung gesammelt ; Michael Günter verfügte in seinem Testament im Jahre 1516 über 20 899 fl.[91] Diese hohe Summe gehört aber schon eher in die Geschichte des 16., als in die des ausgehenden 15. Jh.-s.

*

Auf Grund der Steuerrollen behaupteten wir, daß Kaschau am Ende des 15 Jahrhunderts 4200 Einwohner hatte und eine Mittelstadt war. Auf Grund der festgesetzten Steuer waren die Vermögensunterschiede groß. Als wir diesen Unterschieden nachforschten, konnten wir feststellen, daß die Stadt, deren wirtschaftlichen Basis am Anfang des 14. Jahrhunderts der Weinbau und ein Warenaustausch im unmittelbaren Wirtschaftsbereich war, im Laufe des 14. Jahrhunderts — dank der vorteilhaften geographischen Lage — sich dem Fernhandel anschließen konnte, der von dem Westen nach Osten Gewerbeartikel beförderte und sie gegen östliches Rohmaterial austauschte. Der Handelskontrakt mit Krakau ließ den Kaschauer Handel rasch aufblühen. So wurde er der führende Wirtschaftszweig in der Stadt. Der Fernhandel und der mit ihm verbundene Aufschwung üben einen Druck auf das sich im Entwickeln befindene Gewerbe. Die Konkurrenz der niedrigen Preise wirkte vernichtend und Gewerbezweige, die den niedrigen Preisen nicht gewachsen waren, konnten nur ein kärgliches Dasein führen. Das Textil-

[84] Ebenda 438, 446.
[85] Ebenda 460.
[86] Ebenda 419.
[87] Er wohnte im letzten Bezirk. (L. KEMÉNY a. a. O.)
[88] Der König schuldete z. B. Erasmus Kraidel 640 fl. (Történeti Tár 1902, 299.)
[89] Stadtarchiv `Kaschau 18.103., 479., 19.189.
[90] Das Stadtbuch im Stadtarchiv von Rozsnyó (Rožňava).
[91] GY. KEREKES a. a. O. 37.

gewerbe war besonders durch den Import der westlichen Waren getroffen, es wurde in der Tat stillgelegt. Das gewerbliche Zunftwesen blieb den Handelsorganisationen gegenüber weit zurück. Doch die Kaufleute, die sich in den handelsmäßigen Zünften vereinigten, waren durch Warenkredit von Krakau abhängig geblieben. Es ist ihnen trotz des hohen Prozentsatzes im Gewinn nicht gelungen, größere Kapitalien anzuhäufen. Die Finanzverhältnisse in Kaschau stellen uns eher ein kompliziertes Kreditnetz, als ein mobiles Kapital vor.

Die Institutionen und Personen, die Kapital anhäuften, waren dieselben wie im Westen : Kirche, Stadt und Private erwarben einen Reichtum und wandelten diesen in Kapitalien um. Die Faktoren, die die Kapitalanhäufung ermöglichten, waren auch die gleichen. Und doch ist Kaschau eine osteuropäische Stadt und ihre Wirtschaft eine osteuropäische Wirtschaft gewesen. Wir behaupten das nicht nur deswegen, weil sich das Kapitals langsamer und bedeutend später enfaltete als im westlichen Europa. Wir sehen diese Züge eher in den niedrigen Summen, die angehäuft wurden und in der Weise, in dem das erworbene Kapital benützt wurde. Das osteuropäische Kapital war weniger unternehmungslustig, es strebte nach Ausbeutung und Verwertung des erreichbaren Rohmaterials. Es ist weitaus kennzeichnend, daß die Hutmacher von Frau Dorothea ein Darlehen annehmen, doch gegen das vorgestreckte Rohmaterial eine Zahlung im baren Gelde gefördert wird und nicht die Lieferung fertiger Waren, die im Handel abgesetzt werden konnten. Es ist kein Zeichen eines Verlagssystems nachzuweisen, selbst in Kaschau nicht, wo es an Rohmaterial für gewisse Gewerbe nicht fehlte. Kaschau war eine Mittelstadt, ihrer Größe, der Zahl der Einwohner, dem architektonischen Antlitz nach. Aber eben dem Wesen des westlichen Frühkapitalismus lag es fern.

XII

La formation des villes
et les ordres mendiants en Hongrie

Il y a deux ans, M. Jacques Le Goff lançait dans les *Annales* l'idée d'une enquête dont les résultats s'annoncent féconds :[1] approcher les problèmes d'urbanisation de la France médiévale par le biais de l'implantation des ordres mendiants, car il y a coïncidence, dans la France médiévale, entre la carte des villes et la carte des couvents mendiants. Il y a là une direction de recherche fort intéressante pour l'historien de l'Europe orientale qui a essayé, en vain de définir le caractère urbain d'une agglomération à l'aide de critères juridiques. En vain, car finalement, ce n'est pas la façon dont on la nomme, ni la façon dont elle s'administre qui décident du caractère urbain d'une agglomération. Et l'historien de la Hongrie ne peut davantage déceler le fait urbain à partir d'indices économiques, étant donné le caractère trop fragmentaire de ses sources. Ainsi le rapport entre la population urbaine et les ordres mendiants — aussi bien pour la France que pour la Hongrie — semble être un point de départ qui promet beaucoup, non seulement pour opérer une coupe intéressante en un moment donné, mais aussi pour mieux connaître l'urbanisation en tant que processus. Il y a plus d'une décennie, nous avons nous-même traité le problème de la formation des villes hongroises, en nous efforçant d'utiliser toutes les données disponibles : diplômes et sources descriptives, aussi bien que résultats des fouilles archéologiques et données linguistiques[2]. Mais nous ne croyons pas pour autant avoir épuisé cette question complexe. Ce ne sont pas les connaissances philologiques ni les découvertes archéologiques qui, à elles seules, nous permettront de mieux interpréter notre documentation fragmentaire ; il faut aussi que des idées nouvelles nous aident à reclasser les connaissances déjà acquises. Nous espérons que les analyses suivantes, menées à partir de l'idée lancée par M. Le Goff, contribueront à mieux éclairer le processus de l'urbanisation hongroise.

---

1. J. Le Goff, « Apostolat mendiant et fait urbain dans la France », *Annales E.S.C.*, 23/1968. 335-352.
2. E. Fugedi, « Die Entstehung des Städtewesens in Ungarn », *Alba Regia*. 10/1969.

XII

VILLES ET ORDRES MENDIANTS EN HONGRIE

En se précisant, notre connaissance de l'évolution des villes en Hongrie fera apparaître la divergence avec l'histoire urbaine de l'Europe occidentale. Nous retrouverons les mêmes divergences dans le développement de l'organisation de l'Église et des ordres religieux.

Les ordres mendiants et leurs antécédents.

Avant même que l'organisme ecclésiastique ne fût mis en place par Étienne Ier le Saint (997-1038), il y eut en Hongrie des religieux de rite grec et romain, dont la tâche primordiale était l'évangélisation[1]. Puis les Bénédictins furent suivis par les ordres monastiques — Cisterciens, Prémontrés — comme partout en Europe. Parmi les Bénédictins certains étaient venus directement de France (ainsi des moines de Saint-Gilles arrivèrent à Somogyvar en 1091), mais le nombre de monastères cisterciens et prémontrés affiliés à des monastères français était encore plus élevé[2]. Les fondateurs des monastères étaient les souverains ou des riches familles seigneuriales, pour lesquels l'église monastique servait en même temps de lieu de sépulture familiale[3].

En 1241 le pays subit une catastrophe nationale. Après une bataille décisive, les Tartares envahissent une partie considérable de la Hongrie, et bien que leur occupation ne dure qu'un an, leurs ravages sont immenses. Si nous prenons cette catastrophe comme point de repère nous constatons qu'avant l'invasion des Mongols le royaume de Hongrie comptait soixante-sept couvents bénédictins (dont douze fondés par les rois, les autres par des particuliers), vingt couvents cisterciens et vingt-quatre prémontrés[4]. Mais nos documents mentionnent encore au moins cinquante monastères dont nous ne savons plus à quel ordre ils appartenaient[5]. La majorité — surtout ceux fondés par des particuliers — disparurent vite, bien souvent parce que leurs patrons reprenaient les domaines donnés par leurs ancêtres. Récemment L. B. Kumorovitz a montré un bel exemple de cette « sécularisation » patronale en retraçant l'histoire d'un monastère bénédictin fondé en 1061[6].

Actuellement, nous ne disposons encore que de peu de données sur l'importance de ces monastères, mais nous pouvons affirmer que la plupart ne pouvaient guère entretenir plus de dix à vingt religieux[7]. Du point de vue de leur répartition géographique, il nous faut remarquer qu'en Hongrie, la préférence pour les sites boisés, marécageux, situés loin du « monde » est caractéristique non seulement des Cis-

1. Gy. Moravcsik, « The role of the Byzantine Church in medieval Hungary », *American Slavic Review*, 1947.
2. A Pannonhalmi Szt. Benedek rend története (Histoire de l'ordre de saint Benoît, de Pannonhalma). Par la suite : PRT/XII/B. Budapest, 1912. R. Békefi, *A ciszterci rend története Magyarországon* (Histoire de l'ordre cistercien en Hongrie). *1148-1896*, Budapest, 1896.
3. A. Oszvald, *Fejezetek a premontreiek nyolcszázéves multjabol* (Chapitres de l'histoire huit fois centenaire des Prémontrés), Gödöllö, 1941.
4. D'après l'*Histoire de l'ordre de saint Benoît* citée plus haut note 2.
5. Malheureusement, on ne retrouve ces monastères sur aucun registre permettant de connaître l'ordre auquel ils étaient affiliés. Rappelons que nous connaissons dans le diocèse de Csanád douze monastères qui se trouvent dans le même cas. Cf. K. Juhász, *Die Stifte der Tschanader Diözese im Mittelalter*, Münster, 1927, pp. 165-214.
6. B. K. Kumorovitz, « A zselicszentjakabi alapitolevél 1061-böl » (La charte de fondation datée de l'an 1061 de Zselicszentjakab), *Tanulmányok Budapest multjából*, 16/1964, pp. 43-81.
7. A. Oszvald, « Adatok a magyarországi premontreiek Árpádkori történetéhez », *Művészettörténeti Értesitö* (Contributions à l'histoire des Prémontrés hongrois à l'époque arpadienne, Bulletin de l'histoire de l'art), 1957, p. 252. — Le monastère de Zsámbok passait pour prospère avec ses vingt religieux.

967

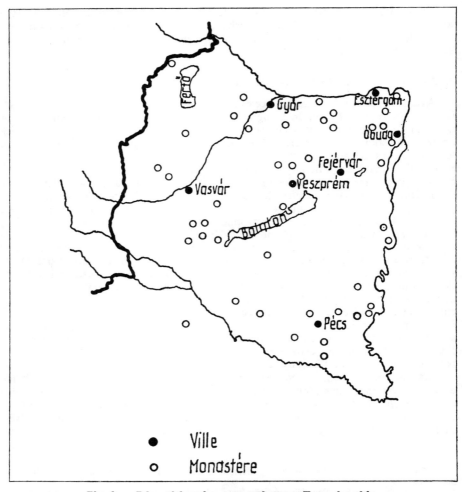

Fig. 1. — Répartition des monastères en Transdanubie.

terciens et des Prémontrés mais aussi des Bénédictins. Nous avons porté sur une carte (fig. 1) les villes et les monastères de la Transdanubie, principal centre économique et culturel du pays au début du XIII° siècle. Un seul coup d'œil permet de voir que nos Bénédictins — pour ne pas parler des Cisterciens et des Prémontrés — préféraient les lieux éloignés de tout trafic. Les plus anciens monastères bénédictins, de fondation royale (Pannonhalma, fondé avant 1002, Bakonybél en 1023, Tihany en 1055), ont été construits à l'intérieur ou à la lisière du massif montagneux de Bakony qui traverse la Transdanubie ; mais nous trouvons des monastères familiaux également dans les forêts, tel par exemple Zselic-Szentjakab. A lui seul le site des monastères révèle qu'ils n'eurent aucun rôle dans le développement de nos

VILLES ET ORDRES MENDIANTS EN HONGRIE

villes primitives. Ainsi, en 1015, le roi fonda un monastère bénédictin à Pécsvárad, presque à une journée de marche de l'importante ville de Pécs [1]. Il existe un même rapport de distances entre la ville de Györ et l'abbaye bénédictine de Pannonhalma, entre Fehérvár et le monastère de Tihany. Autre exemple : Zalavár. L'abbaye est de fondation très ancienne, bâtie sur l'emplacement où, un siècle plus tôt, se trouvait le centre de la petite principauté slave soumise à l'autorité franque [2], et cependant Zalavár n'est pas devenue ville. En bref : en Hongrie les abbayes bénédictines n'ont pas joué le même rôle que sur le sol français, elles n'ont pas contribué à l'urbanisation [3]. Ce rôle incombait aux chapitres collégiaux séculiers, fondés par le roi.

Aux ordres monastiques succèdent les ordres mendiants. Mais en Hongrie apparaît un nouvel ordre d'un caractère spécial, l'ordre des Ermites de Saint-Paul (*Ordo Sancti Pauli primi heremitae*), qui n'est ni ordre monastique ni encore moins mendiant. Sa fondation définitive remonte seulement à 1262, c'est-à-dire postérieurement à l'apparition des deux grands ordres mendiants en Hongrie. Barthélemy, religieux français de Cluny devenu évêque de Pécs, organise des groupes d'ermites vivant dans la montagne Mecsek (1225), tandis qu'Eusèbe, chanoine d'Esztergom, rassemble d'autres ermites sur la montagne Pilis (1246) [4]. L'ordre se développe rapidement (fig. 2). Les fondateurs des monastères étaient des princes ou de grands

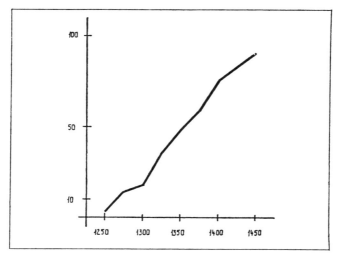

Fig. 2. — Nombre de couvents de l'ordre des Ermites de Saint-Paul.

---

1. G. Gyorffy, *Az Árpád-kori Magyarország történeti földrajza* (La Géographie historique de la Hongrie à l'époque des Arpad), t. I, Budapest, 1963, pp. 356-367.
2. A. Soós, *Die Ausgrabungen Géza Fehérs in Zalavár* (Archeologia Hungarica 41), Budapest, 1963, pp. 33-42.
3. H. Buttner, « Studien zum frühmittelalterlichen Städtewesen in Frankreich, vornehmlich im Loire- und Rhonegebiet », in *Studien zu den Anfängen des europäischen Städtewesen*, Konstanz, 1958, pp. 151-189 ; F. Petri, « Die Anfängen des mittelalterlichen Städtewesens in den Niederländen und dem angrenzenden Frankreich », *ibid.*, pp. 229-259 ; F. Prinz, « Die Ausbreitung fränkischer Reichskultur », *ibid.*, pp. 191-194.
4. E. Kisbán, *A magyar pálosrend története* (Histoire de l'ordre des Paulistes hongrois), t. I, *1225-1711*, Budapest, 1938, pp. 16-20.

XII

propriétaires fonciers, et l'église conventuelle leur servait de lieu de sépulture. Comme les Bénédictins, les Pauliens étaient possesseurs de terre ; leur caractère érémitique tenait à la répartition géographique des monastères ; la plupart étaient construits dans les montagnes boisées ; à la différence des Bénédictins, ils étaient implantés surtout dans la partie montagneuse septentrionale du pays. A l'exemple des ordres monastiques, les Pauliens évitaient les villes. Ainsi le couvent de Saint-Laurent, qui joua aux xive et xve siècles le rôle de centre de l'ordre, s'installa, il est vrai, près de Bude, ville la plus importante du pays depuis le xive siècle, mais pas même dans un des faubourgs : c'est à 5 ou 6 km de la ville, dans la forêt, que le couvent fut bâti [1]. Ces couvents « extra-muros » avaient, certes, des relations avec les gens des villes — Saint-Laurent pár exemple était lieu de pèlerinage — mais ils n'exerçaient pas l'apostolat comme les ordres mendiants. Les Pauliens n'ont donc pas influencé l'urbanisation et leur apparition n'est aucunement le signe de la formation des villes.

Les Dominicains eurent en Hongrie des débuts très prometteurs. Un professeur, de naissance hongroise, de l'Université de Bologne, Paulus Hungarus, ayant pris l'habit de l'ordre, fut chargé de l'organisation de la province dominicaine de Hongrie et revint en 1221 dans sa terre natale, accompagné de quelques religieux. Peu après fut fondé le premier couvent à Györ qui, à cette époque, était la porte occidentale du pays sur la grande route qui allait de Vienne à Esztergom, en longeant le Danube [2]. L'ordre gagna bientôt la faveur du prince héritier, le futur roi Béla IV (1235-1270) et celle de Robert, archevêque d'Esztergom, vraisemblablement d'origine française. Ce prélat énergique, aux vertus austères, s'était voué à l'évangélisation des Cumans païens, voisins des Hongrois, et le champ d'activité primordial des Dominicains fut également l'apostolat vers l'Orient. L'archevêque Robert baptisa en 1227 un des princes des Cumans, et le premier « évêque cuman », auquel il transmit la mitre et la crosse, appartenait à l'ordre dominicain [3]. En 1232 quatre frères prêcheurs partirent retrouver et évangéliser cette portion des Hongrois qui, d'après les traditions conservées dans les chroniques, étaient demeurés dans la patrie primitive. Leur voyage de trois ans, plein de tribulations et de vicissitudes, fut couronné de succès, et en 1235 quatre autres Dominicains se mirent en route. Le rapport où ils relatent leurs expériences constitue un des monuments émouvants du passé hongrois [4]. Survint, en 1241, l'invasion des Tartares. Les Cumans s'enfuirent et vinrent s'installer en Hongrie ; leur conversion devint une des tâches de l'ordre. En 1254, lors d'un chapitre général des Dominicains tenu dans le nouveau couvent bénédictin de Buda, le prince héritier hongrois mena à l'autel une princesse cumane [5]. L'influence de l'ordre à la Cour atteignait son apogée. Mais la disgrâce suivit de près. Bien que nos sources soient muettes à ce sujet, E. Lovas a réussi à expliquer ce revirement royal par des causes politiques [6] : en 1260, les

---

1. M. Zakonyi, « A Buda melletti Szt. Lörinc pálos kolostor története » (Histoire du monastère Saint-Laurent des Ermites de Saint-Paul près de Bude), *Századok*, 45/1911, pp. 513-530, 586-606.
2. M. Pfeiffer, *A Domonkos rend magyar zárdáinak vázlatos története* (Histoire abrégée des couvents hongrois de l'ordre de saint Dominique), Kassa, 1917, pp. 22-26.
3. Z. Makkai, *A milkói kun püspökség és népei* (l'Évêché cuman de Milkó et ses fidèles), Debrecen, 1936.
4. *Scriptores rerum hungaricarum* (éd. E. Szentpétery), II, Budapest, 1938, pp. 535-542.
5. Fr. G. de Frachetes, *Vitae fratrum ordinis praedicatorum necnon cronica ordinis ab anno MCCIII usque ad MCCLIV*, Leovanii, 1896, pp. 337-338.
6. E. Lovas, *Boldog margit történetének részletes forráskritikája* (Critique des sources concernant l'histoire de la vénérable Marguerite), Budapest, pp. 85-86.

VILLES ET ORDRES MENDIANTS EN HONGRIE

intérêts du roi exigeaient que sa fille Marguerite, qui avait pris l'habit dominicain, se mariât. Marguerite s'y refusa, et le roi tint pour responsable le confesseur et les conseillers dominicains de sa fille. Les relations se refroidirent et l'ordre en supporta les conséquences.

Un registre daté de 1303 nous renseigne sur l'origine des couvents dominicains. Malheureusement, il nous est impossible d'identifier quelques-uns des toponymes qui y figurent[1]. Il est certain, néanmoins, qu'en 1277 les Dominicains avaient trente couvents d'hommes et deux de femmes[2], y compris la Dalmatie. Après cette date la cadence de fondation de couvents (trente-cinq en 1303) augmente à peine jusqu'en 1350 (trente-huit couvents) ; un siècle après, l'augmentation n'est que d'un couvent (fig. 3)[3]. Qu'a-t-il pu se passer ? Prenons un exemple. Au début du XIVe siècle, Debrecen, devenu le centre des propriétés d'une grande famille, est en plein essor. Le village devient bourgade et ses habitants exercent une activité commerciale ; en 1316, lors d'une bataille entre le roi Charles et un grand seigneur rebelle, les « bourgeois » de la bourgade de Debrecen sont mentionnés dans l'armée du roi. Parallèlement à sa prospérité économique se développe l'autonomie de la bour-

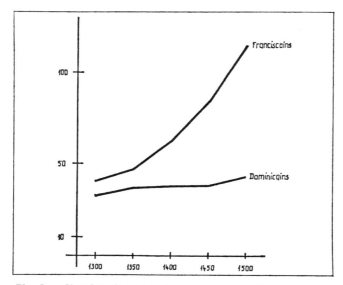

Fig. 3. — Nombre de couvents dominicains et franciscains.

1. N. PFEIFFER, *Die ungarische Dominikanerprovinz von ihrer Gründung 1221 bis zur Tatarenwüstung 1241-1242*, Zürich, 1913, pp. 27-28. Le couvent Saint-Martin en Transdanubie et les couvents dits Alba et Erdély en Transylvanie ne sont pas identifiables.

2. PFEIFFER, *A domonkos rend* (L'ordre de saint Dominique), p. 28.

3. La liste de couvents du registre de l'an 1303 doit être complétée grâce au registre de Pécs (fondé en 1238. Cf. GYORFFY, *op. cit.*, I, p. 360), au registre de Sarospatak (puisque Bodrog, que Pfeiffer identifia avec le couvent de Sarospatak, se trouvait dans le comitat de Bács. Cf. GYORFFY, *op. cit.*, I, p. 712) et au registre du couvent de Beregszász. Concernant le développement ultérieur voir PFEIFFER, *op. cit.*, passim.

gade ; l'évêque diocésain y fait bâtir une belle église, dont il retient les revenus pour sa propre *tabula episcopalis* [1]. Or, avant 1326, des Dominicains avaient assumé la cure et « occupé » l'église ; ils en seront chassés en 1326, sur l'ordre du pape [2]. Il est difficile de juger les événements d'après ce seul diplôme papal. Mais le phénomène qui nous intéresse apparaît là clairement : les Dominicains s'efforçaient de s'introduire dans l'agglomération parce qu'elle était en voie d'urbanisation [3]. Ce même fait est attesté par le choix de l'emplacement des couvents fondés après 1303. Des couvents nouveaux se bâtirent à Szeged (1318), Brassó (1323), Gara (1325) et à Temesvár [4]. L'ordre s'efforce donc de s'implanter dans les centres économiques et politiques du pays, et semble fort bien informé sur les agglomérations en voie de développement. Si le nombre de leurs monastères n'a pas augmenté à la même cadence que les villes hongroises, cela ne tenait pas à eux. Par contre, on peut difficilement croire que la rupture des relations avec la cour royale ait été le seul obstacle à leur expansion ultérieure. Il y avait sans aucun doute d'autres causes, peut-être plus graves, mais nous les ignorons.

Huit ans après les Dominicains, en 1229, arrivent les premiers Franciscains, venus des contrées allemandes ; au bout de neuf années est érigée une province hongroise autonome. L'expansion des Frères Mineurs fut d'abord plutôt lente ; ils s'implantent avant tout dans les agglomérations où vivaient des *coloni latini*, c'est-à-dire des colons wallons, flamands, français ou italiens. Un de leurs premiers provinciaux était d'origine française [5]. C'est seulement après la disgrâce des Dominicains qu'ils connurent un essor rapide. En 1265 le confesseur du roi est franciscain [6]. Quelques années plus tard, malgré une tradition de cent cinquante années, ce n'est plus la basilique de Fehérvar mais l'église franciscaine d'Esztergom qui reçoit la dépouille du roi, qui avait demandé expressément d'y reposer auprès de son fils le plus cher et le plus jeune, et, plus tard, auprès de sa femme [7]. Les Franciscains n'obtinrent le droit de sépulture royale qu'au prix de grands efforts, et durent l'arracher au puissant archevêque d'Esztergom. Ce n'est pas seulement à la Cour que les Frères Mineurs succèdent aux Dominicains. Ils remplacent également les Frères Prêcheurs dans l'évangélisation des Cumans ; et plus tard, c'est à leur ordre que sera attribué le droit d'inquisition. Leur essor s'accélère : le nombre de leurs couvents passe de 41 à 115 entre 1300 et 1500. La remarque que nous avons faite à propos des Dominicains vaut également ici : il est peu vraisemblable que l'expansion rapide et continue des Mineurs n'ait d'autre cause que la seule faveur royale. Mais nous ne connaissons pas les autres facteurs de leur succès.

---

1. G. GYORFFY, *op. cit.*, t. I, p. 611.
2. A. THEINER, *Vetera monumenta historica Hungariam sacram illustrantia 1216-1534*, I, Romae 1859 : « quod fratres ordinis predicatorum commorantes in villa de Broten... propriis commodis inhiantes, cum evidenti eiusdem episcopi et ecclesie sue iactura, ipsius etiam episcopi licentia non petita, parochialem ecclesiam dicte ville... fulti potentia seculari temeritate propria occuparunt et detinent occupatam, dictique sancti [Andree] mutato vocabulo, ipsi parochiali ecclesie vocabulum beate Marie virginis tribuerunt ac usurparunt et exercent omnia iura parochialia... »
3. J. KARÁCSONYI, *Szt. Ferenc rendjének története Magyarországon 1711-ig* (Histoire de l'ordre de saint François en Hongrie jusqu'en 1711), Budapest, 1923, t. I, p. 156.
4. *Monumenta ordinis Fratrum Praedicatorum historica*, Lovanii et Romae, IV, 110, 150. — Le première mention du couvent de Temesvár est de 1329, cf. SCHMITTH, *Episcopi Agrienses Tyrnaviae*, 1768, I, pp. 254-255.
5. KARÁCSONYI, *op. cit.*, pp. 16-17.
6. *Ibid.*, p. 22.
7. *Ibid.*, p. 22.

VILLES ET ORDRES MENDIANTS EN HONGRIE

Si l'histoire des deux grands ordres mendiants présente déjà des lacunes, celle des Augustins en offre encore davantage ; à vrai dire, elle n'est pas encore faite à l'exception d'une seule monographie — assez maigre — écrite au XVIIIᵉ siècle[1]. Il est certain en tout cas que les Augustins furent peu représentés en Hongrie ; ils n'y avaient que huit ou dix couvents au plus, et nous ignorons même la date de leur fondation. Nous devons nous contenter de mentions du XVᵉ siècle qui nous sont parvenues par hasard.

Esquisse du développement urbain en Hongrie[2].

Le développement des villes médiévales hongroises connut trois phases successives. La première prit fin vers le milieu du XIIᵉ siècle, la seconde se termina aux années 1340, la troisième alla jusqu'au milieu du XVᵉ siècle.

Pendant longtemps les historiens ont prétendu que les Hongrois, installés au IXᵉ siècle dans le bassin des Carpates, y menaient une vie entièrement nomade, répugnant à s'enfermer dans des agglomérations ; dans cette hypothèse, toutes les villes hongroises auraient donc été fondées par des étrangers. Mais les documents qui parlent des Hongrois du XIᵉ siècle — que ces informations émanent de religieux occidentaux ou de Musulmans — contredisent cette théorie. Idrisi mentionne les cités hongroises et en donne même des descriptions détaillées[3]. L'œuvre récemment découverte d'un Arabe espagnol, Abu-Hamid al-Andalusi[4] qui passa plusieurs années en Hongrie, compare ces villes — non sans exagération — à Bagdad et à Ispahan. Les chroniques occidentales mentionnent également maintes fois des villes, surtout Fehérvár et Esztergom. « Alba civitas », lisons-nous sur le manteau royal que l'épouse du roi Étienne Iᵉʳ se fit faire pour le sacre[5]. Ces mêmes mots et celui d'*urbs* se retrouvent dans la légende de la vie d'Étienne Iᵉʳ, écrite par Hartwick, dominicain exilé du sol allemand et devenu en Hongrie évêque de Győr[6]. Les sources écrites nous permettent donc d'affirmer qu'au XIᵉ siècle existaient en Hongrie des agglomérations que l'on pouvait qualifier de villes, car elles répondaient aux fonctions économiques d'une cité.

Quels sont les facteurs qui ont présidé à la naissance de ces villes ? Il faut souligner que les Hongrois, après avoir conquis leur nouvelle patrie, et même après leur christianisation, restaient membres de cette unité économique est-européenne dont les centres étaient Byzance et Kiev. Sur la frontière occidentale une zone dévastée à plusieurs jours de marche et une cavalerie mobile assuraient l'isolement hermétique du pays. Aucune route de transit ne traversait le pays, les marchandises byzantines arrivaient tout au plus à Prague, vers le nord-est. Dans ces conditions, du point de vue de l'urbanisation c'est avant tout la division du travail qui a joué le rôle important. Nous savons que des artisans de différents corps de métier se groupèrent

---

1. P. X. SCHIER, *Memoria provinciae Hungaricae augustanae*, Graecii, 1778.
2. Pour plus de détails, nous renvoyons à notre mémoire cité plus haut : « Die Entstehung des Städtewesens in Ungarn ».
3. T. LEWICKI, *Polska i kraje sasednie w świetle « Ksiegi Rogera » geografa arabskiego z XII w. Al Idriesiego* (La Pologne et ses voisins dans « Le livre de Roger » d'Al Idrisi, géographe arabe du XIIᵉ siècle), Prace Komsiji Orientalistycznej 34, Kraków, 1945, pp. 128-130.
4. I. HRBEK, « Ein arabischer Bericht über Ungarn », *Acta Orientalia*. 5/1955, p. 20.
5. « Anno Incarnationis Christi MXXXI Indictione XIII a Stephano Rege et Gisela Regina Casula haec operata et data ecclesiae Sanctae Mariae sitae in Civitate Alba. »
6. *Scriptores Rerum Hungaricarum*, II, pp. 408, 417, 432.

dans des villages séparés. On le vérifie aisément pour la catégorie des forgerons, fournisseurs de l'armée, revêtus d'un caractère sacré à l'époque païenne aussi bien chez les Hongrois que chez les autres peuples nomades et cavaliers[1].

Il faut tenir compte du fait qu'une partie du pays — la Transdanubie — avait vécu durant des siècles sous la domination romaine. Longtemps nos historiens se sont prononcés négativement sur le problème de la continuité, jusqu'à ce que de nouvelles données archéologiques et linguistiques les aient amenés à changer

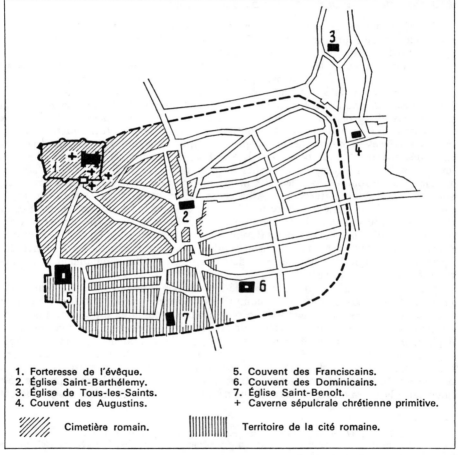

1. Forteresse de l'évêque.
2. Église Saint-Barthélemy.
3. Église de Tous-les-Saints.
4. Couvent des Augustins.

5. Couvent des Franciscains.
6. Couvent des Dominicains.
7. Église Saint-Benoît.
+ Caverne sépulcrale chrétienne primitive.

Cimetière romain.

Territoire de la cité romaine.

Fig. 4. — Plan de la ville de Pécs.

---

1. G. HECKENAST, « A kora arpádkori magyar vaskohászat szervezete », *Történeti Szemle*, 1966, pp. 135-161 (L'organisation de la sidérurgie hongroise à l'époque de la dynastie des Arpads).

VILLES ET ORDRES MENDIANTS EN HONGRIE

d'avis. Aujourd'hui, force nous est de supposer qu'en certains points de la Transdanubie, avant tout dans les lieux boisés et marécageux (que les nomades montés évitaient de préférence) subsistaient des vestiges d'une population romanisée. En deux endroits nous pouvons supposer une évolution analogue à celle de l'Europe occidentale : à Pécs et à Szombathely. A Pécs (fig. 4) le centre de l'agglomération s'est déplacé de la ville romaine jusqu'aux cimetières, aux tombeaux des martyrs chrétiens ; selon la « Conversio Carantanorum et Bagoariorum », une église y fut consacrée au VIIIᵉ siècle [1]. Le changement du nom de la ville est significatif. Son nom romain « Sopianae » étant tombé en oubli, au VIIIᵉ siècle on l'appelle *Quinque Basilicae*, qui veut dire sans doute « *Quinque martyrum basilica* » : « Basilique des cinq martyrs » ; son nom latin du XIᵉ siècle — *Quinque ecclesiae* — rappelle encore cette dénomination, qui traduite du latin passa en allemand et en langue slave. Si nous ajoutons que l'endroit le plus important de Szombathely — le lieu de naissance présumé de saint Martin de Tours — se situait à l'emplacement de la «Saveria» romaine, la continuité de peuplement nous apparaît clairement. L'organisation municipale des Romains ayant disparu en Pannonie de même que dans les provinces rhénanes, nous ne pouvons parler de sa persistance. Mais pourtant, grâce à la population romanisée, subsistent des vestiges de la domination romaine : le réseau routier, des ruines de villes ; au XIIIᵉ siècle encore, c'étaient des pierres milliaires et des aqueducs romains qui marquaient les limites des domaines. Autant de symptômes de la persistance des souvenirs romains et de l'influence des anciens occupants sur le développement des villes. A Bùde et à Pest, c'est-à-dire Óbuda (aujourd'hui un des arrondissements de Budapest), cette influence est connue depuis longtemps. Pest s'étendait sur la rive droite du Danube entre les murs d'un *burgus* romain ; et Óbuda est bâtie exactement à l'emplacement d'Aquincum, chef-lieu de la province romaine dont l'amphithéâtre servait déjà de forteresse aux Lombards, puis devint le bastion de Kurszán, chef des Hongrois. Les fouilles archéologiques des dernières années ont révélé que les murs de la cité de Sopron étaient les murs mêmes de l'ancienne colonie romaine, remis en état au XIIIᵉ siècle [2]. L'héritage des Romains a donc été un facteur d'une influence décisive.

Les premières décennies du XIᵉ siècle sont marquées par la formation du royaume chrétien de Hongrie. Des évêchés, des chapitres se créèrent ; des écoles capitulaires s'ouvrirent. Presque toutes les premières villes hongroises furent le siège d'un évêché. L'administration laïque se développait parallèlement à l'organisation ecclésiastique. Ces villes devinrent chefs-lieux du comitat où résidait le *comes parochialis*, premier magistrat de ce comté, dont les administrés défendaient la ville en cas de danger.

Nos sources documentaires nous apportent très peu de renseignements sur la vie économique, et ils concernent le commerce plus que l'industrie. C'étaient des Grecs, des Musulmans et des Juifs qui assumaient le commerce avec l'étranger. Ils fournissaient aussi des articles de luxe et des épices aux habitants des villes hongroises, plus exactement à une toute petite couche privilégiée. Nous ne savons presque rien sur les artisans ; il est très probable que les monnayeurs (en Hongrie le roi seul avait droit de battre monnaie) s'étaient donné quelque organisation [3].

---

1. Gy. PAULER et S. SZILÁGYI, *A magyar honfoglalás kutföi* (Les sources de la conquête arpadienne), Budapest, 1900, p. 311.
2. I. HOLL, « Sopron középkori városfalai » (Les murs d'enceinte médiévaux de Sopron), *Archeologiai Értesitö*. 94/1967, pp. 155-183.
3. E. LÉDERER, « A legrégibb magyar iparososztály kialakulása » (La formation de la classe industrielle la plus ancienne en Hongrie), *Századok*, 61-62 (1927-28), p. 639.

Les villes avaient un aspect de forteresses ; une partie d'entre elles portaient en effet le nom de *castrum*. Au pied de la butte fortifiée s'étendaient des agglomérations éparses, très peu liées entre elles, éventuellement un ou plusieurs faubourgs. Esztergom et Fehérvár représentent bien ce type de villes. Le *castrum* formant le centre ecclésiastique et laïque d'une part, et de l'autre le *suburbium*, réunissant commerçants et artisans, donnent des agglomérations à double caractère, analogues à celles d'Europe occidentale. De vastes cathédrales occupaient la majeure partie du *castrum* généralement exigu (fig. 5). A l'ombre des clochers vivaient prélats et seigneurs, commerçants hongrois, mahométans et juifs, agents du roi et esclaves, se mêlant en un fouillis bigarré. Devant la porte de la forteresse se tenait le marché hebdomadaire dont l'ordre était assuré par le *comes* royal et ses gens, puisque tous

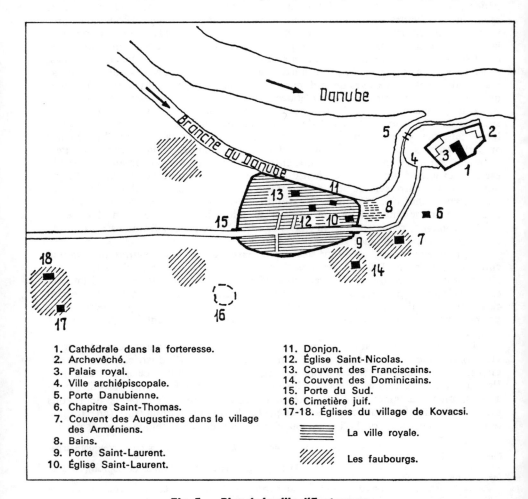

1. Cathédrale dans la forteresse.
2. Archevêché.
3. Palais royal.
4. Ville archiépiscopale.
5. Porte Danubienne.
6. Chapitre Saint-Thomas.
7. Couvent des Augustines dans le village des Arméniens.
8. Bains.
9. Porte Saint-Laurent.
10. Église Saint-Laurent.
11. Donjon.
12. Église Saint-Nicolas.
13. Couvent des Franciscains.
14. Couvent des Dominicains.
15. Porte du Sud.
16. Cimetière juif.
17-18. Églises du village de Kovacsi.

≡≡≡ La ville royale.

▨▨▨ Les faubourgs.

Fig. 5. — Plan de la ville d'Esztergom.

les habitants de la ville étaient sujets du roi. Les premières villes ne se distinguaient des villages que par leurs fonctions économiques et leur forme d'établissement, mais n'en différaient pas juridiquement.

Quel était donc le caractère de ces premières villes ? Leur statut juridique et social étant le même que celui de la campagne, nous ne pouvons les qualifier de villes à l'européenne. N'oublions pas que les Hongrois, avant d'occuper leur nouvelle patrie, vivaient dans l'Empire khazar ; ils y avaient connu un autre type de ville, la ville nomade, dont l'exemple le plus connu (grâce aux sources écrites) est Itil. La description d'Itil [1] montre clairement qu'il s'agit d'une ville, mais ses habitants ne se distinguaient en rien des autres sujets du khan. Malgré la présence de l'Église chrétienne et des organes de l'État féodal, il nous faut considérer les premières villes hongroises comme appartenant à ce type nomade.

La ville nomade a dû subsister tant que le pays est demeuré dans la sphère économique est-européenne, mais elle perdit sa raison d'être au moment où les frontières occidentales du royaume s'ouvrirent vers l'Europe, lors des croisades : dans les dernières années du XIe siècle les armées de la première croisade traversent le pays ; au milieu du XIIe siècle les troupes de la deuxième croisade. Les croisés occidentaux virent un pays peu peuplé, au sol fertile, et, mieux encore (Abu-Hamid en est à nouveau le principal témoin), ils y trouvèrent des mines de métaux précieux. Sur les traces des croisés se dirigeant vers la Terre sainte arrivèrent bientôt des immigrants pacifiques venus de territoire germanophones et francophones. Parmi les premiers immigrés occidentaux il y avait beaucoup d'agriculteurs, mais également des *Latini*, citadins en majeure partie ; on nommait *Latini* les Français, les Wallons ainsi que les Italiens, moins nombreux. Ils s'installèrent dans les résidences royales (Esztergom, Fehérvár) et dans quelques autres villes, formant des groupes dotés d'autonomie. Leur colonie de Fehérvár était sans aucun doute la plus importante du point de vue de l'urbanisation. A cette époque la ville (fig. 6) comprenait le *castrum Albense* — devenu cité plus tard — et plusieurs faubourgs. Dans la cité se dressaient le palais royal ainsi que le centre sacré du pays, lieu de sépulture de la famille royale : la basilique où reposait Étienne Ier le Saint, fondateur du royaume, et son fils Emeric, également canonisé. Dans un des faubourgs les Johannites avaient leurs couvents et leur hôpital ; dans l'autre faubourg — nommé *suburbium* (faubourg de Bude) — étaient l'église érigée en l'honneur de saint Nicolas et son hôpital. C'est dans ce faubourg de Bude que s'installèrent entre 1147 et 1172 les *Latini*, les premiers en Hongrie qui aient joui d'une charte de franchise communale, délivrée par Étienne III (mais attribuée, déjà en 1235, à Étienne Ier). Bien qu'elle ne nous soit pas parvenue, nous savons par les extraits qu'on en connaît : 1° Qu'elle assurait la libre élection du maire ; 2° Qu'elle autorisait le maire et les jurés à juger n'importe quelle affaire ; 3° Qu'elle permettait à d'autres habitants de se joindre aux *Latini*; 4° Qu'elle leur permettait de commercer librement dans le pays entier ainsi qu'aux frontières.

Cette lettre de franchise a ouvert un nouveau chapitre de l'histoire des villes hongroises. Dans les agglomérations que l'on peut considérer comme villes du point de vue économique, même avant cette date, apparaissent les ancêtres des futurs bourgeois, les premiers citadins jouissant d'autonomie et se distinguant même juridiquement des villageois. Au début du XIIIe siècle, la charte de la franchise des *Latini*

---

1. PAULER-SZILÁGYI, *op. cit.*

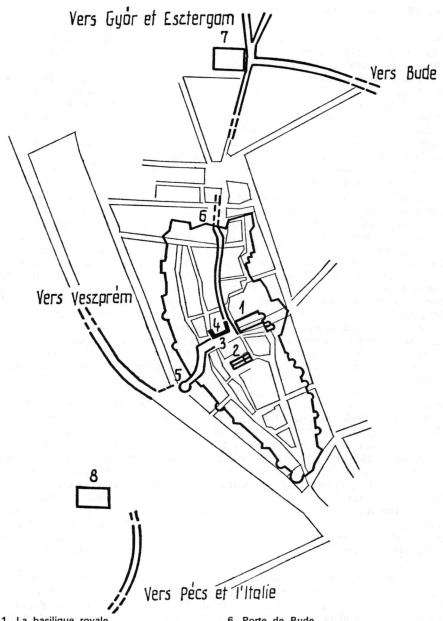

Fig. 6. — Plan de la ville de Fehérvár.

1. La basilique royale.
2. Église Saint-Pierre.
3. Marché.
4. Palais royal.
5. Porte de Palata.
6. Porte de Bude.
7. Église Saint-Nicolas dans le « suburbium ».
8. Église des Johannites dans le faubourg « insula ».

de Székesfehérvár, la « *libertas civium Albensium* », devint le prototype des privilèges municipaux. La charte de franchise des Fehérvarois et leur sceau (portant l'inscription « Sigillum Latinorum Albensium ») sont significatifs des changements économiques et sociaux fondamentaux qui s'accomplissent dans le pays.

Par suite de l'immigration et d'une natalité apparemment forte, l'accroissement de la population s'accélère. Les grandes forêts d'un seul tenant des frontières sont abattues, surtout dans les parties nord et est, et sur les terres défrichées s'installent des villages s'adonnant à la production agraire. De nouvelles mines de métaux précieux sont mises en exploitation ; autour des villes minières apparaissent des villages qui les approvisionnent en vivres et en matières brutes. Même le système des villages se transforme : aux colonies mobiles succèdent des villages sédentarisés, à caractère agraire. Le réseau d'habitants et l'accroissement de la population a augmenté la production marchande ; la condition des paysans se transforme ; leur servitude personnelle est devenue servitude foncière. Les finages des communes sont divisés en manses tributaires d'égales dimensions ; la redevance et l'impôt deviennent proportionnels à la tenure. Au commencement du XIIIᵉ siècle l'aliénation des domaines royaux se fit à une telle cadence que ce n'étaient plus les produits des terres, mais les impôts et autres recettes en argent liquide qui constituaient le gros des revenus du roi. Aussi le roi et les seigneurs exigeaient-ils le tribut qui leur était dû en argent liquide. Au tournant du XIIᵉ et du XIIIᵉ siècle, les ateliers royaux de monnayage ne pouvaient plus satisfaire les exigences accrues ; des deniers de Friesach, de qualité inférieure, inondent le pays, surtout dans sa partie occidentale. Cette transformation affecta aussi le commerce. La Hongrie fournit à l'Occident des produits miniers et des matières brutes, en échange d'articles fabriqués. Le commerce intérieur a pour organe une foire nationale, d'une durée de quinze jours ; elle apparaît pour la première fois à Fehérvár.

Les changements économiques entraînaient des changements politiques. Une classe de grands propriétaires ecclésiastiques apparaît qui persécute la population musulmane des villes, s'efforçant de la convertir à la foi chrétienne.

Les villes à caractère nomade ne pouvaient plus répondre à leur but. Leur transformation était en cours lorsque l'invasion des Mongols vint en accélérer le processus. Béla IV (1235-1270), qui occupa le trône peu avant l'invasion, s'était efforcé, entre 1235 et 1242, de freiner les changements en cours. Mais, en 1241, il perdit la bataille contre les Tartares et toute sa politique s'écroula. Le roi eut le mérite de tirer la leçon des événements, et après la retraite des Tartares, d'adopter une politique toute contraire à la précédente. La protection des villes en faisait partie. Dix-huit lettres de privilège accordées aux villes nous sont parvenues, qui datent de son règne, et certainement plusieurs autres sont perdues.

L'exemple de Pest rend bien compte de tout ce processus. Centre commercial important dès le XIᵉ siècle, des Sarrasins y habitaient encore en 1216 ; ils en furent chassés, semble-t-il, sous la pression des prélats, et à leur place furent installés des Allemands qui reçurent des privilèges vers les années 1230. Selon le témoin oculaire de l'invasion, Pest était « ditissima villa Teutonicorum » quand les Mongols la brûlèrent et exterminèrent une partie de sa population. Après la retraite des Tartares la vie recommença ; le roi renouvela en 1244 la charte de franchise perdue, en y ajoutant de nombreux privilèges ; il en étendit le bénéfice à la petite colonie, formée également d'Allemands, installée sur la rive droite du fleuve, au pied du mont Gellért. Quand en 1246 le bruit d'une nouvelle attaque des Tartares se répandit, le roi Béla transféra les Allemands de Pest sur la colline de la rive droite. Sur le versant nord de celle-ci, autour du château royal, il y avait déjà une petite agglomération de Hongrois, ayant son église et son marché hebdomadaire le samedi. Ce mont (le « Mont du Château » actuel) s'appelait en latin « novus mons castri Pestiensis », mais en hongrois on l'appelait Bude. Les deux agglomérations, fondues en une seule, furent munies d'une fortification commune. La nouvelle colonie éclipsa bientôt l'ancienne Óbuda, prospère au XIe siècle, mais tombée depuis en décadence. Le « Mont nouveau de Pest », nommé Bude devint en cinquante ans la ville la plus importante du pays, mais sa charte de privilège était en réalité la charte de Pest, son sceau était celui de Pest, et sa population allemande provenait de Pest.

Le réseau urbain ancien ne répondant plus aux exigences économiques, la fondation de nouvelles villes était de toute nécessité. Leur population était souvent — du moins en partie — d'origine allemande. La charte de privilège la plus ancienne qui nous soit parvenue est celle de Nagyszombat (Trnava, Tchécoslovaquie, 1238). Cette ville se forma par l'installation d'Allemands auprès d'un village à population mixte, slovaque-hongroise, puis les deux agglomérations se réunirent, la nouvelle ville s'entoura d'une muraille unique et reçut les privilèges de Fehérvár. Dans les régions nord et est du pays, des villes allemandes se fondèrent, surtout dans le pays minier. Grâce aux recherches de M. O. Paulinyi nous connaissons une ville minière type fondée par une société d'entrepreneurs : ceux-ci recevaient, sur la place du marché, des terrains, jouissant de toute une série de privilèges économiques, voire politiques. Ce système favorisait en même temps l'homogénéité de la municipalité du point de vue social et national.

Si nous examinons soit les villes anciennes, soit les villes nouvellement fondées, nous constatons qu'elles n'appartiennent plus au type de la ville-nomade. Une bourgeoisie s'y était constituée, qui s'efforçait de dominer sur l'ensemble du territoire de la ville ; il lui fallait tenir compte des institutions ecclésiastiques implantées dans l'enceinte des villes, dont elle ne réussissait pas toujours à abolir les privilèges. Les municipalités se formaient. La première des villes commerciales était Buda, ses coutumes étaient normatives. La plus importante des villes minières était Selmecbánya.

Un nouveau réseau urbain apparut donc, où Bude jouait le rôle le plus important, entourée de plusieurs villes anciennes ou nouvelles. C'était la Transdanubie qui disposait du réseau urbain le plus dense. Les villes minières aussi bien que les villes commerciales s'installaient aux frontières polonaise et orientale. Cette deuxième période de l'urbanisation est vraiment celle où s'implanta la ville européenne en Hongrie.

Au milieu du XIVe siècle apparaît en Hongrie un nouveau type d'agglomération qui n'est plus un village mais pas encore une ville, et que la terminologie latine, après quelques hésitations, appelle *oppidum*, c'est-à-dire « bourgade », en opposition à « village », désigné par *villa* ou *possessio*, et à « ville » ou *civitas*. Le nombre des bourgades n'a cessé d'augmenter aux XIVe et XVe siècles : au commencement du XVIe siècle, le royaume compte 800 *oppida*. Prenons pour exemple Galgóc (Hlohovec, Tchécoslovaquie), situé dans le comitat de Nyitra, près de la rivière Vág ; deux routes — l'une venant de la ville de Nagyszombat, l'autre longeant la rivière Vág — traversaient la rivière pour s'acheminer vers la résidence épiscopale de Nyitra. Sur la colline qui domine la rivière, il y avait une forteresse depuis le XIIIe siècle. En 1349, le roi Louis donna en fief le domaine de Galgóc, comprenant cinq villages, à son officier du gobelet, Nicolas Kont[1]. Quelques années plus tard, il ajouta encore

---

1. *Anjoukori okmánytár* (Diplomatarium Andegavense), t. V, p. 339.

d'autres villages. Nicolas Kont de son côté s'employa à augmenter sa seigneurie à titre onéreux ou par échanges. Parmi les dons ultérieurs du roi, notons le péage du pont de Vág[1]. Parallèlement à l'agrandissement de son domaine le seigneur commença à faire de Galgóc son centre seigneurial. En 1360, il lui faisait don d'une propriété foncière : « civibus et universis jobagionibus [serfs] nostris de libera civitate nostra Golgoch pro augmentatione utilitatis eiusdem »[2]. Deux ans plus tard, à la demande de Nicolas Kont, le roi lui concéda le droit d'y tenir des foires, et le diplôme porte que les bourgeois de Galgóc avaient qualité pour juger les différends survenus durant ces foires[3]. La charte de privilège proprement dite de Galgóc date de 1365, et elle émane du seigneur Nicolas Kont ; celui-ci fixe le montant des redevances et stipule que les habitants peuvent posséder et cultiver leurs vignes selon le droit coutumier de Nagyszombat[4]. En 1400, la mise par écrit des droits de propriété de l'hôpital fondé peu auparavant nous apprend que dans la bourgade (que les seigneurs continuent d'appeler *civitas*) il y a forteresse, marché, étals, mais ce sont encore les champs et les vignobles qui constituent les sources de revenu les plus importantes de l'hôpital[5]. En 1453, lors du dénombrement de l'ensemble du domaine, Galgóc, nommé dès lors *oppidum*, est le centre économique et administratif d'une seigneurie comprenant quatorze villages[6]. En 1465 le seigneur fonde dans la bourgade un couvent franciscain[7] que son successeur agrandira trente ans plus tard[8].

L'exemple de Galgóc montre bien la constitution, la formation d'une bourgade, mais en même temps les difficultés qu'entraîne le nouveau type d'agglomération. Tout comme il est difficile de définir la ville, de même la bourgade. On a d'abord pris des critères juridiques : outre la dénomination d'*oppidum*, la bourgade a son maire et ses jurés qui ont compétence pour juger toutes les affaires — ou presque toutes. Nous connaissons plus d'une bourgade qui vivait selon les coutumes d'une ville plus considérable, et, dans les cas délicats, s'adressait à celle-ci pour trancher la question[9].

L'un des critères juridiques, c'est le fait que la charte de franchise est le plus souvent octroyée par le seigneur, et non par le roi. Jusqu'à la fin du XIVᵉ siècle, il existe encore beaucoup de bourgades qui sont propriétés royales, mais à partir du XVᵉ siècle la majorité d'entre elles sont tombées en possession de seigneurs[10].

Aucun des critères juridiques que nous avons donnés ne suffit à définir une bourgade ; le seul fait certain c'est que la bourgade jouissait de privilèges juridiques que les simples villages ne possédaient pas, sans pourtant s'égaler aux « villes royales libres », mais ici les différences sont plus estompées.

Au cours des dernières décennies toute une série de chercheurs se sont occupés de la situation économique des bourgades. Ils soulignent tous que les bourgades étaient des agglomérations de caractère agraire, dont la population s'adonnait à

1. *Ibid.*, t. VI, p. 133.
2. Magyar Országos Levéltár Diplomatikai Osztály (Section diplomatique des Archives nationales hongroises, cité plus loin comme suit : DL), 5020.
3. DL 5133.
4. DL 5389.
5. DL 8588.
6. DL 14726.
7. KARÁCSONYI, *op. cit.*, t. II, pp. 52-53.
8. *Ibid.*, p. 53.
9. E. FUGEDI, *Középkori városprivilégiumok. Tanulmányok Budapest multjából* (Privilèges municipaux médiévaux en Hongrie. Études portant sur le passé de Budapest), 14/1961, pp. 67-68.
10. V. BÁCSKAI, *Magyar mezővárosok a 15 Értekezések a történettudomány köréből. Uj sorozat, 37* (Bourgades hongroises au XVᵉ siècle), Budapest, 1965, p. 19.

l'agriculture, et où la viticulture jouait un rôle important [1]. En même temps, l'industrie de la région se concentrait dans ces agglomérations, et les divers métiers (cordonniers, tailleurs, tonneliers) arrivaient souvent au niveau corporatif. L'essor industriel entraîna le développement du marché des bourgades. Ces marchés hebdomadaires, anciens ou nouveaux (souvent fondés par un seigneur), devinrent pour la population des villages environnants d'importants centres d'échange de marchandises [2]. Ajoutons que beaucoup de bourgades payaient à titre d'impôts et de redevances une somme fixée une fois pour toutes, ce qui était avantageux dans les périodes de prospérité [3]. Si, du point de vue juridique, la limite entre le village et la bourgade est nettement tracée, du point de vue économique, il est presque impossible de distinguer une bourgade d'un village prospère.

Les travaux récents ont également éclairé certaines caractéristiques des agglomérations. La grande majorité des bourgades n'étaient pas entourées de murs, et leur grand-rue était généralement assez large pour que le marché pût s'y tenir [4]. A l'opposé des villages où le nombre d'habitants était très bas (100 à 200 têtes), la population des bourgades atteignait de 400 à 500 personnes. Aussi n'est-il point étonnant qu'au début du xvie siècle presqu'un cinquième des serfs habitât une bourgade [5].

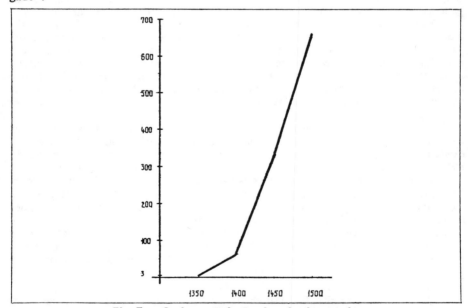

Fig. 7. — Croissance du nombre des bourgades.

1. *Ibid.*, p. 63.
2. *Ibid.*, pp. 69-82.
3. E. MÁLYUSZ, *A mezővárosi fejlödés. Tanulmányok a parasztság történetéhez Magyarországon a 14. században. Szerk. Székely György* (Formation de bourgades. Études portant sur l'histoire de la paysannerie au xive siècle en Hongrie), Budapest, 1933, p. 152.
4. *Ibid.*, p. 140.
5. I. SZABÓ, *La répartition de la population de Hongrie entre les bourgades et les villages dans les années 1449-1586.* Studia historica 49, Budapest, 1960.

V. Bácskai a récemment pu conclure, en employant la méthode quantitative, que le xve siècle a été l'époque de l'évolution en masse des bourgades (fig. 7).

En dernière analyse, nous sommes en présence d'un type d'agglomérations transitoire qui se modifie sans cesse et comprend aussi bien les villages en développement que les villes en décadence. E. Mályusz est allé jusqu'à dire que « les bourgades ont enlevé à des milliers de villages de grandes masses de paysans pour les diriger vers la vie citadine » [1]. Cette constatation s'applique surtout aux villages en voie de développement, mais il ne faut pas oublier que parmi les bourgades se trouvent aussi des chefs-lieux de comitat et même des résidences épiscopales dont le développement s'est arrêté.

En bref, on pourrait dire, pour mieux caractériser les bourgades, qu'elles étaient des agglomérations à caractère agraire, jouissant du point de vue juridique de privilèges spéciaux, et pourvoyant, sur un territoire restreint, à une partie des fonctions économiques et sociales des villes. Leur formation est postérieure à celle des villes, et elles tenaient le milieu entre les villes et les villages. Ajoutons que ce n'est pas leur existence mais leur nombre étonnamment élevé que l'on peut considérer comme spécifique du royaume de Hongrie.

Le témoignage des ordres mendiants.

Après ces pages trop succinctes, venons-en à l'objet essentiel de notre étude : comment la présence des ordres mendiants contribue-t-elle à mieux faire connaître le développement urbain.

Récapitulons brièvement ce qui concerne les Dominicains. Leur expansion — avons-nous dit — s'est arrêtée après 1260, la majeure partie de leurs couvents ayant été fondés avant. Cette date coïncide avec une époque de transformation. Ajoutons que jusqu'à présent nous n'avions pu, dans la période qui va de la fin du XIIe siècle au commencement du XIVe, déterminer les phases d'un processus, mais seulement enregistrer le résultat final. Maintenant l'implantation des Dominicains apporte des lumières sur ce problème. On peut avancer que parmi les villes (soit de fondation ancienne mais transformées avant 1260 en villes de type européen, soit nouvellement fondées) c'étaient les plus importantes — ou, pour mieux dire, celles qui avaient le plus haut degré d'urbanisation — qui attiraient les Dominicains.

En 1270 — nous l'avons dit — la province de Hongrie comptait trente couvents d'hommes et deux de femmes ; si, de ce nombre, on retire les couvents dalmates, il reste vingt-cinq couvents en Hongrie, auxquels il faut ajouter trois couvents qui ne figurent pas sur la liste établie en 1303 mais dont l'existence est prouvée. Malheureusement sur ces vingt-huit couvents, un en Transdanubie et deux en Transylvanie échappent à toute identification. On peut néanmoins affirmer qu'au milieu du XIIIe siècle existaient en Hongrie quelque trente agglomérations d'un caractère analogue à celui des villes occidentales — et cette constatation est significative de la situation économique du pays. La répartition géographique des couvents dominicains est encore plus révélatrice. On constate, là encore, une certaine concentration aux alentours de Bude (Bude, Pest et Esztergom). Seules deux villes limitrophes (Kassa et Nagyszombat) et une ville minière (Selmecbánya) figurent sur la liste. Nous ne trouvons de couvents dominicains ni près des mines de sel gemme, ni à

1. MÁLYUSZ, loc. cit., p. 186.

Radna (en Transylvanie) dont la mine d'argent était déjà exploitée avant l'invasion des Mongols.

La transformation des villes est également bien éclairée par les fondations dominicaines. Une partie considérable de nos villes anciennes avait déjà perdu son importance ; il n'y a donc pas de couvent dominicain à Óbuda — qui était encore résidence royale à l'époque de l'invasion des Mongols — mais il n'y en a pas non plus dans la majorité des chefs-lieux de comitats. Aux frontières occidentales, l'urbanisation en est à ses débuts ; Nagyszombat, dans cette région, est une ville nouvellement fondée, mais ni Pozsony, ni Sopron ne jouent encore de rôle marquant : c'est l'ancien Vasvár qui est la ville la plus importante de la Transdanubie occidentale.

En passant en revue la liste dominicaine, nous ne pouvons échapper à l'impression qu'elle se confond avec la liste des villes de commerce au milieu du XIIIe siècle. Et les couvents fondés au commencement du XIVe siècle sont apparemment dans le même cas (Szeged, Brassó, Temesvár), comme le montre l'échec d'une fondation des Dominicains à Debrecen. Si nous relions les couvents par un trait, nous voyons se dessiner les grandes routes commerciales qui viennent du Bassin tchèque par Nagyszombat, du margraviat autrichien par Vasvár et Györ, qui vont d'Italie à Fehérvár, et qui, par Pécs, convergent au centre, aux environs de Bude. Le marchand de l'époque se dirigeait vers la Russie par Sárospatak et Beregszász, vers la Moldavie par Beszterce. Il fallait traverser Szeged, Temesvár et Nagyolaszi (Francavilla) pour aller à Byzance ; par Szeben et Brassó la route menait en Havasalföld (Valachie). Vers cette époque la route allant de Kassa — par Debrecen et Várad — en Transylvanie était en formation, mais, après une expérience manquée, les Dominicains ne la jalonnèrent pas : les trois points de jonction les plus importants de cette route (Debrecen, Várad et Kolozsvár) n'auront pas de couvent dominicain. Le plus surprenant, c'est que Várad ne figure pas sur la liste. Par contre, l'existence d'un couvent à Szatmár prouve que la route menant de Kassa vers la région au delà de la Tisza avait été déjà ouverte.

Apparemment les Dominicains préféraient les villes de commerce qui attiraient beaucoup de monde sur un rayon étendu. Sur leur liste de couvents figurent — Várad excepté — toutes les villes importantes de Hongrie à l'époque, ce qui prouve à nouveau que, dans cette partie d'Europe, le rôle du commerce l'emportait sur celui de l'industrie pour la formation des villes.

L'attirance exercée par les villes de commerce est attesté également par les premières fondations franciscaines. Avant 1260, les Franciscains fondèrent dix-sept couvents en Hongrie, dont la majorité (dix couvents) s'implantaient dans les mêmes villes que les couvents dominicains [1]. Parmi les lieux choisis certains ne s'avéraient pas durables, et le couvent dépérissait [2]. Si l'on applique aux Franciscains le tableau de l'expansion géographique des couvents dominicains, les seuls changements à introduire tiennent à ce que : 1° Eger et Nyitra sont désormais des villes importantes ; 2° A la frontière occidentale, Pozsony et Sopron ont déjà leurs couvents franciscains. Les implantations des couvents des ordres mendiants montrent nettement que la majeure partie de nos anciennes villes perdirent leur importance et déclinèrent au cours de la première moitié du XIIIe siècle et que, parmi les villes nouvellement fondées, seules les villes de commerce jouèrent un rôle notable.

---

1. Ce sont : Buda, Esztergom, Fehérvár, Györ, Kassa, Nagyszombat, Pest, Pécs, Sárospatak, Veröce.
2. KARÁCSONYI, *op. cit.*, t. I, p. 34.

VILLES ET ORDRES MENDIANTS EN HONGRIE

Autre point sur lequel la répartition des couvents de mendiants peut nous prêter son aide : tenter d'établir une discrimination dans la masse des bourgades. Mais revenons d'abord aux ordres monastiques. Nous avons dit plus haut que les monastères n'eurent pas d'influence dans l'évolution de notre réseau urbain primitif. Mais tel ne fut pas le cas pour le développement des bourgades, surtout si l'on envisage les monastères de fondation royale. Les abbayes bénédictines, cisterciennes et prémontrées constituaient des centres domaniaux plus ou moins grands, et elles remplissaient des fonctions analogues à celles du notaire occidental : mise par écrit des opérations juridiques, interventions en matières contentieuses. Par leur caractère central, par la présence de leurs lettrés, elles contribuaient à ce que le village où elles étaient fondées se transformât en bourgade. Nous ne citerons qu'un exemple de ce rôle paradoxal, celui de Kapornak, en Transdanubie : ce monastère bénédictin était *locus credibilis*, faisant office de tabellion ; et le village où il se trouvait, nommé *oppidum* dès le milieu du xve siècle, devint siège de la chambre de la gabelle et lieu de rassemblement de la noblesse [1].

Pour revenir aux ordres mendiants, nous constatons qu'en général on ne trouve pas de couvent dominicain dans les bourgades. Font exception les agglomérations qui avaient été *civitas* avant le milieu du xiiie siècle, mais dont le développement s'arrêta au cours du xive ou du xve siècle et qui devinrent de simples bourgades. A vrai dire, il n'est pas étonnant que les bourgades n'aient pas eu de couvents dominicains. Ce type d'agglomération ne se développe qu'au milieu du xive siècle, alors que l'expansion des Dominicains en Hongrie était déjà close.

Dans certaines bourgades nous trouvons cependant des couvents franciscains. Leur présence nous pose des questions auxquelles nous ne sommes pas en mesure de répondre. D'autre part la multiplication du nombre des bourgades n'est pas sans paraître étonnante. Quand on en parle, c'est en se référant à l'ouvrage de Csánki, resté inachevé, sur la géographie historique de la Hongrie dans la deuxième moitié du xve siècle. L'auteur considère comme bourgade toute agglomération que les sources latines de l'époque appellent *oppidum*. Il a rangé parmi les bourgades non seulement les agglomérations nommées *oppida* mais toutes celles à propos desquelles il est question de *cives*, c'est-à-dire de ceux qui ont droit au marché hebdomadaire ou à une foire nationale ; également celles où l'impôt était élevé [2]. Remarquons : 1° Que Csánki n'a pas songé à noter quelle est la personne qui qualifie l'agglomération d'*oppidum* ; or le seigneur — simplement pour s'en faire honneur — pouvait appeler un de ses domaines *oppidum* bien avant que ne l'eût fait le roi ou un magistrat ; 2° Que la dénomination d'*oppidum* est une notion juridique, et s'applique seulement à une agglomération qui se distingue des simples villages [3]. Compte tenu de cela, on pourrait introduire des distinctions entre ces nombreuses bourgades selon qu'elles ont eu ou non un couvent franciscain (ou augustin). Établir cette donnée demande un travail de longue haleine, mais nous sommes convaincus de son utilité. Pour ne citer que deux exemples, il existait certainement des différences entre Ujlak et Ilyés dans le comitat de Valkó [4]. A Ujlak les Franciscains et les Augustins avaient des couvents ; Ilyés n'est nommé *oppidum* qu'une seule fois. Encore plus

1. D. Csánki, *Magyarország történeti földrajza a Hunyadiak korában* (Géographie historique de Hongrie à l'époque des Hunyadi), t. III, Budapest, 1897, p. 20.
2. *Ibid.*, t. I, pp. 287-288.
3. Bácskai, *op. cit.*, p. 2, formule également de grandes réserves quant au caractère de bourgade de ces agglomérations qui ne sont appelées *oppidum* qu'une seule fois. C'est lui-même qui a fait remarquer que le nombre de ces agglomérations augmente sans cesse.
4. Csánki, *op. cit.*, t. II, pp. 283 et 288-289.

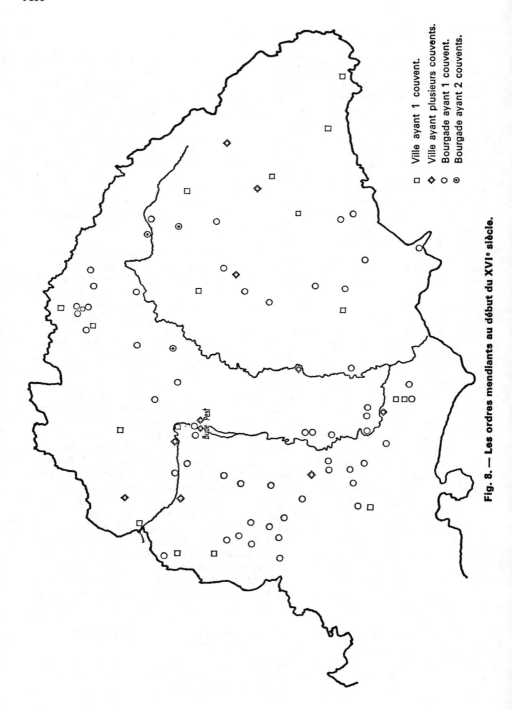

Fig. 8. — Les ordres mendiants au début du XVIe siècle.

□ Ville ayant 1 couvent.
□ Ville ayant plusieurs couvents.
◇ Bourgade ayant 1 couvent.
○ Bourgade ayant 1 couvent.
◉ Bourgade ayant 2 couvents.

Buda Pest

VILLES ET ORDRES MENDIANTS EN HONGRIE

frappant le cas du comitat de Somogy, où Segesd — qui possédait un couvent franciscain — est nommée sur le même pied qu'Atád et Bonya : or bien qu'il y eût des marchés hebdomadaires dans ces deux agglomérations (et même des foires à Atád), aucune d'elles n'est appelée une seule fois « bourgade » [1].

Le développement des bourgades et l'expansion des ordres mendiants pose une question plus complexe encore. Nous avons dit que vers 1240 il y avait tout juste 200 monastères. Jusqu'en 1260 les deux grands ordres mendiants fondèrent 45 couvents, c'est-à-dire qu'en quarante ans — entre 1221 et 1260 — le développement eut une cadence accélérée. Nous ne sommes pas en mesure de connaître le nombre des moines (ce qui serait une indication décisive), mais le seul nombre des bâtiments permet de conclure qu'il y eut un progrès économique. Ce progrès, nous pouvons le suivre. Jusqu'en 1500 le nombre des couvents (qui était de 47, y compris les Ermites de Saint-Paul) est monté à 260 au moins, c'est-à-dire a quintuplé, tandis que, à notre connaissance, la population a seulement doublé. Mais la logique impitoyable des nombres va encore plus loin. Si nous constatons qu'entre 1350 et 1500 le nombre des monastères est passé de 133 à 260, et que le nombre des bourgades — selon l'estimation de V. Bácskai — est passé de 20 à 330, nous devons présumer que la multiplication des bourgades est le signe non pas d'un développement économique mais de la transformation de notre système d'implantation.

Pour conclure, non seulement nous avons vérifié que fait urbain et présence des ordres mendiants sont en rapport étroit, mais nous pensons que l'examen de l'implantation des couvents de mendiants peut, surtout dans les pays où les sources directes ne sont pas très nombreuses, contribuer à la connaissance du développement économique en général.

---

1. *Ibid.*, t. II, pp. 576, 577.

XIII

DIE AUSBREITUNG DER STÄDTISCHEN LEBENSFORM - UNGARNS OPPIDA IM 14. JAHRHUNDERT

Vor vierzig Jahren erschien in einer ungarischen wissenschaftlichen Zeitschrift ein kurzer Artikel von E. MALYUSZ. Auf die schon früher erkannte Tatsache bauend, daß die Führer des Bauernkrieges von 1514 fast alle aus den *oppida* genannten Siedlungen stammten, konnte der damals junge Historiker den Beweis führen, daß diese Siedlungen nach dem Tode des Königs Mathias (1490) von den Aristokraten des Landes unter starken Druck gesetzt, die Bewohner in ihren Rechten bedeutend geschmälert wurden und deswegen sich den Kreuzfahrern anschließend das Heer — anstatt die Türken zu bekämpfen — gegen die Herren geführt haben[1]. Der Artikel stellte die Bedeutung der oppida (von uns schlechthin Marktflecken genannt) auf einen Schlag in ein scharfes Licht, das später noch durch die statistischen Erwägungen von I. SZABO gesteigert wurde, indem er bewies, daß an der Wende des 16. Jahrhunderts schon ein Fünftel des Bauerntums Marktfleckenbewohner war[2].

Die Schwierigkeiten, die sich der Forschung gegenüberstellten, waren nicht geringer als die Bedeutung des Fragenkomplexes. Vor allem konnte der lateinische Ausdruck aus den Quellen der Zeit nicht einwandfrei ausgelegt werden, teilweise deswegen, weil er im Laufe der Zeit seine Bedeutung wechselte. Während bis zur Mitte des 15. Jahrhunderts *oppidum* eine größere, städteähnliche, aber unbefestigte Siedlung bedeutete und das entsprechende ungarische Wort (mezőváros — Stadt im Felde) bis zum heutigen Tag diesen Sinn aufrechterhielt, benützte man das Wort in der zweiten Hälfte des 15. Jahrhunderts im verfassungsrechtlichen Sinn, indem man damit eine privilegierte Siedlung bezeichnete, die aber weiterhin unter grundherrschaftlicher Jurisdiktion blieb.

Eine den heutigen Forschungsbedingungen entsprechende Definition konnte von den Historikern noch nicht aufgestellt werden. In verfassungsrechtlicher Hinsicht befanden sich unter den *oppida* auch frühere königliche Freistädte, die im 13. Jahrhundert mit allen nötigen Freiheiten bekleidet wurden, doch später ihre wirtschaftliche Position eingebüßt haben oder durch Verschenkung bzw. Verpfändung durch den Herrscher in Privatbesitz geraten waren. Die methodischen Fehler, die während der Fertigstellung einer historischen Geographie begangen wurden, steigerten die Schwierigkeiten, indem der Verfasser rund 800 *oppida* aufwies, was den tatsächlichen Verhältnissen keineswegs entspricht[3]. Aber selbst unter den einwandfrei festgestellten Marktflecken konnte man gleichermaßen rege Umschlagplätze, erhabene Bischofsitze und kleine Ackerbürgerstädte finden. Es ist vielleicht kaum nötig zu bemerken, daß manche unter ihnen größer und wirtschaftlich bedeutender waren als die regelrechten königlichen Freistädte. E. MALYUSZ, der 1952 die Frage von neuem aufgriff, bemühte sich, eine klare Definition aufzustellen, mußte aber schließlich darauf verzichten und stellte nur soviel fest, daß sie zwar gemeinsame Züge aufweisen, die sie von den Dörfern trennten, doch können sie nur in einer Hinsicht als homogen betrachtet werden, nämlich hinsichtlich ihrer historischen Funktion, daß sie Tausende von Bauern in die städtische Lebensform einführten[4]. V. BACSKAIS Forschungen ergaben die Definition, daß unter den Marktflecken unbefestigte Siedlungen zu verstehen sind, die unter grundherrschaftlicher Jurisdiktion standen und mit städteähnlichen Freiheiten versehen waren[5]. G. SZEKELY gelang es, darauf hinzuweisen, daß vom wirtschaftlichen Standpunkt aus zwei Typen, nämlich jene Marktflecken, welche (hauptsächlich in der Tiefebene) Mittelpunkte der Viehzucht und des Viehhandels waren, von den grundherrschaftlichen Zentren unterschieden werden müssen[6]. Vor einem Jahr haben wir das Kennzeichen der Urbanität der Städte Ungarns in der Anwesenheit der Bettelorden gesucht und — wir hoffen es — gefunden. Was sich aber als klares Kennzeichen für die Städte erwies, war für die Marktflecken unbrauchbar. In den *oppida* scheinen die Hospitäler Zeichen einer Sozialdifferenzierung zu sein[7].

In der Frage der Marktflecken geriet die ungarische Geschichtswissenschaft in eine Sackgasse, aus der nur durch Anwendung methodischer Schärfe ein Ausweg gefunden werden kann. Wie schon darauf hingewiesen wurde, fand man unter dem einheitlichen Namen *oppidum* verschiedene Typen, und die müssen voneinander abgegrenzt und konsequent auseinandergehalten werden. Die Forschung muß aber auch den praktischen Vorbedingungen Rechnung tragen, indem sie einerseits die stadtgeschichtliche Methode auf die Entstehung der Marktflecken überträgt, andererseits die Entwicklung in mehrere Perioden zerlegt. Aus den bisherigen Ergebnissen ist es klar, daß die *oppida* trotz desselben Ausdrucks verschiedene Entwicklungsphasen durchgemacht haben. Die Grenze liegt um die Mitte des 15. Jahrhunderts. Von dieser Zeit an benützte man das Wort *oppidum* in einem anderen, viel weiteren, vor allem aber in einem verfassungsrechtlichen Sinn.

Angesichts dieser Tatsachen und der methodischen Vorbedingungen möchten wir hier die Marktflecken des 14. Jahrhunderts mit Hilfe zweier Ermittlungen beleuchten, indem wir

a) acht Marktflecken des 14. Jahrhunderts auf ihre Entstehung,

b) die im Laufe des 14. Jahrhunderts erlassenen Freiheitsbriefe untersuchen.

Ehe wir die gemeinsamen Entwicklungszüge der ausgewählten acht Marktflecken zusammenfassen (Einzelheiten sind im Anhang zu finden), muß soviel vorausgeschickt werden, daß prinzipiell von jedem Landesteil je zwei Ortschaften einer Untersuchung unterzogen wurden. Siebenbürgen mußte wegen seiner abweichenden Entwicklung außer acht gelassen werden. Leider konnten bei der Wahl der acht untersuchten Ortschaften die Regeln der statistischen Stichprobenerhebung nicht eingehalten werden, da wir — einerseits wegen des Quellenmaterials, andererseits wegen der zur Verfügung stehenden kurzen Zeit — schlechthin jene als „Stichproben" hinnehmen mußten, deren Geschichte schon geschrieben und deren Geschichtsquellen schon veröffentlicht wurden. Die Schwierigkeiten, die der Forschung im Wege stehen, blieben selbst bei der Berücksichtigung von Literatur und Quellen fast unüberwindbar. Alle drei grundlegenden Angabengruppen, nämlich (1) die wirtschaftliche Entwicklung, (2) die allgemeine und verfassungsrechtliche Lage der Bewohner und (3) die Verfassungstopographie, stehen uns in keinem Fall zu Verfügung. Auf eine Verfassungstopographie mußte im voraus verzichtet werden, da dazu Angaben fehlen. Die Urbare sind meistens späteren Ursprungs, sie stammen aus dem zweiten Drittel des 16. Jahrhunderts und widerspiegeln kaum die Verhältnisse des 14. Jahrhunderts. An ihre Stelle trat der Grundriß der Ortschaft (soweit er ermittelt werden konnte), von dem doch einige Entwicklungszüge herausgeholt werden konnten.

Das Städtenetz Ungarns in der ersten Hälfte des 14. Jh.

An der Wende zum 14. Jahrhundert trug das Stadtnetz Ungarns die Kennzeichen der Entstehung des Städtewesens an sich[8]. Es wurde einerseits durch das Erzvorkommen, andererseits durch die sogenannte „Marktregion" bestimmt, welche sich am Rande der großen Tiefebene und am Fuße der Gebirge befindet. Der Standort der Bergstädte war dadurch ebenso gegeben wie jener der großen Handelsstädte. Eine Folge der letzten Erscheinung war, daß die Städte voneinander weit entfernt lagen. Dabei kann eine gewisse Disproportion festgestellt werden. An der vom Westen aus ins Land führenden Handelsstraße waren viel mehr Städte zu finden als im Osten des Landes. Von der Grenze bis Ofen nahmen Preßburg, Raab und Gran am Warenverkehr teil, während von Ofen bis Kronstadt nur Großwardein, Szegedin und Klausenburg als wichtige Umschlagplätze bezeichnet werden können. Dasselbe gilt von der Straße Ofen—Kaschau, bzw. Kaschau—Großwardein. Handwerk und Handel konzentrierten sich in den Städten und die Entfernungen waren zu groß dazu, daß beide normalerweise funktionieren hätten können. Vor allem litt dadurch der Binnenhandel, der bei so großen Entfernungen weder die Verteilung der im Fernhandel eingeführten, noch den Aufkauf der ausgeführten Waren durchführen konnte, von der Verteilung unentbehrlicher Artikel wie Salz ganz zu schweigen. Vom Standpunkt des Handwerks her ergab sich ein ähnliches Problem. Man konnte nicht einen Tagesmarsch unternehmen, um Stiefel oder Kleider machen zu lassen. Es wurde zur absoluten Notwendigkeit, die großen Entfernungen zwischen den Städten im gleichen Maße zu vermindern, in dem der Landesausbau voranschritt und sich die ungarische Wirtschaft entwickelte. Für Handel und Handwerk mußten kleinere Zentren ins Leben gerufen werden, um die wichtigsten Handwerks- und Handelsprodukte besorgen zu können. Das ist der erste Faktor, der die Marktflecken entstehen ließ.

Die Marktflecken zwischen Theiss und Maros im 14. Jh.

Auf Karte 2 stellten wir den östlichen Landesteil zwischen der Theiß und Maros dar. Die Städte waren hier Großwardein und Szatmár, außer der dargestellten Gegend Ofen, Kaschau und Klausenburg. Die großen Straßen liefen in den Flußtälern, bzw. überquerten das Zwischengebiet, um die Flußübergänge zu erreichen. Aus westlicher Richtung kamen die Fernhandelsartikel, aus dem Osten das unentbehrliche Siebenbürger Salz und Schlachtvieh. Die Entfernung zwischen den Städten war enorm, Kaschau war von Großwardein ungefähr 250 km entfernt. Es nimmt nicht Wunder, daß in diesem großen und bevölkerten Gebiet rund neunzehn Marktflecken entstanden. Schon die Entstehung derselben beweist die oben nur theoretisch aufgestellte Notwendigkeit, kleinere Zentren ins Leben zu rufen. Wenn wir behaupten, daß der erste Faktor für die Entstehung der *oppida* die wirtschaftliche Notwendigkeit war, kleinere Zentren zwischen die Städte zu schieben, so müssen wir zugleich zugeben, daß diese Notwendigkeit nicht erst im 14. Jahrhundert aufkam, sondern schon Jahrhunderte früher bestand. Auf diese Frage kommen wir noch zurück.

Von den auf der Karte angegebenen zwanzig Marktflecken waren neunzehn Mittelpunkte von Grundherrschaften. Für den ausländischen Leser muß hier ganz kurz etwas über die Entwicklung des Großgrundbesitzes im mittelalterlichen Ungarn vorausgeschickt werden. Der ungarische Großgrundbesitz hat im Mittelalter zwei Entwicklungsphasen durchgemacht. In der ersten Phase lagen die Güter verstreut, wie dies besonders kennzeichnend die Untersuchung über die Abtei Pécsvárad ergab. Der Besitz der Abtei stammte aus dem 11. Jahrhundert, war und blieb darum so verstreut, weil sich von den 41 Dörfern, die sie besaß, nur 19 in der unmittelbaren Umgebung der Abtei befanden. Die zweite Hälfte des 13. Jahrhunderts brachte eine jähe Wandlung in der Entwicklung des Großgrundbesitzes mit sich. Die königlichen Güter wurden schon etwas früher größtenteils verschenkt. Als die Anjous auf den ungarischen Thron kamen, organisierten sie die übriggebliebenen und teilweise rückgeforderten Güter in Domänen, die um eine Burg konzentriert, womöglich geographisch eine zusammenhängende Einheit bildeten und von der Burg aus verwaltet wurden[9]. Der im Laufe des 13. Jahrhunderts sich entwickelnde Herrenstand war schon früher bemüht, seine Güter zu konzentrieren, erhielt in seiner Bemühung durch das Vorgehen der Anjous einen neuen Impuls und steckte sich das Ziel, ähnliche zusammenhängende Domänen zu gestalten, um im Gebiet derselben eine der königlichen Macht ähnliche Herrschaft über die Leibeigenen aufzubauen. Vor allem sollten diese neuen Privatdomänen eine geschlossene Einheit bilden. Alle Mittel, von der königlichen Belehnung, zum Tausch und Kauf bis zur Gewalt wurden angewendet, um das Ziel zu erreichen. Abgesehen von dem sozialen Verhalten, das hinter diesen Bemühungen steckt, hatte eine geographisch zusammenhängende Domäne ihre praktischen Vorteile. Die Verwaltung war einfacher und weniger kostspielig, die Güter konnten leichter vor der Gewalt des benachbarten Großgrundbesitzers beschützt, der Transportweg von produzierten Gütern vermindert werden. Wirtschaftliche Vorteile genügten aber nicht. Der Herrenstand setzte sich auch im Rechtswesen und sogar in kirchlichen Angelegenheiten durch. Die Königsrichter der Arpaden, die über alle Untertanen des Königs zuständig waren, waren längst verschwunden, und die Herren wurden allmählich bevollmächtigt, ihre Leibeigenen nicht nur in bezug auf die niedere Gerichtsbarkeit, sondern auch auf das Blutgericht abzuurteilen[10]. Das Patronatsrecht galt schon früher. Nun aber war es Gewohnheit geworden, daß es samt dem Gut an den neuen Besitzer fiel, wodurch die vollkommene Herrschaft über Leibeigene und Boden der Domäne ergänzt wurde[11].

Die geschlossene Herrschaft war ohne Mittelpunkt unvorstellbar. Es mußte einen Punkt geben, von dem aus die Domäne verwaltet werden und wo der Besitzer von Zeit zu Zeit die Urteile über seine Leibeigenen sprechen konnte. Auch wegen der standesgemäßen Lebensführung konnte man den Herrensitz nicht entbehren; hier fällte der Herr seine Urteile, hier wurden die politischen Besprechungen abgewickelt, hier unterhielt der Herr seine Gefolgschaft. In den hügeligen Gegenden zwischen den Bergen und Sümpfen baute sich der Grundherr — falls er es sich leisten konnte — eine Burg. Unter bescheidenen materiellen Verhältnissen mußte er sich oft mit einem „*curia*" genannten Steinhaus begnügen. Hatte er eine Burg, dann ließ er in ihr auch eine Privatkapelle erbauen. War es ein bescheidener Herrensitz, so mußte das Dorf eine dem Ruhm und der Würde des Patronatsherrn entsprechende Kirche als Begräbnisstätte haben.

Debrezin war nicht die einzige Ortschaft, die, an der Bevölkerungszahl gemessen, eine überdimensionierte Kirche besaß und wo die Grundherren dem Pfarrer liegende Güter[12] und andere Pfründen zukommen ließen. Auch die Gründung eines Spitals gehört zu diesem standesgemäßen und zugleich religiösen Ausdruck der Würde des Herrn.

Der Markt war ebenso unerläßlich wie der Herrensitz. Die Domänen waren in vieler Hinsicht auf den Markt angewiesen[13], wo die Leibeigenen ihre Produkte verkauften und sich so das für Abgaben und Steuer notwendige Geld verschafften. Um die landwirtschaftliche Produktion aufrechterhalten zu können mußten Handwerkserzeugnisse zur Verfügung stehen, die teils nicht von den Leibeigenen erzeugt werden konnten und so ebenfalls auf dem Markt gekauft werden mußten.

Wirtschaftliche Interessen des Herrn und die Auffassung, daß die Domäne die Verkörperung der Herrschaft ist, wirkten sich auch auf den Markt aus. Der Herrschaftsinhaber versuchte, den Warenverkehr seiner Domäne auf einen Markt zu konzentrieren, um auf diese Weise den Ertrag der Marktgebühr zu erhöhen und zugleich für sich zu sichern. Wirtschafts- und Verwaltungsmittelpunkt sowie Herrensitz wurden zu Faktoren, die vom Grundherrn ausgingen. Am Markt trafen sich seine Interessen mit jenen der Kaufleute. Der Kaufmann beanspruchte einerseits Ordnung und Schutz, andererseits die Möglichkeit, seine Forderungen auf dem Rechtswege zu realisieren. Dies konnte er nur von dem Grundherrn erwarten, der Recht sprach und die nötige Kraft besaß, um beide zu sichern.

Wir haben zwei Faktoren in der Entwicklung erkannt: den Herrn und die wirtschaftliche Notwendigkeit. Es konnte auch festgestellt werden, daß sie an der Entstehung von Marktplätzen ein gemeinsames Interesse hatten. Dazu gesellte sich noch ein dritter Faktor, nämlich die Bevölkerungskonzentration in den Marktflecken. In manchen Fällen nahm sie die Form eines zielbewußten Ausbaues durch Besiedlung an. Manchmal erscheint sie in klar erfaßbarer Form, wie z. B. in Pécsvárad oder Galgóc, manchmal kann sie nur durch mittelbare Angaben aufgehellt werden, wie z. B. in Debrezin, manchmal erscheint sie in der Form der Verschmelzung mehrerer kleinerer Siedlungen.

Haben wir die Komponenten der Entwicklung erfaßt, so stellt sich die Frage, wie sie zur Geltung kamen, mit anderen Worten, wie es dem Herrn gelang, das geeignete Dorf in seiner Domäne auszuwählen. Vor allem möchten wir hier betonen, daß die absolute Größe der Domäne eine interessante Rolle spielte. War die Domäne klein, so beeinflußte diese Tatsache die Entstehung eines Marktfleckens nicht. War aber die Domäne zu groß, wie im Falle von Gyula und Békés, so entstanden anstatt einem Mittelpunkt zwei, manchmal auch noch mehrere. Es gab sicherlich ein Maß, nach dem diese Teilungen unternommen wurden, doch konnte es nicht ermittelt werden und wird auch wahrscheinlich allgemeingültig nie ermittelt werden können, da in jedem Einzelfall viele andere Komponenten (Gelände, Agrarstruktur, Wegenetz usw.) in Betracht gezogen werden müssen.

Nicht die Größe der Domäne, sondern die Auswahl eines günstigen Punktes spielte die ausschlaggebende Rolle. Das ausgewählte Dorf sollte eine günstige Verkehrslage haben, also — das ist in allen 19 Fällen in dem von uns untersuchten Gebiet gültig — am Handelsweg und womöglich an einem Straßenknotenpunkt oder Flußübergang liegen. Oft besaß dieser Platz schon vor der Entstehung des *oppidum* das Marktrecht. Die Verkehrslage war weitaus wichtiger als die Anwesenheit des Herrensitzes. Als die Báthorys in Ecsed ihre Burg erbauten und damit das Verwaltungszentrum aus Nyirbátor nach Ecsed verlegten, blieb weiterhin Nyirbátor die possessio principalis, denn Ecsed lag inmitten der Sümpfe[14]. Dasselbe bezieht sich auf Bán, wo der Herrensitz in die Burg Ugróc umgesiedelt wurde, da aber Ugróc zwischen den Bergen, von der Hauptstraße abgelegen war, blieb weiterhin Bán der wirtschaftliche Mittelpunkt der Gegend. Ein noch mehr einleuchtendes Beispiel bietet Gyöngyös, das auf der Straße Ofen—Kaschau lag und von der Herrschaft, zu der es am Ende des 13. Jahrhunderts gehörte, losgelöst wurde, dennoch weiterhin *oppidum* geblieben ist[15]. Scheinbar war die Tätigkeit des Grundherrn nur in der ersten Phase beim Entstehen des Marktfleckens unerläßlich, den weiteren Lauf bestimmte sie nicht mehr.

Zusammenfassend möchten wir behaupten, daß wir unter den Marktflecken einen besonderen Typ, nämlich die Mittelpunkte der Großgrundbesitze, aussondern konnten. Bei der Entstehung dieses Typs spielte das wirtschaftliche Erfordernis die Hauptrolle. Dem Großgrundbesitzer bot sie die Gelegenheit, durch Erwerbung des Marktrechts und durch den Ausbau eines seiner Dörfer zum „*caput bonorum*", dieses Erfordernis zu seinem Vorteil zu realisieren. Während er seine Wahl traf, mußte er die Lage seiner Domäne sorgfältig prüfen und die Verkehrslage klar ins Auge fassen. War es ihm gelungen den geeigneten Punkt zu treffen, so konnte sich ein Marktflecken entwickeln, aufblühen und später ein von der Domäne gewissermaßen unabhängiges Dasein führen.

Die Märkte des 11.—13. Jh. in Ungarn nach J. Major

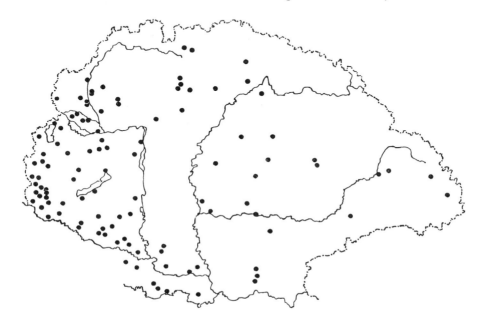

Hier glauben wir auf die schon gestellte Frage zurückkommen zu müssen, daß nämlich die Notwendigkeit, ein Marktnetz auszubauen, nicht erst im 14. Jahrhundert aufkam. Tatsächlich gab es in Ungarn schon seit dem 10. Jahrhundert Märkte neben den Städten. J. Major untersuchte die ältesten Märkte Ungarns auf Grund eines Ortsnamentyps, der den Namen eines Tages mit dem Wort „Markt" verband, z. B. Csütörtökhely = Donnerstagmarkt[16]. Seine diesbezügliche Karte zeigt deutlich, daß in den westlichen Landesteilen, hauptsächlich aber in Transdanubien das Marktnetz viel dichter war als in den östlichen. Mit Hilfe seiner Karte kann festgestellt werden, daß aus einer Reihe dieser alten Marktorte kein *oppidum* geworden ist. Selbst in den östlichen Landesteilen gab es solche. Dabei soll betont werden, daß sie ihr Marktrecht nicht einbüßten, sondern nur ihre wirtschaftliche Bedeutung verloren haben. Die angeführten Tatsachen scheinen darauf hinzudeuten, daß es im Marktnetz im Laufe der zweiten Hälfte des 13. und in der ersten Hälfte des 14. Jahrhunderts zu einer Wandlung kam, die darin bestand, daß einerseits von den alten Marktorten nur jene ihre Bedeutung beibehalten konnten, die *oppida* geworden sind, und daß andererseits das schon bestehende Netz durch neue Märkte der *oppida* ergänzt wurde.

Gab es eine Wandlung, so mußte sie begründet sein. Allgemeine wirtschaftliche Ursache war wahrscheinlich das Wachsen sowohl der Produktion wie der Konsumtion. Dazu gesellte sich aber noch ein schwerwiegendes außerwirtschaftliches Moment. Vor dem 13. Jahrhundert sorgten der König, bzw. sein Gespan (*comes comitatus*), für Aufrechterhaltung der Ordnung und des Friedens in den Märkten. Sie nahmen die Marktgebühr ein und waren für den Rechtsspruch in Handelsangelegenheiten zuständig[17]. Dieser königliche Graf verschwand im Laufe des 13. Jahrhunderts, als nach den schweren inneren Kämpfen um den Thron in lokaler Hinsicht der Grundherr an seine Stelle trat. Vom Beginn des 14. Jahrhunderts an war es der Grundherr, der die unentbehrliche Sicherheit und Recht zu bieten vermochte. Das war auch ein Grund, der die Umschichtung und den weiteren Ausbau des Marktnetzes förderte.

Bevor wir uns von diesem Typ des Marktfleckens trennen, sei noch darauf hingewiesen, daß der größte Teil der *oppida* des 14. Jahrhunderts aus solchen grundherrschaftlichen Mittelpunkten bestand. Vielleicht ist das Verhältnis 20 : 19 nicht für das ganze Land charakteristisch, denn in anderen Landesteilen dürfte der Prozentsatz niedriger sein. Sicher ·ist es aber, daß dieser Typ des Marktfleckens die häufigste Erscheinungsform darstellt und daß sein hoher Prozentsatz durch die allgemeine wirtschaftliche und soziale Entwicklung des Landes begründet war.

In dem von uns dargestellten östlichen Landesteil bleibt nur eine Ortschaft, Belényes, deren Entwicklung zum Marktflecken nicht durch die Grundherrschaft erklärt werden kann. Belényes bildet einen Spezialfall, der eine besondere Untersuchung verdient. Im 13. Jahrhundert befanden sich in der Ortschaft Silbergruben, die aber rasch erschöpft waren. Aus dem 14. Jahrhundert stehen uns über den Bergbau keine Angaben mehr zur Verfügung[18], die Ortschaft war im Begriffe, zu einem unbedeutenden kleinen Dorf abzusinken. Trotzdem bewahrte sie ihren *oppidum*-Charakter, und zwar deswegen, weil zwischen den Waldungen um die einstige Bergbausiedlung durch Rodung neue Dörfer im Herrschaftsbereich des Grundherrn von Belényes, des Bischofs von Großwardein, entstanden[19]. Es scheint, daß die ursprünglichen Bewohner Belényes verließen, an ihre Stelle traten neue, wahrscheinlich Rumänen[20]. Die so wiederbelebte Siedlung wurde der Mittelpunkt einer Herrschaft, in dieser Weise konnte sie den Charakter eines Marktfleckens retten und am Anfang des 15. Jahrhunderts vom Grundherrn einen neuen Freiheitsbrief erhalten[21].

Aus dem Beispiel von Belényes dürfen zwei Folgerungen gezogen werden: 1. daß der Bergbau der betreffenden Siedlung ebenfalls den Charakter eines *oppidum* verleihen konnte, und 2., daß das durch den Bergbau geschaffene höhere Niveau selbst nach dem Erschöpfen der Gruben beibehalten werden konnte, wenn die Siedlung inzwischen zum Mittelpunkt einer Herrschaft geworden war. Tatsächlich gab es eine Reihe von Bergstädten in Ungarn, die nie bedeutende Städte geworden sind, sondern Marktflecken blieben, und zwar einesteils, weil sie nicht Edelmetalle erzeugten wie z. B. die Marktflecken bei den Eisengruben im Komitat Gömör[22], und anderenteils, weil ihre Silber- oder Goldproduktion nicht die Hoffnungen erfüllte oder aber die Gruben noch vor dem Aufblühen der Ortschaft erschöpft waren wie bei Rimaszombat, das ebenfalls im Komitat Gömör[23] liegt. Leider stehen uns von den Letztgenannten keine Untersuchungen zur Verfügung, weshalb wir die Art und Weise, warum sie Marktflecken geblieben sind, nicht darstellen können. Ein sehr schönes Beispiel liefert dagegen Modern (unweit von Preßburg), wo sich anfangs ebenfalls eine Goldgrube befand, die rasch erschöpft war[24]. Auf den Bergen, wo bis dahin Gold abgebaut wurde, haben die (neuen?) Bewohner Wein angebaut und dadurch den Charakter eines Marktfleckens gerettet[25].

Im mittelalterlichen Ungarn war der Weinbau als Monokultur imstande, aus einem Dorf einen Marktflecken zu gestalten. Er ermöglichte größere Bevölkerungskonzentration, wirtschaftliche Blüte und — wie wir noch sehen werden — eine größere Unabhängigkeit in Verwaltungs- und Rechtsfragen. Die Marktflecken im Tokajer Gebirge verdankten ihre Prosperität diesem Umstand[26].

Fassen wir unsere Ergebnisse über die Entstehung der Marktflecken zusammen und vergegenwärtigen wir uns noch einmal die Faktoren, die ihre Entstehung ermöglichten, dann scheint es, daß es sich hier eigentlich um neue Kleinstädte handelt, die geeignet waren, die Funktionen der Städte in bezug auf Handel und Handwerk in einem begrenzten Raum zu versehen. Die Teilnahme am Warenverkehr und die auf dem Marktplatz versammelten Handwerker scheinen darauf hinzuweisen, daß wir es mit Siedlungen zu tun haben, die im Begriff waren, Städte zu werden. Ob sie diesen Status erreichten, hing von der Gunst der Verhältnisse ab, berührt aber den Charakter der Entwicklung nicht.

Aus dem 14. Jahrhundert werden in der ungarischen Geschichtswissenschaft insgesamt eineinhalb Dutzend Urkunden als Marktfleckenprivilegien in Evidenz gehalten[26a]. Diese Zahl bezieht sich auf ganz Ungarn. Für die von uns untersuchten zwanzig Ortschaften heißt dies, daß nur zwei einen Freiheitsbrief aufweisen können. Eine erstaunlich kleine Zahl, an die der ungarische Historiker gewöhnt ist, da in unseren Nachschlagewerken auf Schritt und Tritt die Feststellung zu lesen ist, daß das Privileg des betreffenden *oppidum* nicht erhalten geblieben ist. Im ersten Moment möchte man an die Verheerungen der Türkenherrschaft denken, doch finden wir in Oberungarn dieselbe Lage vor. Scheinbar besaß die überwiegende Mehrheit der *oppida* nie einen regelrechten Freiheitsbrief. Dazu gesellt sich noch die Tatsache, daß die ungarische Geschichtswissenschaft der Tradition der Marktflecken folgend schlechthin jene Urkunden als Freiheitsbriefe hinnahm, die von den einstigen *oppida* als solche aufbewahrt wurden. Die im 13. Jahrhundert erteilten Stadtprivilegien weisen trotz mannigfaltiger Abweichungen und Varianten gewisse einheitliche Züge auf. Diese grundsätzliche Einheit fehlt in den Freiheitsbriefen der Marktflecken, bei denen man einige wiederkehrende, voneinander gänzlich abweichende Typen vorfindet. In einer dieser Typen wird das Recht auf Befestigung und die Übernahme schon bestehender Stadtrechte genehmigt. Sie sind keine Marktprivilegien im wahren Sinne des Wortes, da sie eigentlich nur zwei Verfügungen enthalten; einerseits ermächtigen sie den Grundherrn, eine seiner Siedlungen zu befestigen, andererseits ermöglichen sie den Bewohnern, nach einem gewissen Stadtrecht zu urteilen. Trotz der eineinhalb Dutzend Urkunden, die als Freiheitsbriefe der *oppida* angesehen werden, sind es im Grunde genommen nur zwei, nämlich jene von Eisenstadt und Modern, die die Sonderrechte der Bewohner in einem den Stadtprivilegien ähnlichen Sinn regeln. Alle übrigen geben nur lückenhafte Informationen, doch kann aus ihnen der Rechtszustand der betreffenden Siedlungen ermittelt werden. Deswegen versuchen wir, die in den Freiheitsbriefen gesicherten Sonderrechte einzeln und nach ihrem wirtschaftlichen bzw. rechtlichen Charakter zu untersuchen. Dabei soll stets auch die wirtschaftliche und rechtliche Stellung der Städte berücksichtigt werden, weil die ungarische Geschichtswissenschaft einerseits in den Marktflecken werdende Städte sah, und weil andererseits die Untersuchung ihrer wirtschaftlichen Entwicklung auch von uns mit der Feststellung beendet wurde, daß sie städtische Funktionen in einem geographisch begrenzten Umkreis ausübten und in vielen Hinsichten als Keime werdender Städte betrachtet werden können.

Wenden wir uns den wirtschaftlichen Sonderrechten der Marktflecken zu, so stellt sich vor allem die Frage nach dem Marktrecht. Wir haben schon darauf hingewiesen, daß zu Ende des 14. Jahrhunderts jedes *oppidum* das Recht des Wochenmarktes, manche sogar schon das Recht Jahrmärkte abzuhalten, hatten. Von unserem jetzigen Standpunkt aus scheint es belanglos, ob dieses Marktrecht schon seit früheren Zeiten bestand, wie z. B. in Pécsvárad, oder ob es im Laufe des Domänenausbaus vom Herrscher durch den Grundherrn erworben wurde. Der Unterschied gegenüber den Städten lag nicht in diesem zeitlichen Ablauf, sondern in den Besitzverhältnissen des Marktrechtes. Wurde das Marktrecht schon früher, als der betreffende Ort noch königliches Gut war, erteilt, so kam es bei der Verschenkung samt Gut an den neuen Grundherrn; noch mehr bildete es seinen Besitz, falls er das Marktrecht vom König erworben hatte. Während also in den Städten das Marktrecht ausschließlich den Bürgern gehörte, war es in den Marktflecken immer Eigentum des Grundherrn. Das Sonderrecht haftete zwar am Gut, war aber — natürlich samt dem Markteinkommen — im Besitz des adeligen Gutsherrn.

Bei den Städtegründungen wurde nicht nur das Marktrecht den Bürgern überlassen, sondern auch die Gemarkung der neuen Stadt. Es lag an den Bürgern, wie sie die Gemarkung unter sich teilten, weshalb in dieser Hinsicht verschiedene Formen aufkamen. Demgegenüber blieb der Grund und Boden des Marktfleckens weiterhin im Besitz des Grundherrn und weiterhin in Bauernhöfe (*sessiones*) aufgeteilt. Von dieser Regel gibt es anscheinend nur eine Ausnahme, obzwar wir — wegen des Fehlens von Spezialuntersuchungen — nur die Erscheinung, nicht aber die dahinter steckende Rechtsentwicklung erfassen können. Diese Ausnahme bilden die fast ausschließlich oder ausschließlich Weinbau treibenden Marktflecken, wo hohe Investitionskosten und der relativ große Wert des Weins einen Einbruch in das adelige Besitzrecht erlaubten. Dazu soll bemerkt werden, daß in Ungarn nur der Adel (bzw. der Klerus und die königlichen Freistädte als Genossenschaften) berechtigt war, liegende Güter zu besitzen. Sie konnten in der Regel nur vor dem König, den hohen Richtern des Landes oder vor Stiften, denen hierzulande als „glaubwürdige Orte" *(loca credibilia)* notarielle Eigenschaft zukam, veräußert werden. Das Übertragen eines Bauernhofes konnte z. B. auf zwei verschiedene Weisen erfolgen: a) änderte sich nur der bäuerliche Inhaber des Hofes, so war das vom besitzrechtlichen Standpunkt her belanglos, da ein Wechsel nur in der Person des Pächters (des Leibeigenen) eingetreten war, nicht aber in der Person des Besitzers, in diesem Fall wurde kein Schriftstück ausgestellt; verkaufte oder verpachtete dagegen ein Edelmann einen seiner Bauernhöfe, so änderte sich der Besitzer, weshalb ein Schriftstück ausgefertigt werden mußte. In den Monokultur treibenden Marktflecken können zwei Einrichtungen beobachtet werden, die diesen Grundsatz durchbrochen haben. Es war einerseits allgemeiner Brauch, daß auch der Wechsel in der Person des bäuerlichen Pächters (Fall a) vor einem glaubwürdigen Ort schriftlich durchgeführt wurde, andererseits deuten gewisse — teilweise spätere, aus dem 15. Jahrhundert stammende — Zeichen darauf hin, daß sich in diesen Marktflecken ein Gewohnheitsrecht ausgebildet hat, sei es von einer anderen, größeren Stadt übernommen (wie z. B. im Falle von Galgóc das Recht von Tirnau oder in der Tokajer Gegend jenes von Kaschau) oder in einer eklektischen Weise entstanden.

Die städtischen Grundstücke mußten vor dem Magistrat veräußert werden, ungeachtet dessen, ob die Käufer oder Verkäufer Bürger oder Fremde (oft kirchliche Institutionen und Adelige) waren. In einem einzigen Fall finden wir das auch in Steinamanger vor, können aber leider nicht sagen, ob es schon im 14. Jahrhundert allgemein war. Da — wie schon oben ausgeführt — der Grund und Boden weiterhin dem Grundherrn gehörte, scheint dieser Fall eher eine unter westlichem Einfluß entstandene Ausnahme zu sein.

Die meisten Freiheitsbriefe der *oppida* erwähnen kaum etwas über die grundherrschaftlichen Abgaben. Sie bestanden in Ungarn in den Dörfern aus dem Zins *(census)*, aus den meistens in Naturalien geleisteten Geschenken *(munera)* und aus der Fronarbeit. Zins und Fronarbeit sollten nach dem Bauernhof *(sessio)*, die Geschenke gemeinschaftlich entrichtet werden. Anstatt dieser drei wurde jetzt für Modern, später auch für andere Marktflecken eine einheitliche, von der Zahl der Bauernhöfe unabhängige, ein für allemal in einer Summe festgestellte Steuer eingeführt. Dies war im Grunde genommen ein städtisches Sonderrecht, es lag an den Einwohnern, die Steuer unter sich zu verteilen. Die für die *oppida* vorteilhafte Lösung bildete den größten Vorteil, den diese Orte in wirtschaftlicher Hinsicht erreicht haben.

In zwei Fällen wurde auch Zoll-, bzw. Außenhandelszollfreiheit an Bewohner von *oppida* erteilt. Es ist jedoch durchaus kennzeichnend, daß in einem Fall diese Exemtion in der späteren königlichen Bestätigung zurückgezogen wurde, im zweiten Fall sich nur auf eine Zollstätte bezog.

Es wird der Aufmerksamkeit des Lesers kaum entgangen sein, daß wir über die wirtschaftlichen Sonderrechte der Marktflecken im 14. Jahrhundert nur geringe und lückenhafte Kenntnisse besitzen. Dennoch scheinen diese Kenntnisse eine gewisse wirtschaftliche Charakteristik klar aufzuzeigen. Ein *oppidum* — ob Mittelpunkt einer Grundherrschaft, ein an Weinbau emporgekommenes Dorf oder ein bescheidenes Bergstädtchen — soll in wirtschaftlicher Hinsicht die Funktion einer Stadt erfüllen, ohne aber dadurch den Grundherrn in seinem Besitzrecht oder Machtkreis zu stören oder in seinen Einkünften zu schmälern. Das Marktrecht und die daraus fließenden Einnahmen sollen ebenso im Besitz des Herrn bleiben wie Grund und Boden. Die einzige Ausnahme bildet die Erleichterung in den Abgaben, doch ist selbst diese kein tatsächlicher Verzicht seitens des Grundherrn, da er das Pauschale ausschließlich oder fast ausschließlich in barem Gelde bestimmte und dadurch einerseits die Sorgen um den Verkauf der eingetriebenen Naturalien los wurde, andererseits nicht um die Organisation der Fronarbeit sorgen. mußte. Der Marktflecken soll wirtschaftlicher Mittelpunkt seiner Domäne werden wie die Städte im Lande, ohne aber die Nachteile der Städte (Selbständigkeit, fremder Rechtskörper, persönliche Freiheit, usw.) mitzuziehen.

Untersuchen wir die verfassungs- bzw. privatrechtlichen Verhältnisse in den Marktflecken, so kann das bisherige Bild noch schärfer gestellt werden. Verfassungsrechtlich standen die Bürger unter der Zuständigkeit des selbst erwählten Richters und der Geschworenen in allen Streitfragen, also auch in jenen der höheren Gerichtsbarkeit. Von da führt der Appellationsweg zum König, bzw. dessen Beauftragten in städtischen Angelegenheiten, zum Tarnakmeister. In einem der frühesten Marktfleckenprivilegien, jenem für Csetnek und Pelsöc, fügt der König zum Grundsatz, daß die Bewohner die Sonderrechte von Karpfen genießen, erklärend zu, daß alle Angelegenheiten, selbst jene der hohen Gerichtsbarkeit in den Ortschaften „erledigt" werden sollen. Es wird jedoch weder der frei gewählte Richter, noch seine Zuständigkeit erwähnt, so bleibt es aus der Urkunde unklar, wer diese Streitfragen zu „erledigen" ermächtigt ist.

Die unklare Wortführung des Privilegs wurde nicht ohne Absicht geschrieben. Drei Jahre später erhielt Nyirbátor seinen Freiheitsbrief, der übrigens nur aus fünf Paragraphen besteht. Im ersten werden die Bewohner von der Zuständigkeit des königlichen Gespans befreit, im dritten verordnet, daß die Grundherren „*Quibuslibet in articulis semper iustitae complementum exhibere et impendere ... teneantur*" und endlich ihnen das Recht auf Blutgericht erteilt. Die Gedankenführung ist klar. Der königliche Gespan war der zuständige Richter für die Leibeigenen. Wurden sie von seiner Kompetenz befreit, so trat an seine Stelle der Grundherr, der — um seinen neuen Wirkungskreis erfüllen zu können — mit dem *ius gladii* ausgestattet wurde.

Eine Abweichung bedeutet der erste Freiheitsbrief von Debrezin, in dem alle Streitfragen dem Richter überlassen werden. Scheinbar geht es hier um ein richtiges städtisches Sonderrecht. Nur ein Ausdruck ist verdächtig, daß nämlich die Urkunde vom Richter und Geschworenen nicht als den „*electi*", sondern als „*per ips*os (nämlich den Debrezinern) *constituendi*" spricht. Der Verdacht wird nur gesteigert, wenn wir im zweiten, 1405 erlassenen Privileg lesen, daß der Richter und die Geschworenen frei gewählt werden können, ohne daß sie jemandem vorgestellt werden müssen. Dem Anschein nach war die Richterwahl im 14. Jahrhundert dadurch beschränkt, daß dieser sein Amt nur nach Vorstellung beim Grundherrn (*praesentatio*) und dessen Genehmigung antreten durfte. Es ist überflüssig zu betonen, daß so eine Vorstellung auch den Urteilsspruch beeinflußte.

Der Freiheitsbrief von Modern ergänzt unsere Kenntnisse, da in ihm der Rechtsspruch eingehender geregelt wurde. Hier gibt es einen erwählten Richter, der in allen Fällen urteilen durfte, aber nur mit dem grundherrschaftlichen Beamten *(unacum officiali ipsorum)* zusammen, der den Vorsitz führte. Das Privileg beschrieb auch den Appellationsweg und regelte ihn in zweifacher Weise. In kreditrechtlichen Angelegenheiten und „anderen kleineren Prozessen" sollte die Stadt Tirnau, in besitzrechtlichen dagegen Preßburg das Appellationsgericht bilden. In beiden Fällen sind sie letzte Instanz.

Den Freiheitsbrief von Modern lesend gewinnt man den Eindruck, daß der König die Sonderrechte der Städte keinesfalls an Marktflecken verleihen wollte. Daß es sich hier nicht um einen Irrtum handelt, sondern daß der Herrscher selbst in dieser Frage gut unterrichtet war, beweist ein Befehl, den er an den Kastellan von Ugróc erließ. Er teilte dem Kastellan (der übrigens ein Aristokrat war) mit, er habe „*villam nostram Ban*" von der Domäne ausgenommen und zwischen seine Freistädte eingereiht *(in numerum aliarum liberarum civitatum regalium aggregavimus)*, weshalb der Kastellan die Bewohner nicht daran hindern dürfte, ihre Prozesse vor den Tarnakmeister zu bringen. Dieser Befehl entsprach der darin ausgesprochenen Absicht, Bán zu einer königlichen Freistadt zu erheben. Erteilte daher der König das Blutgericht den Besitzern, anstatt die Zuständigkeit des Richters zu erweitern, dann beschränkte er die Marktflecken in der Gerichtsbarkeit, indem er sie dem Grundherrn oder ihren Bevollmächtigten unterstellte, und seine Absicht kann nicht die Erteilung einer städtischen verfassungsrechtlichen Sonderstellung gewesen sein. Wenn sich der König, als natürlicher Verbündeter des Bürgertums, gegenüber den Marktflecken so verhielt, dann scheint es selbstverständlich, daß die Grundherren noch weniger geneigt waren, ihren Leibeigenen echte städtische Sonderrechte und verfassungsrechtliche Unabhängigkeit zu gewähren.

Schon die Freiheitsbriefe von Pelsöc und Csetnek deuten darauf hin, daß die Entwicklung in privatrechtlicher Hinsicht jener der verfassungsrechtlichen schroff entgegengesetzt war. Ungeachtet dessen, ob der Richter in einem Marktflecken auch in Fragen der hohen Gerichtsbarkeit zuständig war oder ob der Appellationsweg zum Grundherrn führte, wurden die meisten *oppida* mit Stadtrechten ausgestattet, die ihre Zuständigkeit in privatrechtlichen Prozessen enthielten. Es wurde darin andererseits auch geregelt, wo sie in komplizierten, schwer entscheidbaren oder unentscheidbaren Rechtsfragen Rat und Gutachten einholen konnten. Dieses Sonderrecht wurde für die Städte des Landes durch den Gesetzartikel 1405: 12 zur allgemeinen Praxis erhoben[27]. Daß es sich aber in diesem Fall nicht nur um Städte, sondern auch um Marktflecken handelte, beweist die Geschichte von Debrezin, wo der Rat öfters das Gutachten Ofens eingeholt hat[28]. Dadurch entstand ein Netz von Stadtrechten, die an Marktflecken verliehen wurden. Ofens und Karpfens Recht wurde im Laufe des 14. Jahrhunderts je dreimal[29], das Recht von Eperjes und Ödenburg je einmal[30] an Marktflecken übertragen. Einen sicherlich absurden, doch hochinteressanten Fall bietet Modern, das sich in „kleineren" privatrechtlichen Fragen an Tirnau, in besitzrechtlichen an Preßburg wenden konnte, obwohl diese beiden Städte zugleich Appellationsgerichte waren[31].

Wenden wir uns dem Grundherrn zu, so müssen wir feststellen, daß er in seinem Verhalten gegenüber Rechtsangelegenheiten ein Doppelgänger war. In verfassungsrechtlicher Hinsicht achtete er scharf auf seine Interessen. Er behielt die höhere Gerichtsbarkeit für sich, da sie ein Machtmittel war, und zugleich die Erhaltung einer stadtähnlichen Siedlung im Rahmen seiner Domäne sicherte. War er in verfassungsrechtlicher Hinsicht geizig, so war er in privatrechtlicher Hinsicht großzügig. Hier soll darauf hingewiesen werden, daß es z. B. im Falle von Galgóc der Grundherr war, der in den besitzrechtlichen Angelegenheiten der Weingärten seinen Leibeigenen das Tirnauer Recht zugesprochen hat[32]. Es kann auch kein Zweifel darüber bestehen, daß in all jenen Fällen, in welchen der König die Anwendung eines Stadtrechts genehmigte, seine Verordnung mit den Absichten des Grundherrn im Einklang stand. Der Grundherr fand es eben angenehm, komplizierte handels- und privatrechtliche Fragen, die fast ausschließlich in den Bereich der niederen Gerichtsbarkeit fielen, nicht nur seinen Leibeigenen zu überlassen, sondern ihnen in solchen Angelegenheiten auch die besten Sachverständigen zu sichern. Übrigens verstand der Grundherr, der nach den adeligen Rechtsgewohnheiten lebte, herzlich wenig von solchen Sachen.

Wenden wir die Münze und betrachten wir dieselben Züge vom Standpunkt der Marktflecken, dann ergibt sich ein davon vollkommen abweichendes Bild. Die Übernahme eines schon bestehenden Stadtrechtes bedeutete für die Bewohner der *oppida* unschätzbare Vorteile. Es bedeutete geordnete Rechtspflege, Sicherheit im wirtschaftlichen Schaffen, letzten Endes einen Anschluß an die bürgerliche Lebensführung. Leider kann die Frage, ob die Bewohner der Marktflecken ein Wort bei der Auswahl des erteilten Stadtrechtes gehabt haben, wegen Mangels an entsprechenden Angaben nicht beantwortet werden.

Fassen wir die Untersuchung der Privilegien zusammen, so kommen wir zu dem Ergebnis, daß das Entstehen der Marktflecken diesbezüglich ebenfalls die Leistung des Grundherrn war. Er war es, der das Marktrecht erwarb, die sogenannten Marktfleckenprivilegien wurden oft für ihn und in seinem Interesse erlassen. Er wollte eine städteähnliche Siedlung in seiner Domäne ins Leben rufen, die hinsichtlich der wirtschaftlichen Funktion die Rolle einer Stadt erfüllte, d. h. ein Umschlagplatz war und zugleich seine handwerklichen Bedürfnisse erfüllte. Nichts aber lag ihm ferner als die Absicht, eine wahre Stadt hinsichtlich der Sonderrechte entstehen zu lassen. Ungeachtet dessen, ob der Grundherr König, Prälat oder Laie war, war man sich darin einig, das höchste Machtmittel — nämlich die hohe Gerichtsbarkeit — nicht den Leibeigenen zu überlassen. Man behielt all diese Einkünfte weiterhin für sich. Mit Ausnahme von Thomas von Szécsény und der Kanizsais[33] — die es sich erlauben konnten — dachte keiner daran, sein *oppidum* zu befestigen. Dadurch wäre die Siedlung regelrecht unabhängig geworden. In privatrechtlicher Hinsicht überließ er jedoch die Initiative seinen Leibeigenen und ließ Stadtrecht walten. Das ermöglichte einen Anschluß an die Städte des Landes.

Die Bilanz kann nach dem bisher Gesagten so gezogen werden, daß die Marktflecken im 14. Jahrhundert Siedlungen waren, die wirtschaftliche, verwaltungs- und rechtsmäßig städteähnliche Funktionen ausübten, aber nie den städtischen Charakter in den erwähnten drei Hinsichten erreichten. Sie bildeten eine unabhängige Kategorie zwischen den Dörfern und den Städten. Dennoch glauben wir behaupten zu dürfen, daß ihre Entstehung und ihr Wirken eine Ausbreitung des Städtewesens und der bürgerlichen Lebensform bedeutet hat. Abgesehen von den eben geschilderten Stadtrechtsübernahmen möchten wir hier vor allem daran erinnern, daß der Handel ohne sie nicht flüssig abgewickelt hätte werden können. Auch hier fanden die Einwohner einen Anschluß an die Städte.

Aus dieser frühen Zeit stehen uns zwar nur lückenhafte Angaben über die soziale und Vermögensverteilung in den Marktflecken zur Verfügung, doch jene, welche uns erhalten geblieben sind, zeigen eine ziemlich vorgeschrittene Differenzierung in beiderlei Hinsicht. Auch die Gründung der Spitäler deutet darauf hin[34]. Die Vermögenden waren hier reicher als reiche Bauern in den Dörfern, die Armen noch ärmer. Es waren natürlich Reiche, die den Anschluß an die Städte fanden. Um nur ein einziges Beispiel anzuführen, soll hier ein gewisser „comes Gregorius" aus Pécsvárad erwähnt werden. Sohn eines Klemens „magnus", kaufte er der Reihe nach Mühlen, Weingärten und Felder in und um Pécsvárad, wurde Richter des Marktfleckens und war sicherlich der reichste Mann in der Ortschaft[35]. Ein Mann mit solchem Vermögen und — allem Anschein nach — mit solchen Ambitionen konnte nicht für immer in einem Marktflecken bleiben. Überblicken wir die Neubürger der Städte oder die bürgerlichen Namensverzeichnisse, so finden wir überall Leute, die den Namen eines sich in der Nähe befindenden *oppidum* tragen[36]. War es ihnen gelungen, ein Vermögen anzuhäufen, so zogen sie in die Stadt.

Interessanterweise war es nicht allein die wirtschaftliche Tätigkeit, die Marktfleckenbewohner zu städtischen Bürgern werden ließ, sondern auch ein kultureller Weg, und zwar die kirchliche Laufbahn. Offensichtlich gab es in den Marktflecken häufiger und vielleicht auch bessere Schulen als in den Dörfern. Dieselbe Erscheinung, die wir in den Bürgerverzeichnissen entdeckten, begegnet uns in den Namensverzeichnissen der Stifte und in den vereinzelten Angaben über Kleriker. Ein beträchtlicher Teil dieser Pfründen wurde durch Söhne von Marktfleckenbewohnern besetzt[37].

Die hier geschilderten zwei Möglichkeiten stellen persönliche Bande, die Stadtrechtsübernahme ein institutionelles dar. Selbst die königlichen Urkunden und überhaupt das Latein des mittelalterlichen Ungarn waren sich dessen bewußt, daß es hier nicht um einfache Leibeigene ging. Man nannte sie oft *cives*, d. h. städtische Bürger, obzwar sie keine *civitas*, sondern nur ein *oppidum* bewohnten.

Anhang

Debrezin

Das Dorf lag an der Grenze der Komitate Bihar und Szabolcs in einem Tiefland, das im 12. bis 14. Jahrhundert noch teilweise waldig und von mehreren Bächen durchquert war. Die heutige Ortschaft befand sich in der Nähe eines Bächleins, in ihrer Mitte lag noch am Ende des Mittelalters ein kleiner, Paptó genannter See.

Debrezin lag in einer Gegend, wo teils mittelmäßig begüterte, teils kleinadelige Familien ihre Güter hatten. Die Gegend war im Westen von den Besitzungen des Geschlechts der Gyóvad, im Osten von jenen der Gutkeled und Ákos umgeben[38].

Die kleine Siedlung erfreute sich einer äußerst günstigen Verkehrslage. Die Straße, welche die beiden größten Umschlagplätze Ostungarns, nämlich Großwardein und Kaschau miteinander verband, lief in der Nähe Debrezins der Theiß-Überfahrt bei Tokaj zu, und unmittelbar vor dem Paptó See zweigte aus ihr ein Weg nach Nyirbátor und Mátészalka ab. Ebenfalls beim See kreuzte diese wichtige Straße eine andere, nicht minder bedeutungsvolle, die von Szalacs. Dort befand sich ein großes königliches Salzdepot (Salzkammer). Von Szalacs führte die Straße zur Theiß-Überfahrt bei Poroszló und nach Erlau. Hier entstand also ein regelrechter Straßenknotenpunkt, der einerseits die Verbindung zwischen Siebenbürgen und Oberungarn (sogar auf zwei Linien, durch Tokaj und durch Poroszló), andererseits zwischen den Dörfern der Theißebene ermöglichte[39].

Der Grundriß von Debrezin

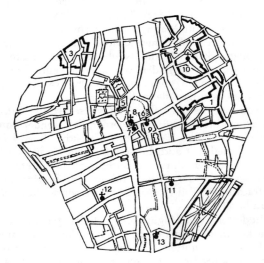

1. Das Dorf Debrezin	7. Allerheiligenkapelle	▬▬ Frühmittelalterliche Dörfer
2. Das Dorf Szentlászló	8. Elisabethkapelle	── Gassen im 13.–14. Jh.
3. Das Dorf Szentmihály	9. Franziskaner	
4. Das Dorf Torna	10. Ladislaikirche	── Heutiges Straßennetz
5. Andreaskirche	11. Annakapelle	
6. Herrensitz (curia)	12. Nikolaikapelle	
	13. Joachimskapelle	

Die wenig, oder höchstens mittelmäßig begüterte Familie, die sich von Debrezin nannte[40], schuf binnen einer kurzen Zeitspanne eine Grundherrschaft, diè nach dem Aussterben der Familie 27 Dörfer und eine Reihe von verlasssenen Siedlungen umfaßte[41]. Aus den Quellen läßt sich leider nicht in jedem Fall ermitteln, wann und wie diese Siedlungen in die Hände der Familie fielen. Sicher ist, daß eines der Dörfer (Macs, 1285) vom König an das erste hervorragende Familienmitglied, einen gewissen Rafain „banus" geschenkt[42], vier andere (Gáborján, Keresztur, Szentpéterszegi, Boldogasszonyfa) — darunter ein unmittelbarer Nachbar von Debrezin — erwarb Rafain durch Kauf[43]. Weitere königliche Schenkungen erfolgten an seinen Neffen Dózsa, der als Anhänger König

Karls I. die höchste weltliche Würde, jene des Palatin, erreichte (Máta, Elep 1307)[44]. Sein Besitztum vermehrte sich auch durch Konfiskation (Haláp, Csalános)[45] und Kauf (Zám)[46] von Gütern. Von einem anderen Gut wissen wir nur, daß es königliches Geschenk war und vor 1351 in Familienbesitz kam (Hatház)[47]. Von den 27 Dörfern können also nur elf mit Gewißheit als spätere Erwerbungen qualifiziert werden, doch scheint es unwahrscheinlich, daß die übrigen 16 schon am Ende des 13. Jahrhunderts der Familie gehörten. Ohne hier auf die weiteren Einzelheiten des Prozesses einzugehen, soll nur darauf hingewiesen werden, daß innerhalb von zwei Generationen eine ausgedehnte Herrschaft entstand, die sich mit Ausnahme von Gáborján und den dazugehörenden zwei Siedlungen, geschlossen um den ursprünglichen Familienbesitz ausdehnte. Zwar war Debrezin nicht die einzige Mautstelle, denn es sind noch fünf andere am Anfang des 15. Jahrhunderts bekannt[48], doch erreichte keine die Bedeutung von Debrezin, da alle übrigen nur den in eine Richtung laufenden Verkehr verzollen konnten.

Zu einem nicht bekannten Zeitpunkt, doch allem Anschein nach vor 1299, als die Kaufleute des Rafain zuerst erwähnt werden[49], erwarb die Familie auch das Recht, in Debrezin einen Wochenmarkt abzuhalten[50]. Das Dorf war auch in dieser Hinsicht sehr begünstigt, denn die nächsten großen Wochenmärkte befanden sich in einer Vorstadt von Großwardein, im Dorf Bihar und im Marktflecken Szalacs (1374)[51].

Die Würde des Palatins brachte es mit sich, daß Dózsa in Debrezin ständig Residenz hielt, dort seine Urteile fällte und mehrere Komitate zu Versammlungen zusammenrief[52]. Zu seiner Residenz gesellte sich (im Laufe des 14. Jahrhunderts) eine königliche Salzkammer[53], von der aus einerseits die Ortschaft und ihre unmittelbare Umgebung mit Salz versehen, andererseits das Salz nach Erlau (durch Poroszló) transportiert wurde.

Der Grundriß von Debrezin zeigt dieselbe Entwicklung. Zwischen den späteren Grenzen des Marktfleckens und um den Straßenknotenpunkt standen vier Dörfer, von denen das eine Debrezin, die anderen Szentlászló, Torna und Szentmihály genannt wurden. Debrezin war wahrscheinlich das kleinste, denn es hatte anfangs keine Kirche. Zwischen den Dörfern, beim Paptó, lag der Marktplatz, dessen nördliche Seite von einer am Ende des 13. Jahrhunderts angelegten großzügigen (50 m langen und 17 m breiten) Andreaskirche, der Pfarrkirche von Debrezin[54], und dessen Ostseite vom Herrensitz *(curia)* umgeben war[55]. Dadurch entwickelte sich ein Zentrum, das eigentlich zu keinem der vier Dörfer gehörte, sondern zwischen ihnen lag. Nach einem mißglückten Versuch der Dominikaner wurde 1322 gegenüber dem Herrensitz ein Franziskanerkloster gegründet[56]. Wir wissen, daß auch die königliche Salzkammer ein größeres Objekt war[57], können aber ihren Platz im Grundriß nicht bestimmen. Das Ausfüllen des zwischen den Dörfern und dem Zentrum stehenden Terrains geschah durch Einberufung neuer Siedler, vielleicht auch aus der Domäne, da die Dörfer der Umgebung sich rasch entvölkerten[58].

Den ersten Freiheitsbrief erhielt Debrezin 1361 von König Ludwig I. Laut dieses Freiheitsbriefes waren Richter *(iudex)* und Geschworene *(iurati)* in allen Streitfällen zuständig. Den Freiheiten der königlichen Freistädte entsprechend durften die Bürger und Gäste *(cives et hospites)* nicht anderswo wegen Verbrechen ihrer Mitbürger verhaftet, bzw. ihr Hab und Gut beschlagnahmt werden[59]. Nichtsdestoweniger hören wir schon 1332 von den *iudicibus* (!), *iuratis, hospitibus et mercatoribus de Debrezen*[60]. 1395 erließen Richter und Rat samt den Grundherren einen Freiheitsbrief für die Weberzunft[61]. Nach dem Aussterben der Familie von Debrezin fiel der Marktflecken an die Krone heim. 1405 erteilte König Sigismund einen Freiheitsbrief, in dem er, um den Aufbau der Stadtbefestigung zu fördern, der *„civitas Debrechen"* die freie Richterwahl zusicherte, sie mit den Rechten Ofens bekleidete und sogar Ofen als Appellationsforum bezeichnete[62].

Damit war prinzipiell der Weg geebnet, um Debrezin zu einer königlichen Freistadt zu machen, doch hat derselbe Sigismund die Herrschaft samt ihrer *„Civitas"* verschenkt[63] und damit in rechtlicher Hinsicht die Entwicklung abgebrochen. Debrezin blieb nichtsdestoweniger eine wahre Stadt mit blühendem Handel und etwas Gewerbe.

Nyirbátor

Unweit von Debrezin, ebenfalls in der Tiefebene, befindet sich ein Bátor genanntes Dorf, das König Ladislaus IV. 1279 den Mitgliedern des damals schon mächtigen Geschlechts Gutkeled schenkte[64]. Das Geschlecht war in diesem Landesteil schon bekannt, die Begräbnisstätten der verschiedenen Zweige und zugleich Abteien standen schon vor dem Tatareneinfall (1241) hier in der Gegend[65]. Am Beginn des 14. Jahrhunderts war die Geschlechtsverfassung schon überholt, die gemeinsamen Güter wurden zwischen den selbständig gewordenen Familien geteilt, und so kam Bátor in den Besitz einer Familie, die sich nach diesem Dorf Báthory nannte[66].

Die Besitzteilungen waren nicht immer gelungen, und es bedurfte weiterer 25 Jahre bis die Angelegenheit abgeschlossen war[67]. Die durch Teilungen zustande gekommene Herrschaft wird 1354 detailliert beschrieben, als Bátor schon *„possessio principalis et capitalis"* war und zu ihr elf Dörfer und weitere zwölf kleinere Güter gehörten[68]. Nicht alle Güter hatte das Geschlecht geerbt, einige von ihnen wurden am Anfang des 14. Jahrhunderts durch Kauf erworben (Pocs 1321, Ecsed 1322—29, Fábiánháza, Tereme vor 1341)[69]. In Ecsed bauten die Báthorys zwischen 1334—1354 eine Burg, doch blieb weiterhin Bátor die größte Siedlung. 1354 bestand sie aus sieben Gassen (davon fünf als *vicus* oder *platea*, zwei als *viculus* bezeichnet). Am Marktplatz standen 18 Fleischbänke. Natürlich fehlte weder die Pfarrkirche noch der Herrensitz[70].

Wie F. Maksay darauf hinwies, verdankte Bátor sein rasches Aufblühen der geographischen Lage. Die aus Siebenbürgen in dem Szamos-Tal nach dem Westen führenden Straßen mußten den großen Sumpf von Ecsed umgehen und vereinigten sich hier in Bátor, um von hier aus nach Debrezin und weiter nach dem Westen bzw. zu der Theiß-Überfahrt bei Rakamaz zu führen[71]. Die Marktverhältnisse waren ebenfalls günstig, denn die nächsten Märkte lagen hinter dem Ecseder Sumpf und nur jener von Kálló befand sich in der Nähe[72]. Von Siebenbürgen kamen die Kaufleute mit Schlachtvieh (Ochsen) und die Bürger von Szalacs mit Salz[73].

Der mittelalterliche Grundriß kann leider heute noch nicht rekonstruiert werden. Pfarrkirche und Herrensitz sind einwandfrei lokalisierbar und scheinen die trichterförmige Straßengabel an dem Marktplatz zu umgeben, jedoch konnten

die Straßen von 1354 nicht mit den heutigen identifiziert werden. Vielleicht kam es beim Ausbau des Minoritenklosters (1480—84) auch zu bedeutenden Änderungen. Sicher ist, daß die Siedlung unbefestigt war[74].
Wie das Marktprivileg, so wurde auch der erste „Freiheitsbrief" von den Báthorys erworben. König Karl I. befreite die Bewohner von der Zuständigkeit der königlichen Richter und erteilte den Báthorys das Blutgericht *(ius gladii)*[75].

Freistadt

Der Freistadt (Galgóc, Hlohovec) genannte Marktflecken des Spätmittelalters lag an einem wichtigen Übergang des Waag-Flusses, der Neutra mit Tirnau, bzw. Preßburg und Trentschin verband. Im 12. bis 13. Jahrhundert stand hier eine Galgóc genannte, bedeutungsvolle königliche Burg, zugleich der Sitz einer königlichen Gespanschaft, die urkundlich 1113 *(castellani Golgocienses)*[76], während die Mautstelle 1270 erwähnt wird[77]. Letzte ist sicherlich viel älter, da der Zehnte der Mauteinkünfte dem Bischof von Neutra gebührte. Die Burg wurde zwischen 1274 und 1294 vernichtet[78].

Der Grundriß von Galgóc

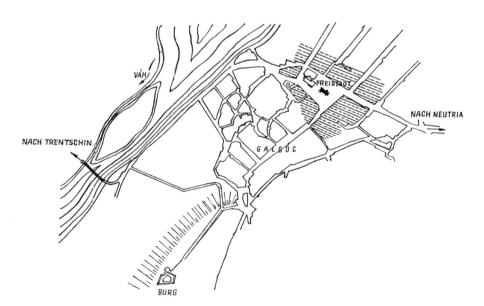

An der Wende des 14. Jahrhunderts war das Gebiet im Besitz von Aba, eines Anhängers von Matheus Csák, der sowohl die Grundlagen der späteren Herrschaft schuf, indem er die in unmittelbarer Umgebung der *„villa Galgoch"* liegenden drei Dörfer erwarb (Ujlak 1261, Udvarnok und Dics vor 1349)[79]. Wegen Abas Untreue kamen diese Güter in königlichen Besitz[80] und wurden erst 1349 an die Familie Kont (Ujlaki) verschenkt[81]. 1353 kam auch die königliche Maut in den Besitz der Familie Kont[82]. Die neuen Grundherren bauten die Burg wieder auf und erwarben vier weitere Dörfer (Zöldvár 1352, Jalsó 1353, Pásztó 1364, Tövis 1362) teils als königliches Lehen, teils durch Kauf und Tausch[83] und durch Rückforderung im Gerichtswege (Kelecsény 1360)[84]. Durch ihre Siedlungstätigkeit riefen sie noch zwei Dörfer ins Leben (Csened, Szentpéter eine Wiederbesiedlung vor 1369)[85]. Galgóc mitinbegriffen, entstand in dieser Weise eine Herrschaft von zwölf Dörfern.

Das alte Galgóc war ein kleines Dorf unterhalb der Burg. Zwischen 1349—60 ließen die Ujlakis deutsche oder mährische Einwanderer ansiedeln und gründeten neben dem alten Dorf eine ungarisch Uj-Galgóc (= Neu-Galgóc), deutsch und slowakisch Freistadt (Frišták) genannte Siedlung, deren Entwicklung sie mit allen Mitteln förderten[86]. 1360 schenkten sie den Bewohnern ein Gut (Váracs)[87], 1362 erwarben sie das Marktrecht[88], gründeten ein Spital[89] und später 1465 auch ein Franziskanerkloster[90]. Aus den Angaben des 15. Jahrhunderts scheint es, daß Freistadt dreimal so groß war als das weiterhin Dorf gebliebene Alt-Galgóc[91].

Die Topographie von Freistadt ist von V. Mencl geklärt worden[92]. Sie zeigt neben dem alten, unregelmäßigen Dorf unterhalb der Burg einen regelrecht angelegten Stadtgrundriß. Befestigungen gab es keine.

Der Freiheitsbrief von Freistadt ist nicht bekannt, doch kennen wir ein an die Leibeigenen von Alt-Galgóc 1365 von Palatin Nikolaus Kont erlassenes Privileg, in dem er die grundherrschaftlichen Abgaben der Einwohner regelte und in bezug auf den Weinbau die Übernahme der Tirnauer Rechte sicherte[93]. Aus einer 1400 ausgefertigten Urkunde erfahren wir über Freistadt, daß die „civitas" (!) in „sessiones hostach" aufgeteilt war, daß in ihr Steinhäuser und Fleischbänke standen. Die Einkünfte des Spitals sicherte man weiterhin aus dem Ertrag von Feldern, Wiesen und Wäldern, also aus der Landwirtschaft[94]. Aus dem 15. Jahrhundert sind allerdings „iudex et iurati" von Freistadt belegt[95].

B á n

Bán war schon im 11. Jahrhundert ein bedeutender Ort am Übergang des Neutra-Flusses, wo die Straße Böhmen—Trentschin—Neutra—Gran den Fluß überquerte und eine Burg stand. Bán war zugleich Mittelpunkt eines Archidiakonats[96]. Am Ende des 13. Jahrhunderts war die schon weiter abgelegene Burg Ugróc Zentrum einer Privatherrschaft geworden, die außer Bán noch sieben Dörfer in sich schloß[97]. Leider schweigen unsere Quellen über die Entstehung dieser Domäne. Am Anfang des 14. Jahrhunderts kam sie in den Besitz des Oligarchen Matheus Csák und fiel nach dessen Tod an die Krone heim. Später erscheint die Ugrócer Herrschaft 1389, als sie an Stibor verschenkt wurde und außer den schon erwähnten aus zwölf weiteren Dörfern bestand. Nur in drei Fällen kennen wir die ungefähre Zeit, in der das Dorf an die Herrschaft angeschlossen wurde (Brezolup vor 1323, Benóc nach 1345, Timorác vor 1355)[98].

Von Bán selbst wissen wir nur soviel, daß — laut eines Befehls — König Ludwig I. die Absicht hatte, das Dorf in die Reihe der königlichen Freistädte aufzunehmen[99]. Tatsächlich wird 1375 Bán als „civitas regis" erwähnt[100]. Die Schenkung von 1389 vereitelte diese Pläne.

Auffallenderweise zeigt der Grundriß des Marktfleckens eine regelmäßige Anlage mit einem großen viereckigen Marktplatz in der Mitte[101]. Man kann sich nicht des Eindrucks erwehren, daß die Ortschaft des 11. bis 13. Jahrhunderts näher bei Fluß und Kastell lag und erst später mit Hilfe von Zuwanderern ihre planmäßige Anlage erhielt.

Der Grundriß von Bán

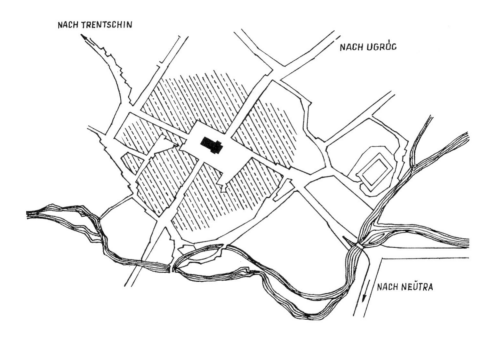

NACH TRENTSCHIN

NACH UGRÓC

NACH NEÚTRA

Pécsvárad

1015 gründete Stephan I. eine der frühesten Abteien an den Abhängen des Mecsek-Gebirges in Pécsvárad. Er hat diese reichlich mit liegenden Gütern ausgestattet. Die Abtei wurde insgesamt mit 41 Dörfern belehnt, von denen jedoch nur 23 im Komitat Baranya und nur 19 in der unmittelbaren Umgebung der Abtei lagen, die übrigen — und auch die späteren Schenkungen — befanden sich im benachbarten Komitat Tolna oder noch weiter jenseits der Donau[102]. Die Abtei und ihre sie unmittelbar umgebenden Dörfer lagen an der großen und bedeutenden Straße von Stuhlweißenburg bzw. Ofen nach Fünfkirchen. Die Entfernung zwischen Fünfkirchen und Pécsvárad beträgt ungefähr 15 km. Die Abtei wurde bei ihrer Gründung auch mit dem Marktrecht ausgestattet, und zwar mit zwei Wochenmärkten in Pécsvárad (Montag und Mittwoch). Die unmittelbar unter der burgartig ausgebauten Abtei gelegene Siedlung hieß

Váralja (= suburbium) und hatte eine dem heiligen Petrus geweihte Pfarrkirche. Noch vor 1258 ließ der Abt „latini" (= Wallonen und Franzosen) ansiedeln, die ihrer Siedlung den Namen Olaszfalu (=Welschdorf) und Uj-Pécs gaben und eine dem heiligen Nikolaus geweihte Pfarrkirche bauten[103].

Der Grundriß von Pécsvárad nach G. Györffy

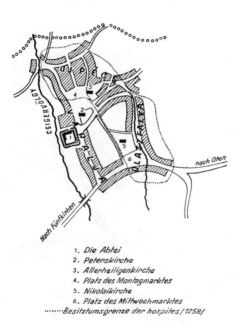

1. Die Abtei
2. Peterskirche
3. Allerheiligenkirche
4. Platz des Montagmarktes
5. Nikolaikirche
6. Platz des Mittwochmarktes
······Besitzhumsgrenze der hospites/1258/

Der Grundriß zeigt diese Entwicklung. Váralja kann an Hand eines Prozesses, den die „latini" gegen den Abt geführt haben, von den anderen beiden Siedlungen abgegrenzt werden, doch ist es unklar, warum Olaszfalu und Uj-Pécs einen besonderen Namen führten. Im 14. Jahrhundert nannte man schon beide zusammen civitas Waradiensis und unterschied sie manchmal mit der Bezeichnung civitas inferior, bzw. superior, was den Höhenverhältnissen tatsächlich entsprach[104].

Obzwar die Freiheitsbriefe nicht erhalten geblieben sind, ist es sicher, daß die Bewohner von Olaszi und Uj-Pécs im Besitz von Sonderrechten waren. Die Tatsache ist nicht nur durch den erwähnten Prozeß von 1258 erwiesen; auch später entschied der Abt in den Angelegenheiten des Marktflekkens „habito unanimi consilio et pari tractatu nostro unacum hospitibus eiusdem civitatis Waradiensis"[105].

Die wirtschaftliche Bedeutung von Pécsvárad lag nicht im Handwerk oder Handel, sondern im Weinbau. Aus einer 1439 stammenden Schätzung der Einkünfte des Abtes geht hervor, daß die Weinabgaben (600 fl.) beinahe die Hälfte des Gesamtertrags (1400 fl.) bedeuteten[106].

Siklós

Unter der Regierung König Andreas II. stieg die Macht des Gyula aus dem Geschlecht Kán immer höher. 1222—26 bekleidete er die höchste weltliche Würde des Königreichs, jene des Palatins[107]. Er wurde unter anderem mit einer großen königlichen Domäne im Komitat Baranya, um den Ort Siklós belehnt. Obzwar wir die zur Domäne gehörenden 49 Dörfer nur aus den Schriftstücken des ausgehenden 15. Jahrhunderts kennen, besteht kein Zweifel, daß sie schon zur Zeit der Belehnung zur Herrschaft gehörten, die nur in geringem Maße erweitert wurde, da die Familie nach dem Sturz Gyulas Ansehen und Reichtum eingebüßt hat[108].

Interessanterweise liegt Siklós verkehrsgeographisch nicht besonders glück-
lich. Es gab hier weder einen Flußübergang noch einen Straßenknotenpunkt und
dennoch wurde hier eine Burg aufgebaut. Siklós ist aber Mittelpunkt eines an
den Südhängen der Hügeln liegenden Rebenlandes[109].

Das Dorf besaß schon 1294 das Marktrecht, ein Szombatszeg (Samstagflur)
genannter Teil wird 1344, ein Wall (fossatum) ein Jahr später erwähnt[110]. Im
Marktflecken stand auch ein 1333 zuerst erwähntes Kloster der Augustiner
Chorherren. Sein Grundriß konnte leider nicht ermittelt werden.

Gyula

An dem Flusse Fehér-Körös, der zugleich die Grenze zwischen den Komitaten Békés und Zaránd, bzw. zwischen den Diözesen von Groß-Wardein und
Erlau bildete, gründete ein nicht näher bekannter Gyula ein Benediktinerkloster,
nach dem der Ort Gyulamonostora genannt wurde[111]. Dieses Kloster und das

Rekonstruktion des Grundrisses von Gyula

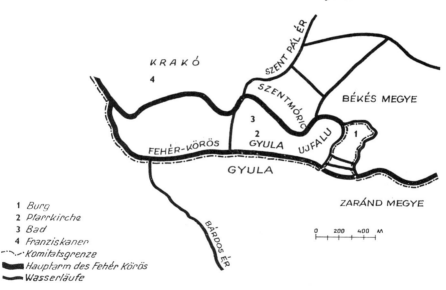

1 *Burg*
2 *Pfarrkirche*
3 *Bad*
4 *Franziskaner*
-`.`-`Komitatsgrenze*
▬ *Hauptarm des Fehér Körös*
➤ *Wasserläufe*

später unweit desselben stehende Dorf befanden sich an jenem wichtigen Punkt,
wo der aus Groß-Wardein nach Temesvár führende Weg den Fluß überquerte.
Das Benediktinerkloster wurde aus unbekannten Gründen aufgehoben. Der Ort
aber wurde in der Regierungszeit Karls I., und zwar sicherlich vor 1313, Mittelpunkt einer Herrschaft[112]. Leider schweigen die Quellen über die Entstehung der
Domäne ebenso wie über die Entwicklung ihres Mittelpunktes. Als 1387 die
Herrschaft an den Siebenbürger Woiwoden Ladislaus von Losonc verschenkt
wurde, bestand die Domäne aus 43 Dörfern und Weilern[113].

Der Marktflecken Gyula erscheint zum erstenmal in den päpstlichen Zehnten-registern, als der Pfarrer der Ortschaft 20 Groschen als ein Zehntel seines Ein-kommens bezahlt, das auf einen hohen Ertrag schließen läßt[114]. 1396 kaufte ein „civis de Gyula" ein Gut in der Umgebung[115], und es nimmt daher nicht Wunder, daß schon vor 1435 ein Siegel des Marktfleckens mit der Umschrift „Sigillum civium de Giula Johannis de Maroth bani" verfertigt wurde[116]. Sicherlich hielt man vor 1405 jeden Montag einen Wochenmarkt ab[117]. Da es sich um eine königliche Herrschaft handelte, finden wir keinen Herrensitz. Anstatt dessen brachten archäologische Forschungen den Beweis, daß der Turm (donjon) der 1438—1445 erbauten Burg aus dem 14. Jahrhundert stammt[118].

Die Topographie des Ortes konnte teilweise aus den Quellen der Türkenzeit (16. bis 17. Jahrhundert), teilweise auf Grund von Ausgrabungen in großen Zügen festgestellt werden[119]. Die ganze Siedlung stand auf den nebeneinander-liegenden Körös-Inseln. Auf der kleinsten war die Burg zu finden und ihr gegenüber lag der Marktflecken, doch — wie es die Pfarrkirche beweist — nicht dicht neben der Burg, sondern etwas ferner. Das Zwischengebiet wurde durch eine Ujfalu (Neudorf) genannte Siedlung ausgefüllt, die im Marktflecken auf-ging und schon 1422 als eine Gasse (vicus) von Gyula erwähnt wird. Allem Anschein nach kam es hier zu einer planmäßigen Ansiedlung, doch kann das nicht bestimmt behauptet werden, da das mittelalterliche Straßennetz wegen der Verheerungen der Türkenzeit nicht ermittelt werden konnte.

Békés

Am Zusammenfluß der zwei Körös-Flüsse, bei einem wichtigen Übergang, stand schon im 10. Jahrhundert eine Burg, die im 11. Jahrhundert Sitz eines Komitats geworden war[120]. Das unter der Burg liegende Dorf wurde schon sehr früh, spätestens im 12. Jahrhundert, mit einem Marktrecht belehnt[121]. Das wei-tere Schicksal der Burg ist unbekannt. Scheinbar kam sie im Laufe des 13. Jahr-hunderts ab. Das Dorf wurde in die Domäne von Gyula einverleibt, blieb aber dennoch bedeutend, da es während des 14. Jahrhunderts der einzige Marktort im ganzen Komitat Békés war[122]. Da die Domäne von Gyula zu groß war, um von einem Mittelpunkt her geleitet zu werden, wurde Békés das zweite Zentrum der Domäne[123]. Anfang des 15. Jahrhunderts wurde dort auch ein Herren-sitz erbaut[124]. Daß Békés im 14. Jahrhundert eine der größten und bedeutend-sten Siedlungen war, beweist die Tatsache, daß der Pfarrer 1333—35 den höchsten Betrag als päpstlichen Zehnten zahlte (15 Groschen)[125]. Wahrscheinlich gehörten zu Békés als Zentrum jene elf Dörfer, die im 16. Jahrhundert bei der Teilung der Herrschaft Gyula eine eigene Domäne um Békés gebildet hatten[126]. Leider kann der Grundriß der seit 1405 oppidum genannten Siedlung nicht ermittelt werden.

Anmerkungen

1 E. M á l y u s z, Az 1514. jobbágyháboru okai (Die Ursachen des Bauernkrieges vom Jahre 1514), Társadalomtudomány 1926.

2 I. S z a b ó, La répartition de la population de Hongrie entre les bourgades et les villages dans les années 1449—1526, /Studia historica Acad. Sc. Hung. 49/, Budapest 1960.

3 D. C s á n k i, Magyaroszág történeti földrajza a Hunyadiak korában (Die historische Geographie Ungarns im Zeitalter der Hunyadis) I—III., V., Budapest 1890—1913. Vgl. E. F ü g e d i, Koldulórendek és városfejlödés Magyarországon (Bettelorden und Stadtentwicklung in Ungarn), in: Századok C/1971, S. 85—87.

4 E. M á l y u s z, A mezövárosi fejlödés (Die Entwicklung in den Marktflecken), in: Tanulmányok a parasztság történetéhez Magyarországon a 14. században (Studien zur Geschichte des Bauerntums in Ungarn im 14. Jahrhundert), Budapest 1953, S. 186.

5 V. B á c s k a i, Magyar mezövárosok a XV. században (Ungarns Marktflecken im 15. Jahrhundert), (Ért. a törttud. köréböl. Uj folyam /Abhandlung aus der Geschichtswissenschaft/, Neue Folge 37), S. 19.

6 Gy. S z é k e l y, Vidéki termelöágak és az árukereskedelem Magyarországon a XV—XVI. században (Dörfliche Produktionszweige und Warenverkehr in Ungarn im 15.—16. Jahrhundert), in: Agrártörténeti Szemle, 1961, S. 309—322.

7 F ü g e d i, a. a. O.

8 E. F ü g e d i, Die Entstehung des Städtewesens in Ungarn, in: Alba Regia 10/1969, S. 101—118.

9 B. H ó m a n - Gy. S z e k f ü, Magyar Történet (Geschichte Ungarns) II, Budapest 1939⁶, S. 89—92.

10 K. S z o i k a, A földesuri biráskodás az Árpád-kori Magyarországon (Die grundherrschaftliche Gerichtsbarkeit in Ungarn in der Arpadenzeit), Budapest 1944, S. 62—69.

11 F. K o l l á n y i, A magánkegyuri jog hazánkban a középkorban (Das Privatpatronatsrecht in Ungarn im Mittelalter), Budapest 1906.

12 Im Zeitalter der Arpaden (1000—1301), als die Dorfkirchen im allgemeinen sehr klein, also wahrscheinlich der Bevölkerungszahl angemessen waren, finden wir in den Marktflecken im Verhältnis zur Einwohnerzahl sehr große Pfarrkirchen. So z. B. in Sztropkó, Rimaszombat, Rosenberg (Rózsahegy, Ružomberok) usw. Vgl. M e n c l, a. a. O., S. 107, 117, 147.

13 M á l y u s z, a. a. O. (wie Anm. 4), S. 128—133.

14 F. M a k s a y, A középkori Szatmár megye (Das Komitat Szatmár im Mittelalter), Település- és népiségtört. ért. (Studien zur Siedlungs- und Volkstumsgeschichte) 4, Budapest 1940, S. 132.

15 Als 1301 die Herrschaft aufgeteilt wurde, war Gyöngyös der Mittelpunkt mit einer Pfarrkirche, einer Gottleichnamskapelle und einem Wall, bzw. mit einem befestigten Herrensitz. AO, I, 2.

16 J. M a j o r, A magyar városok és városhálózat kialakulásának kezdetei (Die Anfänge der Entwicklung des ungarischen Städtewesens und Stadtnetzes), in: Településtudományi Közlemények 18/1966, S. 48—90.

17 E. F ü g e d i, Középkori magyar városprivilégiumok (Ungarische Städteprivilegien des Mittelalters), in: Tanulmányok Budapest multjából 14/1961, S. 28—31.

18 Z. B. Rimaszombat, wo 1270 mehrere „*aurifodine*" erwähnt werden, ÁUO XII, 34.

19 Zs. J a k ó, Bihar megye a török pusztitás elött (Das Komitat Bihar vor der Türkenherrschaft), Település- és népisétörténeti értekezések (Studien zur Siedlungs- und Volkstumsgeschichte) 5, Budapest 1940, S. 168—170.

20 Ebenda, S. 210.

21 Ebenda, S. 210.

22 Csetnek, Dobsina, Rozsnyó.

23 Nach dem Jahre 1270 wird in Rimaszombat nie mehr eine Goldgrube erwähnt.

24 Magyarország vármegyéi és városai. Pozsony megye (Die Komitate und Städte Ungarns. Das Preßburger Komitat), ohne Ort und Jahr, S. 563.

25 Ebenda, S. 202—203.

26 K u b i n y i, Tállya levéltára (Das Archiv von Tállya), Levéltári Közlemények.

190

26a Es wurden die folgenden Freiheitsbriefe benützt:
Pelsöc und Csetnek 1327, F e j é r, CD VIII/3, 265.
Nyirbátor 1330, ebenda VIII/3, 406.
Hanusfalva 1332, C. W a g n e r, Diplomatarium comitatus Sarosiensis, 447.
Szécsény 1334, AO III, 71.
Rimaszombat 1335, ebenda III, 73.
Gyöngyös 1334, F e j é r, CD IX/2, 324.
Modern 1360, Dl. 6173.

27 Art. 12: 1405: „... cives civitatum ... quibusque aliarum civitatum contulimus libertates: si de iudicatu et sententia iudicum et iuratorum suorum noluerint contentari, ad illam civitatem cuius libertate funguntur ... valeant appellare."

28 B. I v á n y i, Debreczen és a budai jog (Debrezin und das Ofner Recht), Debrecen 1924, S. 19—35.

29 Das Ofner wurde an Szécsény, Rimaszombat und Gyöngyös, das Karpfener an Pelsöc, Csetnek und St. Martin in Turz verliehen, vgl. P. F l o r e k, Turčiansky Svätý Martin v stredoveku (St. Martin im Mittelalter), Turč. Sv. Martin 1936.

30 Hanusfalva wurde mit dem Recht von Eperjes, Eisenstadt mit jenem von Ödenburg belehnt.

31 „Si qui vero de eorum iudicio in facto rerum debitorum et aliarum minutarum causarum ... non contentaretur, tunc iudici civitatis nostre Tyrnaviensis requiratur; si autem in facto possessionum et hereditatum, domorum videlicet et vinearum ipsorum iudicatu non contentaretur, tunc ad iudicium civium nostrorum Posoniensium recurratur", Dl. 6173.

32 Dl. 5389.

33 Das oben zitierte Privileg (Anmerkung 26a) ermächtigte Thomas von Szécsény sein Gut Gyöngyös mit Wehrbauten zu befestigen. Dasselbe für Eisenstadt: Sopron megyei oklevéltár (Urkundenbuch des Komitats Ödenburg) I.

34 F ü g e d i, Bettelorden (Anmerkung 3), S. 91—92.

35 AO V, 117, 222, 260, 67, 360, 560.

36 So z. B. finden wir in dem Verzeichnis der Kaschauer Neubürger Personennamen, die aus dem Namen der umgebenden Marktflecken gebildet wurden, vgl. E. F ü g e d i, Kaschau, eine osteuropäische Handelsstadt am Ende des Mittelalters, in: Studia Slavica II/1957.

37 Vgl. Die Namensverzeichnisse des Raaber Stiftes in dem Rechnungsbuch (Kapitelarchiv Raab, ohne Signatur).

38 Zs. J a k ó, Bihar megye a török pusztítás elött (Das Komitat Bihar vor der Türkenherrschaft), Település- és népiségtörténeti értekezések (Studien zur Siedlungs- und Volkstumsgeschichte) 5, Budapest 1940, S. 78—79, J. K a r á c s o n y i, A magyar nemzetségek a XIV. század közepéig (Die ungarischen Geschlechter bis zur Mitte des 14. Jahrhunderts), Budapest 1901, II, S. 91—94.

39 G y ö r f f y, I, Kartenbeilage.

40 A. K o m á r o m y, Dózsa nádor és a Debreczeni család (Palatin Dózsa und die Familie von Debreczin), Turul 9/1891, S. 1—9, 64, 78.

41 O. Z i c h y, S. 146, 318, 370.

42 G y ö r f f y, I, S. 640.

43 O. H é d e r v á r y, 127, O. Z i c h y, I, S. 128—129.

44 AO, II, S. 354, Fejér, CD VIII/1, S. 320.

45 AO, II, S. 23, J a k ó, a. a. O., S. 320.

46 O. Z i c h y, I, S. 88.

47 O. Z i c h y, I, S. 45.

48 In Csalános, Böszörmény, Szoboszló und Téglás, vgl. O. Z i c h y, VI, S. 146.

49 G y ö r f f y, I, S. 611.

50 Ebenda.

51 O. Z i c h y, III, S. 491.

52 G y ö r f f y, I, S. 611.

53 O. Z i c h y, IV, S. 387.

54 I. B a l o g h, Debrecen, Budapest 1958, S. 10, 17—18, G y ö r f f y, I, S. 610.

55 Ebenda, S. 13.

56 E. F ü g e d i, La formation des villes et les ordres mendiants en Hongrie, in: Annales Economies, Sociétés, Civilisations 25/1970.

57 F e j é r, CD X/5, S. 79.

58 I. B a l o g h, Adatok az Alföld régészetéhez (Beiträge zur Archäologie der Tiefebene), in: Archeológiai Értesitö 80/1953, S. 141—150.

59 I. S z ü c s, Sz. kir. Debreczen város történelme (Die Geschichte der königlichen Freistadt Debrezin), Debreczen 1870, I, S. 56.

60 G y ö r f f y, I, S. 610.

61 S z ü c s, a. a. O., I, S. 58.

62 Zsk. O, II, Nr. 3767.

63 F e j é r, CD X/5, S. 79. Vgl. Zsk. O, II, Nr. 7655.

64 F. M a k s a y, A középkori Szatmár megye (Das Komitat Szatmár im Mittelalter), Budapest 1940, S. 113.

65 J. K a r á c s o n y i, A magyar nemzetségek a 14. század közepéig II, S. 24—32.

66 Ebenda.

67 A Nagykállói Kállay család levéltára (Das Archiv der Familie Kállay von Nagykálló. Regestenband), Budapest 1943, Nr. 1085.

68 AO, VI, 160.

69 M a k s a y, a. a. O., 132, 135, 220.

70 Ebenda, 114.

71 Ebenda, 114.

72 Ebenda, 114.

73 Ebenda, 114.

74 G. E n t z - B. S z a l o n t a i, Nyirbátor, Bp.

75 F e j é r, CD VIII/3, 406.

76 E. F ü g e d i, Nyitra megye betelepülése (Die Besiedlung des Komitats Neutra), in: Századok 72/1938, S. 288.

77 Kapitelarchiv Preßburg, Capsa 13, Fasz. 2, Nr. 5.

78 ÁUO X, S. 136.

79 A p p o n y i O. I., S. 6, F e j é r, CD V/1, S. 309.

80 A p p o n y i O. I., S. 53.

81 AO, V, S, 339.

82 AO, VI, S. 109.

83 AO, VI, S. 136. J. V á g n e r, Adalékok a nyitrai székeskáptalan történetéhez (Beiträge zur Geschichte des Neutraer Domkapitels), Nyitra 1896, S. 392; Dl. 39, 204.

84 Dl. 1, 869.

85 A p p o n y i O. I., S. 35. Dl. 5, 728.

86 Die Unsicherheit hinsichtlich der Nationalität ist dadurch begründet, daß zwar die Siedlung einen deutschen Namen trägt und auch eine „*via Nemethwt*" (deutsche Straße) belegt ist, doch die Grundstücke schon 1400 „*hostach*" heißen. Dies bedeutet eine slawisierte Form des deutschen Wortes „Hofstatt".

87 Dl. 22, 479.

88 Dl. 5, 133.

89 F e j é r, CD X/2, S. 815.

90 J. K a r á c s o n y i, Szt. Ferencz rendjének története Magyarországon 1711-ig (Die Geschichte des Franziskanerordens in Ungarn bis 1711), Budapest 1923, II, S. 52—53.

91 Dl. 44, 649.

92 V. M e n c l, Stredoveka mesta na Slovensku (Die mittelalterlichen Städte in der Slowakei), Bratislava 1938, S. 129—133.

93 Dl. 5, 389.

94 F e j é r, CD X/2, S. 815.

95 Staatsarchiv, Familienarchiv Pongrácz 4—22.

96 A. F e k e t e N a g y, Trencsén megye (Das Komitat Trencsén), Magyarország történeti földrajza a Hunyadiak korában IV. (Die historische Geographie Ungarns im Zeitalter der Hunyadis), Budapest 1941, S. 84—85. Cosmas, II, cap. 48 „*locus qui dicitur Banow iuxta castrum nomine Trencin*".

97 F e k e t e N a g y, a. a. o., S. 81—82.

98 Ebenda, S. 82, 97—98.

[99] Levéltári Közlemények 14/1936, S. 231 „villam nostram Baan vocatam . . . in numerum aliarum liberarum civitatum nostrarum regalium aggregavimus".
[100] F e k e t e N a g y, a. a. O., S. 97—98.
[101] M e n c l, a. a. O., S. 131, 133.
[102] G y ö r f f y, I, S. 364.
[103] Ebenda, I, S. 366.
[104] Ebenda, I, S. 365.
[105] AO, IV, 410.
[106] Pannonhalmi Szt. Benedek rend története (Die Geschichte des Benediktinerordens von Pannonhalma), XII/B, S. 26.
[107] Karácsonyi: A magyar nemzetségek a XIV. század közepéig (Die Geschlechter Ungarns bis zur Mitte des 14. Jahrhunderts), Budapest 1901, II, S. 282.
[108] Ebenda, S. 283—285.
[109] Zuerst 1395 erwähnt. Dl. 8087.
[110] AO, IV, 435, 481.
[111] F. S c h e r e r, Gyula város története (Die Geschichte der Stadt Gyula), I, Gyula 1938, S. 89.
[112] Zwischen dem 19. und 22. Juni 1313 datierte König Karl I. hier seine Urkunden. Damals muß die Herrschaft schon organisiert gewesen sein.Vgl. J. K a r á c s o n y i, Békésvármegye története (Die Geschichte des Komitats Békés), Gyula 1896, S. 138.
[113] S c h e r e r, a. a. O., I, S. 44.
[114] K a r á c s o n y i, a. a. O., II, S. 138.
[115] Ebenda, S. 139.
[116] S c h e r e r, a. a. O., I, S. 47.
[117] Ebenda, I, S. 47.
[118] Ebenda, I, S. 55—56.
[119] Ebenda, I, S. 84—88.
[120] G y ö r f f y, a. a. O., S. 504.
[121] Ebenda, S. 504.
[122] K a r á c s o n y i, Békés vármegye története, II, S. 35.
[123] G y ö r f f y, a. a. O., S. 504.
[124] K a r á c s o n y i, a. a. O., S. 36.
[125] G y ö r f f y, a. a. O., S. 504.
[126] K a r á c s o n y i, a. a. O., S. 36.

BIBLIOGRAPHY
OF THE WRITINGS OF ERIK FÜGEDI
1937-1984

The arrangement within years is alphabetic. Reviews are set in smaller type. For the sake of economy, foreign language titles of books reviewed were not translated.

ABBREVIATIONS:

Bp. [as place of publication]= Budapest.

Periodicals:

AÉ	*Archaelógiai Értesítő* [Archaeological Bulletin], Bp.
AH	*Acta Historica Academiae Scientiarum Hungaricae*, Bp.
AgtSz	*Agrártörténeti Szemle* [Journal of Agrarian History], Bp.
Dem.	*Demográfia*, Bp.
StSl	*Studia Slavica Academiae Scientiarum Hungaricae*, Bp.
Száz.	*Századok. A Magyar Történelmi Társulat közlönye* [Centuries. Journal of the Hungarian Historical Association], Bp.
TBM	*Tanulmányok Budapest Múltjából* [Studies on the past of Budapest], Bp.
TStÉ	*Történeti Statisztikai Évkönyv* [Historical Statistical Yearbook], Bp.
TSz	*Történelmi Szemle* [Historical Journal] Bp.

1937

a. [Rev.] Ethey, Gyula: *Vágvölgyi krónika* (Komárom-Komarno, 1936), Száz. 71:386.

b. [Rev.] Ethey, Gyula: *A Zoborvidék múltjából* (Nyitra, 1936), Száz. 71:386.

c. [Rev.] *Nitra. Dejiny a umenie nitrianského zámku. Na pamiatku knieza Pribinu* (Trnava, 1933), Száz. 72: 116-7.

1938

a. [Rev.] Eisner, Jan: *Slovensko v pravéku* (Bratislava, 1933), Száz. 72: 106-7.

b. [Rev.] Frankenberger, Zdenko: *Antropologie starého Slovenska* (Bratislava, 1934), Száz. 72: 106-7.

c. "Nyitra megye betelepülése", Száz. 72: 273-319, 488-500.

2

1939

a. [Rev.] Belitzky, János: *Sopron vármegye története I*, (Bp., 1938), Száz. 73: 360-2.

b. [Rev.] Jansák, Stefan: *Praveké sidliská s obsiadianovou industriou na Vychodnom Slovensku* (Bratislava, 1936), Száz., 73: 232.

c. [Rev.] *A podmanini Podmaniczky-család oklevéltára, I (1361-1510)* ed. I. Lukinich (Bp., 1937), Száz. 73: 82-4.

1941

a. "A Felvidék településtörténetének újabb német irodalma" [Recent German writings on the settlement history of Slovakia], Száz. 75: 405-21.

1944-46

a. "Középkori település és egyházi szervezet az egykori nyugati Felvidéken" [Medieval settlement and ecclesiastical organisation in former north-western Hungary], *Regnum* 6: 117-40. [cf. 1959/f.]

b. [Rev.] Sikura Jan St.: *Miestopisne dejiny Turca* (Bratislava, 1944), Száz. 79-80: 247.

1946-48

a. "Avares et slaves moraves" AÉ Ser. III, 7-9: 328-38.

b. "Avarok és morva-szlávok", *Ibid.* 312-37 [cf. 1946-48/a.]

c. [Rev.] Markov, Josef: 'Prehlad literatury právnych dejin ... 1939-45', *Právny obzor 1947*, Száz. 81: 267.

1951

a. "Levéltáraink sorsa a felszabadulás után" [The fate of our archives after the liberation], *Levéltári Híradó* 1: 34-7.

1952

a. [Co-ed., with B. Bottló, St. Kniezsa, P. Király], *Stredoveké české listiny. Középkori cseh oklevelek* ... [Medieval Czech charters], Bp. Akadémiai K., 207 pp.

1953

a. "'Németjogú' falvak települése a szlovák és német nyelvterületen" [Settlement of villages *iure theutonico* in Slovak and German surroundings], in: *Tanulmányok a parasztság történetéhez Magyarországon a 14. században* [Studies to the history of the peasantry in Hungary in the 14th C.], Gy. Székely, ed.

1955

a. "K otázka uzivania slovenského jazyka na panstvách v 17. storoci" [Concerning the spread of the use of Slovak language on a 17th century estate], StSl 1: 179-226.

1956

a. [Rev.] Pelikán, Josef: *Rozmberské dluhopsy z let 1457-1481* (Prague, 1953), Száz. 90: 805-7.

1957

a. "Kaschau, eine osteuropäische Handelsstadt des 15. Jahrhunderts", StSl 2: 185-213.

1958

a. "Középkori várostörténetünk statisztikai forrásai" [Statistical sources for Hungarian medieval urban history], *Történeti Statisztikai Közlemények* I (1957) 1:43-85, 2:16-75; II (1958) 1-2:33-46.

1959

a. "Kirchliche Topographie und Siedlungsverhältnisse im Mittelalter in der Slowakei, StSl 5: 363-400

b. "Majthényi Mártonné szóbeli végrendelete 1517-böl", [Verbal last will of Mrs Márton Majthényi from 1517] *Magyar Nyelv* 55: 425-6.

c. Topográfia és városi fejlödés a középkori Óbudán [Topography and urban development in medieval Old-Buda], TBM 13: 7-56.

1960

a. [Rev.] Balogh, István: *Debrecen* (Bp., 1958), Száz. 94: 430-2.

b. [Rev.] Dercsényi, Dezsö, Zolnay, László: *Esztergom* (Bp., 1956), Száz. 94:430-2.

c. "Az esztergomi érsekség gazdálkodása a XV. század végén" [cf. 1961/e.], Száz. 94: 82-124, 505-555.

d. [Rev.] Fitz, Jenö: *Székesfehérvár* (Bp., 1957), Száz. 94:430-2.

e. [Rev.] Gerö, László: *Eger* (Bp. 1957), Száz 94: 430-2.

1961

a. [Rev.] *Historica: Les sciences historiques en Tchécoslovaquie I* (Prague, 1959), Száz. 95: 414-5.

4

b. [Rev.] Két könyv a cseh és morva parasztság XVI. század eleji helyzetéről: A. Mika, *Poddany lid v Cechách* (Prague, 1960), F. Matejek, *Feodalni velkostatek a paddany*...(Ibid. 1959), AgtSz 3: 583-91.

c. "Középkori magyar városprivilégiumok" [Medieval Hungarian urban charters of liberty], TBM 14: 17-108.

d. [Rev.] K. Mollay, ed.: *Das Ofner Stadrecht, eine deutschsprachige Rechtssammlung* ... (Bp., 1959), Száz. 95: 398-400.

e. "Die Wirtschaft des Erzbistums von Gran am Ende des 15. Jahrhunderts", AH 7: 253-95.

1962

a. [Rev.] *Az árpádházi királyok okleveleinek kritikai jegyzéke / Regesta critico-diplomatica regum Arpad. II,2-3 (1272-1290)*, Száz. 96: 255-7.

b. [Rev.] Hamilton, E. J., *The History of Prices before 1750* (XIe Congr. Int. Sc. Hist.), Száz 96:656-8.

c. Henry, L., *Developpements récents de l'étude de la démographie* (XIe Congr. Int. Sc. Hist.), Száz. 96: 300-1.

d. A Magyar Történelmi Társulat Közgyűlése" [Convention of the Hungarian Historical Association], Száz. 96: 353-60.

1963

a. [Rev.] *Historica. Les sciences historiques en Tchécoslovaquie II* (Prague, 1960), Száz. 97: 207-9.

b. [Co-ed. with Gy. Székely] *La Renaissance et la Réformation en Pologne et en Hongrie. Conférence Budapest-Eger, 10-14 oct. 1961*, Bp., Akadémiai K. 562 pp.

c. "A XV. századi magyar arisztokrácia demográfiai viszonyai" [Demographic conditions of the Hungarian aristocracy in the 15th C.], TStÉ 1963-64: 35-71.

1964

a. [Rev.] Györffy, György, *Az Árpád-kori Magyarország történeti földrajza I* (Bp., 1963), AgtSz 6: 568-72.

b. "Megjegyzések a budai vitáról" [Comments on the discussion regarding Buda], Száz. 98: 772-81.

c. "Ujabb történeti demográfiai irodalmunkról" [On our recent historical demographic literature], Száz 98: 1252-64.

5

1965

a. "Beiträge zur Siedlungsgeschichte der Slowaken im 18. Jh. auf dem Gebiet des heutigen Ungarn", StSl 11: 289-329.

b. "Eperjes város hetipiac-jövedelme 1497-1526" [Income from the weekly fair in Eperjes between 1497 and 1526], TStÉ 1965-66: 3-26.

c. "Fehérvár középkori alaprajza" [The medieval ground plan of Székesfehérvár], *Fejér megyei Szemle* 2,1: 3-14

d. "Hungarian Bishops in the Fifteenth Century (Some Statistical Observations)", AH 11: 375-91.

e. "Jelentés a II. Várostörténeti Konferenciáról" [Report on the II. Urban History Conference], *Arrabona* 6: 249-308.

f. "A XV. századi magyar püspökök" [cf. 1965/d], TSz 8:477-98.

g. "A XV. századi magyar arisztokrácia demográfiai viszonyai", TStÉ 1965: 35-71.

1966

a. "Agrár jellegű szlovák település a török alól felszabadult területen" [Agrarian Slovak settlement in the region liberated from the Ottomans], AgtSz 8: 313-31.

b. [Rev.] Edit Lettrich: *Esztergom, a dorogi iparvidék városa* (Bp. 1964), Száz. 100: 536-8.

c. "Zur demographischen Entwicklung vier slowakischer Dörfer im Pilis-Gebirge im XVIII. und XIX. Jahrhundert", StSl 12: 139-45.

1967

a. "Alsáni Bálint, a pécsi egyetem második kancellárja" [B. Alsáni, second chancellor of the University of Pécs], in: A. Csizmadia, ed. *Jubileumi kiadványok. A pécsi egyetem történetébol* (Pécs 1967) 97-109.

b. "Székesfehérvár korai története a város alaprajzában" [cf. 1969/e.], *Székesfehérvár évszázadai* 1: 27-34.

c. "Székesfehérvar középkori alaprajza és a polgárság kezdetei Magyarországon" [cf. 1969/e.], *Településtudományi Közlemények* 20: 31-45.

1968

a. "A telekkatonaság kérdése a középkorban." [The problem of the *militia portalis* in the Middle Ages] *A magyar hivatalos statisztika történetébűl* (Bp., 1968) 293-8.

b. "A 18. századi lélekösszeírások története" [History of 18th Century Censuses of 'Souls'], Dem. 9: 366-80.

c. "Történeti demográfiánk kérdései."[Problems of our historical demography], Száz. 102: 364-7.

1969

a. "Békéscsaba újratelepítése" [The resettlement of B.], *Békési Élet* 4: 56-65.

b. "Magyarország külkereskedelme a XVI. század elején" [cf. 1971/a.], AgtSz 11: 1-19.

c. "A középkori Magyarország történeti demográfiájának mai állása" [cf. 1969/d.], Dem. 12: 500-7.

d. "Pour une analyse démographique de la Hongrie médiévale", *Annales: ESC* 24: 1299-312.

e. "Der Stadtplan von Stuhlweissenburg und die Anfänge des Bürgertums in Ungarn", AH 15: 103-36.

1970

a. "Die Entstehung des Städtewesens in Ungarn", *Alba Regia: Annales Musei Stephani Regis* 10: 101-18

b. "La formation des villes et les ordres mendients en Hongrie" *Annales: ESC* 25: 966-87.

c. *A 15. századi magyar arisztokrácia mobilitása* [Social mobility of fifteenth-century Hungarian aristocracy] Bp., Történeti Statisztikai Kötetek, 233 pp.

1971

a. "Der Aussenhandel Ungarns am Anfang des 16. Jahrhunderts", in: *Der Aussenhandel Ostmitteleuropas*, hrsg. I. Bog (Cologne-Vienna, 1971) 56-85.

b. "Győr városának 1271. évi kiváltságlevele" [The urban privilege of 1271 for the city of Gy.], *Várostörténeti Tanulmányok* (Győr) 1971: 109-17.

c. [Rev.] Struzek, B.: *Historia rolnictwa na zemiach polskich...*(Warsaw, 1966), AgtSz 13: 550-3.

1972

a. "Die Ausbreitung der städtischen Lebensform — Ungarns *oppida* im 14. Jahrhundert", in: W. Rasch, ed. *Stadt und Stadtherr im 14. Jahrhundert* (Linz, 1972), 165-92.

b. A bártfai XVI. sz. eleji bor- és lókivitel néhány kérdése [Some questions concerning wine- and horse-export from early 16th C. Bártfa], AgtSz 14: 41-89.

c. "Koldulórendek és városfejlődés Magyarországon" [cf. 1970/b.], Száz. 106: 69-94.

d. "Mezővárosaink kialakulása a XIV. században" [cf. 1972/a.], TSz 15: 321-42.

e. "A Szentgyörgyi Vincze család" [The family Sz.-V.], A Veszprém megyei múzeumok közleményei 11: 261-9.

1973

a. [Rev.] Bakás, István, Hont vármegye Mohács előtt (Bp., 1971), Száz. 107: 1239-42.

b. [Rev.] Maksay, Ferenc: A magyar falu középkori településrendje (Bp., 1971), Ibid.: 983-7.

1974

a. Mályusz, Elemér: Egyházi társadalom a középkori Magyarországon, (Bp., 1971), Száz. 108: 1254-8.

b. "The meeting of the Commission for Urban History, Székesefehérvár, 26 March 1972", Alba Regia 13: 303-4.

c. "Das mittelalterliche Königreich Ungarn als Gastland", in: W. Schlesinger, ed. Die deutsche Ostsiedlung des Mittelalters als Problem der europäischen Geschichte [Vorträge und Forschungen XVIII] (Sigmaringen:Thorbecke) 471-507

d. Uram, királyom... A XV. századi Magyarország hatalmasai [My lord, my king...: The Powerful Men of Fifteenth Century Hungary] Bp., Gondolat, 253 pp.

1975

a. [Rev.] Csapodi, Csaba: The Corvinian Library: History and Stock (Bp., 1973), Száz. 109: 195-7.

b. [Rev.] Kristó, Gyula: Csák Máté tartományúri hatalma (Bp., 1973), Száz. 109:421-5.

c. [Rev.] Püspöki Nagy, Péter: Rozsnyó város címere...(Bratislava, 1973), Száz. 109: 1153.

1976

a. [Rev.] Bak, János M.: Königtum und Stände in Ungarn im 14.-16. Jahrhundert (Wiesbaden, 1973), Száz. 110: 571-2.

8

b. "Gabonaárak a 19. sz eleji sajtóban. (Megjegyzések Ny. Straub Éva Közleményéhez)" [Grain prices in early 19th C. press (Comments on an article of E. N. Straub)], AgtSz 18: 550.

c. [Transl. & ed. with afterword] *Kimondhatatlan nyomorúság. Két emlékirat a 15.-16. századi oszmán fogságról* [Unspeakable misery: Two Memoirs on 15th-16th C. Ottoman captivity], Bp., Európa K., 254 pp.

d. [Rev.] *Magyar műemlékvédelem 1971-72* (Bp., 1974) Száz. 110: 149-50.

e. [Rev.], Josif Pataki: *Domeniul Hunedoara la inceptul sec. XVI.* (Bucharest, 1973) AgtSz 18: 5665-7.

f. "Tájékoztató a KSH Könyvtár Történeti Statisztikai Kutató Csoportjának agrártörténeti irányú munkálatairól [Information concerning the agrarian history-related activities of the Hist. Statistical Res. Group at the Central Stat. Off. Library]. AgtSz 18: 140-7.

1977

a. [Rev.] Antonius de Bonfinis: *Rerurm Ungaricarum decades, IV/2* (Bp., 1976). Száz. 111:603.

b. [Rev.] Franc. Döry, Georg. Bónis, Vera Bácskai: *Decreta Regni Hungariae ... 1301-1457* (Bp., 1976), Száz. 111:1049-52.

c. "A dunántuli városok fejlődése 1767-1848 között" [Development of western Hungarian towns between 17667 and 1848], *PAB VEAB Értesítő* 1977: 125-34.

d. "Jakó Zsigmondról, legfrisebb könyve nyomán" [Concerning Zsigmond Jakó, à propos his recent book], Száz. 111: 1231-40.

e. "Kapisztránói János csodái. A jegyzőkönyvek társadalomtörténeti tanulságai" [Miracles of John of Capestrano: Social historical lessons from the protocols of canonisation] Száz. 111:847-87.

f. "Kapisztrán János csodái. Találkozás a középkori népi vallásossággal" [The miracles of John of Capestrano: Encounters with medieval popular religiosity], *Ethnográfia* 88: 555-64.

g. *Vár és társadalom a 13.-14. századi Magyarországon* [Castle and society in 13th-14th C. Hungary], Bp. Akadémiai K., 233 pp. [Értek. a tört. tud. kör., NS 82]

1978

a. "Beszámoló a XVIII-XIX. századi háztartás- és családszerkezettel foglalkozó két tanulmány vitájáról" [Report on the discussion about two studies on 18th-19th C. household- and family structure], AgtSz 20: 292-300.

b. "Korona és hit" [Crown and faith], *Confessio* 1978: 79-85.

1979

a. "The *'avus'* in the medieval conceptual framework of kinship in Hungary", StSl 25: 137-42.

b. "A befogadó: a középkori magyar királyság "[cf. 1974/c], TSz 22: 355-76.

c. [Rev.] *Die Burgen im deutschen Sprachraum. Ihre rechts- und verfassungsge-schichtliche Bedeutung* 2 vols. (Sigmaringen, 1976), Száz. 113: 1113.

d. "A Csáky család szepesmindszenti levéltára", *Levéltári Közlemények* 50: 93-131.

e. [with K. Benda] *A magyar korona regénye* [Story of the Hungarian crown] Bp., Magvető K., 254 pp.

f. Ransanus, Petrus: *Epithome rerum Hungaricarum*, ed. P. Kulcsár (Bp., 1977), Száz. 113: 151-2.

1980

a. "Beiträge zur Siedlungsgeschichte einiger slowakischer Dörfer auf dem Gebiet des heutigen Ungarns", StSl 26: 245-305

b. "Coronation in medieval Hungary", *Studies in Medieval and Renaissance History* NS 3 [13] 159-89.

c. "Középkori rokonsági terminologógiák kérdéséhez" [Comments on medieval kinship terminologies], *Ethnográfia 91: 361-71.*

d. "Steuerlisten, Vermögen und soziale Gruppen in mittelalterlichen Städten", *Städtische Gesellschaft und Reformation*, hrsg. I. Bátori (Stuttgart) [Tübinger Beiträge zur Geschichtsforschung 12] 57-96.

1981

a. *Kolduló barátok, polgárok, nemesek. Tanulmányok a magyar középkorról* [Mendicant friars, burghers and nobles, studies on the Hungarian Middle Ages] Bp., Magvető K., 565 pp. [contains 1960/d., 1961/c., 1965/f., 1969/c., 1970/a.,1972/c., d., 1977/e., 1979/b., 1984/c.]

b. [Rev.] Novák, Gyula, Sándorffy György, Miklós Zsuzsa: *A Börzsöny hegység őskori és középkori várai* (Bp., 1979), Száz. 115: 219-21.

1982

a. "Királyi tisztség vagy hűbér?" [Royal office or fief?], TSz 25: 482-509.

b. "Das Königreich Ungarn (1458-1541)", *Schallaburg '82: Matthias Corvinus und die Renaissance in Ungarn 1458-1541, 8. Mai − 1. Nov. 1982* (Vienna, 1982), 17-32.

c. "Medieval Castles in Existence at the Start of the Ottoman Advance" in: J.M.Bak, B.K.Király, eds. *From Hunyadi to Rákóczi: War and Society in*

Medieval and Early Modern Hungary (Brooklyn, Atlantic Monographs) 59-62 & 2 maps.

d. "Mátyás király jövedelme 1475-ben" [Revenues of King Matthias in 1475], Száz. 116: 484-506.

e. [Rev.] Simon de Proxenus a Sudetis: *Commentarius de itinere Francogallico* (Bp., 1979), Száz. 116: 164.

f. "Some characteristics of the medieval Hungarian noble family", *Journal of Family History* VII (1982), 27–39.

1983

a. "Das Baumkirchnerbild in der ungarischen Geschichtsschreibung", *Andreas Baumkirchner und seine Zeit: Symposium im Rahmen der 'Schlaininger Gepräche'*, hrsg. R. Kropf, W. Meyer (Eisenstadt) 257-62.

  b. [Rev.] Steinmann, Judit: *Die Benedikterabtei zu Fraumünster und ihre Verhältnis zur Stadt Zürich 853-1524* (s.l., 1980), Száz. 117: 667-8.

c. [Rev.] *Johannes Vitéz de Zredna opera quae supersunt*, ed. I. Boronaki (Bp., 1980), Száz. 117: 462-4.

1984

a. "Emlékezés Paulinyi Oszkárra" [In memoriam Oszkár Paulinyi], *A Ráday Gyüjtemény Évkönyve* 3: 335-7.

b. "A középkori magyar nemesség rokonsági rendszerének két kérdése", *Történeti antropológia. Az 1983. április 18-19-én tartott tudományos ülésszak előadásai*, 217-26.

c. "Verba volant... Középkori nemességünk szóbelisége és az írás" [Verba volant: Oral culture and literacy among the medieval. Hungarian nobility] in: *Emlékkönyv Mályusz Elemér 80. születése napjára* [also in 1981/a. 437-62].

(Compiled with the assistance of Gyula Benda)

INDEX

This index, as usual in this series, contains a selection of personal and place names mentioned in the studies. Variant (Latin, German, Slovak, Romanian, etc.) forms of place names are included for orientation. Considering the character of the studies, persons were occasionally mentioned merely as examples for a social or political issue; such names are, as a rule, omitted. Names of modern scholars appear in italics.

ABBREVIATIONS:
abp.= archbishop;   bp.= bishop;   H.= Hungary;   k.= king

Abu Hamid al Andalusi: **VIII** 477-8; **IX** 105
Alba Regia *see* Székesfehérvár
Albert I, k. of H.: **I** 160, 171
Alexander de Hungaria: **VII** 10
Andreas Pannonius: **VII** 10
Andrew II, k. of H.: **I** 184-5; **III** 6, 8
Andrew III,k. of H.: **I** 177-9, 185; **IV** 1; **V** 140
Anne of Châtillon, queen of H.: **VII** 2
Anonymus [Notary] **IV** 7
Aquincum: **IX** 102

Bácskai, Vera: **XII** 983, 987; **XIII** 166
Bakócz, Ferenc, bp.: **II** 377, 380
Bakócz, Tamás, abp.: **II** 375, 380, 382-3; **III** 266
Bán, town: **XIII** 171, 177, 184-5
Banská Bystrica *see* Besztercebánya
Banská Stavnice *see* Selmecbánya
Bartoniek, Emma: **I** 160, 173, 175
Bastian, F.: **IX** 103
Báthory, aristocrats: **II** 382; **IV** 18

Beckensloer, Johann, abp.: **II** 379-80; **VIII** 495
Békés, town: **XIII** 188
Béla III, k. of H.: **I** 176; **VII** 2
Béla IV, k. of H.: **I** 159, 184; **III** 8; **IV** 2-3, 6, 9;**V** 140; **IX** 110-1; **XII** 979
Belényes, town: **XIII** 172-3
Belgrade: **II** 376
Berthold of Merania: **VIII** 495
Betrand, bp.: **VII** 4
Besztercebánya (Neusohl, Banská Bystrica): **IX** 115-7
Bethlen, Gergely: **IV** 13
Bratislava *see* Pozsony
Brassó (Braşov, Kronstadt):**VIII** 502, 505; **XII** 984, 972; **XIII** 167
Bonfini, Antonio: **I** 160-1, 165, 168; **IV** 14
Bónis, György: **IV** 19-20
Bosnia: **II** 376, 380
Buda (Ofen): **IV** 2, 23; **VIII** 491, 500-1, 515; **IX**102-3, 105, 113-6; **XII** 975, 983; **XIII** 167

Callimachus   Experiens

III 12; **IV** 23

Siklós, town, castle: **XIII** 186-7

Sopron (Ödenburg), town: **VIII** 505; **IX** 102, 114-5; **XII** 984; **XIII** 177

Stephen I, St., k. of H.: **I** 159, 162, 167, 178-81, 188-9; **IV** 2; **VII** 2; **X** 110, 113, 115; **XII** 967, 973, 977

Stephen III, k. of H.: **IX** 111; **X** 123; **XII** 977

Stephen V, k. of H.: **I** 185; **III** 2; **V** 138

Stuhlweissenburg *see* Székesfehérvár

Sylvester II, Pope: **I** 159, 180

Szabó, István: **III** 261-2; **XIII** 165

Szalkai, László, bp.: **II** 380-1; **VII** 13

Szatmári, György, abp.: **II** 378

Széchy, Dénes, abp.: **I** 172

Szeben (Nagyszeben, Hermannstadt, Sibiu), town: **VIII** 498, 502, 503

Szeged, town: **XII** 972, 984; **XIII** 167

Székely, György: **III** 261; **XIII** 166

Székesfehérvár (Alba Regia, Stuhlweissenburg), town, **I** 161, 163, 166; 176-7, 179-81; **IV** 3, 23; **VII** 4; **VIII** 492; **IX** 106, 110, 112, 117; **X** *passim;* **XII** 973, 977-9

Szentkereszt (Heiligenkreuz, Sv. Kríz n/Hr.), estate: **III** 258

Szerém, bishopric: **II** 376, 380, 381

Szombathely (Steinamanger), town: **IX** 102; **X** 105

Tallóci, aristocrats: **III** 12

Temesvár (Timişoara): **XII** 972, 984

Thúróczy, Johannes: **IV** 14

Transylvania (Siebenbürgen): **II** 381; **VIII** 482, 486

Trnava *see* Nagyszombat

Tubero, Ludovico: **I** 160

Ujlak, town: **XII** 985-6

Vác (Waitzen), bishopric, town: **II** 381; **IX** 106-7

Várad (Nagyvárad, Wardein, Oradea), bishopric, town: **II** 381; **IX** 110, 113; **XI** 207; **XIII** 167-8

Várdai, aristocrats: **II** 391; **IV** 15

Várdai, István, abp.: **IV** 17-8

Venceslas III, k. of H.: **I** 179

Veszprém, town, bishopric **II** 381; **VIII** 8; **X** 106, 108, 113

Vienna: **VII** 11

Visegrád, castle: **III** 3

Vitéz, János (Johannes) de Zredna, abp.: **II** 379; **III** 284; **IV** 18; **VII** 9, 11

Werböczy, István: **IV** 9, 24

Wladislas I, k. of H.: **I** 159, 171-2, 179

Wladislas II, k. of H.: **I** 160-2, 168, 173, 183

Zagreb (Agram), bishopric,town: **IX** 110

Zalavár: **XII** 969

Zsolna (Sillein, Zilina), town: **VIII** 500; **IX** 118